FIRST AMONG UNEQUALS

THE AUTOBIOGRAPHY

FIRST AMONG UNEQUALS

The Autobiography

Viv Anderson MBE
with Lynton Guest

FullBack
Media

First published in Great Britian 2010 by Fullback Media Ltd

Fullback Media Ltd
26 Eton Close,
Datchet,
Berks,
SL3 9BE

ISBN 978 184226 015 9 HB Arsenal

ISBN 978 184226 016 6 HB Manchester United

ISBN 978 184226 017 3 HB Notts Forest

ISBN 978 184226 018 0 HB England

ISBN 978 184226 019 7 PB

ISBN 978 184226 021 0 HB Sheffield Wednesday

Typeset by: Bookcraft Ltd, Stroud, Gloucestershire

Printed by Dolman Scott
www.dolmanscott.com

Front cover design by: PR3

TO:
Mam, Dad, Donald, Nichole, Debra, Charlie,
Gabrielle, Freddie and our new baby due soon

CONTENTS

ACKNOWLEDGMENTS

Very Special Thanks To:

Bill Hill, Les Molloy, John Kaufman, Roger Grime, Dean Morter, Chris Lloyd and his team, Orca Distribution, Richard Chalmers, David Landau, Harriet Lester, John Speer, Dave Clarke, David Wood, Graham Bell, Tony Stanley, Brian Longmuir, Alex Fynn, Lynton Guest, David Wood, Peter Law, Nottingham Forest F.C., Brian Clough, Gordon Taylor, Trevor Braithwaite, Danny Lynch, Arsenal F.C., Manchester United F.C., Sir Alex Ferguson, Sheffield Wednesday F.C., Bryan Robson, Tony Woodcock, Barnsley F.C., Middlesbrough F.C., The Alex Stepney Fund, Paul McGarvey at JP3, Norman Whiteside, John Sumpter @ PA Action Images, Danny Wilson, Steve Bruce, Martin O'Neill, John Robertson, Kevin Keegan, Bob Latchford, Shelagh Aitken, Debra Anderson, Nichole Burton, Bert Bowery, Michael Wykes, Glyn Saunders, Peter Wells, Michale & Kevin Byrne, Trevor Kershaw, Colin Wragg, Kevin Rodgers, John & Paula, Bert Johnson, Trevor Brooking, Pedro Richards, Robin Fox, Sacit and Monica Amorim Molloy.

PHOTO ACKNOWLEDGEMENTS

All photographs are from the author's personal collection.

The Author would like to thank the following photographers:

Bob Thomas, H. Barlow, *Manchester Evening News*, AllSports Photographic, County Press, Charles A. Noble, Doug Poole, Steve Ellis, P. Spencer, Ken Prater, Barnsley F.C., Middlesbrough F.C., Getty Images

Every effort has been made to contact the copyright holders of the photographs used in this book, unfortunately some were not reachable. The publishers would be grateful if those concerned would contact Fullback Media.

PREFACE

It is now more than thirty years since I became the first black footballer to be capped by England. I was the first among unequals! In those days the number of black players was limited and we – the original generation – had to fight every step of the way to be recognised. How that has changed. Today, you would be surprised to see an English professional side without a full complement of ethnic minority players. What a difference from when I started.

With the approach of the thirtieth anniversary itself, in the 2008–09 season, a raft of celebrations were planned. It was pointed out to me that there were huge numbers of people out there who wanted to mark the occasion. It was fantastic to realise that my milestone meant so much to so many. One of the events suggested to me was an all-star charity football match, featuring some of the greatest players over the last thirty years. Another was for me to write a book about my experiences both in the game and in life. The match didn't take place in the end, for reasons you will see as you read on. The book, however, was completed and this is the result.

The first thing you need to know is that my memory

for detail is not the best in the business. Anyone who knows me will tell you that. Dates, times, even years are a mystery to me sometimes. Because of that I have tried to check all the facts in this book to make sure they are correct. If one or two fall outside that boundary, well I apologise but I'm sure you'll find your enjoyment of my story is in no way diminished.

In these pages you will read tales of some of the great footballers and managers I have worked with and played against. I've tried to give a proper opinion of them, for good or ill. I'll tell you about my time with England and my unique contribution to World Cup history. I have also written about being made an ambassador for our bid for the 2018 World Cup. I think you'll find that my views on our efforts to date are forthright, to say the least.

The clubs I played for form a large part of the book. Most of you will know the list: Nottingham Forest, in the most successful period they've ever had, under the incomparable Brian Clough; Arsenal, at the very beginning of the George Graham revolution which put the club back on top of the pile; Manchester United, where I was Sir Alex Ferguson's first signing; Sheffield Wednesday with Big Ron Atkinson in his pomp and Trevor Francis in the wings; Barnsley, the family club which gave me my first experience as a player-manager alongside Danny Wilson; with Bryan Robson at Middlesbrough, when we brought some of the world's greatest stars to the Riverside. All of these and more come under my microscope.

Rather than write a comprehensive account of my life,

I've included stories and incidents which I hope will keep you entertained and tell you a story about football. Many of them you will not have heard about before. There is a huge cast of characters in this book and I have tried to bring them all to life. At the same time I offer you my thoughts and opinions on the players and the events. What I haven't written is a compendium of games and seasons; you can get that elsewhere. Instead, I want to tell you about those personalities who shaped the world of modern football, most of whom I knew personally.

Much of my adult life has been lived in the public eye. In *First Among Unequals* I talk about what that's like and the effects it can sometimes have. I have also included aspects of my personal life which have made headlines over the years. I set the record straight wherever I can.

The most important element I have tried to sustain throughout the book is honesty. I've done my very best to tell it like it is. I've not gone out of my way to criticise anyone unnecessarily but I make no apologies for giving my views where appropriate. Parts of this book will be controversial, there's no question about that. But I think overall you will find it a riveting account of the life of a professional footballer in the today's world. I hope you enjoy it.

Viv Anderson MBE: Manchester, 2010

Chapter One

ENGLAND MY ENGLAND

As the day broke on Monday, May 18 2009, I was feeling pretty good. Making my way to Wembley was a joy I had felt many times before when I played at the old ground. I also loved attending matches there after my retirement. But this time was different. It wasn't a game I was going to see, nor was I simply visiting the new Wembley – probably the best stadium in the world – with its fantastic arch that you can see from miles away. It was none of these things. I was to be present at the public launch of England's bid to stage the 2018 World Cup. But what should have been a memorable occasion soon turned into a disaster and, as far as I am concerned, shows exactly why we have more to accomplish in this country, even though we have already achieved so much.

I couldn't fail to notice there were no black or Asian faces in the main group. That led me to remember my invitation had not come direct from the Football Association (FA) or the bidding committee. I didn't think about it too much at the time but I was there, if you like, by default. I had been asked if I wanted to attend by one of the companies for whom I carry out promotional work. They had been allocated a number of tickets. Maybe the fact that my invitation hadn't arrived direct from the FA should have alerted me but, to be honest, I never really gave it a second thought. I was pleased to be included, whatever route the invite took. But there was Prince William, along with the Prime Minister, Gordon Brown; there was David Beckham; there was Wayne Rooney for God's sake. But of black England players, there was not a sign. No Rio Ferdinand, no Ashley Cole, no Emile Heskey. It was the same with the speeches, which were broadcast and commented on throughout the media.

Now I know David and Wayne are box-office, I've got no problem with that. They should have been there and prominently displayed. But surely room could have been found at the main table for some of the black footballers who have contributed to England's cause over the years. It was not the only sour note. Hardly commented upon in the next morning's back pages was the fact that the England manager, Fabio Capello, was also noticeable by his absence. It seemed to me a strange way to announce our bid to the waiting world. Yet again, just like a previous attempt to secure the 2006 tournament, when the English delegation committed just about every mistake in the book, our nation got off on completely the wrong foot.

Suddenly, as I was taking everything in, a murmur went around the assembled dignitaries near where I was sitting. I didn't realise it at the time but it turned out that the FA had invited a London Assembly member from the racist British National Party to the event. How this happened I really don't know. I don't think the FA knows either. In fact the FA was caught cold. The next day, the stories in the press were as much concerned with the BNP member as they were about the bid. To me, it was sad and the truth is the whole thing left a nasty taste.

Those people who know me would tell you I am an optimistic, humorous, happy-go-lucky kind of person. Alex Ferguson once attempted to buy me back from the club he sold me to – Ron Atkinson's Sheffield Wednesday – because I was such a positive influence in the dressing room. Fergie felt he needed my presence for Manchester United's first European campaign in many years. For someone like me to say what I have about my experience at Wembley tells you that something about our 2018 bid is seriously wrong.

The debacle was felt well beyond our shores. The influential FIFA Vice President, Jack Warner, who is also the controversial President of the Central American Football Federation, Concacaf, and who has often been a thorn in England's side in the past, could hardly have been any clearer, when he said: "I'm quite sure the FA will recognise an error when one is made and they will correct it. I hope they will do it quickly." My old mate Garth Crooks was even more forceful when he declared: "What I find so desperately sad is that whatever your views (are) about the BNP being there, there is a bigger view. If it had been a really diverse event, if there had been a selection of black multi-ethnic groups there, we could have got over this. We've spent twenty years trying to drive the

BNP out of football and they are getting an invitation to the launch of our World Cup bid." Now Garth, who I played against many times, takes some stick for the length of his pronouncements, but here I think everyone would agree that he was absolutely spot on. At the time of writing this, the FA has made some efforts to right its terrible wrong but I remain worried that the damage has already been done.

Soon afterwards, a football conference took place at Stamford Bridge, during which Jack Warner again made his feelings known. Among other observations, he said the England bid was "lightweight". This was an implied criticism of the bid leader, Lord Triesman (who is also Chairman of the FA), and his bid team. Since Warner, as a close ally of FIFA President Sepp Blatter, wields some considerable influence on the votes to decide who gets World Cups, this was as bad as it could get. Later, it turned out that Australia, which is also bidding for 2018, had stolen a march on England by providing those attending the conference with goody bags promoting its bid but there was no sign of any English equivalent. For this, the England bid team were derided in the press.

As you will see later in this book, I have some experience in the ways of the press. One aspect of what I have learnt is that if the media has decided something is a shambles, everything that happens from then on is reported in that light. So when it became known that England had spent £24,000 buying expensive Mulberry handbags to give away to FIFA delegates' wives (including Mrs. Jack Warner), the same papers that had taken the FA to task for not providing goody bags at Stamford Bridge blasted the organisation for its extravagance over the handbags. The point is that the FA, in its desperate attempts to respond to the negative comments in the press, merely made everything worse. The association's expensive PR machine should have realised this way before it got out of hand.

In response to the unfavourable publicity, the FA decided to recruit fifty "ambassadors" to help promote the 2018 bid. Huge dossiers were sent to each ambassador explaining the party line. I was one of those chosen. I still have the 100 page email. I was happy to accept the invitation. I want to do all I can to bring the World Cup to my country. That is part of the reason why I believe far more transparency is required on the part of the bid team. The good thing about the ambassadors is that we are made up of many different nationalities, all of us having made an impact on the English game at one time or another. However, I do not feel that our role has been properly thought through or developed over time. What was a good idea in principle is, in my view, in danger of being squandered.

I want to say right here that I am fully committed to helping England win the right to stage the 2018 World Cup. Like every other Englishman, I desperately want this country to host the tournament once again. It's been far too long. However, as one who accepted the role of ambassador for the bid I believe I should speak freely, both to the powers that be and the public at large. With the matter to be decided in December 2010, time is running out. The

FA has made mistakes and continues to make them. The belated move to create the panel of ambassadors might have been honourably meant but – since little has been asked of us – it appears to be a case of both tokenism and a failure to understand the nature of the beast they are dealing with. Sending out David Beckham is an obviously good move. He is a global icon. He will woo crowds and delegates wherever he goes anywhere in the world. We need him. But we ambassadors are not being used to anything like the same effect. I am ready to talk to anyone, anytime to help my country. But I only get the occasional email with requests to perform an ambassadorial duty. The role is undefined. As one of the players who was at the centre of England's change from an all-white game to a game of all the talents, I would have thought the FA would have found a way to use my status – and that of the others who came afterwards – to promote the bid, particularly around the world. The bid team needs to resolve these issues – and fast – if we are to stand any chance of bringing the World Cup back to these shores.

As if to vindicate my position, I heard from a colleague one day in November, 2009, that there were serious disagreements within the bid committee and that Jack Warner would soon be back to haunt us. Within a couple of days the Warner story was public knowledge and it wasn't very pretty. Mr. Warner decided to return his wife's Mulberry handbag, accusing the FA of giving her a present which was "a symbol of derision, betrayal and embarrassment for me and my family." Accepting the handbag had, according to Warner, caused him to suffer all manner of "indignities" from "all kinds of persons". It seemed he was objecting to negative coverage in the media which implied his wife's acceptance of the gift and the FA's giving of it was somehow evidence of corruption. He went on, in a letter to Lord Triesman, to say, "When these insults touch my wife, it represents an all time low." As if that wasn't enough damage to inflict in one day, Warner directly accused Lord Triesman of failing to stand up to those who were making the allegations of wrong-doing.

However much we might not agree with the interpretation put on the Mulberries by either the press or Warner, we must respond to the criticisms of those who have the vote. Not capitulate, but learn. I am told that panic ensued at the FA after the series of terrible articles and broadcasts following Mr. Warner's outburst. Again my information proved correct and by the middle of November the whole bid committee had been restructured. I was pleased to see the former Chelsea player, Paul Elliot, drafted in. Paul has long campaigned against racism and is a welcome addition. The question is: will he be deployed in a way that will best use his talent? The rest of the restructuring exercise smacked of indecision.

Sometimes I think there is a sense of entitlement in this country (or at least in those that run football). It goes like this: because we haven't had the World Cup here since 1966 and we are the home of football, it is our right to have it now. Others, we point out, like Germany, have hosted two World Cups since it was last held here. Frankly, this kind of thing cuts no ice with FIFA and the notion needs to be rapidly abandoned if we are to have any hope of winning. If we don't grasp these issues and deal with them, our bid will go the same way as our attempt to get the 2006 tournament. Nowhere!

After the experience of Wembley and its aftermath, my mind went back to earlier times; to growing up a black kid in Nottingham. I can't say I particularly suffered from racism in my youth but of course I knew it was out there. I spent the whole of my energy trying to make it in the cut and thrust world of professional sport. In those days casual racism did exist in the dressing room and on the training pitch. It was the 1970s, remember. Life on Mars and all that! And there weren't many professional black players back then. I remember Clyde Best at West Ham and Albert Johansson of Leeds, that's about it. But I just didn't have the space, mentally, to deal with the world's prejudices. I'm not saying I was oblivious to it all, just that if I'd have let it get to me, my career would have been that much harder and may not have happened at all. Even when I won my first England cap I refused to be sucked into the media frenzy that came with it. Well, not too much anyway!

Whether I like it or not, I will always be remembered as the first black player to be capped by England. The accolade is an honour and I will always treasure the memory of my achievement. The match, against Czechoslovakia on a freezing cold night in November 1978, was a run-of-the-mill friendly, so the emphasis placed by the media on my appearance was magnified. I don't recall too much about the game to be honest, except that I had a hand in the solitary goal which brought England victory. I remember that alright. I thought I did well on the night, particularly when I spotted Tony Currie ahead of me down the right and played the perfect pass to release him. Tony, one of the most skilful players I ever saw but who never really had enough chances at international level to show what he was capable of, put in a great cross for Steve Coppell to score. Despite the hysteria, for me, that night wasn't a case of me being the first black England player, no matter what the media said. I was a professional footballer and I wanted to reach the very top. I had just won the First Division Championship with Nottingham Forest, now I was an international. I was really pleased with my progress.

Many people at my club thought I would get my England chance earlier than I did. They felt that the player who occupied the position, Liverpool's Phil Neal, was no longer the best. But I had to bide my time. Phil was still a great full-back, no question, and it was up to me to dislodge him. When the call came, I was determined to show I could be a fixture in the England team. That's what I was thinking about. I wanted to lay down a marker. It would be some years before I could seriously consider the wider issues that were undoubtedly raised by my elevation to the national team. At the time I thought about my mother and father, hoping they would be proud of me. Like everybody, I wanted their approval. As fate would have it, on the day after the game my mother was involved in a car accident that required a stay in hospital, so my celebrations were cut short. I was at first worried sick about her condition and only perked up when it was explained to me that her injuries were not too serious. Nothing, however, could take away the inner glow I felt over my achievement.

Like everybody else, I didn't get to choose the era in which I played. I always regarded myself as a footballer, not a black footballer, and I wanted to be judged on my ability and performances, not the colour of my skin. However, as a player who helped open up football to black players, I suppose it was inevitable that the race issue would be uppermost in many people's minds, even if not in mine. I can say now that I am proud of the role I played. It helped pave the way for the huge improvements in football that have occurred since then. I am also pleased to have helped the game move away from the prejudices that stood in the way of black footballers when I started.

Of course, in those days, crowds at games were often blatantly racist. Nowhere was free from the scourge. I suffered as much as anyone from the hate but most of the time I was able to shut it out and concentrate on my game. Perhaps it even spurred me on to be a better player. There was no room for complacency, certainly, because you never knew what was around the corner. The next away game could bring the most disgusting chants by the crowd and racist comments from individual supporters. I learned this lesson early. In only my second game for Forest I was subjected to a mass taunt – and that was before the game even started. It was a League Cup tie away to Newcastle. Now the St. James' Park regulars could be intimidating to any footballer but what I experienced that night went way beyond the boundaries of acceptable behaviour. Before the match, the then Forest manager, Dave Mackay, took us pitch-side to get a flavour of the atmosphere. As soon as the crowd got a glimpse of me the baiting started. I froze. As a teenager I must admit I was totally unprepared for the taunting. I told Dave Mackay I didn't want to play. He took me aside and gave me a good talking to. He didn't mince his words. "If you want to be a footballer, son, you've got to learn to cope with stuff like this," he said. I played.

It was only with the support of the management and the other Forest players that I came through it. Maybe it was better to have that experience so early on in my career. It probably made me a stronger person. In the future I would always refuse to be intimidated. My tactic was to concentrate even harder on my game. But it should never have happened in the first place. No player should have to deal with that. To be fair to the Geordies, Newcastle was one of the first grounds where this kind of thing was eradicated. I have since found the Geordie supporters nothing but fair in the way they give me stick.

I don't think the reaction of the Newcastle crowd on that day was any different to what went on at other grounds. It was simply that at St. James' Park the noise was deafening and the antagonism immense. I shut it out. I had to, otherwise my career would have been over there and then. Of course I shouldn't have had to do that but I found out that night that I could cope. No crowd ever really got to me again, even as things turned nastier when eighties hooliganism took hold of the game and almost destroyed it.

After my first appearance against Czechoslovakia the media gave me rave reviews for my performance. The manager, Ron Greenwood, also praised my contribution, saying he was "very pleased" with me. His assistant, Don Howe, was even more impressed and told me I could become a fixture in the England team. This was all I wanted to hear. However, I wasn't picked for the next match or the five after that. Footballers have to learn quickly that no matter how well you think you have done you can suddenly be out of the team. By the time I first played for England I had already learned the lesson. In my short time in the game I had been rejected by the club I had always supported, Manchester United, and been ignored by the great Brian Clough when he first arrived at Forest. I had come back from those disappointments to more than prove my worth. You just have to believe in yourself and work your way back any way you can. The higher you go the more this applies. In my case, Phil Neal came in for me in the England team and when he wasn't available for one match, Trevor Cherry of Leeds got the nod before me. I could have been forgiven for thinking my England career was over almost as soon as it had started.

Happily, this proved not to be the case, although I had to wait until the following June before I got another chance to show what I could do for the national team. Seven months! Today, I can look back with satisfaction on my record for England. I won over thirty caps at right-back in an era when there were quite a few exceptional full-backs about. That's a pretty good return. Not only that, I managed to score two goals in my international career, one against Turkey, one against Yugoslavia.

When he first selected me for England, the manager, Ron Greenwood, didn't really give me any individual advice as to how to approach the game. He just briefed the team as a whole. It was as if he kind of expected you to know what you were about because he had selected you. He sort of floated above it all, smiling. I will always be grateful to Kevin Keegan and Bob Latchford, who took me aside for a chat.

"Just remember you wouldn't be playing if you weren't good enough," Kevin said, while Bob told me to "make sure you do what you do for your club every Saturday." While what they said might seem a cliché, let me tell you that their intervention made all the difference to me. So much so it's something I tried to pass on to younger players when I was established, both for club and country. These are the incredible values that do exist in the world of football. Beyond the cynicism, there are people prepared to take time out to reassure a newcomer; to let him know he is accepted for what he is. Kevin Keegan and Bob Latchford were living examples of this tradition.

Until then, I had only known the training and management team at my club, Nottingham Forest. With England I was finding out that Brian Clough and Peter Taylor were not typical. This was brought home to me, not only through the methods of Ron Greenwood and his assistant, Don Howe, but also in the stories I heard from the other players. I had sampled something of this when I had been called up to the "B" team or age-based squads previously. But nothing compared to the education I received with the senior boys. Management, media interest and competitive instinct fuelled a completely different atmosphere. I discovered that other managers and coaches had very different ideas from Clough, including hard physical training during the season, something Clough thought pointless. That's why he often used to take us off to Mallorca or somewhere where relaxation was the objective and precious little training was carried out. I was soon disabused of the notion that this was the norm.

As time went on, more black players were called up for England, first Laurie Cunningham, who so tragically died in a car crash in Spain some years later, then Cyrille Regis and bit by bit, many, many others. I think I can speak for all of us when I say we are pleased we blazed the trail in the way we did. Today, it would be inconceivable for any English team – whether club or country – not to field its fair share of black players. Nothing is so eloquent a testament to the way our country can respond to change as that.

There is no question that throughout the game and its supporters the issue of racism has improved immeasurably since I began playing. But resting on our laurels should not be the order of the day. While the launch bid for England 2018 was going on under the full glare of publicity at Wembley, other events were unfolding, much more personal to me and relevant to every decent football follower, which showed just how much further the game has yet to travel. Nothing of what was happening found its way into the media. I am going to tell everything in this book, but that incident, which really shows where the game is at in this country, will come later.

First, I want to tell you about my involvement – if you can call it that – in a couple of previous World Cups.

Chapter 2

WORLD CUPS

It is every footballers dream to play in a World Cup. It's the pinnacle of the game and the summit of any career. But those highs don't just arrive after a few good performances for your club. Before I made it into the full England team I played in the under-21s and the "B" team. Before I got into a World Cup squad I played in friendly games, various qualifiers and one match in the European Championships. What I found was that international football is at best unpredictable, as you'll see from my experience.

After my initial appearance in the England first team in 1978 and my seven month wait for another cap, I was in and out of the side. However, as the 1980 Euro Championships in Italy approached, I played in the qualifying games and considered myself the number one choice. I had, after all, just won the European Cup for the second time. In the event I was included in the squad for Italy but I was only selected for one game, the last group match against Spain. By that time we were already out of the tournament so it was a dead match. It was, however, the only game we won, by two goals to one. This wasn't the progress I had hoped for following my performance against Czechoslovakia two years before. Still, I was an international novice in 1980, so when I thought about it later I realised that playing in the one game wasn't too bad. I obviously would have preferred more minutes on the pitch. But then I thought I should have been in the team for every game. I decided it was all part of learning about the international set-up.

When we qualified for the 1982 World Cup in Spain I was hopeful of getting more of a chance than I had received in Italy. Four years on from my debut I really felt I was at the top of my game. I was finally established as Greenwood's right-back, or so I thought. It soon began to dawn on me, however, that things were not going my way. They were not going my way at all.

International football is nothing like playing for your club, where you can get in the team, do reasonably well, and be fairly sure you will keep your place. It was different with the national team. For instance, England international managers in my time were notorious for chopping and changing the side. There were always lots of players withdrawing from England squads in those days – not always through genuine injury but often at the request of their managers, who wanted to keep them ready to play for their clubs. This unnerved England's managers. They rarely seemed to know what their best eleven was. So it was no real surprise to me when Liverpool's Phil Neal would sometimes be drafted in by Ron Greenwood. But now, with the World cup approaching, I felt it was my time. With Nottingham Forest, I had won promotion from the old division two, the First Division title, and two European Cups back-to-back. It was time to go to the next level.

But I wasn't selected for the first game. I had to sit and watch as, after a great start to the tournament, things started to go horribly wrong.

Two of our most creative players, Kevin Keegan and Trevor Brooking, were injured going into the campaign. I think any side which had those two fit could have achieved great things. Without them, we were severely lacking in the playmaker department and up front. We had Glenn Hoddle, who could unlock opposing defences, but he was never really trusted in the role by either Greenwood or his successor, Bobby Robson. Keegan became a great player through commitment and determination and he was one of the few English players at the time who had played on the continent. In his time at Hamburg it was obvious he had developed an under-standing of the European game. Brooking, who played under Greenwood at West Ham, was simply top-draw, all silky skills and great passing. Without those two, it was always going to be tough.

Ron Greenwood got the England job when just about everyone thought my boss at Forest, Brian Clough, should have been given the crown. And if Clough had been appointed I'm pretty sure I would have been in his first eleven. Instead, in Spain, Greenwood's preferred right-back was Mick Mills of Ipswich. Now don't get me wrong, but at that time – good though they were

– Ipswich had hardly reached the heights that I had achieved with Forest. Mick Mills was effective but I had stopped some of the greatest wingers in the world. In truth I was devastated. I couldn't understand the manager's decision and he didn't explain it to me. Mr. Greenwood was not always the best communicator, especially when there was bad news to be broken. I tried to stay optimistic and be a good member of the squad. But it still hurt.

Despite the injuries to Brooking and Keegan, things looked good after the first game. We beat the French 3–1, with Robbo scoring the fastest-ever World Cup goal, 27 seconds after we kicked off. I watched with the dawning realisation that the manager was unlikely to want to change a winning team. What was worse and what really filled me with foreboding was that with Kevin Keegan injured, Mick Mills had not only taken my position, Greenwood made him captain.

To be fair, the win against the French had been a good performance. We had beaten the side which would get to the semi-final in this tournament then win the European Championships two years later. From the French game, England's performances looked to have got even better as the team triumphed in their two remaining group matches. It was looking bad for me as we beat Czechoslovakia and Kuwait without conceding a goal.

The injuries meant an awful lot of hopes rested on the shoulders of Bryan Robson and Ray Wilkins, with occasional support coming from Glenn Hoddle. Hoddle, however, played in just one and a half matches, a full game against Kuwait and half a game against the Czechs. Brooking and Keegan, both obviously unfit, only managed appearances as substitutes in our final game against Spain, when it was a case of either score or go home. I kept my natural optimism, though, and I was hopeful I would be included at some stage.

But it didn't happen. It turned out to be worse than Italy. I didn't get to play in even one game. I didn't get on the pitch at all. Not one minute of one game. This kind of disappointment became a recurring feature of my time in international football. I loved being an England player. That's why I would get dejected when I was left out. In Spain, just as in Italy, the worst thing about my omission was that the team was not pulling up any trees. Apart from a very good first match and a reasonable showing in the group, we were nothing more than average. It wasn't as if we won the tournament or even got close. Yes, the defence was solid but ...

The problems for England and Greenwood came in the next round when we failed to score a goal in two games, against West Germany and the hosts, Spain. In the Spanish World Cup, the second round was not a knockout stage as it is today. The teams emerging from the first round entered a second group phase. Each group contained three teams with only the winners progressing. England's performances, which had at first stirred hope, began to fade badly. The defence looked rock-solid but we couldn't score goals. Both of England's matches in the second round ended

0–0. This meant we were out – without losing a match and I never got to kick a ball in anger.

After Spain, Ron Greenwood's tenure as England manager came to an end. He was a man who often couldn't make up his mind, as in the famous rotation of the two goalkeepers, Peter Shilton and Ray Clemence. Maybe he just wanted to keep both of them happy, I don't know. This indecision hindered us at the highest level. But he was also a man who believed football should be played in the right way and he earned the trust of the players. I certainly learned a lot from him. As I mentioned earlier, he was sometimes reticent. When he omitted me from the team in Spain, he hardly offered a word of encouragement. That was left to the coaching staff, especially Don Howe, who told me that he thought I was the best right-back around. Still, I remember Greenwood with fondness. He may not have found room for me in his stab at winning the World Cup but he was the man who gave me my big opportunity for England. For that I owe him an awful lot.

I was selected in the squad for new manager Bobby Robson's first big match, a friendly against the old enemy, West Germany. Robson had been recruited after performing heroics for Ipswich over many years. They may not have matched Forest's epic feats but they had gradually become more impressive under Robson, eventually winning the UEFA Cup. Like all players when a manager is replaced, I was apprehensive at first. I needn't have worried. Robson made it clear he rated me and said I would be in the team for his first game.

However, in football, just as you think you've got it worked out, fate can take a hand, for better or worse. In my case it was definitely for the worse. In training on the day before the West Germany game I was marking a promising young winger called John Barnes. I attempted to tackle him, landed badly and dislocated my knee. I was out for four months. After I recovered and made it back for my club, it took me a further year to get back into the England team. During my absence, qualification for the 84 Euros went badly and we didn't make it to the tournament in France. Today that would not be tolerated, as Steve McClaren discovered to his cost when he failed in his attempts to qualify for the 2008 tournament.

But after the disaster of the 1984 Euro-qualifiers, Bobby Robson kept his job, despite mutterings in the press. The FA was more tolerant of failure back then. I was fit again and back in favour under the new man. Going into the Mexico World Cup of 1986 I really thought my time had come. I had put the disappointment of Spain behind me and played regularly throughout the qualifying competition. We won our group with something to spare and as is often the case when England are about to enter a big tournament, the nation's expectations were high and the team was performing well. It didn't turn out as we would have liked, both for me and the team.

I saw Mexico as an opportunity to put matters right after the experience of Spain. I was also desperate to put my injury behind me. However, exactly the same thing happened in Mexico as in Spain. This time it was Everton's Gary Stevens who became a fixture in what I thought should have been my position. I might be bigging myself up here but I think I could have made a good fist of stopping Maradona when he went on that mazy run through the England defence for Argentina's second goal in the quarter-final. Well! Maybe!

I stopped George Best once and he was the closest thing to Maradona this country has ever seen. In the seventies I was a youngster at Forest when we went to Craven Cottage to play a resurgent Fulham, who boasted the combined talents of Best, Bobby Moore and Rodney Marsh in their team. I've got to admit that as the game drew closer I got more and more nervous. I have never been one to suffer with nerves, either before or since, but the thought of facing the legendary Best was getting to me. He may have been at the fag-end of his career but he was still the man. He was the player most people regarded then and still believe now to be the best footballer the British Isles has ever produced.

By the time we went onto the pitch I was a nervous wreck. I just didn't want George to make a fool of me like he had so many full-backs all round the world. That was what was in my mind. "Don't let him make a fool of you ... . Don't let him make a fool of you." I kept repeating the phrase to myself. For just about the only time in my whole career, the old red mist came down. When, as half-time approached, Besty received the ball at his feet I steamed in. I creamed him. He almost went into orbit. When he landed he gave me a rueful smile but to his credit he got up and got on with the game. He didn't trouble us too much for the rest of the match, though, and eventually had to limp off the pitch. I almost felt guilty.

There was no doubt it was a bad tackle. As a defender you always want to be hard but fair. But at the same time you do everything you can to make sure the winger doesn't get past you. You might try to send him outside or force him to go inside, depending on how good he is with his left or right foot. Or the manager's tactics might dictate which way you tried to shuffle your winger. With George (and Maradona) it didn't matter, he had a hundred ways of going past you and was equally good with both feet. He could also ride a tackle better than anyone I have played against. I suppose my extreme youth is my excuse for mullering him. In subsequent years I tried to stop the opposition in a more stylish fashion. But the fact is, as everyone knows, there are bad tackles in football, plenty of them, and I'll describe one or two more during the course of this book. That one of mine against Best stands out, though, as the crudest chop I ever meted out. But back to Mexico 86. In that one run, Maradona made a fool of virtually the whole England team. Someone should have creamed him like I did Besty.

There were many excellent full backs around during the time I played. Initially, there was Phil Neal, Mick Mills and myself competing for one place in the national side. Later we were joined by Gary Stevens, a good defender in a very good Everton team, and others, including Mike Duxbury from Manchester United. I thrived on this sort of competition. I thought I could more than hold my own. But I suppose it didn't help my cause that by the time the World Cup came round I was experiencing turmoil at my club. I had been playing for Arsenal for two seasons, having been transferred from Forest in the summer of 1984. Arsenal had not done as well as expected under Don Howe and a new manager was liable to be appointed in the summer of the Mexico World Cup. We were a club in transition and had won nothing, which did little to advance my case with England.

Just as my thoughts were turning to Mexico, Arsenal were parting company with Don Howe and installing George Graham in his place. Graham had been making a name for himself as manager of Millwall but we didn't know much about his managerial style beyond that. Although Arsenal had not made much of an impact in the League under Don Howe, I felt sure my perform-ances over the season had been good enough for me to get the nod for England. Also, I had been selected for our two warm-up games and felt I had played really well. But no, when we got to Mexico, Robson decided to go with Stevens. Surely this couldn't be happening again. I was gutted. I went back to my hotel room and took it out on my room-mate, Terry Butcher. Normally, I roomed with Bryan Robson but in Mexico I was teamed up with Terry. He took the brunt of my outburst.

I railed against the manager to Butch, telling him that Robson was "fucking useless" and "didn't know what he was doing." I didn't really believe this, of course, but players just can't help reacting badly when things like that occur. It's part of the competitive instinct. Butch – who was the first choice centre-half and therefore always in the team – told me to "get over it and go to sleep." It was probably the best advice I could have got. The experience produced an odd combination of emotions. I was pleased for Butch that he was in the team, yet annoyed and despondent because I wasn't. I felt the determination to compete and win back my place and I wanted to help the team win. It's the strangest feeling.

Like Greenwood, Robson said nothing to me about the reasons I was left out. He just muttered "this is the team." Any bad feeling this kind of thing might bring about is stopped in its tracks because, at the end of the day, all players are in it together. And nothing is more important than the England team doing well. So you are saved from your self-pity by the camaraderie and the desire for the team to win.

Unlike Spain, England's start in Mexico was disastrous – a 1–0 loss to Portugal and a terrible 0–0 draw against Morocco, when Bryan Robson injured his shoulder (it was an injury he had sustained previously) and Ray Wilkins was sent off. I thought there might be wholesale changes to the team to face Poland in a must-win last game. Well, there certainly were changes, but not at right-back. In defence, the only player to come in was

Alvin Martin for Terry Fenwick. Most of the changes were in midfield and up front, two of them enforced because of Robbo's injury and Butch Wilkins's sending off.

Before the Poland encounter some of the senior players, particularly Peter Shilton and Peter Reid, argued for a change of formation. Until then we had been playing four in the middle of the park but it wasn't working and we were often overrun. Bobby Robson listened and a general discussion took place involving the whole squad and the management. Eventually, Robson agreed that we needed a change. So half-way through the tournament the manager altered his team and his tactics. It didn't make any difference to my situation. For me, there was still no place in the starting line-up.

No-one was more overjoyed than me that England notched up a brilliant win against Poland courtesy of a Gary Lineker hat-trick, but I realised it meant I was now unlikely to be considered for the rest of the tournament. And so it proved. I still say that if I had been on the pitch against Argentina I would at least have anticipated and come across when Maradona went on his run for the second goal. If I had been there ... who knows. As it was, England failed to reach the country's expectations and couldn't get beyond the quarter-final.

Although Maradona's second goal was brilliant by any standard, I got a good view of the so-called "Hand of God" goal. I wasn't even on the subs' bench so I was positioned in a different part of the stadium, right on top of the area where Maradona was operating when he handled the ball. It was just on the edge of our penalty box. I don't think I've ever seen anything so blatant on a football field as Maradona's cheating that day. How none of the officials saw it is beyond belief. To this day most of us, players and fans alike, believe that had it not been for that terrible mistake by the referee and his assistants, we could have beaten Argentina and progressed to the semi-final. But then football is often a case of what might have been.

If I was upset when I didn't get a game in Spain, I was totally traumatised by my experience in Mexico. At first I thought my time was up with England. Although it's always an honour for any footballer to play for his country I kind of lost faith in the whole thing after that. However, a footballer cannot harbour those types of thoughts for too long. Football is always about the next game, not the last. So I moved on and decided to knuckle down and try to win back my place. In England's first game post-Mexico, I came in for the injured Gary Stevens in a 1–0 defeat to Sweden. Despite the loss I felt I had put in a good display. Once again I was proud when both the press and the manager singled me out for praise. Robson said I was "the one real plus" and described my performance as "terrific". Maybe I was back.

But football being football, nothing is that simple. I made a dream move to Manchester United in the summer of 1987 (I loved my time at Arsenal and I can honestly say there was no other club I would have joined except United). But I picked up an Achilles injury early on and struggled for most of my first and second seasons. The injury just wouldn't heal properly and I played many times when I probably shouldn't have. Despite the injury, in that last stage of my England career I went on to gain another nine caps. I was playing well enough to be first choice once again during the qualifying stage for the 1988 European Championships in Germany. I had done more than enough to be selected in the squad. This time, though, I realised I wasn't really fit enough for tournament football. I didn't think my heel had recovered enough to stand up to three matches in the first week. However, Bobby Robson said he wanted me in the squad anyway, even if I could only make a limited contribution. Being someone who has always been ready to answer my country's call, I agreed to Robson's request and once again packed my bags for a major tournament. But yet again I didn't make an appearance, although this time I wasn't too displeased. In the event, England crashed out in the first round, losing every game, including the first match against Jack Charlton's Republic of Ireland. In my whole career as an England international, the only tournament fixture I actually played in was that final group game of the 1980 Euro competition in Italy, after we were eliminated.

I was with Sir Bobby Robson for his first six years of international management. He was a lovely man and he knew how to fill you with his enthusiasm. It is well known that he mangled the English language from time to time, particularly when it came to people's names. He used to call Mark Hately "Tony." Mark would reply, "that's my dad," but it didn't seem to make any difference. Once he was reading out the team. "Bluther's number nine," he said. "Who the fuck's Bluther?" someone asked from the back. It turned out he meant Luther Blissett. I've left the best one till last. I was chatting to the Newcastle player Shola Ameobi not long after Robson became manager. "How's everything going with Bobby?" I asked him. "Great," came Shola's reply. "Except that he thinks I'm Carl Cort."

Before our first game in Mexico, Robson organised a screening of a qualifying match that one of our opponents – Portugal – had won. They were playing Turkey. After about 40 minutes watching Portugal destroy the Turks, Robson opened the curtains and said "Those Turkey's are chickens." He didn't mean it as a joke, of course, but the whole room collapsed in laughter.

Following Euro 88, it was time to retire from international football. I had never been one to suffer too many injuries and was not what you'd call injury-prone. But during my time at Old Trafford I seemed to suffer injury after injury and my heel continued to be a problem. This turn of events certainly impacted on my international career. It was also the case that by then my knees were taking longer to recover. It was time to recognise that World Cups were a thing of the past. But my contribution to England's World Cup history is unique. I went to two consecutive tournaments and didn't play for one single minute. If you include the Euros, I went to four tournaments and played one game. Still, nothing, let me tell you, feels like playing for your country.

There would be plenty more amazing experiences for me in football before I hung up my boots. Before I tell you about some of those, however, I would like to say a thing or two about how I got there in the first place.

Chapter Three

IN THE BEGINNING

My Dad, Audley Anderson, arrived in the UK from Jamaica in 1954. He was part of the first big wave of immigration to this country from the Caribbean. How the people who came to these shores in those days had the courage to leave everything behind and travel halfway round the world in search of a better life is something for which I have the greatest respect and admiration. Dad, for some reason I still don't fully understand, decided not to follow most immigrants from the West Indies to Notting Hill, Brixton or towns where there was an established Jamaican population. Instead, he made his way to Nottingham, where he was one of the first arrivals in the city from that part of the world. It must have been unbelievably hard for him but to this day I have never heard him complain. Not once.

Before long, he managed to secure a job as a porter at a local hospital in Nottingham. He was on his way. My mother, Myrtle, arrived from Jamaica a few months later to join him. She was a nurse and, like a number of her compatriots, a mainstay of the National Health Service for decades to come. The NHS might well have collapsed without their contribution. While Dad was quite philosophical about the different life here, Mam was intensely homesick. She had been used to land and space in Jamaica, as well as fine weather. In England she had to make the best of life in cold, cramped accommodation in the city. And what was worse for her was that – in the days before regular transatlantic calls, let alone mobile phones – she missed her friends and family terribly. Many were the nights she cried.

I arrived in this world in 1956. My brother Donald came two years later. I think, although I have never been told, that our births made our parents really happy and helped them become totally committed to their new homeland. Ours was a Christian family and for my brother and me, our early years were centred round the church, especially Sunday school. Although I never admitted it to my team-mates when I became a professional footballer, I was also something of a choirboy in my youth. It was, with some ups and downs, a great upbringing.

Perhaps the most difficult event I had to come to terms with in my childhood years was the serious illness which overtook Donald. I am not looking for sympathy here, not least because Donald was the one who really suffered. But I saw the pain on the faces of my mother and father, much as they tried to hide it. I had come down with a cold or the flu, which I recovered from quite easily. Donald then started to display similar symptoms. To this day I wonder if he caught it from me. But instead of getting better as I had done, Donald's condition got worse. My lovely younger brother's life was in the balance. He had, in fact, contracted a condition that was the scourge of Britain in the 1950s and 60s, Poliomyelitis. Now, polio was a killer until a vaccination was invented. Donald was lucky to be alive but was extremely unlucky to be left disabled. I don't know how I would have coped with that. Yet Donald has always remained an optimist, an outlook on life which I think I gained from him. Not only that, he refused to go into his shell like many would have done. To this day he has asserted his independence. Maybe he could have been a sportsman too. As it was, through no fault of his own, he was denied the possibility of finding out.

Perhaps it was this experience which later led me to question many of the certainties with which I was brought up. I'm no expert but I asked myself time and again over the years how this could happen. How could Donald to be so struck down? I don't know what I think or believe today to be honest, but the memories can haunt me still. It was such a cruel suffering to be inflicted on both Donald and my parents.

I was always more interested in sport than anything else. If my parents had stayed in the Caribbean, maybe I would have been a cricketer or a track and field athlete. Or maybe not! I've played other sports over the years and I have to say that football was made for me. I played for my school, for local clubs around Nottingham and when I wasn't playing matches or with my mates I was kicking a ball against the wall that occupied one side of our house. Although my mother made sure I worked at school, my heart wasn't really in it. I wanted to be a footballer, pure and simple. As a youngster I was a striker, scoring goals for fun. If you had told me then I would become a full-back I would have questioned your sanity. If you'd told me I would become a pro footballer, I'd have believed you totally.

For whatever reason – and I don't know to this day what it was – I turned away from my two local teams, Forest and County, and decided to support Manchester United. In those days United fielded the Best, Law and Charlton team and they captivated my imagination to the point that it overwhelmed any real interest in the Nottingham clubs. In those days most kids tended to support their home-town team. I was the odd one out being a United fan in Nottingham. I dreamed of playing for United, of course. But so did thousands of others. Little did I know it would become a reality for me before too long.

When I was fourteen or so the unimaginable happened. The family had gone to Bridlington for our summer holidays. One day I was playing football on my own on the beach. This bloke approached me and said he was a scout for Sheffield United (life was more innocent in those days). Was I interested, he said, in a trial at Bramall Lane? My parents didn't really want me to go, they thought I was too young and needed to pay more attention to schoolwork. And anyway a professional footballer lived a precarious and not very well-paid life. It wasn't what parents would want for their kids. But I had a desire to be a footballer, I think they knew that deep down. We eventually came to an agreement: if I did another year at school I could then go for the trial. I didn't like it but there was nothing I could do.

In the meantime, I played football whenever and wherever I could. I won trophies in schoolboy competitions and honed my skills against the wall while I tried to keep up in school. I wasn't bad at English but I had to work hard at most other subjects. Then, out of nowhere, Manchester – not Sheffield – United came knocking. One of their scouts saw me playing at a soccer camp and recommended me to Old Trafford. My parents made sure I went to these summer camps for kids, so you can see how they really did encourage me. I enjoyed the trips away and the games of football, around which everything was organised. I'm told there were always a few scouts from League clubs on the look-out for promising youngsters at the camps. Thrilled to have been singled out, I now had the chance to go to what I thought was the centre of the football universe, Manchester – and United's youth set-up. Even my parents were impressed and said I could go. It was there that they turned me into a proper footballer, and a defender at that.

I had a wonderful time in the year I spent at United. I loved it. I remember watching those great players train. I can see them now if I shut my eyes. They were an inspiration to the young guys. This was a dream come true. Every time I travelled up to Manchester from Nottingham I was full of anticipation. There was suddenly nothing I couldn't achieve. And when I stayed in Manchester, I lived with the parents of John Aston, the brilliant United winger. It was the experience of a lifetime. Many years later, Garry Birtles was transferred from Forest to Manchester United. At Forest he was on fire and scored bundles of goals, many against world-class defences, but for United he could hardly get a kick, let alone score a goal. I think part of his problem was that he was homesick. He didn't enjoy life in the big city. He loved getting back to Nottingham whenever he could to be with his old mates, playing snooker and going to pubs. Even at my young age, I never suffered that type of homesickness. I took in everything I could in Manchester, both at the club and in the city.

But when I reached sixteen, the powers at United decided I was not good enough to be offered a contract and they let me go. I don't know who made the actual decision or why. Maybe I hadn't asserted myself enough. I certainly didn't feel that I was way behind the other kids in footballing ability. I was as good as any of them. But with that decision going against me I felt all my dreams of being a professional footballer were shattered. I wasn't told and therefore I didn't realise, that this was only one club, no matter how big. Nor did anyone point out that the majority of those in the youth set-up would eventually be let go. I simply believed I had no future in the game. I returned home to Nottingham with my tail between my legs. My mother was right. I should get a 'proper' job. My world had collapsed. I looked at what I might do for a while. For some reason I still can't fathom I decided to become an apprentice silk screen printer. That's what my life would be from now on. A solid trade! I would play football for fun.

Yet within six months I was offered a second chance, and this time I told myself to really go for it. Once again I was spotted by a scout, this time while I was playing amateur football in Nottingham. I was invited into the Forest youth programme. It was a lifeline that would shape my destiny. I made friends early on with another aspiring youngster, Tony Woodcock. Woody and I struck up an instant friendship which has lasted to this day. I'm certain we helped each other achieve the success that came our way. Along with Kevin Keegan, Woody was one of the first English players of the modern era to ply his trade in Europe. Like Keegan, Woody went to Germany. He learned the language and immersed himself in German culture. When he later played in the same Arsenal side as me and whenever he turned out for England he brought all that to his game. In my opinion should have won many more caps than he eventually did. He scored his fair share of goals at all levels but probably not quite enough to become England's long-term centre-forward. But he was a fantastic footballer with great vision.

I had been long-time childhood friends with a couple of other kids in the youth scheme at Forest. There was goalkeeper, Peter Wells and defender, Glyn Saunders. We all lived on the same council estate in Clifton and played for the same school team. They went to Forest before me and tipped me the wink about how I should behave. I was the new kid on the block and they helped pave the way for me. Peter, Glynn, Woody and me all became apprentices together.

The trouble for all of us was that in the early seventies Forest were going nowhere. They were a run-of-the-mill second division side which had known better days. The first team showed no signs of being able to challenge for promotion back to the top flight under the manager, Matt Gillies. It seemed the committee members who ruled the club at the time were content with mediocrity. Gillies soon departed, to be replaced by the legendary Dave Mackay, who, after a great career as a player, was making his way in management. Mackay only lasted a year, however, during which time the club drifted further into obscurity. Allan Brown took over from Mackay and initially the team picked up. But it was soon facing a dogfight against relegation once more.

This period for me, however, was the end of the rainbow, the possibility once again of realising my dream. No, no, no! I was a silk screen printer, I was bound, surely, for a life in that solid trade. But gradually I progressed through the ranks alongside Woody, until I ended up in the reserves. I still have a copy of the written invitation which tells me I was selected for the Forest "A" team to play Coventry "A". At last I had a chance. This was it. Do or die!

I must have done something right because I soon came to attention of the manager. He brought me, along with Woody, into the senior set-up. I made my debut for the Nottingham Forest first team in August 1974, in a pre-season friendly at Walsall. The 1–1 draw was played out in front of only 1700 spectators. I didn't think I performed particularly well but then neither did anyone that day. Martin O'Neill was in the team and Tony Woodcock was a substitute. It may not sound much but to me it could have been a Wembley Cup Final. The feeling was electric. I realised at that moment that I was in my element, this was what I was here for.

I didn't make my full League debut for another six weeks. During that period the team made a poor start to the season, winning just twice in our first nine games. We drew a fair number, including a 2–2 at Old Trafford in front of 40,000 people. Manchester United had suffered the unthinkable the previous season when they were relegated from Division One. It had shocked their fans and the nation to the core. They were still drawing huge crowds to Old Trafford, though, and would eventually run away with Division Two to make an immediate return to the top flight. My turn came in the tenth game of the campaign. It was an away match at Sheffield Wednesday which we won 3–2. Wednesday was a club I would come to love many years later when I was part of Ron Atkinson's and Trevor Francis's successful spells in charge. I kept my place for the next three matches but they brought two defeats – against Newcastle and Aston Villa – and a 1–1 draw with Sunderland. It was no wonder I was dropped and Liam O'Kane made it back into the team in my position.

No matter what I said about my feelings when I was left out of various England teams, actually, being dropped is experienced at some point by 99% of footballers. You have to work out a way of dealing with it and come back stronger. I have since found out, of course, that young players often lack the consistency to maintain a high level of performance week in, week out. I probably fell into that category.

But sometimes poor management or coaching plays its part. Whatever combination the manager, by then Allan Brown, sent out, the team just couldn't put any kind of run together and the relegation places were staring us in the face. The low point came in a massive Christmas game played at the City Ground against our neighbours by the Trent, Notts County. Now Forest fans don't even consider matches against County to be proper derbies, since County are supposed to be far inferior to Forest. Our derbies are against Derby or Leicester, not County. But as the end of 1974 beckoned County came to our place ahead of us in the division. In front of a 20,000 crowd, in a complete debacle of a game, they beat us 2–0. It proved to be Allan Brown's last match in charge. It could have been far worse. We were lucky to get nil. I didn't play in the match but I shared the terrible feelings with the rest of the squad. The result was too much even for the Forest committee to bear and they were forced to act. Brown was sacked before the New Year and a new manager installed. That manager was, of course, Brian Clough.

Clough arrived following his disastrous 44 days in charge of Leeds, a time made famous recently in the book and film, *The Damned United*. His exploits at Derby, when he won the League and reached the semi-final of the European Cup were no more than a distant memory after the Leeds business. He was still a big name, though, the first Forest had employed for quite some time. We weren't too sure what to expect. Looking back, I can see that the pressure was actually on him. The Forest job was probably his last chance to really prove himself again. But at the time he appeared to be oozing with confidence and knowhow. If he ever had doubts about his ability to make us the best he never, ever showed it.

I can't quite remember if Clough was in place when we played in the third round of the FA Cup, at home against First Division Spurs. He certainly selected the team for the replay, which was necessary after we somehow managed to draw the first game 1–1. I had to come off with cramp. I couldn't train afterwards but was fit to play when the replay was due. I wasn't included in the squad that went to London. We won the game, incredibly, 1–0. I wondered if Clough thought I was any good as he had left me behind. I said to myself: "if the great man doesn't fancy me, I'll soon be on my way."

But we had beaten the mighty Spurs. At that moment, the legend that was Clough was up and running again. He showed no bias against me in training, even encouraging me from time to time, so I began to believe I had a future. And if someone with such a massive name as Brian Clough thought so, it must be true. It took another six weeks before the boss decided I was ready for an extended run in the side. However, from the end of February I was more or less a fixture in the team. At last I was a real footballer.

We managed to pull ourselves clear of the threat of relegation and finished 16th in the table, two places behind County. Manchester United won the division at the first time of asking, nine points ahead of the second placed team, Aston Villa. Norwich City secured the third automatic promotion spot (there were no play-offs then).

For the new season, the manager brought in two players who had been with him at Derby and Leeds, John McGovern and John O'Hare. His plan, he told us, was to put his faith in youngsters like myself and Tony Woodcock, and ally us to the experience of McGovern and O'Hare. Both of the old boys relished the new challenge Clough presented to them. For us, they knew exactly how Clough worked, what he wanted from players and they could pass all that information on. For Clough, his old boys would reinforce his beliefs to the younger generation while he hollered at all and sundry from the sidelines.

That next season was one of consolidation. Clough stabilised the team and we finished a creditable but unspectacular eighth. It was far better than the threat of relegation, though. Sunderland were top, with Bristol City and West Bromwich Albion filling the other promotion positions. That season was noticeable for the emergence of John Robertson on the left wing. John Robbo had been in and out of the side in midfield before Clough came. I think even he would admit that he was overweight and his game was going nowhere. But the manager saw something no-one else had seen and converted John to a wide man. He became a classic winger, not of the type that goes past defenders with speed. John Robbo could shift the ball a yard to create space behind the full-back. He would then put in a succession of pin-point crosses. Near post, far post, you name it, he did it. At the same time Clough got on Robbo's case to lose weight and get fit, which, to his credit, he did.

Also coming into his own was Martin O'Neill, who operated along the right in front of me. Martin always claimed that the work he put in up and down the line made me the player I was. It is a feature of Martin that he can make ironic, tongue-in-cheek comments which are both humorous and wrong but contain a tiny bit of truth. It doesn't surprise me that Martin has become such a spectacularly good manager. Mind you, Clough used to really get on his case sometimes, telling him he didn't like him because he had a law degree and he was Irish. In truth I was lucky to have someone like

Martin playing in front of me. But equally, he was lucky to have someone like me playing behind him. Martin is a lovely man. In later years, both he and his wife, Geraldine, were very kind to me at a very difficult time.

During that first full term under Clough I played for the first half of the season but lost my place to Colin Barratt for the second. As I said before, I think I was an example of how young players often struggle to maintain their form in their first and second seasons. But back then I was inconsolable. I told myself it was temporary but I could see the Manchester United experience repeating itself. By now I had thoroughly joined the world of the professional footballer. I did not want to go back to being a silk screen printer. The only way out was to do enough to convince the great Brian Clough that I was worth a place in his team. I wanted to be crucial to his plans. I was not going to be a printer ... I was not going to be a printer.

The defining season for the players and the club was not when we won the League. It wasn't even when we won the European Cup. No! What decided all our futures was the season we won promotion to the First Division. The seventies! For me, the year 1976–77 was the year of all years. It was the year that made everything else possible.

First, and most important, I was back in contention for the team. I must have done something right in pre-season. Again though, it was some time before I really nailed down my place. Clough insisted that pre-season was about getting the players fit and ready to accept his every word and decision without question. It was psychological moulding as much as it was about getting fit for football. Once he made us run through stinging nettles. We did it without question. After pre-season, Clough didn't believe in anything other than light training and five-a-sides. With lots of walks. And some drinking. And some trips to Mallorca. He never paid much attention to the opposition. We went into the season ready.

And yet it came so close to going wrong. We were there or thereabouts for most of the campaign but we were not playing well enough be sure of our place in the promotion mix. No-one was tipping us to go up, that was for sure. We had some good results but had setbacks too. However, changes were taking place which later made promotion seem inevitable. Of course nothing in football is inevitable, it just seems like that now. Clough was increasing his influence in all areas. But perhaps the most important of these changes was the arrival of Peter Taylor as Clough's assistant.

Taylor had been Clough's right-hand man at Derby but had stayed at Brighton when Clough went to Leeds. Now the great duo were reunited. Taylor brought an immediate contrast to the boss. Where Clough was aloof, Taylor was your friend. And Taylor, it was reputed, could spot a player like no other. He drafted in three who would make a huge difference to our prospects. First there was the uncompromising centre-forward, Peter Withe, who grabbed sixteen goals that season; then there was Larry Lloyd, who was massive at the centre of the defence; finally, there was the surprising figure of Frank Clark, the grizzled pro deemed too old by Newcastle but who graced the City Ground for the next four seasons. Frank was never happier than when he spent time telling us youngsters a hundred stories from his hundred years in the game.

So although we didn't take the division by storm, we were now a team to be reckoned with, we thought. As the season came to its business end we began to get more consistent. We scraped into third place, behind Wolves and Chelsea. That was enough for promotion. We finished one point in front of both Bolton and Blackpool, both of whom missed out. For us, it was a massive achievement. No-one had thought we were promotion material. But the momentum was ours and it was to stay that way for many a year. I didn't get a game until the middle of October, when I scored in a 6–1 rout of Sheffield United. I had actually scored a goal. In the professional game! I was walking on air. I began to feel times were changing.

And even better, after that October victory over Sheffield United, I stayed in the team for the rest of that momentous season. Of our last four games, we won three, while the other was drawn. Most of our goals in the run-in were supplied by Woody, Martin and Peter Withe. We could at last feel we were going places. Never in our wildest dreams could we have known exactly how far we would get. The stage was set. We didn't know it yet but we were about to tear up the script of football and write our own. It wouldn't have made it past the first editor if it was fiction. It was too ridiculous.

Chapter Four

YEARS OF BLISS

No-one: not the media, not the Forest fans, not the players, thought that we would or could win anything in our first season back in Division One. The only exception to this opinion was Brian Clough, who told us we were winners. Mind you, he said it through his schoolboy smile.

There were some new arrivals in the dressing room, both in the close season and during the campaign itself. One of them was Peter Shilton in goal, who the manager described to anyone who would listen as the best keeper in the world. No-one was prepared to disagree with Clough's statement, but no-one had Shilts in the frame for a top club either. Clough said that Peter would win us points. This is what we wanted to hear. In training he would point to Shilton and say that he "frightened the life" out of opposing centre forwards. I think it is fair to say that Peter himself gained considerably from the manager's faith in him and his performances just got better and better. At last he began to fulfil the potential he had showed when he first broke into the Leicester side as a sixteen-year-old (at the expense of Gordon Banks). To me, that was entirely due to Brian

Clough's influence and Peter's recognition that he at last had someone to believe in him, not just as a goal-keeper but as a person.

Archie Gemmill also arrived to add some bite to the midfield. But perhaps the most surprising acqui-sition was the Bad Boy of Birmingham, Kenny Burns. Burns started out as a forward but was converted into a centre half. His fiery Scottish temperament got him into all sorts of trouble on the pitch. His stock in trade was getting sent off. All told, he had been dismissed seven or eight times in his career. Somehow, Clough and Taylor believed, they could keep the best of Kenny, who was a very good defender, and eliminate the worst, his habit of violently assaulting opponents. Virtually the whole of the football world thought Clough had lost it when he signed Kenny. Once again, the manager had not only brought someone to the club who could play, he also knew how he could garner massive publicity at the same time. Clough and controversy walked hand in hand. He loved it. I was still a young lad, I didn't appreciate many of these things at the time, understanding only came with experience, both of football and of life. Then, I just wanted to please the manager and keep my place in the team.

For our return to the top flight, our pre-season went well. We were undefeated on a tour of Germany. Our first game in the League was a real test, however, away to Everton, who would finish the season in third place. They were a good side who would get better and better over the next ten years. The match at Goodison Park, in front of over 38,000 fans, went better than we could have dreamed. We won 3-1 with goals from Peter Withe, Martin O'Neill and John Robertson. We were off and running.

The high that everyone felt after that beginning was just unbelievable. In some ways it defined our whole season. John Robbo and Martin were a revelation. Football reporters everywhere gave them rave reviews. The triumph over Everton was followed up with three straight wins, including a 5-0 thrashing of West Ham in the League Cup. To say we were on a roll would be an understatement. We were flying. So were Clough and Taylor and that made them even better at what they did.

As summer turned to autumn we kept up with the pack. Liverpool, the country's leading club by far in the seventies and eighties, were up there, as they always were. Bill Shankly and Bob Paisley had created a giant out of nothing. What we at Forest got annoyed by, though, was that Liverpool had become a machine which was expected to win all the big match-ups as if it were their right. Clough didn't like that. Everton and Manchester City posed a threat and Arsenal were showing signs of resurgence. But no-one looked any further than the Scousers for the eventual title winners.

In what was by any measure a most remarkable season, perhaps the match that really made us believe we could topple Liverpool came just before Christmas when we went to Old Trafford to face Manchester United. Going back to the club that had rejected me just a few years earlier was emotional for me. I had missed the game in Manchester when we met in the second division. Stepping out at the Theatre of Dreams was certainly a dream to me. A dream come true. I was now firmly established as the number one right-back in Clough's scheme of things.

What was totally unexpected was that by the time we visited Old Trafford, Forest were top of the table. We had already beaten United at the City Ground. But what was about to unfold was something really special. We produced our best display of the season, filmed by the *Match of the Day* cameras, and ran out 4–0 winners. Now, even though United were not the force they had been previously or would become again, it was still an incredible result and from there, we never looked back. To beat them in their own lair was one thing, to win by four goals was unprecedented.

Confidence just flooded through the team after that. It came in the middle of a period when the manager could do no wrong. The result at Old Trafford only served to magnify the mystique of Brian Clough and what he could drive his side to achieve.

Kenny Burns was a sensation, curbing his excesses and becoming an extremely accomplished defender, indispensible even. He didn't get sent off once. The press couldn't believe the transformation that took place before their very eyes. The Clough magic was working again. Looking back I can see that with every game, the ghost of Clough's disastrous time at Leeds was receding. Even his exploits with Derby might be bettered. Nottingham Forest was the project of his life. This was his – and therefore our – destiny.

After a 1–0 defeat to Leeds in November, we didn't lose another match all season and the title was ours. To write that now hardly conveys the immensity of our achievement. That season has been talked and written about ever since. It is the stuff of fantasy that in these days of the Premier League and its riches seems about as real as Harry Potter. I don't think anything like our League campaign that year could happen again. The game has changed so much. A provincial side storming to the title the season after promotion – you couldn't make it up. Forest weren't the only team to do it in that era. I must give respect to a club that paved the way over fifteen years before. In the early sixties, Ipswich Town managed the same feat. Having said in an earlier chapter that Ipswich didn't reach the heights of Forest, I am happy to give their earlier side the credit they are due. That team was managed by Alf Ramsey and it was enough to make him the only candidate for the England job when it came up. Ramsey, of course, went on to win the World Cup. Shouldn't Brian Clough have been similarly rewarded for his Herculean effort? I think so. Anyone who can achieve such success from such modest beginnings – and only Ramsey and Clough have done it in the modern era, although Bill Shankly came close – is an obvious candidate for higher things. Ramsey won the

World Cup, something no other England manager has come close to. I think Clough would have done the same. It is to the eternal shame of the FA that they snubbed Clough and I believe it set the England cause back for more than a generation.

Even though our League campaign that season was immense, I think you can see what the team was all about by looking at our Cup runs. Clough and Taylor wanted to win every match, there was no let up. In the FA Cup we beat Swindon, Manchester City and Queens Park Rangers (in a second replay). We went out of the competition in the sixth round with our worst display of the season, losing to West Brom 2–0. The Ipswich side of Bobby Robson won the trophy when they beat Arsenal in the final.

For all our success over the next few years, the FA Cup always eluded us. Funnily enough, the FA Cup was the one trophy Brian Clough couldn't win, either as a player or manager. In the last years of his time in football and long after our great team had broken up, Clough finally got a Forest team to the final – the 1991 showpiece against Spurs. But somehow the gods were against him in the FA Cup. The match was bizarre, with Gazza's reckless tackle early doors which put him out of the game. Stuart Pearce gave Forest the lead with an incredible free-kick. But we somehow contrived to lose 2–1, with Spurs' winning goal coming from Des Walker's head. In all the years I was with Forest – and for years after I left – the FA Cup was always just beyond our reach.

If we floundered in the FA Cup, we more than made up for it in the League Cup. It was our run to the final of this competition that sealed our growing reputation. In our amazing story, this was the first trophy the team won. The success set us up for the rest of the season. And it taught us to win. These days, the League Cup is often devalued by the top clubs, except for Jose Mourinho when he was in charge of Chelsea. Mourinho decided that it was important for his side to win a trophy as soon as possible and it is no coincidence that in his first season in the Premier League his Chelsea side won the League Cup. It set them up for the league title, as it did us twenty-five years earlier. It seems strange to me that more managers don't seem to understand the importance of trying to win the League Cup. Bryan Robson and I gave it a good go in the nineties with Middlesbrough. The only modern top division manager I know who really takes it seriously is Martin O'Neill, who won the competition twice as manager of Leicester. And where was it that he learned of its importance?

We overcame West Ham, Notts County, Aston Villa, Bury and Leeds on our way to Wembley. Our opponents, Liverpool, were hot favourites, as they always were in those days. No-one could beat them, let alone the upstarts of Nottingham Forest. But we snuffed them out and took them to a replay. The second game was as tight as they come. A John Robertson penalty, which, to be honest, was a bit dubious, won it. Liverpool beaten! Yes!

In the first game our star performer was our goal-keeper: not Peter Shilton, but the young Chris Woods, who was playing because Shilton was cup-tied. Brian Clough made Woods feel as if he were second only to Shilts in the world, not just Nottingham Forest. I have to say, if Chris felt any nerves going out at Wembley he didn't show it. Shilts helped gee him up before the game, while Clough just kept telling him that if he were in any other team he would be first choice. Chris's performance guaranteed us the replay. The replay was ours. We now knew how to win.

We were unstoppable. Clough was in his element. He was, once again, the talk of the nation. We won the League before April was out, with an anticlimactic 0-0 draw at Coventry. Technically, Liverpool could have caught us if they won a game in hand due to be played on the Monday. We had a midweek game against Ipswich on Tuesday. But Liverpool failed to win and Nottingham Forest were League Champions. We spent the next few hours celebrating like it was 1999. Needless to say, there was very little in the way of training for the Ipswich game (which we won 2-0). In the event, we ended up seven points clear of Liverpool, which in the days of two points for a win was an immense gap. It was an achievement of the most incredible proportions. Brian Clough was God.

We had done the impossible. Throughout that season, our exploits were marvelled at. Woody and I were just on cloud nine. We thought football would always be like this. Woody scored 27 goals. What a return that was. It was an unbelievable season for him. He was without doubt the top English goalscorer. Our other striker, Peter Withe, scored 20 goals and his partnership with Woody was the most potent in the country. Brian Clough, of course, was worshipped. The media could not get enough of him. His estimation of his own worth, high enough previously, went through the roof. Trips to Mallorca were planned.

However much praise was heaped upon our achievements, it was still Liverpool that the country looked to as the best team in the English game. While we triumphed in the League and the League Cup, Liverpool somehow managed to retain the European Cup they first won in 1977. I think it was someone called Dalglish who got the winner. Looking ahead to the next season, few pundits could see beyond Liverpool to find the likely European Champions. Yet again, we were the upstarts who would soon be 'found out' and put in our place. And the reason for that view was that Forest had no tradition in Europe and because few people realised how desperately Brian Clough wanted to win European Cup.

On the eve of the following season – 1978-9 – Clough called us together. We were going to retain the League title, he said. We would win both domestic cups and move heaven and earth to win the European Cup. Provided, of course, we listened to no-one else but him. It was him who had brought us to this place and it would be him who would take us to even greater deeds. Once again he mesmerised us. It was like a religion, with us players as the apostles and the fans as the followers. I was brought up in the church. Brian Clough was like the fiery preacher. When he spoke, we listened.

Our statement of intent came in the Charity Shield at Wembley against the Cup winners, Ipswich. Bobby Robson's team had out-thought and out-fought Arsenal in winning the Cup 1–0. In the Charity Shield we swotted them aside, beating them 5–0. Martin O'Neill grabbed two goals, while John Robbo, Larry Lloyd and Peter Withe scored one each. In the space of a year, we had gone from second division nobodies to the only side in the land that could really challenge Liverpool. Clough told us we shouldn't worry about any other team. We were going to make history.

After that, surprisingly, Peter Withe only played in the first League game before he was shipped out. He was replaced in the beginning by local boy Garry Birtles. Before long Garry and Woody were joined by the country's first player to command a transfer fee of one million pounds, Trevor Francis. Clough caused another sensation when he announced that he had paid the massive fee. We were a bit put out when Withey left. He not only notched up goals, he was a great player to be around as he took on the burden of roughing up opposing defences and making space for everyone else. But Birtles and Woodcock were altogether more refined and began to forge another great partnership. Garry ended the season our top scorer. Trevor Francis, however, was on another plane. He was not only naturally gifted, he also scored goals at the most important moments.

Despite Clough's predictions, there would be no repeat League title that season. The crown went back to .... damn it .... Liverpool. We finished a distant second, eight points adrift, with West Bromwich Albion third. Nevertheless, it was a superb campaign in many ways, consolidating our position and ensuring we weren't one season wonders. We notched up notable wins, especially in the two games against Chelsea in March, which we won 6–1 and 3–1. It is difficult to conceive today, but that season Chelsea finished bottom, fourteen points from safety. I managed to score four goals that year, the best return of my career so far. Clough wasn't always pleased when I scored. "Good goal young Mr. Anderson", he would say. "But it's defending I pay you for." It wasn't that I didn't have a licence to get forward. I like to think I was one of the first English full-backs to make driving runs into the opposition's half. I tried to model that part of my game on Terry Cooper, the left-back of the great Leeds team of Don Revie and the brilliant Celtic full-back, Danny McGrain. I think the manager didn't want me to get ahead of myself. He wanted to remind me of what my primary duty was: to stop the opposing winger.

Once again, the FA Cup proved a step too far. At first we looked good, with convincing victories in the third and fourth rounds, against Aston Villa and York City. We were well set up for our fifth round tie at home to

Arsenal. But the Gunners stifled the life out of us and knocked us out 1–0. They did to us what we had done to Liverpool in the League Cup Final.

It was in the League Cup that we again showed our mettle. We won it. Again! Now no-one could dismiss us as a flash in the pan. Our best win in terms of performance in that season's competition came at Goodison Park, against Everton in the fourth round. As usual, the manager refused to let us train too much before the game. Not only that, he never said anything at all, except that we had to go for a walk along the banks of the River Mersey. Still, we won 3–2. We defeated Southampton in the final by the same score. Again, training before the game was banned. Garry Birtles loved this non-training stuff; he scored two in the final with the other coming from Woody.

We returned to Nottingham as heroes. It was nothing compared to what we were about to achieve. We would soon be bigger in Nottingham than Robin Hood.

Yes, we might have been tearing up the domestic script but, so went the accepted wisdom, we did not have the resources to make waves in the European Cup. British teams had suffered in Europe over the years and in the major competition, the European Cup, it was only in the last two years that Britain had punched its weight. I remember the great, great Celtic team. I was a young football fanatic when they became the first British side to win the Cup in 1967. Manchester United had also won it with the great side of 68 but for nine years after that the country floundered in the major European competition. Until Liverpool, with Kevin Keegan rampant, destroyed Hamburg in 1977 and retained the Cup the following year with a 1-0 win in the final against Bruges. But that was because they were Liverpool. Wasn't it? There was no club like Liverpool, the way they did things, the continual record of success, even when managers departed. Shankly to Paisley, it made no difference. If anything, Liverpool got better. As Manchester United discovered when Matt Busby left Old Trafford, maintaining success is no easy task when an icon departs. Not at Liverpool. Liverpool, Liverpool, Liverpool!

It was a simple equation. Only a country's champions played in the European Cup plus the holders. There was no seeding, no groups, just straight knockout ties played over home and away legs. You could draw anyone from the first round on. We, of course, drew Liverpool. From the moment that improbable draw took place the players, like the fans, couldn't help but talk about it. I remember Peter Shilton saying he thought we would win it but most of us were somewhat apprehensive. We might have beaten Liverpool to the title and in the League Cup Final but this was Europe, where they reigned supreme and untroubled. We had not managed to beat them in League matches in our title-winning season, with both games ending in draws. If we read the press, it told us that Liverpool were overwhelming favourites. Strangely, Bob Paisley was one of the few who gave us a chance, saying Forest were the one club who could prevent Liverpool from emulating Bayern Munich and Ajax and win three European Cups in a row.

Brian Clough hardly mentioned Liverpool as the first leg at the City Ground approached. He did, however, let us know in no uncertain terms that he expected nothing less than for us to win the European Cup. If we listened to him, we would realise we were more than good enough to reach that objective. Peter Taylor told us how their Derby side had reached the semi-finals, only to be thwarted by poor refereeing and official corruption. There was, we realised, really good European experience in our management team. Just about the only thing that Clough had to say was that "Liverpool couldn't beat you in four matches last season. You beat them in a final (the League Cup). There is no way for them to win." In the absence of Peter Withe – and before the arrival of Trevor Francis – we were a bit light up front. That's when Clough pulled his masterstroke and threw Garry Birtles into the team. Birtles was a completely unknown player who was signed from Long Eaton. The first leg against the Scousers was only his second game in Forest colours. I remember seeing him with a grin from ear to ear when he realised he would be playing.

The tie against Liverpool has passed into folklore. It was Forest's first ever game in Europe, Liverpool's one hundredth. For one of the only times during Clough's reign, he dropped Martin O'Neill for the game. All of us were shocked. Martin had come to display all of the things that were the hallmark of Clough and Taylor at Forest: industrious, skilful and prepared to adapt his game to the boss's wishes. In his place was Archie Gemmill, on the face of it to hamper Liverpool's progress down our right side. I think it was one of the manager's eccentricities, designed first to throw us off-guard, then to bind us as a team in the belief that he could do no wrong. We were also pleased – and Clough knew this – that it was none of us that had been dropped.

Woody instigated the breakthrough. We were playing the ball on the left side of Liverpool's defence when he took the ball beyond the defenders in the inside-right channel. I watched as he put in a pass to Garry Birtles and Garry did the rest. 1–0. We were unimpressed by Liverpool's response. They didn't seem too bothered about going back to Anfield losing by a goal. It was a fatal mistake. It spurred us on. We talked to each other throughout the game and told ourselves that at this rate, we could get another and kill the tie stone dead. Sure enough, in the 87th minute, the most junior player on the field, the Long Eaton dead-eye, Garry Birtles, went past a couple of defenders. He found Woody, who headed the ball back across the goal for Colin Barrett, playing at left-back in place of Frank Clark, to conjure a volley and make it 2–0 on the night. That goal gave Liverpool a mountain to climb.

Fourteen days later we went to Anfield for the return. Clough had a way to prick the balloon of hype that often overcame away teams at Liverpool before the match even started. "You know that sign – the one you see when you run onto the pitch saying 'This is Anfield,'" he said. "Well, so fucking what."

Chapter Five

SLAYING DRAGONS

I f Manchester United were the Red Devils, Liverpool were the dragons, breathing fire and invincible on their own patch. English pretenders or European giants – it didn't matter – they all came to grief at Anfield. It needed someone like St. George to slay them. For St. George read Brian Clough. He sent us into the cauldron believing we were about to dispatch the European champions. Without that, even a 2–0 lead might not have been enough. That was the measure of how Liverpool unnerved their opponents. Ever since our victory at the City Ground, the press and television, both at home and across Europe, were forced to reassess their analysis of Forest. It was an upset to them, that's for sure. Still they couldn't see beyond Liverpool. To us, that win was one more fact to prove there was nothing we couldn't achieve. It was bred into us by the manager and reinforced by the results his methods were bringing. As long as we remained loyal and committed to his way of doing things, we thought we were invincible.

His way of doing things in the return game was unbelievable. First, he refused to let the bus leave the hotel until the last possible moment. His excuse was that he wanted the traffic to clear so we could have a "nice ride" to the ground. Then, once on board, he produced wine and beer and told us to get stuck in. It was only a friendly, he assured us. Clough was showing us that he would be the only one to decide when we were under pressure. Not the press; not the opposition; certainly not the Anfield hordes. Only Clough! This wasn't pressure, this was the European Cup.

The return match against Liverpool was a damp squib as we intended it to be. To be honest, we were happy for the game to stay at 0–0. If Liverpool scored one, it would only inflame the Kop and pass the advantage to the opposition. If we scored it might do the same thing. No! 0–0 was perfect.

I was involved in the game's two talking points. The one player we – and anyone else who faced Liverpool – were concerned about was Kenny Dalglish. That night he was perfectly played by Larry Lloyd, a former Liverpool player with something to prove to his old team-mates. Larry was outstanding all game, ensuring Kenny could not employ his trademark turn which often left defenders for dead. Then, for one moment, Kenny got the better of Larry. I saw it coming and decided to retreat to give the rest of the defence some cover. Kenny got his head to the ball and it looped towards our goal. I was in the right place at the right time and managed to head the ball off the line. It was the last time Kenny came anywhere near getting a goal. Later in the match, I saw the opportunity to break forward. The Liverpool defence backed off so I let fly. I'm sure, even to this day, that the ball was heading into the Liverpool net. Then the arm of Phil Thompson came out. It was like slow motion. I watched with delight as the ball struck his hand inside the box. I was sure it was a stick-on penalty. His hands were so far away from his body it looked like a crucifixion scene. But the referee waved it away. A home decision! The danger for Liverpool had been averted but it showed they could take nothing for granted – except gifts from the referee. No problem! We were hardly in trouble at all towards the end of the game and won the tie embarrassingly easily.

We had sent a message to the whole of Europe. None of them could halt the Liverpool march but we had done it. The Scouse dragon was vanquished. The English as a football nation, not just Liverpool, were back. It gave us a massive psychological advantage over the rest of Europe. We must be some team. We were.

In the next round we were drawn against the Greek team, AEK Athens. If the Liverpool tie was an unusual pairing, this was uncanny. The reason was we had already played Athens on their own ground in a pre-season friendly, which ended in a 1–1 draw in front of a partisan crowd numbering some 30,000 Greeks. We therefore knew exactly what to expect in the first leg, which was at their ground. We knew what the pitch played like, what the crowd sounded like. It was a huge advantage. Martin O'Neill was back in the side and we attacked them from the start. We ran out 2–1 winners. Garry Birtles scored again, along with John McGovern.

The return at the City ground was a goal-fest. It was a party. We won 5–1. Yet again, Garry Birtles was the scourge of Europe with two well-taken goals. Woody grabbed one for himself and David Needham, coming up from centre-back, scored another. But this was my night. It belonged to me. I picked the ball up just inside their half, found no-one barring my way, so off I went forward. The Greek defence seemed to ignore me. As I advanced towards the penalty area I looked for a pass. None was available so I hit it from twenty-five yards. It screamed into the net. I had scored in the European Cup. For those of you not lucky enough to have played professional football it is difficult to find the words to explain the feeling that goal gave me. It was, simply, indescribable. Some great banter went around the dressing room afterwards, most of it started by me, talking about my incredible goal again and again.

Results elsewhere in the competition went in our favour. It was as if the destination of the trophy was pre-ordained. Was our name on the Cup? Juventus, the Italian champions, were already out at the hands of Rangers, while Bruges, who had reached the final the year before, when they lost to that Kenny Dalglish winner at Wembley, were also removed from the competition. Perhaps most important, Real Madrid, who would have been the most difficult of opponents, were knocked out in the first round by the minnows from Switzerland, Grasshoppers of Zurich. We drew Grasshoppers in the third round and saw them off quite comfortably with a 4–1 win at home and a 1–1 draw in Switzerland. Garry Birtles yet again scored a goal in the first leg, Martin O'Neill securing the draw in Zurich. Of the teams that remained, only the West German champions, Cologne, were a side to be feared. It goes without saying that we drew them in the next round, the semi-final.

I missed the first game against the Germans. I had been booked in the second leg against Grasshoppers for a nothing foul, which meant I was banned for one match. It was hell watching when I should have been playing. We were also without Trevor Francis, who was injured. Among a number of talented players, Cologne boasted the brilliant Bernd Schuster, a player who could really hurt any side. It proved to be an incredible game.

It was the only time we underestimated our opponents. Brian Clough often used to belittle the opposition in team meetings. The way he did it, though, made you understand that you could only exploit the opposition's weaknesses if you worked to implement what Clough told you to do. Before the home tie against Cologne, Clough decided to hand over the team talk to Peter Taylor. Taylor tried the same tactics as Clough, telling us Cologne were basically useless. But, great though Taylor was in his own sphere, he was not Clough when it came to the psychology of playing. He made the side feel that all they had to do was turn up. Knowing I was not playing, I took the time to look at our players and I could see the overconfidence.

Twenty minutes into the first half we were 2–0 down and facing a rout. I watched aghast from my seat in the stands. But our success was built on some intangible quality that you might call spirit or belief. Gradually, Ian Bowyer and John Robbo began to get a hold of the midfield. They hauled us back into contention. Both of them scored, as did Garry Birtles and suddenly we were 3–2 up. Maybe if Cologne hadn't scored their goals so early on in the match they might have beaten us. As it was we had both the time and the ability to come back. We couldn't hold on to the lead, however. With ten minutes to go, Cologne's substitute, the Japanese player, Okudera, hit a speculative shot from distance. For one of only a very few times that I witnessed, Peter Shilton made a mistake and let the ball go under his body and into the goal. The match ended 3–3 and the general view was that we would be defeated in the return leg and be out of the European Cup.

Within the camp, we were not so pessimistic. Clough was convinced we would win and told us in no uncertain terms that nothing but a win would do. He informed the press that we would win the tie. The players were quietly confident. Our defending was poor in the first leg, which was unlike Forest under Clough. We felt we would not play so poorly again and we would certainly not gift them any goals this time.

My suspension over, I came back in for the second leg, which we had to win (or gain an improbable 4–4 draw) to go through. As usual, the management refused to overplay the importance of the game and we spent most of our time in Cologne walking round the old city, looking at the cathedral, things like that. We were also encouraged to have a few, but not too many, beers. We did a little light training and that was it.

"What I want you to do," went Clough's team talk, "is to ensure they don't score in the first half. Then in the second half you will score the winning goal. End of story." The game went exactly as Clough demanded, with Ian Bowyer getting the winner. In the dying moments, Peter Shilton redeemed his mistake in the first leg with interest when he pulled off an incredible save which prevented a certain equaliser. We had dumbfounded British critics and the whole of European football, just as we had done in winning the League the previous season and in knocking Liverpool off their pedestal.

The final in Munich against Malmo of Sweden was a bit of an anticlimax in terms of the football. But it meant everything to us. In many ways it was the minnows' final. Neither Malmo nor Forest possessed any European tradition. For once, we weren't underdogs but we weren't favourites either. No-one was more pleased with the prospect of playing in a European final than Trevor Francis. He was the wonder-kid at Birmingham but he had come to Forest with a million pound price-tag round his neck. As John Robbo put in one of his immaculate crosses from the left, which bamboozled the entire defence and the goalkeeper, Trevor stole in on the blindside and headed home from two yards. Never can one goal have justified such a high transfer fee.

Champions of England! Champions of Europe! I must admit those phrases have a certain ring to them. Hundreds of thousands of people turned up to watch us return to Nottingham. We had put the club and the city on the map and we had shown that you didn't have to be one of the big boys to win the glittering prizes. What you did need, if you were good players in the first place, was a manager like Brian Clough, whose determination to succeed overcame all obstacles, provided he had compliant players who were in awe of him, as we were. It turned out there was no mystery as to why he had failed so miserably at Leeds. The players there had already enjoyed unbelievable success under Don Revie. Brian Clough's methods just left them cold and he could never use the argument that all they had achieved was due to him, as he could with us.

These days, when managers are asked to account for success, they generally say it's down to 'hard work', as if the opposing side did not work so hard. Don't get me wrong, we worked as hard at Forest as anyone, particularly in pre-season, but during the regular season, Clough recognised when to put in the hard yards and when to keep the training light and interesting. Sometimes, as you will have gathered, it was weird. Most of the time when we were away from home, the only training we did was by way of walking past local beauty-spots and enjoying the odd recreational drink. Some of today's managers might do well to take a leaf out of Clough's book and go to Mallorca on a whim. Trips to foreign resorts these days are usually part of some pre-planned strategy when there is an international week or something. The trouble is, too many confuse 'hard work' with a lack of talent. To Clough, football was simple: you passed it to a player in a red shirt and the rest would take care of itself if you had good players.

As the new season – 1979–80 – approached, there was only one thing anyone could say: follow that! Clough and Taylor had already answered that to their own satisfaction. They were now ploughing their own furrow and they had the once-sceptical media eating out of their hands. I was to miss only two games throughout the season, which pleased me no end. In a move which left the rest of football reeling, the boss signed the legendary Stan Bowles. Now for anyone who saw him, Stan Bowles was the most naturally gifted footballer you could wish to see. In his heyday at Queens Park Rangers he was a revelation in what was anyway a good team. The trouble with Stan was, as everyone knows, he had an off-field lifestyle which wasn't compatible with that of a professional athlete. With Stan, his particular vice was gambling. He would bet on anything. He probably would have made a great bookmaker, so extensive was his knowledge of odds. He could give you odds on anything. As they say, if he could have passed a betting shop the way he passed a football he'd have been an all-time great.

Having experienced Clough and Taylor over some years by then, I got the feeling they were making a statement when they signed Stan. They had rehabilitated Kenny

Burns and got the best out of him when others scoffed. They had told anyone who would listen that Peter Shilton was the best in the world while others wavered. They had shown their intent when they became the first in this country to splash out a million on a single player. Now they would get the best out of one of England's most talented but wayward post-war footballers. They soon added to their reputation for left-field decisions by bringing in another veteran, Charlie George, on loan.

Unfortunately, Stan never really reached the level he was capable of at Forest. He was sporadically brilliant, that's for sure, and when he turned it on he was fantastic. But I think Stan would be the first to admit that his days at Forest were inconsistent at best. His behaviour was also often erratic. Stan being Stan, one game when he really turned it on was in the away leg of the European Super Cup, when we faced the mighty Barcelona in front of 90,000 fanatical supporters. Stan hadn't played in the first leg at the City Ground. We edged it 1–0 with a goal from, you've guessed it, the on-loan Charlie George. Yet again our chances were written off. We might have performed amazing feats but Barcelona were an entirely different proposition.

Clough found us plenty of entertainment and walks in the Catalan capital but didn't want us to do too much training. He wanted us "nice and relaxed". His master-stroke was to tell Stan Bowles that this was his stage and he brought him in for Ian Bowyer. To select a flair player in place of a solid performer when you are defending a 1–0 lead in such circumstances was a staggering move.

It was typical of Clough's readiness to make bold decisions which went against football wisdom. He was busy creating a new wisdom all his own.

Running out at the Camp Nou was one of the highlights of my career. The emotion streams from the crowd in a way that Liverpool can only dream of. It comes in waves from those mile-high stands. But it was us who were in heaven. We were underdogs in the home of our opponents, just like Cologne, just like Liverpool. Stan ran the second leg. Responding to the occasion he was like some returning matador. He was absolutely brilliant. He was responsible for us getting a 0–0 draw and we were applauded off the pitch. We had won the European Super Cup in one of Europe's most iconic stadiums. Incredible!

Our League form was not what any of us wanted. It is amazing to think that only a couple of years before we were happy with second division respectability. Now, we were disappointed to finish fifth in Division One. Yet again, Liverpool won it. In the FA Cup, we were as bad as ever, flattering to deceive. We smashed Leeds at Elland Road 4–1 in round three, then we were drawn at home to ... Liverpool.

It wasn't as simple as that, though. We had already been paired against the Scousers in the semi-final of the League Cup, the first leg of which came three days before the FA Cup tie. Two of the three games before the Anfield leg of the League Cup tie were the Super Cup matches against Barcelona. "This is what success means", was what the manager had to say about it all.

We saw off Liverpool 1-0 in the first leg of the League Cup semi-final. So far so good! That gave us confidence for the FA Cup game the following Saturday. There was little in the way of rotation then. Pretty much the same team turned out in all competitive matches with a couple of exceptions like Stan Bowles at the Camp Nou. All us regulars played in one game in the sequence which could have been a chance to give some hard-pressed players a breather. It was a home League match against Bristol City. Clough would have none of that. He approached the game against Bristol in exactly the same way as the matches against the more illustrious opponents. However, that old FA Cup demon still had it in for us no matter what Clough did. Liverpool beat us on our own turf 2-0.

We had won the League Cup two years running. We almost felt it belonged to us. There was no way we would surrender that to Liverpool, particularly after the FA Cup reverse. We managed a 0-0 in the second leg, to go through to our third Wembley final in a row. We were favourites but not by much. Our opponents, Wolves, finished only a point behind us in the League and were a more than decent side. For the first time in a major final, we failed to function properly at Wembley and Wolves beat us 1-0. None of us liked the taste of defeat. Clough liked it least of all.

Over the previous few months, in fact it was probably longer than that when I look back on it, Woody had been talking about going abroad. It wasn't that he was fed up with Forest or had anything against the manager.

He just wanted to lift his sights to other challenges. We used to get together a lot and he would tell me how he wanted to experience more than Nottingham had to offer, more than England had to offer. I didn't try to talk him out of it, his mind was made up. Much as I enjoyed his company and what he brought to the team, I understood his ideas even if I didn't share them. Then all of a sudden, the deal was done and Woody was gone. To Cologne, would you believe!

The defeat by Wolves was even worse for us and our fans because ten days earlier we had been beaten by Dynamo Berlin in the home leg of the third round of the European Cup. Was our campaign to defend our most treasured trophy about to founder so early? The game in Berlin was only four days after the League Cup Final, which of course we had lost. We went to Germany for the return, our European status hanging by a thread.

Lots of praise has been heaped on the quality of our victories over Liverpool and Cologne in our glory years. But our performance in Berlin is to me the greatest of them all. We were on the floor. The manager refused to accept that the two defeats we had suffered at the hands of Berlin and Wolves had occurred at all. He acted as if nothing were any different to usual. He took us for walks, gave us history lessons about Berlin and wouldn't let us train too much. We won 3–1. Trevor Francis got two of the goals. I felt I put in one of my best ever performances that night. Their winger never got a kick. We had confounded our critics one more time.

To be fair to the pundits – and someone needs to be – that win in Berlin turned us from upstarts to a team with genuine European pedigree. You would have thought winning the European Cup and the Super Cup would have achieved that. But no, it took that comeback against Berlin to establish our place among the greats of Europe. Now even the media finally took Clough at his word when he told them how good we were.

That win pitched us against the Dutch masters, Ajax, in the semi-final. Ajax had won the trophy three times in a row in the seventies, with the legendary Johan Cruyff pulling the strings. True, the 1980 vintage might not have been as good as that team but they were still a force to be reckoned with. In the first leg, played at our place, we ran out good winners, 2–0. It was the same score as our famous first leg against Liverpool the previous season and we knew how to defend it. In Amsterdam, Clough took us for a walk by the canals and then to the city's famous red-light district. About half-an-hour into the trip, the manager stopped us and announced that "if anyone wants a quick one the club's paying". We didn't know how serious he was and to my knowledge no-one took him up on the offer. Instead, we had a few drinks. One thing we didn't do too much was train.

In front of a crowd of 65,000, we lost the return leg 1–0, taking a bit of a battering in the process. That meant we were in the final. Again! Only the dreaded Liverpool among English clubs had managed that, two appearances on the spin. Now, we had to win.

1980 was more of a glamour final than the previous season. The game was to be staged in the incredible Bernabeu Stadium in Madrid, home of Real, the club who are a byword for European greatness. Clough waxed lyrical about Spanish culture and tried to tell us about a civil war or something. We were housed in a lovely hotel in the hills outside the city. Our wives and girlfriends were in 5-star accommodation in downtown Madrid, quite close to the stadium. It was not often that those in charge of Forest were so generous. We were a bit put out, though, that our spouses were in a hotel which was quite a distance from us. Any time we spent with them would be controlled by the manager.

We were up against SV Hamburg, a top team of the time. Kevin Keegan was their most famous player, Felix Magath their best. They had disposed of Real Madrid in the semi-final. Clough hardly mentioned Keegan or Magath. He took us to Mallorca before the game. Stan Bowles, in one of his more inexplicable bouts of erratic behaviour, didn't show up for the flight. So he missed what could have been a reprise of his display in Barcelona, a chance of glory on the ultimate stage. If Clough was put out by Stan's non-appearance, he didn't let on. He ensured we stayed relaxed. Not much training took place. Playing at the Bernabeu was another milestone. If the Camp Nou was inspiring, the Bernabeu was the ultimate. The match itself was a tight encounter. John Robertson provided the only moment of class. Weaving his way forward he cut in from the left and passed the ball into the net. If winning the European Cup once was immense, this was beyond awesome.

It was a magnificent climax to the season. We were now among the greats. Nothing could ever diminish this achievement. However, after the game, the manager delayed our reunion with our wives and girlfriends by keeping us in the mountain retreat for the night. It was a strange way to reward us for our efforts. Some of us, including myself, Martin and John Robbo, decided to defy the manager and slip out of the hotel. In the end, John Robbo bottled out, for which he took some serious stick. The rest of us made our way to Madrid. We weren't caught, thank God. We did celebrate with the management but something didn't feel right. In many ways, it was never the same again at Forest. The great team had already lost Withey and Woody. Soon it would begin to break up completely.

Chapter Six

THAT MAN

When Brian Clough arrived at Forest, the whole world wondered if he could recapture the magic he had performed at Derby. At the Baseball Ground he had won the League and reached the semi-final of the European Cup. He felt he was cheated of the opportunity to reach the final by corrupt administrators and referees. That was an issue which would impact on us further down the line, as you'll see later. Clough's Derby side was the most successful in the club's history. At first sight, it didn't seem likely he would be able to regain that kind of success ever again, especially not with us. Many thought his experience at Leeds had worn him down. He was, it was said, a busted flush. Some busted flush.

We soon found out that with Clough, we should always expect the unexpected. I have played under some great managers. And I really mean great. Each of them possessed special characteristics that marked them out. If they had anything in common it is that they all seemed as if they were born to be in football. But you got the impression with Brian Clough that he would have been just as successful whatever he had done in life. And he would have ended up a celebrity even if he'd been a chartered accountant. His fame spread way beyond our shores and the world of football. It's fair to say that the players at Forest, used to the more conventional approaches of coaches like Allan Brown and Dave Mackay, were immediately blown away.

On the first day, the new boss called us together and told us we were hopeless. He went on to say that we could do well or we could be also-rans. We would only get anywhere, he said, if we listened to him and followed his instructions to the letter. If he had been in any way humbled by his time at Leeds it didn't show. He took great pains to make it clear that he wasn't there just for an easy pay day and neither were we. He was there to win. He was mesmerising.

It's a bit of a riddle how footballers respond to managers. If you are winning games, then of course players think their boss is brilliant. But what about when a manager first arrives? If he has been successful elsewhere as the main man, an assistant or a coach, he has a head start. If he has been a top player, won championships, cups or international caps, he automatically gets respect from the players. But footballers are a funny bunch. Unlike many jobs, the integrity of the group is the most important thing. One or two disaffected guys can cause all kinds of problems for the team and when it comes down to it, football is about winning games as a team. The trouble is, there is no set method for success, nor is there just one type of manager who can inspire the necessary loyalty and level of performance. Some managers gee you up, tell you how good you are or could be if you did things their way. The trouble is, for most of them, 'their way' is not that different to lots of others. Believe it or not, the vast majority find it difficult to deal with even simple issues, such as the fact that some players react to a bollocking while others need to be cajoled.

Brian Clough was most definitely a one-off among managers. You couldn't fit him into any category. I think everyone knows that. His short spell with Leeds had been an unmitigated disaster, no question. But he had created that Derby side. His reputation for strange behaviour had, of course, preceded him. We were, I think it's safe to say, a bit wary when he pitched up. The difference between him and the manager who had been sacked to make way for him, Allan Brown, was immense. Whereas Brown was an old-school coach who was good on the training ground but somehow couldn't motivate the group beyond second division mediocrity, Clough was like a whirlwind.

I hadn't been in the first team squad for long when he arrived so I didn't have too much experience of how managers operate. I soon discovered from players at other clubs that Clough was different. He was adamant from day one that his ambitions reached the stratosphere and yours had to be the same. Otherwise you would be out. He would often stoop to insults, which he repeated again and again. John Robertson was "too fat and lazy", Martin O'Neill "had no skill" and so on. He rarely, if ever, praised you directly. Or if he did, it was either to make a wider point (as when he named Peter Shilton the 'Best Goalkeeper in the World' in order to intimidate his own players and opponents alike) or to pave the way for a sometimes savage put-down.

In fact, you never knew where you were with Brian Clough. Sometimes he would talk to you, sometimes he wouldn't. When I was left out of the team for that cup replay at Spurs there was no explanation. On other occasions he went out of his way to explain himself. The fact that I was injured in the first leg of the Spurs FA Cup game gave him ample opportunity to tell me that because I hadn't trained, he couldn't risk me in such an important match. But no! There was nothing. Just a great big empty silence. I thought I had been doing quite well up to then but there I was left behind in Nottingham for the Spurs match. Mind you, in hindsight, that was better than what happened to Tony Woodcock.

As I've already said, Tony and I came up through the ranks together. We remain the best of friends to this day. Then, we were both young teenagers who broke into the side at more or less the same time. Tony thought he was in favour when he was included in the squad for the cup replay against Spurs and naturally thought he had a good chance of playing. Clough didn't let on what the actual team would be but that only increased Woody's expectations. After all, why would the manager take him if he wasn't going to throw him into the game at some point.

That was Woody's reasoning. But no-one realised at that time quite what Clough was really like. As it happened Woody came back to Nottingham from London without making an appearance in the game. He told me what happened.

When the squad arrived in London, the new manager called everyone together, seemingly for a team talk. First, he turned to Woody.

"I've got a special job for you, young man," he began. Woody's expectation level went up another notch. Then Clough delivered the punch-line. Handing Tony a small package, he continued: "There's a brush and polish, go and clean my shoes." Tony looked blank but Clough was deadly serious. Woody was there to clean his shoes. And that was the closest Woody came to the action that night. It did, however, establish the way things were going to be from then on.

We were soon to find out that it was best never to try and second guess Clough. You had no idea what he was going to do. This carried on throughout my time with him. If anything, that aspect was intensified when Peter Taylor arrived as Clough's assistant. Clough and Taylor used to egg each other on. I don't know which of them came up with this little wheeze. In one of many, many examples of Clough's unique approach to football management, we were staying at a hotel near London the night before a big game. It was a very big game indeed. It was the League Cup Final. We enjoyed a good meal and were sent to bed at 8pm. Soon afterwards, we each got a phone call from the manager summoning us to a private room downstairs. Clough stood up and banged his spoon on a plate to shut us all up and get our attention.

"Right you lot," he said (this was a favourite phrase of Clough's). "Everyone here is going to have a drink. I've got champagne laid on for you. But not one of you leaves this room until you have all told us a joke." So one by one we each had to deliver a gag. I was never that good at telling jokes and really struggled. But the boss persisted and I managed to mumble some rubbish. That was pretty much the extent of the pre-match talk. I finally made it to bed around midnight. Needless to say I woke up with a hangover, as did quite a few of the other players. At the game the next day Clough hardly said a word. Wolves beat us 1-0. Andy Gray scored the only goal. Clough never asked us to tell any jokes again.

There was never too much talk about tactics or the opposition with Cloughie. There were certainly no dossiers on the strengths and weaknesses of opposing players. Nonetheless, you wanted to play for him, you would do anything to please him. If he put a hand on your shoulder after a match you knew he was bestowing high praise and you walked on air for days. Just a hand on your shoulder! It didn't mean you would be in the team for the next game, though.

I've never experienced, before or since, the kind of training sessions which Clough and his trainer, Jimmy Gordon employed (Peter Taylor was rarely involved in coaching. Come to think of it, Clough didn't do much coaching either. It just seemed like he did). As you will have already seen, during the season there wasn't much training at all. There were walks, there was eating and a bit of drinking, but very little training beyond five-a-sides. Clough always liked his players to work with the ball if they were working at all. Anything else, to him, was a waste of time. It came as a shock when I moved to other clubs and found out first-hand how most coaches approached training, with work-outs and endless talk about tactics.

One thing Clough did spend time telling us, especially defenders, was his ownership of the goal. By this I mean he would point to the goal in training and say: "That there is MY net. Keep the ball out of MY net, that's what I pay you for." That was Clough's coaching method. He had this knack of coming up with a phrase – like 'MY net' or 'just pass the ball to someone in a red shirt' – which was so memorable it imprinted the idea on your mind. There may have been little in the way of what could be called team talks but somehow his insistence on passing the ball and keeping possession were instilled until they became second nature. And Clough made it abundantly clear that we were never, ever to argue with referees or question their decisions. A knock-on from this order was that of course we were never allowed to question him either.

That first season we were coming to terms with a man, the like of whose methods and personality we had never seen before. Even John Robbo started to take notice. I gradually saw a difference when we came in for training. More often than not, the manager wasn't there, he left things to his assistant, Jimmy Gordon. We didn't know where he was but the idea of his all-knowing presence somehow caused us to sharpen up. He would suddenly turn up, claim to have been playing squash, make a few observations, then disappear again. Sometimes Peter Taylor would be there, sometimes he wouldn't. Bit by bit, Clough's way of doing things paid dividends and we began buying into his dream and our own future.

At the beginning of Clough's second full season, the boss made it clear he expected nothing less than promotion. It was a kind of ultimatum. We either got promotion or he'd get players in who would. So it was with relief as much as anything else when we managed to achieve his command by scraping into third place. No-one gave us much chance of surviving in the top flight that first season, let alone win anything. No-one, that is, except the manager. Clough had no interest in the way many teams played in those days. He particularly didn't like long balls lumped to a big man up front. Speculative balls into the channels were for teams with no talent as far as he was concerned. We would live or die playing his way: keeping possession; getting the ball out to the wide players; lots of crosses; midfielders who didn't lose the ball. No matter how other sides played, we were to play Clough's way. For us there was no other.

The manager took us all to Mallorca towards the end of that first season in the top division, as he often did at moments of pressure. Sometimes he went himself and left us to get on with things back home. Clough was one of those managers who believed that football at the highest level, like in all sport, is won and lost by the small things, the one or two percent that makes the difference between victory and defeat. Part of this is the way players deal with the relentless pressure that accompanies the striving always to improve. There is no standing still in football. If you don't keep improving you are going backwards. Some players take to this reality better than others. The best managers develop strategies to enable their players to cope and even use the pressure as a means of improvement. There is no one way of doing it, all great managers are different. Brian Clough used it by pretending it didn't exist. To him, football was a simple game played by idiots. The idiots couldn't fail to be successful provided they did what they were told by someone who was a genius, that is, Clough himself. Pressure, what pressure? "Pressure," he would say, "is going down a pit everyday to dig coal."

Clough's eccentric approach can be seen in the build up to our first European Cup Final. We flew to Munich for the game against Malmo on the Monday, with the match due to take place in Bayern Munich's fantastic Olympic Stadium on Wednesday. We arrived in the evening. We stayed at a nice but hardly great hotel in the Bavarian mountains outside the city. It was in the middle of nowhere really. The first thing we noticed as we drew up outside was that the hotel had no training pitches or anything much in the way of outdoor facilities. Once we were installed in our rooms, Clough called us together. "Right, you lot," he said. "This is what you're going to do. Tomorrow morning I want you in the lobby at nine o'clock in your tracksuits. I've organised training." This was unusual. At other clubs it might be normal but with Clough it was highly abnormal. What kind of training could he mean?

So there we were the next day, all bright-eyed and expecting at most a light training session. We should have known better. There was nothing planned at all that related to football as far as any of us could see. Then he gave us our orders. He began pointing at various indoor facilities: "There's a dart board, there's a pool table, there's the bar but there's no drinks in it. Just relax. I'll see you at six o'clock." And with that he was gone. It turned out that Clough, who often encouraged a bit of social drinking, had decided that because we had all been drinking the week before, when we were on one of our Spanish getaways, there would be no alcohol in Germany.

Not only that, he wouldn't let us train the whole time we were in Munich. The one player this affected more than any other was goalkeeper, Peter Shilton. Shilts had a pathological aversion to not training. He simply had to train every day, otherwise he became unbearable. He'd been doing his routine for years and needed to keep it going. He begged Clough to organise something for him. In Shilton's case, Clough relented, perhaps because he knew and understood Peter's needs and he respected him as the best goalkeeper in the world. Or he may have been making a point to the rest of us. If that was the case, none of us knew what the point might be. Anyway, he got Jimmy Gordon to find Shilts a 'suitable' place to train on his own. Whether the venue was chosen by Clough or Gordon I don't know. It turned out to be on a traffic island at the junction of two busy roads. It was almost bare of grass with just a smattering of rough shrub in the middle. On driving by, local motorists were surprised to see the world's number one goalkeeper going through his training routines on the patchy grass which made up the island. The rest of us were banished to the bar with no drinks. That was pure Clough and of course we won the European Cup. Malmo never stood a chance.

Perhaps here I can explode a myth that has grown up about the manager and his relationship with Peter Taylor. Clough and Taylor were a team. A brilliant team! But there was no doubt who was boss, never ever! However, Clough's relationship with Taylor was hugely important to the success that both of them achieved. Look at each one's performance when the other was not at their side. It was never that good. Taylor at Brighton and later at Derby – and Clough at Leeds – had all been failed experiments in one way or another. Together, they were an irresistible force. When Taylor finally left Forest, his reasons for breaking up the partnership – so he told Clough – were that he wanted to retire and live with less stress (Taylor suffered from heart problems). Clough understood and was sympathetic. Then suddenly, out of nowhere, Taylor took the manager's job at Derby, of all places. Since that moment it has become an established 'fact' that Taylor's actions destroyed the relationship between the two men. It is said that the mutual antagonism was so great they never spoke to each other again. Now there was bad feeling, sure. Clough saw Taylor's actions as a terrible betrayal, no question. But it was far more complex than that.

Towards the end of my time at Forest, and after Taylor had become Derby's manager, I began to suffer a few niggling injuries, which was unusual for me. I also got that bad injury on England duty. So concerned did Clough become at the length of my absences that he bought a replacement right-back, Kenny Swain, from Aston Villa. Gradually, however, I began to return to fitness and was ready to reclaim my place. Then one day the boss called me and another player, Mark Proctor, into his office.

"Will you two go out on loan?" Clough began.

This was a shock but we had no choice but to listen to what the boss had to say.

"Where to?" I asked.

The gaffer shuffled a little and didn't answer straight away, which was unusual for him. He was seldom lost for words. He looked a bit shifty, to be honest. Then he blurted it out. "I've been talking to Peter and he needs a couple of players of your calibre."

"You mean Derby?"

"Yes."

Now as a Nottingham boy there was no way I was going to Derby. Mark wasn't too keen on the move either.

Anyway, no disrespect to Derby, but I saw it as a step down, which I could not accept. I told Clough this. A pained expression came over his face. "Look," he said. "Let me drive you over to Pete's house, have a word with him, then make up your mind. If you're not interested in going there you can tell him yourself." I didn't want to do it but agreed only because it was Brian Clough doing the asking. So Clough drove Mark and me to Taylor's house, way out in the middle of the Nottinghamshire countryside, not even near a village. When we arrived, Clough went into the kitchen for a cup of tea with Peter's wife, Lillian, while Peter made his pitch. The talks went on for a couple of hours before both of us told him we were going to stay at Forest. Neither Clough nor Taylor was too pleased at this turn of events.

"Well you can find your own way home then," Clough said. Then he softened. "Could you give us a couple of minutes? I want a quick word with Pete. Go and have a cup of tea in the kitchen." We duly went to the kitchen where Taylor's wife made us a lovely cup of tea. While we were doing this, Clough and Taylor secretly left the house. Like two naughty boys, they scuttled off to do who knows what and left us out in the sticks with no transport.

We went to speak to Taylor's wife. "What's the matter, love?" she asked me. We told her what had happened and could see a grin begin to form on her face. "Never mind," she continued. "Have another cup of tea and call a cab." Well, two hours later, the cab had still not arrived. We didn't know if Clough and Taylor had instructed the cab company not to pick us up or what had happened. It was now past eight in the evening and we decided to leg it. Over styles and fields we went, cutting ourselves on the undergrowth and tearing our clothes. Eventually we reached a village pub where we had a couple of drinks to calm us down. From there, we managed to get a taxi home to Nottingham, arriving about midnight, exhausted and bemused. If Clough and Taylor had really fallen out to the extent that everyone now believes, no-one had told them on that day. We never did find out what they got up to but I'm sure they must have been having a right laugh.

There are so many stories about Brian Clough. To me, he was a complicated man who gave the impression that everything was simple. He often had a bit of a cheeky smile but that was an expression of his satisfaction at his own genius rather than an encouragement to a player. Nonetheless, he was central to my whole career. I respected him but I'm not sure to this day if I liked him. I still haven't worked him out and I was at his side for ten years. Since then I've played under other great managers. I've been a manager myself. Still, Brian Clough looms the largest of all. He wasn't like Bobby Robson, who treated you like a son. He wasn't like Sir Alex Ferguson, an equally huge personality of whom you'll hear a lot more later. He wasn't like George Graham, the great disciplinarian or Ron Atkinson, the great comedian of football managers. He was Clough.

For all of us footballers who came under Clough's influence, he took us on a mind-boggling journey, one that will probably never be repeated. I can only liken him to the Pied Piper. To lead a team out of the second tier and win the League at the first attempt would today be the stuff of childish fantasy. As for back-to-back European Cups – forget it. But Clough did it. With us! The more peaks we conquered, the more we wanted to please him. We ran through stinging nettles for him. We would have run through a wall into a nuclear reactor if he asked us to. I think it is true to say we will never see his like again.

Chapter Seven

THE ROAD TO LONDON

Somehow – and I can't say how – the start of the 1980–81 season just didn't feel the same as before. That may seem a strange thing to say given that we had won the European Cup for the second time just a few short months before. But the feeling became more certain as the great Forest team began to break up over the course of the next eighteen months. What had started with Woody the previous year proved not to be a one-off but a trend. The season saw the departure of quite a number of other players as the boss tried to construct a new side to take the club forward.

The highest profile transfer out was Garry Birtles, who went to Manchester United for £1.25 million. Garry was never the same player again. Having played with him and seen him at close quarters turn some of the best defenders in the business I can tell you he was an absolutely top-draw striker. Quite why he failed at Old Trafford is a mystery, except to say that Brian Clough knew how to play to Garry's strengths and I don't think the same can be said of United. Also, as I found out some years later, Manchester United is a massive step up, no matter what clubs you've played for in the past. It's not easy for some players to manage. The only thing I can put it down to is that Garry – as I've said previously – was continuously homesick for Nottingham and his old mates. He would return whenever he could, which couldn't have been good for his form. Maybe this homesickness meant he was unable to really embrace his new status as number one striker at one of the world's biggest clubs. He just preferred to be in the town of his youth rather than in one of the big cities of Europe.

For me, the saddest departure was that of Martin O'Neill, who left for Norwich. Not only had we played together down the right side for so long with such incredible success, I regarded Martin and his wife, Geraldine, as close friends. The team would definitely lack something big without him in it. Our talisman, Kenny Burns, and his partner at the centre of defence, Larry Lloyd, both moved on, as did the midfielder, Archie Gemmill. Kenny had become one of the most consistent defenders in the country. With him, the Clough method paid massive dividends. In the strikers' department, John O'Hare, whose opportunities to play were becoming less and less as age crept up on him, called time on his period at the City Ground. It wasn't that long before Trevor Francis joined the exodus. Just as Trevor's arrival for a million pounds sent out a message to the world, so his departure said something about where we were heading. There would still be some marquee signings but, as I said, it just wasn't the same.

In their places came good players but the question was: could we all gel to produce another great team? One of those marquee signings was Justin Fashanu. His transfer from Norwich was very high-profile. Poor Justin would later be the first footballer to come out as gay and there is no question he suffered for it. Such was the pressure on him he eventually committed suicide. When he arrived at Forest, I was at first detailed to room with him on away trips. At the time, I didn't know he was gay, none of us did. Sometimes the manager called him a "poof" in training but we thought that was an example of Clough's use of insult rather than the reality. After all, Clough insulted everyone in one way or another. Looking back, I can see the lengths Justin must have gone to in order to disguise his sexuality – and what it cost him.

On the first occasion we shared a room, during a pre-season tour of Spain, I was blissfully asleep. I awoke to the sound of a very loud banging on the walls or something. It was a huge commotion. Then I saw the door. It was a thick, strong door but it had a huge hole in it. I jumped out of bed, now fully awake and rushed to open the door. It looked like the room was under attack. There was no sign of Justin. I flung the door open to see doors opening all down the corridor and half-asleep players putting their heads out demanding to know what was going on. I went back into the room and heard the sound of sobbing coming from the bathroom. I went in. Justin was bathing his hands – covered in blood – in the sink, and was moaning. He had smashed through the door with his fists. They were bruised and bloodied. I thought it was someone with an axe trying to get in, not someone trying to get out. He didn't appear to be fully awake, almost like he was in a really bad dream. I got the impression he was reliving some dark incident from his boyhood but I have no idea what it was. A doctor was summoned and Justin was helped back into bed. Needless to say I didn't get another wink of sleep for the rest of the night.

Such was football culture in those days that I never discussed the night's events with Justin. You didn't talk about those sorts of things back then. It felt awkward and unmanly. Of, course everyone knew what had happened. And being footballers, some of the comments were a bit close to the edge. Perhaps I should have been more sympathetic but as a professional athlete I could not afford to have my sleep disturbed like that. I didn't dislike Justin, we always got on OK. But what if it was the night before a big match and he did that again? I refused to spend another night in the same room as him. Incidents like this soured relations between Justin and the manager. Clough realised his methods just didn't work with Justin. That's not surprising given that Justin was a disturbed individual in many ways, as his door-smashing showed. Instead of his football improving, his form dipped, which in turn led to even fiercer criticism from the press and the manager. He eventually left Forest for Notts County, but not before being forcibly escorted from the training ground by burly policemen following yet another altercation with the manager.

At first, the season looked to be going well. We went on an unbeaten run – which included a 5–0 demolition of Stoke – and felt good. It seemed our whole season caved in, though, when we crashed out of the European Cup in the first round. For two years, the greatest of all club prizes had been ours. It had made us famous wherever football was played. We expected to do better than this. We were confident enough going into the first match, the away leg, against CSKA Sofia of Bulgaria. The truth is we were very poor on the night, while the Bulgarians surprised us with the strength of their display. We lost 1-0.

Like a wounded tiger, we roared straight back, beating Leicester 5-0 in the League and Bury 7-0 in the League Cup. But then we lost to Arsenal. Consistency, which had been one of our hallmarks in the previous three years (we established a record for going the most games undefeated), was beginning to desert us. Nothing could be a better example of this than the return leg against CSKA. It was a disaster. We just couldn't get going, they scored on the break and we again lost 1-0.

The Bulgarians went absolutely wild. No-one blamed them. We were back-to-back European Champions, after all. It felt terrible. We were out. Forest under Brian Clough were a team I loved playing in. I loved the type of attacking football Clough encouraged. I loved the way we played. I loved the belief we had. After the defeat by CSKA, I asked myself whether we could salvage our season. As a team, I don't know if we believed we could. It was a massive blow.

As if to rub salt in our wounds, we were out of the League Cup before Christmas. Like the European Cup, we had made the League Cup our own. Three years in the final, two of them won. In our worst performance in the competition since our days in the second division, we were dumped out by the emerging Watford side put together by Graham Taylor. I was out injured but I felt the defeat as much as anyone. Watford's style of play was all direct football, getting the ball up front as early as possible with long, hopeful punts. It was the opposite of what Clough – and therefore the rest of us – believed was the right way to play the game. That made it all the worse when they beat us 4–1. This was ominous.

For once, the FA Cup provided our best performances of the season. We knocked out Bolton, Manchester United and Bristol City in a run to the sixth round. However, at that stage we went out in a replay, beaten by Ipswich. We also relinquished the European Super Cup, to Valencia on away goals. In December, we travelled to Tokyo for the World Club Championship against Nacional Montevideo of Uruguay. Once again, we were beaten. In a bad-tempered game, full of niggling fouls and off-the-ball incidents, the Latin Americans edged it 1–0.

Aston Villa came from nowhere to win the League. They went all the way in the European Cup the next season and won it with one of Forest's old boys, Peter Withe, getting their winner in the final. At least it wasn't Liverpool. We finished seventh that season, nowhere near good enough considering what we had achieved. But I remembered where we were three years earlier. Expectations in Nottingham were probably unrealistically high. But you couldn't get away from the fact that we won nothing that season and worse, would not have a

European campaign to look forward to. We didn't finish high enough in the League to qualify. At the end of the season another bond with the past was broken when Jimmy Gordon retired. He was replaced by the veteran, Ron Fenton.

Throughout their time at Forest, Clough and Taylor were not content just to bring in players on big transfers. They enjoyed plucking footballers from non-league clubs, such as Garry Birtles or, later, Stuart Pearce. They also liked bringing youngsters through the ranks, like myself and Woody. We were followed by the likes of Peter Davenport, Colin Walsh and Steve Hodge. One of the youngsters who stepped up during this time was Danny Wilson, who would remain a friend of mine. Danny and I often discussed the idea of coaching when we left the game, which was unusual for a young player. Many years later, I installed him as my assistant when I became manager of Barnsley. Some of the fees Forest received when many of the young players who came through the system were transferred were huge. However, we needed immediate results, not future profits.

We didn't get them. The season 1981–82 saw a further decline. It wasn't by much. But at the very top there is only a small gap between success and failure. We did quite well in the first half of the season. Our League form was good and we started making inroads into the League Cup once again. We cruised through the first three rounds against Birmingham, Blackburn and Tranmere. After Christmas it all started to go wrong. It wasn't that we or the management were doing anything different. Success just wasn't happening for us and for once Clough couldn't do anything about it. I was now a senior player and took it upon myself to help youngsters and newcomers whenever I could. I noticed that they looked to me for inspiration more and more. I was always happy in the dressing room, I loved the banter and I knew I could help gee-up the next generation of players. So that is what I did and the manager seemed to appreciate it, although he never said as much.

My efforts didn't help at first. In the New Year we lined up to face Wrexham in the third round of the FA Cup. It was at the City Ground. It should have been a home banker. But that FA Cup hoodoo struck again and Wrexham knocked us out 3–1. We had always been able to recover quickly from defeats in the past but this time we took a knock to our confidence and we went ten League games without a win. Spurs knocked us out of the League Cup and we finished eleventh in the First Division. Once again we couldn't qualify for Europe. The manager was not pleased.

Peter Shilton left in the summer, to be replaced by Hans van Breukelen. It was another piece of the old team to disappear. Perhaps the departure that had the biggest effect, though, was Peter Taylor, who retired to many tears then promptly took the job as Derby manager. I continued talking to many of the players who had moved on. I met up with a few of them on England duty. Woody often told me how great his life had become since his move to Germany. For the first time I started having the odd thought about leaving myself. Also, my contract was up soon.

In early 1980 I embarked on a relationship with Debra, a Nottingham girl who came from the same area of the city – Clifton – as me. We had been virtually insepa-rable since we first met. She was the reason I wanted to slip out of our mountain hotel after the European Cup Final in Madrid. Two years later we were thinking more seriously about our future. The prospect of marriage was in the air and we both wanted children. It was time to take stock and do what was best for both of us. Before, it had always been what suited me. Now there was more to consider.

In the end, I decided to sign a two-year extension to my contract. Two more years to see if I could help raise the club back up to the very top. Half-way through what was until then another mediocre campaign, Clough seemed to get the old magic working again and we got better and better as 1983 went on. We finished fifth, only two points behind Watford, who themselves were second. Needless to say, Liverpool won the title – for the second year running. While we did poorly in both cup competitions, our disap-pointments were more than made up for by our League position, which meant we qualified for the UEFA Cup. That was a real achievement for a side with more than its fair share of young players. This was the season I was injured and Kenny Swain came in. After I turned down the loan move to Peter Taylor's Derby I won back my place. My reappearance coincided with the team's revival. I was back.

My final year at Forest was fantastic. I played in virtually every game. Yes, we made early exits from both cup
competitions but our form in the League was back to
near its very best. We were top goalscorers in the division, with Peter Davenport getting seventeen. We hit five
goals on four separate occasions. Our attacking style won
over a whole new set of fans. We finished third, which
was pretty astounding. Who finished first? Who else?
Liverpool, again!

It was in the UEFA Cup, though, that we really shone.
We had been out of Europe for two years. I was so proud
to be back playing at that level. I was really pleased I had
stayed for the extra two years. If I had left when we were
at a low, I always would have wondered what might have
been. This way, I was again fighting at the top. We put
a huge effort into our European campaign. It ended in
massive controversy, with Clough stalking the training
ground muttering about "conspiracies" and "fucking
cheating – again".

There were enough of us remaining from the games
against CSKA who felt we still had something to prove in
Europe. For our season in the UEFA Cup, the manager
was really up for it. During the two years of drought,
Clough had often seemed more detached than I had ever
seen him in the past. Whether his drinking was getting
the better of him I don't know. The prospect of the
break-up with Peter Taylor must have also affected him.
But when Taylor actually left, after a short period, for
whatever reason, Clough was rejuvenated. He promoted
people from within to his coaching staff and ruled the

roost even more. For the first time, he was succeeding without Peter Taylor by his side.

Routine victories against Vorwaerts of Hamburg and PSV Eindhoven of Holland got us back in the European groove. Then came the dream draw. Forest versus Celtic! First leg at the City Ground! Yes!

At first, things didn't go to plan. Celtic did a job on us and got out of Nottingham with a 0-0 draw. That made them firm favourites to go through. But that was only if you forgot our European pedigree. We were never more dangerous than in situations like this. Having to go away in Europe and get a result. Clough was flying. It could have been Cologne all over again. As we went up to Glasgow, the manager was more relaxed than I had seen him in years. We were back in the old routine, going for walks, not doing much training, drinking at the manager's command. I had been through it all before. Along with a few other senior players, I continued to help the young players understand the ways of the manager and what they had to do to please him.

Before the away leg against Celtic, Clough told anyone who would listen that his new Forest team were as good as before. We were, he said, the "new, improved version." Walking out at Parkhead was the most deafening experience I had known since Barcelona. The atmosphere was absolutely unbelievable. If ever we needed to produce a disciplined performance, this was it. And produce it we did. It was a big effort. We gave a great account of ourselves. I don't think it's an exaggeration to say we played them off the park. In the process we broke their supporters' hearts. Goals from Colin Walsh and Steve Hodge gave us a 2–1 win. Both players had come through the ranks like me. It was a special moment.

Brian Clough once again held court for the world's media. He was the hero. He could do no wrong. He confidently predicted we would win the UEFA Cup.

There is no doubt that Clough had a talent for getting up the noses of the powerful. That was why he had been kept out of the England job when he was clearly the most qualified candidate. He was the kind of character who the men in suits wanted to 'take down a peg or two.' Part of what irked his critics was that the press lapped him up. He was a natural performer and always controversial. His predictions of triumph could not fail to be heard in Switzerland, the headquarters of UEFA.

Clough's pronouncements looked to be coming true as we eased past Sturm Graz in the next round. We were then drawn against the Belgians of Anderlecht in the semi-final. They were a reasonable enough side but we didn't see anything to frighten us. Everything looked to be going according to plan when we brushed them aside 2–0 in the first leg. We were more than confident of getting through to the final. However, in the return leg, everything went wrong for us and matters got so bad that the integrity of UEFA itself was called into question.

First of all let me say that we did not play well in the game in Brussels. Sometimes this happens. Sometimes opponents do better than you on the day. But still, our 2–0 lead from the first leg should have been enough to see us through. In the game, however, the referee – one

Mr. Guruceta – seemed to be making a few strange decisions as the match progressed, all of them in favour of our opponents. We were 3-0 down and in danger of crashing out of the competition when Paul Hart scored a late goal which would have won us the tie on away goals. Everyone could see it was a perfectly good goal. Everyone, that is, except Mr Guruceta. We were convinced we had done it. Our celebrations, however, were cut short when, to our horror, the ref ruled out Paul's goal. He disallowed it for no reason whatever that anyone has ever been able to see, either at the time or since. It was perhaps the only occasion when the Forest players questioned a referee's decision. We were, to be honest, outraged.

As a senior player, I thought it right to approach the official. But as he waved me away I gave him a mouthful. I can't remember exactly what I said but it probably shouldn't be repeated here anyway. Of course my intervention had no effect on the decision and we were denied our rightful victory. None of us thought it was an honest mistake. Taken alongside other decisions the referee had made, we were sure we had been cheated.

The fall-out from that match is still going on to the present day. At the time, Forest complained to UEFA and they were forced to investigate, although we got the distinct impression they didn't want to. After months, it was admitted by the directors of Anderlecht that they had paid money to bribe the referee. I think it was about £20,000. The appeals lasted years. The directors of Anderlecht changed. Eventually, no punishment of any consequence was handed down. In recent times Forest have been going through the relevant tribunals and courts to try to win compensation for the loss we suffered through that bit of corruption. So far, the club have not received a penny although they continue to press their case. At this rate, Forest may receive something in about fifty years time.

Of course, the biggest way Anderlecht profited from their crime was that they reached the final of the UEFA Cup. It wasn't the first time something like this had happened and it won't be the last. But as the main victims on this occasion, the ejection from Europe probably affected Forest badly for years afterwards.

For me, that season was the end of the line at Forest. It felt so good that I could leave the club on a high. After discussing my future with Debra and a few close friends and family, I decided to pursue new pastures. At about the same time Don Howe got in touch. He was manager at Arsenal, where he had helped win the double as assistant to Bertie Mee back in 1971. He was now back and this time in the manager's chair. Howe let me know he was interested in signing me for the Gunners.

This was a turn up for the book. Arsenal! Wow! The idea of playing for them was fantastic. And I knew the Don from my time with England. What a challenge. The money was good, too, much better than I was getting at Forest. Arsenal were a club for whom I had the greatest respect. They did things the right way. The Arsenal players I met on England duty were always full of praise for the club. Better still, Howe had brought Woody back from Germany and the prospect of renewing our friendship and playing with him again was another reason for considering Howe's offer extremely seriously.

I talked to Debra. We were from Clifton. We were born and brought up in Nottingham. Did we want to go to London? All those people? All those bright lights? Yes we did.

Before that, though, there was the little matter of getting married.

Chapter Eight

LONDON

Debra and I had been together for over four years by the time my transfer to Arsenal went through in the summer of 1984. We were living happily in Nottingham and had built ourselves a good life. But when we talked about moving south, one of the things we both wanted to do was get married. We spoke about it and decided to tie the knot before we departed for London. Unfortunately, we left the details to the point where there wasn't much time to organise the nuptials. I began to panic as the arrangements became more and more complicated and the date for our move to London got closer. And we hadn't told anyone yet.

In the end we threw all the plans out, just went to the registry office in Nottingham and got hitched. Only a photographer was invited to attend. The photographer was the Forest club cameraman, John Sumpter. I told him to bring a friend to be our witness. He brought his brother. Although he acted as a witness to our wedding, I've not seen John's brother from that day to this. I'm ashamed to say that Debra and I didn't tell our parents we were about to be wed, mainly at my urging. For some reason I just couldn't cope with it. Afterwards, we drove first to Debra's parents' house and told them what we had done. They were really great about it and gave us their blessing and their congratulations. When we arrived at my folks' house my Dad was there but Mam was at work. This wasn't how it was supposed to be. Dad seemed genuinely pleased although somewhat taken aback by the news. He too gave us his congratulations, which was lovely. The trouble was I was getting more and more worried when I couldn't get my mother on the phone. At that precise moment she was somewhere in the hospital but no-one knew where. I tried again and again, to no avail. Mam discovered the wedding had taken place when a patient told her he had heard it on the news. It wasn't how I wanted her to find out. In fact I was mortified that it was even on the news. It wouldn't be the last time the press would get to my family with a personal story before I did, as you'll see later. Anyway, as far as the wedding was concerned, you can imagine the stick I got, all of it deserved. I can't totally account for our behaviour, even at this distance in time, but the formalities all seemed to get on top of us, especially me.

My journey to Arsenal began when Don Howe phoned me during the long summer of 1984 when there was no England team in the European Championships. If I remember it right, it was July and we were due to report to Forest for the pre-season any day. "I'd like to talk to you, can we meet?" Howe said, in a cloak-and-dagger sort of way. I pressed him for more information but he didn't want to talk too much on the phone. For some reason or other, I wondered whether it was anything to do with England. After all, it was with England that I had worked with Howe in the past. I found out what was on his mind when he drove up to Nottingham and we met in semi-secrecy at my house. Don looked this way and that, making sure no-one was observing him. When we got into the house he sat down, had a cup of tea as we exchanged hellos and began his pitch. "I want you with me at Arsenal," he said, "and I'm ready to talk terms." He looked this way and that again as though he half-expected someone to be listening at the window or the door. I was flattered. And the thought of working with the Don excited me. I enjoyed training sessions with him when I was on England duty – as much as I enjoyed any training at all, which I didn't. Don was steeped in football, he could remember everything, lots of it from before the war, or that's how it seemed. He was a fountain of knowledge.

The Don told me he had big plans for Arsenal. He was going to make the team an attacking force in the First Division once again. He also made an attempt to sell the club to me, but Arsenal needed no selling. They were a great club. Always have been, always will be. We quickly moved on to other matters like my wages. The contract details were thrashed out there and then and that was it. The days of agents and long, drawn-out negotiations had not arrived in football back then. It was generally just you and the manager. My thoughts went back to the club I was leaving. I had to talk to Clough. So I arranged to meet him just before the lads were due off on a pre-season trip. I told him I wanted to go. Although he at first said I would be a fool to leave, he soon realised I was serious. He was ready to offer me a new contract to stay at Forest but my mind was made up. Eventually, Clough was fantastic about it and allowed me to leave for a reasonable fee – £250,000. Forest were the club that had nurtured me, had taken me on a journey of success and which I had come to love. But I was no longer responding to the ways of Brian Clough. I was also pretty much the last player from the glory days still remaining at Forest and I really needed this new challenge.

Moving to London was fantastic. Yes, I had travelled the world with Forest but it was now time to see whether I could cut it living and working in the capital. It wasn't so much the football, I was pretty sure I could cope with that. No, it was the fact that there are many distractions in a city like London. There is so much to do, and the bright lights had turned the heads of so many people who thought they could handle it. I wasn't going to be one of them. I was happy in myself and my relationship and plunged into my new life with gusto. One thing that really pleased me was the article Brian Clough wrote about me in his column in Nottingham's local newspaper when I departed. "As I see it," he said, "Viv left the club simply because he wanted a change after ten years at the City Ground. And who can blame him? He gave Forest magnificent service." It was also great to know that I would be linking up with Woody once more. Don Howe had brought him brought him back from Germany and intended him to be one of Arsenal's main strikers.

The first thing I noticed that was different at Arsenal

Mam and Dad.

Me and my brother Donald.

Winning my first football award.

The Legendary duo of Peter Taylor and Brian Clough.

Cloughie, not known for pulling his punches, presents me with the player of the year trophy.

Forest team, bikes and all, outside City Ground.

Training with Trevor Francis before Munich final 1979.

Winners of The European Cup, Munich 30th May 1979.

Champions of Europe.

Lining up with the Nottingham Forest Team and European Cup.

The European Cup.

Celebrating at the Player of the Year Awards' Gala with a few mates including
Tony Currie, Peter Shilton, Garry Birtles, John Robertson, Derek Statham,
Cyrille Regis, Laurie Cunningham.

Best ever Forest team voted by the fans: Back row left to right: Ian Storey-Moore,
Kenny Burns, Stan Collymore, Peter Shilts, John Robbo, Viv Anderson, Big Larry
Front row left to right: Martin O'Neill, Tony Woodcock, Archie Gem, Steve Stone,
Des Walker, Trevor Francis. (Stuart Pearce was also voted in, but couldn't attend.)

"Hot shot" defender signs for the Gunners!

Tackling Clive Allen in a heated Arsenal v Spurs North London Derby.

With Pat "God" Jennings and former Forest team mate Tony Woodcock.

Sharing a joke with the great Don Howe.

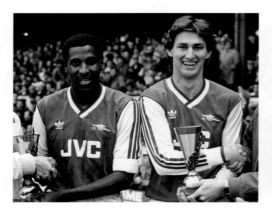

Shoulder to shoulder with Tony Adams, one of the greatest defenders I had the honour to play alongside.

Receiving the player of the month award from Arsenal manager George Graham.

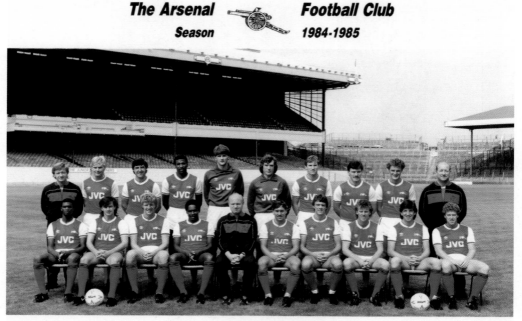

The Arsenal Football Club Season 1984-1985

STANDING (left to right), Terry BURTON (Coach), David CORK, Brian TALBOT, Viv ANDERSON, John LUKIC, Pat JENNINGS, Stewart ROBSON, Ian ALLINSON, Colin HILL, Roy JOHNSON (Physio)
SEATED (left to right), Paul DAVIS, Charlie NICHOLAS, Tommy CATON, Raphael MEADE, Don HOWE (Manager), Kenny SANSOM, David O'LEARY, Graham RIX, Paul MARINER, Tony WOODCOCK

Arsenal team 84–85.

was the feel of Highbury when you walked through the doors. It wasn't just the famous 'marble halls'. You could taste the atmosphere of tradition and success in every corner. As I came to understand, this could sometimes weigh heavily on the players. In Arsenal's case, whatever you did tended to be compared to the exploits of the double-winning team of 1971 (before that, I'm told, it was the team of the 1930s but only Don Howe could remember that far back). Now admittedly, the double-winning team were brilliant but it seemed to me that many at the club just couldn't let it go. To them, nothing could ever be as good as that. I think this negative attitude finally began to change after George Graham's championship-winning campaigns in 1989 and 1991 but was only finally laid to rest in the Arsene Wenger era.

If Highbury, with its unique atmosphere, was the first difference I noticed, the main change from what I had been used to was Don Howe's training methods. Under Clough, training, especially during the season, was minimal, with lots of walks and a few five-a-sides. Don Howe was more mainstream. We went for hard runs, trained with weights and were strictly monitored all the time. Luckily for me, I had been exposed to some of this way of doing things with England. Howe was the number two to both Ron Greenwood and Bobby Robson, so I thought I had a good idea of what to expect. Believe me, it was hard. For someone like me who was not the greatest trainer unless it was ball-work, training under the Don was especially difficult.

On my first day at Arsenal for pre-season training, Howe

sent us on a five mile run. What an introduction! All of us started together bar the manager. After four miles I was way, way behind everyone else. I hated long-distance running, especially the cross-country. I was slogging away and doing my best but it was a real effort. Suddenly I heard footsteps and regular puffs of breath coming up behind me. I turned round. It was Don Howe, who had started running forty-five minutes after the rest of us. Now here he was about to overtake me. I had to sprint flat-out over the last hundred metres in order not to be beaten in a cross-country by a sixty-five year-old man who remembered the thirties. I have to say that as prepared as I thought I was, that run was a rude awakening.

The manager told me Arsenal had needed a replacement for Pat Rice at right-back for at least a couple of years. Since he had retired it was something of a problem position. This was what I wanted to hear. I knew I could fill Pat's shoes, and he was good, very good. It all meant my position in the team was secure, at least if I performed as I knew I could. Don Howe had been Bertie Mee's assistant during the double-winning season and he was very ambitious to take Arsenal back to the top. He had got the job after Terry Neill's unsuccessful spell in charge and he seemed determined to bring back the good times. We had some very good players, notably the great Pat Jennings in goal. Pat was as calm, cool and collected as anyone could possibly be. For a goalkeeper, he was like Buddha. In fact we called him 'God'. Not for him the shouting and finger-pointing at defenders when an opponent shoots from 45 yards. Although he was nearing the end of his career when I arrived (he was replaced by John Lukic) some of the saves I saw him make were simply out of this world. One-on-one with a forward he was the best. He could be looking one way, stick a foot out the other way, and save a shot he had no right to get anywhere near. No problem!

Kenny Samson was a left-back of total class. His natural ability never ceased to amaze me and he worked hard on his game so he could make those surging runs up the left flank that were his trademark. He held off a strong challenge for his England place by another very good English full-back, Derek Statham of West Brom, and ended up with over eighty England caps. We had Brian Talbot running the midfield, with Tommy Caton (who sadly died young) and the incomparable David O'Leary at the heart of the defence. Up front with Woody was Paul Mariner, another top striker who had played for England. In addition, the talented Charlie Nicholas was brought down from Scotland to add some flair to the team going forward. On the face of it, we looked like we had a solid enough side to push for honours.

Charlie had been a sensation at Celtic. As a Glasgow boy himself he was revered on the terraces at Parkhead. He was so, so gifted and the fans loved him for that as much as his goalscoring feats. The year before he came to Arsenal he had scored forty-odd goals for Celtic, which cemented his already huge reputation and brought the club the Scottish League title. As a reward, Charlie told me, the always stingy Celtic board had offered him an increase in wages – of eight pounds a week. We all couldn't believe it. It was such an insult. He would have loved to have continued playing for his boyhood club, but they did absolutely nothing to entice him to stay there. So off he went, into the waiting arms of Don Howe and the five mile runs. Charlie was a catalyst for us. He was the one we looked to, the one who could turn it on, who could produce something a bit special and win us games.

Charlie and Paul Mariner had the two loudest voices I have ever heard. When either of them spoke they could break glass a hundred yards away. It wasn't that they shouted as such, they just had extremely loud voices. They were so loud you couldn't tell what they were saying half the time. If you watch Charlie on TV these days, you'll see that although he's managed to tone it down a bit, that voice still goes some when he gets excited. Whenever Charlie and Paul were together, it was best to stay well clear. One day, for some reason I can't remember, we were training on the Highbury pitch. At Highbury, the dressing room had a window that looked out onto the street. After training Charlie and Paul struck up a conversation by the open window. As one of them bellowed something, so the other bellowed even louder. I can't remember what the conversation was about. It could have been the weather. So loud did their dialogue get we all had to leave the room. We heard later that a neighbour across the street had heard them and thought there was some kind of riot going on. They complained about the noise to the club, who had to explain that no-one was hurt or killed. Either one of the two players could have found a job as a fairground barker if they hadn't been so good at football.

As often happens in football, as soon as I joined Arsenal, we had to play my old club at the City Ground. It was only the second game of the season. I wondered what kind of reception I'd get from the fans. I asked myself if I'd be able to concentrate on the game. I wished I'd had a few more matches for the Gunners under my belt before this fixture came round. In the event, the crowd was fantastic and gave me a great reception. It was an emotional return. Perhaps too much so! We didn't perform too well on the day and Forest beat us 2–0.

That first season was in and out. On our day we could beat anyone but we could also lose to anyone on another day. Inconsistency was our defining characteristic, to the frustration of our supporters, who turned up in fantastic numbers week after week. I remember one Saturday we were away at Villa, who by then had won the European Cup. We hammered them 6–0. The week after that we meekly succumbed to West Brom at home. Don Howe began tinkering, always looking for what he called the "right blend". The Don, a brilliant coach, could often be uncertain when it came to picking his best team, particularly after a couple of bad results. Some of that was because he loved talking football and swapping opinions, some of which became his own. As a manager he didn't always know when to give a player a bollocking and when to put his arm round him. Motivation of players was a bit of a mystery to him. The uncertainty was felt in other ways too. When we got a good result playing poorly, Don was never sure whether to praise the result or get on our backs for the performance. Everything had to be black or white. When there were shades of grey, which was a lot of the time, the Don was lost. In the end it did for him. If there was one thing George Graham brought to Arsenal it was the certainty that he, George Graham, and he alone, knew who the best eleven were and how they should be treated.

I was pleased with my own performances under Howe and I was generally left out of much of the criticism the team took from the papers, which, when you are a huge club like Arsenal, dissect every error, every point dropped. I knuckled down to the harsher training methods and made sure I never slacked, even for a moment. My attitude began to pay off as I put in some of the best displays of my career. I settled into the Arsenal way of doing things easily and soon felt I had been there all my life. I only missed three games in three years.

I got my first goal for my new club at the end of September, in a League Cup game against Bristol Rovers, which we won 4-0. Somehow, I found myself bounding forward as the great Graham Rix put in a perfect cross from the left. I continued into the six yard box and I nodded it in. Simple!

Debra and I also settled well into life in the capital. There were dinners at the best restaurants and hours spent at the most famous night clubs in the world. I was never a playboy or anything like that – and more often than not when I went out I would be accompanied by my wife – but I think it's fair to say that both of us loved the London life. We took to it like ducks to water.

Clubbing would sometimes prove to contain more drama than football. One Friday night (we had no game that Saturday) Debra and I were at Tramps, partying with Simon Le Bon (the singer of Duran Duran) and George Best. Now wherever you went with Bestie, you could be sure the drink would be flowing. This particular night was no exception, in fact George seemed to be drinking more than ever – if that was possible. By about 5am he was paralytic. Then he let us know he wanted our attention and tried to make what turned out to be a slurred announcement. "I'm supposed to be getting married today," he said. At first we didn't believe him but it soon became clear he was serious. He was actually due to marry his fiancé, Angie, later that morning. "What are we going to do with him?" Simon asked. Debra said we had to get him into some kind of better shape. So Simon Le Bon, Debra and I tried to get him sobered up, at least to the extent that he would be able to make it to his wedding. This was easier said than done with George, who had more ways of finding an alcoholic beverage than anyone I've known. We tried coffee, we tried walking him about. In the end, the task proved impossible. George passed out and that was it. He failed to show up for his own wedding. Thankfully, he did manage to make it for the rearranged ceremony, which took place a few weeks later.

Back on the pitch, the season was turning into one of missed opportunities. We just couldn't put together any kind of decent run to challenge for the title. It was all the more annoying because we had good players who were playing reasonably well. Don Howe was providing dossiers on the opposition, not that it did much good. We went over every little detail again and again. By the end of these talks we knew what our opponents had for breakfast. I suppose at Arsenal, the pressure was far greater on the manager than it had been at Forest. There, Clough was king. At Highbury, you always felt the manager's job was only lent out for a limited time. A few bad results and the boss would be out. It wasn't as cut-throat as today, when a manager can be sacked only a few matches into a season, but at the big clubs in those days there was always speculation concerning the manager's position if the team was faltering. And always there was pressure to win.

The effect of the detailed attention on the opposition was that we became a bit more defensive than necessary at times. This was not what Howe wanted. His instinct was to encourage us to attack at every opportunity. But we became known as a team that first of all looked to stop our opponents from playing. It was around that time that the 'boring Arsenal' tag became commonplace. I didn't think we were boring – how could we be with Charlie Nicholas in the team – but we certainly did not find it easy to play the expansive football that Don Howe craved. More often than not, we were praised for keeping clean sheets far more than we ever were for producing a great piece of skill or scoring a wonderful goal. The Don had wanted his Arsenal to play flowing, attacking football. But instead our reputation was for organisation and a good defence.

It's funny but my own performances were top-notch all season, in a team that was stuttering at best. The problem was that, despite the dossiers and the hard training, the manager chopped and changed our team and our system depending on what his thoughts were that week or how the opposition was set up. Often, we would have no idea of our likely formation week to week. At a club like Arsenal, the team was expected to challenge for League titles and lift at least a cup every season. So our League finish of seventh (Everton won it, thirteen points clear of Liverpool) and our poor showing in the cups – which might not have been a bad return at some clubs – was not good enough for Arsenal. There would have to be a big improvement.

Chapter 9

COMETH THE HOUR

At the beginning of my second season at Arsenal, Don Howe's assistant, John Cartwright, decided to alter our style of play completely. It was a most un-Arsenal type of change and it didn't bring the required improvement. For a few seasons, the English football world had marvelled at the way Graham Taylor had lifted Watford from the depths of the old fourth division to the heights of the first, where they finished second and secured a place in the UEFA Cup. They had also reached the FA Cup Final in 1984 although they were beaten by Everton. All in all, Taylor had performed wonders at Watford. There were arguments, though, over the way that success had been achieved.

The problem was, football purists – and I would include myself in their number – thought that Watford's system was old-fashioned, not to say Neanderthal. That is, they played long balls up to the front players – particularly Luther Blissett – in what was termed the direct style. In this method, the midfield was often bypassed as defenders hoofed the ball upfield. Even with two wingers of pace and skill, one of them John Barnes, Watford more often than not continued to overuse the long ball. It was, at best, a percentage game. At its worst, it was ugly anti-football. The problem was that in England, it was proving to be very successful and it provoked huge debate within the game and in the media. At Watford, although Taylor played with wingers, it is for the long ball that he is most remembered.

John Cartwright and Don Howe became convinced that this was the way Arsenal should play. Now while it is acceptable for teams who cannot afford to buy the best players to adopt this sort of tactic, for Arsenal and the club's fans it was beyond the pale. Arsenal supporters were used to seeing midfield players of the calibre of Liam Brady pulling the strings. Neither our midfielders nor our forwards, both of whom had to change their game, were best pleased. Charlie Nicholas suffered most. His whole game was based on his skill when the ball was played to his feet. He was no good when he had to run down the channels all day. Brian Talbot, who had learned his football under Bobby Robson at Ipswich, and Steve Williams, who had been bought to bring his midfield skills to the team, both expressed their strong disapproval, as did Graham Rix, our wide player on the left. Indeed, Williams voiced his discontent at every opportunity and was dropped from the side.

I didn't like these tactics, I was used to playing in tandem with right-sided wide players and had become adept at using the space they provided. I also liked looking for a pass, short or long, playing out from the back. Now when I got the ball I was expected to bang it up into the channel or onto the heads of the forwards. That left little opportunity for crafting attacks through the opposition's midfield. It wasn't as bad for us full-backs, though, as it was for the likes of Steve Williams, who found his particular talents were almost worthless in such a style. Although I told the Don I didn't like it, I felt it was my job to play in whatever style the manager dictated and I was, after all, paid to get on with it and give it my best shot, which I did.

That season, 1985–86, was again one of treading water for Arsenal. The fans weren't too pleased and attendances at Highbury started to dip. In fairness, this wasn't just a problem in North London. Throughout the 1980s, terrace hooliganism had been getting worse. The terrible events at the Heysel stadium in Brussels, when a clash between Liverpool and Juventus supporters at the European Cup Final resulted in many deaths, sent a signal to the decent fan that football stadiums were dangerous places to be. English clubs were banned from playing in Europe. It was a bad time. For a while, football lost its place in the hearts of those who made up its huge mass of support. There was even the prospect that the game would wither on the vine and die. It is difficult to imagine now, but during that season, football was no longer shown on television as the two big companies, BBC and ITV, refused to screen it.

At Arsenal, the malaise was felt hard. We were a club in the best traditions of English football. We had players who would draw big crowds anywhere. But during this period, it seemed like our performances on the pitch mirrored the disillusion of our fans.

Liverpool lifted the title (again), by two points from Everton, who had won it the previous season with a great side put together by Howard Kendall. They were denied their opportunity to test themselves in Europe because of the ban. I know it always rankled with Peter Reid, because he told me. I don't know how I'd have felt if I had won the League then been unable to go into the European Cup and have those fantastic experiences. Through no fault of your own! I sympathised with Peter and the rest of his team.

Whether or not there was a ban on English clubs in Europe, Arsenal wouldn't have made it into continental competition anyway. We finished seventh. Again! Even West Ham were above us. That meant there had been no improvement on the previous season. That is simply not good enough at a club like Arsenal. We had a tilt at both the FA Cup and the League Cup, but after starting well we were knocked out of both competitions at the quarter final stage. In the FA Cup we went out to Luton after a second replay, while in the League Cup Aston Villa beat us 2–1 in a replay at Highbury after we had gained a hard-fought 1–1 draw at Villa Park. It wasn't why I had come to the club.

Don Howe was a good coach, there is no doubt about that. I experienced his methods with England and Arsenal and I think I can say he was second to nobody in his coaching skills. As a manager, I don't think he developed the necessary feel for the top job. Perhaps also his best days were behind him. Put it this way: at the end of the 1985–86 season change was in the air. The Arsenal board needed a new man to take them back to the level they expected of their team. They also needed someone who could galvanise the club's fan-base.

George Graham had played in the double-winning team. He was, by all accounts, an extremely cultured and mild-mannered midfield player, one of only a few to have played for both Arsenal and Manchester United (I would become a member of this select club soon enough). He also played for Chelsea. When he was nearing the end of his career at Crystal Palace, Terry Venables convinced him to become a coach. His first managerial job had been at Millwall, where he excelled. He arrived at Highbury with the coaching reputation of a defensive-minded disciplinarian. I don't know how or when the transformation from stylish football player to tough, no-nonsense manager occurred, but I will say this: it was always hard to swallow the line that Graham was as nice a player as he would have us believe.

When he arrived, Graham showed great skill in dealing with the departure of Don Howe. He called us together as a group and looked at us for a few moment with that square jaw of his. "I know some of you will be upset that Don has gone," he said. "But all of you now have to look to the future. You have to look forward. I'm here. That's that. Work hard and you'll be OK with me." He said it in that gentle, rolling Scottish tone. It was perfect. It said everything that needed to be said.

He used to tie us defenders up. Literally! The back-four were often roped together in training so that we couldn't be pulled apart from each other beyond a certain distance. So when one moved to the left, we all moved to the left. If you didn't go when the rope was on you would soon be made to look a fool as you slithered around on the ground. Does that make sense? Me neither! However, as time went by, the back four started to develop an uncanny collective move-ment. We became a unit, always sure of where each other was and what we had to do. Unlike at Forest, the full-backs played out wide but just in front of the centre-backs, with the job of stifling anything the oppo-sition tried to do in our area of the pitch. We were supposed to usher our wingers inside so they never got the chance to cross. At Forest it didn't matter if the winger went outside as long as you prevented him from getting a cross in. At Arsenal, George Graham wanted the winger inside before he could go on a run. He didn't want even the smallest percentage that gave the winger a chance to cross. I felt confident enough to challenge him on this philosophy from time to time but, as I said before, it is the boss who dictates the system of play. At least George was prepared to debate the matter with me but I wasn't able to change his mind. We had our ups and downs but I have to say that George was proved right. With the squad he had it was an effective way of playing. At least he knew what he wanted, which was a refreshing difference from the Don Howe period.

Another change Graham made to the defence was to get us to play higher up the pitch. If an opposing midfield player had the ball, our midfield was expected to pressure him. The full-backs would advance up the pitch to stop the ball played out wide. If he tried to knock it over the top we would more often than not catch one of their forwards offside. The only option left would be a pass to another midfield player, where the move could be strangled, or back, where it posed no problem.

Around that time, some very good young players were beginning to emerge from the youth system, including Paul Davis, David Rocastle and Michael Thomas, players who would take the club to new heights. Graham always encouraged the youngsters. He recognised that Arsenal's youth set-up was one of the club's greatest strengths. He gave the rest of the players the respect he felt was due to senior professionals – as long as we were prepared – after discussions if need be – to accept his way of doing things.

The one player Graham didn't seem to rate was his fellow Scot, Charlie Nicholas. It was because of Graham's unwillingness to put his trust in Charlie that the manager became known as someone who had no faith in flair. That wasn't the whole story though. Graham was always obsessed with his team controlling the midfield and having an organised defence. But once that was achieved, he liked to attack with panache. He brought plenty of flair players up front in his time at the club, whether in the transfer market (Ian Wright) or from the youth team (Paul Merson). But, for some reason, he just didn't get Charlie. Now Charlie is the first to admit that when he originally came to London from Scotland he made some bad decisions which gave him what was an undeserved reputation as 'Champagne Charlie'. He never took to staying in a hotel. We both stayed in the same place for a time while we were looking for houses and I always got the impression that Charlie didn't really like it. On the pitch he rarely produced the consistency he should have. It had also been difficult for him when John Cartwright brought in the direct style of play. At the time George Graham came, Charlie's confidence was low. But trust me, Charlie was a special talent, as even Graham would have to admit before the season was out.

One of the youngsters Graham brought through was Tony Adams. When Tony was added to the defence it was obvious from the word go that he would have a great career. It wasn't simply his physical strength that imposed itself on you but his attitude. He displayed an absolute determination to succeed in every tackle. He also possessed another rare quality: leadership.

1986–87 was due to be the last season of my three year contract with the Gunners. It was George Graham's first campaign in charge. I felt I had unfinished business with Arsenal. I had come to Highbury for a number of reasons: the challenge; the money, to play for one of England's great clubs. All played a part. But most of all I came to win trophies and medals. As the new season got underway I really did think we could achieve success with Graham. He had something of the Clough about him. However, I thought it would take at least a couple of years to get into a position to win something – especially since the manager was beginning to put his faith in the production line of young players. I began to think about renewing my contract. I was entering my thirties and knew that my next deal needed to be a good one. Graham indicated that a new offer would be made to me at the end of the season. That could never happen today, where new contracts are sewn up (or not) well before the expiry date of the old one. In those days, even when a player decided to leave at the end of his contract, a transfer fee was payable. That has now changed completely.

We started the season quite well, but it was the period between November and the end of January that really announced the club's revival. During that time we went seventeen League games unbeaten, with thirteen wins. It was incredible. The fans loved it. George Graham loved the fact that we were hardly conceding any goals even more. Arsenal were back. As February dawned we were top of the table. For the first time since I arrived, there was a real buzz around the place.

As the senior player, when I looked around the team, I wasn't sure it was ready to win the League. It was talented, yes, and strong. But it generally takes a bit of time for

132

youngsters to come good. Even when we were top of the table, I felt this. I was as excited as everyone else that we had got this far but I could see the younger players were getting tired at times. That made me redouble my efforts. I was the one who had won the medals. I was the one who had won the title and European Cups. I had to lead by example. The way that young team managed to find the strength to carry on, in that and the following seasons, amazes me to this day.

Our form in the League dipped towards the end of the season. We were soundly beaten at Manchester United, when David Rocastle got sent off following a clash with Norman Whiteside. Somehow, that adversity affected the players more than it should have and we lost five of the next eight games. The other three were drawn. We also went on a goal drought, scoring one in nine. We fell to fourth, which is where we remained until the end of the season. Despite the end-of-season downturn, it was Arsenal's best finish for years. Everton lifted the title once more for the second time in three seasons. What was worse, much worse, for our north London fans, however, was the fact that Spurs had stolen a march under the management of David Pleat and had finished ahead of us in third. This wasn't in the script at all.

Again, our performances in the FA Cup flattered to deceive. I can hardly even remember the games now. I do know that Watford defeated us 3–1 at Highbury in the sixth round and we were out. To this day, the FA Cup is the one medal missing from my collection.

It was in the League Cup that we showed exactly what we were capable of and I can certainly remember that. All of us at the club were aware that we needed to give our long-suffering fans something to cheer. We did that by letting them get their first sniff of a trophy for seven years. It was the League Cup that gave the team the platform to go on and perform great deeds.

Of all our matches on the way to Wembley that year, the one that is most fondly remembered by Arsenal fans is the semi-final victory over Spurs. And remember, this was the Spurs team of David Pleat which reached – but lost – the FA Cup Final that year. They had the country's leading goalscorer of the day, Clive Allen, who hit 49 goals that season. They also possessed two absolutely brilliant talents, Chris Waddle and Glenn Hoddle. They were hot favourites. We were a young side. Also, some of our best players, including Charlie Nick and Graham Rix, had suffered injuries throughout the season. But this was Spurs. It meant an awful lot.

We lost the first leg at home by a slender margin, 1–0, with Clive Allen scoring their goal. That was a deflating result. Spurs fans were cock-a-hoop, ours dejected. If Spurs were favourites before the game they were now odds-on. The manager didn't panic though. He told us we could still win, that we hadn't played too badly. Somehow, his belief transferred to us.

As the second leg unfolded at White Hart Lane, Allen again scored and Spurs were in control. To all intents and purposes, we were out. It was simply a matter of playing out time, surely. We would have to pull something big out of the hat if we were going to turn this round. That night, though, that steely determination that George Graham had begun to instil was running through the side.

I played a massive part in our revival in the tie. It was probably the best thing I ever did for Arsenal. I went up for a long throw from David Rocastle, hoping to steal in unnoticed. The ball eluded everybody except big Niall Quinn who got a head on it. The ball landed at my feet. I forced it into the net. That lifted the whole team. We were on top and Spurs began to look jittery. In the blink of an eye, Quinny got his toe to a ball, and he swept it into the net. Cue pandemonium. The crowd went berserk. The players went wild. We were 2–1 up at their place and the tie was all-square.

That goal broke Spurs and energised us. It meant the game would go to extra time. We pressed and pressed during the extra thirty minutes but could not make another breakthrough. Spurs also had a couple of chances. I think both sets of players were drained at the end. I described my goal again and again to everyone after the game. The forwards got fed up with me telling them they couldn't hit a barn door. I was in heaven.

In those days there was no away goals rule in the League Cup so we had to go to another replay. The venue was chosen by the toss of a coin and Spurs won it. So it was back to White Hart Lane for the decider. The atmosphere across North London was electric. Everywhere I went – shopping, in petrol stations, at restaurants, in the

streets – members of the public would either be congratu-
lating me and urging me on (if they were Arsenal fans) or
telling me we would lose big-time (if they were Spurs).

Yet again, Clive Allen was the danger man. Rarely can
someone have scored three goals in a cup tie and ended
up on the losing side. He put Spurs in front. First blood
to them. Their fans seemed to settle back, ready for the
win. But we conjured an equaliser from Ian Allinson and
it was game on. The tension inside White Hart Lane was
incredible as the match approached its climax. Inside the
last ten minutes, we went forward and the young David
Rocastle put us ahead for the first time in the tie. We had
been playing for 250 minutes and now, at last, we were
in the lead with just a few minutes to hang on. Gone was
the recent downturn, we were now on a roll. Spurs gave
it a go and we had one or two scares but we powered
into the final. For our fans, it was a double celebration.
Not only had we reached a major final for the first time
in some years, we had beaten their greatest enemy to get
there.

As I mentioned earlier in this book, games between
Forest and County were never what you would call proper
derbies. Arsenal and Spurs, however, is the real thing,
one of the best. I loved playing in games against them.
When I scored that goal – one of seven I managed that
term – I fully realised what it meant to the fans. I was the
toast of our half of north London for weeks. What's not
to love about that?

Having said that, for me personally there was another
game on the road to Wembley that meant an awful

lot. It was the fifth round tie in January 1987 against Nottingham Forest. It was one game, winner take all, at Highbury. In the three years I spent at Arsenal I was never on the winning side against Forest in the League. I didn't like that. I wanted my new team to beat them. Any professional feels the same, that's why you often get great performances out of players when they line up against their old clubs. But for Arsenal, I either lost or drew every game against Forest. Except for that League Cup tie. We were superb that night, it came in the middle of our unbeaten run and we walloped them 2–0 in front of a capacity crowd. Stuart Pearce missed a penalty. Our goals were scored by Charlie Nick and Martin Hayes. The fans were back now as well. They were buying into George Graham and the team in a big way. It was a fantastic turnaround from the nowhere days of Don Howe.

And so to the showpiece at Wembley. Against Liverpool (aaaargh)! I was in my element, letting the youngsters know exactly how I'd knocked the Scousers out of the European Cup single-handed, as well as seeing them off in the League Cup Final. Liverpool – to echo Brian Clough – so what!

Ian Rush put them in front and the crowd waited for the inevitable victory that would follow. After all, it was oft repeated in those days that Liverpool never lost when Rush scored. And until that match it was true. But no-one had told Charlie Nicholas. He at last showed his class. On the biggest occasion since his move to London from Celtic in 1983, Charlie bagged the two goals that won us the Cup. For perhaps the only time, Champagne Charlie had come up trumps when it mattered. It couldn't have happened to a nicer bloke, even if he is Mr. Motormouth at times.

This was what I had come to Arsenal for. To feel once again the thrill of winning. It was obvious to me that this team could really achieve something big in the next few years. I wanted to be part of it. Then I got a phone call from Bryan Robson.

Chapter Ten

FIRST FOR FERGIE

It was the most I could do to keep looking at the floor. There we were on the training ground ready for our normal workout. But Fergie was having none of it. He was not a happy bunny. Sir Alex Ferguson is one of those managers who make it their business to know every little thing that goes on in their club. He does it better than anybody. You can't hide anything from his gaze. When you know him, you understand this way of operating. And there is no escape. So why would you want to hide anything from him? That's how he maintains such a high level of performance in his players. They come to realise there is nothing that he doesn't know.

Fergie felt the need to be aware of what his players were up to when they were on their own time as well as when they were on club business. He had spies and informers all over Manchester who kept him up to speed. If he hadn't been a football man he would have made a great head of MI5. This was the opposite of what I was used to under Cloughie, who seemed to know everything anyway without anyone having to tell him, or George Graham, who simply expected you to follow his commands. For Ferguson, there was no 'own time'. And when anyone transgressed in a way he didn't like he came down on you like a ton of bricks. It was the whole building. His rage was like a hurricane not a hair-dryer.

The problem really was that we were all frustrated. When I was transferred to United, it soon became clear that Ferguson was fed up with the behaviour of some of those he considered over-paid players who were failing to perform. He wanted to infuse his team with youngsters, trained from an early age in the United cause. The trouble with the first crop in the late eighties was that there were some talented individuals but collectively they were not really good enough. Not like the Aberdeen players he had brought through in his previous job, who had conquered Scotland and Europe. Don't get me wrong, there was a sprinkling of excellent players but the team just wasn't producing on the pitch. It would take a couple more years yet before the FA Cup came back to Old Trafford, followed by the Cup Winners' Cup and the incredible success that came in its wake.

Anyway, on this occasion on the training ground, it seemed the young Lee Sharpe came in for the most criticism, although I think it fair to say that Lee was a bit of a pussycat compared to Norman Whiteside, Bryan Robson and me. Now Robbo could (and did) put his drink away, mostly with Norman Whiteside and yours truly. Lee wasn't in the same class. But we all felt the vicious side of Fergie's tongue at one time or another. We often got grassed up for drinking and staying out late. This time, having heard about a drunken binge the day before, Fergie had obviously had enough.

If I remember it correctly, Fergie started by berating all of us as time-wasters. Moreover, he bawled: "You are time-wasters who can't hold your drink. You wouldn't last five minutes in Glasgow." Looking at Sharpey, the manager's eyes narrowed. Then he exploded. The rant lasted a good five minutes. All I can remember of it were the last few words. "As good as you are I've got someone better in your position. And he doesn't drink. If you're not careful, next week he'll be in and you'll be out." None of us, least of all Sharpey, thought he was serious. Then we saw Ryan Giggs ....

I was Alex Ferguson's first signing for Manchester United. I was also the last player to be transferred from Arsenal to Old Trafford, the previous one being George Graham. The move came out of the blue. I had been all set to negotiate a new contract at Arsenal when I got the call from Bryan.

"Your contract's up isn't it?" Robbo enquired.

I had roomed with Robbo on a number of England away games and he and I discovered we had similar ideas on the way football should be played and the way players should be motivated. Robbo was dubbed 'Captain Marvel' by the media for his no-holds-barred style. But he was also an extremely gifted footballer. Sometimes this got overlooked because of his all-action approach to the game. I identified straight away with his views: they were the same as mine. Robbo was

141

never content simply to be a player; even for England he made sure he always had his say. At United, he was extremely proactive. When Ferguson arrived from Scotland, he was shrewd enough to recognise that Robbo could be an asset over and above what he contributed on the pitch.

"Yeah, but the boss said I'd be offered a new one," I replied.

"Look," Robbo continued, "The manager said he needs a right-back. He also said he wants some proper experience. I told him you were the man. He agreed. I said I'd phone you to see what your situation was."

Was this real? I thought. "Come on Robbo, you're having a laugh," was the best I could manage. I was thirty-one years old. Now here was the greatest club in the land courting my services, through my mate, Bryan Robson.

"If you're up for it, the boss wants to meet you."

"I'm there."

Ferguson had not long been put in charge of United after the departure of Ron Atkinson. He was in no mood to let Manchester United's years of underachievement continue. He bristled with intent. "We need a right-back and you're the one I want," was all he said when I spoke to him on the phone.

I was surprised to say the least. And flattered! In a nanosecond hundreds of thoughts flashed through my mind. I was a United supporter, man and boy; the club had rejected me as a youngster, surely this was vindication, the most fantastic turn of events; if

Arsenal were big, United were massive. I had come to love Arsenal, the way they did things was superb and the intensity of the supporters was never anything less than impressive. And I like to think I gave them three good seasons which helped them to the success they have maintained to the present day. The only club that could have tempted me away was Manchester United. It was personal.

Fergie, would you believe, wanted to meet me at a motorway service station. I was immediately impressed with the way he conducted himself. On top of that he made me a fantastic financial offer. It was far in excess of what I was being paid by Arsenal, and my wages there weren't bad. But more than that, I wanted to play for him.

George Graham was a bit put out when I told him. But there was nothing he could do. My contract was up, I could sign for whomever I liked. If I had been offered a new contract at any time before Robbo's approach I probably would have accepted it. I would have been more than happy to stay at Arsenal. But it never occurred to me that a club of United's stature would want to sign me. After all, I was 31. Maybe it never occurred to George Graham either because he didn't really enter into serious contract talks with me. Perhaps he took it for granted that no club bigger than Arsenal would come in for me so he thought he could bide his time.

George got his own back when it came to the transfer fee United would have to pay. He demanded £450,000, which was ridiculous for a defender of my age. I'm afraid I went public and criticised him in the press. "I accuse George Graham today of sheer greed in attempting to screw a £450,000 transfer fee out of my move to Manchester United," I told the Daily Mirror. "Nearly £500,000 for a full-back who will be 31 next month? Come on, George, you've got to be kidding. Arsenal's demand is extortionate," I continued.

Back then, when a player came to the end of his contract, he was free to move. But a transfer fee was payable. If the two clubs in question couldn't agree the fee it went to a tribunal which tended to split the difference. In the end, the tribunal decreed that United pay Arsenal £250,000 for my services. This meant that the Gunners recouped their outlay on me when I left. Despite the arguments over my departure, I still retain a great affection for the club and its fans. Overall, I really enjoyed my time at Highbury and I definitely helped in the club's revival after years without success.

My manager was now Alex Ferguson. The knighthood came later. I had played under Clough, Howe and Graham. I thought I had seen it all. I had seen nothing.

In the years since he arrived at Old Trafford, enough has been written about Sir Alex Ferguson to fill a large library. His deeds are legendary and his character and motivation have been analysed to death. Just about everyone on the planet has an opinion about him. Scores of players who played under him have had their say, as has the man himself. Let me make this clear. Sir Alex has always treated me – both as a football player and a man – with the utmost kindness and courtesy, sometimes beyond the call of duty.

Let me give you an example. At one point in the middle of my career with United I was becoming more and more frustrated. Injuries had plagued me. I'd be out, get back in for a few games then get injured again. It was something I wasn't used to. And when I did play I didn't do myself justice. The trouble was, the team had not been progressing as everyone had hoped and my poor performances were not helping. I had been picked for a televised game. It was against Liverpool. I don't remember too much about the match, except that I played so badly I was substituted early doors. I was furious, as much with myself as with the decision to take me off in such a way in front of the TV cameras. Without really thinking, I committed one of football's cardinal sins: I ran straight to the dressing room, collected my things and went home, without saying a word to anyone. This you don't do. No-one did it to Ferguson and got away with it. Players were transferred out for less.

My wife Debra almost had a heart attack when she heard the keys opening the front door to our house. She was watching the game on television and naturally thought I was still at the ground. When she saw it was me she was flabbergasted. I couldn't remember driving home, I was in that much of a state. I knew I had done wrong but I was too angry to know how to put it right. It was Debra who convinced me to apologise to the manager. I went in on the Monday and rather sheepishly asked to see him. I was regretting what I had done big-time as I waited for Fergie's reaction. There would surely be fireworks and some severe disciplinary penalty. It might be the end of me at United.

Instead, Ferguson was sympathetic. "I understand your state of mind," he said. "I know you want to do well and you've had some bad injuries." He went on to say there would be no action taken against me. He put his arm round my shoulder. But he let me know in no uncertain terms that if anything like that happened again, "that will be it for you here". Needless to say, nothing like that ever happened again.

At all times he was a gentleman in his dealings with me. Even in the incident with Sharpey I described earlier, Fergie did not turn his wrath on me too much.

Our first meeting after Robbo's call was one of those motorway service stations, Watford Gap or Leicester Forest East or somewhere. Agents were not a force in the game back then. As I have said previously, transfer matters were generally conducted between manager and player. Unfortunately, Fergie had not bought wads of cash but did offer me a lucrative deal, including a substantial increase in the salary I was getting at Arsenal. This was confirmed some time later when I met Fergie and the United Chairman, Martin Edwards, in a hotel in Nottingham. Edwards seemed in awe of Fergie, which was unusual in a Chairman. In my experience, most Chairmen hate their manager. The feeling is generally mutual.

Even if the Gunners had offered me a new contract, it was extremely doubtful they could match the amounts on offer from United. Fergie had been lured from Aberdeen, where he was extremely successful, partly because he was promised the funds to buy the players of his choice by Martin Edwards. I was his first choice. Maybe that's why we have such a good relationship. Anyway, it wasn't just the money. Ferguson let me know forcefully his vision for the club. He pointed to the success in Europe he had brought to Aberdeen. He dismissed United's recent performances as "rubbish" and told me how he was going to make the club great again. There was no doubting him. Where George Graham cajoled you into believing he could bring back the good times, Fergie was just adamant. It would happen. No question. United were not then in the position that they are now. They had not won a League title for over twenty years and had got nowhere in Europe in about as long. Yet I could do nothing but believe him. It was an incredibly passionate sell. I was hooked. I agreed there and then.

At first, Debra wasn't too keen on moving north. She loved it in London, as did I. She even made a good case for staying at Arsenal for football reasons. Arsenal under George Graham, she said, were the team to watch, Fergie had a mountain to climb. No-one had done it at United since Matt Busby. I had to agree. But in the end I couldn't turn Fergie down. To be fair, Debra knew that and supported me. Now, even though we have been divorced for some years, Debra has not taken the opportunity to move back to London and has stayed in the north-west, which she now loves.

It was pleasing to me that much later George Graham said that he wished he could have kept me at Arsenal. He tried lots of players in my position after I departed, including the left-footed Nigel Winterburn, but never found a proper replacement until he signed Lee Dixon. It is comments like that one that become part of a footballer's most treasured memories. After all, George had every reason to resent me after my outburst in the Daily Mirror, even if what I said was true. But he was big enough to give me credit. I was sorry he left Arsenal under a cloud following the 'bung' he received from a transfer fee. In my dealings with him there was never any question of dishonesty. I have witnessed far worse in my many years in the game than anything George Graham ever did. None of their crimes, though, were ever investigated, let alone punished.

Obviously, the team I went into at Old Trafford was not Fergie's side. It was, in the main, Ron Atkinson's construction. Of the players Fergie inherited, one stood out like a colossus. The rock, the player on which the side was based, was the incomparable Bryan Robson. For me, Robbo was the complete midfield player. He could do everything: tackle; track back; pass short or long and he scored goals. His will to win was extraordinary and if a few more of United's players had shown his determination, success would have been guaranteed. The only player who could come anywhere near him at the modern Manchester United is Roy Keane. Keano was lucky in the sense that he had a great team around him and so achieved the kind of success at Old Trafford that eluded Robbo.

Robbo always thought about the game and liked to swap opinions with all the other players all the time. Robbo and I became the greatest of friends. We spent lots of time together discussing tactics: how the team was performing, what we could do to improve, things like that. We also spoke about how we might make a great management team one day. We agreed that once our playing careers were over, if one of us was ever offered a management role, the other would come along as well. Some years later, as most football followers will know, I answered the call to be Robbo's number two at Middlesbrough.

There were some good young players coming through at United. Norman Whiteside was the first and the most notable. Unfortunately for him, his knees could not take the pressure put on them and continually gave him problems. It was because of this that he never really fulfilled his undoubted potential. He was a superb player when he was fit, so powerful and full of menace for opposing defenders. There were others too, like Mark Robins, who scored a memorable goal in the FA Cup against Forest in 1989–90, which, many say, kept Fergie in his job when things were looking bleak.

Debra and I had not long moved into a new house in Hertfordshire when the call came from United.

It took some time to organise a move north. In the meantime, I commuted up the motorway or stayed in hotels. That is not the best way for a footballer to live but sometimes it is a necessary evil. I was never fazed by that kind of situation. It wasn't what I would have liked in a perfect world but I made the most of it. Some players completely lose their form after a few weeks in a hotel. The best managers try to take this into account, even though it's not always easy. All the time I was living in the hotel, Fergie did his best to make me feel at home. Once again, he was proving as good as his word.

The one thing Fergie always seemed to want to achieve was good, attacking football in the Manchester United tradition. He was proud of the way his Aberdeen side not only won, but won with real style. This is one of the reasons the crowd took to him. It was never enough at United merely to win. Like a handful of clubs around the world – Real Madrid for instance – the United fans demanded their team play with flair and entertain them. I could understand this; they had, after all, been brought up on the Busby Babes, then the great team of Best, Law and Charlton. I would have been the same as a supporter. But I had been schooled in the ways of Clough and Graham and I saw winning as the only thing. Of course I would prefer to win with style – who wouldn't – but winning was the primary aim, never mind anything else. It was so long since United had occupied the highest levels of English football that a whole generation of supporters had grown up since they last won the League. To me that had to change. It wasn't as if they had played brilliantly either. For little spells they looked good but it always ended in tears.

Fergie understood all of this. It was his genius that he saw no contradiction in creating a team which could both entertain and win. It took him some years and I was gone by the time his plans came to full fruition. But I believed in his vision. Only Fergie could have seen the value of Eric Cantona and had the nerve to put his faith in him. Only Fergie would have gone into a season with a team brimming with talented kids, as he did with the Beckham generation. Look at the way Fergie supported Bryan Robson's input. His masterstroke with Cantona was to make the Frenchman a kind of father-figure to that young generation, all of whom worshipped him. For my part, I like to think that in my time there I contributed something important to the culture of success on which the modern Manchester United is built.

Fergie's approach can be seen in the difference between defending for United and defending for Arsenal. There was no rigid plan like there had been under George Graham. We worked on defending, yes, but we weren't expected to play the other side in one fixed way. We had to improvise a bit and we were expected to get forward at every opportunity. Attack was as important as defence, not merely a bonus. And we didn't look to play the offside game which was such a feature at Highbury. It was also a more open approach than had been the case at Forest. There, I would know where everyone was on the pitch at any given time. Under Fergie, for instance, my wide player, who should have been in front of me when I got the ball, was often somewhere else entirely. It took me a while to adjust. But it was exciting. To play this way, though, good players were required in every position.

This won't surprise you. In Alex Ferguson's first seasons at United (mine as well), Liverpool, with John Barnes recruited from Watford, won just about everything. The only relief came in the FA Cup when they were the hottest favourites for years but got beaten by the other long-ball gurus of English football, Wimbledon. Liverpool's persistent success niggled with Fergie even more than it did with me. Finishing second to them in my first season at United should have been a source of pride but I'm sure Ferguson seethed. Second. Not bad to most. To Fergie, nowhere!

It was no surprise to me that some years later he ditched his plans to retire. When anyone asks what could possibly continue to motivate him, now he has won two Champions League trophies and any number of domestic honours, you could do worse than tell them that more than anything he wants to beat those eighteen Liverpool titles. He has a burning desire to vanquish the Anfield dragon once and for all, like Forest did in the European Cup. In his darkest days when he faced the sack he was continually confronted with Liverpool's success, not just on the pitch but as a club. Liverpool always gave the impression of being morally superior to everyone else. I don't know how they managed it but they did. What better climax to a career could there be than doing what for years was believed could never be done and overthrowing the Scousers' record. This, I believe, is what drives him on. He is already immortal.

Fergie allowed a culture of alcohol at United. Where Clough had encouraged social drinking and Graham had simply expected his players to regulate their intake, Fergie's Glaswegian roots and old-school career made him tolerant to the point where it sometimes got out of hand. That was when he would come down like a ton of bricks as in the story at the beginning of this chapter. I'm not sure whether this did any of us any favours in the long run, but then Fergie's record speaks for itself.

I don't think Fergie actually approved of his players' drinking habits. In his autobiography he said that when he first arrived at United he was shocked to discover the extent of the drinking. However, he also admits that he didn't want to impose a complete ban and let players – Paul McGrath was one – promise to give up the booze without actually doing it. It was the one area where he sent out mixed messages. He didn't like it but he never stopped it. Maybe that's why he needed his spies.

As I went into my first season at United, all those type of thoughts could not have been further from my mind.

What I wanted was to show what I could do on one of the greatest stages in the world of football. I could not have imagined some of the dramas that were about to occur at the club.

Chapter Eleven

UNITED

The team I joined at Old Trafford was a work in progress. Alex Ferguson had arrived the previous season after the reign of Ron Atkinson failed to reach the goal set out for him – winning the League title. It probably wasn't Big Ron's fault: the trophy had eluded United since 1967. During the initial half-season Fergie spent at Old Trafford, the team were down to 21st place and were staring relegation in the face. By the end of the season, though, Fergie managed to lift the side to mid-table respectability. That was quite an achievement considering how bad things had got but it was nowhere near good enough for United. The mini-revival towards the end of the campaign, however, ensured that expectations remained high. Most people thought the improvement Ferguson had brought during the second half of the season would be continued and taken forward.

I felt extremely proud that such a high-profile manager had made me his first signing. I also knew I would be the first of many. Sure enough Ferguson soon brought in a number of new recruits, the most noteworthy being Brian McClair from north of the border. Already at United was a player Fergie had discovered, Gordon Strachan. Gordon had been central to Fergie's all-conquering Aberdeen side. He was a busy and skilful midfield player, something United had been missing for a while. For some reason, the manager and Gordon seemed to suffer from some sort of mutual resentment. You could feel it when they spoke to each other but neither of them let on what exactly the cause was.

During the course of the season, Fergie also bought the sixteen year-old Lee Sharpe from Torquay. His transfer fee, said to be £200,000, was the highest ever paid for a player on the Youth Training Scheme. This programme, part-funded by the government to help reduce unemployment among youngsters, was the main route into professional football for the majority of young players in those days. Sharpey was the highest-profile product of the system. He was always likely to come to a big club like United, after getting rave reviews for his performances in the West Country. In December, Steve Bruce arrived from Norwich after some protracted negotiations over his transfer fee, which in the end reached over £900,000.

The players I teamed up with who were already at United were a great bunch of individuals but had not been moulded into a team. Some were outstanding, like Bryan Robson. Others had shown enormous promise, like Norman Whiteside, who was still only 21, although he had been playing in the first team for five years. There was also the old-stager, Paul McGrath, and my team-mate from Forest, Peter Davenport. Jesper Olsen, one of the players Ron Atkinson thought would transform United, was also still around. Jesper captivated the Old Trafford crowd when he was on his game but I don't think he was really a Fergie type of player for whatever reason. It wasn't too long before he was on his bike.

Before I settled in there was a bit of a problem to overcome. When I was at Arsenal, we played a really bad-tempered game against United at Old Trafford. United won it 1–0 but that in itself wasn't really the trouble. It was the sending off of David Rocastle that really rankled. I felt Norman Whiteside had provoked him beyond what was acceptable. David was a teenager and although he was only a couple of years older, Norman was far more street-wise, having been in the first team since he was a sixteen year-old. He had also played in a World Cup. When Norman slyly trampled on David for about the third time, David reacted, kicked out at Norman and was dismissed by the referee. I was incensed, as were the rest of the Arsenal team. As the game progressed, the two sides went at each other even more ferociously. At one point, while the ball was at the other end of the pitch, I squared up to Norman and, believe, me, I was ready to have him. Norman wound me up even more when he laughed and said: "Hit me, go on hit me, I'd love you to hit me." He knew that if I did, I too would be sent off and Arsenal would be down to nine men.

Something inside stopped me from laying him out. But I was still fuming. It kicked off again in the tunnel at the end of the match, with more players joining in and Norman again coming on strong. It was an unsavoury encounter. And I felt Norman was the main contributor to the mayhem.

When I was next on England duty and met up with Robbo again, I took him aside and gave him a mouthful. "That Whiteside," I said to him, "he's a fucking wanker." Robbo laughed until he saw I was deadly serious. "Norm didn't mean anything by it," he said, "I bet we've both done worse in our time." I wasn't too sure.

Fast-forward to my first appearance at the United training ground. Robbo, the captain of the side, was the undisputed leader of the players at United off the pitch as well as on. He was involved in many behind-the-scenes activities, as I think you will know from his part in my transfer. Anyway, on that first day he took the trouble to introduce me to each member of the squad individually. When we got to Norman, Bryan suddenly turned to me and said: "Tell him what you said to me about him, tell him what you think of him." I was a bit embarrassed but I had to repeat my insults and why I made them. In response, Norman stood his ground. We indulged in a bit of banter and left it at that. However, the atmosphere between us remained strained.

A couple of weeks later Norman approached me after training. "Listen," he said, "let's try and sort this out. Let me take you out for a drink. I know a great pub down the road where they serve the best bitter in Manchester." I was impressed that the youngster had made the first move. So off we went for a drink.

I think it's fair to say that the modernisation of pub interiors that had been taking place across the country for a few years had passed the Pamona Palace on the Chester Road by. It had sawdust on the floor and you could imagine the spittoons hadn't long been removed. Its customers fitted the place perfectly. They looked like they'd kill you as soon as look at you. There were more tattoos than in a Hannibal Lector film. Norman seemed quite at home.

"Two pints of bitter please," he said.

"Can I have some lime in mine?" I asked.

Uproar!

Having lime in your beer not only insulted the so-called 'best bitter in Manchester' but was also badly received by the other customers in the bar. To them, no man had lime in his beer. Ever! They started making noises. Norman saved the day by telling them I had been ordered to dilute any alcohol I drank by the manager. He said it was to get me fit enough to play for Manchester United. They appeared to accept his explanation. Norman and I had a right laugh when we left the pub. The ice was broken.

From that day to this, Norman and I have been the best of friends. I have spent some great times with him and I've been skiing with his son. After we both retired I helped with a golf tournament that bears his name.

There were never any problems between us again. Fair play to him for taking the bull by the horns and trying to sort out the bad feeling between us.

It was still the old days. I had seen – and been part of – drinking sessions at Forest and Arsenal, but they were nothing compared to what went on in Manchester. On a given day, often the Monday following a Saturday match, Robbo would declare that after training he wanted all the players to come along to what he called a 'team meeting'. Everyone had to attend, even the overseas players who weren't used to it. These 'team meetings' would take place at various bars and drinking clubs in the centre of Manchester. We didn't favour one place over any other. We tried them all. We would be there all day and sometimes into the evening and beyond.

Now, when footballers get together they tend to talk about – football. Even when they are pissed. Robbo would instigate discussions on what we were doing wrong on the pitch, what we were doing right and what we could do to improve. Everyone was expected to have their say. Sometimes the chat centred on one person's performance. Other times we were fixated on the team and our roles in it. The more we drank, the more we knew how to win the League.

These sessions may seem crazy now. But back then society was different, not just football. Then, more or less everyone drank and there was something suspicious about you if you didn't. There is no way that could happen today. The drinking culture is not what it was in football, what with the introduction of scientific measures to test fitness and the modern emphasis on things like nutrition and fluid intake. I don't even drink much myself anymore. Not only that, everybody has camera phones today. If such gatherings as those at Manchester United were going on it would not take long before the press got hold of pictures. They would then be plastered all over the papers, accompanied by unfavourable and lurid headlines. Back then, few knew about our 'team meetings'. One of those who did, of course, was the manager and to him, they must have been useful. He never took measures to ban them. He only didn't like it if he thought we couldn't hold our drink or if we were partying rather than talking football. With his spies all over the place he generally knew what was going on. Although he didn't like it, he tolerated drinking provided it didn't affect performances or bring the club into disrepute in some way.

As I've mentioned before, Robbo was right up there as a drinker. A number of us weren't far behind. Poor Paul McGrath suffered from terrible problems with alcohol. He loved his drink. The trouble was, he only had to have a couple of pints and he was tipsy. After four he was blind drunk. He passed out more times than he passed the ball. It was an accepted part of the day-to-day routine in those days that we would get regularly merry. But the truth is we were always ready for training and always sober on the days leading up to a game and on match day itself. Fergie himself was not a huge drinker, preferring his Bordeaux Clarets to anything stronger. But his background meant he was well up to speed with how footballers behaved and he made it his business to know as many of the details as he needed.

Another thing about the old days: as I wrote previously, crowds had gone down with the rise in hooliganism and the ban on English clubs playing in Europe. Our gates averaged around 38,000 in the League, which was well down on what United had been used to over the years. Our biggest League attendance that season was 48,000 for the game against Spurs. That brought our average up a bit but there was no question the game was suffering. It was big games in the FA Cup that brought out mass support. Today, the opposite is the case, which I think is a shame. It was fantastic to see the crowds flock back in the 1990s but no-one could have predicted that the League would end up as so much more important than the FA Cup. In my first season at United our largest crowd was the fifty-odd thousand that turned up for the FA Cup fifth-round game against Chelsea, which we won. Other clubs were suffering from the downturn too. They also relied on the FA Cup for the really big gates. For instance, the competition provided Arsenal with their largest number of spectators that season, 54,000 for our visit in the sixth round.

We started the 1987–88 season with two draws, 2–2 away to Southampton, when Norman Whiteside bagged both our goals, followed by a 0–0 at home to my old club, Arsenal. It wasn't a great beginning but as soon as we recorded our first win, a 2–0 defeat of Watford, with goals from McClair and McGrath, we picked up big-time.

That season was the best of my three-and-a-half years at Old Trafford. We finished second in the League, with Brian McClair scoring twenty-four League goals, the highest total for the club since George Best over twenty years before. Unfortunately, that would not mean we could play in the UEFA Cup because of the European ban. The worst thing was – you've guessed it – Liverpool secured another title, nine points ahead of us. We drew both games with them that year, with the match at Anfield being remarkable because we came back from 3–1 down at half-time to level the score at 3–3. We were never really in with a realistic shout of finishing first, though. Liverpool were just too good, although it hurts me to say it. Forest took third spot, eight points adrift of us.

Although everyone knew Liverpool were on a different plane to the rest of us – they had the team of John Barnes and Peter Beardsley – finishing second led the supporters to think we would be in a position to mount a serious challenge to the Scousers the following season. However, the good times had to be postponed for a while as we went backwards in the next campaign. Still, the feeling among the players and the management was that it was only a matter of time.

Norman Whiteside was suffering a bit that year, although he weighed in with his fair share of goals.

His build meant that his body was under too much stress and his form and fitness began to suffer. The Old Trafford pitch was a quagmire back then. You couldn't play football on it. It was that bad. So Norman had to chase long balls, win headers and scrap. He was always willing but it did his body no favours. It got so bad that half-way through the season he opened a rift with the manager by asking for a transfer, which the rest of us didn't know about at the time. It was not granted by the board but the writing was on the wall for Norman. He was a likeable guy and a very good player. Had it not been for his physical frailties he would have been a great. As it was, it would not be too long before he was shipped out to Everton and was never the same force again.

As I said, the FA Cup provided the huge crowds. They were games which produced the most fantastic atmosphere. Having beaten Chelsea, we were confident of getting a result at Highbury. I once again looked forward to visiting one of my old stamping grounds. This was especially true with Arsenal as I looked on the club as the place where my career had taken off for the second time. I think I had exorcised any Forest ghosts by then. We didn't do ourselves justice on the day, though, and we lost 2–1. There was to be no FA Cup run that season. As for the League Cup, we made it to round six before going out to an Oxford side who were then in the top flight. It is hard to imagine today since Oxford are no longer even in the Football League, let alone the First Division. In those days they were riding high and actually won the League Cup in 1986.

I made thirty appearances in the League that term. My personal highlight was when I scored my first United goal, the opener in a 3-1 victory over West Ham at Old Trafford in March. I also got on the score-sheet in the away League game at Oxford, which we won 2-0.

But it was the twelve games in which I didn't play that proved to be an omen. It was the beginning of a period for me the like of which I had not experienced before in my career: a prolonged spell of being plagued by injury and out of the team.

Alex Ferguson took many things into account when he signed a player. Would the player fit into the team well? Could he make the step up to the plate and perform for a big club like United? What was his character like? That type of thing. One of the manager's most important considerations was how many games you had missed through injury. He believed that some players, no matter how good, were injury prone and he would never get the best out of them. I had missed only three games in three years for Arsenal. I had sustained only one major injury in my career – the dislocated knee which I got on England duty while I was at Forest – so I was a very good bet indeed.

Halfway through my first season I got kicked on the heel during a game. I can't remember the exact circumstances. What I do remember is that the pain was terrible and would not go away. More often than

not I couldn't train and could only play with corti-
sone injections. Sometimes it was so bad I couldn't
put my foot down. When I failed to respond to the
attentions of the club's medical team, I went to a
series of doctors and hospitals to find a cure. Lots
of different treatments were tried, including radio-
therapy. Nothing worked. At one consultation I was
told that bone fragments had become detached and I
needed an operation. Then a doctor informed me that
scar tissue resulting from the operation could make
matters worse. I didn't know what to do. The injury
just wouldn't heal. I was on the verge of having the
operation. Just before I was due to go under the knife
I was referred to Dr. Basil Hallal, who was doctor
to the British Olympic team. He said he thought it
might be a simple problem and prescribed a course
of anti-inflammatory tablets. Within forty-eight hours
the pain had reduced by so much I could jog for the
first time in months. It was remarkable. But it made
me wonder why none of the other medics who had
examined me could find out what the real cause of
the injury was. I was very grateful to Dr. Hallal. I was
still not a hundred percent pain-free but I made it to
the end of the season and hoped that by the next pre-
season, I would be over it. It didn't quite work out
that way.

After reporting back for pre-season in July, everything
seemed to be OK. I had no pain in my heel and felt good
about going into the new season. Then one day, after
training, I was doing some ball-work by myself. I think I

was tired and shouldn't have been doing it. I heard my knee go. I knew what it was. I had done it before and that time I was out for months. I had dislocated my knee. Again!

The following season, 1988–89, I managed only five starts in the League. It turned into the worst season of my career. I was continually on the treatment table and putting in rehabilitation work. I know it all helped in my eventual recovery but at the time it seemed to be making no difference at all. I think I became a bit depressed. I saw the guys most days and, even if I couldn't participate, they always made me welcome. That was important as it kept me feeling included and stopped any depression in its tracks. Fergie encouraged me to remain part of the squad and go to all the games. He always made time to ask me how I was coming along. I appreciated the manager's way of dealing with it, I can tell you. It was still, by a long way, the most frustrating part of my career.

In the time I was out of the side, United's performances on the pitch became erratic. The outlook was so promising at the start. The great Mark Hughes came back from Barcelona, via a stint at Bayern Munich. His return was welcomed by players and fans alike. He was a legend at United and everyone fully expected him to pick up where he had left off: scoring goals and making a nuisance of himself to opposing defences. We heard rumours – which found their way into the press – that the young Newcastle prodigy, Paul Gascoigne, was coming to United. Fergie told us that Gazza was "99% sure" he would be joining us at Old Trafford. Then suddenly, out of the blue as far as we were concerned, he decided to join Spurs. There's been a lot of comment over the years as to whether Gazza – given his problems – would have been better served coming to Old Trafford. Who can say, but I do think he was one of those individuals who succumbed to the distractions London has to offer to a well-paid young man.

The team did manage a couple of good spells that season. They got themselves up to third in February. Fergie was determined to try the crop of youngsters he had at his disposal alongside the more experienced players like Sparky Hughes and Robbo. During the campaign, the manager gave the seventeen-year-old Lee Sharpe his debut, alongside Mark Robins, who I think was only a couple of years older than Sharpey. The one who made the biggest impact, however, was Russell Beardsmore, who stole the show in a game against Liverpool and scored a great goal. He was the toast of Manchester for a time but – skilful though he was – he could never replicate his early great performances. Although these young players paved the way for the great team of the 1990s, it's strange, but all of them faded from the game before their time, for one reason or another.

From third place in February, United's season crashed. Our wins dried up and we dropped like a stone to eleventh, which is where we finished. That was appalling for a club like United and doubts about Fergie started creeping into the press and onto phone-in shows on the radio. These doubts would turn into a full-blown campaign for his head before too long. I was frustrated that I wasn't fit enough to help out the team, which I'm sure my experience would have done. The players had no doubts about the manager, we believed in his dream. Never once during this dark period did his confidence waver. He was working to a plan, which may have taken longer than outsiders thought it should to work, but Fergie always gave the impression that he knew exactly what he was doing.

Once again, our two biggest crowds of the season were in the FA Cup. First up was a fifth round home tie, not against one of our big rivals, but lower-division Bournemouth. Bournemouth had knocked United out of the competition not many years before so interest in the match was intense. Over 52,000 came to Old Trafford to watch Brian McClair score the winner in a tight match. The game I really wanted to play in but couldn't because of my damn injury was the sixth round tie at home to Forest. This drew a massive 54,000. The noise was deafening from the Stretford End that day. I listened from the stands, tingling. But Forest nicked it 1–0. Our FA Cup dream was over yet again. But not for long!

There was one consolation in what had been an extremely disappointing season for me. My old mates at Arsenal pipped Liverpool to the title in that famous game at Anfield, which they won with a goal from Alan Smith and that late, late strike from Michael Thomas. I could have hugged them. It did make me think, though, if I had stayed at Highbury, whether I would have avoided those injuries and been part of a title-winning team again. Those thoughts did not last too long. As I've said before, football is about the next game, not the last. I had no idea when my next game would be. What I had to do was get fit and hope matters would improve the following season. They did for United, after a few scares. They definitely didn't for me at all.

Chapter Twelve

TRIUMPH AND TRAGEDY

During the summer of 1989 my injury problems seemed to ease a bit. It's one thing to feel OK out of season, though, and quite another to be match-fit for football. The question in my mind was: could I get myself really fit for the new campaign? Having missed so much of the previous season I was desperate to get over my injuries and back in the team. I had been at United for two years and while the first of them had gone well, the second was an injury-plagued disaster for me. As I think you will be aware by now I was never a great one for training. I did what was necessary and I always tried to be enthusiastic but I didn't enjoy it like some players. The worst thing for me was cross-country running, as you'll know from my Arsenal experience. When I ran, I liked to have a football at my feet. At Forest, I was always last when we did a cross-country during pre-season. Larry Lloyd, who was not the quickest I've ever seen, would beat me. At Arsenal on that first day, even Don Howe almost beat me. But this particular summer was different. I had been out for virtually the entire season and I felt I had to do something extra to make sure I gave myself every chance of a successful return. So I decided that I would not use pre-season training to get fit, I would be super-fit by the time pre-season started.

To achieve full fitness I went on cross-country runs by myself. Lots of them! Believe me, they took some doing. I didn't like them but I knew I had to work super-hard to achieve what I wanted – a full come-back. It worked. By the time the players met up I had been training on my own for over a month. The rest of the squad couldn't believe the condition I was in. They had to play catch-up through the whole of July. I breezed through the pre-season and thought I had done enough to impress the manager. I was pretty pleased with myself.

I had also drawn quite a bit of controversy because of a quote I gave to the author, Andrew Longmuir, who had written a book about me published the previous season. In it I said – and I later repeated it to the press – that "If a forward is going through, I'll try to get the ball first, obviously. But if I have to I would upend him. In that case I would expect punishment from the referee." The statement didn't seem to me to be anything particularly out of the ordinary but the authorities didn't like it at all and I had the prospect of FA charges hanging over me for months. In the end, no action was taken. Somehow, the fact that I had been out injured for such lengthy periods made the story more newsworthy. I don't know why. It was really a storm in a tea-cup. It came around the same time as I was embroiled in another massive showdown, this time with John Fashanu of Wimbledon. I'll tell you all about that later. What I do know is that it took me some time to put the matter of the quote behind me.

I was sad when Norman Whiteside was allowed to go to Everton. Norman and I may have got off on the wrong foot but I had come to enjoy his company and appreciate his talent. I liked the way he played the game. He was like an early version of Wayne Rooney when he was on form and firing on all cylinders. But Fergie wasn't satisfied. Not so much with Norman's playing contribution as the state of his fitness, particularly his knees. When he sold Norman it was an example of the manager's methods and the standards he expected. I also wonder if Norman asking for a transfer had anything to do with it. I don't think there was ever any question of Norman's ability but his tendency to suffer from continuing physical niggles meant he was not a Ferguson-type player. He did well enough for Everton but he never recaptured the form he had shown in his early days at United.

Paul McGrath left too, going to Aston Villa, at the time managed by Graham Taylor. He was another player whose injury record was suspect. Everyone thought Paul's combination of bad knees – which left him unable to train on a regular basis – and his fondness for Pernod would signal the end of his time in the game. But Paul proved everyone wrong. At Villa Park he extended his career beyond what any of us thought was possible. Graham Taylor made special arrangements for Paul and let him miss training on a regular basis so he could play in games. I think he also got him a minder to ensure Paul's drinking didn't get out of hand. That would never have happened at United. No-one was more pleased than me that Paul had a great time at Villa and enhanced his reputation as a top-quality defender. He even won more caps for the Republic of Ireland. I knew the examples of Norman and Paul could happen to me if I didn't remain fit. Their experience was a lesson for me. If you were constantly out of the team, it wouldn't be too long before you were out of the club as well. I had become more prone to injury than at any time in my career. Fergie just didn't fancy players who were continually out injured and he moved to replace them as quickly as possible. I was pleased I had put in all that extra training by myself in the summer. But I still feared my time would be called if my physical condition wasn't one hundred percent.

Perhaps the most surprising departure was that of Gordon Strachan, who went to Leeds. He first helped them to promotion then won a League title with them two seasons later in 1991–92. Strachan was an extremely creative midfielder and was one of United's few real successes at the time. He was a busy player with lovely ball-skills and he had been the most important part of Ferguson's side at Aberdeen. We became aware, however, that some problem had developed between Strachan and the manager but we never actually knew what it was. Even if Gordon had told us, we probably wouldn't have understood a word he was saying. Gordon goes into the broadest of Scots accents when he doesn't want to engage. What made this endearing rather than annoying was that he could be extremely funny as well as enigmatic. So we assumed there was some sort of contractual dispute but we never found out what really went on. Both Fergie and Gordon blamed each other for the falling-out, as you can see by reading both of their auto-biographies. Fergie felt Gordon had misled him over a new contract, Gordon denied he had ever agreed to one. It turned out that Fergie believed and supported Martin Edwards, who claimed Strachan agreed to stay at United. He disbelieved Strachan's word – that he had not agreed to anything. Martin Edwards would later repay Fergie for his loyalty with interest. All we knew was that Gordon was gone. His success at Leeds led to comparisons with Johnny Giles, a similar player to Strachan who had left United for Leeds in the early sixties and had become the final piece in the jigsaw of Don Revie's well-oiled machine of a side.

As usual, there were a number of signings both in the summer and during the season. Neil Webb, an elegant midfielder, arrived from Forest and Paul Ince, all combat-iveness and 'up-and-at-em' mentality, came from West Ham. Incey suffered a lot of criticism over his move to United because he foolishly let himself be photographed in a United shirt while he was still technically a Hammers player. Participating in the photo-shoot might have been a bit immature of him but as a player, Incey was second to none. He had a bit of the Bryan Robson about him. He was full of menace. The forward, Danny Wallace, and the ace defender, Gary Pallister, were also added to the squad. But for me, it was the fact that Fergie brought in a midfielder who could also play right-back, Mike Phelan, that began to be a bit of a worry. It occurred to me again that the manager didn't think my fitness and form could be relied upon. I really shouldn't have been surprised. I was thirty-three years old. Maybe my age told against me. I thought I could overcome any physical problems because I had looked after myself as well as anyone during my time in football. Also, earlier on in my career, I had seen off Kenny Swain when Brian Clough thought I couldn't do it anymore. I believed I was good for another couple of seasons at the top at the very least.

The bitter truth is I was never first-choice right-back for Manchester United again. That season I played in only fourteen League games, an improvement on the season before but not what I wanted at that stage of my career. However, I recognised that I had decided to play for one of the biggest clubs in the world and competition for places was bound to be intense. If you were out for a long period injured, then it was just tough. Get over it! It went with the territory. I was one of the senior players and I commanded some respect for that and for my achievements in the game. For my part, I did everything I could to contribute to the team through the encouragement of other players and expressing my opinions. It seemed to be appreciated and I was often sought out by younger players for advice, which I was always happy to give. However, what I really wanted was to play.

Since I went to every game while I was injured, I was in a good position to gauge how the side was performing. I had many talks with Robbo about this. Once again, in my absence, the team was not looking as if it could get anywhere near winning the title. In fact the opposite was the case. One day, Robbo called a 'team meeting'. He was not pleased with some of Gary Pallister's defending and asked me for my opinion. I agreed with him. Poor Pally! As the drink flowed we pulled his game apart, told him he shouldn't be doing this, should be doing that, and generally gave him a hard time. We pointed out the defects we thought he had in his positional play and what he should do to put them right. To be fair to him, he took everything we said on board and went on to become one of the best defenders in the game. Pally wasn't the only one who suffered this treatment. We all went through it at one time or another. It was a way we could get things off our chests and try to take responsibility for our performances. Yes, those meetings were fuelled by alcohol, but we all reckoned we gained a lot from them, as well as a hangover.

The 1989-90 season began with a bang, in more ways than one. Our first match was at home to the Champions, Arsenal. It was good to see players who were so recently my team-mates again, although I was a bit embarrassed by events that day. As for the match, we brushed them aside and won comfortably 4-1. It was a great start against the team who had foiled Liverpool so brilliantly just a few short months earlier. There was talk afterwards that with performances like that we could win the League ourselves this time. But it was what occurred before the match kicked off that preoccupied the nation rather than our magnificent performance. What happened was bizarre. I've never seen anything like it before or since. And, through no fault of our own, it made us something of a laughing stock across the whole country. Some – although not me – said the incident blighted our whole campaign.

I had met our Chairman, Martin Edwards, on a number of occasions. He had been part of my discussions with Alex Ferguson when I first came to the club. He came across as a decent, if somewhat distant man. You could never be sure what he really wanted from his term as owner of the club. His attitude to both the players and the manager, however, was impeccable. He was a real, old-school gentleman. There were those around Old Trafford who remembered his father, Louis, who sounded to me like a completely different type of character – ruthless and uncompromising as opposed to Martin's more reserved way of conducting himself. Along with Matt Busby, Louis created the modern Manchester United. Busby gave the fans the team, Edwards gave Busby the money to pay for them. The two of them oversaw the progress of the club to the position where it was one of the top three football clubs in the world and perhaps the most famous. It was a hard act to follow for any son. Edwards senior died suddenly after a TV programme, *World in Action*, questioned his business methods in gaining control of United in the first place. Upon his father's death, Martin, instead of selling his interests, decided to take up the reins himself.

By the end of the eighties, though, we were told that Martin Edwards had grown disillusioned with his ownership of United and wanted to sell. We didn't pay much attention to the rumours, footballers don't really concern themselves with such things as ownership – unless their wages aren't paid or the best players are sold. None of this was likely to happen at United. And no matter what

Patron:
HER MAJESTY THE QUEEN
President:
H.R.H. THE DUKE OF KENT
Chairman:
SIR HAROLD THOMPSON, C.B.E., F.R.S.
Secretary:
E.A. CROKER

INTERNATIONAL COMMITTEE

R. Wragg (Chairman)	L.T. Shipman, C.B.E.
Sir Matt Busby, C.B.E.	L. Smart
N.W. Hillier	P.J. Swales
E. Kangley	J.C. Thomas
J.B. Mears	J.F. Wiseman
F.A. Millichip	

* * * * * * * *

TEAM MANAGER . . . . R. Greenwood
COACH . . . . W. Taylor (Manchester City)
ASSISTANT COACH . . . . G. Hurst (Telford United)
PHYSIOTHERAPISTS . . . . F. Street (Arsenal)
N. Medhurst (Chelsea)
TEAM PHYSICIAN. . . . . . Dr. P.J. Burrows (Luton Town)
ADMINISTRATION OFFICER. . . . . A. Odell

INTERNATIONAL MATCH

ENGLAND

v.

CZECHOSLOVAKIA

To be played at the
Empire Stadium, Wembley
on
Wednesday, 29th November, 1978
Kick-off 7.45 p.m.

ENGLAND SQUAD

1.	R. Clemence	–	Liverpool
2.	P. Shilton	–	Nottingham Forest
3.	V. Anderson	–	Nottingham Forest
4.	P. Neal	–	Liverpool
5.	E. Hughes	–	Liverpool
6.	D. Watson	–	Manchester City
7.	M. Mills	–	Ipswich Town
8.	P. Thompson	–	Liverpool
9.	T. Cherry	–	Leeds United
10.	R. Wilkins	–	Chelsea
11.	T. Brooking	–	West Ham United
12.	R. Kennedy	–	Liverpool
13.	A. Currie	–	Leeds United
14.	S. Coppell	–	Manchester United
15.	K. Keegan	–	S.V. Hamburg
16.	R. Latchford	–	Everton
17.	P. Barnes	–	Manchester City
18.	A. Woodock	–	Nottingham Forest

HEADQUARTERS

West Lodge Park Hotel

Cockfosters Road

Hadley Wood

Hertfordshire

(Tel: 01-440 8311)

ARRANGEMENTS FOR TRAVEL AND ACCOMMODATION

SUNDAY, 26TH NOVEMBER, 1978
ASSEMBLY. All players should make their own arrangements in order to arrive at West Lodge Park Hotel by 6.00 p.m.

7.00 p.m.   Dinner at West Lodge Park.

MONDAY, 27TH NOVEMBER, 1978
10.30 a.m.   Training session at Dame Alice Owen School Playing Fields, Whetstone.

N.B. THIS TRAINING SESSION WILL BE OPEN TO PRESS AND PHOTOGRAPHERS.

1.00 p.m.   Lunch at West Lodge Park.

Arrangements for the remainder of the day will be announced at Headquarters.

TUESDAY, 28TH NOVEMBER, 1978
9.30 a.m.   Depart from West Lodge Park Hotel by motor coach for Bisham Abbey National Recreation Centre, nr. Marlow, Bucks.

11.00 a.m.   Training session at Bisham Abbey.

1.00 p.m.   Lunch at Bisham Abbey.

2.30 p.m.   Training session at Bisham Abbey.

N.B. THESE TRAINING SESSIONS WILL BE PRIVATE.

4.00 p.m.   Depart from Bisham Abbey by motor coach for West Lodge Park.

7.00 p.m.   Dinner at West Lodge Park.

WEDNESDAY, 29TH NOVEMBER, 1978
Arrangements for the morning and afternoon will be announced at Headquarters.

6.00 p.m.   Depart from West Lodge Park by motor coach with police escort for Wembley Stadium.

7.45 p.m.   ENGLAND v. CZECHOSLOVAKIA

Players will be free to disperse after the match if they wish, but accommodation will be reserved at the London Euro-Crest Hotel, Wembley, for any players who wish to stay over the Wednesday night.

SPECIAL NOTES FOR PLAYERS

1. **Fitness to play.** All players must acknowledge receipt of these arrangements, and signify their fitness to play. In the event of a player being subsequently unfit to play, he must telegraph or telephone immediately to The Football Association.

2. **Fees and Expenses.** In addition to travelling expenses all players in the squad will receive the match fee of £100.

3. **Equipment.** Shirts, shorts and stockings will be provided by The Football Association. Players are requested to bring with them athletic slips, shin guards and football boots, which must be properly studded. All players are advised to take with them soap and towels for personal use.

4. **Exchange of Shirts.** Please note that any players wishing to exchange shirts with opponents after the match should do so after both teams have returned to their dressing rooms and in no circumstances should this exchange of shirts take place on the filed of play.

5. **Press Reports.** Players are forbidden to comment upon the match in television or radio programmes or in Press Reports before or after the game. The Football Association regulations are that players selected to play in International and other Representative matches under the jurisdiction of The Football Association must neither write nor allow to be written under their signature articles in which criticism of match officials or players is expressed, or the result of any match forecast.

16 Lancaster Gate,
London, W2 3LW.
Telephone: 01-262 4542

Ted Croker

Secretary

My debut game for England: England v Czechoslovakia Players FA Match Itinerary Booklet (note the mis-spelling of "A Woodock").

On the training ground with Dave Sexton, the former Chelsea, Q.P.R., Man Utd, Coventry City and England Under 21 manager.

Fred Street examines my damaged knee.

Wearing my first of 30
England caps.

England Senior Squad 1979.

Me, Tony Woodcock and Les (F.A.Security man) look on at Egyptian defender
Rabei Yassin and team mate in prayer after the match.

Bobby Robson tests the "pyramid formation", without much success!

Tension brews as we line up before kick off for England. England Tour of
USA/Mexico 1985.

Istanbul 14.11.84 Scoring for England v Turkey.

On the ball for England.

Training session for England.

England team fly out to the World Cup Finals. Luton Airport 1982.

Beating Roy Aitken to the ball. England v Scotland.

Splashing about with John Barnes, Mexico.

Ambassadorial, for England World Cup Bid 2018.

club you are at and whoever is in control you still have to perform the same on the pitch. This time, though, we had no choice but to take notice.

A couple of days before the opening game it was announced to the public that the Chairman had indeed concluded a deal to sell his shares to some bloke we'd never heard of called Michael Knighton. We found out at the same time as the rest of the world, through the media. Knighton, we read in the press, was a businessman who was ready to pay ten or twenty million pounds, or some such figure, to become owner of United. He was also quoted as saying he wanted to invest in the team. United fans were a bit fed up with the Edwards dynasty by then. They felt the Chairman wasn't spending enough on players. So they were ready to take this new owner to their hearts. It was only when we arrived at Old Trafford for the first game of the season though, that we realised exactly what this meant for us.

Knighton came into the dressing room before the match and was introduced to each of us as the new owner. We were all polite as we exchanged pleasantries. Knighton acted like he was one of the players, all enthusiasm and banter. We thought that was a bit strange to start with. Then, out of nowhere, the podgy Knighton produced a bag in which he had an extra-large United kit. "I want to run out with you when you go onto the pitch," he said. Fergie didn't look too pleased and the players were a bit bemused. We glanced at each other trying to suppress our amusement. But he was the new owner. And if the new owner wanted to make a prat of himself then so be it.

As everyone saw on that night's *Match of the Day*, we took to the pitch with the deafening roar of the Old Trafford faithful ringing in our ears. Only this time, we were led out by a tubby, middle-aged guy in full kit and boots, who ran into the penalty area, did some keepy-uppy in front of the Stretford End and fired a couple of shots into the net. He milked the applause but looked knackered. To be honest, us players took the piss out of him. None of us had ever experienced anything remotely like it before. Robbo was particularly scornful. "What was that fucking idiot doing?" he said as we lined up to kick off. None of us could answer his question, partly because we were still laughing. Thank God we won. I don't want to think what the crowd might have chanted if we'd gone a goal down.

Fergie didn't like it at all. To him it was a "tawdry side-show" that interfered with his preparations. He didn't think Knighton had any class doing something like that. I could see his face turning purple. I don't think he thought much of Knighton as a person, either. He certainly never had a good word to say about him. Knighton showed up at the training ground a couple of times but the manager made it clear that in his realm, even owners were unwelcome if he said so. It was a bit of a gamble on Fergie's part and I wonder if he would have stayed had the Knighton deal gone through.

As it happened, the Knighton deal did not go through.

He had difficulty coming up with the promised finance and the whole agreement to buy the club disintegrated. The revelation that Knighton didn't have the money, along with his preposterous appearance at Old Trafford before the Arsenal game, made us the butt of every comedian's jokes. However, Knighton's inability to seal the deal was probably the luckiest thing to have happened to Martin Edwards. He made tens of millions of pounds more than he ever would have done in the Knighton deal when he floated the club on the Stock Exchange and later sold out completely to the Glazer family. At the time, when we saw Edwards around Old Trafford, he often looked pained, as if he was aware that his error of judgment over Knighton had made United a laughing stock and sullied his own name. To be honest, it was a bit sad.

After the Arsenal win, our League campaign turned into United's worst since the relegation season back in the seventies. It was capped by a dreadful performance at Maine Road in September, when City beat us 5–1. At one point we were again down to twenty-first in the division and relegation was a real possibility. Our finishing position of thirteenth was not what had been expected and it brought increasing calls for the manager's head. Despite the four we managed in the first game, we continually struggled to score enough goals. Sparky was our top scorer with thirteen in the League – not a great return really! I hate to have to write this but who do you think were Champions yet again. I'm not even going to say their name.

Fergie's position looked very insecure, with a raging clamour building for him to be given the sack. Having got nowhere in the League, gone out of League Cup early on in a terrible 3-0 defeat at home by Spurs, attention turned to the FA Cup, our last possibility to salvage something from the season. The shrewd bets were on the manager departing sooner rather than later.

Incredibly – and this is one of the reasons he is a great – Fergie took it all in his stride. If the speculation was affecting him he never let it show to the players. I was sure there would be no change of manager, despite what the press whipped up. Martin Edwards continued to treat everyone, including Fergie, with great respect and made it clear that the manager had his full backing. When he said it, it didn't sound like one of those 'votes of confidence' which often precede the sack. We never believed Fergie would be fired, even though the press were convinced he was only days away from picking up his P45.

I still continued to feel niggles during the season and I didn't make too many League appearances. Fergie did include me in the team for four of our FA Cup ties, though, all of which we won. Whether that was because I happened to be fit when the Cup came around or Fergie now saw me as a fringe player no longer up to playing in a large number of games I don't really know. Whatever, the first game in the Cup that season was a third round tie against Forest. This match is widely credited with saving the manager's job. In the days leading up to the game at the City Ground, the press was full of stories that if United failed to win, Fergie would be out. There was a feeling among a section of the fans that employing the Scotsman had just not worked and a change was needed. There were even predictions that Howard Kendall, who had left Everton, was being lined up to take over. Whether any of this was true or not, I cannot say. I can only repeat that none of us thought he was on his way out. But there was no question the pressure was on to save our season.

It was a game we could easily have lost. Instead, a Mark Robins goal took us through to the next round, after the game had swung this way and that. Mark's strike has been referred to ever since as the goal that saved Ferguson. I'm not so sure that this was the case but it did make a great talking point. I'm convinced the Michael Knighton episode scarred Martin Edwards. The last thing he wanted was more upheavals and his judgment questioned again. On top of that, I think he genuinely respected Fergie and thought he was still the only man for the job. Then there was the store Martin Edwards put on Fergie's backing for him in the Strachan affair. I don't believe the board would have sacked the manager even if we had lost the Cup tie at Forest.

After playing a full part in wins against Hereford and Newcastle in the fourth and fifth rounds, we went to Bramall Lane for the quarter-final against Sheffield United. Although we won the tie 1–0, for me it was to be the end of the line that season. Both my injury plague and my FA Cup hoodoo struck at the same time like a perfect storm. I landed awkwardly after a tackle and something went in my knee. It didn't feel like it had when I dislocated it but there was definitely something seriously wrong. I limped out of the game. It turned out I had tweaked a ligament. This injury was not one of those career-threatening knee ligament problems. And it wasn't bad enough to warrant an operation. But any ligament injury is serious and in my case the only cure was rest and rehabilitation. I would be out for a while. So I missed the semi-final against Oldham. We won that in a replay. I was back in contention for the final against Crystal Palace. But Fergie not only didn't pick me, I wasn't even on the bench. We won the final in a replay. I wasn't picked for either game. In the team's moment of triumph I was left dejected. Worse, the boss decided to play midfielder Paul Ince at right-back. Now Incey was a very good player but to me he was no kind of full-back. He basically had no idea of how to play in the position and was badly exposed in the first game.

I watched the two games with mixed emotions. The first match, a 3–3 draw after extra time was a magnificent spectacle. Ian Wright, just coming back from a broken leg, got two for them and Sparky Hughes scored two for us, his first FA Cup goals of the season. Fergie showed how ruthless he could be once again when he dropped goalkeeper Jim Leighton for the replay. Jim, who was Scotland's first-choice keeper, had made some bad mistakes in the match. So Fergie left him out. The press said it was the most monumental gamble of Fergie's career but the manager knew what he was doing. After the first match he realised he couldn't rely on Jim any more. So in came the veteran Les Sealey, who had come to United on loan from Luton as cover. Les pulled off at least three great saves in the second game, vindicating Fergie's decision. The replay didn't live up to the excitement of the first game and we shaded it 1–0, courtesy of a goal from another of Fergie's youngsters, Lee Martin. It was as bad-tempered as the first match was free-flowing. Amazingly, the eccentric Les Sealey gave his Cup-Winners medal to Jim Leighton. Of course I was pleased that United won the Cup but I was frustrated that I wasn't a part of it. I celebrated with the rest of the lads and don't get me wrong, I enjoyed it. But I had been at United for three years, I had only one year left on my contract and deep down I was wondering what my future now held.

Chapter Thirteen

REAL LIFE

A funny thing happened at the start of the 1990–91 season. England had done really well in that summer's World Cup in Italy, reaching the semi-finals for the first time since the triumph of 1966. I had been involved in all international tournaments since 1980 but this time I was watching like everyone else. I knew how much it took to get within a penalty kick of a World Cup Final and I felt for the English lads, most of whom were friends. Amazingly, England's performances had a huge affect on the country and its football supporters. Following years of decline, suddenly the crowds were back and there was a new optimism in the air. United's average gate topped 40,000 for the first time in years. After hooliganism, Heysel, Hillsborough, the European ban and the appalling fire at Bradford, all of which occurred in the 1980s, football had reached its lowest point anyone could remember. Now, with Gazza's tears and Lineker's goals, the whole atmosphere lifted.

More good news came before the start of the season. UEFA, at its annual meeting in Switzerland, relaxed its ban on English clubs. This meant that Manchester

United were back playing in Europe in the Cup Winners' Cup following the replay victory over Crystal Palace. It made all the difference to players to know the country was back in the mainstream, not shunned, as it had been for those past few years. The ban had a terrible effect on the English game. It set us back years and cut us off from the rest of the world of football. With UEFA's decision and the World Cup semi-final, we could all look forward to better times at last.

Amid the upturn in the country's fortunes I was presented with a new problem. Despite the fact that I felt fit again, Fergie paid over £600,000 to bring Denis Irwin to the club from Oldham. Irwin could play either side of the defence but it was obvious to me that he was first in the pecking order for the right-back spot. My position in the team was under its greatest threat since I had arrived. The feeling grew that I was on borrowed time at Old Trafford.

Despite the arrival of Denis, the manager went to great pains to keep me feeling included. He never made me false promises about my position in the side. Nevertheless, he encouraged me to play the role of senior professional, which helped keep my enthusiasm intact. For my part I was always a bit of a bubbly character around the dressing room and I made it my business to keep smiling and contribute in any way I could. This wasn't a forced attitude; it is just the way I am. I would rather think about the positives. After all, there might be suspensions, transfers, injuries ... ... then who knows? I might get back.

It wasn't to be. I played in only four matches up to Christmas and one of those was a pre-season friendly against Waterford in the Irish Republic. I scored a goal in that one. But when the proper action started I was again out in the cold. I managed one game in each of three competitions, the League, the Cup Winners' Cup and the League Cup. But Denis Irwin was installed as the number one right-back and he occupied that position in most games, with Clayton Blackmore on the left. If there was an injury to Irwin, Mike Phelan came in. Phelan was often on the substitutes' bench, which meant there was no room for me. The one good thing was that my injuries seemed to be over. I was now fit and would stay that way for quite a while. At the time, it wasn't much of a consolation.

I didn't sulk: that is just not my style and it rarely gets you anywhere. I threw myself into training, turning out for the reserves and helping the team in my role as senior pro. Although I didn't know it at the time, I scored my final goal for United on 10 October in a 2–1 home win against Halifax in the second leg of a second round League Cup tie. It was an emotional goal for me for more reasons than the obvious. A week before the Halifax match, the great Peter Taylor died. He was a huge influence on my life and career. He was also much undervalued for his contribution to the game. I felt the loss. My mind went back to the day Taylor and Cloughie ran away and left me and Mark Proctor at Taylor's house. I smiled to myself.

It was typical of Fergie that he brought me into the team

for the next match. I think he knew I would want to play well for Peter. I was pleased to be in the team at last and very pleased indeed to have scored. I even thought there might be a way back into the side after what I thought was a good performance. That one game, however, came back to haunt me as the season progressed, as you'll see later.

My problem was that the team was doing much better in the League than we had managed in the previous two seasons, when we finished eleventh and thirteenth. My first season, where we ended up second, now seemed like a long time ago. In 1990–91 the club came in sixth, which wasn't fantastic but a massive improvement on what had gone before. Arsenal won the League again under George Graham. By then I had flown the Old Trafford nest.

I could see that Fergie was now determined to push on. Never mind that I had been injured for much of the last two years and wasn't part of the team which had displayed such poor form. I suppose I was tarred with the same brush. With me, the manager was never less than supportive, even when he was letting me know that if the right offer came along, I should consider it seriously. He told me I still had a future in the game. I suppose that what he meant – but was too kind to say – was that I had no future at Manchester United. This was typical of his dealings with me. He had decided I was now a fringe player and there is no way he would ever compromise on what he thought was best for the team. That is one of his greatest strengths as a manager. He is unafraid to ring the changes when he thinks it necessary. Remember the Jim Leighton-Les Sealey saga in the Cup Final. But he never put any pressure on me to leave and, it was reported in the press, actually tried to get me back on loan after I had moved on to Sheffield Wednesday.

Fergie really doesn't care if his decisions raise eyebrows elsewhere! Neither does he flinch at going out on a limb in public. He will berate officials and defend his players if he thinks it is to the team's advantage. He is a warrior-manager who loves "feisty encounters" with big-name opponents. He loved the battles, the mind games, the feeling he got when his decisions proved to be correct in the face of criticism. He was never afraid to ship a player out, no matter how big they were. In later years he saw off David Beckham when he let him go to Real Madrid. That was a time when David was one of the most famous people – let alone sportsmen – in the world. It was a massive call but Fergie came out of it so well, United went from strength to strength. Ruud van Nistelrooy seemed to be at the top of his game when he was transferred out but Fergie had spotted a player becoming more injury-prone. And when he was displeased, as with Gordon Strachan or later Jaap Stam, the player was on his way, no matter how good he was. With me, he let me know he still valued my input to the squad and wanted the best for me. Looking back, I think Fergie and I had a special bond. He also went out of his way to let Debra know he had my best interests at heart.

When I consider that period now, I think the fact

190

that Fergie let Mike Duxbury go to Blackburn before the season started was, in its own way, a vote of confidence in me. Or perhaps it was a sentimental act on Fergie's part. If it was, it would probably be the only one he ever made in his football career. Duxbury had been my only rival for the right-back position before Mike Phelan and Denis Irwin came in. That he sold Duxbury and kept me showed, I think, that he still retained some faith in my abilities. The point was, I could no longer compare myself in skill and talent to other full-backs and find them wanting. There were any number of youngsters coming through in the game. But they were rookies, even Denis Irwin (although I have to admit that Denis became one of the great full-backs after he took over from me). It was now simply a question of fitness for me. I knew my position inside out and I had played for enough different managers to realise I could change my game according to the way a manager wanted to play. If anyone thought it was my age rather than my injuries which blunted my opportunities, they were mistaken. I wasn't prepared – yet – to entertain any thought of ending my career. I was still, I believed, one of the best right-backs in the game and had plenty left to offer.

As Christmas drew closer, I got the nod that something was in the wind. Over the holiday, an approach was made by Ron Atkinson, who was then managing Sheffield Wednesday. In another act of friendship and kindness, Fergie said that I could have a free transfer, which meant I could negotiate a good signing-on fee if I took up the offer.

I still had six months to run on my contract. Fergie recommended to the board that they let me leave for nothing. They agreed, and the decision on whether to go or stay was passed to me for consideration.

I think Fergie's empathy with me went beyond his admiration for my football skills. His boyhood in the toughest of neighbourhoods of Glasgow, his time in the industrial grime of the Clyde in the steel industry, both made him a natural socialist. Even today, when he is rich beyond belief, he has hung on to the philosophy that he took in with his mother's milk back then. That, I think, is what enabled him to identify with the son of a Jamaican immigrant. He knew how difficult it was for me to forge a career in the days when there were hardly any black footballers or role models. In his own way, he too had developed the strength of mind to overcome humble beginnings. We had that in common and I think he recognised it long before I did.

There was another side to Fergie's concern for my wellbeing, which extended into my my time with my next club, Sheffield Wednesday. Debra and I had been together since 1980. We were married just before my move to Arsenal in 1984. We enjoyed a great lifestyle and we were happy together. We went to the best restaurants and hotels, were driven about in limousines and travelled all over the world on holidays. You could say we had all the trappings of luxury. The one thing that we didn't have, and both of us wanted – desperately – was children. Unfortunately, however hard we tried – and believe me we did try – it just wasn't happening. Bit by bit, this began putting a strain on our marriage. I think my injuries also had an effect. I must have been difficult to live with as I sustained knock after knock in my time at United and put so much of my focus into getting fit. Anyway, after various tests we were told that the only option open to us was *in vitro* fertilisation, or IVF. It was a big step but we decided to give it a go. We were upset when at first it didn't work. But we were told this was not unusual so we persisted and eventually were thrilled when Debra became pregnant – with twins.

I have rarely spoken of the heartache that followed. Even now, it is difficult to put into words the pain we lived through in the following nine months. We were absolutely ecstatic that twins were on the way. Scans showed they were a boy and a girl. I was walking on air. For me, it was the icing on the cake, the one thing in my life that was missing would now be filled. The same was true, I think, for Debra. We had success, a fabulous lifestyle and public recognition. Now we would have children. It was the only thing we wanted. It was perfect.

Debra's pregnancy went well for the first few months. Then, one day in March 1991, it's all a bit hazy now, but I think we were due to play a big match. Debra was told by doctors that something was wrong. Our beautiful daughter was not developing properly. Tests showed her lungs were not working as they should. She was, the doctors said, unlikely to survive outside the womb. This was the most devastating thing I had ever heard.

Missing Cup Finals and being out of the team, things which seemed so important before, meant nothing. Debra tried to protect me. She didn't know how or when to tell me the terrible news. She understood that I had to be focused to play professional football. But after she let me know what the doctors had said how could I focus on anything other than this tragedy? I don't even remember how we got through those times. We decided to name the two children there and then. We called our son Charlie and our daughter Gabrielle. The name Gabrielle came from the archangel Gabriel in the bible. On reflection, I don't think I gave Debra the support she needed at that time. However bad it was for me, what must it be like for a woman to hear that? And if anything could be worse this was: Debra had to carry both babies to full term in order for our boy, Charlie, to have a chance to survive.

In virtually her last act on this earth, when the time came, Gabrielle rolled over to allow Charlie to be born normally. I can't account for that. Nor, I think, can anyone else. Gabrielle hung on for an hour then passed away. We didn't know what to feel. We were so happy to have Charlie yet were destroyed at the death of Gabrielle. Nothing prepares you for the loss of a child. And you never get over it.

My manager at Wednesday, Ron Atkinson, along with Alex Ferguson and his wife, were absolutely incredible to us at this awful time. Fergie and his wife had twins. Maybe they also experienced problems, I don't know. Maybe they realised the risks being pregnant with twins can pose. Either way, they understood somehow the trauma we suffered better than anyone else. To this day, when Fergie sees Debra, he asks after Charlie.

Perhaps I should have been left out of the team in the wake of these events. At the time I thought I was fine to play. Maybe I was. I believed I was. You learn to hide your vulnerabilities when you are a professional footballer. But I could not possibly have been in the right frame of mind, even if I didn't know it myself at the time.

Looking back, perhaps that Christmas was the right moment to leave United. A new start, that's what we needed. The chance came when Ron Atkinson came calling that December. Wednesday, suffering from an injury crisis, needed short term help in defence. Big Ron was convinced I could do a job. "You can do great here," he said. "This club can revive your career." I was interested, not least because my old team-mate from the European Cup win with Forest, Trevor Francis, was the team's senior player. Danny Wilson was there too. I would be going back among friends.

Wednesday had been relegated the previous season and were in Division Two. But they looked as if they could get back up to the top flight at the first attempt if they had a good second half to the season. This was where I came in. I was wanted to bring some much-needed know-how to their quest for promotion. Dropping down a division? Suddenly, that didn't seem important in the scheme of things. I was promised first-team football, which, I think, was what I needed at that point. Over Christmas, after talking it over with Debra, I decided to leave the club of my dreams for a new challenge across the Pennines. I signed for Wednesday in the first week of January 1991, two months before the bombshell of Gabrielle's situation hit us.

Fergie was still looking out for me. I was owed some money in bonus and loyalty payments. It could have dragged on and on with United wanting Wednesday to pay and vice-versa. Fergie stepped in and not only organised the payment, he convinced the board to pay me more than I was actually due.

It was a wrench to leave United. They were my boyhood club. I always wanted to play for them. But in the end, the life of a professional footballer is not governed by such things. The days of the one-club footballer were being left behind. And, as I had discovered so painfully, there were things in life that were far more important than football.

I still kept in touch with the players at Old Trafford, particularly Robbo. Debra and I continued to live in the Manchester area and I commuted to Sheffield. I watched as United made it all the way to the Cup Winners' Cup Final. I felt sure they could beat the mighty Barcelona. I was as pleased as they were when two goals from Sparky – the second was one of the great goals of all time – won the trophy for my old mates. Having appeared in one match during the European campaign, I felt I had made at least some contribution to the triumph in Europe. That success was as important for England as it was for United. For England, it showed we could still compete on the European stage after being isolated during the time of the ban. For

United, winning their first European trophy since the European Cup in 1968 paved the way for the even greater victories to come. Much as I could share the feelings of achievement over United's accomplishment, though, I was now playing for the team of a potential rival. Only I wasn't allowed to be there when the two clubs clashed for one of the country's big prizes, all because of that game at Halifax.

Chapter Fourteen

BAD TACKLES IN THE
TUNNEL OF HATE

Bryan Robson was a hard bastard, no question. I mean no disrespect to those other Manchester United enforcers, Nobby Stiles and Roy Keane. Both of them could put themselves about. They could look after themselves too. Roy even had the audacity to tell the world about how he deliberately went after Alf-Inge Haaland in retaliation for some supposed offence against him. I'm sorry, Keano, but Bryan was way ahead of you. He didn't just crock any old midfielder who couldn't fight back. He went after players with big reputations who were renowned for mixing it.

We were playing Wimbledon in their heyday during the eighties. The game was held at their old Plough Lane ground, where the stands were so close to the pitch you felt you could reach out and shake hands with their supporters. Not that you'd want to, mind you. Their fans were definitely not the type you got at the tennis, that's for sure. In the match, Wimbledon, as was their way, kicked us all over the park. Robbo was not best pleased. He was in an even worse mood when Terry Gibson, an ex-United forward, put the Dons ahead. He said he was going to do something "special". He snarled instructions to Mark Hughes and Norman Whiteside, telling them exactly what he wanted them to do when they kicked off. This is how it went: Hughes to Whiteside, Whiteside back to Robson, standing on the edge of the centre circle, directly opposite Vinnie Jones.

Now I don't think it's an exaggeration to say that Vincent Jones was one of the most brutal tacklers the game has ever seen. Throughout the circle of ex-players, stories are rife of Vinnie's tackles, none of which involve any finesse on his part. Broken bones and torn ligaments were the order of the day when you faced Vinnie. And that was when he was on his best behaviour. Paul Gascoigne can testify to his dark side, having been on the receiving end of Jones's testicle squeezing act, carried out on the blind side of the referee but caught by an alert photographer from the tabloid press. Contrary to popular opinion, Vinnie could play a bit too. I think he just preferred not to most of the time. I'll tell you what, though: none of us ever thought for a moment that Vinnie would end up conquering the movie world, appearing in major films in both London and Hollywood and becoming an international star. He's even been on Celebrity Big Brother for God's sake. He's brilliant at it isn't he? Fair play to him for all of that.

Anyway, on this occasion the ball was rolled back to Robbo, who deliberately miscontrolled it, allowing it to drop about a yard in front of him. He knew Vinnie would be unable to resist giving him the charge on the pretext that the ball was there to be won. Sure enough, Vinnie careered towards the ball. Just as he reached it, however, Robbo's boot came over the top and his studs crashed into Vinnie's leg, almost snapping it in two. Vinnie was carried off. Robbo not only put Vinnie out of the game, he had done it such a way that the referee couldn't get a good view. He pleaded innocence and wasn't even booked. To Vinnie's credit, he could take it as well as dish it out, unlike some players I could name. Whenever he saw Bryan after that he'd say, "That was a great tackle, Robbo, the best anyone has ever managed on me.".Then he would smile ...

Bad tackles are a fact of life in football. I've put in a few myself. As I mentioned in a previous chapter, I got into trouble with the FA for saying that I'd foul an opponent rather than let them get past me. I didn't mean it literally. Or maybe I did. Well, it had a degree of truth. Very occasionally, though, bad blood goes further. Think Zidane's head-but in the 2006 World Cup Final. Sometimes it gets personal. Apart from the incident with Norman Whiteside, which was soon resolved after I went to United, there was one other incident in my career that falls into this category. It created untold column inches in the press, arguments at FA headquarters in Lancaster Gate and a law suit at the High Court in the Strand.

Again, it was United versus Wimbledon. Now, Wimbledon played in a certain way: the Wimbledon way. Under the stewardship of first Bobby Gould then Dave Bassett and Joe Kinnear, they played aggressive, in-your-face football. They had nurtured Vinnie Jones, remember. The Wimbledon side took up the long ball game that had brought success to Watford and they perfected it. On top of that they were very physical and tried everything they could to intimidate opponents. We all like a good physical battle with no quarter given or expected. But Wimbledon played right on the edge. It was often ugly. The club had come from non-league nowhere to the top flight, where they did well year after year. They definitely punched way above their weight. This didn't mean that they attracted too many supporters to their games – on the contrary, their crowds were the lowest in the division – but they seemed to revel in their outsider status. In 1988 they gave me a right laugh when they won the FA Cup, beating what was supposedly an unbeatable Liverpool side containing John Barnes and Peter Beardsley. They had a few tasty players on the pitch and some you wouldn't want to spend much time with off it. For such underdogs, they were strangely unloved in the world at large. Supporters of football respected their achievements but hated their methods. And they always seemed to up the aggression factor when they played one of the big teams. And they came no bigger than Manchester United.

The big one occurred after a Wednesday night League Cup third round match at Plough Lane in November 1988, during my second season at United. Despite all our run-ins, I was genuinely sorry when Wimbledon later had to leave Plough Lane to lead a nomadic life around the grounds of the other clubs of South London.

The game was a bad-tempered affair from start to finish. The most bad-tempered player of all on the pitch that night was John Fashanu, Wimbledon's centre-forward and the brother of Justin. For the record, we lost the game 2–1. I had been suffering from the heel injury that was such a blight on my time at United. I wasn't really fit enough to start but Fergie gave me a seat on the bench. In the second half he brought me on as a substitute to help shore up the defence. From the moment I hit the field Fashanu started giving me the verbals. I don't know why he singled me out. He appeared totally out of control. He called me a 'big-time Charlie' among other things and kept urging his team-mates to put me out of the game. He complained to the referee whenever I went near him, saying I was 'fouling bastard'. Now I may have many faults but I don't think anyone who knows me thinks I'm a 'big-time Charlie' or a 'fouling bastard'. From some of his comments, I got the impression Fashanu resented the fact that I was a regular England player, something I thought he wanted to be more than anything. He won three caps or so in his career, I believe. "Think you're an international eh?" he said at one stage. "We'll see about that. You won't be an international for long when I've finished with you."

There had been running feuds going on the whole game. It was an unsavoury performance by both sides to be honest. I mean, we were prepared to mix it ourselves when necessary but this time it went further than that. For some reason – and I don't know what it was – matches between us had simmered with trouble for some time. Two weeks before the Plough Lane encounter in the Cup we met in a League game at Old Trafford. Among other assaults that took place that day, our goalkeeper Jim Leighton was roughed up and lost one of his teeth. Before that, in the League game at their place, Robbo had his nose broken. Then there was the incident between Robbo and Vinnie Jones. Normally, you just accept these things, as Vinnie did when Bryan crocked him, but we got the distinct feeling that Wimbledon were deliberately setting out to bend the rules as far as they could in their matches against us. We responded in kind and I think it's safe to say that by the time we met in the League Cup tie both teams were a car crash waiting to happen.

The arguments continued after the final whistle. As we went towards the tunnel there was all manner of shouting, pushing and shoving. I tried to confront Fashanu.

"What's your fucking problem, John," I asked.

"Fuck off," was Fashanu's reply and he tried to push me away.

I stood my ground and we eye-balled each other for a moment or two. Then Fashanu exploded. Without any warning his arms came up like a boxer and he punched me twice in the face – hard. I went backwards and down and all hell broke loose. I kind of came to and saw Fashanu running away down the tunnel. God knows how, but I got to my feet and chased him. I tried to kick the door open but by then I was feeling the effects of Fashanu's assault. Someone fell over me as I was half lying on the floor. The next thing I remember is staggering into the dressing room with the help of the United players. It was pandemonium. When I came to my senses, I saw everyone fussing around me but it was hard to take it all in. A policeman came into the dressing room and started asking me questions. Apparently, Fergie had witnessed the fracas and had summoned the law. At the time I just wanted to get out of there. I put it down to a momentary rush of blood on Fashanu's part and when I was asked if I wanted to press charges, I said no.

If I thought that would be the end of the matter I was sadly mistaken. First, the story was all over the next day's papers. "The Tunnel of Hate", they dubbed it. At that point it was only known that some kind of fight had broken out but no-one knew who the participants were. When fights occur on the pitch, everyone can see what has happened but in the tunnel after a match there are no members of the public or the media present to witness anything going off. The press filled this gap in their knowledge with speculation. It soon came out that I was the victim of a punch but Fashanu failed to own up to his part in it. In fact he denied it was anything to do with him, saying: "Don't point the guilty finger at me." All those at Wimbledon closed ranks and for a while refused to reveal who was involved or what had occurred. At first suspicion fell on the Wimbledon centre-back, Eric Young, but that was because he was the player who had tripped over my body while I was half on the floor. Eric, an honest pro, hadn't done anything.

Although the Wimbledon people knew what had happened, they continued to refuse to identify Fashanu. Their manager at the time, Bobby Gould, was particularly cagey and everyone took their lead from him. This didn't surprise me as Gould's first instinct would have been to protect his own player. What shocked and saddened me was that Don Howe, one of my mentors in football and Wimbledon's coach at the time, didn't speak up. I suppose he was under orders.

It was United's manager who broke the silence and put the press straight. The police confirmed that Fergie himself had made a complaint to them, hence the constable's appearance in the dressing room. Our manager issued a statement, saying: "I saw exactly what happened and John Fashanu hit Viv with two punches that knocked him back yards. If that had been a Manchester United player he would have been on the first train home and finished with this club." That brought the FA into the picture. The Chief Executive, Graham Kelly, insisted that Fergie tell the governing body what had happened. "Alex Ferguson is an official of a club and as such he has a duty to report misconduct to the FA. It's his obligation under FA rules," Kelly said.

The FA's stance forced Fergie to prepare a witness statement in writing and send it to them. After they received his evidence they asked Wimbledon to respond. Once they considered both submissions they charged both Fashanu and me with bringing the game into disrepute. I couldn't believe it. Nothing I had said during the match or after it was any worse than the banter you would hear on the pitch every week but Fashanu claimed he had been "provoked". The truth was he assaulted me. If players hit out after the kind of clash that took place between Fash and me, there would be punch-ups after every game. Nevertheless, a hearing was arranged at which we would all have to give our side of the story. I was the victim. Now I too would have to defend myself. It was a disgrace.

In the wake of the FA's decision, Fashanu started giving interviews to the press. He continued to protest his innocence of throwing a punch but when that was exposed as a sham he shifted his position, saying "Viv started it." Then he did something unforgiveable. In a press interview he said that we had been feuding for a long time and I was jealous of him. He implied, although he didn't say it directly, that I was envious because he had, in the past, embarked on an affair with my wife, Debra. This was a totally untrue comment and, quite naturally, infuriated both Debra and I. He also told The Daily Star that I had lied in my version of what had happened in the tunnel. The paper printed Fashanu's remarks it as if they were true. We sued the newspapers who carried these stories, eventually won the case in the libel court and were awarded £35,000 in damages, which was a lot of money in those days. It didn't get that far with The Daily

Star. The paper admitted it had been duped by Fashanu and, to be fair, printed a fulsome apology.

In the middle of all this, Fashanu did the most unbelievable thing. He rang my house. Debra took the call. Fashanu told her that "if we play our cards right" we could keep the story going and make a fortune from the press. He actually wanted to turn the whole thing into a money-making opportunity by conspiring together with us to invent further stories which we would sell to the newspapers. Debra gave him short shrift. She was furious and so was I but we decided not to report Fashanu's approach. With the FA hearing due, we didn't want to escalate the dispute.

Before the hearing at FA headquarters took place, Manchester United announced that they would be taking ten witnesses to Lancaster Gate to speak on my behalf. The party included a United board member, Maurice Watkins, who is also a lawyer. Watkins gave both Debra and I incredible support during this period, especially in the libel case. He explained procedures to us, told us what we should focus on and generally helped in every way he could. I was pleased he was coming to the FA.

When it became known that one of United's team was a solicitor, Fashanu asked the FA if he could be legally represented as well. The FA turned him down. At first, he denied that he had made any such request. But it was confirmed by the FA themselves, who explained to the press that Fashanu had indeed asked them if he could bring his solicitor to speak for him. But, the FA explained, legal representation was not allowed. They went on to say that their rules stated that if a witness or club director also happened to be a solicitor, they could attend, but only in a non-legal capacity. Otherwise, Fashanu was not entitled to have his solicitor in attendance. Today, there would be no question that all parties involved would have their own legal representatives in any disciplinary proceedings. In the nineties, when I was at Middlesbrough, we had the celebrated advocate, George Carman, speaking for us in front of the FA when we were deducted three points for not fulfilling a fixture. But back in the eighties, the FA operated by rules which had been in force for decades, a time when the notion of the parties having any legal rights would have appeared absurd.

The hearing was a farce. The panel listened to the evidence, found Fashanu guilty, and gave him what was effectively a slap on the wrist. He got a three match ban and a £2,000 fine. They also found me guilty of "provocation". I received a one match ban and a fine of £750. I was at first surprised and then angry that this was happening. The verdicts and punishments bore no relation to what had occurred. It was a complete fudge on the part of the disciplinary panel and, to me, the FA didn't come out of the case very well.

The outcome was particularly infuriating for the Arsenal midfielder, Paul Davis. He had been banned for nine matches – including two England games – after he had been caught on camera punching Southampton's Glenn Cockerill and breaking his jaw. He had also pleaded provocation but in his case the FA wasn't interested. He couldn't understand how Fashanu got off so lightly. He never really recovered from the incident. Fashanu was lucky by comparison. It was a distasteful end to a very distasteful business.

Chapter Fifteen

FLYING HIGH WITH OWLS

Sheffield Wednesday was just what I needed. After all that had happened in my time at United, both personal and professional, going to Hillsborough was a breath of fresh air. First of all, Ron Atkinson had assembled a very talented group of players. They were far better than I realised. In my time at Wednesday, in addition to Trevor Francis and Danny Wilson, there was Nigel Pearson, who was a leader if ever I saw one, Nigel Worthington, Carlton Palmer, David Hirst, Peter Shirtliff, the American John Harkes, and the superb Chris Waddle, among a number of other quality performers. Second, I had been so happy to go to Manchester but it never occurred to me that most of my time at Old Trafford would be spent fighting injuries. Perhaps a change of scene would help.

Wednesday's regular right-back, Roland Nilsson, had suffered a long-term injury and it looked fairly serious at the time. That's why Ron Atkinson wanted to sign a replacement for the rest of the season at least. I spoke to both him and Fergie before I made up my mind. I also talked to Debra, who was enthusiastic and thought it could be a good move at that

stage of my career. Atkinson offered me an eighteen
month contract, promised me regular first-team football and told me: "We can definitely get promotion if
you come here." That was music to my ears. Only an
hour's drive from my home, Sheffield Wednesday –
traditionally one of the big clubs of England – looked
to be the ideal place for me to relocate to. It was a
great opportunity.

Another reason for having a good feeling about
Wednesday was Atkinson himself. Larger than life,
Big Ron's personality ruled supreme over the playing
side of the club. The board were anonymous: Ron
happily fronted everything. The team had been relegated on goal difference the previous season but that
had not dented the manager's confidence or vitality.
He was convinced we would get back into the First
Division straight away and when we got there, he
told us, we'd do well. That season there would be
automatic promotion for the top four clubs, which
reduced the odds on us a bit. The First Division
was being increased in numbers from twenty to
twenty-two, so two teams went down and four went
up. That situation was tailor-made for someone like
Atkinson, who had the ability to motivate his players
when push came to shove. Just like those days when
I started at Forest, the second tier of English football
was competitive and you needed to scrap to get out of
it. Big Ron revelled in it.

Atkinson's teams also played the kind of football I liked.
It was similar to the way we operated under Clough at

Forest and Ferguson at Manchester United. We got the ball on the floor and played a passing game. We were encouraged to attack, and that included the defenders. The full-backs were told to overlap as much as possible. It was perfect for my game and I knew straight away I would enjoy it.

Big Ron Atkinson was a massive student of the game. If you asked him any football question, no matter how obscure, he knew the answer ninety-nine percent of the time. On the rare occasions he didn't know he would be so annoyed with himself he would make a point of finding out. He was a wannabe player and loved to participate in the five-a-sides. To be absolutely honest, he wasn't very good and always ended up the last pick. His football career had been as a central defender in the lower leagues so his skills left something to be desired. He took the jokes we made about his playing ability in good heart, though, and they didn't do anything to curb his enthusiasm. He was an open person who spoke his mind and was very good with words. His appearances in the media, where he was continually in demand as a television pundit, added to his aura. As a manager, he was one of the best. It was easy to see why he had been poached by Manchester United.

I was both shocked and surprised when, some years later, he made a racially-charged comment on TV about Marcel Desailly when he thought the microphone was switched off. To me, Ron Atkinson is not a racist. He always treated me with complete respect. He was known throughout the game as the manager who had done more than any other to bring the first generation of black players into the English game when he was manager of West Brom. He took the down-at-heel midlands club and made it into one of the most exciting outfits in the English game by selecting the first clutch of British black players and building his team around them. No-one had the nerve to do this before Atkinson. I don't know what he was thinking of when he made the comment about Marcel but it is something for which he paid a heavy price. He was public enemy number one for a while and the controversy killed his career in the media stone dead.

Amazingly, as soon as I left Manchester for Sheffield, my injury problems ceased. I felt better, physically, than at any time since my days at Arsenal. And the more I played for Wednesday, the greater the improvement in my performances. Within a couple of months I was playing as well as I had ever done. It was around that time that it was reported that Fergie wanted me back at United on loan to help them in the final stages of their Cup Winners' Cup campaign. I couldn't go in the end because Wednesday needed my services. It was an unbelievable transformation. I don't know what to put it down to: maybe the injuries had run their course anyway; maybe the change of scene helped me to recover; or maybe I was getting over the trials and tribulations of my personal life. I don't know. But whatever was happening I felt as if I had been given a new lease of life.

I played in most of Wednesday's League games from the moment I arrived in January 1991 to the end of the season. We finished in third place and were promoted back to the First Division, just as Big Ron had predicted. However, the game I played for Manchester United against Halifax in the League Cup meant I couldn't appear in the competition that season for Wednesday. I was cup-tied. Such was our form, though, that in my absence the team ploughed through the rounds, beating Chelsea in the two-legged semi-final, and made it all the way to the final. At Wembley they were to face who else but Manchester United. And I couldn't play.

United were massive favourites, obviously. They were First Division; they were on their way in the Cup Winners' Cup; they were Manchester United. How could they fail to win?

But against the odds, Big Ron got the drop on Fergie in that final. I think it started before the game. We had a coach trip from our hotel to the stadium which was due to take around forty-five minutes. Big Ron organised entertainment for the journey. He arranged for a popular comedian of the day, Stan Boardman, to join us on the coach. Boardman didn't stop cracking jokes for the whole of the time we were on the road. We were in stitches at Stan's antics from start to finish. We were still laughing when we got off the coach and walked into the stadium. It really set us up for the game and was a ploy worthy of Brian Clough at his best. Big Ron was showbiz, there is no question about that.

As I think back to the match at Wembley – and remember, my powers of recall are not the best – it was a fantastic game settled by one outstanding goal from John Sheridan. For United, Robbo and Paul Ince were magnificent but Nigel Pearson, especially, and the rest of our team, were better. Sheridan was a skilful player who never really got the credit I think he merited. He was bought by Brian Clough for Forest but Clough decided early on he didn't fancy him and left him in the reserves for months on end before selling him to Wednesday. Clough also publicly questioned John's ability. His goal that day at Wembley was a beauty, one that was fit to win any match and a great answer to Clough's criticism of his game. It came after a free kick from Nigel Worthington was headed out by Gary Pallister. Sheridan, just outside the box, caught it on the volley perfectly and it screamed into the net. I think Les Sealey got a hand on it but couldn't keep it out. We could have had more but the one goal proved to be enough. Wednesday had beaten the mighty United. I was as enthusiastic as the most diehard Wednesday fan as I watched Nigel Pearson lift the trophy, the club's first for over fifty years. The city of Sheffield was buzzing.

After the game at Wembley, I took a six-pack of beer to share with Steve Bruce and Bryan Robson, partly in commiseration, partly to enforce my bragging rights. Brucie and his wife had been very supportive of Debra and me in our troubles and it was good to spend some time with him that day. As you will have gathered, Robbo and I were friends from day one. Neither Robbo nor me is surprised Steve has turned into a top manager. He just knew what was right and what was wrong and although he could be uncompromising he always played it straight. That's something Robbo and I have always loved about Brucie. He was also the most dependable centre-back you could wish for. How he never played for England is a complete mystery to me.

At the end of the season we had hardly finished our celebrations over promotion and our cup win when we began to hear a disturbing rumour on the grapevine. Big Ron was wanted by Doug Ellis to be his manager at Aston Villa following the departure of Graham Taylor. We didn't want to believe it. Atkinson was the club at that time. But it was true. I don't know what went on between Ron and the Wednesday board but he left for Villa Park that summer. As we contemplated the upcoming season with the big boys, our manager upped and left. For a while we were in a bit of turmoil, so much did we believe in Big Ron's influence over our success. But being footballers, before long the players turned their attention to who might be recruited to take on Atkinson's job as manager.

Danny Wilson got it spot on, I don't know how. "I phoned Trevor (Francis)," he told me. "I said to him, you know who's gonna get the job don't you? He said he had no idea. I said .... it's you, Trevor, it's you." Danny was sure Trevor would be the board's choice, even though he was still a top player and had no experience of management. I don't know how he worked it out but Trevor was indeed appointed player-manager a few days later. We all wondered what Danny knew that we didn't. In fact, he's like that. He just knew.

As it turned out, the departure of Big Ron didn't have a negative effect on the team. We raised our game and went from strength to strength. The players took responsibility and Trevor grew into the managerial job overnight. He began to limit his own appearances as a player as he assumed the mantle of manager and boss. He was also shrewd enough to realise that he had inherited a good team from Ron Atkinson. He had trained, played and relaxed with the group of players at his disposal and he understood our strengths and weaknesses from that experience, a knowledge he used extremely well. Of course, I had known him since our glory days at Forest. I can still see that header in the European Cup Final. Trevor and I always got on well and we knew where each other was coming from. One of the first things he said to me after becoming player-manager was that he didn't intend to make any major changes. He'd carry on playing in the same way as Atkinson, with essentially the same players. It was an intelligent way to begin his career as a manager. If I remember right, he was true to his word and the only significant new player he added to the squad in my time was Paul Warhurst from Blackburn.

Although the ban on English clubs playing in Europe had been partly lifted, the new policy did not yet extend to the UEFA Cup. So our League Cup win did not automatically bring European football to Hillsborough.

Under different circumstances we might have been frustrated at missing out on Europe but this particular season was dominated by thoughts of being back in the top flight. In the event, our first season after promotion to Division One, 1991–92, was absolutely fantastic, better than anyone associated with the club could have imagined. For me, it felt great. I was back in the groove. Being free from injury was fantastic and I was enjoying my football again. Roland Nilsson returned from his injury earlier than expected but he couldn't dislodge me from my position. Then, Trevor Francis went one step further than any manager I had played under. He made me captain when Nigel Pearson wasn't playing. I loved the role. I had become something of a leader at Manchester United but this was just brilliant. I liked it. A lot!

We started with a bang and won four in a row during September. One of those wins was against Forest at the City Ground, which we won 2–1. It was one of the few times I finished on the winning side in the League against them. Cloughie said hello but I don't think he was too pleased at the end. Clough was coming to the end of his illustrious career and would suffer relegation before too long in his final season at Forest. He never did anything by halves.

When we played Manchester United at Hillsborough that season, I was captain of Wednesday and Robbo was captain of United. It was a wonderful occasion for both of us. The game was a close-fought encounter which ended in a 1–1 draw. As fate would have it, both

United and Wednesday were right up there with the leading pack for most of the season. For United, it was nothing less than expected and they had high hopes of lifting the title. We were the surprise package, having our best season since 1961. In the end we were both beaten to the crown by Leeds, who won the League under the management of Howard Wilkinson. United finished second and we were third. It was my best season in years.

By this time, the European ban was totally ended. It was the final recognition that English football was back, free now from the problems of violence and ready to embrace all-seater stadiums. It was only three years since the dreadful events at Hillsborough when over ninety Liverpool fans were killed at the FA Cup semi-final against Forest. In those three years, we had entered a new era, where such tragedies would hopefully be in the past. It was fitting that one of the first English clubs back was Sheffield Wednesday. Our League position ensured that we were in the UEFA Cup. I even chipped in with a fair quota of goals in our League campaign to help us get into Europe.

I also played some games as a centre-back. It started when we had injuries in defence. I think the first time was the away game at Forest. At the age I was then, it proved to be quite easy for me in that position and I took to it like a natural. Playing at full-back demands more running, you have to get forward and back, forward and back. You have to make crosses on the overlap and be able to put in crunching tackles to stop your opposing winger.

As a central defender I concentrated on defending and reading the game, which I always loved and tried to perfect. I only tended to get forward at set pieces when I was playing centre-back, which saved my legs. It was all the better because we were winning and the crowds at Hillsborough were fantastic. I was loving it. And playing in a new position ... amazing!

While I was enjoying life again following our tragedy, Debra was left to look after Charlie most of the time, which was a full-time job. I did my share when I was home – I loved being with Charlie – but Debra bore the brunt of the work. He, poor thing, suffered quite a lot in his childhood, particularly with a sleep disorder which left him awake and active for much longer periods than is usually the case. He had so much energy it was incredible. A footballer's life, though, entails regular trips away from home and at the times when I was wasn't there, Debra had to cope alone. She did a magnificent job but a rift in our relationship was appearing, I think, due to these new circumstances and the trauma of our experiences. We tried to keep our marriage working but I suppose the truth is that, little by little, we were growing further apart. Eventually there would be huge consequences.

My contract with Wednesday ran out at the end of the 1991–92 season. At the grand old age of thirty-five I thought I was playing better than ever. So did Trevor Francis, who offered me a one year deal and told everyone that I was central to his plans. He said I would be "invaluable" in the European campaign. He was so enthusiastic about my contribution, I couldn't say no. Not that I wanted to. It wasn't nostalgia for Forest, he told me, it was because I still had what was required. I took the offer, looking forward to at least another year at the top and maybe more. All the woes of my footballing life at United were well and truly behind me. I had come back, good as new. And I had joined a club which was geared for life at the top after a period in the doldrums. It was a fabulous two and-a-half year swansong.

There had been enormous debates in English football around that period about the best way to move the game forward and take advantage of the upsurge in interest following Italia 90. There was talk of a European Super League with the big clubs of each nation breaking away from their national leagues. Vast amounts of money were said to be on offer from the new satellite television service, BSkyB. In response to these developments, the football authorities formed the Premier League, to be introduced for the 1992–93 season. It was the decision that transformed the game in this country and the lives of the top players. From that moment on, the money pouring into football increased in a way I had never seen in all my years as a professional and it changed the game forever. Bit by bit, players had moved from being like serfs, totally at the mercy of unscrupulous chairmen, to being in the box seat when it came to their careers. It wouldn't be long before agents ruled the roost. I had seen the old world. Now I could see the new world. I straddled both eras. Believe me, for the top players, the new one was better.

In the first season of the new Premier League, we again did well at Sheffield, though not quite as well as the previous year. We finished seventh. At last, Manchester United fulfilled Fergie's quest and won the title for the first time in a quarter of a century. I was pleased for them and took some pride in my contribution to the club's resurgence.

Wednesday's UEFA Cup run was not what we would have wanted, however. In the first round we easily beat the part-timers, Spora Luxembourg 10–2 on aggregate. In the next round we drew a very good team, Kaiserslauten. The first leg in Germany sealed our fate. Despite a good goal from David Hirst, we lost 3–1. In the return, we got a creditable 2–2 draw with goals from John Sheridan and Danny Wilson. It wasn't what we had hoped for when the season started. However, I was pleased for Danny that he got a European goal. While we were together at Hillsborough, we renewed the friendship that we had begun all those years before at Forest. Danny, also coming towards the end of his career, loved to talk about the game, just like Robbo and me. Our friendship would be cemented in an unforeseen way at the end of the season.

The lack of a good European run, however, was completely overshadowed by a unique set of circum-stances that unfolded as the season progressed. The domestic campaign that year will be remembered for the way Sheffield Wednesday and Arsenal, locked together in mortal combat, dominated both Cup competitions.

Wednesday began to progress in the FA Cup. So much so, we made it all the way to Wembley. It was fantastic to play in an FA Cup Final at last. Even better, was that I led the team out as captain. After all my years of suffering that old FA Cup hoodoo, this was a turn up. Who would have thought I would get there with Sheffield Wednesday, a team that, when I joined, had not appeared in an FA Cup Final since 1966? Promotion, third in the League and an FA Cup Final, all in three years! It was like Forest in the old days. As fate would have it yet again, we were facing one of my old teams: this time it was Arsenal.

Ian Wright gave the Gunners the lead in the first half but David Hirst grabbed a great equaliser after an hour. If I thought my FA Cup hoodoo was laid to rest, what about this: I was injured and had to come off. After playing for over two years without a serious injury I had to limp off in the showpiece game of the season. Can you imagine? The match ended 1–1 so a replay was required. Of course, my injury had not healed so I was still out when it took place. I missed the game, which Arsenal won 2–1. I was gutted. What made the defeat so much worse was that Arsenal had beaten us by the same score in the League Cup Final earlier in the season. That was another choker. That year remains the only time both finals have been contested by the same two teams. Fair play to Arsenal, they probably just about deserved their wins. We felt we could do it. We had got so near but just couldn't get across the line in either final.

By the summer of 1993, my contract had again run out. Trevor was keen to keep me and I was keen to stay. But I was coming up to thirty-seven and I needed to pay some attention to my long-term prospects. I'd had a fantastic career as a player, spanning almost twenty years. I had reached heights no-one would have thought possible. I had played for some of the greatest clubs in the land. What was the best thing to do now? I could carry on at Wednesday but could anything get any better than the last two-and-a-half years? I was pondering all this when I got a call from a certain Mr. John Dennis.

Chapter Sixteen

IT'S JUST LIKE WATCHING BRAZIL

John Dennis, it turned out, was the Chairman of Barnsley Football Club. Barnsley, known as the Tykes, had for most of their existence been consigned to the lower divisions of the Football League. There was something about the club, though, that was appealing. The feeling was homely if a bit ramshackle. It was more like a family than anywhere else I had ever been. Barnsley had lived in the shadow of more famous Yorkshire clubs like Leeds and Sheffield Wednesday for ever. There were also any number of other smallish Yorkshire sides doing the same thing. Like them, Barnsley's roots are in the local community and they are as strong at Oakwell as they are anywhere in the land.

John was a local businessman. I think he made his money in the fruit and veg trade. When he rang me, Barnsley were in the renamed First Division but what in fact, before the advent of the Premier League, was called the second division. This was the summit of their ambitions before Dennis became involved with the club. John asked if we could meet. Now I had been offered a new contract by Trevor Francis that I was inclined to take. But I agreed to the meeting, out of courtesy more than

anything else. I couldn't see myself playing in the second
tier again, unless it was with a team with great potential,
like Wednesday had been when I joined.

When we got together, Dennis told me he didn't want
me solely as a player. He thought I would make a great
manager and he offered me the dual role at Barnsley.
I was taken aback. I had been thinking about management with Robbo for years but at the time of Dennis's
approach we were both still players. I hadn't thought
about being a player-manager. I was intrigued and pleased
by John's approach, even more so when he said I was his
first choice. It was a magnificent gesture. At the time, the
only black manager in the professional game was Keith
Alexander at Lincoln. My appointment would be more
high-profile. I had been one of the first successful black
players. Could I be the first successful black manager? It
was a tempting thought.

When I was working on this book I contacted Barnsley's
official historian, David Wood. He told me that Barnsley
were known as an "all-white club". I hadn't known this
at the time. "The fans were also notorious for making
things tough for black footballers," he continued. "I
don't know if there was an all-white policy on the part
of the board but we didn't sign any black players after
Winston Campbell left in 1986." So I not only broke the
mould as far as black managers were concerned, I did it
with a club who were living in the dark ages before John
Dennis appointed me.

Whether I would have gone if I'd known that ... well, who
can say? But good financial terms were on offer. John said

there was not a lot of money for signings but they had the nucleus of a decent side. He told me that he could find the backing for a manager who could show potential. He wanted to take the club into the Premier League before too long. And he insisted that promotion should be achieved with the team playing attractive football, even if it took a bit of time. He didn't want to do a Watford or a Wimbledon and play long balls to big strikers. No, his Barnsley would – for good or ill – be known for watchable football. I have to admit I was flattered. I decided to give it some thought and talk it over with Debra.

As I've said, Bryan Robson and I had been discussing going into management for years. It was something we had talked about endlessly and we agreed that, if at all possible, we would do it together. I spoke to Bryan on the phone. He said he reckoned he had two years of playing left in him. "I think you should go to Barnsley," he said. "It will be a great learning process for you and we can team up when I retire in a couple of years. You'll have had all that experience by then." Debra, who had encouraged me to go to Wednesday in the first place, was also positive about Barnsley. She thought it was the perfect move at that time. And as it was just up the road from Sheffield, I could still keep my home in the Manchester area since the journey didn't take long.

Still, it was a big step. Was I ready to take on the task? The more I thought about it, the more I believed I was. Having played with such success down the years this was the chance to prove myself in another sphere. I pretty much talked myself into it and informed Trevor that I would be leaving. He tried to persuade me to stay, which was nice but he also realised that an opportunity like Barnsley might not come around for me again. And realistically, how long could I keep performing at a high level in the Premier League? I was sorry to say goodbye to Trevor and the players and they were sorry to say goodbye to me but it was time to move on.

I had a word with Danny Wilson. I wanted him as my assistant. He was really enthusiastic which helped cement my decision. I had already spoken to John Dennis and told him I would accept his offer provided he also took Danny on as number two. He immediately agreed and the new adventure began.

I wasn't quite prepared for the culture shock. I had spent my career at top clubs, all of which had great facilities. Of course I knew there was a different world on the other side of the tracks but the reality was something I was not totally prepared for. The dressing rooms were in a dreadful state, the training facilities were rudimentary to say the least and there weren't even any biscuits for the lads. I have to say that when I brought all these matters to the attention of the Chairman his response was always fantastic. He changed everything I asked him to, spending his own money in the process. Even the dressing rooms at Oakwell were upgraded. Well the home dressing room anyway.

The whole atmosphere of the place was friendly, like a close-knit family should be. There was never any hint of racism. Some of the back-room staff had been there for years. Nothing was too much trouble and John Dennis proved to be a wonderful Chairman. Debra was right. It was, in its way, the perfect job.

A great example of the family-type nature of Barnsley was Norman Remington. Norman, in his seventies then, had been at the club from the year dot and had done every job going. When Danny and I arrived he was the groundsman. One day in deep midwinter, when it was absolutely freezing, we saw him faithfully doing his best to keep the pitch in shape and decided it was time to offer him a new role. He was a lovely man as well as being a great servant of the club. It was something we really wanted to do. We made him kit man. He absolutely loved it, travelling with the first team and being part of things again. And the players loved him. We literally brought him back in from the cold, like you would with family.

In one respect, taking the job proved to be a baptism of fire. The previous management had accepted an offer to play in a pre-season tournament on the Isle of Man. It was the first time I had been in charge of a team, let alone a team on a trip away from home. I was a bit nervous. One night I sent the players to bed and was having a drink with Danny downstairs. Suddenly an official looking woman came into the bar.

"Who's in charge of the Barnsley footballers," she said, in a loud voice.

"I am," I replied.

"Could I have a word with you please?"

It turned out she was looking after a group of teenage girls who were staying at the hotel. They were young offenders, I think. Their trip had been paid for by the government to help in their rehabilitation.

"I've got a complaint," she continued.

"What kind of complaint?"

She came right out with it.

"One of my girls says that two of your players raped her."

I was staggered. Having obtained more details from the lady, including the identity of the players concerned, I told her I would immediately deal with the matter. I asked her to wait while Danny and I had words with the individuals named. My assistant and I were well prepared for football-related problems. But having to cope with something like this before we had really started on our management careers was not what we had expected. Nonetheless, it had to be confronted.

We went up to the room the two players were sharing and told them about the allegation as bluntly as we ourselves had been told. We wanted to see how they would react. Both Danny and I could tell from the expressions of complete and utter surprise on their faces that they knew nothing about any rape. Either that or they were great actors – which they weren't. They totally denied raping the girl in question and were adamant she had made the whole thing up.

Danny and I returned to the bar and reported our conversation to the woman downstairs. "My two players say there was no rape at all," I told her. She could have called the police there and then but she didn't. She was silent for a moment or two as if she had some inkling that the girl was lying. Then, instead of calling the police she and her staff decided to question the girl again. This time she asked us to stay in the bar while she enquired further. We spent quite some time worrying while we waited for her to return.

When she came back she looked grim. "The girl has admitted she made it up," she said. We breathed a big sigh of relief. So did the players when we told them. The woman looked uneasy and made an attempt at an apology which wasn't very convincing. Still, the tension that had been building up was relieved now the truth was out. The issue had been resolved in an hour or so. It could have been much worse for the guys involved if the girl had stuck to her story. If that had happened there would have been no way of keeping the police out of it. Once the police were summoned, the press would get hold of it and all hell would break loose. Luckily for the players, none of that happened. The next day it was made known to us that the girl's holiday had been terminated and she had been sent back to the mainland. It was a close call, that's for sure. But Danny and I had passed our first big test.

Expectations are not that high at a place like Barnsley. The fans have seen too many years go by without even a sniff of success for it to be any different. You can't compare working there in any way with the likes of Arsenal or Manchester United, where the loss of a couple of games on the spin is a full-blown crisis. Those clubs might as well be on a different planet. Nonetheless, John Dennis set targets and it was my job as manager to achieve them. Up until that point, Barnsley had always been a lower league club. The second (or new first) division was the highest they could realistically hope for in the short term. John Dennis wanted their position in the First Division consolidated and for the team to finish as high as possible. Mid-table was the minimum, anything higher a bonus. A couple of wins in one of the cup competitions would be welcome too. After that .... who knew? John dreamed of life in the Premier League one day. So a good campaign in my first season was expected to be followed by improvements year-on-year. It was a challenge on the budget we had.

Player-manager is not an easy role to get right. You tend to be harder on yourself as a player and not hard enough as a manager. You need the input of those around you. I was lucky to have had the experience of watching Trevor Francis because, apart from him, I had no experience of how a player-manager should operate. For instance, a big problem is the half-time talk. This is when the manager, who has been watching the match from his vantage point, really earns his money. Games are won and lost in the second half. The half-time talk can help the players consolidate a winning position or have a big influence on turning a game around if you are losing. How you approach the second half is the most important thing whatever the state of the game; even if you're losing 6–0. When you're playing, you have to concentrate on your own performance. You can't see the big picture so it's difficult to communicate anything meaningful to the players at the interval. In our case at Barnsley, Danny Wilson would normally have been expected to carry out the half-time talk. But he was also brought in as part player, part my assistant manager, so he couldn't do it either. We asked the long-standing coach, Eric Winstanley, to do the job. He did it willingly and made a useful contribution. But it was not an ideal solution, that's why Eric was not a manager.

I believed the existing squad of players, bolstered by myself and Danny, was almost – but not quite – good enough to do well in the division. Only two seasons before they had missed out on a promotion place only on goal difference. But that near-success had not been built upon. It was that failure, I think, which led to the departure of the manager, Mel Machin. After looking at them in training I decided that we needed to strengthen upfront. The Chairman found enough funds for me to secure the services of Andy Payton from Celtic to give us some goalscoring options alongside the striker, Neil Redfearn. Apart from that I left things much as they were.

I was right about the team in one way but wrong in another. When they were going forward they could play some great stuff, especially after Danny, Eric and I got them on the training ground. Andy Payton scored goals. The defence, however, was all over the place. Collective and individual mistakes cost us goals in game after game and we slumped down the table. These defects at the back surprised me. I couldn't leave myself out of the criticism although my own game wasn't too bad after I had adjusted to the difference between Division One and the

Premier League once more. We also had Gerry Taggart in the side and he was one of the most uncompromising defenders in the game. It was all very odd. Neither Danny nor I could put our finger on what was going wrong.

Gerry Taggart had been bought from Manchester City by Mel Machin in what was a very strange deal. Barnsley got Gerry on the cheap but if Barnsley sold him, City would get eighty percent of the fee. I got plenty of offers for Gerry, he was an outstanding defender, but I tried to stall them all because I knew that if we sold him, we wouldn't get enough out of our twenty percent to be able to buy a decent replacement.

During the first half of the season we lost five straight home matches and shipped thirty-eight goals in eighteen games. It was horrible and at one stage, after losing at home to Grimsby through a last-minute penalty, we dropped to twenty-first in the table. There were calls for me to be sacked. I knew now what Alex Ferguson must have gone through when it happened to him. But the Chairman stuck by me. He refused to listen to the critics and backed his judgment of me. That gave me the confidence to carry on.

While we were in the grip of those poor performances one of the senior players, Gary Fleming, came to see me. He said he thought that some of our problems stemmed from a poor attitude towards training on the part of the players.

"I reckon everything goes back to when the last manager was here," he told me.

"What do you mean?"

"Well, to be honest, boss, the players got to the point where they hated coming in for training."

"Go on."

"It wasn't Mel Machin himself, it was the coaching staff. They hardly ever had us doing stuff with the ball or working on different skills or tactics. They just had us running for stamina and practising how far we could kick the ball. That's pretty much all we did. It was horrible. Towards the end some of them (the players) wouldn't turn up."

I hadn't known about the training methods of Mel's coaching staff but from what Gary had said it appeared they had alienated the players to the extent that it had spilled over onto my watch. I talked to Eric Winstanley and he confirmed what Fleming had said in regard to the methods that were employed at the time. But he hadn't known about the players' reactions or how it affected them.

I spoke about the matter to Danny Wilson. We got together every day after training in a local pub and would analyse everything about what we were doing. We not only decided to put a new training programme in place but we would also change the team's style of play. On the training side, the first thing we did was to bring in loads of five-a-sides, which the players loved. Then we made sure the coaching staff laid off practising the long balls.

Under Machin, Barnsley played a sweeper system, which at first sight might seem at odds with what the training was trying to achieve. I couldn't pay too much attention to that, though, I had work to do. Danny

and I had been brought up on 4-4-2 so that was naturally our preferred way to play. But we realised that this
particular group of players were much more comfortable playing with a sweeper. Machin had instilled it into
them. Switching them straight to 4-4-2 and expecting
them to just understand its requirements had confused
them. It was a lesson to me. Although you would think
that a professional footballer can seamlessly switch from
one system to another, this is not necessarily the case.
Footballers need to have their role explained to them in
great detail and they need to practice it again and again.

Danny and me decided on two major changes. First,
we would revert to playing with a sweeper. Second, I
decided to play less and manage more. I could still keep
up with the younger lads on the pitch. But we thought
the manager's briefings, especially the half-time talk,
were more important. It couldn't be left to one of the
coaches.

I began to see improvements in the team's performances. After Christmas, results started to go in our favour
as well. The turnaround occurred when we scraped
through the third round of the FA Cup against non-
league Bromsgrove. The performance wasn't very good
that day, in fact it was embarrassing. I thought Gerry
Taggart got the winning goal but that just shows you what
my memory is like. Recently I was out with Gerry for a
night in London. He told me that, actually, it was Owen
Archdeacon. Shows you how much I know. Whoever got
the goal, we were lucky to win it and from there, confidence returned to the players and we strung together

some good results. Not long after the Bromsgrove game, Andy Payton got the winner against Peterborough in our first home victory for three months. Gradually, Payton, along with Andy Rammell, began scoring more goals. The new work we were doing on the training ground was paying off. I could see the players enjoying it. At the business end of the season we won eight out of ten games and finished well clear of the drop zone in mid-table. We had reached the Chairman's minimum requirement.

It was around this time that an odd chant started to be heard on occasion from the fans: "It's just like watching Brazil," they sang.

Believe it or not, we played in a European competition that season. But we didn't play any European teams, which is of course a bit of a contradiction. It was in a weird tournament called the Anglo-Italian Cup, devised for teams in the second tier of each country's football leagues. The format comprised an initial group stage followed by semi-finals and a final. There were three teams in each group and they were only from your own country. So there was an English group and an Italian group. The winners and runners up went through to the knockout stage where they played teams from the other country. Then there was a final which might or might not be between an English and an Italian team. If it sounds mad, it was, and it didn't last for long before it died a natural death.

Unfortunately, the competition came in the first half of the season when we were at our worst. We played two games, against Middlesbrough and Grimsby. Very

Italian! We won one and lost one but finished bottom of our group on goal difference. So we never got to play any Italian side. I don't think anyone mourns the passing of the Anglo-Italian Cup.

Our improvement coincided with the FA Cup. We were drawn away to Plymouth in the fourth round. The Pilgrims were managed by my old Forest team-mate, Peter Shilton. Although they occupied a place in the division beneath us, Shilts had them playing well and they were pushing for promotion.

Plymouth took their good form into the game against us. Andy Payton put us ahead against the run of play but our opponents came back with two wonder goals. We were thankful to Gerry Taggart who came up for a set-piece and grabbed us an equaliser. The tie had to go to a replay, which would generate some money for the Chairman. An Andy Payton goal just before half-time won us the replay and set us up for a fifth round match-up away from home against Oldham.

Although Oldham knocked us out 1–0, Barnsley's mini cup run was the club's best performance in the FA Cup for some time. It gave the fans some much-needed cheer and the players new belief. The Chairman was pleased too.

All told, John Dennis was happy with our season. He didn't have much money to spend so we certainly couldn't buy our way out of trouble. He did what he could, though, and backed me all the way. At the end of the season he wanted to sit down with me and plan the next campaign.

By then, though, I had been having a number of conversations with Bryan Robson. Robbo had seen the writing on the wall. Fergie thought he had passed his sell-by date as a player. The time was right to leave, he said, because he had received a management offer. He wanted to know if I was still up for it.

He began to tell me about Middlesbrough and the club's new Chairman, Steve Gibson. Robbo was impressed with Gibson's ambitions for the club, which included, among other things, a new stadium which was already being built. That was a statement of intent for Robbo. He wanted a manager's job at a club whose ambitions matched his own. That club, he insisted, was Middlesbrough.

Was I up for it? You bet I was. At last it looked like the perfect opportunity had arrived. But I had an obligation to Barnsley, especially John Dennis. I talked about it with Debra. She didn't want me to take the Middlesbrough job. I don't think she was ever so against a move. Her arguments were that I was number one at Barnsley and would be number two at Middlesbrough. And she thought that even though we could continue to live in the Manchester area and I would be able to commute, Middlesbrough was much further away than either Sheffield or Barnsley. That meant I would spend even more time away from home. She liked the way I was treated at Barnsley and doubted whether this aspect could be the same anywhere else. She was also a bit worried about me and Robbo's drinking when we got together socially. Having said her bit, she was happy to leave the decision up to me.

I agonised for a couple of days but really my decision was never in doubt. I couldn't not go, if you know what I mean. However much I fancied finishing what I started at Oakwell, this was what me and Robbo had been talking about all these years. Reluctantly, I broke the news to John Dennis. He wasn't pleased but he wished me well. He also asked me to recommend my successor.

Chapter Seventeen

STARS IN OUR EYES

I enjoyed my time at Barnsley. It was a fantastic period and I thought the team responded to my methods and were definitely on the up. I would have loved to have worked with the players some more. I wouldn't have gone anywhere if anybody else but Robbo had been the one to ask me. I had a last conversation with John Dennis.

"The man you need to take my place is Danny Wilson, he can take this team forward."

John looked at me, scrutinising my face as if to see if I meant what I was saying or was just putting a word in for my old mate. I meant it alright. I couldn't see any manager being able to do as well as Danny could. I was pleased when John decided to give Danny his chance, it was exactly the right decision. Danny knew the players, he could provide some continuity from my period in charge and, I believed, he was good enough to be a success in the number one job.

Danny turned out to be the perfect successor to me at Barnsley. I cannot praise his achievements there enough. He took them into the Premier League with good football and the chants of 'It's just like watching

Brazil' ringing round Oakwell. There were no better times to be a Barnsley supporter than when the club got promotion then spent a season in the top division. Although that term in the Premier League ended in relegation, it was the best thing to happen to the Tykes in many a long year. Unfortunately, after relegation, finances suffered and John Dennis had to place the club into administration in 2002. Happily, a revived Barnsley are now doing well in the Championship. The fans will remember their adventure in the Premier League forever.

Robbo was full of praise for the set-up at Middlesbrough. A new stadium, the Riverside, was rising on the banks of the River Tees and would be the first major new football ground to be built in England for over seventy years. The chairman, Steve Gibson, told Bryan he intended to make Middlesbrough a top team. There would be big money for the best players. He had recruited Keith Lamb as Chief Executive. Lamb helped save the club when he worked for the administrators, who had been called in during Middlesbrough's darkest hour. The club were bankrupt in the mid-eighties and were forced into administration. They actually came within a whisker of folding completely. Now, thanks entirely to Gibson's efforts, Middlesbrough was a phoenix rising from the ashes. The club was a symbol of the new world of English football, ready for success with luxurious facilities and money to spend.

Responding to Robbo's invitation, I really had no hesitation in swapping Barnsley for Middlesbrough, despite

In the dug out with United's new goal scoring sensation Brian McClair who went on to score 24 goals in his first season.

Leaping for a header with Kevin Moran, putting Liverpool under pressure, as Match of the Day's Alan Hansen looks on. Man Utd. v Liverpool 1987.

Avoiding the sliding tackle.

Can you spot all the future Premier League managers?

Before kick off with my good friend Bryan Robson.

Goal celebration with David Hirst against
Blackburn.

All for the Wednesday cause.

"Big" Ron Atkinson talks tactics on the training ground.

Barnsley team photo 1993–94
Back row: L to R: David Currie, Adrian Moses, Gareth Williams, David Watson,
Lee Butler, Jamie Robinson, Andy Rammell, Charlie Bishop. Middle Row L to R:
Colin Walker (Youth Coach), Eric Winstanley (First Team Coach), Mark Feeney,
Ian Bryson, Robert Hanby, Brendan O'Connell, Deiniol Graham, Gary Fleming,
Mark Burton, Gerry Taggart, Wayne Biggins, Martin Bullock, Steve Stafford (Physio)
Front row L to R: John Clegg, Owen Archdeacon, Andrew Liddell, Danny Wilson
(Player Coach), Viv Anderson (Player Manager), Glynn Snodin, Nicky Eaden,
Neil Redfern, Greg Morgan.

The Barnsley player manager in action!

I was only sent off once at Barnsley, but the cartoonist still found this sketch necessary!

Terry Venables, the master tactician, with Bryan Robson and myself pondering the Middlesbrough team selection.

Middlesbrough FC team management: Terry Venables, Bryan Robson and I direct from the sidelines.

Out for a duck!

Relaxing with my partner Nichole.

With, Charlie and
Freddie, my boys.

I'm a huge fan of the
Rolling Stones. Here
I am with the original
bass player supreme,
Bill Wyman.

With a few football legends for the National Football Museum held at the
Reebok Stadium 2007. In attendance were Bert Trautmann, Roy Hartle,
Mike Summerbee, Jackie Charlton, myself, Frank Worthington, Bryan Robson,
Phil Neal, Tom Finney, Alan Ball, Pat Crerand and Peter Reid.

Proudly collecting
my MBE with my wife
Debra and my eldest son
Charlie. January 2000.

Still winning trophies, with the
Manchester United Masters, at the Malaysia Cup 2009.

Debra's misgivings and the great relationship I had developed with John Dennis and the Barnsley fans. This was always what Robbo and I had agreed we wanted to do. Happy that I had done my very best for the Yorkshire club, I struck out for Teesside. In more ways than one, it was to prove a fateful decision.

Middlesbrough is a club with a long and proud tradition. However, when I went there they had never won a major trophy and had existed under the shadow of their fellow north-eastern clubs, Newcastle and Sunderland, for many years. Some success had come their way in the seventies when Jack Charlton was manager, but that first trophy had still proved elusive. They had some great players down the years, none more so than Brian Clough, who scored bagfuls of goals for Boro in the fifties. When I joined up with Robbo they had been suffering from the financial meltdown of the 1980s. Steve Gibson, however, intended to end all that. The fact that Middlesbrough still exists is down to Gibson. He is the founder and Chairman of a company called Bulkhaul Ltd., which transports dangerous substances such as liquids, gases and powders all over the world. He made his fortune available to the club, as a life-long fan would. Nothing was too good for his Middlesbrough.

Along with me and Robbo, we took the great Scottish defender Gordon McQueen with us to Boro. He had been a team-mate of Robbo's at Manchester United and both Bryan and I thought we could bring his experience to the younger players. After that, Robbo immediately set about breaking the club's transfer record, signing Neil Cox from Aston Villa for £1 million, the first time Middlesbrough had paid seven figures for a player. We also brought in Nigel Pearson from Wednesday to be our leader on the pitch. Amazingly, Manchester United let us take Clayton Blackmore on a free transfer. That was a real coup. I remained registered as a player and Bryan was player-manager. But while Bryan still wanted to play I didn't intend to make regular appearances. So it would be down to me to be Robbo's eyes and ears when he was on the pitch and handle the all-important half-time talk. In the unlikely event that we had a run of injuries, I would play. Otherwise I was now a full-time assistant manager.

When we arrived the team had spent one unsuccessful season in the new First Division, having been relegated from the Premier League the year before. Lenny Lawrence was the manager during that time and he resigned when it became clear that his methods were not working. Steve Gibson was a massive fan of Robbo's. He was prepared to back his judgment and give Robbo the chance to prove he could be a manager at a big club. He made it clear that Bryan was the only man for the job.

Our first season in management together – 1994–95 – was incredible and we stormed to the First Division title. We were the best team by far. A loan player we brought in, Uwe Fuchs, was particularly successful, scoring nine goals during the run-in.

Needless to say, the unlikely happened. Late in the season we suffered a spate of injuries and suspensions, particularly in the defence. So I was forced to make my full playing debut. We were away to West Brom and pushing for promotion. I was the grand old age of 39. How I managed to stay fit enough to appear in the first team at that age is beyond comprehension. Robbo also played in the game and he was the same age as me. I had a great game marking Andy Hunt and we ran out 3–1 winners. I was knackered afterwards, though, especially my feet and ankles. Robbo, on the other hand, couldn't get enough of the action. He was not only a player and manager for us, he also did some coaching with England. How he managed to keep it all together amazed me. It did mean, though, that I felt it my duty to keep an eye on him in case there were any signs of burnout.

Since the start of the Premier League, a play-off system of promotion had been adopted. For our first season at Middlesbrough, there was only one automatic promotion spot as the Premier League was once again tinkering with its format. This time the number of teams in the top flight was being reduced back to twenty. So four teams went down and two came up: The teams to be promoted were to be the winners of the First Division and the side that won the play-offs. Given our profile and the money Robbo and I spent, that one automatic place had to go to us. Some thought Wolves were favourites. They had also spent some big money and recruited ex-England boss, Graham Taylor, to be their manager. Like us they had a rich owner who was prepared to pay out on transfer fees and wages. But the lottery of the play-offs was not an option as far as Robbo and me were concerned. As things turned out, we blitzed the division and Wolves could not keep up with the pace we set. The expectations at Middlesbrough brought pressure but we were more than ready for the challenge.

Steve Gibson was in ecstasy as we clinched the First Division title. He saw it as his first objective achieved, right on schedule. What made Steve even happier was that we were going back to the Premier League with the Riverside ready to open for business. It would be a great showcase for the club. He wanted a team fit to grace the new stadium. He called me and Robbo together and asked us about our plans for the top flight.

In the close season, as we contemplated the Premier League, the work began in earnest. Robbo and Keith Lamb left me to look after team matters while they flew to Brazil. They went to see if they could persuade the Brazilian footballer of the year, Juninho, to come to the Riverside. We wanted him as our marquee signing. Steve Gibson agreed the £4.5 million transfer fee with Juninho's club and Robbo and Keith entered into talks with the player and his advisors. What clinched the deal, as would be the case time and again at Middlesbrough, was a combination of Gibson's money and Robbo's reputation.

Bryan wanted Juninho. He was convinced the little midfielder had what it took to be a major star in Europe and a massive performer for Middlesbrough. His plan was to build his team round the Brazilian. There was not much history of Brazilian players coming to England in those days and certainly none who achieved any great success. But Robbo loved the skills a player like Juninho showed on the pitch. He said from the outset, and I agreed with him, that Juninho was just the sort of player who could help produce the type of football we wanted to play. For his part, Juninho knew all about Bryan Robson even if he'd never heard of Teesside. His enthusiasm was obvious. When Robbo arrived home he was convinced he'd done the right thing. When I saw Juninho play, so was I.

We also bought Nick Barmby from Spurs for a massive £5.3 million. Barmby had been a really talented youngster who had lost his way a bit with Tottenham. The size of the fee shows the regard in which he was held in the football world. We had to fight off a number of other clubs to get his signature. By now the town was jumping. Middlesbrough had suffered untold hardships during the eighties. Both the football club and the town itself were victims of a sharp decline in fortunes. Now, the football club were leading the way back. Our emergence was the talk of the country and the town was right behind us. It was a feel-good factor the like of which the citizens of Middlesbrough hadn't seen for years. For a time, Middlesbrough was the centre of the football universe.

In the meantime, both Robbo and I were spending more and more time on the club's business. Yet we both lived in Manchester with our spouses. The drive to Middlesbrough took at least two hours, often much longer. On occasion, Steve Gibson provided us with the use of a private plane, which made things a bit easier. But most of the time we either got home late or had to stay in hotels. Looking back I can see I was hardly at home for huge periods of my time at Middlesbrough. This in turn led to the bonds with Debra loosening that little bit more.

But back at the football club, we were on a roll. By October we were up to fourth in the Premier League. Surely we couldn't do a Forest – could we? But the football gods were not to be so kind. Our away form was not great from the moment we got back into the top division. We were sustained by our performances at the new Riverside. Moving there just as Juninho arrived was unbelievable. Crowds were flocking to the new stadium and, with an opening capacity of just over 35,000, it was proving too small to accommodate all those who wanted to attend matches. Steve Gibson had thought about this, and built into the design was the possibility of increasing the capacity year-on-year. In the first three months there we blew teams away with Juninho turning it on. But away from home, we were a bit of a soft prospect, and couldn't score goals. We only managed eight all season. This began to put pressure on us at home. After getting up to fourth we went on a terrible run and even our home form deserted us. Nonetheless, we finished a very creditable twelfth. As Middlesbrough's last season at the top finished in relegation, I think we all would have taken that at the beginning of the campaign.

It was the next season – 1996–97 – that football threw everything it had at us. What could happen did happen. First and biggest came when Robbo, Keith and me found ourselves in Turin. We were meeting with the management of Juventus, the European Champions and one of the world's greatest clubs. The meeting was held to talk about the possible transfer of an ageing Juventus forward, Vaili, to Middlesbrough as cover. We also wanted to establish a relationship with the Italians and we spoke to them about the business of football and where there might be any common interests between us.

After some initial small talk, we all congratulated them on their European Cup win. I decided to play the cheeky chappie, asking them "And how much will you sell us Fabrizio for?" This was a reference to the brilliant Fabrizio Ravanelli, one of the best strikers in the world and the scorer of Juventus's winner in the Euro-final. Instead of laughter at the obviously ludicrous request, the assembled Juventus management went silent before exchanging knowing glances. "Ten million pounds" came the reply. This was getting interesting. We couldn't believe our ears, really. Could it be true that the club was prepared to let someone of Ravanelli's stature go? It was only a joke question from me, now things had turned very serious indeed. We jumped in and immediately agreed their valuation, even if it was an outrageous price. We weren't about to let this opportunity slip away. The deal was done there and then.

There is no question that Ravanelli was shocked when he found out that Juventus were prepared to sell him behind his back. He could have rejected us out of hand; no-one would have blamed him for insisting on Champions League football at the very least if he were forced to leave. But again, Robbo's reputation held sway. And Steve Gibson made Ravanelli an offer he couldn't refuse. It made him probably the highest paid player in Europe. We now had the best from Brazil and the best from Italy lining up for Middlesbrough.

These days the great players from every country queue up to come to England. In the mid-nineties, when the Premier League was still in its infancy, that was not yet the case. We blazed the trail. Lots of the metropolitan media made fun of the sophisticated Italian coming to Teesside. But the truth is, just a short drive from the industrial landscape of the town there is some exquisite countryside and Fabrizio, when he came to visit, immediately fell in love with English village life. Having secured the great Italian, Robbo went for another Brazilian, the midfielder Emerson, who was playing in Portugal at the time. Once Emerson heard that Ravanelli had joined Juninho at Middlesbrough (and when he found out the size of the salary on the table), he couldn't wait to come to England. I think he was shocked when he saw Teesside. That's not what his image of England was. But he was still enthusiastic. We now had a team to really stamp our mark on the Premier League. And Middlesbrough, who had never won a League trophy or appeared in any Cup Final, were making huge waves in what was then still a very traditionally-minded Premier League. For Robbo and me it was the highest point in our managerial career.

Ravanelli was a revelation, scoring goals for fun and working as hard in training as anyone I've ever seen. The fans loved him, particularly when he pioneered the shirt-over-the-head goal celebration. Juninho also excelled himself and drew rave reviews. The media adored him.

They weren't so keen on Emerson but he was our best player on many occasions. Unfortunately, his manner made the press constantly question his commitment, which got on all our nerves I can tell you. We only had two problems with Emerson. The first was when he failed to return from a trip to Brazil on time. This was interpreted by the press as evidence that Emerson wanted away and it is true that his agent was hoping to engineer a move to Barcelona. Maybe he did find it hard in the northeast, but as a player he always gave it everything. And his failure to come back from Brazil on time was easily dealt with by our disciplinary procedure. I think Emerson was a great success. The other problem occurred one day as we prepared to go onto the pitch for a big Premier League game, I forget who we were playing. Bryan wanted a last minute word with the players and called them together. All were there except Emerson.

"Where is he?" Robbo enquired.

No-one knew. Some of us went off to find him.

I looked in the toilets, thinking that was the most likely place to find him. Maybe he was ill. Then something alerted my nostrils. It was tobacco smoke.

"Emer," I called. "Are you in there?"

I heard a few Brazilian-type grunts then Emerson appeared. He had been having a crafty cigarette. We didn't know he was a smoker. Although in years past smoking was common among footballers, our generation frowned upon it. As managers, both Robbo and I expected our players to be non-smokers.

"What?" he asked.

"The boss wants to talk to all the players, get in there and don't let me catch you having a fag again." He looked at me as if he didn't quite understand. But we never found him smoking after that.

It didn't help that the press were constantly speculating that our overseas stars hated life in the north-east and couldn't wait to move on. Even though these stories were a long way from the truth, the English contingent could never really be sure and team morale – or rather confidence – suffered as a consequence. We slipped down the League and found ourselves in a battle against relegation, to the delight of the cynics.

We would have won that battle but for a disastrous error of judgment on the part of all of us in positions of responsibility at the club. Coming into the Christmas programme we were struck down by the flu. The virus went through the whole squad like a dose of salts. Both Robbo and I caught it. So did the backroom staff and several directors. This wasn't just a cold or man-flu. This was full-blown influenza. I had never seen anything like it at a football club. We were going down like ninepins. And it had a really horrible effect on all who contracted it.

By the time we were due to face an away game at Blackburn we were really struggling to field a team. We sought permission to have the match postponed but this was not forthcoming. There was no national epidemic, it seemed to be a localised problem and the Premier League were unsympathetic. Meanwhile, on the day of the game, we lost even more of the few players who remained. Keith Lamb spoke on the phone to someone at the Premier League – I don't know who it was – and asked them what the penalty would be if we failed to fulfil the fixture. The word came back that we would incur a hefty fine.

On the basis of that phone call, Robbo and I recommended to Keith Lamb and Steve Gibson that we pull out of the game. Gibson authorised it. Quite why we did it on the basis of a phone call with nothing in writing I can't explain to this day, to be honest. Whatever, we didn't turn up to play at Blackburn. That turned out to be a big mistake.

The disciplinary panel took a very dim view of our actions. Failure to fulfil a fixture is a very serious offence in football. All the medical evidence in the world couldn't save us and as well as a fine we were docked three points. Never mind what we had been told in that phone call, it cut no ice. Those three points made the difference between staying up and going down. It was a terrible end to the season.

We appealed the decision and the punishment. At the appeal hearing we were represented by one of the most famous barristers in the country, the legendary George Carman QC, who was a big Manchester United supporter. Carman's fee was £13,000 a day (you think footballers are overpaid). The great lawyer couldn't believe the way the tribunal conducted itself. At one point he turned to Steve Gibson and said: "In a real court of law you would win your case hands down. But these people: they have their own set of rules and you will never win your case with them. I can tell."

At the time we felt we had been unfairly treated but with hindsight we really should have known better than to take such a major step as not playing a fixture on the basis of a phone call. It was just too big a risk. In our defence, I think we were all suffering from the effects of the flu. But still, it would have been better to recruit a bunch of lads off the streets than not play the game. Perhaps we had got ahead of ourselves. We had to take our share of responsibility for the fiasco. We certainly never thought for a moment that we would be docked points. Until it happened! Now, all our plans were in tatters. Not only would we have to start again in the First Division, we were bound to lose our stars. They would not be prepared to play in the lower league. We really would have to go back to square one. Although we managed to rally in the following two years, nothing was ever the same again.

To rub salt in our wounds, we lost the League Cup Final to Martin O'Neill's Leicester in a replay. We also got to the FA Cup Final but were well beaten by Chelsea. Before the League Cup Final the town was absolutely humming as we had become the first side in Middlesbrough's history to get through to a major final. Not only that, we were hot favourites. Not because we had performed better in our League campaign than Leicester – on the contrary, they finished way above us in the final table. No, it was the money we had spent, the stars we had in our team and our aura of success which made us odds-on (at the time of the final, we had not been relegated and most football-watchers thought we would survive). A very tight first game at Wembley seemed to be going our way when Fabrizio put us ahead in extra time. But Emile Heskey got a scrappy equaliser with virtually the last kick of the match and we had to go to Hillsborough for the replay. We were not very good that night and a solitary Steve Claridge goal won the Cup for Leicester.

Neither me nor Robbo were in a great frame of mind. Things on the field had collapsed. We would have to put in some serious hard work and regroup for the future. But there were other things collapsing in my life that would have more profound effects than anything on a football pitch could manage.

Chapter Eighteen

REAL LIFE - 2

Telling all of you who read this book about my football career, even the bad or controversial bits, is easy. No matter what, it's still just football, which is not real life. It's a game we have played and enjoyed since we were toddlers. Much as we love it, it is only a game. Being good at sport, however, doesn't necessarily equip you with the skills to deal with other things in life. For example, you have to be able to deal with the press, which is not an easy thing to do. I learned early on in my career that the attention you get from the media as a top player is intense and you can't do anything to change it. Maybe you don't want to, particularly when you are getting regular praise for your deeds on the field. There will always come a time, though, when you'll have to take some stick. That's the way it works. Some people handle that better than others. I like to think that I have always stood up for what I believed when I've been criticised in the media and refused to be intimidated. This was the case when there were calls for my resignation at Barnsley. But I've never challenged the right of reporters to do their job. Like in any field of work, some do it better than others. And some are more honest than others.

There are huge numbers of people who loved playing football when they were kids. For most, their lives take various courses and they go on to other careers. But the game remains a passion throughout their lives. They are interested in every story, every bit of gossip about the game they love. Those of us who progress to the ranks of the professional – whether we like it or not – become role-models for all who stay in love with the game they once played with their mates. That has produced a press that is hungry for any story, whether or not it has anything to do with football. And the scrutiny is getting scarier with every passing year. Ask John Terry. It's no good complaining about this. Footballers get paid well, receive the adoration of fans and generally live a blessed life doing what we love. That doesn't mean, however, that we are any good at anything else. We are expected to be experts on family matters, be brilliant at interviews in the media and to possess thrilling personalities. As the Americans might say: we can just play ball.

By the time I linked up with Robbo I should have been well aware of how the media operates. Not only had I been subjected to my fair share of positive and negative stories, I had also seen how any number of other players and mangers dealt with the intrusions that come with a high profile. What I wasn't prepared for was my personal life being splashed all over the newspapers. I still find it difficult, even now, to talk about it. But given that so much appeared in the press about my life during the time I was at Middlesbrough, I feel I would not be giving the reader a fair deal if I wasn't prepared to say something about what went on. I would not do this under normal circumstances and certainly not without the consent of some of the people involved. So I asked both my current partner, Nichole, and my former partner, Debra, what their thoughts were regarding me speaking about this part of my life. Both said they felt it should be included. They were even prepared to help with their recollections. That tells you what kind of people they are. They have both made a significant contribution to this book and I thank them for that.

As I have stated previously, by the time I went to Middlesbrough, my marriage to Debra was feeling the strain of events that had happened over the years. Our protracted attempts to have children and the consequences that came from them had a big effect on our relationship. It's not something you realise when it's happening because it occurs so slowly, but you can see it when you look back from a decent distance in time. The John Fashanu incident might have contributed to our problems but I don't think it did. It actually made us stronger as we fought against his misinformation, but the togetherness we displayed during that period only masked what, in the end, proved fatal to our marriage.

Outwardly, we presented a united front but really a distance had grown between us. The strain of trying for children and the bittersweet experience of Debra's pregnancy had taken their toll. Also, the footballer's lifestyle includes lots of time away from home. As a manager, more so. This can lead to a couple starting to drift apart. Absence doesn't make the heart grow fonder in my experience. There is no special pleading here. The kind of strains we suffered happen in many marriages up and down the land. Knowledge of that, though, doesn't lessen the impact when matters go wrong. Nevertheless, I would never have wanted things to turn out the way they did, with our personal lives plastered across the tabloids and the press-pack camped outside our house.

Everything came to a head after I took the Middlesbrough job. I wasn't seeing as much of Debra as before and, as I said earlier, the absences undoubtedly contributed to the problems. And she had advised me against taking the job in the first place, in part for that very reason. Robbo and I were spending an awful lot of time after training analysing every aspect of what was going on at the club. This wasn't anything new. We had always done it as players and I continued to do it with Danny Wilson at Barnsley. But with Robbo and me, those talks took up quite a bit of time. What was different was that at that moment in our lives we were also needed at home. There was also the task of going to other games to watch players. All this was compounded by a never-ending round of business meetings, reports to the Chief Executive, reviewing the progress of construction at the new stadium and dealing with the usual disasters that befall professional footballers. We had also resumed our drinking after work was finished for the day. I wouldn't say we were problem drinkers (although some might argue otherwise) but it did take up more time than it ought to have done. Perhaps we should have spent more of our hours relaxing with our families. On the other hand, if my life had not taken this turn, I would never have forged a new life with Nichole, nor would I have had the pleasure of another child.

Robbo and I often used to wind down at a restaurant, which had a night-club attached, close to the Riverside. That's where I met Nichole, who at the time was the club's manager. It was a busy and successful rendezvous, with a nice, relaxed atmosphere. It was always full and was a fun place to be. Nichole and I hit it off immediately. There was a connection and a chemistry between us and before long the inevitable happened. We started an affair that soon blossomed into a fully-fledged relationship. I had never been a womaniser – despite having every opportunity down the years – and didn't really know how best to deal with the situation. I am the first to admit that I could have managed it better than I did.

I am ashamed to say that I didn't tell Debra what was going on. I just couldn't. I don't know why. And anyway, it didn't become certain that Nichole and I would make a life together for some time after we started our affair. It was wrong of me not to deal with it there and then but now I can only hold my hands up, admit the fact, and apologise for the pain I caused.

As someone who had been schooled in the ways of the press over many years, I should have realised they would get hold of the story sooner or later. Who tipped them off, I don't know. These days it is impossible for anyone in the public eye to go to a restaurant, a club, a theatre or anywhere else for that matter, without being snapped by either the paparazzi or a member of the public's mobile phone. In my case I can only guess whether this was how the press found out about my affair with Nichole. The first any of us knew that the newspapers were onto it was when Debra got a knock on the door one morning to find two reporters there. I think they were from the Sunday Mirror or the Sunday People. They wanted to know what Debra had to say about the fact that I was having an affair with another woman in Middlesbrough. They had assumed she was aware of it. Debra, of course, knew nothing about it. Her surprise must have been obvious. She thought they were joking. When the reporters realised she was ignorant of my affair, it only served to whet their appetites even more.

Debra decided to say nothing further and got on the phone to me. I was with Robbo, I think we were driving. She was understandably extremely upset. Both Robbo and I tried to calm her down without much success. It was a shock for which I was totally unprepared and my reaction was at first defensive. I had no idea the media had been sniffing about. The reporters were clever. They had not yet approached me or Nichole at this point.

I denied it all at first. It was a silly thing to do. The game was up. I raced home to see what I could salvage from the mess but it was too late. After talking around the issue for what seemed like an eternity with Debra, I at last admitted my affair. Debra was stunned.

"Do you love her?" she asked.

I don't know why but this question threw me.

"No, I don't know," was my inadequate reply.

Nothing now was going to stop the media in all its

glory reporting what had happened. The papers had a field day, printing all manner of lurid stories. Once the floodgates were opened, we were swamped. Loads more journalists door-stepped our house in an attempt to get Debra to give them an interview. What they were after was a comment that sounded like a 'betrayed wife'. It wasn't very pleasant. She was in too much turmoil to respond to anything at that point. When she collected her thoughts she tried to give the press a wide berth. In fact she never gave them anything they could use against me, much to her credit in my view.

Meanwhile, two other reporters descended on Nichole's restaurant pretending to be ordinary members of the public. What they really wanted was to get a picture of her they could splash all over the paper. They claimed they had heard of the place from a friend and were there to see if it was a suitable club to hire for a private party they were organising. Nichole, not realising what was going on, was taken in by the deception. She showed them around like a good manager would when presented with a possible booking. She was happy to answer their questions. They even duped her into letting them take photographs – with Nichole included in them – on the pretext that they wanted to show their friends what the venue and its staff looked like. The photos, along with a highly-dubious article, duly appeared in the papers. This led to a deluge of reporters and paparazzi descending on Nichole. She, of course, had no experience at all in the ways of the press. The tactics they used were unbeliev-able. For instance, I had bought Nichole a watch for her birthday. When the newspapers got hold of this they published it in a way that sounded awful. 'Viv Anderson lavishes expensive jewellery on his mistress' was the spin they hit us with. It was a completely untrue interpretation but it sounded scandalous. The tabloids loved it; they couldn't get enough.

The thing is, Nichole and I were serious about each other. I think we both knew that. I was in love with her. But, at this stage, with this level of intrusion, we wanted to do the right thing. After a lot of soul-searching we agreed that I would try to patch up my marriage and we wouldn't see each other, at least for a time.

While Debra and I made a doomed attempt to save our marriage – we even went to New York for a holiday, staying at one of the city's finest hotels and flying back on Concorde – the press approached Nichole dangling huge amounts of money. It was on offer, they said, if she would tell her side of the story. As she resisted, the figure they were prepared to pay went up and up. Eventually, it reached over £100,000. It looked at this point as if the relationship between us might be over so it is not surprising that she was tempted. Sensing a foot in the door, the press put her under enormous pressure to kiss and tell. All the attention had made it ever more difficult for her to do her job and it looked like she would have to leave. This might have given her even more incentive to sell her story. But she refused to fall for the media's advances and that is something I will always be grateful to her for.

As for Debra, she also handled the difficult situation

with class. Of course there were times when she must have felt as if she wanted to take revenge on me for my infidelity and I wouldn't have blamed her if she did. I think she knew by then, though, even if I didn't, that the marriage was finished. When we returned from New York we just couldn't seem to relate to each other in the way we had in the past. Also, I missed Nichole. Eventually, Nichole and I began seeing each other again. Why I thought I could keep it secret after all that had happened I just can't say. When Debra found out she was, not surprisingly, angry. She decided to take drastic action.

It sounds funny now, and I suppose it was at the time, although I didn't think so. Debra ordered removal men to go to our house. She packed up all my stuff and when they arrived told them to take it to Middlesbrough's training ground and dump it there. We can laugh about it today, but can you imagine my embarrassment when, going through a serious training exercise with the players, this lorry turned up? It was unusual at the very least to see a removal van driving onto a football club's training ground. We thought it had got lost. Everyone stopped what they were doing and gave their attention to the truck. That's when the driver rolled down the window, stuck his head out and said:

"Is Mr. Anderson here?"

I stepped forward. "Yeah, I'm here," I replied, still not understanding what was going on.

"We've got your belongings here, mate. Where do you want us to put 'em?"

"What do you mean, you've got my belongings?"

"Your missus told us to move 'em."

"What?"

"Your missus, mate. And she said don't come back. Where shall I put it?"

I got the message.

So did the players. They looked at each other, then at the coaching staff. They started shuffling about. I thought I heard a stifled laugh. I wasn't going to live this down in a hurry. I had to store my things and arrange to get them taken somewhere else. At least the press weren't around to witness what happened. Thank heaven for small mercies.

I moved out of the house as quickly as I could and found my own place. Debra and I were now, without any doubt, finished. We went through a bit of a messy and drawn-out divorce. As this went on, Nichole and I resumed our relationship. We didn't set up home together at first. That came later, after Nichole became pregnant with our son, Freddie.

This period of my life was not easy for anyone involved. For that I take full responsibility. I caused a lot of pain, especially to Charlie, there is no question about that. I am sure there are millions of people out there who have been through similar experiences and suffer similar remorse. I am luckier than most in that everybody managed to do something the majority of people find impossible. They put aside the past, moved on and gave me the benefit of the doubt. That, at least, I think I deserved. Now, Nichole and I enjoy a family life I could never have thought possible when things were at their worst. I am pleased to say that Debra has also found a fantastic new partner, Geoff, with whom she is very happy. Nichole and I are proud to count them amongst our friends. We see each other regularly and Debra often helps out with Freddie. I am lucky indeed.

As I said at the beginning of this chapter, it has not been easy to tell this story. But even if at times it shows me in not the best of lights, I felt it had to be said. While it was all going on, of course, I had to continue working at Middlesbrough and, as the assistant manager, maintain a degree of detachment from the players. It was not so easy when that lorry turned up, let me tell you. Robbo gave me immense support throughout, as did a number of others. One thing I learned: when you are on top, as I was for so much of my life, everyone is your friend; it's only when you suffer adversity that you really know who your friends are. Again I was lucky in that plenty of people helped. And, if that wasn't enough drama for one lifetime, the roller-coaster ride that was my life was being mirrored in the affairs of the club which employed me. The unheard of was about to happen.

Chapter Nineteen

STRANGE DAYS

I couldn't believe my ears. In all my years in football I'd never heard anything like it. As far as I'm aware, nothing approaching Robbo's suggestion has ever happened in the game before or since, certainly not in England. And in the time Robbo and I had been discussing management, going back to our England and Manchester United days, we never considered a possibility like this.

"Run it by me again, Bryan," I said.

Bryan Robson spelled it out and even then it didn't really register. It didn't compute.

"I don't think I can go on like this, I just don't seem to be able to do it anymore," he continued.

"Of course you can, Robbo. If anyone can, you can. Look, we can get out of this, we really can. We've done it before. We just need to keep our heads and continue working hard."

But there was no shifting him. He never compromised as a player and he wasn't going to start now. There was something both tragic yet noble about what he was proposing.

"Have you told the Chairman?"

"I'm going to see him this afternoon. It's got to be

done, Viv. You know it and I know it. We can resign but that would leave the club in too big a hole and who knows what kind of manager they'd be lumbered with. I don't want to leave with us relegated. At least this way we know we'll have the best man for the job."

I tried to form an argument against what he was saying but all I could come up with was the comment that "he could sack us anyway."

"He is the best Chairman in the Premier League. No, make that the whole of football," Robbo said. "He's the best in the world. He stood by us when we went down for Christ's sake."

"I know, but ...."

After we were relegated, at the end of the 1996–97 season, Robbo and I survived in our jobs. At most clubs, relegation would have brought us the sack. But Steve Gibson was made of sterner stuff. I think he also recognised his own role in the three point deduction fiasco and, like the gentleman he is, didn't want to make Robbo and me the scapegoats. That alone shows the difference between him and the vast majority of football chairmen. Still, for all the mistakes of the backroom staff and the club's executives, there is no denying we should never have been in that position with the players we had. They were more than good enough to hold their own in the Premier League. Maybe getting to two cup finals did us no favours. Remember, Middlesbrough had never been in any final in the whole of their history. Everyone, I think, got carried away with the cup runs and we took our eyes off our main task – to prosper in the top division.

It broke our hearts that, because of relegation, we had to let what should have been the nucleus of a great side leave the club. That team should have gone from strength to strength. The two cup finals ought to have been the springboard for greater things. Instead, they were mill-stones round our neck.

Despite the ridicule heaped on us for buying Fabrizio Ravanelli, his signing put the Premier League in the frame to be counted as the best league in the world. It also put Middlesbrough right up there with the best of them. It set the template for so much that came after-wards. To the press we were gatecrashers. They said the great Italian had only come to Middlesbrough for a big pay day. But the same could be said for any high-profile transfer. They just thought that when so-called lesser teams had the audacity to think big, they were getting above their station.

I think the truth about Ravanelli can be seen in the fact that we sold him to Olympique Marseille for far more than we paid for him. As for Juninho, he was in great demand. There were any number of clubs all over Europe who came in for him. In the end we received more than double the amount we had laid out for the Brazilian, with Atletico Madrid stumping up over £12 million to take him to Spain.

Juninho loved it at Middlesbrough. So much so that he came back twice more, once on loan while Robbo and me were still at the club and later after Steve McClaren had taken over. With the departure of such world names as Ravanelli and Juninho, though, it was the end of an era. We had to re-examine our project and start all over again. To his credit, Emerson wanted to stay and prove himself to be a loyal team member.

Not that Steve Gibson and Keith Lamb were about to take things lying down. They were still prepared to spend big to bring the best players possible to the Riverside. Players who could get us back up at the first attempt and maintain the faith of the fans, who, quite naturally, were on the verge of being totally disillusioned. We recruited Paul Merson, who may have dropped down a division to play for us but whose performances were so good that the England manager, Glenn Hoddle, took him to the 1998 World Cup in France. He was the only player from the second tier to make it into Hoddle's squad. Merson was a brilliant playmaker and goalscorer for our team, helping to push us to promotion. Ravanelli for Merson wasn't such a bad swap. Paul did the same for Harry Redknapp's Portsmouth a couple of years later. Then there were players like the Australian goalkeeper, Mark Schwartzer, who still graces the Premier League to this day.

We only stayed in the First Division for a single season. Once again, we managed to stop the slide and get the team back to winning ways. We didn't win the division this time like we had in our first promotion season in 1994–95, but went up automatically in second place. The Premier League had finally sorted out its format and had brought in the system we know today. Forest won our division, having been relegated with us the year before. Again we were pleased to have avoided the play-offs. At one point between October and November we won five games on the spin, scoring sixteen goals and conceding just three. Emerson was absolutely brilliant during this spell. On the eve of a game against fellow high-flyers Forest, the Nottingham Post became one of the first newspapers to at last give Emerson the credit he was due, saying: "Perhaps the public rehabilitation of the complex Brazilian this season serves as an adequate symbol for the club's positive change of direction."

Our season got even better when we went on a run and reached the League Cup Final yet again. As a second division side, we were underdogs this time and playing against a resurgent Chelsea, who beat us 2–0 after extra time. Given that we started the campaign in such a depressed state, that term saw probably the very best of the resilience the Robson-Anderson management team possessed. We re-energised the side, gave the fans a memorable season, and in my view proved our capabilities to anyone who cared to look. In perhaps our most audacious coup to date, we also persuaded the greatest player of his generation to revive his career at the Riverside. Paul Gascoigne came from Rangers for over £4 million. Having spent time in Italy, he had surprisingly moved to Scotland. During his Scottish period he shone for England in Euro 96. It was a massive boost to bring him back to the English league, where he surely belonged. The fans loved him. He made his first appearance for us in the final against Chelsea, when he came on as a substitute.

Gazza was both brilliant and troubled by turns. As a fellow Geordie, prodigy and mega-drinker, Robbo was convinced he could get one last master-class from the England star. I agreed. It was a joy working with him. His level of skill was as high as anything I'd ever seen and his enthusiasm was infectious. The rest of the lads took to him immediately. Mind you, he was still daft as a brush.

I think Gazza would agree that he was not always fit in his time with us. He was also suffering from his drink-related problems and troubles in his marriage. He was hardly ever out of the headlines and that was something with which I could sympathise. However, he turned in some great performance for us and wherever we went, fans paid money to watch him. When he was 'injured', the whole squad suffered from his absence. In his time with Middlesbrough, it is my opinion that he more than repaid every penny the club invested in him. He became extremely depressed after Glenn Hoddle decided not to take him to the World Cup in France during the summer and I think that affected him more than anything else in his career. I don't think he ever recovered from the setback. He only made occasional appearances for us after that and before too long we sold him to Everton.

One game he did play in when we were back in the Premier League was an away match against Derby, which we eventually lost 2–1. From the moment the lads kicked off, Gazza was all over the place. When he passed it, he gave the ball away; when he tried to trap it, he put it out of play; when he went for headers, he was nowhere near the ball. It was a terrible display.

I looked at Robbo. He looked at me. I said to him, "What's he doing?"

"I don't know what he's doing," was Robbo's reply.

"We've got to get him off," I said.

Robbo looked into the middle distance. Then he said "we can't take him off. It's only fifteen minutes into the game. It will destroy him."

I went along with the manager's opinion for another quarter of an hour. Gazza didn't improve, in fact he got worse. He couldn't run, he couldn't control the ball, he looked as if he couldn't even walk.

"Get him off, Robbo, get him off."

Robbo nodded. We substituted him. It was only thirty minutes into the game. As he walked past me I went up to him and told him to get in the bath and I'd come and have a chat. Gazza looked spaced out. Dazed and confused would be a good description of his state of mind.

I went to find him and ask him some questions. "What the fuck were you doing out there Gazza, what's going on?"

"I don't know boss, I just can't get me act together."

"Were you out last night?"

"No, I promise."

I looked at him closely. His drinking was legendary. Could I believe him when he said he hadn't been out on the lash? It looked like he had been. But he was adamant he had drunk nothing alcoholic.

"What have you eaten?" I asked him.

"The chicken and beans like everyone else, that's all."

"Nothing else?"

"Nothing."

"Have you drunk anything?"

"No ... .well just some Red Bull, they sent me a crate. They want to know if I'll promote it."

"How many Red Bulls did you drink, Paul?"

"Six."

Now Red Bull contains the stimulant caffeine. Any more than two cans and you'll fail a drugs test. Gazza had drunk half a crate, one after the other. If you drink six in a short amount of time you can be completely disoriented, if you are an athlete. Paul was out of his head. He could hardly talk. He didn't sleep for three weeks. It's not surprising after all those Red Bulls. That's why he's daft as a brush.

When he got frustrated, Gazza did some silly things, both on and off the pitch. Remember that terrible tackle on Gary Charles in the 1991 Cup Final when he almost destroyed his career. While he was with us he got himself banned for three games following an elbow attack on George Boateng of Aston Villa. He injured himself at the same time and was out for about eight weeks in total. After that, the press wrote him off completely. There was talk of him being frozen out at the Riverside. I was having none of it. I told the press "Nobody is shutting the door on him. He's mad, not bad." I had no idea why Gazza sometimes lost it, it just happened when you least expected it – or sometimes when you did expect it. Paul didn't know why he did it either. No matter how much he tried to control himself, he was only storing up the explosion that would come sooner or later.

When we first went to Middlesbrough, the club had already been relegated and we started from a low-point for both players and fans alike. I suppose our latest experience of being relegated from the Premier League affected Robbo and me in many ways and when we got back to the top flight we were less prepared to take chances than we had before. The result was two seasons of reasonable but undramatic performances, finishing mid-table in both seasons. My biggest recollection during this period, and remember, this was when my personal life was at its most tumultuous, was winning 3–2 at Old Trafford, although I'd be hard-pressed to give you any details of the game. I'm told we were 3–0 up at one point but, to be honest, I can't remember it.

Having grown used to a comfortable position in the table, our fans now expected us to push on. I expected us to push on. Somehow we couldn't do it. On the plus side for me personally, around this time I received some unexpected good news. In the New Year's Honours List of 1999–2000 – the millennium – I was awarded an MBE for services to football. You would have thought I'd seen it all, what with European Cup wins and England appearances, but receiving that medal from the Queen was the proudest moment of my life. To be recognised by my country in such a way was extra-special. I even enjoyed the endless rehearsals of protocol before the event itself. We had to learn to bow so that we behaved properly in front of Her Majesty. To be the son of immigrants and now invited to Buckingham Palace to receive one of the nation's highest accolades was the stuff of dreams. Something to be cherished. Forever!

In the same Honours List MBEs were awarded to a number of England's 1966 World Cup heroes, who had somehow been forgotten when it came to dishing out the gongs. Nobby Stiles, Alan Ball, Roger Hunt, George Cohen and Ray Wilson were all recognised. I was so happy to receive my medal in the same list as those great performers. Other footballers who received recognition were Ian Wright (then playing for Celtic), the Wolves veteran Steve Bull and Mansfield's Tony Ford, who broke Terry Paine's record for the most number of games played, reaching the incredible number of 825. Henry Cooper and Stirling Moss were both awarded knighthoods.

During the following campaign the harsh realities of football came back to bite us. Far from pushing on, we were struggling again. As Christmas approached, we were odds-on for relegation. Our results were appalling from almost the moment the season began. After two years of consolidation this was unexpected. For some reason, we just couldn't get the team to function as we wanted. Whatever happened, though, Robbo did not want to put the club, and particularly Steve Gibson, through the trauma of relegation again. His solution, though, was extraordinary.

That was when Robbo and I had the strange conversation I referred to at the beginning of this chapter. He wanted to bring in another manager/coach to work with the players. He also wanted that person to be a big name. Not only had I never heard anything like Robbo's proposal before, I also understood that, whether it was successful or not, it spelt the end of the

road for us at Middlesbrough. If it ended up in relegation, we would be blamed and sacked anyway. If we
stayed up, it wouldn't be us who got the credit, but the
newcomer. But Robbo was adamant that he wanted to
do the unthinkable. He would take more of a back seat,
he said. He felt he had lost his powers of motivation, at
least for the moment. Maybe he had been around for
too long. Maybe I had failed to recognise the symptoms
of burn-out which I knew might be a possibility when
we first went to Middlesbrough. As defeat followed
defeat, Robbo seemed to withdraw into another world.
It was a place we'd never been before and not a very
nice one at that.

I have to say that in my opinion the answer Robbo
came up with was far from an act of weakness, which is
the way it was portrayed in the media. On the contrary,
it was an act of the greatest possible strength. Bryan
may have seemed to be in his own world – and television pictures of him in the technical area during games
reinforced this view – but he had actually analysed the
situation coolly and knew what was required. No matter
how unconventional it might be he would recommend
it to the Chairman. He was prepared to resign if necessary, but neither of us thought it would come to that. It
hardly needed saying that I would have gone with him
had he taken that decision. Instead, he convinced Steve
Gibson to open negotiations with none other than Terry
Venables, one of England's greatest managerial and
coaching talents of the modern era.

Robbo had worked under Venables when he was

England manager and rated him as one of the greatest coaches in the world. So did a lot of other people in the game. In addition, Venables was a household name, possessed charisma in bucket-loads and was someone who would command the respect of the players. Robbo believed the former England manager was the only man who could turn performances around and stave off the drop. He also knew Steve Gibson could afford to pay Venables's huge asking price: £1 million for half a season's work, no matter what the outcome.

This colossal amount of money caused considerable controversy, especially on Teesside, where many people had lost their jobs in the recent past, particularly in the steel industry. The popular view expressed in the pubs and working men's clubs, as well as on the local media, was that giving an already rich southerner such a massive pay-day was obscene. I had some sympathy with that view. But at the same time I knew what Venables could do and if that is what it took to get him, then so be it. The public naturally thought Gibson was already employing a team to carry out the job of managing the club. Us! So we came in for more than our fair share of the brickbats. There was a lot of local pressure on Steve, some of it pro-Venables, a lot of it anti. Gibson, though, continued to rate Robbo's judgment and he was still, at heart, a Boro fan who would do anything if he thought it would help the club. He agreed to pay Venables the money he demanded.

Robbo was proved right. I don't know how he did it

but Venables displayed all the qualities that had earned him success in the past and he saved us from relegation. Maybe it was simply the case of a new man with new ideas to freshen up performances. But I don't think it was just that. Terry had his own way with players. He could sum up their strengths and weaknesses after he had the merest glimpse of them playing. And he was rarely wrong in his assessments. He was also a breath of fresh air and brought all his experience and personality to bear on the situation. He was always jovial on the training ground yet he knew what he wanted from day one and he made sure the players delivered.

Our salvation was confirmed when we went to Arsenal and won 3-0, our best performance of the season by far. Terry loved putting one over on the Gunners. Whether or not Robbo and I could have achieved a position of safety without Venables, no-one will ever know. I like to think we could have. I'm not sure, even today, if I disagreed with Robbo's view or whether it was just so unprecedented it was difficult to take in. But we had genuine achievements to our name at Boro. I believe we had what it took to see the club through the choppy waters in which it found itself. But it wasn't to be.

Having survived – just – in the Premier League with Terry Venables at the helm, it was obvious that Robbo and I would have to be on our way. We had been at the Riverside for six great years. We had put the team in the limelight and, we felt, had taken it to the next level. We had reached three Cup Finals and left the club established in the top division. Steve Gibson was almost in tears when the time came but he knew as well as we did that the parting of the ways could not be put off. What concerned Bryan and I, of course, was what we were going to do next.

Chapter Twenty

LIFE AFTER FOOTBALL

When Bryan and I left Middlesbrough, we knew we had to take stock of our situation. But first, we needed to rest and re-charge our batteries after such a long time on the frontline. So we took some time out. I went on a couple of holidays, the first I had taken during the summer for twenty-odd years. Christmases and the July-August holidays are forbidden to the British footballer. After a while you almost forget what they are like.

Steve Gibson was more upset than either Robbo or me at our departure. We knew the score but Steve was strangely depressed about it all. For a time I thought the club might spiral down or Steve might lose interest. But, to give him his due, he came back stronger than ever with his commitment to Middlesbrough intact. I was pleased he managed to pull off what was then a bit of a coup. He enticed Steve McClaren from the assistant's job at Manchester United, where he was a key figure in the treble-winning season. McClaren – who is now most remembered for his ill-starred period as England manager – built upon what Robbo, Terry Venables and I had constructed on Teesside and took them to greater success than even we had managed. He won the club the first trophy in their history and got them to the UEFA Cup Final the next year. That was a truly amazing achievement which he is continuing with his new club, Twente Enschede of Holland. His time with England may have been a disaster but his record in club football speaks for itself.

Following our Middlesbrough experience neither Robbo nor I applied for any managerial jobs. It was a decision both of us took together. If anything was offered, we would consider it on its merits but we weren't going to chase another position. We had spent six tumultuous years on Teesside and we both needed to take a step back. Sometime later, Bryan was offered the manager's job at Bradford. He decided to take it. I was never going to go to there so in many ways; it represented the end of the road for Robbo and me. We had fulfilled our ambition of being joint managers of a great club with money in the bank and a Chairman who was prepared to spend it. We achieved substantial progress with Middlesbrough. When we went to Teesside the club had been relegated and was going nowhere. When we left, Middlesbrough were established in the Premier League – albeit with help from Terry Venables – had reached three cup finals and had brought some of the most exciting players in the world to the north-east. Whoever took over would have something solid to build on, far more than we did when we started. Steve McClaren was exactly the right man to take it forward. Did I want to do it all over again? I wasn't sure.

Far from being out in the cold, almost as soon as I left football I received offers of other work. I had owned a stake in an events company for many years and upped my role in its day-to-day operations, becoming more hands-on. I worked on hospitality packages at sporting events and on the creation and implementation of new events, such as a golf classic named after Norman Whiteside. In later years I formed a company with my old friend, Tony Woodcock. In partnership with the Jebel Ali Hotel in Dubai, we set up the Jebel Ali Centre of Excellence, a coaching facility in the sun. The centre came into existence after we took the owners of the hotel to Manchester United's training ground at Carrington and Arsenal's at London Colney, where they could see how football training works in the modern age. The centre now provides warm-weather facilities for a number of clubs and international teams, including Aston Villa, Blackburn and Portsmouth from the Premier League and the national teams of Russia, Ghana and Nigeria. Russian club sides come for their pre-season. In all, approximately ten or more teams use the centre every year at present.

These developments in my life meant that I did not miss the cut and thrust of daily involvement in the game nearly as much as I thought I would. I have really enjoyed the new challenges these activities have thrown up for me. It wasn't always like that for former pros.

The nineties was an era when the media, especially television and radio, were opening up. This led to far

more ex-footballers being in demand by the broad-
casters than had been the case previously. By the
time I left management in 2001, there was a whole
industry devoted to football. I did some work for Sky
when I departed from Middlesbrough but I was soon
poached by ESPN, which in those days was not available in Britain but was extensively broadcast to the
rest of the world. Now, of course, the company is a
major player in the negotiations for TV rights to the
Premier League. I have been a regular on ESPN in
the far-east for some years and was their main pundit
in 2009 for the FA Cup Final and the Champions
League Final. I also appear regularly on the in-house
channel, Manchester United TV.

I enjoy the TV work and I think I've got a natural
flair for giving my opinions in an interesting way, even
if many of them turn out to be wrong. I was convinced,
for instance, that United would beat Barcelona in the
2009 Champions League Final. I gave my views live to
millions of viewers on ESPN. I thought Barcelona's
injury problems would leave them fatally exposed to
the likes of Ronaldo and Rooney. How wrong can you
be?

My promotional work has increased through the
years. I was appointed as an ambassador for the Victor
Chandler betting empire, which entails attending
sporting events around the world and giving my take
on things to the company's clients. This year I teamed
up with some high-tech guys to market a new, internet-
based gambling product called Passoker. Designed by

John Carr, who is a systems designer for major automobile manufacturers, Passoker lets players bet in real time on the next incident to happen in a sports event as they watch it live on TV or their computer.

It works is like this: if the event is a football match, it is split into its component parts. So as the game progresses, the next incident will be, say, a throw-in, a goal, a corner, a free-kick, a goal-kick etc. You can bet money on what incident on the list of possibilities will occur next. The odds are instantaneously reset after every incident. You can bet against the house or other players in a poker-style format. There is even a championship version of the game with prizes of sporting memorabilia. By the time you read this, Passoker should just about be on the market, in time for the South Africa World Cup.

Another consultancy contract is with the Dubai-based global transportation company, GAC. This company is involved in a number of sports-related activities. For instance, it is shirt sponsor of Crystal Palace and sponsors one of the stands at Bramall Lane, home of Sheffield United. GAC is also a logistics partner to one of the world's leading Formula One racing teams.

It is a different world from the one in which I first started playing. Then, footballers had no capital behind them or pension to see them through the long retirement years. That was why so many opened shops, became landlords of pubs or looked for employment anywhere they could find it. Many ended up with nothing. Even George

Cohen was forced to sell his World Cup winners medal to make ends meet. The unbelievable transformation since those times has opened up a whole new set of possibilities for players and ex-players. The hospitality industry, for instance, has been one of the fastest growing areas in all sport in recent times and large numbers of old pros earn a decent living from it.

When I won the European Cup for the first time with Forest my basic wage was eighty pounds a week. Sure, there were bonuses for winning but still we made about as much as a skilled worker in a car factory. This meant we felt close to the community who supported us. We were a part of it. Everyone knows that situation has been completely turned on its head since the inception of the Premiership and the Champions League. But things were changing before these two mega-competitions were established. In fact, the new order was the result of the changes rather than the cause. And I was right there when they happened.

By the time I left Forest there had been significant improvements to the negotiating position of players, especially at the top level. There wasn't yet total freedom of contract, that would come later, but neither could clubs any longer retain a player against his will once his contract had expired. The new club a player went to still had to pay a transfer fee but if the two clubs couldn't agree it would go to a tribunal to decide, as it did when I left Arsenal for Manchester United. No longer was it possible for clubs to completely control a footballer's playing career, telling them where they could or couldn't play.

This change gave players the confidence to promote their interests further. Our union, the Professional Footballers Association, under the astute leadership of Gordon Taylor, took up the long fight to gain true freedom of contract like every other worker. Before long the Bosman case gave us real freedom at last. We weren't asking for anything more than the conditions everyone else takes for granted. It is true that the money on offer these days to the best players is so huge that many ordinary people find it fundamentally wrong. But the vast majority of professional players do not make these massive amounts. They deserve to be protected. And they have every right to negotiate the best possible deal for themselves that they can.

After two European Cups, a League title and three League Cup Final appearances for Forest my pay had gone up but it was nowhere near the amounts on offer at bigger clubs, even those who were not winning things. My basic was around £250 a week by that time. There was also some bad feeling at Forest because towards the end of my period there, the players were disillusioned when expected bonuses did not materialise. Although my move to Arsenal was prompted by the need for a new challenge and a desire to experience life in the capital, I cannot deny that money played its part. Arsenal offered me double what I was getting with Forest. This level of payment allowed some footballers to leave the world of the factory worker I mentioned earlier far behind. We were starting on the road towards bigger rewards.

We were also examining things like private pensions. Change was in the air.

After three years at Arsenal, my wages reached about £1000 a week, which was a fortune compared to what I was getting before at Forest. I realise that this level of salary was outstripping by far the income that most people could expect from their work. But if the income generated within the football industry doesn't go to players where would it go? I don't think it would help to reduce prices for spectators or build better facilities. It would more likely be spent on even higher transfer fees than you see at the moment. Agents and greedy owners would take more money out of the game. It is, don't forget, players who bring crowds through the turnstiles, whatever the level of football.

The three most important reasons for improving the lot of the professional footballer are, in my view, these: first, you live and work with the possibility of a career-threatening injury every day; second, even if you avoid serious injury, your life as a professional player is over when you are in your thirties. It is difficult for anyone in a conventional job to understand the impact this can have. Most people start at the bottom, if you like, and over the length of their working careers climb the ladder of experience, success and remuneration. For an athlete, the opposite occurs. You can be on the scrapheap at 35. The third reason is historical: for decades, the footballer was little more than a serf. For years there was an income-ceiling of £20 a week – the maximum wage – which applied in no other area of business that I know of. Footballers – as most people are probably aware – were very badly treated by their employers, the clubs. They might, if they were lucky, receive a testimonial match in recognition of long service but even this morsel was at the discretion of the club's directors.

The long-time secretary of the Football League, Alan Hardaker, once said: "I wouldn't hang a dog on the word of a footballer." That tells you all you need to know about the attitudes of the time. Everything the modern player has gained has had to be fought for, often through the courts in the teeth of fierce opposition from clubs. All players in this country owe a debt of gratitude to those who paved the way, like Jimmy Hill, who fought for the abolition of the maximum wage, and Gordon Taylor, who single-handedly ensured that players' rights are taken into account at every stage and who raised the role of the PFA to unprecedented influence. There are those who might say that things have gone too far in the other direction, with players and their agents now too powerful. However, I make no apologies for the advancement of players' terms and conditions of employment and my small part in the process that brought it about.

Although every professional footballer's main motivation is a love of the game, it soon becomes clear that you have to take steps to look after your interests. This is particularly true when you have a family. You have to do everything you can for your loved ones in what is at best a precarious profession, where you are only as good as your last game and can be discarded before you know it.

Arsenal, one of the biggest clubs around, were paying good wages when I went to Highbury. As I said, they paid me far more than I could ever have received at Forest. But when I went to Manchester United, my pay packets went through the roof. Even though United were not, at the time, anything like the force they have since become, they still paid more than anyone else. They were always the glamour club. And I was in the top group of earners there. Only Robbo and Jesper Olsen were paid more than me. So you can see that during my time as a pro there was beginning to be a player revolution.

When the Premier League, soon to be followed by the Champions League, started in the nineties, they were the authorities' response to these and other changes that were occurring in the world of football. For example, along with player-power, the Chairmen and Presidents of clubs throughout Europe lobbied for competitions to be reorganised for their benefit and to the detriment of the smaller clubs. I doubt if a club like Forest could ever hope to win the Champions League today. All these changes came about in the wake of the players increasing their power. The consequence was that the new competitions helped the top players increase that power even more.

With the advent of the Premier League, far more of the world's best players began to come to England. To make this happen, the financial packages on offer had to be immense. I played a pivotal role in this development. Our quartet at Middlesbrough – Steve Gibson, Keith Lamb, Bryan Robson and yours truly – put together the team of Ravanelli, Juninho and Emerson. One had scored in the final of the Champions League just a few months previously to win the Cup for Juventus, another was Brazil's footballer of the year and the third was one of the most exciting prospects in the world. To bring such players to England was unheard of at the time: to bring them to unfashionable Middlesbrough was impossible.

In the main, even the biggest clubs in England could only attract good Scandinavians or East Europeans and continentals whose careers were coming towards their end. When Manchester United bought Eric Cantona from Leeds, the fee was modest, his wages not outrageous and because he was the wild child of French football he was seen as drinking at the last chance saloon. He had lost his place in the French team. Howard Wilkinson was one manager among many who failed to get the best out of him. Manchester United was his final throw of the dice. He turned out to be probably the most important signing of Fergie's career. Cantona's subsequent influence on United's destiny made Robbo and me realise that if we could entice Europe's best players we could make Middlesbrough a force to be reckoned with.

How did we do it? How did we convince these top performers to come to the Riverside? Well, as I think you already know, we raised the bar in terms of transfer fees. More important, we paid these players a king's ransom, far more than they could have earned anywhere else in the world. That's how far Steve Gibson was prepared to go in his backing of Robbo and me. Our plunges into the transfer market set in motion a game of catch-up by the big boys and smaller clubs alike. That meant that even journeymen Premier League players began to see their weekly pay reach the thousands of pounds level. After our outlay at Middlesbrough, the face of English football changed forever and it wasn't long before the Premier League began to be talked of as the most exciting league in the world. Its value to TV and to sponsors multiplied a hundredfold. New stadiums were built and the crowds went up every year. It is all a long way from my days as a teenager trying to break in to the Forest first team, when facilities for players and fans were primitive to say the least. I believe the changes, for the most part, have been positive developments.

But for all the talk of money, it is the game that means so much to all of us, players and supporters alike. I have called this chapter Life After Football but these days there is no life after football, really. For ex-players there is now more football to take part in than ever before. There has been, for instance, the emergence of veterans' – or Masters – tournaments going on all round the world to wildly enthusiastic spectators both live and on TV. I myself have recently appeared in a number of these events so you can see that even us old-uns can still draw an audience and play to a reasonable level ... provided the matches don't last too long. I captain the Manchester United Masters team all round the world and have appeared in tournaments from South Africa to Vietnam.

My most recent outing for the United old boys came in a tournament in Kuala Lumpur, Malaysia. The reason I am telling you this will become clear in a moment. The competition comprised various English sides, one a Premier League Select X1 captained by Ray Parlour. The other participants were Sheffield United, with Brian Deane still putting himself about and ... yes ... Liverpool. Another go at the old enemy. That's why I had to include it here.

We had the brilliant Andy Cole playing for us. It was good to see Clayton Blackmore again after knowing him both at United and Middlesbrough. In addition, we had Russell Beardsmore, one of Fergie's early youngsters who scored that great goal against the Scousers all those years ago. We had Paul Parker, another of United's great full-backs. Ronnie Johnsson and Jesper Blomquist made up our outfield, Frazer Digby was in goal.

For the dreaded Liverpool, who had made so many teams' lives a misery but whom I had managed to get the better of on the odd important occasion, there were some ominous names: Mark Walters, who could make mincemeat of the best full-back; the stylish Don Hutchinson; Michael Thomas, an old team-mate from my Arsenal days, who, after breaking Scouse hearts with that winning goal at Anfield in 1989 which took the title to Highbury, actually joined the club he had demolished; and last but by no means least, there was Mark Wright and Jason McAteer. We were all set.

The Liverpool veterans generally win most tournaments they enter, just like they did when they were regular players. This time, they faced us in the final. A magnificent match ended 3–3 and we went to penalties. We beat them in the shoot-out. Nothing could have given me greater pleasure than to triumph over them again, especially on penalties. It was a great moment when I lifted the trophy. My thoughts drifted back to that night in Nottingham long ago, in the first round of the European Cup. Against Liverpool! Liverpool the undefeated! Liverpool the best! Liverpool the destroyers of other clubs' dreams!

2–0!

The rest, as they say, is history.

POSTSCRIPT

Along with the whole nation I was absolutely delighted when England, under the watchful eye of Fabio Capello, qualified for the 2010 World Cup in South Africa. As the first black player to be capped by England, the choice of an African country, let alone one with such a history of racism, was a poignant reminder to me of what can be achieved with belief and commitment.

South African football has long been the province of the black majority in the country. Traditionally, the white minority favoured rugby and cricket. It was a pleasant surprise for all of us within the game that FIFA rewarded the reconciliation that has taken place within South Africa since apartheid came to an end. It brought home to me the full extent of the change the world has undergone since I first began to ply my trade as a professional footballer. Back then, you wouldn't have used football and South Africa in the same sentence. Now, the country is a football nation as well as a rainbow one.

2010 is truly a world event, the biggest sporting spectacular on the planet. By taking it to South Africa, football has given the South Africans the opportunity to show the world how far their country has come in the last two decades.

At first I was a bit worried that England would find it difficult to qualify. Our previous campaign to reach the European Championships under Steve McClaren ended in abject failure, as we are all too well aware. What was worse about our attempt to qualify for South Africa was that we again drew our nemesis from the Euro qualifiers – Croatia – in the same group. What I hadn't quite appreciated was the difference Capello would make. It shouldn't, perhaps, have been such a surprise. Hadn't I believed for years that managers make a difference? Wasn't this what Robbo and I had been discussing for so long? The trouble is, as every fan knows, when it comes to your country, it is easy to lose your sense of perspective. In the event, we qualified so easily that complacency is what we have to avoid.

Now that we are certain of participating in the next World Cup, I've had a chance to bring my experience and knowledge of the game to bear on the situation. I'd like to share my thoughts with you about how I think the South Africa tournament will pan out. I realise I'm giving you all a hostage to fortune here. At least anything I say can be checked against what actually happens. And my predictions are in truth no more likely to come to pass than someone sticking a pin in the fixture list. Still, you might be interested in my insider knowledge, offered to you here with no guarantees. If you want those, get Russell Grant.

How far can England go? That is the question all of us in this country are most concerned with. The last two World Cups have ended in quarter-final disappointment. Can we really expect to do any better this time round? Having seen World Cup campaigns from the inside I know what kind of things influence the outcome. Of course, tactical nous and motivational skill are very important. But there is more to it than that. As you settle down to watch the greatest tournament in the world, here is what I make of it all.

Well, I'm optimistic on England's behalf. I know the team has let us down in the past but I really believe it will be different this time. Fabio Capello will ensure there is no repeat of the WAGS debacle that occurred in Germany, when attention shifted away from the football and onto the shopping sprees of the wives and girlfriends. And the atmosphere he will create will be geared to winning. England could go all the way, you know. They should, in my opinion, make it to the semi-finals at the very least. Not that anything can be taken for granted. For England to do well, a number of things have to happen.

The first, and to me the most important requirement, is that Jermain Defoe is fit and firing. Although he has not always been first choice for Capello, I believe that will change. He can score goals at any level and if he is on his game, he will make the difference. Although the manager has often used Emile Heskey or Peter Crouch up front with Wayne Rooney, I think Jermain is our most natural goalscorer. To progress in a World Cup you need someone you can rely on to score you the goals you need. Gary Lineker was supreme in this role. When I played with him for England, the team just knew Gary could get you a goal, no matter what the circumstances. Having someone like that breeds a lot of confidence throughout the side. Rooney, Steven Gerrard, Frank Lampard and John Terry will be important in South Africa, obviously, but I think the key is Defoe. If he is below par for any reason, or not picked, I think we will struggle.

The hotels and facilities are also extremely important. Having been to two World Cups, I can tell you that boredom can be the biggest problem. You can't just take a stroll these days because of security concerns so you don't get to see much of the country you're in. Good relaxation time, however, is crucial. There have to be distractions and they must be relevant to today's young adults. You should also have old stand-by attractions like pool tables, dart boards, table tennis and video games. There must be lots for the players to do, because boredom actually causes fatigue, which is the last thing you want at a World Cup. You have to be ready for three games in a short space of time then be able to switch your focus onto the knock-out format. It is the manager's job to see that the players are fresh by the time each game comes around.

In terms of training, Capello will have a balancing act to deal with. Some of the players, particularly those from the most successful club sides, will have played a lot of games of high intensity throughout the year. Their season might not finish until the end of May if they are involved in the later stages of European competitions. This group doesn't need too much training, they need to be nursed along. Then there are the players who might have been out for some of the campaign, perhaps only playing 30 odd games at clubs whose season finished at the beginning of May. They may need more intensive training sessions. It is in these little things that Cups are won and lost.

Any team that wins the World Cup will have had a bit of luck somewhere along the way. Fortune, though, cannot be predicted. You just need a bit now and again. Remember, every team is there on merit and on any given day one of them could beat a so-called superior team or at least get a draw. It can happen. It has happened, too many times for comfort in England's case. I believe Fabio Capello will deal with all these issues better than previous managers. That is why I am optimistic.

In the group stage – which we really should qualify for without too many scares – we need to pay special attention to the USA. If we are not right on our game, they will beat us. Increasing numbers of the USA's players now operate in Europe, like Donovan Landon and Clint Dempsey in the Premier League, so they know how we play our game. The USA would love to put one over on the English, make no mistake. If we can perform to the standards we did in the qualifying competition, though, there will be no problem.

If you know anything about the remaining countries in the tournament, you will agree that none of them will fancy being drawn against England in the later stages. Of the countries who can win it, there are question marks against them all.

The European Champions, Spain, have a fabulous team that can play fantastic football. If Fernando Torres is fit, and their immensely talented midfield performs, their chances are sky-high. But can they raise themselves on the biggest stage of all when they have underperformed on so many occasions in the past? If they can, they must be favourites. But if they can't, the door is wide open for everyone else.

Argentina are an enigma. I think their chances depend on whether Lionel Messi can step up to the plate in the way the team's current coach – Diego Maradona – did back in Mexico 86. In the last World Cup, Argentina played some wonderful football early on but collapsed when it mattered. That could happen again if Messi doesn't perform. However, Messi is the World Player of the Year and that alone makes Argentina dangerous. I know they had difficulty qualifying for this tournament but that may make them hungrier. They may feel they have something to prove. In the end I don't believe they will have enough to win it but they will be nobody's fools.

Brazil are always a threat, we know that only too well. If we have to play them, we will find it difficult. They showed in the recent friendly against England in Doha that they are still a force. These days many of their best players are based in Europe and they have added extra dimensions to their game over the years. And you can never write off the most successful country in World Cup history. If England are to triumph, they will have to gain victory over Brazil somewhere along the line. Sometimes I think Brazil beat teams before they even get on the pitch. Their reputation can intimidate opponents.

If England face them, the players have to remember that this is not the Brazil of Pele or Zico. They are good but they are beatable.

As for the best of the rest, Italy are an ageing team and I don't think they will successfully defend their title. I don't mean to be dismissive but they were a bit lucky to win last time in my opinion. You always have to watch out for the Germans, every one of us knows that. They regularly seem to be in a state of transition but they always do better than you would think at the outset. The Germans are supreme at tournament-play. They will not be easily brushed aside. If we have to face them we have the players to win but ... mmm ... it's Germany ... I don't know.

This time round, I believe there is a possibility that an African team could do well. The accepted wisdom is that the African sides are not yet good enough. That view is maybe a bit premature. It would be fitting if one of them won it the first time the tournament has come to their continent. I don't think the hosts, South Africa, have any chance. Cameroon and Nigeria could cause upsets here and there but the African team with the best prospects is, in my view, Ivory Coast. I know they underperformed in the last African Cup of Nations but I don't think you can read too much into that. They possess one of the best goalscorers in the world in Didier Drogba. If he plays to his potential, Ivory Coast have a chance. I'm sure Drogba would enjoy facing England at some point. If that happens we will have to snuff out his menace, otherwise he will have a field day.

My last team to watch is something of a nostalgic and left-field choice. No-one who witnessed them will ever forget the exploits of North Korea in 1966. Their performances lit up the tournament, seeing off Italy in the process. The Italians went home to be bombarded with rotten fruit at the airport. It would be great to see that again. And when North Korea led a Portugal side featuring the great Eusebio 3–0, it seemed miracles could really happen. Eusebio, of course, dragged his team back into contention in that match on his own and the 5–3 win for Portugal is still one of the greatest-ever games in World Cup history. But no-one really knows the strength of the North Koreans. So my off-the-wall prediction is that North Korea will at some point in the tournament give us cause for celebration by upsetting one of their so-called betters.

That's my view of the 2010 World Cup. How much of it proves to be accurate remains to be seen. That is why the World Cup is such a fantastic tournament. But perhaps more important in the long term is how things are progressing in our quest to be hosts of the 2018 tournament.

As I wrote in the first chapter of this book, I have some reservations about the conduct of our bid. Looking at it objectively, we shoot ourselves in the foot far too often for our own good. There has been a lot of activity during the latter half of 2009 and I hope it pays dividends. I desperately want the World Cup to come here once again. I think you can see from the things I have written how committed I am. In the absence of a real plan to use the ambassadors, I concentrated on getting Nottingham selected as one of the host cities. This we managed to achieve, even though there is no stadium in the city at present that could put on a World Cup game. It has been a leap of faith on the part of the FA to accept that if England wins the bid, a new stadium will be built. The only shame is that Nottingham is the only venue in the East-Midlands to be chosen. When London could have three venues, Manchester two and there looks like being two in the north-east, it seems wrong somehow that our bid had to be at the expense of Leicester and Derby. The three cities of the East Midlands will always maintain their intense rivalry but in this case it would have been nice if the region – which has excellent hotels and great transport links – could have been awarded two venues. And the owners of the Derby and Leicester clubs have already invested in new stadiums.

The bid team for 2018 has undergone some changes since the avalanche of criticisms of its operations. The most notable has been the resignation of Sir Dave Richards, who runs the Premier League. His departure has not, in my opinion, been adequately explained. We are still on a knife edge and I don't yet believe we have got it right. With the decision coming up this December, all those things which I wrote about at the start of this book are still issues to be resolved. Will we win it? Maybe, by the skin of our teeth. A great performance in South Africa might tip the scales. I travel on football-related business all over the world and from what I've heard I have to tell you that for England, it's nowhere near a done deal.

As I have explained, much has been accomplished in the years since I began my life as a professional footballer. But unfortunately, racism does keep rearing its head. We have to be vigilant. We have to listen to ex-players who know more about this than anyone else. And racism must be tackled in those European countries like Spain who pay lip service to the cause but in effect do little to combat it and often seem to condone racist behaviour.

At the end of the first chapter, I wrote that around the time of my visit to Wembley for the launch of the 2018 bid, certain other things were taking place which affected me personally. This is what happened.

I have always been there for Nottingham Forest. When they have wanted reunions of the European Cup-winning team I have continually made myself available. The club has made huge amounts of money from the players who gave them the most successful period in their history. The same treatment, though, has not been forthcoming from the club to me and the other members of that history-making team.

The season 2008–9 marked the thirtieth anniversary of my ground-breaking debut in the England team. I was approached by a consortium who believed my appearance thirty years ago should be commemorated with an all-star charity football match. The event would celebrate the progress this country has made in overcoming racism over the last three decades. It would also show how England has led the way in the world of football.

The consortium contained some important names from the sports business. We received fantastic support from the PFA – from Gordon Taylor personally – and the anti-racist charity, Kick It Out, which would have been a beneficiary of some of the income.

A number of television channels were prepared to bid for the rights to screen the match, which told me that it would really resonate with people. It was a chance for the nation to feel good about itself and the changes that have taken place over the last thirty years in regard to racism. Sponsors were also queuing up to get involved. Players rushed to pledge their attendance. It was a no-brainer.

The FA offered notional support but didn't fall over themselves to get proactive. If you think about it, the FA could have used the event to promote the 2018 bid; they could have invited key FIFA delegates and shown them just how much this country has embraced multi-cultur-alism and fought racism over the years. They could have shown how England is in the vanguard of the anti-racist cause. It would have played so well with FIFA that their delegates would have been lining up to vote for England. Instead, the FA missed a golden opportunity by offering only lukewarm support and not spotting what everyone else could see. Everyone else, that is, except Nottingham Forest.

With all the backing we had, the only remaining issue was the venue at which the match would be played. Our first thought, you won't be surprised to hear, was Wembley, where my debut took place. Now, I thought that Wembley was under the control of the FA but it turned out that due to the way the stadium was financed, it is operated by a subsidiary company whose brief is to make as much money as possible in order to service the debt incurred when the stadium was built. The FA were powerless to intervene. As it happened, at the time we wanted to schedule the game, Wembley was due to have its pitch taken up so we were forced to look elsewhere. It still seemed odd that a game which had been received with enthusiasm from every quarter did not seem to register with the one organisation that could benefit the most from it: the FA.

Then we had a brainwave. Of course: it should be in my home town at the place where I achieved so much. The City Ground, Nottingham. I found out that the local council was establishing a sports facility for deprived kids from the inner city and I arranged for some of the proceeds from the match to go to the new building. In return, Nottingham Council offered their full co-operation and support.

It was a fantastic feeling for me to contemplate what it meant to hold the game in Nottingham. I have great affection for all the clubs I played for: Forest, the first and the most revolutionary; Arsenal, all class from top to bottom; Manchester United, the world's favourite club; Sheffield Wednesday, tradition, success and great football; Barnsley, just like a family; Middlesbrough, world stars, great fans, what a Chairman. I cherish all these clubs. But taking the match to my home town, where I grew up, where I had so many memories, was a very special idea.

We attended a meeting about the proposed event with representatives of Nottingham Forest. We came away with a handshake on a deal. For the club, Forest would get some much-needed income and be seen hosting a major event by a huge television audience. It would have been a great advert for the campaign for a new stadium and the 2018 World Cup matches that would come with it. The profile of the city and the region would immediately be raised. The consortium was to receive a reasonable – but not excessive – return on its investment, the designated charities would receive funds, while TV, sponsors and spectators would be participating in a massive, feel-good event. Fantastic!

Almost immediately, Forest began to shift their position. They wanted to impose impossible conditions, including taking over the administration of all charitable donations from the match. This included a demand that their own preferred charity – Childline – received a significant donation. Now, I've nothing against Childline, I'm sure it is a worthy cause. But this match was about celebrating the fight against racism and we had already put in place the charities which would benefit from the event, Kick it Out and Nottingham's facility for inner-city kids. Forest went on to make more inexplicable demands and continually refused to negotiate in good faith. I have no idea to this day why they changed their attitude after that handshake. As someone who has done more to put Forest in the top drawer of great football clubs than any of the current directors, I find their actions reprehensible. In the end, although we offered a number of compromises,

Forest's intransigence made it impossible for the game to go ahead.

I said at the beginning of this book, that we have come a long way, but we still have a long way to go. I think the events I've described surrounding the commemorative game illustrate that perfectly. It wasn't me who lost out. It was the charities, the game, the people, the club. Everyone lost the chance to celebrate our achievements as a nation.

Still, I remain optimistic, as ever. I prefer to dwell on what's gone right rather than what's gone wrong. For instance, I've given my criticisms of the FA in this book so it's only fair that I give credit on something the organisation is trying to get right. During the last couple of years the FA has been subtly changing the make-up of its disciplinary panels by bringing in ex-players who are closer to the modern game than the committee men who acted as judges in the past. I was one of the first to be asked to participate and I have now sat in judgment on a number of cases of alleged player or managerial indiscipline. It's ironic, given the times I was taken to task myself while I was a player. Maybe that's the point. I am the poacher turned gamekeeper. In my life I have to say that far more has gone right than wrong. I have played for some wonderful football clubs. I've had a fantastic career. It has been an incredible journey. I wouldn't have missed it for the world.

INDEX

THE LOVE OF COOKING

*To be a good cook means the knowledge
of all fruits, herbs, balms and spices;
and of all that is healing and sweet in
field and groves; savoury in meats. It
means carefulness, inventiveness,
watchfulness, willingness and readiness
of appliance. It means the economy
of our great-grandmothers and the
science of modern chemists; it means
much tasting and no wasting; it means
English thoroughness, French art, and
Arabian hospitality; it means, in fine,
that you are to see that everybody has
something nice to eat.*

John Ruskin (1819–1900)

THE LOVE OF COOKING

Sonia Allison

COLLINS

GLASGOW & LONDON

Italian style lamb (see page 63)

First published in 1972
by William Collins Sons & Co Ltd
London · Glasgow · Sydney
Auckland · Johannesburg
New edition (tenth reprint) 1986

© Sonia Allison 1972, 1986

ISBN 0 00 411288 1

Designed and edited by Youé & Spooner Ltd
Filmset by Sir Joseph Causton & Sons Ltd
Printed and bound in Spain by
Graficromo S.A., Cordoba

Contents

Introduction

To be a good cook means the knowledge of all fruits, herbs, balms and spices; and of all that is healing and sweet in field and groves; savoury in meats. It means carefulness, inventiveness, watchfulness, willingness and readiness of appliance. It means the economy of our great-grandmothers and the science of modern chemists; it means much tasting and no wasting; it means English thoroughness, French art, and Arabian hospitality; it means, in fine, that you are to see that everybody has something nice to eat.

John Ruskin (1819–1900)

I am delighted to introduce this latest edition of *The Love of Cooking*. Writing this book for Collins, over ten years ago, gave me immense personal pleasure, but it is you, the public, to whom I owe all my thanks and appreciation, for it was enthusiastic cooks – from every walk of life – who bought my family book and used it, turning it into the classic it has now become.

Food fashions come and go, as do customs, and over the last few years we have all witnessed many changes in the culinary world. All the same, seeing that 'everybody has something nice to eat' remains my personal philosophy and your steady stream of letters through the years has endorsed this view and assured me that good food, prepared with love and enthusiasm, is still one of the finest ways of bringing people together. I hope that the recipes in this latest edition of *The Love of Cooking* will continue to find favour with all of you who buy the book and that the satisfaction of eating well will prove once more to be a happy and rewarding experience.

Sonia Allison, 1986

Raspberry cream layer sandwich (see page 206)

Meal starters

Starters can be whimsical, down-to-earth, filling, light, hot, cold, simple, exotic, cheap, expensive, traditional, unusual, colourful or muted. By their very nature, they are capable of creating the mood for the meal to follow and while chilly grapefruit on an equally chilly day does little to lift the spirits and encourage a cheerful atmosphere, a bowl of piping hot soup or dish of spaghetti instead would do more than enough to gladden the heart and spread a comfortable—and comforting—feeling of well-being and bonhomie to all. A good start to a good meal!

For soup lovers, I have given in this section a reasonable selection from which to choose, including chilled fruit soups from northern Europe which, on a blazing summer's day, are deliciously refreshing. Those less enthusiastic about soups will also find recipes for all the old favourites—prawn cocktail, egg mayonnaise, vol-au-vents, pâté and mixed hors d'oeuvre—together with specialities from abroad such as risotto, Italian pancakes and taramasalata. Even steak tartare, the glorious concoction of raw minced beef, egg yolk and capers, has found a place here because it is one of my own particular loves. When choosing any starter, consider the rest of the meal carefully and if the main course and sweet are light, a fairly filling starter should be served. If, on the other hand, the meal is on the robust side, settle for an uncomplicated and non-rich starter, otherwise everyone will be too full too soon. If the meal is hot, give a cold starter; if the meal is cold, a hot one.

Broths and cream soups

Scotch broth

Serves 6

1lb (½ kilo) middle neck of lamb
2 pints (approximately 1 litre) water
2 onions, coarsely chopped
1 medium carrot, diced
1 small turnip, diced
1 medium celery stalk, coarsely chopped
1 small leek, slit and chopped
2 level teaspoons salt
good shake of pepper
2 level tablespoons barley
finely-chopped parsley to garnish

1. Divide lamb into neat pieces and trim away surplus fat.
2. Put into a saucepan with stock or water.
3. Bring to boil and remove scum.
4. Add all remaining ingredients except parsley.
5. Cover and simmer 2 hours or until meat is tender, stirring occasionally.
6. Sprinkle each serving with parsley.

Paté, devilled potato salad and mixed hors d'oeuvre (see page 18)

Beef broth

Serves 4 to 6

Make exactly as for Scotch broth, (see page 8) substituting 8oz (200gm) stewing beef, cut into tiny cubes, for the lamb. Cook for 2½ hours.

Creamed vegetable broth

Serves 4 to 6

Make exactly as for Scotch broth, (see page 8) omitting meat and adding 1lb (½ kilo) root vegetables, cut into small dice, 2 medium onions, chopped, 2 celery stalks and 1 slit and chopped leek. Stir in 4 tablespoons double cream just before serving.

Chicken or turkey broth

Chicken or turkey broth

Serves 4 to 6

1 cooked chicken carcase

2 pints (approximately 1 litre) chicken stock or water

2 onions, coarsely chopped

2 medium carrots, diced

2 medium celery stalks, coarsely chopped

2 level teaspoons salt (or less if using seasoned stock)

good shake of pepper

2 level tablespoons uncooked long grain rice

finely-chopped parsley to garnish

1. Break up carcase and put into a saucepan with stock or water.
2. Bring to boil and remove scum.
3. Add all remaining ingredients except rice and parsley.
4. Cover and simmer for 2 hours, stirring occasionally.
5. Remove carcase and add rice. Simmer 20 to 30 minutes or until rice is tender.
6. Sprinkle each serving with parsley.

Cream of artichoke soup

2oz (50gm) butter or margarine

2lb (1 kilo) Jerusalem artichokes, peeled and cut into chunks

1 medium onion, peeled and chopped

1 celery stalk, chopped

2 pints (approximately 1 litre) stock or water

1 to 2 level teaspoons salt

pepper to taste

1 level tablespoon flour or cornflour

¼ pint (125ml) milk

2 to 3 tablespoons double cream

nutmeg or finely-chopped parsley to garnish

1. Heat butter or margarine in saucepan.
2. Add artichokes, onion and celery.
3. Fry gently, with lid on pan, for 10 minutes. Shake pan frequently to prevent vegetables from sticking.
4. Add stock or water, salt and pepper.
5. Bring to boil and lower heat.
6. Cover and simmer for 1 hour.
7. Either rub vegetables and liquid through a fine sieve or blend until smooth in electric blender.
8. Return mixture to saucepan.
9. Mix flour or cornflour to a smooth cream with milk.
10. Add to soup.
11. Cook, stirring continuously, until soup comes to the boil and thickens.
12. Simmer 5 minutes. Remove from heat and stir in cream.
13. Serve each portion sprinkled lightly with nutmeg or parsley.

Cream of asparagus soup

Serves 4

1 can (approximately 10oz or 250gm) asparagus

chicken stock

½ pint (250ml) cold milk

1oz (25gm) butter or margarine

1oz (25gm) flour

salt and pepper to taste

green food colouring

finely-chopped parsley to garnish

1. Drain asparagus, reserving liquor.
2. Make liquor up to ½ pint (250ml) with chicken stock. Blend in milk.
3. Melt butter or margarine in saucepan.
4. Stir in flour and cook 2 minutes.
5. Remove from heat and gradually blend in liquid.
6. Cook, stirring continuously, until soup comes to the boil and thickens.
7. Simmer 5 minutes then season to taste with salt and pepper.
8. Tint pale green with food colouring.
9. Chop asparagus and add.
10. Heat through a further 5 minutes.
11. Serve each portion sprinkled lightly with parsley.

Cream of carrot soup

Serves 4 to 6

2oz (50gm) butter or margarine

1 medium onion, chopped

3lb (1½ kilo) carrots, peeled and sliced

2 medium celery stalks, chopped

2 pints (approximately 1 litre) stock or water

2 level teaspoons salt

pepper to taste

1 level tablespoon flour or cornflour

¼ pint (125ml) cold milk

2 tablespoons double cream

finely-chopped parsley to garnish

1. Heat butter or margarine in saucepan.
2. Add prepared vegetables and fry gently, with lid on pan, for 10 minutes. Shake pan frequently to prevent vegetables from sticking.
3. Add stock or water and salt and pepper to taste.
4. Bring to boil and lower heat.
5. Cover pan and simmer gently for 1½ to 2 hours or until vegetables are tender.
6. Either rub vegetables and liquid through a fine sieve or blend until smooth in electric blender.
7. Return mixture to saucepan.
8. Mix flour or cornflour to a smooth cream with milk.
9. Add soup.
10. Cook, stirring continuously, until soup comes to the boil and thickens.
11. Simmer 5 minutes. Remove from heat and stir in cream.
12. Serve each portion sprinkled lightly with parsley.

Cream of celery soup

Serves 4 to 6

Make exactly as for cream of carrot soup, above, substituting 1 large head of celery (2lb or 1 kilo) for the carrots. Wash and scrape celery thoroughly then coarsely chop. Omit the 2 medium sticks of celery included in the carrot soup recipe. Garnish each portion by sprinkling very lightly with nutmeg.

Cream of potato soup

Serves 4 to 6

Make exactly as for cream of carrot soup (see this page), substituting 2lb (1 kilo) potatoes for the carrots. Simmer 45 minutes to 1 hour. If preferred, 2 leeks may be used instead of the onion and the soup garnished with scissor-snipped chives.

Cream of onion soup

Serves 4 to 6

Make exactly as for cream of carrot soup (see left), substituting 2lb (1 kilo) onions for the carrots. Omit all other vegetables but, if liked, add a small bay leaf which should be removed before the soup is sieved or blended. Garnish each portion by sprinkling lightly with finely-chopped watercress or parsley.

Cream of green pea soup

Serves 4 to 6

Make exactly as for cream of carrot soup (see left), but substitute 2lb (1 kilo) shelled green peas (or the equivalent weight in frozen peas) for the carrots and omit celery. Simmer 30 minutes for fresh peas but only 5 minutes for frozen ones. Garnish soup with a small quantity of finely-chopped fresh mint or some lean ham, cut into fine shreds.

Cream of tomato soup

Serves 4 to 6

Make exactly as for cream of carrot soup (see opposite page), but substitute 2lb (1 kilo) skinned tomatoes for the carrots. Include onion and celery plus 2 sliced carrots and 2 rashers chopped lean bacon. Add 1 level teaspoon sugar and 1 teaspoon Worcestershire sauce at the very end with the cream. Garnish by sprinkling each serving with finely-chopped parsley.

Cream of mushroom soup

Serves 4

8 to 12oz (200 to 300gm) mushrooms, sliced	
2oz (50gm) butter or margarine	
1oz (25gm) flour	
$\frac{3}{4}$ pint (375ml) milk	
$\frac{1}{4}$ pint (125ml) water	
salt and pepper to taste	
paprika to garnish	

1. Put mushrooms into a pan with butter or margarine. Fry gently for 5 minutes.
2. Stir in flour. Cook 3 minutes.
3. Remove from heat and gradually blend in milk and water.
4. Cook, stirring or whisking continuously, until soup comes to the boil and thickens. Simmer 5 minutes.
5. Season with salt and pepper.
6. Serve each portion lightly sprinkled with paprika.

Cream of green pea soup

Cream of chicken soup

Serves 4

1oz (25gm) butter or margarine	
1oz (25gm) flour	
$\frac{1}{2}$ pint (250ml) chicken stock	
$\frac{1}{2}$ pint (250ml) milk	
4 to 6oz (100 to 150gm) cooked chicken, chopped	
pinch of nutmeg	
salt and pepper to taste	
2 to 3 tablespoons double cream	
4 level tablespoons cooked peas to garnish	

1. Heat butter or margarine in saucepan.
2. Stir in flour and cook 2 minutes without browning.
3. Remove from heat and gradually blend in stock and milk.
4. Cook, stirring, until soup comes to boil and thickens.
5. Add chicken, nutmeg and salt and pepper to taste. Heat through for 10 minutes.
6. Remove from heat and stir in cream.
7. Add a tablespoon of cooked peas to every serving.

Consommé

Mellow, clear and golden brown stock, which is the basis for classic consommé, belongs, strictly speaking, to the expert chef and caterer. To make it as it should be—without a trace of fat and completely clear—requires patience, expertise and time and these days most of us turn to the very excellent canned consommés which are generally available from most supermarkets and grocers, or to stock or bouillon cubes, which make a fair substitute for the real thing. Canned consommé requires no treatment whatsoever for it is already a good colour and flavour. Beef stock, however, made from beef cubes, lacks the necessary colour and strength and the following recipe is one way of making a well-tasting stock from cubes.

Easy consommé

Serves 4 to 6

2 beef stock cubes	
1½ pints (approximately $\frac{3}{4}$ litre) water	
1 level teaspoon meat extract	
1 carrot, grated	
1 medium onion, grated	
1 small celery stalk, coarsely chopped	
1 to 2 tablespoons dry sherry	

1. Put all ingredients except sherry into saucepan.
2. Bring to boil, stirring.
3. Lower heat and cover.
4. Simmer 30 minutes.
5. Strain into a bowl and leave until cold.
6. Cover and refrigerate.
7. Skim off any fat that rises to the surface.
8. Before serving, re-heat soup and stir in sherry.

Like sauces, consommé has many classic variations and a few are listed below. They may be made either from canned consommé or from the basic recipe given above for easy consommé.

Consommé Aurore

Serves 4 to 6

Re-heat consommé with 1 level tablespoon tomato paste, a dash of sugar and 4 level tablespoons cooked chicken, cut into fine strips. Stir in sherry at the very end.

Consommé Julienne

Serves 4 to 6

Just before serving, add to consommé 4 to 6 heaped tablespoons of cooked mixed vegetables cut into thin strips. Choose carrots, cabbage, celery, leeks and a little turnip.

Consommé niçoise

Serves 4 to 6

Re-heat consommé with 2 heaped tablespoons chopped tomatoes (minus seeds), 2 heaped tablespoons freshly-cooked green beans and 1 heaped tablespoon finely-diced cooked potatoes.

Consommé solange

Serves 4 to 6

Re-heat consommé with 3 rounded tablespoons cooked barley and 2 level tablespoons cooked chicken, cut into thin strips. Just before serving, stir in 2 heaped tablespoons finely-shredded lettuce.

11

Jellied consommé

Serves 4 to 6

This is a cool and elegant way of eating consommé on a hot summer day and it is perfectly simple to prepare.

Make up the easy consommé as directed (see page 11). Before re-heating soup, stir in 3 level teaspoons gelatine softened in 2 tablespoons cold water. Heat consommé gently until gelatine dissolves then stir in sherry. Leave in a cold place until lightly set then break up with a fork and transfer to 4 or 6 individual bowls. Sprinkle with finely-chopped parsley and serve well-chilled with thin crisp toast.

Soups from abroad

Princes' soup

Serves 4 to 5

3 hard-boiled eggs

3oz (75gm) cold cooked chicken

2oz (50gm) cooked ham

2 tablespoons dry sherry

1½ pints (¾ litre) well-seasoned chicken stock

chopped parsley to garnish

1. Chop eggs, chicken and ham.
2. Put into soup tureen.
3. Add sherry to stock and bring to the boil.
4. Pour into tureen and stir well to mix.
5. Sprinkle with parsley and serve straight away.

Minestrone

Serves 4 to 6

2 medium celery stalks, chopped

1 medium leek, trimmed and chopped

2 medium onions, chopped

2 medium carrots, diced

1 small cabbage, shredded

4oz (100gm) raw green beans, sliced

1 can (approximately 1lb or ½ kilo) tomatoes

2oz (50gm) dried haricot beans, soaked overnight

1 level teaspoon dried basil or ½ level teaspoon mixed herbs

1 level teaspoon sugar

2 level teaspoons salt

1½ pint (approximately ¾ litre) cold water

1 knuckle of shin, chopped (optional)

2oz (50gm) elbow macaroni

2 heaped tablespoons finely-chopped parsley

grated Parmesan cheese to serve

1. Put prepared vegetables into large saucepan.
2. Add can of tomatoes, haricot beans, basil or herbs, sugar, salt, water and knuckle of shin if used.
3. Bring to boil, stirring. Lower heat and remove scum.
4. Cover and simmer very gently for 2½ hours.
5. Add macaroni and continue to simmer for 20 minutes.
6. Stir in parsley then serve each portion sprinkled with grated cheese.

Austrian vegetable soup

Mulligatawny soup

Serves 4

2 medium onions, chopped

1 medium carrot, finely diced

2 medium celery stalks, finely chopped

1oz (25gm) butter or margarine

1 dessertspoon salad oil

½ to 1 level tablespoon curry powder

1½ pints (approximately ¾ litre) beef stock or water

1 level teaspoon salt

2 medium cooking apples, peeled and cored

1 level tablespoon cornflour

¼ pint (125ml) cold milk

2 heaped tablespoons cooked rice

1 heaped tablespoon cooked chicken, finely diced

2 level tablespoons sultanas to garnish

1. Slowly fry onions, carrot and celery stalks in the butter or margarine and salad oil until soft and pale gold—about 10 minutes.
2. Stir in curry powder then blend in stock.
3. Add salt and the grated apples.
4. Bring to boil, stirring. Lower heat and cover pan. Simmer 1½ hours.
5. Strain soup or blend until smooth in electric blender.
6. Return soup to clean saucepan.
7. Mix cornflour to a smooth cream with the milk.
8. Add to soup and bring to boil, stirring continuously.
9. Add rice and chicken and simmer gently for 10 minutes.
10. Adjust seasoning to taste and serve each portion sprinkled with sultanas.

Austrian vegetable soup

Serves 4 to 6

1oz (25gm) butter

2oz (50gm) fine semolina

¾ pint (375ml) chicken stock

1 medium onion, chopped

2 medium carrots, grated

8 leaves of spring greens, shredded

pinch of mixed herbs

1 pint (approximately ½ litre) milk

1 carton (¼ pint or 125ml) natural yogurt

salt and pepper

chopped parsley or scissor-snipped chives to garnish

1. Melt butter, add semolina and cook over low heat for 2 minutes. Stir in the stock and simmer 15 minutes, stirring occasionally.
2. Add onion, carrots, greens and herbs.
3. Simmer 10 minutes and remove from heat.
4. Whisk in all the milk and yogurt and re-heat gently without boiling.
5. Season to taste with salt and pepper.
6. Serve each portion sprinkled with chopped parsley or chives.

Hungarian goulash soup

Serves 4 to 6

1 large green pepper, de-seeded and chopped

1 large onion, chopped

1oz (25gm) lard

1lb (½ kilo) stewing beef, cut into small cubes

1 level tablespoon paprika

1 level tablespoon tomato paste

1 level tablespoon cornflour

¼ level teaspoon caraway seeds

2 pints (approximately 1 litre) beef stock or water

4 medium potatoes, cooked and diced

4 to 6 dessertspoons soured cream or yogurt to garnish

1. Slowly fry green pepper and onion in the lard until pale gold.
2. Add beef and fry a little more briskly, stirring, until meat is brown and sealed.
3. Stir in paprika, tomato paste, cornflour and caraway seeds.
4. Gradually blend in stock or water.
5. Cook, stirring continuously, until soup comes to the boil.
6. Lower heat and cover. Simmer 2 to 2½ hours or until meat is tender, stirring occasionally to prevent sticking.
7. Add potato dice and heat for 10 minutes.
8. Top each portion with a spoonful of soured cream or yogurt.

Russian bortsch

Serves 4 to 6

1 large onion, chopped

1 large carrot, coarsely grated

1lb (½ kilo) raw potatoes, peeled and grated

1½lb (¾ kilo) raw beetroot, peeled and coarsely grated

½ medium head of cabbage

2 pints (approximately 1 litre) water

1 knuckle of shin, chopped

2 to 3 level teaspoons salt

shake of pepper

handful of parsley

1 egg white, stiffly beaten

juice of 1 small lemon, strained

red food colouring (if necessary)

4 to 6 heaped teaspoons soured cream to garnish

1. Put prepared vegetables into large saucepan with water and knuckle of shin.
2. Add salt, pepper and parsley. Bring to boil.
3. Lower heat and cover pan.
4. Simmer gently for 2 hours.
5. Strain soup into clean saucepan.
6. Add stiffly-beaten egg white.
7. Bring to boil and strain again.
8. Add lemon juice and a little red food colouring to heighten the colour if necessary. Re-heat.
9. Top each portion with soured cream.

Alaska soup

Spanish tomato soup

Serves 4 to 6

1oz (25gm) butter or margarine

1 dessertspoon salad oil

1 large onion, chopped

1 large carrot, chopped

2 medium celery stalks, chopped

2 rashers lean bacon, chopped

2lb (1 kilo) skinned tomatoes, chopped

1½ pints (approximately ¾ litre) water

1 bay leaf

1 blade mace

2 level teaspoons sugar

1 teaspoon Worcestershire sauce

2 to 3 level teaspoons salt

pepper to taste

2 level dessertspoons cornflour

5 tablespoons cold water

2 or 3 slices white bread

butter or bacon dripping for frying

1. Heat butter or margarine and oil in large saucepan.
2. Add onion, carrot, celery and bacon and fry slowly until soft and pale gold—10 minutes.
3. Add tomatoes, water, bay leaf, mace, sugar, Worcestershire sauce, salt and pepper to taste.
4. Bring to boil, stirring.
5. Lower heat and cover pan.
6. Simmer gently for 1½ hours, stirring occasionally.
7. Rub soup and vegetables through a sieve or remove bay leaf and blade of mace and blend until smooth in electric blender.
8. Return to clean saucepan and stir in cornflour mixed to a smooth cream with the water.
9. Bring to boil, stirring continuously.
10. Simmer 5 minutes.
11. Serve with tiny cubes of bread, fried in butter or bacon dripping until crisp and golden.

Alaska soup

Serves 4 to 6

3 egg yolks

2 tablespoons single cream

2 egg whites

1½ pints (approximately ¾ litre) chicken stock

1. Beat egg yolks lightly with cream.
2. Whisk egg whites to a stiff snow.
3. Bring stock almost to boil and add about 1 breakfast cup to egg yolk mixture. Return to saucepan of stock, stir well and remove from heat.
4. Divide stiffly-beaten egg whites equally among 4 large soup plates then carefully pour in the stock so that the whites float on top.
5. Serve straight away.

Bouillabaisse

Serves 4

A warm and flavourful fish soup from the south of France. The real thing is made from fish freshly caught in the Mediterranean but for everyday purposes one has to compromise and use what is readily available. Therefore I have included an assortment of cod, haddock, mussels, scallops and lobster which together produce a delicious and appetising substitute.

2 tablespoons olive oil

1 large onion, chopped

2 medium garlic cloves, chopped

¾ pint (375ml) fish stock or water

1 can (1lb or ½ kilo) tomatoes

½ level teaspoon finely-grated orange peel

½ to 1 level teaspoon salt

½ level teaspoon saffron strands

pinch of dried oregano and thyme

1 bay leaf

1 level teaspoon sugar

8oz (200gm) cod fillet

8oz (200gm) haddock fillet

2 scallops

1 dozen mussels, well-scrubbed

8oz (200gm) fresh, frozen or canned prawns or lobster

4 thick slices French bread, toasted

1. Heat oil in saucepan.
2. Add onion and garlic and fry gently until pale gold.
3. Add fish stock or water with tomatoes, orange peel, salt, saffron, oregano, thyme, bay leaf and sugar.
4. Bring to boil, cover pan and simmer 45 minutes.
5. Cut cod and haddock into 1-inch cubes. Cut each scallop into 4 pieces.
6. Add to soup with mussels. Stir well and simmer 5 minutes.
7. Add prawns or lobster (first divided into pieces) and heat through for 5 minutes.
8. Put each slice of toasted bread into a large soup plate.
9. Fill each plate with bouillabaisse and serve very hot.

Easy shellfish bisque

Serves 4 to 6

1½ pints (approximately ¾ litre) cold water

1lb (½ kilo) fish trimmings

1 large onion, sliced

2 medium celery stalks, coarsely chopped

2 level teaspoons salt

2 cloves

1 bay leaf

3 peppercorns

2oz (50gm) butter or margarine

2oz (50gm) flour

½ pint (250ml) milk

12oz (300gm) cooked lobster, crab-meat or prawns, already shelled

4 tablespoons double cream

finely-chopped parsley or scissor-snipped chives to garnish

1. Put water into pan with fish trimmings, onion, celery, salt, cloves, bay leaf and peppercorns.
2. Bring to boil, cover and simmer gently for 1 hour. Strain.
3. Melt butter in clean saucepan. Stir in flour and cook 2 minutes without browning.
4. Gradually blend in fish stock and milk.
5. Cook, stirring continuously, until soup comes to the boil and thickens.
6. Add shellfish and re-heat a further 5 minutes.
7. Remove from heat and stir in cream.
8. Adjust seasoning to taste and serve each portion sprinkled with parsley or chives.

Fish soup

Serves 5 to 6

1 cod or haddock head

2oz (50gm) butter or margarine

1 large onion, chopped

3 medium celery stalks, chopped

3 level tablespoons flour

2 pints (approximately 1 litre) fish stock

1 small packet saffron

salt and pepper to taste

¼ pint (125ml) milk

2 level tablespoons finely-chopped parsley

12oz (300gm) cod or haddock fillet

1. Cover fish head with 3 pints (1¾ litres) water and simmer 25 minutes. Drain, reserving 2 pints (1 litre) fish stock.
2. Heat butter or margarine in saucepan.
3. Add onion and celery and fry quickly until transparent but not brown.
4. Stir in flour and cook 2 minutes.
5. Add fish stock, saffron and salt and pepper to taste.
6. Simmer 10 minutes.
7. Stir in milk and parsley.
8. Skin fish and cut into cubes.
9. Add to soup and simmer 5 minutes.
10. Adjust seasoning, add a squeeze of lemon juice and serve.

Smoked haddock and vegetable chowder

Serves 4

Chowders are thick, satisfying and typically American soups which usually contain bacon, milk, potatoes, other vegetables to taste and either meat or fish. Clams are the traditional fish to use (New England clam chowder is world famous) but on the other side of the Atlantic there is nothing to touch smoked haddock for making this soup-cum-meal one of the most heart-warming winter feasts I know.

6oz (150gm) back bacon, coarsely chopped

1 medium onion, chopped

1oz (25gm) butter or margarine

1½oz (37gm) flour

¾ pint (375ml) milk

½ pint (250ml) water

4 medium potatoes, diced

4 medium carrots, diced

2 medium celery stalks, chopped

8 to 12oz (200 to 300gm) smoked haddock fillet, skinned

salt and pepper to taste

1. Slowly fry bacon and onion in the butter or margarine until soft and pale—about 7 to 10 minutes.
2. Stir in flour and cook 2 minutes.
3. Remove from heat and gradually blend in milk and water.
4. Cook, stirring, until soup comes to the boil and thickens.
5. Lower heat and cover.
6. Add potatoes, carrots and celery. Simmer very gently 25 to 30 minutes or until vegetables are tender.
7. Cut haddock into 1-inch cubes and add to soup. Simmer 5 to 7 minutes.
8. Season to taste with salt and pepper and serve piping hot.

Chilled soups

Fruit soups are extremely popular—and justifiably so—in Austria, Germany, Yugoslavia, Poland and Scandinavia. They are simply a mixture of fruit, water, sugar, cornflour or semolina to thicken and sometimes wine or liqueur and spice. I place them somewhere between stewed fruit and fruit juice and, provided they are well-covered, the soups will keep in the refrigerator up to 3 days. There are two types of fruit soups—those made with stoned fruit such as apricots, plums or cherries, and those made with berries such as blackcurrants or gooseberries.

Fish soup

Berry soup

Serves 4 to 6

1lb (½ kilo) black or redcurrants or fresh cranberries

2 pints (approximately 1 litre) water

2 strips of lemon peel

1 teaspoon vanilla essence

4oz (100gm) granulated sugar

1oz (25gm) cornflour or semolina

3 tablespoons cold water

1 wine glass sweet red wine

1. Put currants or cranberries into a saucepan with water, lemon peel and essence.
2. Cover and simmer 20 to 30 minutes or until fruit is tender.
3. Rub through a fine sieve (do not blend in electric blender because it is not always effective in crushing pips).
4. Return to clean saucepan, add sugar and re-heat until dissolved.
5. Stir in cornflour or semolina, mixed until smooth with the cold water.
6. Cook, stirring, until soup comes to the boil and thickens. Simmer 5 minutes.
7. Remove from heat and stir in wine.
8. Transfer to large bowl and chill thoroughly before serving.

Black cherry soup

Serves 4 to 6

Make exactly as for apricot soup (see this page) but if blending in an electric blender, make sure that all stones are removed first. Omit the glass of wine or apricot brandy. Add a liqueur glass of cherry brandy and serve the soup with macaroons.

Plum soup

Serves 4 to 6

Make as apricot soup (see this page) but include a cinnamon stick when simmering the fruit. If blending in an electric blender, make sure that all the stones are removed first. Add a wine glass of sweet red wine instead of the white wine or apricot brandy.

Vichyssoise

Serves 4 to 6

This is a deliciously smooth and creamy chilled potato and leek soup.

2 medium leeks

1 medium onion

1½oz (37gm) butter

1lb (½ kilo) potatoes, peeled and thinly sliced

½ pint (250ml) chicken stock

½ pint (250ml) milk

1 level teaspoon salt

white pepper to taste

¼ pint (125ml) double cream

2 level tablespoons scissor-snipped chives or parsley to garnish

1. Trim leeks so that white part only remains. Slit, wash thoroughly and chop.
2. Chop onion.
3. Melt butter in saucepan. Add leeks and onion and fry very gently, with lid on pan, for 10 minutes but do not allow vegetables to brown.
4. Add potatoes, stock, milk and salt and pepper to taste.
5. Slowly bring to boil, stirring.
6. Reduce heat and cover pan.
7. Simmer slowly for about 30 minutes or until potatoes are tender.
8. Rub vegetables and liquid through a fine sieve or blend until smooth in an electric blender.
9. Transfer to a bowl and refrigerate until completely cold.
10. Just before serving, whip cream until thick and gradually blend soup into it.
11. Transfer to 4 or 6 soup bowls and sprinkle tops with chives or parsley.

Note

If soup seems to be on the thick side, thin down with a little milk before combining with cream.

Strawberry soup

Serves 4

1lb (½ kilo) ripe strawberries

juice of ½ a large lemon

¾ pint (375ml) water

3oz (75gm) granulated sugar

1 level dessertspoon cornflour

1 large wine glass sweet red wine

1. Crush strawberries and put into saucepan with lemon juice and water.
2. Boil slowly for 5 minutes.
3. Add sugar and stir until dissolved.
4. Either rub liquid and fruit through a fine sieve or blend until smooth in an electric blender.
5. Return to clean saucepan.
6. Add cornflour, mixed until smooth with the wine.
7. Cook, stirring, until soup comes to the boil and thickens. Simmer 5 minutes.
8. Transfer to large bowl and chill thoroughly before serving.

Apricot soup

Serves 4 to 6

1lb (½ kilo) ripe apricots

2 pints (approximately 1 litre) cold water

2 strips of lemon peel

3 to 4oz (75 to 100gm) granulated sugar

1oz (25gm) cornflour or semolina

3 tablespoons cold water

1 wine glass sweet white wine or a liqueur glass apricot brandy

1. Halve apricots and remove stones.
2. Put into saucepan with water and lemon peel.
3. Slowly bring to boil. Cover and simmer until fruit is tender.
4. Remove lemon peel. Add sugar and stir until dissolved.
5. Either rub fruit and liquor through a fine sieve or blend until smooth in an electric blender.
6. Return to clean saucepan. Add cornflour or semolina mixed until smooth with water.
7. Cook, stirring, until soup comes to the boil and thickens. Simmer 5 minutes.
8. Remove from heat and stir in wine or liqueur.
9. Transfer to large bowl and chill thoroughly before serving.

Chilled asparagus soup

Serves 4 to 6

¾ pint (375ml) chicken stock
½ pint (250ml) milk
3 level tablespoons instant mashed potato powder
1 can (10oz or 250gm) asparagus
¼ level teaspoon onion salt
good shake of white pepper
¼ pint (125ml) double cream
green food colouring
about 1 tablespoon finely-chopped mint or 2 level tablespoons finely-chopped parsley to garnish

1. Bring stock and milk to boil.
2. Gradually stir in instant mashed potato powder.
3. Simmer gently for 7 minutes.
4. Drain asparagus. Mash finely and add to potato mixture.
5. Season with onion salt and pepper then transfer to bowl.
6. Refrigerate until completely cold.
7. Just before serving, whip cream until thick and gradually blend soup into it.
8. Tint pale green with food colouring and transfer to 4 or 6 bowls.
9. Sprinkle with mint or parsley.

Gazpacho

Serves 4 to 6

A highly-flavoured, chilled, tomato-based soup from Spain.

1 medium can (approximately 14oz or 350gm) tomatoes
3oz (75gm) fresh white breadcrumbs
1 medium can (approximately 14oz or 350gm) tomato juice
4 tablespoons salad oil
3 tablespoons wine vinegar or lemon juice
4 tablespoons water
½ level teaspoon garlic salt
½ medium unpeeled cucumber
1 medium onion
1 medium green pepper
salt and pepper to taste

1. Rub tomatoes through a sieve or blend until smooth in electric blender.
2. Put into large bowl.
3. Stir in breadcrumbs, tomato juice, oil, vinegar or lemon juice, water and garlic salt.
4. Grate cucumber and onion. De-seed green pepper and chop finely.
5. Add cucumber, onion and pepper to bowl.
6. Season to taste with salt and pepper and refrigerate until ice cold.
7. Just before serving, stir well to combine ingredients and transfer to 4 or 6 soup bowls.

Chilled tomato soup

Chilled shrimp and corn soup

Serves 4 to 6

1 tablespoon olive oil
1 medium onion, chopped
2 medium potatoes, diced
1 garlic clove, finely chopped
½ pint (250ml) dry cider
¾ pint (375ml) water
salt and pepper to taste
1 level teaspoon paprika
1 can (approximately 12oz or 300gm) sweetcorn
4oz (100gm) shelled shrimps or prawns
1 level dessertspoon cornflour
¼ pint (125ml) cold milk
4 tablespoons double cream

1. Heat oil in saucepan.
2. Add onion, potatoes and garlic and fry very gently until oil is absorbed by the vegetables.
3. Add cider, water, salt and pepper to taste and paprika.
4. Bring to boil, lower heat and cover pan. Simmer gently for 15 minutes.
5. Add undrained sweetcorn and simmer a further 10 minutes.
6. Reserve 12 shrimps or prawns for decoration. Chop remainder and add to soup. Simmer 5 minutes.
7. Either rub soup through a fine sieve or blend until smooth in electric blender. Return to saucepan.
8. Mix cornflour to a smooth cream with milk and add to soup.
9. Cook, stirring, until it comes to the boil then simmer for 5 minutes.
10. Transfer to large bowl and refrigerate until cold.
11. Just before serving, whip cream until thick.
12. Transfer soup to 4 or 6 soup bowls and top each with cream and remaining shrimps or prawns.

Chilled tomato soup

Serves 4

1lb (½ kilo) tomatoes, skinned
½ large cucumber, peeled
1 pint (approximately ½ kilo) chicken stock
1 bay leaf, 6 peppercorns and 1 blade mace, all tied in muslin bag
1oz (25gm) butter
1oz (25gm) flour
salt and pepper to taste
red food colouring (optional)
1 level dessertspoon golden syrup
4 level teaspoons scissor-snipped chives to garnish

1. Roughly chop tomatoes. Chop ½ the cucumber, reserving remainder for garnish.
2. Put tomatoes and cucumber into pan with stock and bag of spices.
3. Bring to boil. Lower heat and cover. Simmer 30 minutes.
4. Remove bag of spices.
5. Either rub vegetables and liquid through a fine sieve or blend until smooth in electric blender.
6. Melt butter in a clean saucepan. Add flour and cook 2 minutes without browning.
7. Gradually add tomato and cucumber purée.
8. Cook, stirring, until soup comes to the boil then simmer 10 minutes.
9. Season to taste with salt and pepper and if liked, heighten the colour by stirring in a little red food colouring.
10. Blend in syrup then transfer soup to bowl.
11. Refrigerate until cold.
12. Just before serving, cut rest of cucumber into tiny dice.
13. Transfer soup to 4 bowls and add equal amounts of cucumber to each.
14. Sprinkle top of each with chives.

Chilled blender beetroot soup

Serves 4

8oz (200gm) cooked beetroot
4 tablespoons hot water
juice of 1 medium lemon
½ small onion, sliced
2 tablespoons wine or cider vinegar
2 standard eggs
1 level teaspoon salt
3 tablespoons soured cream
white pepper to taste
4 slices of lemon

1. Cut beetroot into large dice.
2. Put into blender with all remaining ingredients except pepper and lemon slices.
3. Blend until smooth.
4. Pour into large bowl.
5. Season to taste with pepper and chill thoroughly before serving.
6. Transfer to 4 bowls and stand a lemon slice (slit from centre to outside edge) on the rim of each.

Hors d'oeuvre and other starters

Shrimp tartlets

Serves 4 to 6

$\frac{1}{4}$ pint (125ml) freshly-made white sauce (see page 94)

6oz (150gm) peeled shrimps, fresh, frozen or canned

1 level tablespoon finely-chopped parsley

salt and pepper to taste

6 fairly deep tartlet cases, already baked

1 skinned tomato to garnish

1. Combine sauce with shrimps (reserving about 12 for garnish).
2. Stir in parsley then season to taste with salt and pepper.
3. Transfer equal amounts to tartlet cases.
4. Garnish with remaining shrimps and the tomato, cut into wedges.

Shrimp tartlets, seafood ramekins and prawn cocktail

Seafood ramekins

Serves 4

4oz (100gm) prawns, fresh, frozen or canned

4 small plaice fillets

$\frac{1}{2}$oz (12gm) butter or margarine

$\frac{1}{2}$oz (12gm) flour

$\frac{1}{4}$ pint (125ml) single cream

salt and pepper to taste

1 level dessertspoon chopped parsley

2oz (50gm) strong Cheddar cheese, finely grated

1. Pre-heat oven to moderately hot, 375 deg F or gas 5 (190 deg C).
2. Put equal amounts of prawns on to skin side of plaice fillets.
3. Roll each fillet up and put into 4 individual buttered heatproof dishes or ramekins.
4. Melt butter or margarine in saucepan. Stir in flour and cook 2 minutes without browning.
5. Gradually blend in cream and return to heat.
6. Cook, stirring, until sauce comes to the boil and thickens.
7. Simmer 2 minutes then season to taste with salt and pepper.
8. Spoon equal amounts over fish in dishes and sprinkle with cheese.
9. Cook in centre of oven for 25 minutes then brown under a hot grill immediately before serving.

Prawn cocktail

Serves 4

6 heaped tablespoons shredded lettuce

6 level tablespoons mayonnaise

2 level tablespoons tomato ketchup

1 teaspoon Worcestershire sauce

dash of tabasco

2 tablespoons double cream

2 teaspoons lemon juice

2 level teaspoons bottled horseradish sauce

8oz (200gm) peeled prawns, fresh, frozen or canned

4 slices of lemon and 4 parsley sprigs to garnish

1. Divide lettuce equally among 4 large wine glasses.
2. To make cocktail sauce, combine mayonnaise with all remaining ingredients except prawns and garnish.
3. Put equal amounts of prawns on top of lettuce then coat with sauce.
4. Garnish each with a slice of lemon and parsley sprig.

Pâté

Illustrated on page 9

Serves 8

8oz (200gm) streaky bacon

8oz (200gm) lambs' liver

8oz (200gm) belly of pork

1½oz (37gm) butter or margarine

1 dessertspoon oil

1oz (25gm) plain flour

½ level teaspoon salt

freshly-ground pepper

½ pint (250ml) milk

1oz (25gm) fresh white breadcrumbs

1 tablespoon Worcestershire sauce

1. Pre-heat oven to moderate, 350 deg F or gas 4 (180 deg C).
2. Remove rind from bacon then flatten rashers by rolling with a rolling pin.
3. Line a 1lb (½ kilo) loaf tin with the bacon, leaving the ends overhanging the edge.
4. Remove skin and/or gristle from liver and pork. Chop both into small pieces.
5. Fry gently in the hot butter or margarine and oil for about 5 minutes. Remove from pan. Mince finely.
6. Mix flour, salt and pepper well together.
7. Stir into remaining fat and oil in pan then gradually blend in milk.
8. Cook, stirring, until sauce comes to the boil and thickens.
9. Add liver, pork, breadcrumbs and Worcestershire sauce.
10. Press mixture into prepared tin, flatten surface and fold over the ends of bacon.
11. Put into a roasting tin half-filled with water.
12. Bake in centre of oven for 1½ hours.
13. Leave to cool, turn out of tin and serve with either freshly-made toast and butter, with devilled potato salad (see below) and/or an assortment of mixed salads.

Devilled potato salad

Illustrated on page 9

Serves 4 to 6

1lb (½ kilo) cold cooked potatoes or equivalent weight in canned potatoes

1 small onion

2oz (50gm) margarine

1 large apple, peeled, cored and sliced

4 to 6 level teaspoons curry powder

salt and pepper

1 banana, sliced

2oz (50gm) seedless raisins

1. Cut potatoes into slices and finely chop the onion.
2. Melt margarine in a large frying pan.
3. Add potatoes and onion and fry 5 minutes.
4. Add apple with curry powder and salt and pepper to taste.
5. Cook slowly a further 5 minutes.
6. Add sliced banana and raisins.
7. Fry gently for 3 minutes then increase heat to brown the potatoes.
8. Serve hot.

Sardine filled lemons

Serves 4

4 medium lemons

1 can (approximately 4oz or 100gm) sardines, drained

4oz (100gm) butter, softened

1 egg, separated

salt

freshly-ground black pepper

1 level tablespoon chopped parsley

1. Cut tops off lemons and scoop out the insides.
2. Chop up the pulp but retain juice (which can be used in drinks or cooking).
3. Mash sardines finely.
4. Stir in lemon pulp then beat in butter.
5. Add egg yolk, salt, pepper and parsley.
6. Beat egg white to a stiff snow and fold into mixture.
7. Return mixture to lemon cases, top with lemon caps and serve with crisp toast or brown bread and butter.

Note

Should there be any left-over mixture, spread it on to fingers of hot toast or savoury biscuits and serve separately as a cocktail snack.

Sardine filled lemons

Mixed hors d'oeuvre

Illustrated on page 9

Mixed hors d'oeuvre, as their name would suggest, contain an assortment of savoury appetisers and the following are suggestions for 15 basic ideas. Arrange hors d'oeuvre on small plates or dishes with serving spoons or forks. Accompany with crisp rolls and butter.

1. Sliced salami garnished with cucumber.
2. Canned or home-made potato salad garnished with chopped parsley.
3. Buttered savoury biscuits, topped with sliced liver sausage, tomato wedges, slices of cucumber and strips of canned pimiento.
4. Thinly-sliced ham, rolled up with a filling of cream cheese and chopped chives, refrigerated until required then cut into ½-inch wedges.
5. Halved hard-boiled eggs, the yolks mashed finely with 1 or 2 level dessertspoons chopped celery, seasoning to taste and sufficient cream to bind. Pipe or spoon mixture back into egg white halves then garnish with sliced radishes and chopped parsley.
6. Canned whole beetroot, diced and mixed with tarragon vinegar.
7. Stuffed green olives.
8. Rice-stuffed vine leaves (canned) garnished with sliced cucumber.
9. Sliced tomatoes, coated with French dressing.
10. Cocktail onions.
11. Whole sardines.
12. Cooked rice mixed with diced carrots, peas, shrimps and French dressing.
13. Small gherkins.
14. Canned asparagus.
15. Canned sweetcorn, either plain or mixed with chopped red or green pepper.

Egg mayonnaise

Serves 4

lettuce leaves

4 hard-boiled eggs

4 to 5 level tablespoons mayonnaise

8 rolled anchovy fillets

paprika

1. Arrange lettuce leaves on 4 individual plates.
2. Shell eggs and halve lengthwise.
3. Stand 2 halves on each plate, cut sides down.
4. Coat with mayonnaise.
5. Garnish with anchovies and a light sprinkling of paprika.
6. Serve with brown bread and butter.

Left: mixed hors d'oeuvre
Below: pizza

Steak tartare

Serves 4

1lb (½ kilo) rump or fillet steak, finely minced

1 to 2 level dessertspoons drained capers, finely chopped

1 to 2 teaspoons Worcestershire sauce

salt and freshly-milled pepper to taste

1 small onion, finely chopped

4 egg yolks

1. Combine meat with capers, Worcestershire sauce and salt and pepper to taste.
2. Divide into 4 equal portions and place on 4 individual plates.
3. Shape each portion into a neat mound, then make a well in the centre.
4. Sprinkle wells with chopped onion then drop an egg yolk into each.

Pizza

Serves 6 to 8

8oz (200gm) white bread dough (see page 230)

1½lb (¾ kilo) tomatoes, skinned and chopped

2 medium onions, chopped

2 garlic cloves, chopped

1 tablespoon salad oil

1 level teaspoon dried basil

2 tablespoons tomato paste

1 level teaspoon sugar

salt and pepper to taste

3 to 4oz (75 to 100gm) Bel Paese cheese

1 small can anchovies in oil

1 dozen black olives

1. Pre-heat oven to moderately hot, 400 deg F or gas 6 (200 deg C).
2. Put tomatoes, onions, garlic, oil, basil, tomato paste and sugar into a saucepan.
3. Cook, uncovered, over a low heat until mixture becomes very thick and purée-like. Stir occasionally and season to taste with salt and pepper.
4. Roll out risen bread dough into an 8-inch round and stand it on a greased baking tray.
5. Cover, to within ¼ inch of edges, with the tomato mixture.
6. Cut cheese into thin slices and arrange on top then garnish with a trellis of anchovies. Stand olives round the edge.
7. Leave to rise in a warm place for 20 minutes then bake near top of oven for half an hour.
8. Cut into wedges and serve while still warm.

Spaghetti Bolognese

Serves 4

3 tablespoons salad oil

1 large onion, finely chopped or grated

1 medium celery stalk, chopped

1 garlic clove, chopped

2 rashers lean bacon, chopped

8oz (200gm) lean minced beef

1 can (5oz or 125gm) tomato paste

8oz (200gm) peeled and chopped tomatoes (or same amount of canned)

¼ pint (125ml) beef stock or water

1 bay leaf

½ level teaspoon mixed herbs or dried basil

2 level teaspoons granulated sugar

salt and pepper to taste

12oz (300gm) spaghetti rings or long spaghetti, freshly cooked

grated Parmesan cheese to serve

1. Heat salad oil in saucepan.
2. Add onion, celery, garlic and bacon.
3. Fry slowly, with lid on pan, for 10 minutes. Remove lid and continue to fry until onion is pale gold.
4. Add minced beef. Increase heat and fry until beef is well-browned, breaking it up with a fork all the time.
5. Add remaining ingredients except spaghetti and Parmesan cheese.
6. Bring to boil, stirring. Lower heat and cover. Simmer 35 to 45 minutes, stirring occasionally.
7. Toss drained spaghetti with a little butter then divide equally on 4 warm plates.
8. Coat with sauce and pass cheese separately.

Scandinavian melon

Buttercup mould

Serves 4 to 6

1 pint (approximately ½ litre) aspic jelly

3 hard-boiled eggs, sliced

⅓ of a cucumber, peeled and diced

3 medium celery stalks, diced

2 eating apples, peeled, cored and diced

1 medium can pilchards

juice of ½ lemon

mayonnaise or salad cream (see pages 99 or 161)

1. Make aspic jelly following instructions on packet.
2. Lightly oil or rinse with water a 1½ pint (¾ litre) ring mould then overlap egg slices round base.
3. Cover with a little aspic jelly and refrigerate until set.
4. Chill rest of aspic jelly until it is just beginning to thicken and set then stir in cucumber, celery and apples.
5. Spoon into mould then chill until firm and set.
6. Dip mould for a few seconds into very hot water then turn out on to a plate.
7. Fill centre with mashed pilchards mixed with lemon juice and mayonnaise or salad cream.

Scandinavian melon

Serves 4 to 6

4oz (100gm) long grain rice

½ pint (250ml) water

½ level teaspoon salt

1 medium melon

maraschino, cognac or apricot brandy

1 small can fruit cocktail

1 banana, peeled and sliced

12 grapes, black and green mixed

1 orange, skinned and diced

finely grated peel and juice of ½ lemon

½ pint (250ml) double cream

5 level dessertspoons caster sugar

few drops vanilla essence

1. Put rice, water and salt into a saucepan.
2. Bring to the boil and stir once.
3. Lower heat and cover.
4. Cook 15 minutes, or until rice is tender and liquid absorbed. Leave to cool.
5. Cut off the top of the melon and take out the seeds.
6. Hollow out the melon and cut the flesh into bite-size pieces.
7. Sprinkle melon with maraschino, cognac or apricot brandy and chill for at least an hour.
8. Drain fruit cocktail and mix with the bananas, grapes, orange, melon and rice.
9. Add lemon peel and juice and a few drops more liqueur or brandy.
10. Chill 1 hour.
11. Before serving, whip cream.
12. Add sugar and vanilla and gently fold into the fruit mixture.
13. Fill the hollowed out melon with the fruit salad and stand it on a platter. Garnish with fresh fruits.

Buttercup mould

Tuna timbales

Serves 4 to 5

1 can (approximately 8oz or 200gm) tuna, drained and flaked

1 small onion, chopped

2 tablespoons salad oil

3 beaten egg yolks

6oz (150gm) fresh white bread, decrusted and cut into ¼-inch cubes

2 teaspoons lemon juice

2 level teaspoons finely-chopped parsley

salt

½ teaspoon Tabasco

3 egg whites

½ pint (250ml) freshly-made white coating sauce (see page 94)

2 level tablespoons canned red pimiento, drained and chopped

1 green pepper, deseeded and chopped

1. Pre-heat oven to moderate, 350 deg F or gas 4 (180 deg C).
2. Lightly brown the tuna and onion in the heated salad oil.
3. Remove from heat and add egg yolks, bread cubes, lemon juice, parsley, salt and Tabasco.
4. Fold in egg whites, beaten to a stiff snow, and turn the mixture into 4 or 5 greased ramekins or dariole moulds.
5. Stand moulds in a tin containing 2 inches of hot water and bake in centre of oven for 30 minutes or until firm.
6. Unmould and serve with the sauce, heated through with the pimiento and green pepper.

Tuna timbale

French rice salad

Serves 4

6oz (150gm) long grain rice

¾ pint (375ml) water

¾ level teaspoon salt

6oz (150gm) blue vein cheese, crumbled

¼ pint (125ml) soured cream

1 tablespoon lemon juice

½ small head of celery, finely chopped

½ unpeeled cucumber, cubed

1 bunch radishes, sliced

2 heaped tablespoons scissor-snipped chives

salt and pepper

4 tomatoes, cut into wedges

dill (if available), parsley or watercress to garnish

1. Put rice, water and salt into saucepan.
2. Bring to the boil and stir once.
3. Lower heat and cover.
4. Cook 15 minutes or until rice is tender and liquid absorbed.
5. Mix cheese, soured cream and lemon juice.
6. Combine rice with celery, cucumber, radishes, half the cheese mixture and chives.
7. Season with salt and pepper then stir in tomatoes. Chill.
8. Before serving, transfer to 4 bowls and coat with remaining cheese mixture.
9. Garnish with dill, parsley or watercress.

Swiss-style cheese puff flan

Serves 4

6oz (150gm) short crust pastry (see page 108)

3 standard eggs, separated

4 level tablespoons grated Gruyère cheese

4oz (100gm) cream cheese

2 level teaspoons finely-chopped parsley

salt and pepper to taste

parsley to garnish

1. Pre-heat oven to moderately hot, 400 deg F or gas 6 (200 deg C).
2. Roll out pastry and use to line an 8-inch flan ring standing on a greased baking tray.
3. Prick pastry lightly with a fork then line with aluminium foil to prevent pastry from rising as it cooks.
4. Bake near top of oven for 20 minutes.
5. Meanwhile, beat egg yolks with 3 tablespoons Gruyère cheese, cream cheese, parsley and salt and pepper to taste.
6. Beat egg whites to a stiff snow and fold into cheese mixture.
7. Remove flan case from oven and carefully lift out foil.
8. Fill with cheese mixture, sprinkle over remaining Gruyère cheese and bake a further 20 minutes.
9. Serve hot.

French rice salad

21

Chicken vol-au-vents

Cold game soufflé

Serves 4 to 6

1 level tablespoon gelatine

3 tablespoons boiling water

2 tablespoons dry sherry

½ pint (250ml) freshly-made suprême sauce (see page 97)

8oz (200gm) cold cooked game, minced

2oz (50gm) ham, minced

2 egg whites

¼ pint (125ml) double cream

¼ pint cold and set aspic jelly

radish slices to garnish

1. Tie a 4-inch strip of folded greaseproof paper round a 1 pint straight-sided soufflé dish, making sure the paper stands 1½ to 2 inches above edge of dish. Tie securely with string then brush inside of strip with oil.
2. Put gelatine and water into a saucepan and stand saucepan over a low heat until gelatine dissolves. Add sherry.
3. Stir gently into sauce then leave in a cold place until just beginning to thicken and set. Stir in game and ham.
4. Beat egg whites to a stiff snow. Whip cream until thick.
5. Fold both into sauce mixture.
6. When smooth and evenly combined, transfer to prepared soufflé dish and chill until firm and set.
7. To serve soufflé, remove paper band carefully. Tip aspic jelly out on to a sheet of damp greaseproof paper and chop with a knife.
8. Arrange in round top and centre of soufflé then decorate with radish slices.

Cold game soufflé

Chicken vol-au-vents

Serves 4

1 packet (12) deep frozen vol-au-vent cases

egg to glaze

1oz (25gm) butter or margarine

2 level tablespoons flour

¼ pint (125ml) chicken stock

¼ pint (125ml) milk

2 cooked chicken joints, boned and chopped

4 level tablespoons chopped, canned pimiento

2 tablespoons single cream

½ teaspoon Tabasco

additional seasoning to taste

chopped parsley to garnish

1. Bake the vol-au-vent cases according to packet instructions.
2. To make the filling, melt butter or margarine in a saucepan and stir in flour.
3. Cook 2 minutes without browning.
4. Gradually add stock and milk and bring to the boil.
5. Simmer 3 minutes. Add chopped chicken, pimiento, cream, Tabasco and any additional seasoning to taste.
6. Fill the vol-au-vent cases with the chicken mixture and sprinkle with parsley.
7. Serve hot.

Greek taramasalata

Serves 4

6 large slices white bread

hot water

8-oz (200gm) jar smoked cod's roe

2 small garlic cloves

1 small onion

¼ pint (125ml) corn oil

4 tablespoons strained lemon juice

pepper to taste

chopped parsley to garnish

1. Remove crusts from bread and discard.
2. Cut remaining bread into cubes and cover with hot water. Leave to soak 2 to 3 minutes.
3. Squeeze dry and put into bowl.
4. Beat with a fork until smooth then gradually beat in cod's roe.
5. Very finely chop garlic. Finely grate onion.
6. Add both to bread mixture and stir well to mix.
7. Slowly beat in oil alternately with lemon juice and continue beating until mixture is smooth and creamy.
8. Season to taste with pepper and pile into a serving dish.
9. Sprinkle with parsley then serve with fingers of hot toast.

Note
Alternatively, put ingredients into blender goblet and blend at low speed until smooth.

Danish blue mousse

Serves 6

4oz (100gm) Danish blue cheese

4oz (100gm) Samsoe cheese

½ pint (250gm) double cream

1oz (25gm) toasted almonds, chopped

½oz (12gm) gelatine

2 tablespoons boiling water

2 eggs whites

salt and pepper to taste

maraschino cherries and small lettuce leaves to garnish

1. Finely grate both cheeses into large bowl.
2. Partially whip cream.
3. Add to cheese with almonds.
4. Dissolve gelatine in boiling water.
5. Add to cheese mixture.
6. Leave until cold and just beginning to thicken and set.
7. Fold in egg whites beaten to a stiff snow.
8. Season to taste with salt and pepper then transfer to 1lb (½ kilo) loaf tin.
9. Chill until firm and set.
10. Turn out on to a plate and garnish with cherries and lettuce leaves.
11. Serve with Melba toast or crisp biscuits.

Austrian cheese and anchovy ramekins

Austrian cheese and anchovy ramekins

Serves 6

2 standard eggs

2oz (50gm) Cheddar cheese, grated

½ pint (250ml) milk

salt and pepper to taste

2 large slices white bread

1½oz (37gm) butter

6 anchovy fillets, halved lengthwise

paprika

1. Pre-heat oven to moderately hot, 375 deg F or gas 5 (190 deg C).
2. Beat eggs thoroughly then stir in cheese, milk and salt and pepper to taste.
3. Cut bread into cubes and fry in the butter until crisp and golden.
4. Butter 6 individual dishes and put equal amounts of bread cubes into each.
5. Fill with egg mixture then arrange 2 strips of anchovies on top of each.
6. Sprinkle with paprika and bake in centre of oven for 15 to 20 minutes or until golden and firm.
7. Serve straight away.

Creamed chicken and ham mould

Serves 4 to 6

1 level tablespoon gelatine
3 tablespoons boiling water
1 level dessertspoon cornflour
4 standard eggs, separated
¾ pint (375ml) milk
salt and pepper
Worcestershire sauce
Tabasco
pinch of nutmeg
6oz (150gm) cold cooked chicken, minced
4oz (100gm) ham, minced
¼ pint (125ml) double cream
lettuce leaves
radish and cucumber slices, strips of green pepper, and sprigs of watercress to garnish

1. Put gelatine into a saucepan with the boiling water. Leave over a low heat until gelatine dissolves completely. Stir all the time. Remove from heat and leave on one side.
2. Mix cornflour, egg yolks and milk well together.
3. Put into the top of a double saucepan or into a basin over a pan of gently simmering water. Cook, stirring until sauce thickens.
4. Remove from heat and stir in dissolved gelatine.
5. Season well to taste with salt, pepper, Worcestershire sauce, a dash of Tabasco and pinch of nutmeg.
6. Leave in the cold until just beginning to thicken and set then stir in chicken and ham.
7. Beat egg whites to a stiff snow. Whip cream until thick.
8. Fold both alternately into chicken and ham mixture.
9. When smooth and well-combined, transfer to a 2 pint (approximately 1 litre) fancy mould, first rinsed with cold water or lightly oiled.
10. Chill until firm and set then turn out on to a lettuce-lined plate.
11. Garnish with radishes, cucumber, green pepper and watercress.

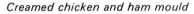

Creamed chicken and ham mould

Spanish rice

Spanish rice

Serves 4

3 dessertspoons salad oil
1 clove garlic, crushed or finely chopped
1 medium celery stalk, chopped
6oz (150gm) long grain rice
1 can (about 1lb or ½ kilo) tomatoes
3 level tablespoons tomato paste
1 level teaspoon salt
1 small bay leaf
½ pint (250ml) hot water
8oz (200gm) raw minced beef
1 small green pepper, de-seeded and chopped
½ teaspoon Tabasco
1 level teaspoon sugar
½ a beef stock cube, dissolved in ¼ pint (125ml) boiling water
parsley to garnish
little grated cheese to serve

1. Pre-heat oven to moderate, 350 deg F or gas 4 (180 deg C).
2. Heat the oil in a frying pan.
3. Add garlic and celery and fry gently until golden brown.
4. Mix the rice, tomatoes, tomato paste, salt and bay leaf with the hot water.
5. Add to garlic and celery in the frying pan.
6. Stir well and cover.
7. Bring to the boil, lower heat and simmer gently for 10 minutes.
8. Put beef and green pepper into a saucepan and brown over a fairly brisk heat, stirring with a fork all the time.
9. Stir in Tabasco, sugar and beef stock.
10. Combine the rice and meat mixtures in a 3 pint (approximately 1½ litre) greased ovenproof dish.
11. Cover and cook in centre of oven for 30 minutes.
12. Remove from oven and sprinkle with grated cheese.
13. Brown under a hot grill.
14. Serve straight away, garnished with parsley.
15. Accompany with grated cheese.

Avocado with seafood

Seafood risotto

Avocado Quacamole

Serves 4

2 medium ripe avocados

1 tablespoon wine or cider vinegar

1 tablespoon lemon juice

1 small garlic clove

1 small onion

1 small green pepper

2 heaped tablespoons chopped parsley

3 tablespoons olive oil

salt and pepper to taste

12 stuffed olives to garnish

1. Halve avocados and remove stones.
2. Spoon flesh into bowl but reserve avocado shells.
3. Add vinegar and lemon juice and mash finely with a stainless fork.
4. Finely chop garlic. Grate onion. De-seed and chop green pepper.
5. Add to avocado mixture with parsley.
6. Gradually beat in oil then season to taste with salt and pepper.
7. Spoon mixture into avocado shells and garnish with halved olives.
8. Transfer to 4 individual plates and serve straight away.

Avocados with seafood

Serves 4

2 medium avocados

lemon juice

4 level tablespoons peeled prawns, flaked crabmeat or lobster

4 to 6 tablespoons cocktail sauce (see page 100)

lemon and parsley to garnish

1. Halve avocados lengthwise and remove stones.
2. Brush flesh with lemon juice to prevent discoloration.
3. Fill cavities with fish then coat with cocktail sauce.
4. Serve straight away, garnished with lemon and parsley.

Peach-topped pork and beef loaf

Seafood risotto

Serves 4

1 lb (½ kilo) cod or haddock fillet

1 medium onion, chopped

1 small green pepper, de-seeded and chopped

1 small red pepper, de-seeded and chopped

1 oz (25gm) butter or margarine

1 dessertspoon salad oil

8 oz (200gm) long grain rice

1 pint (approximately ½ litre) chicken stock

¼ level teaspoon saffron strands

salt and pepper to taste

4 oz (100gm) peeled prawns

2 level tablespoons chopped parsley and 2 whole prawns to garnish

1. Poach cod or haddock for 7 minutes in gently simmering salted water. Drain and flake fish with 2 forks, discarding skin and bones if any.
2. Fry onion and green and red pepper in the butter or margarine and salad oil until pale gold.
3. Add rice and fry a further 2 minutes, stirring all the time with a fork.
4. Pour in stock then add saffron. Season to taste with salt and pepper.
5. Cook, stirring, until rice grains are plump and tender and have absorbed most of the moisture—about 15 minutes.
6. Add flaked fish and peeled prawns. Fork in thoroughly then heat through a further 5 to 7 minutes.
7. Turn out on to a warm dish and garnish with parsley and whole prawns.

Peach-topped pork and beef loaf

Serves 4 to 6

8 oz (200gm) pork sausagemeat

8 oz (200gm) raw minced beef

1 small onion, grated

1 dessertspoon tomato ketchup

4 level tablespoons fresh white breadcrumbs

1 level teaspoon salt

pepper to taste

1 egg, beaten

1 small can (approximately 8oz or 200gm) sliced peaches, drained

watercress and tomato halves to garnish

1. Pre-heat oven to moderately hot, 400 deg F or gas 6 (200 deg C).
2. Mix together sausagemeat, beef, onion, ketchup, breadcrumbs and salt and pepper.
3. Combine with beaten egg.
4. Shape into a loaf and place in a baking dish.
5. Cook in centre of oven for 1 to 1¼ hours.
6. Remove from dish and allow to cool.
7. Before serving, decorate with peach slices, watercress and tomato halves.
8. Slice thinly and serve with hot buttered toast or crisp rolls and butter.

Note
Any left-over loaf makes an excellent sandwich filling.

Potato beef nests

Serves 4

A quickie starter, especially if the Duchesse potatoes are made with a packet of instant mashed potatoes.

Duchesse potatoes (see page 151)

lightly-beaten egg white

1 can (about 1lb or ½ kilo) minced steak

1. Pre-heat oven to moderately hot, 400 deg F or gas 6 (200 deg C).
2. Using a star-shaped tube and forcing bag, pipe 4 nests of potato mixture on to a buttered baking tray. Brush with egg white.
3. Bake near top of oven for 15 minutes or until golden brown.
4. Fill with hot minced steak and serve straight away.

Potato beef nests

Egg and bacon patties

Devilled spicy ring

Serves 6

1oz (25gm) butter or margarine

1oz (25gm) flour

½ pint (250ml) milk

salt

freshly-ground black pepper

2 teaspoons Tabasco

1 level tablespoon curry powder

juice of ½ lemon

1lb (½ kilo) cottage cheese

2 celery stalks, chopped

1 level tablespoon chopped parsley

2 egg yolks

½oz (12gm) gelatine

2 tablespoons boiling water

2 egg whites

¼ pint (125ml) double cream, whipped

cubed ham and cheese

slices of cucumber

watercress

French or other dressing to taste (see page 161)

1. Melt butter or margarine in saucepan.
2. Stir in flour and cook 2 minutes without browning.
3. Gradually blend in milk. Cook, stirring, until sauce comes to the boil and thickens.
4. Season with salt and pepper then add Tabasco, curry powder, lemon juice, cottage cheese, celery, parsley and egg yolks.
5. Dissolve gelatine in boiling water and add.
6. When cold and just beginning to thicken, beat egg whites to a stiff snow. Whip cream until thick.
7. Fold both into gelatine mixture then transfer to a ring mould.
8. Chill until firm and set.
9. Unmould on to a plate and fill centre with ham and cheese.
10. Arrange cucumber round inner edge and watercress round outer edge.
11. Accompany with dressing.

Egg and bacon patties

Serves 4 to 6

1lb (½ kilo) frozen puff pastry

beaten egg or egg yolk beaten with a little milk for glazing

4oz (100gm) lean bacon

½oz (12gm) butter or margarine

4 large hard-boiled eggs

½ pint (250ml) freshly-made coating white or béchamel sauce (see pages 94 and 96)

salt and pepper to taste

1. Pre-heat oven to hot, 425 deg F or gas 7 (220 deg C).
2. Roll out pastry and cut into twelve 2½-inch squares.
3. Place pastry squares on a wet baking tray.
4. Using a 1¼ to 1½ inch round cutter, cut three-quarters of the way through each square of pastry.
5. Brush tops with beaten egg or egg yolk and milk. Bake near top of oven for 10 minutes. Reduce temperature to moderate, 350 deg F or gas 4 (180 deg C), and continue to bake for a further 10 minutes.
6. Meanwhile, chop bacon and fry in the butter or margarine until soft. Remove from heat. Chop hard-boiled eggs and add.
7. Stir both into sauce. Five minutes before patties are ready, heat sauce through over a low heat. Season to taste with salt and pepper.
8. Take patties out of oven and remove round lids and any soft pastry remaining inside each.
9. Fill with sauce mixture and serve straight away.

Salmon pâté

Serves 4 to 6

An unusual fish pâté, which makes an interesting starter with hot buttered toast.

1 medium can (7oz or 175gm) red salmon

2oz (50gm) fresh white breadcrumbs

2oz (50gm) butter, melted

juice and finely-grated peel of ½ a medium lemon

1 small onion, very finely grated

salt and white pepper to taste

1 tablespoon brandy or dry sherry

1 level tablespoon very finely-chopped parsley

pinch of ground nutmeg

1 standard egg, beaten

1. Pre-heat oven to moderate, 325 deg F or gas 3 (170 deg C).
2. Finely mash salmon after first removing bones.
3. Stir in crumbs, butter, lemon juice and peel, onion, salt and pepper to taste, the brandy or sherry, parsley, nutmeg and beaten egg.
4. Mix thoroughly to combine then transfer to a 1lb (½ kilo) loaf tin lined with foil.
5. Smooth top with a knife then cover with more foil.
6. Bake in centre of oven for 1¼ hours or until firm and set.
7. Remove from tin and leave until cold. Refrigerate until needed.
8. Before serving, cut into slices and serve with toast.

Devilled spicy ring

Cheese and sultana flan

Cheese and sultana flan

Serves 4 to 6

6oz (150gm) short crust pastry (see page 108)

6oz (150gm) Gruyère cheese, cut into thin slices

2oz (50gm) sultanas

¼ pint (125ml) plus 5 tablespoons milk

¼ pint (125ml) double cream

3 level tablespoons clear honey

grated peel and juice of ½ lemon

3 standard eggs

salt and pepper to taste

4oz (100gm) ham, sliced

parsley to garnish

1. Pre-heat oven to moderately hot, 400 deg F or gas 6 (200 deg C).
2. Roll out pastry and use to line an 8-inch flan ring standing on baking tray.
3. Prick the base of pastry.
4. Arrange alternate layers of cheese slices and sultanas in flan case.
5. Whisk milk, cream, honey, lemon peel and juice, eggs and salt and pepper to taste well together.
6. Pour over cheese and sultanas.
7. Cook in centre of oven for 30 to 40 minutes or until filling is set.
8. Leave until cold then before serving decorate with small cornets of ham and parsley.

Israeli-style starter

Serves 4

4 medium courgettes

3 tablespoons salad oil

1 medium onion, grated

2 medium tomatoes, skinned and chopped

1 large garlic clove, crushed and finely chopped

1 small bay leaf

½ level teaspoon coriander seeds (optional)

¼ level teaspoon paprika

1 level teaspoon salt

1 tablespoon lemon juice

1. Top and tail courgettes. Wash thoroughly then cut into slices.
2. Heat oil in saucepan.
3. Add onion, tomatoes, garlic, bay leaf, coriander seeds (if used), paprika and salt. Cover. Simmer 10 minutes.
4. Add courgette slices and cook fairly gently for a further 20 minutes, shaking pan from time to time.
5. Stir in lemon juice and serve hot or cold with lamb, veal, poultry and fish dishes.

Italian pancakes

Serves 4

8 cooked pancakes

1 recipe Bolognese sauce (see page 102)

8 tablespoons stock or dry white wine

1 recipe freshly-made cheese sauce (see page 94)

2 tablespoons tomato ketchup

2oz (50gm) strong Cheddar cheese, grated

fresh herbs to garnish

1. Pre-heat oven to hot, 425 deg F or gas 7 (220 deg C).
2. Fill pancakes with equal amounts of Bolognese sauce and roll up.
3. Arrange in heatproof dish, spooning any left-over Bolognese sauce between pancakes.
4. Add stock or wine and coat with cheese sauce.
5. Sprinkle with cheese then trickle tomato ketchup over the top.
6. Re-heat and brown towards top of oven for about 15 minutes.
7. Serve garnished with fresh herbs.

Italian pancakes

Fish

Broadly speaking there are three groups of fish: white fish, which includes cod, haddock, hake, plaice, sole, turbot and coley; oily fish, which includes mackerel, herrings, eels and salmon; and shellfish, which includes crab, lobster, scallops, prawns, mussels and oysters.

Fish from all three categories provide an excellent source of first-class body building protein and oily fish also contain vitamins A and D. Now there is a wide variety of frozen fish readily available, seasons are less important than they used to be. However, it is useful to know that, although most of the popular fish are available all the year round, cod is at its best from October to May, haddock from September to February, hake from midsummer to New Year, plaice throughout the year but particularly during May, sole and coley all the time, turbot from March to late summer, herrings from midsummer to Christmas, mackerel from April to early summer, eel from autumn to March and salmon from March to late summer. Shellfish have their own seasons as well and while the best time for crabs and lobsters are the summer months, mussels, oysters and scallops are at their peak from autumn to spring.

White fish is light and easy to digest but has not the same 'body' as oily fish or as protein foods such as meat and cheese. Therefore it is best to allow between 6 to 8oz (150 to 200gm) raw weight of white fish on the bone per person, 1 or 2oz (25 to 50gm) less if the fish is filleted; 4 to 6oz (100 to 150gm) oily or shellfish is usually adequate for a single serving.

All fish should be bought as fresh as possible from a reliable fishmonger and cooked as soon as possible after purchase. It should never be left lying about in a warm kitchen but put into the refrigerator until needed and washed quickly under cold running water before cooking.

When choosing fish look for bulging eyes, a stiff body and tail, plenty of shimmering scales and reddish gills. The skin of flat fish should be unwrinkled and the spots bright.

Fish may be steamed, poached, grilled, baked or deep or shallow fat fried. Poached fish acquires a better flavour if it is cooked in fish stock or court bouillon.

Salmon summer salad (see page 37) served in a tall glass, quicky herring au gratin (see page 35) decorated with strips of pimiento, tuna mould (see page 37) garnished with lemon and parsley, two bowls of prawn provençale (see page 42), and kipper and egg pie (see page 36)

28

Fish stock

1lb (½ kilo) fish trimmings, cleaned (heads, tails, bones and so on)

1 large onion, quartered

2 carrots, thinly sliced

1 bay leaf

2 cloves

1½ pint (¾ litre) water

2 level teaspoons salt

good shake of pepper

1. Put all ingredients into a saucepan.
2. Slowly bring to boil. Lower heat and cover pan.
3. Simmer 45 minutes.
4. Strain and use as required.

Court bouillon

This is a more flavoursome stock, especially suitable for salmon, salmon trout, halibut, turbot and sole.

1½ pint (¾ litre) water

¼ pint (125ml) dry white wine (for economy, dry cider may be used if preferred)

1 large onion, quartered

2 large celery stalks, broken into pieces

2 medium carrots, thickly sliced

½ teacup parsley

1 bay leaf

1 blade mace

2 cloves

1 level dessertspoon pickling spice

2 level teaspoons salt

1. Put all ingredients into a saucepan.
2. Slowly bring to the boil. Lower heat and cover pan.
3. Simmer 45 minutes.
4. Strain and use as required.

Egg and crumbed fried fillets

Serves 4

8 fillets of plaice or sole (sole should be skinned)

1 level tablespoon flour, well-seasoned with salt and pepper

1 standard egg

2 teaspoons water

toasted breadcrumbs

shallow fat or oil for frying

lemon slices to garnish

1. Wash and dry fish then coat each piece with flour.
2. Dip in egg, beaten with water, then toss in crumbs.
3. Fry in hot fat or oil for 5 to 6 minutes, turning once.
4. Drain on soft kitchen paper then serve straight away garnished with lemon.

Note
Plaice fillets should first be put into the pan with skin side uppermost.

Deep-fried fish

Serves 4

1½lb (¾ kilo) white fish cutlets, steaks or fillets (cod, hake, haddock, rock salmon, coley, halibut or wings of young skate)

salt and pepper

deep oil for frying

coating batter (see page 105)

lemon wedges to garnish

1. Wash and dry fish then sprinkle lightly with salt and pepper.
2. Heat pan of deep oil (which should be no more than half-full) until a cube of bread, dropped into it, turns golden in 1 minute and floats to the top.
3. Coat fish with batter then lift, a few pieces at a time, into pan with kitchen tongs.
4. Fry until golden brown and crisp, allowing about 5 minutes for fillets and skate and 7 to 8 minutes for cutlets and steaks.
5. Drain thoroughly on soft kitchen paper and serve hot, garnished with lemon.
6. Accompany with chips and tartare sauce (see page 100).

Note
When deep frying batter-coated fish, do not use a basket because the fish cooks more satisfactorily if allowed to float about in the oil.

Soft roe fritters

Serves 4

Coat 1lb (½ kilo) soft roes in savoury fritter batter (see page 105). Fry as for deep-fried fish, above, allowing about 5 to 6 minutes. Drain and serve with lemon wedges.

Fried whitebait

Serves 4

These tiny fish are always cooked and eaten whole. Wash 1lb (½ kilo) whitebait and dry in a cloth. Put into a paper bag containing 3 level tablespoons flour, well-seasoned with salt and pepper. Hold the bag firmly at the top and shake up and down until the fish are completely coated. Transfer to a fish basket and lower into a deep pan half-full of hot oil. (When a cube of bread is dropped into it, it should turn golden in 1 minute and float to the top.) Fry 3 minutes, lift out of pan and tip on to crumpled kitchen paper. Drain thoroughly, sprinkle with salt and garnish with wedges or slices of lemon. Serve with brown bread and butter.

Fish cakes

Serves 4 to 6

1lb (½ kilo) freshly-boiled potatoes (raw weight)

½oz (12gm) butter or margarine

8oz (200gm) freshly-cooked and flaked cod, haddock, coley, canned salmon or tuna

1 level tablespoon finely-chopped parsley

1 small onion, finely grated (optional)

salt and pepper to taste

2 standard eggs

2 teaspoons cold water

toasted breadcrumbs

shallow fat or oil for frying

1. Finely mash potatoes with butter or margarine.
2. Add fish, parsley, onion (if used) and salt and pepper to taste. Mix thoroughly.
3. Bind with 1 egg, beaten, and leave until cold.
4. Turn out on to a surface lightly dusted with flour and shape into a thickish roll.
5. Cut into 8 slices then coat with remaining egg, beaten with water.
6. Toss in crumbs then fry in hot fat or oil until golden brown and crisp on both sides, turning once.
7. Drain on soft kitchen paper and serve hot with a sauce to taste.

Fish quenelles mornay

Serves 4 to 6

1lb (½ kilo) white fish

1 recipe choux pastry (see page 112)

2 tablespoons double cream

salt and pepper to taste

freshly-made mornay sauce (see page 96)

1. Cook fish in gently-simmering salted water for about 8 to 10 minutes or until tender.
2. Drain thoroughly and mash very finely with a fork.
3. Beat into choux pastry with cream then season well with salt and pepper.
4. Transfer to a bowl then cover and refrigerate for 2 hours.
5. Half-fill a large pan with water and add 1 to 2 level teaspoons salt. Bring to boil.
6. Lower heat so that water simmers.
7. With 2 wet dessertspoons, shape fish mixture into ovals and lower, a few at a time, into pan of water.
8. Poach 10 minutes or until quenelles puff up and float to the top.
9. Remove from pan, drain on soft kitchen paper and keep hot.
10. Transfer to a warm serving dish and coat with sauce.
11. Serve straight away.

Foil-baked fish steaks

Serves 4

4 fish steaks (cod, haddock, hake, salmon, salmon trout, turbot or halibut)

salt and pepper

lemon juice

parsley

1oz (25gm) butter

1. Pre-heat oven to moderately hot, 375 deg F or gas 5 (190 deg C).
2. Wash and wipe steaks then place each on a fairly large square of buttered aluminium foil.
3. Sprinkle with salt, pepper and lemon juice then top each with parsley and flakes of butter.
4. Wrap up loosely into parcels and stand parcels in a baking tin.
5. Cook in centre of oven for 20 to 30 minutes.
6. Unwrap and transfer to 4 warm serving plates.
7. Serve with any suitable sauce chosen from sauce section (see page 92).

Cod cardinal

Serves 4

1½lb (¾ kilo) filleted cod, in one piece

1oz (25gm) butter

1 large onion, chopped

1 can (14oz or 350gm) peeled tomatoes

salt and pepper to taste

1 tablespoon Worcestershire sauce

6oz (150gm) Cheddar cheese, finely grated

lemon slices and chopped parsley to garnish

1. Pre-heat oven to moderate, 350 deg F or gas 4 (180 deg C).
2. Wash and skin fish and arrange in lightly-buttered heatproof dish.
3. Heat butter in saucepan. Add onion and fry gently until golden.
4. Stir in tomatoes, salt and pepper to taste and Worcestershire sauce.
5. Simmer gently for 5 minutes. Stir in 4oz (100gm) cheese and leave over low heat until melted.
6. Arrange sauce in a line down centre of fish then sprinkle rest of cheese on either side.
7. Cook in centre of oven for 30 minutes.
8. Garnish with lemon and parsley to serve.

Cod cardinal

Fish casserole

Serves 4

1½lb (¾ kilo) cod or haddock fillet

1 medium lemon

salt and pepper to taste

4oz (100gm) mushrooms, chopped

1 medium onion, chopped

1 small green pepper, de-seeded and chopped

2 medium leeks, well-washed and cut into chunks

8oz (200gm) tomatoes, skinned and chopped

1 level tablespoon soft brown sugar

1oz (25gm) butter

1. Pre-heat oven to moderate, 350 deg F or gas 4 (180 deg C).
2. Divide fish into portions and arrange in buttered casserole.
3. Squeeze lemon juice over fish and season well to taste with salt and pepper.
4. Sprinkle mushrooms, onion and green pepper over fish then add pieces of leek.
5. Add two-thirds of the tomatoes then scatter brown sugar over the top.
6. Dot with flakes of butter and cover with lid.
7. Cook in centre of oven for 30 minutes or until leek is tender.
8. Remove from oven and garnish with remaining tomatoes.
9. Serve straight away.

Above: cod steak braise
Below: fish casserole

Cod steak braise

Serves 4

3 small carrots, peeled and diced

8oz (200gm) pickling onions

½ pint (250ml) chicken stock

4 cod steaks

2oz (50gm) mushrooms, sliced

1oz (25gm) butter

1oz (25gm) flour

1 garlic clove, chopped (optional)

3 tablespoons Pernod

4 tablespoons double cream

salt and pepper to taste

1 level tablespoon chopped parsley to garnish

1. Cook carrots and onions in the stock for 15 minutes.
2. Add fish and mushrooms and simmer gently for 10 minutes or until fish is cooked through but still firm.
3. Remove fish from stock, taking care not to break it.
4. Drain stock and reserve for sauce.
5. Put onions and carrots into a shallow, well-buttered serving dish. Arrange fish pieces on top and keep warm.
6. To make sauce, melt butter in a pan and stir in flour. Cook 2 minutes without browning.
7. Gradually blend in strained stock.
8. Cook, stirring, until sauce comes to boil and thickens. Add garlic (if used) and the Pernod.
9. Stir in cream, season to taste with salt and pepper and pour over fish.
10. Sprinkle with chopped parsley.
11. Accompany with plain boiled rice or boiled potatoes.

Fish steaks morpheus

Fish steaks morpheus

Serves 4

¼ pint (125ml) pale ale

½ level teaspoon salt

pepper

juice of ½ lemon

few drops Worcestershire sauce

8 small cod steaks (about 1½lb or ¾ kilo)

1 medium cucumber, peeled

2 large potatoes

1oz (25gm) flour, seasoned with salt and pepper

6 tablespoons salad oil

4oz (100gm) butter

12oz (300gm) mushrooms, sliced

4 medium tomatoes, skinned

3oz (75gm) stuffed olives

1. Put ale, salt, pepper, lemon juice and Worcestershire sauce into a shallow dish.
2. Add fish, cover and marinate in a cold place for 1 to 2 hours, turning occasionally.
3. Cut cucumber in half lengthwise, remove seeds with a spoon and cut flesh into ¼-inch cubes.
4. Cut potatoes into ¼-inch cubes and leave in cold water until required.
5. Drain fish thoroughly then coat with seasoned flour.
6. Heat 4 tablespoons oil in pan, add fish and fry until golden brown, turning once.
7. Melt 1oz (25gm) butter in another pan, add cucumber and fry gently for 5 minutes.
8. Transfer cucumber to a serving dish and keep hot.
9. Wipe out pan and add a further 1oz (25gm) butter and 2 tablespoons oil.
10. Add potatoes (drained and well dried) and fry gently until golden and tender.
11. Remove from pan, drain on soft kitchen paper and combine with cucumber.
12. Fry mushrooms and tomatoes in remaining butter for 3 minutes or until tender.
13. Arrange fried fish steaks on top of cucumber mixture then garnish with mushrooms and tomatoes.
14. Add olives before serving.

Creamed fish in spinach ring

Serves 4

2lb (1 kilo) spinach

3oz (75gm) butter

3oz (75gm) flour

1 pint (½ litre) milk

salt and pepper

3 egg yolks

good pinch of nutmeg

1lb (½ kilo) haddock or cod fillets

3 to 4oz (75 to 100gm) Cheddar cheese, grated

halved tomato slices to garnish

1. Pre-heat oven to moderately hot, 375 deg F or gas 5 (190 deg C).
2. To make spinach ring, cook spinach in a very little salted water. Drain well and chop.
3. Make a thick sauce with 2oz (50gm) butter, 2oz (50gm) flour and ½ pint (250ml) milk then season well to taste with salt and pepper.
4. Stir in egg yolks and nutmeg then add the drained spinach.
5. Pour into a buttered 1-pint (approximately ½-litre) ring mould and place in roasting tin containing 1 inch of water.
6. Cook in centre of oven for 30 to 40 minutes or until firm.
7. Meanwhile, simmer fish in remaining milk until cooked—about 10 minutes.
8. Drain and use liquid to make a white sauce with remaining butter and flour.
9. Season to taste with salt and pepper and stir in half the grated cheese.
10. When spinach ring is cooked, turn out on to a warm plate.
11. Fill centre with flaked fish and pour over the cheese sauce.
12. Sprinkle with rest of grated cheese and garnish with tomatoes.

Fish cutlets with tomato and caper sauce

Serves 2

2 cutlets of hake or haddock

1 small onion

1 small can (approximately 6oz or 150gm) peeled tomatoes

salt and pepper

2 level teaspoons capers

1oz (25gm) butter

lemon wedges and parsley to garnish

1. Pre-heat oven to moderately hot, 375 deg F or gas 5 (190 deg C).
2. Place fish in buttered heatproof dish.
3. Grate onion finely. Rub tomatoes through a sieve or liquidise in blender.
4. Combine with onion, salt and pepper to taste and capers.
5. Spoon round fish then top with flakes of butter.
6. Cover and cook in centre of oven for 30 to 35 minutes or until fish is cooked.
7. Garnish with lemon and parsley.

Creamed fish in spinach ring

Hashed haddock

Serves 4

1½lb (¾ kilo) cooked smoked haddock or cod fillet

6 streaky bacon rashers, chopped

1½lb (¾ kilo) finely-diced raw potatoes

2 level tablespoons chopped onion

2 level tablespoons finely-chopped parsley

good shake of pepper

2 tablespoons bacon fat or salad oil

¼ pint (125ml) water

paprika

parsley sprigs to garnish

1. Remove skin and bones (if any) from fish and flake up flesh with 2 forks.
2. Fry bacon until crisp then combine with potatoes, onion, parsley, pepper and fish.
3. Heat bacon fat or oil in large frying pan.
4. Add fish mixture then pour water over top.
5. Cover and cook over a moderate heat for 7 minutes.
6. Turn the mixture in pan and cook, uncovered, for a further 6 to 8 minutes or until lightly brown.
7. Stir occasionally to mix in the browned potatoes.
8. Serve in a warm dish, sprinkled with paprika, and garnished with parsley sprigs.

Fish cutlets with tomato and caper sauce

Spaghetti with fish and apple balls

Spaghetti with fish and apple balls

Serves 4

12oz (300gm) cod or haddock, cooked

3 eating apples

1oz (25gm) butter

2oz (50gm) flour

¼ pint (125ml) milk

salt and pepper to taste

1 tablespoon salad oil

1 small onion, peeled and chopped

1 tube tomato paste

1 level dessertspoon cornflour

½ pint (250ml) water

1 teaspoon each, sugar and basil

8oz (200gm) tomatoes, skinned and chopped

coating batter (see page 105)

deep oil for frying

8oz (200gm) freshly-boiled spaghetti

1 level tablespoon finely-chopped parsley to garnish

1. Mash cod or haddock finely. Peel 2 apples and chop.
2. Melt butter in pan. Add 1oz (25gm) flour and cook 2 minutes without browning. Gradually blend in milk and cook until mixture thickens sufficiently to leave sides of pan clean.
3. Beat in fish and apples then season well to taste with salt and pepper.
4. Leave until cold, shape into small balls and toss in 1oz (25gm) flour, well-seasoned with salt and pepper. Leave on one side.
5. To make sauce, heat oil in saucepan. Chop third apple finely and add to oil with onion. Fry gently until pale gold.
6. Stir in tomato paste and cornflour then gradually blend in water.
7. Add sugar, basil and tomatoes. Season to taste with salt and pepper then simmer, covered, for 15 minutes.
8. Meanwhile, coat fish balls with batter.
9. Heat pan of deep oil until a cube of bread, dropped into it, turns golden brown in 1 minute and floats to the top.
10. Add fish balls, a few at a time, and fry until golden and crisp.
11. Drain on soft kitchen paper.
12. Line a platter with spaghetti, arrange fish balls on top then coat with the sauce.
13. Sprinkle with parsley and serve straight away.

Midsummer fish mould

Serves 4 to 6

1½ level tablespoons gelatine

3 tablespoons cold water

1½ pints (approximately ¾ litre) fish stock, well-strained

¼ pint (125ml) white wine

salt and pepper to taste

2lb (1 kilo) smoked haddock, cooked

peel of 1 medium lemon, cut into matchstick lengths

2 medium onions, peeled and thinly sliced

3 medium tomatoes, skinned and quartered

watercress to garnish

1. Soak the gelatine in cold water for 5 minutes then add fish stock, heated until hot.
2. Stir until gelatine dissolves.
3. Add white wine and season to taste with salt and pepper.
4. Pour gelatine liquid into an oiled 9-inch ring mould to a depth of approximately ¼ inch. Set until firm. Cool remaining gelatine.
5. When gelatine in ring mould is firm, arrange about 8oz (200gm) of smoked haddock in chunks and half the lemon peel on top.
6. Pour over a few spoons of gelatine mixture and allow to set.
7. When firm, carefully pour in about ½ pint (250ml) cold gelatine mixture and allow to set again.
8. Arrange about 8oz (200gm) of fish and remaining lemon peel round the ring mould and gradually add remaining gelatine mixture.
9. Leave to set in a cool place until firm.
10. Turn out on to a suitable serving dish and fill centre with remaining haddock pieces mixed with onion slices and quarters of tomatoes.
11. Serve garnished with sprigs of watercress.

Midsummer fish mould

Scots herrings

Serves 4

4 medium herrings, cleaned and boned

salt and pepper

1 large egg

1 dessertspoon lemon juice

2oz (50gm) rolled oats

2oz (50gm) lard or 4 tablespoons salad oil for frying

1. Sprinkle herrings with salt and pepper.
2. Dip into egg, beaten with lemon juice.
3. Coat with oats, pressing on to fish with palms of hands.
4. Fry in hot lard or oil for 3 minutes on each side.
5. Drain on soft kitchen paper and serve straight away.

Soused mackerel or herrings

Serves 4

4 large mackerel or herrings, skinned and boned

1 large onion, sliced

2 level dessertspoons mixed pickling spice

1 crumbled bay leaf

5 tablespoons water

4 tablespoons mild vinegar

4 tablespoons lemon juice

1 level teaspoon golden syrup

½ to 1 level teaspoon salt

good shake of pepper

1. Pre-heat oven to cool, 300 deg F or gas 2 (150 deg C).
2. With skin side outside, roll up each fish from head end to tail.
3. Arrange in a 1 to 1½-pint (approximately ½ to ¾-litre) heatproof dish.
4. Sprinkle with pickling spice and bay leaf.
5. Combine all remaining ingredients well together and pour into dish over fish.
6. Cover with lid or foil and cook in centre of oven for 1½ hours.
7. Cool in dish then chill thoroughly before serving.

Grilled mackerel or herrings

Serves 4

4 mackerel or herrings

salt and pepper

½oz (12gm) butter, melted

lemon wedges to garnish

1. Pre-heat grill pan.
2. Remove heads from fish. Clean mackerel or herrings thoroughly.
3. Make 2 or 3 diagonal slits on either side of fish to allow heat to penetrate. Sprinkle with salt and pepper.
4. Stand fish in grill pan and brush with half the melted butter.
5. Grill 5 to 7 minutes. Turn fish over, brush with rest of butter and grill a further 5 to 7 minutes.
6. Serve garnished with lemon and accompany with gooseberry sauce for mackerel or mustard sauce for herrings.

Crab stuffed plaice

Serves 4

4 large fillets plaice

4oz (100gm) fresh or frozen crabmeat, cooked

salt and pepper

butter and little oil

4oz (100gm) button mushrooms

squeeze of lemon juice

2–3 slices white bread

lemon slices

1. Pre-heat oven to moderate, 350 deg F or gas 4 (180 deg C).
2. Butter an ovenproof dish. Melt a little butter.
3. Place 2 fish fillets in dish side by side to form the shape of the fish. Spread crabmeat on fillets, leaving a slight border all round edges. Season and cover with the other fillets. Brush over with melted butter.
4. Cover with foil and bake for about 20 minutes, or until fillets are cooked.
5. While fish is cooking wash and slice mushrooms and cook in a little water and lemon juice.
6. Make croutons by cutting bread into small dice and frying in a mixture of oil and butter until golden.
7. Drain on kitchen paper and keep hot.
8. Remove fish from oven, lift off foil and serve garnished with mushroom slices, croutons and lemon slices.

Crab stuffed plaice

Fish puffs

Serves 3

6 baked vol-au-vent cases, each 3 to 4 inches in diameter

½ pint (250ml) freshly-made white coating sauce (see page 94)

1 can (8oz or 200gm) drained and flaked salmon, pilchards or tuna

1 dessertspoon lemon juice

1 medium celery stalk, chopped

2 level teaspoons grated onion

salt and pepper to taste

chopped parsley and tomatoes to garnish

1. Pre-heat oven to moderate, 325 deg F or gas 3 (170 deg C).
2. Stand vol-au-vent cases on baking tray and heat through for 10 to 15 minutes.
3. Meanwhile, place sauce over a medium heat.
4. Stir in flaked fish, lemon juice, celery and onion.
5. Season to taste with salt and pepper.
6. Heat through, stirring, until hot.
7. Remove vol-au-vent cases from oven and fill with fish mixture.
8. Sprinkle with parsley and serve straight away. Garnish with tomato quarters.

Note

1. If preferred, 8oz (200gm) finely-chopped chicken, ham or tongue may be used instead of the canned fish.
2. Alternatively, use 8oz (200gm) cooked and flaked white fish combined with ½ pint (250ml) cheese or tomato sauce (see page 94 or 102).

Quicky herring au gratin

Illustrated on page 29

Serves 2

1 small can spinach purée

1 can (approximately 8oz or 200gm) herring fillets in savoury sauce

2oz (50gm) Cheddar cheese, grated

strips of canned red pimiento to garnish

1. Spread spinach over the base of a small heatproof dish.
2. Arrange herring fillets on top, coating with sauce from can.
3. Sprinkle with cheese and place under pre-heated hot grill until golden and bubbly.
4. Garnish with strips of pimiento and serve straight away.

Fish puffs

Creamed red fish

Serves 4

2½lb (1¼ kilo) red fish or three 8-oz (200gm) packets deep frozen red fish fillets

¼ pint plus 4 tablespoons dry white wine

¼ pint plus 4 tablespoons water

1 bouquet garni (parsley stalks, 1 bay leaf, pinch of thyme)

1½oz (37gm) butter or margarine

1 small onion, finely chopped

1 blade mace

salt

5 white peppercorns, freshly ground

½ medium lemon

2 level tablespoons flour

6 tablespoons top of milk or single cream

1 level tablespoon chopped parsley

freshly-fried bread to serve

1. Clean red fish and cut off head and tail.
2. Cook trimmings, in covered pan, with wine, water and bouquet garni for 20 minutes. Strain and reserve.
3. Grease flameproof dish with half the butter then sprinkle base with onions.
4. Cut fish into 1½-inch pieces and add to dish with mace and 4 tablespoons strained stock.
5. Season to taste with salt and ground peppercorns then sprinkle with lemon juice.
6. Cover and poach gently for 15 minutes.
7. Meanwhile, melt rest of butter in pan. Stir in flour and cook gently for 2 minutes.
8. Gradually add rest of strained stock.
9. Cook, stirring, until sauce comes to boil and thickens. Simmer 2 minutes then stir in top of milk or cream.
10. Adjust seasoning to taste.
11. Remove blade of mace from fish.
12. Pour sauce over fish then sprinkle with parsley.
13. Serve straight away with triangles of freshly-fried bread.

Note

Cod or haddock may be used instead of red fish.

Tomato caskets

Serves 3

6 large tomatoes, skinned

4 canned pilchards or 1 can (approximately 8oz or 200gm) red salmon

mayonnaise (see page 99)

2 teaspoons lemon juice

2 level tablespoons Cheddar cheese, grated

1 teaspoon Worcestershire sauce

salt and pepper

scissor-snipped chives and watercress to garnish

1. Cut tops off tomatoes and scoop out the insides (reserve for soups or stews). Turn tomato cases upside down to drain on soft kitchen paper.
2. Flake fish finely and mix with just sufficient mayonnaise to bind.
3. Stir in lemon juice, cheese and Worcestershire sauce then season to taste with salt and pepper.
4. Pile back into tomato cases and sprinkle with chives.
5. Transfer to a platter and garnish with watercress.
6. Allow 2 tomatoes per person.

Pilchard pilaf

Serves 4

2oz (50gm) butter or margarine

1 large onion, chopped

8oz (200gm) long-grain rice

1 pint (½ litre) water

½ level teaspoon dried thyme

1 teaspoon Worcestershire sauce

salt and pepper to taste

3 tomatoes, skinned and cut into wedges

1 can (1lb or ½ kilo) pilchards

parsley and midget gherkins to garnish

1. Heat butter or margarine in flameproof pan.
2. Add onion and fry gently until soft but not brown.
3. Add rice and fry a further 2 minutes, turning all the time.
4. Add water, thyme, Worcestershire sauce and salt and pepper to taste.
5. Bring to boil, stir once and cover. Simmer 15 minutes.
6. Arrange pilchards and tomato wedges attractively on top.
7. Re-cover and cook a further 7 minutes.
8. Garnish with parsley and gherkins and serve at once piping hot.

Tomato caskets

Kipper and egg pie

Illustrated on page 29

Serves 4

1oz (25gm) butter or margarine

1oz (25gm) flour

¼ pint (125ml) plus 3 tablespoons milk

2 level tablespoons chopped parsley

1 can (7oz or 175gm) kipper fillets, drained and cut into pieces

2 hard-boiled eggs, sliced

salt and pepper to taste

1 large packet frozen puff pastry (thawed)

a little beaten egg for brushing

1. Pre-heat oven to hot, 425 deg F or gas 7 (220 deg C).
2. Melt butter or margarine in saucepan. Add flour and cook 2 minutes without browning.
3. Gradually blend in milk.
4. Cook, stirring, until sauce comes to the boil and thickens.
5. Add parsley, kippers and egg then season to taste with salt and pepper.
6. Line a 7-inch lipped sandwich tin with about two-thirds of the rolled-out pastry.
7. Fill with sauce mixture.
8. Moisten edges of pastry with water then cover with lid, rolled from rest of pastry.
9. Brush with beaten egg and bake near top of oven for 20 minutes.
10. Serve hot or cold.

Left: creamed red fish
Right: pilchard pilaf

Curried fish

Curried fish

Serves 4

Freshly-made curry sauce (see page 103)

1½lb (¾ kilo) cooked flaked fish, which may be fresh or canned

1 level tablespoon desiccated coconut

8oz (200gm) long-grain rice, freshly cooked (raw weight)

1 level tablespoon sultanas

2 medium bananas

lemon juice

1. Place curry sauce over low heat.
2. Add fish to sauce with coconut. Heat through gently.
3. Arrange rice on warm platter.
4. Pile fish curry in the centre then sprinkle with sultanas.
5. Slice bananas thinly, sprinkle with lemon juice and arrange in a border round the dish.
6. Serve with a mixed salad.

Tuna mould

Illustrated on page 29

Serves 4 to 6

½ pint (250ml) tomato juice

2 level teaspoons gelatine

2 cans (each 7oz or 175gm) tuna, drained and flaked

2 hard-boiled eggs, sliced

2 teaspoons lemon juice

salt and pepper to taste

lemon and parsley to garnish

1. Put tomato juice and gelatine into a saucepan and stir over a low heat until gelatine dissolves.
2. Remove from heat and leave until cold and just beginning to thicken and set.
3. Stir in tuna, eggs, lemon juice and salt and pepper to taste.
4. Transfer to a 1½ to 2-pint (approximately ¾ to 1¼-litre) fancy mould, first rinsed with cold water or lightly oiled.
5. Chill until firm and set then turn out.
6. Garnish with lemon and parsley.

Salmon summer salad

Illustrated on page 29

Serves 4

1 can (approximately 8oz or 200gm) red salmon

1 small lettuce, washed and coarsely shredded

1 small red-skinned apple, cored and sliced

4 level tablespoons mayonnaise (see page 99)

1 orange, cut into segments

1oz (25gm) blanched almonds, toasted and coarsely chopped

1. Drain salmon and break into chunks.
2. Divide lettuce between 4 glasses.
3. Toss salmon and apple slices in mayonnaise.
4. Arrange on top of lettuce.
5. Border each glass with orange segments and sprinkle almonds over the top.

Sole à la crème

Sole à la crème

Serves 4

4 large sole fillets, skinned

salt and pepper

juice of ½ medium lemon

¼ pint (125ml) double cream

¼ pint (125ml) single cream

4 level tablespoons grated Parmesan cheese

½ level teaspoon paprika

1oz (25gm) butter

parsley to garnish

1. Pre-heat oven to moderate, 350 deg F or gas 4 (180 deg C).
2. Arrange sole fillets in buttered heatproof dish.
3. Sprinkle with salt, pepper and lemon juice.
4. Beat both creams together to combine then stir in cheese and paprika.
5. Season to taste with salt and pepper then pour over fish.
6. Dot with flakes of butter and cook in centre of oven for 20 minutes, basting at least twice.
7. Garnish with parsley and serve.

Sole duglère

Serves 6

12 small sole fillets, skinned

salt and pepper to taste

¾ pint (375ml) fish stock

2oz (50gm) butter

2oz (50gm) flour

¼ pint (125ml) dry white wine

¼ pint (125ml) double cream

12oz (375gm) tomatoes, skinned

1 level tablespoon chopped parsley

1. Sprinkle fillets with salt and pepper to taste and fold each into three.
2. Put into pan and add fish stock. Cover and poach for 7 minutes or until sole is opaque.
3. Carefully lift out of pan and keep hot. Strain liquor and make up to ½ pint (250ml) with water, if necessary.
4. Melt butter in clean saucepan. Add flour and cook 2 minutes without browning.
5. Gradually blend in fish liquor and wine.
6. Cook, stirring, until sauce comes to boil and thickens.
7. Add cream and simmer 5 minutes. Season to taste with salt and pepper.
8. Meanwhile, quarter tomatoes and remove seeds and juice. (Reserve for stews and casseroles.) Cut tomato flesh into strips and add to sauce with three-quarters of the parsley.
9. Arrange fish in warm heatproof dish and coat with sauce.
10. Sprinkle lightly with rest of parsley and serve straight away.

Sole meunière

Serves 4

4 medium soles, skinned on both sides

2 level tablespoons flour, seasoned with salt and pepper

3oz (75gm) butter

2 teaspoons olive oil

2 level dessertspoons finely-chopped parsley

juice of 1 medium lemon

lemon slices to garnish

1. Wash soles and wipe dry with soft kitchen paper.
2. Toss in seasoned flour.
3. Melt 2oz (50gm) butter in large frying pan.
4. Add oil and heat until hot.
5. Add fish, one or two at a time, and fry 4 to 5 minutes on each side or until crisp and golden.
6. Remove from pan, drain on soft kitchen paper and transfer to a warm serving platter. Keep hot.
7. Clean the pan in which fish was fried by wiping with soft kitchen paper.
8. Add rest of butter and fry until it turns a deep gold.
9. Add parsley and lemon juice and pour over fish.
10. Garnish with lemon slices and serve straight away.

Note
Small plaice may be used instead of sole.

Steamed plaice or sole

Serves 2

2 medium plaice or sole fillets
½ to 1oz (12 to 25gm) butter or margarine
salt and pepper to taste
1 tablespoon milk

1. Arrange fillets in buttered enamel plate.
2. Place plate over a saucepan of gently-boiling water.
3. Top with flakes of butter or margarine then sprinkle to taste with salt and pepper.
4. Pour milk over fish then cover with a second plate.
5. Cook approximately 10 to 15 minutes or until fish is opaque and flakes easily with a fork.

Stuffed sole in Pernod sauce

Serves 4

4oz (100gm) button mushrooms
2 shallots or 1 small onion
2oz (50gm) fresh white breadcrumbs
2 tablespoons Pernod
juice of 1 medium lemon
½ pint (250ml) fish or chicken stock
salt and pepper to taste
8 sole fillets, skinned
½ pint (250ml) double cream
4oz (100gm) peeled prawns
chives and chopped parsley to garnish

1. Pre-heat oven to moderately hot, 375 deg F or gas 5 (190 deg C).
2. Finely chop mushrooms and shallots or onion.
3. Mix well with breadcrumbs and moisten with 1 tablespoon Pernod and the lemon juice.
4. Add a little stock if the mixture is too dry then season to taste with salt and pepper.
5. Spread sole fillets with breadcrumb mixture then roll up loosely.
6. Secure by spearing a cocktail stick into each fillet.
7. Place fillets in buttered heatproof dish.
8. Pour stock into dish and cover with a piece of buttered greaseproof paper to prevent drying.
9. Bake in centre of oven for 15 minutes.
10. Meanwhile, heat the cream through gently without boiling.
11. Add remaining Pernod and peeled prawns, reserving a few for decoration. Season to taste.
12. To serve, remove cocktail sticks from sole and arrange on a warm serving dish.
13. Coat with sauce and sprinkle with chopped chives and parsley.
14. Decorate with remaining prawns.
15. Serve with button mushrooms.

Stuffed sole in Pernod sauce

Rice-stuffed sole

Serves 4

4 small soles, skinned on both sides

2 level tablespoons flour, well-seasoned with salt and pepper

1 large egg

2 teaspoons cold water

toasted breadcrumbs

deep oil for frying

12oz (300gm) cooked long-grain rice (cooked weight)

4oz (100gm) peeled prawns

1 small onion, finely grated

salt and pepper to taste

1oz (25gm) butter

lemon slices and parsley to garnish

1. Wash soles and wipe dry.
2. Make a cut down the backbone of each then ease fish gently away from either side of bone with a sharp knife.
3. Coat soles with seasoned flour then dip in egg, beaten with water.
4. Toss in breadcrumbs and leave to stand 10 minutes for coating to harden.
5. Heat pan of deep oil until a cube of bread, dropped into it, turns golden brown in 1 minute and floats to the top.
6. Add fish, one or two at a time, and fry for about 7 to 10 minutes (depending on thickness) until golden brown.
7. Turn out on to crumpled kitchen paper then, using scissors, gently ease out backbone from each sole.
8. Put rice, prawns, onion, salt and pepper and butter into a saucepan and heat through gently, stirring frequently with a fork.
9. Fill cavities in fish with a line of rice stuffing, and serve straight away, garnished with lemon and parsley.

Deep-fried whole plaice

Serves 4

Prepare as for rice-stuffed sole, above, using plaice instead of sole—do not make a slit along backbones of plaice. After frying, drain fish on soft kitchen paper and serve garnished with lemon wedges and parsley.

Poached salmon steaks

Serves 4

Put 4 salmon steaks into a large frying pan and cover with court bouillon (see page 30). Slowly bring to boil and cover. Lower heat and poach gently for 7 to 10 minutes. Lift steaks out of pan, drain on soft kitchen paper and remove skin. Serve straight away with hollandaise sauce, (see page 98). Alternatively, leave salmon to cool in the cooking liquor and afterwards drain thoroughly. Remove skin then serve cold with mayonnaise or suitable variation (see page 99).

Rice-stuffed sole

Grilled halibut Colbert

Serves 4

4 slices halibut, each about 6 to 8oz (150 to 200gm)

1oz (25gm) butter, melted

salt and pepper to taste

Colbert butter (see page 101)

lemon wedges and watercress to garnish

1. Trim, wash and dry fish with soft kitchen paper.
2. Place in grill pan then brush with melted butter.
3. Sprinkle with salt and pepper and place under a pre-heated hot grill.
4. Grill 8 minutes. Turn fish over, brush with more butter and sprinkle with more salt and pepper.
5. Grill a further 7 minutes then top each piece with a pat of Colbert butter.
6. Serve straight away, garnished with lemon wedges and watercress.

Note

Instead of Colbert butter, maître d'hôtel or anchovy butter (see page 101) may be served with the fish.

Grilled turbot or salmon steaks

Serves 4

Cook as for grilled halibut, above. Serve with hollandaise or any other suitable sauce to taste (see page 98).

Fried trout with almonds

Serves 4

4 trout, cleaned but with the heads left on

2 level tablespoons flour, well-seasoned with salt and pepper

4oz (100gm) butter

1 dessertspoon olive oil

2 to 3oz (50 to 75gm) almonds, flaked

juice of ½ lemon

1. Wash and dry trout then dust lightly with seasoned flour.
2. Heat 2oz (50gm) butter and the oil in a frying pan.
3. Add trout, two at a time, and fry 10 minutes, turning once.
4. Drain well on soft kitchen paper and keep hot.
5. Wipe pan clean with soft kitchen paper.
6. Add rest of butter and almonds and fry gently until butter begins to turn golden brown.
7. Remove from heat and add lemon juice.
8. Pour over trout and serve straight away.

Grilled trout

Serves 4

4 trout, cleaned but with the heads left on

salt and pepper

1½oz (37gm) butter, melted

lemon wedges to garnish

1. Wash and dry fish and sprinkle with salt and pepper.
2. Place fish in grill pan and brush with butter.
3. Grill 6 to 7 minutes.
4. Turn fish over, brush with more butter and grill a further 5 to 6 minutes.
5. Serve straight away with wedges of lemon.

Baked whole salmon

Serves 10 to 12

1 whole salmon weighing about 5lb (2½ kilo)

1 large onion, sliced (optional)

1 breakfast cup parsley sprigs

salt and pepper to taste

1. Have salmon cleaned and scaled. Pre-heat oven to moderately hot, 375 deg F or gas 5 (190 deg C).
2. Wash salmon and wipe dry then stand it on a large piece of buttered aluminium foil.
3. Top with sliced onion (if used) and parsley.
4. Sprinkle with salt and pepper.
5. Wrap up loosely but securely, stand parcel in a large roasting tin and bake in centre of oven for approximately 45 minutes.
6. Serve hot with hollandaise sauce (see page 98), or cold with mayonnaise or suitable variation (see page 99).

Poached whole salmon

Serves 10 to 12

If preferred, whole salmon may be wrapped loosely in muslin, put into a fish kettle, covered with court bouillon (see page 30) and poached gently (with lid on pan) for 8 to 9 minutes per lb (½ kilo).

Baked salmon trout

Serves 6 to 8

Treat in the same way as whole salmon but cook salmon trout in the oven for 30 minutes or poach in water for 6 minutes per lb (½ kilo).

Buttered skate

Serves 4

2lb (1 kilo) skate wings, divided into 4 portions

fish stock

1 tablespoon vinegar

2oz (50gm) butter

1 tablespoon lemon juice

1 level tablespoon chopped parsley

1. Put fish into a shallow pan and cover with stock.
2. Add vinegar then slowly bring to boil.
3. Lower heat and cover pan. Simmer gently for 25 minutes.
4. Drain and keep warm.
5. Heat butter in a pan until it turns a deep gold.
6. Remove from heat and stir in lemon juice and parsley.
7. Pour over skate and serve straight away.

Moules marinière

Serves 4

4 pints (2½ litres) mussels

2oz (50gm) butter

1 medium onion, chopped

1 garlic clove, chopped

½ pint (250ml) dry white wine

1 level tablespoon flour

3 tablespoons cold water

salt and pepper to taste

2 level tablespoons chopped parsley

1. Remove mussel beards with scissors.
2. Put mussels into a colander and wash under cold running water, shaking colander all the time to prevent the shells from opening. Scrub each one with a stiff brush and wash again.
3. Melt butter in a pan. Add onion and garlic. Cover pan and simmer gently for about 7 minutes or until onion is soft but still white.
4. Add wine and mussels. Bring to boil and boil for 5 to 6 minutes.
5. Lift mussels immediately into a dish, discarding the empty half shells. Cover and keep hot.
6. Mix flour to a cream with cold water. Add to saucepan.
7. Cook, stirring, until liquid comes to the boil and thickens. Season to taste with salt and pepper and simmer for 2 minutes.
8. Pour on to mussels then ladle into 4 warm soup plates.
9. Sprinkle each with chopped parsley and serve straight away, with white bread.

Prawn provençale

Illustrated on page 29

Serves 2

1oz (25gm) butter or margarine

1 small onion, chopped

1 small garlic clove, chopped

8oz (200gm) tomatoes, skinned

1 level teaspoon tomato paste

salt and pepper

½ level teaspoon sugar

2 level teaspoons cornflour

1 tablespoon cold water

6oz (150gm) peeled prawns

6oz (150gm) long-grain rice, freshly cooked (raw weight)

1 level tablespoon chopped parsley to garnish

1. Melt butter or margarine in pan.
2. Add onion and garlic. Cover and cook slowly for 10 minutes.
3. Roughly chop tomatoes and add to pan with tomato paste, salt and pepper to taste and sugar.
4. Cook 5 minutes.
5. Blend cornflour to a smooth cream with water and stir into pan.
6. Cook, stirring, until sauce comes to boil.
7. Add prawns and stir well to mix.
8. Arrange rice in a ring on a warm serving dish.
9. Transfer sauce with prawns into centre and sprinkle with chopped parsley.

Prawn fiesta

Serves 4

8oz (200gm) peeled prawns

1 standard egg, beaten

2oz (50gm) fresh white breadcrumbs

12oz (300gm) tomatoes, skinned

2oz (50gm) butter

2oz (50gm) mushrooms, finely chopped

2oz (50gm) lean ham, finely chopped

1 tablespoon dry sherry

¼ level teaspoon paprika

salt and pepper to taste

3 unpeeled prawns to garnish

1. Toss prawns in beaten egg then coat with crumbs.
2. Peel and quarter tomatoes and remove seeds. Keep for tomato juice or to add to soups and stews.
3. Cut quarters into fairly fine shreds.
4. Melt butter in a flameproof frying pan.
5. Add mushrooms and cook gently for 3 minutes.
6. Add ham, crumbed prawns and shreds of tomato.
7. Heat slowly together, turning frequently.
8. Stir in sherry and paprika, then season well to taste with salt and pepper.
9. Garnish with whole prawns and serve straight away from the pan.

Dressed crab

Serves 2 to 3

Buy a medium to large freshly-boiled crab from the fishmonger. Stand the crab on its back and twist off legs and claws. Separate body from shell by pressing upwards from tail flap. Remove stomach bag (below head) from shell together with feathery gills. Discard also any green matter. Spoon brown meat into a basin. Crack claws (except tiny ones) then remove white meat. Put into separate basin with white meat from body. Break off rough edges round shell then wash thoroughly and dry. If liked, shell may be wiped with a little salad oil to give it a shine. To the brown meat, add 2 level tablespoons fresh white breadcrumbs, ½ level teaspoon prepared mustard, 1 tablespoon double cream and 1 dessertspoon lemon juice. Mix thoroughly and arrange in centre of shell. Season white meat with a little pepper and salt. Arrange in shell on either side of brown meat. Garnish with lines of finely-chopped parsley, chopped hard-boiled egg white and sieved hard-boiled egg yolk. Serve with salad.

Prawn fiesta

Baked crab

Serves 2 to 3

Prepare as for dressed crab, left, but combine both white and dark meats in a basin. Add 4 level tablespoons fresh white breadcrumbs, 1 teaspoon Worcestershire sauce, ½ level teaspoon prepared mustard, 2 tablespoons double cream, ½oz (12gm) melted butter, 1 dessertspoon lemon juice and salt and pepper to taste. Return to washed and dried shell, sprinkle lightly with salt and pepper and dot with small flakes of butter. Heat through near top of moderate oven, 350 deg F or gas 4 (180 deg C), for 15 to 20 minutes.

Fried scampi

Serves 4

Allow 1lb (½ kilo) frozen scampi for 4 people. Coat with savoury fritter batter (see page 105) and deep fry as fried fish (see page 30), cooking 3 to 4 minutes. Serve with tartare sauce (see page 100) and lemon wedges. If preferred, coat scampi with beaten egg and toasted breadcrumbs instead of batter.

Scallops in cream sauce

Scallops in cream sauce

Serves 4

8 scallops

cold water

1 level teaspoon salt

1oz (25gm) butter or margarine

1oz (25gm) flour

$\frac{1}{4}$ pint (125ml) single cream

1 level tablespoon finely-chopped parsley

salt and pepper to taste

1 egg yolk

1 tomato, skinned and cut into wedges, and parsley to garnish

1. Put washed scallops and orange roes into saucepan.
2. Cover with cold water and add salt.
3. Bring to boil and at once lower heat. Cover and poach 5 minutes.
4. Drain, reserving $\frac{1}{4}$ pint (125ml) fish liquor.
5. Cut each scallop into 4 pieces and leave on one side.
6. Melt butter or margarine in saucepan. Add flour and cook 2 minutes without browning.
7. Gradually blend in fish liquor and cream. Cook, stirring, until sauce comes to the boil and thickens.
8. Add parsley, salt and pepper to taste and the scallops.
9. Heat through gently for 5 minutes. Remove from heat and stir in egg yolk.
10. Transfer to 4 clean scallop shells or individual dishes and garnish with wedges of tomato and parsley.

Lobster thermidor

Serves 4

2 cooked lobsters, each about 1 to 1$\frac{1}{2}$lb ($\frac{1}{2}$ to $\frac{3}{4}$ kilo)

2$\frac{1}{2}$oz (62gm) butter

1 small onion, grated

6 tablespoons dry sherry

$\frac{1}{2}$ pint (125ml) béchamel sauce (see page 96)

4 tablespoons double cream

2 egg yolks

4 level tablespoons grated Parmesan cheese

$\frac{1}{2}$ level teaspoon French mustard

salt and pepper to taste

2 level tablespoons toasted breadcrumbs

1. Remove lobster meat from shells and cut into fairly small, neat cubes.
2. Melt 2oz (50gm) butter in a saucepan. Add onion, cover and fry very gently until soft but not brown.
3. Add the sherry and sauce and heat through gently for 10 minutes.
4. Stir in lobster meat and cream and heat through a further 5 minutes.
5. Add egg yolks, half the cheese, mustard and salt and pepper to taste.
6. Transfer to lobster shells, sprinkle with rest of cheese and crumbs then dot with flakes of remaining butter.
7. Brown under a hot grill and serve straight away.

Lobster newburg

Serves 4

2 cooked lobsters each about 1 to 1$\frac{1}{2}$lb ($\frac{1}{2}$ to $\frac{3}{4}$ kilo)

3$\frac{1}{2}$oz (87gm) butter

5 tablespoons dry sherry

$\frac{1}{4}$ pint (125ml) double cream

5 tablespoons single cream

3 egg yolks

salt and pepper to taste

2 level tablespoons white breadcrumbs

1. Remove lobster meat from shells and cut into fairly small, neat pieces.
2. Melt 3oz (75gm) butter in pan.
3. Add lobster and cook gently for 5 minutes.
4. Add sherry and cook a little more briskly until reduced by half.
5. Beat cream and egg yolks well together then season to taste with salt and pepper.
6. Add to pan of lobster and heat very gently without allowing mixture to boil until it thickens.
7. Transfer to lobster shells and sprinkle with crumbs.
8. Dot with flakes of remaining butter and brown quickly under a pre-heated grill.
9. Serve straight away.

Oysters

Make sure shells are tightly closed and allow 6 oysters per person. Open carefully and serve oysters in the deep half shells surrounded by their own liquor. They should be placed on crushed ice and accompanied with cayenne pepper or Tabasco and brown bread and butter.

Meat, poultry and game

Meat

General hints and tips

1. All meat is an excellent source of body-building protein and vitamins of the B group. The cheaper cuts are just as good nutritionally as the more expensive ones and in some cases have a better flavour.

2. When buying beef, make sure the flesh is bright red and 'marbled' or flecked with fat (which indicates that the meat will be tender) and that the fat surrounding the joint is creamy-yellow and firm. For lamb, the flesh should be pinky-red and the fat white, crumbly and fairly hard. For pork, the flesh should be pinky-beige and the fat soft and white. For veal, the flesh should look almost the same as pork if grass-fed; or very pale pinky-beige if milk-fed. There should be minimal fat surrounding the meat but white connective tissue (which cooks into jelly) is to be expected.

3. Choose prime cuts—which tenderise readily—for grilling, frying and roasting. The more muscular, coarser and sometimes bony cuts for stewing, casseroling and braising.

4. For boneless meat, allow between 4 and 8oz (100 to 200gm) per person; for meat with a moderate proportion of bone, between 8 and 12oz (200 to 300gm) per person; for meat which is very bony, up to 1lb (½ kilo) per person.

5. As soon as you have bought meat and reached home with it, unwrap it, stand it on a plate or in a shallow dish and put immediately into the refrigerator. Most meat may be kept for 2 to 3 days under refrigeration but minced meat, veal, pork, offal and sausages should be cooked within 24 hours.

6. All meat should be left uncovered in the refrigerator so that cold air from the cabinet is able to circulate round it satisfactorily.

7. Meat from the refrigerator should be allowed to reach room temperature before it is cooked.

8. When boiling any cut of meat, choose a large piece rather than a small piece; the latter is likely to lose flavour and become stringy.

9. To remove excess salt from a piece of salted meat or bacon, cover with cold water, bring to the boil and drain. Repeat once or twice more if meat is very salty. This is more effective than soaking in cold water.

10. Never turn grilled or fried meat by spearing it with a fork. This releases juices, resulting in loss of flavour and moisture. Cooking tongs are the best tool to use for turning steaks, chops, hamburgers and so forth.

11. Always make sure meat for frying is washed and wiped dry very thoroughly with paper towels. Wet meat put into hot fat causes dangerous spluttering.

12. When grilling meat, remove the grill pan from underneath the heating element before pre-heating the grill itself. If raw meat is put into a hot grill pan, it will stick to it immediately.

13. To make carving easier, leave a joint of roast meat to stand for about 5 to 10 minutes after it has come out of the oven.

14. To prevent dryness, left-over joints or small pieces of meat should be wrapped in foil before being refrigerated.

15. All stews may be pressure cooked for speed. Follow instruction booklet for time guide but as a general rule allow 10 to 15 minutes at 15lb (7 kilo) pressure.

Veal and tomato stewpot
(see page 76)

Beef

Roasting
All the rib cuts, sirloin, topside, aitch-bone and rump in one piece.

Grilling
Rump, fillet, Chateaubriand, tournedos and sirloin cuts to include porterhouse, T-bone and minute steaks.

Frying
Sirloin cuts.

Pot roasting
Topside, unsalted brisket and flank.

Boiling
Salted and unsalted silverside and brisket.

Stewing, braising, casseroling
Blade, chuck, leg, shin, flank, aitch-bone and topside.

Roast beef

Roast beef

Allow 8 to 12oz (200 to 300gm) of beef with bone, or 6 to 8oz (150 to 200gm) of beef without bone per person. Roast beef with bone in the centre of a moderate oven, 350 deg F or gas 4 (180 deg C), for 25 minutes per lb ($\frac{1}{2}$ kilo) and 25 minutes over; beef off the bone for 30 minutes per lb ($\frac{1}{2}$ kilo) and 30 minutes over. Well-cooked beef should be given an extra 5 to 10 minutes roasting time per lb ($\frac{1}{2}$ kilo); rare beef should be given 5 to 7 minutes less cooking than the standard time per lb ($\frac{1}{2}$ kilo). Place beef in roasting tin with fat side uppermost. Brush with melted dripping and roast for required amount of time, basting frequently.

Foil-wrapped joints should be loosely wrapped in foil and baked in centre of hot oven, 425 deg F or gas 7 (220 deg C), for length of time given per lb of unwrapped joints. No extra overtime, however, should be added. The foil should be opened up during the last 30 minutes to brown the meat.

Serve with Yorkshire pudding, gravy, horseradish sauce (see page 103), roast and boiled potatoes and green vegetables to taste.

Yorkshire pudding

Family size

4oz (100gm) plain flour
$\frac{1}{4}$ level teaspoon salt
1 standard egg
$\frac{1}{2}$ pint (125ml) milk
1oz (25gm) dripping

1. Pre-heat oven to moderately hot, 400 deg F or gas 6 (200 deg C).
2. Sift flour and salt into bowl.
3. Mix to a thick, creamy batter with unbeaten egg and half the milk. Beat thoroughly until air bubbles rise to the surface then gently stir in rest of milk.
4. Heat dripping in a 7-inch square roasting tin.
5. Pour in batter and bake 35 to 40 minutes or until well-risen and golden. Cut into portions and serve straight away.

Note
If cooked with unwrapped joints, where oven temperature is moderate, place as high up in the oven as possible. If cooked with wrapped joints, place pudding below centre of oven.

Boiled salted brisket served cold with salad and hard-boiled eggs

Boiled salted brisket

Serves 6 to 8

3 to 4lb (1½ to 2 kilo) salted brisket, rolled and tied

4 cloves

2 large onions

2 large carrots, each cut into 3 pieces

1 medium celery stalk, broken into 4

1 bay leaf

1. Put brisket into a large saucepan and cover with cold water. Bring to boil and drain. Repeat once more.
2. Cover brisket with fresh cold water. Press cloves into onions and add to pan with carrots, celery and bay leaf.
3. Bring to boil and remove any scum that rises to the surface.
4. Lower heat and cover. Simmer gently, allowing 45 minutes per lb (½ kilo) and 30 minutes over.
5. Drain and serve hot or cold, with vegetables to taste.

Note

If preferred, piece of brisket may be pressure cooked for 45 to 50 minutes at 15lb (approximately 7 kilo) pressure.

Boiled silverside with dumplings

Serves 6 to 8

Cook 3 to 4lb (1½ to 2 kilo) fresh, unsalted silverside as for boiled salted brisket, above, but do not boil up twice as directed. Instead, cover meat in pan with water, bring to boil and remove scum. Add 4 medium onions, 3 medium carrots, 2 medium celery stalks, ½ teacup parsley and 2 to 3 level teaspoons salt. About 30 minutes before beef is ready, make dumplings. Sift 4oz (100gm) self-raising flour and 1 level teaspoon salt into a bowl. Add 2oz (50gm) finely-shredded suet then mix to a soft dough with 3 to 4 tablespoons cold water. Shape into 12 small balls with floured hands and drop into saucepan. Cook 15 to 20 minutes or until dumplings are well-risen and float to top of pan. Transfer meat to a platter and surround with vegetables and dumplings. If liked, accompany with parsley sauce (see page 95).

Pot roasted beef

Serves about 6

4lb (2 kilo) unsalted brisket, thick flank or topside

salt and pepper

1oz (25gm) dripping

1 medium onion, peeled

2 cloves

1 small bay leaf

¼ pint (125ml) water (or for luxury touch use half water and half red wine)

2 level dessertspoons cornflour

½ pint (250ml) beef stock

1. Sprinkle meat with salt and pepper.
2. In heavy flameproof casserole, heat dripping until hot. Add meat and brown all over.
3. Add onion, cloves, bay leaf and water, and bring to boil.
4. Lower heat and cover. Cook approximately 3 hours or until tender, turning meat about 3 times.
5. Transfer joint to a warm dish and keep hot.
6. To make gravy, skim off all the fat from the casserole and remove onion, cloves and bay leaf.
7. Gradually mix cornflour to a smooth cream with beef stock.
8. Add to casserole. Cook, stirring, until gravy comes to the boil and thickens.
9. Season to taste with salt and pepper and, if necessary, deepen colour by adding a little yeast or beef extract.
10. Serve meat accompanied with the gravy.

Braised beef

Serves about 6

Choose same cuts and weight of beef as given in pot roasted beef (see this page). Sprinkle with salt and pepper. Brown in 1½oz (37gm) dripping or margarine in large flameproof casserole. Remove to plate. Thinly slice 1½lb (¾ kilo) mixed root vegetables, 2 medium onions and 2 celery stalks. Add to casserole, cover and fry slowly for 10 to 15 minutes or until lightly browned. Strain off excess fat then place beef on top of vegetables. Add 2 level tablespoons coarsely-chopped parsley and enough water just to cover the vegetables. Cover closely and simmer very gently for 2½ to 3 hours or until tender. Uncover and finish cooking in centre of hot oven, 425 deg F or gas 7 (220 deg C), for 30 to 45 minutes. Serve beef sliced with the braised vegetables.

Note

If liked, thicken liquor in pan by adding 1 level tablespoon cornflour blended until smooth with 1 tablespoon water. Bring to boil, stirring, and simmer 2 minutes.

Boiled silverside with dumplings

Pot roasted beef with vegetables

Serves 6

Make as pot roasted beef, above, but before cooking, surround meat with 2 sliced carrots, 2 sliced onions, 2 coarsely-chopped celery stalks, 1 small peeled and sliced turnip and 1 small peeled and sliced parsnip. Serve meat with the vegetables.

Note

If preferred, both the above dishes may be cooked in a cool oven, 300 deg F or gas 2 (150 deg C), for 3 to 3½ hours, instead of on top of the cooker.

Mixed vegetable stew

Stewed beef

Serves 4

1½ to 2lb (¾ to 1 kilo) stewing steak

2 level tablespoons flour, well-seasoned with salt, pepper and dry mustard

1oz (25gm) dripping or margarine or use 3 dessertspoons salad oil

2 medium onions, chopped

2 medium carrots, sliced

1 pint (approximately ½ litre) beef stock or water

salt and pepper to taste

1. Cut beef into 1-inch cubes and coat well with seasoned flour.
2. Heat dripping or margarine or salad oil in a saucepan. Add onions and carrots.
3. Cover with lid and fry gently for 5 minutes. Uncover and continue to fry until vegetables are deep gold.
4. Add meat and fry a little more quickly until pieces are brown and well-sealed.
5. Pour in stock or water then slowly bring to boil, stirring continuously.
6. Adjust seasoning to taste, lower heat and cover pan.
7. Simmer very gently for 2 to 2½ hours or until meat is tender.
8. Stir frequently and add a little more boiling stock or water if stew seems to be drying up too much.
9. Serve with boiled potatoes and vegetables to taste.

Note

1. If liked, use ¼ pint (125ml) red wine or tomato juice in place of ¼ pint (125ml) stock or water.
2. If wished, beef stew seasoning mix may be used, following directions on the packet.

Beef stew with dumplings

Serves 4

Make as for stewed beef (see this page). About 30 minutes before meat is ready, sift 4oz (100gm) self-raising flour and ½ level teaspoon salt into a bowl. Add 2oz (50gm) finely-shredded suet then mix to a soft dough with 3 to 4 tablespoons cold water. Shape into 12 small dumplings with floured hands and drop into stew. Cook 15 to 20 minutes or until dumplings are well-risen and float to the top of the pan.

Note

If liked, when making dumplings, ½ level teaspoon mixed herbs or 1 level dessertspoon chopped parsley may be added with the suet.

Mixed vegetable stew

Serves 4

Make as for stewed beef (see this page), but fry 2 to 3 slices of unpeeled courgettes and 3 or 4 skinned and chopped tomatoes with the onions and carrots.

Cobbler of beef

Serves 4

Make up stewed steak and turn into casserole dish. Leave until cold. To make cobbler topping, sift 8oz (200gm) self-raising flour, 1 level teaspoon dry mustard, pinch of Cayenne pepper and 1 level teaspoon salt into bowl. Rub in 2oz (50gm) margarine finely. Mix to a soft dough with ¼ pint (125ml) cold milk. Turn out on to floured surface and knead lightly until smooth. Roll out to ½ inch in thickness and cut into rounds with 1½-inch biscuit cutter. Place on top of meat, brush with egg and bake just above centre of hot oven, 425 deg F or gas 7 (220 deg C), for 15 minutes or until meat is hot and scones are well-risen and golden.

Brisket braise with apricots

Serves 6 to 8

4lb (2 kilo) rolled and unsalted brisket

2 level tablespoons flour

1½oz (37gm) dripping or margarine

2 large celery stalks, chopped

1 medium onion, chopped

1½ level teaspoons salt

good shake of pepper

1 level tablespoon tomato paste

¼ level teaspoon dried thyme

1 can (approximately 1lb or ½ kilo) apricot halves

½ pint (250ml) water

1½lb (¾ kilo) potatoes, peeled and quartered

liqueur glass of brandy (optional)

1. Pre-heat oven to moderate, 325 deg F or gas 3 (170 deg C).
2. Coat brisket all over with flour.
3. Melt dripping or margarine in a large heavy saucepan. Add brisket and fry fairly briskly until well-browned. Transfer to a large casserole dish.
4. Add celery and onion to remaining dripping or margarine in saucepan.
5. Fry slowly until pale gold then add salt, pepper, tomato paste, thyme, apricots (including syrup from can) and water.
6. Bring to boil then spoon into casserole around meat.
7. Cover with lid or aluminium foil and cook in centre of oven for 3 to 3½ hours or until meat is tender.
8. About 45 minutes before meat is ready, par-boil potatoes in boiling salted water for 5 minutes. Drain and add to casserole with brandy, if used.
9. Re-cover and return to oven.
10. Accompany with broccoli or French beans.

Belgian carbonnade of beef

Serves 4

1½ to 2lb (¾ to 1 kilo) stewing steak

1½oz (37gm) margarine or 2 tablespoons salad oil

12oz (300gm) onions, chopped

1 garlic clove, chopped

3oz (75gm) lean bacon, chopped

½ pint (250ml) brown ale or stout

½ pint (250ml) beef stock

1 to 2 level teaspoons salt

1oz (25gm) flour

2 to 3 level tablespoons chopped parsley

1. Cut meat into 1-inch cubes.
2. Heat margarine, dripping or oil in a saucepan. Add onions, garlic and bacon and fry gently until onions are pale gold.
3. Add meat and fry a little more briskly until pieces are browned and well-sealed.
4. Pour in ale or stout and all but 5 table-spoons stock.
5. Add salt then bring to the boil.
6. Lower heat and cover pan. Simmer gently for 2 hours or until meat is tender, stirring from time to time.
7. Mix flour to a smooth cream with remaining stock. Add a little hot beer liquid then return to saucepan.
8. Cook, stirring gently, until carbonnade thickens then stir in parsley.
9. Serve with freshly-boiled potatoes and green vegetables to taste.

African beef stew served with creamed potatoes and peas

African beef stew

Serves 4

1½ to 2lb (¾ to 1 kilo) stewing steak

1½oz (37gm) butter or margarine or 2 tablespoons salad oil

2 medium onions, chopped

2 medium carrots, sliced

1 to 2 garlic cloves, chopped

2 level tablespoons tomato paste

¼ level teaspoon each ground cloves and ginger

pinch of Cayenne pepper or shake of Tabasco

1 to 2 level teaspoons salt

1 teaspoon vinegar

½ pint (250ml) beef stock or water

2 level tablespoons smooth peanut butter

1 level dessertspoon flour

1. Cut beef into 1-inch cubes.
2. Heat butter or margarine or oil in saucepan.
3. Add onions, carrots and garlic and fry very gently until pale gold.
4. Add beef cubes and fry a little more briskly until well-sealed and brown.
5. Stir in tomato paste, cloves, ginger, Cayenne pepper or Tabasco, salt and vinegar.
6. Pour in stock or water then bring to boil.
7. Lower heat and cover. Simmer gently for 2 hours or until meat is tender, stirring from time to time.
8. Mix peanut butter and flour well to-gether.
9. Add, a little at a time, to the simmering stew and stir until stew thickens. Serve with creamed potatoes and peas.

Hungarian goulash served with potatoes

Hungarian goulash

Serves 4

2oz (50gm) lard or dripping

1lb (½ kilo) onions, chopped

2 garlic cloves, chopped

1½ to 2lb (¾ to 1 kilo) stewing steak (or mixture of stewing steak and pie veal)

1 large green pepper, de-seeded and cut into thin strips

2 level tablespoons paprika

1 level tablespoon tomato paste

½ level teaspoon caraway seeds

8oz (200gm) tomatoes, skinned and chopped

1 dessertspoon lemon juice

1 level teaspoon soft brown sugar

1 carton (¼ pint or 125ml) soured cream

4 tablespoons soured cream and paprika to garnish

1. Heat lard or dripping in large saucepan.
2. Add onions and garlic and fry very slowly, with lid on pan, for 15 minutes or until golden.
3. Cut beef (or beef and veal) into small cubes.
4. Add to pan and fry until well-sealed and brown.
5. Add green pepper strips and fry 5 minutes.
6. Stir in all remaining ingredients, except soured cream and garnish, and bring to boil, stirring.
7. Lower heat and cover. Simmer gently for 2 to 2½ hours or until meat is tender, stirring occasionally.
8. Remove from heat, stir in soured cream and transfer to a warm dish.
9. Spoon remaining soured cream over the top and dust lightly with paprika.
10. Accompany with freshly-boiled pota-toes.

Note
No additional water or stock should be necessary when making a goulash, as the meat and vegetables provide sufficient liquid of their own.

Steak pie

Serves 4 to 6

Cook stewed steak with 1½lb (¾ kilo) beef. Transfer to a 1 pint (approximately ½ litre) lipped pie dish, doming meat up in the centre. Leave until cold. Roll out 6oz (150gm) frozen puff pastry as directed on the packet or flaky pastry made with 8oz (200gm) flour (see page 111) to ¼ inch in thickness. From it cut a lid, about 1½ inches larger all the way round than edge of dish. Moisten lip with cold water and line with pastry strips, cut from trimmings. Cover with lid then press edges well together to seal. Flake up with the back of a knife then press into flutes. Brush with egg and decorate with pastry leaves. Brush leaves with more egg then bake pie just above centre of hot oven, 425 deg F or gas 7 (220 deg C), for 15 minutes. Lower heat to moderate, 350 deg F or gas 4 (180 deg C), and bake a further 15 to 20 minutes or until pastry is golden brown and crisp.

Steak and mushroom pie

Serves 4 to 6

Add 4 to 6oz (100 to 150gm) lightly fried, sliced mushrooms to the stewed beef.

Beef stroganoff with rice

Steak and kidney pudding

Serves 4

suet crust pastry made with 8oz (200gm) flour (see page 110)

12oz (300gm) stewing steak, cut into small cubes

6oz (150gm) ox kidney, cut into small cubes

2 level tablespoons flour, well-seasoned with salt and pepper

1 medium onion, chopped

3 tablespoons water, dry red wine or stout

1. Roll out two-thirds of the pastry and use to line a well-greased 1½ pint (approximately ¾ litre) pudding basin.
2. Coat meat and kidney with seasoned flour.
3. Put into pastry-lined dish with onion.
4. Add water, wine or stout then moisten edge of lining pastry with water.
5. Cover with rest of pastry, rolled into a lid, then press edges of pastry lining and lid well together to seal.
6. Cover with a double thickness of greased greaseproof paper or greased aluminium foil and tie to basin with fine string.
7. Steam in saucepan of steadily boiling water for 3½ to 4 hours.
8. Remove foil from saucepan and uncover.
9. Serve from the dish with a clean napkin tied round it.

Note
Watch the water carefully in the saucepan and replenish with more boiling water when necessary.

Beef stroganoff

Serves 6

1½lb (¾ kilo) fillet or rump steak

3oz (75gm) butter

1 small onion, grated

12oz (300gm) mushrooms, sliced

salt and pepper to taste

3 tablespoons dry sherry

½ pint (250ml) soured cream

8oz (200gm) freshly-boiled long grain rice (raw weight)

or 1lb (½ kilo) freshly-cooked ribbon noodles

chopped parsley to garnish

1. Cut steak into slices, ¼ inch thick, and beat until very thin.
2. Cut slices, across grain, into strips, ½ inch wide.
3. Melt half the butter in a large frying pan.
4. Add onion and fry gently for 5 minutes.
5. Add steak strips and fry 5 minutes, turning all the time. Remove to a plate and keep hot.
6. Add rest of butter to pan and melt.
7. Add mushrooms and fry fairly briskly for 4 minutes.
8. Return steak to pan and sprinkle with salt and pepper to taste.
9. Pour sherry over meat then stir in soured cream.
10. Re-heat without boiling and serve straight away with rice or noodles, garnished with parsley.

Note
If preferred, beef stroganoff seasoning mix may be used following directions on the packet.

Boeuf bourguignonne

Serves 6

$2\frac{1}{2}$lb ($1\frac{1}{4}$ kilo) chuck steak or topside

2 level tablespoons cornflour, well-seasoned with salt and pepper

$1\frac{1}{2}$oz (37gm) butter or margarine

2 teaspoons olive oil

1 large onion, chopped

1 garlic clove, chopped

4oz (100gm) lean bacon, chopped

bouquet garni, tied in muslin bag, made from 1 sprig parsley, 4 black peppercorns, 1 bay leaf and a pinch of dried thyme

$\frac{1}{2}$ pint (250ml) burgundy

$\frac{3}{4}$ pint (375ml) beef stock

12 tiny onions or shallots, peeled and left whole

6oz (150gm) mushrooms, thinly sliced

2 level tablespoons chopped parsley

1. Cut meat into 1-inch cubes and coat with seasoned cornflour.
2. Heat butter or margarine and oil in saucepan. Add onion, garlic and bacon and fry gently until pale gold.
3. Add beef and fry a little more briskly until well-sealed and brown.
4. Add bouquet garni, burgundy and stock.
5. Cook, stirring continuously, until mixture comes to the boil. Adjust seasoning to taste.
6. Lower heat and cover. Simmer gently for 2 hours, stirring occasionally.
7. Add tiny onions or shallots and cook a further 20 minutes.
8. Add mushrooms and cook a further 10 minutes.
9. Transfer to a warm serving dish and sprinkle with chopped parsley. Accompany with freshly-boiled potatoes.

Grilled steak

Serves 4

Choose 4 slices, each 1 inch thick, of suitable steak (see page 46), each weighing about 6oz (150gm). Brush with melted butter or salad oil and place in grill pan. Put under pre-heated hot grill and grill under medium heat, allowing 6 to 7 minutes for rare steaks, 10 minutes for medium rare steaks and 15 minutes for well-done steaks. Turn twice, using kitchen tongs. Serve topped with suitable savoury butter or accompany with béarnaise sauce (see page 99). Garnish with watercress, grilled tomatoes and mushrooms.

Note

If steaks are thicker, allow an extra 2 minutes' cooking time. If thinner than 1 inch, allow 1 to 2 minutes less cooking time.

Pepper steak

Follow instructions for grilled steak, above, but before cooking, crush 2 level tablespoons black peppercorns with a rolling pin and press into steak with palms of hands. Brush with melted butter or oil and cook as directed.

Ingredients for boeuf bourguignonne

Steak Diane

Serves 4

3oz (75gm) butter

2 teaspoons olive oil

4 minute steaks (thin steaks cut from upper part of sirloin)

1 to 2 tablespoons Worcestershire sauce

2 level tablespoons finely-chopped parsley

1. Melt butter in large frying pan. Add oil.
2. When hot and sizzling, add steaks and fry briskly, allowing 1 minute per side.
3. Remove to a warm platter and keep hot.
4. Add Worcestershire sauce and parsley to rest of butter in pan and heat through gently.
5. Pour over steaks and serve straight away.

Tournedos

Serves 4

4 tournedos (round steaks cut from fillet) each about 2 inches thick and 5oz (125gm) in weight

4 rounds of white bread, a little larger than fillets

2oz (50gm) butter, melted

béarnaise sauce (see page 99)

Follow instructions for grilled steak (see this page), but grill the tournedos an extra 1 to 2 minutes to allow for the additional thickness of the steak. Fry bread in butter until golden and crisp on both sides. Transfer to 4 warm plates and top each round of bread with a cooked steak. Coat with béarnaise sauce and serve straight away.

Tournedos Rossini

Prepare as for tournedos, above, but place a slice of pâté de fois gras on each fried bread round before adding the cooked steak. Surround each with Madeira sauce (see page 98).

Fillet of beef in pastry

Serves 6

2lb (1 kilo) fillet of beef, in one piece

3oz (75gm) butter

1 small onion, finely chopped

4oz (100gm) mushrooms, finely chopped

$\frac{1}{2}$ level teaspoon mixed herbs

salt and pepper to taste

2oz (50gm) good quality pâté de fois or soft German liver sausage

1 large packet (approximately 9oz or 225gm) frozen puff pastry, thawed

beaten egg for brushing

1. Pre-heat oven to hot, 425 deg F or gas 7 (220 deg C).
2. Trim fillet to a neat shape then sauté in the butter for 10 minutes or until brown and well-sealed.
3. Remove to a plate and leave until cold.
4. Add onion to remaining butter in pan and fry very gently until soft and pale gold.
5. Add mushrooms and fry a further 3 minutes, turning all the time.
6. Stir in herbs then season well to taste with salt and pepper.
7. Roll out pastry into a rectangle large enough to enclose meat completely. Trim edges and reserve.
8. Place meat on one side of pastry then spread top of beef with pâté or liver sausage and mushroom mixture.
9. Moisten edges of pastry with water then wrap round meat, pressing all joins well together to seal.
10. Brush with beaten egg then decorate with pastry leaves, rolled and cut from trimmings.
11. Brush leaves with more egg then bake fillet just above centre of oven for 40 minutes (a little longer for well-done beef).
12. Cut into slices and accompany with Madeira sauce (see page 98).

Curried beef in rice ring

Curried beef in rice ring

Serves 4

2lb (1 kilo) stewing steak, cubed

2oz (50gm) butter or lard

1 small onion, chopped

1 garlic clove, chopped

1 cooking apple, peeled and chopped

2 to 4 level tablespoons curry powder

1 pint (approximately ½ litre) beef stock or water

1 level teaspoon salt

1 small bay leaf

2 level tablespoons mango chutney

juice of ½ lemon

2 level tablespoons raisins

1 level tablespoon cornflour blended until smooth with 2 tablespoons cold water

8oz (200gm) freshly-cooked long grain rice (raw weight)

2 heaped tablespoons cooked peas

2 heaped tablespoons cooked and diced carrots

2 level tablespoons canned red pimiento, chopped

1. Brown beef cubes in the hot butter or lard. Remove to a plate.
2. Add onion, garlic and apple to remaining fat in pan and fry gently for 5 minutes or until pale gold.
3. Stir in curry powder then gradually blend in stock or water.
4. Bring to boil, stirring, then add salt, bay leaf, chutney, lemon juice, raisins and beef.
5. Lower heat and cover pan then simmer gently for about 2 hours or until meat is tender. Stir occasionally.
6. Remove bay leaf and stir in blended cornflour.
7. Bring to the boil, stirring, then simmer 2 minutes. Leave over low heat while finishing rice ring.
8. Combine rice with all remaining ingredients.
9. Press into a 2½ pint (1½ litre) ring mould and invert on to a warm plate (rice should hold its shape).
10. Fill centre with beef curry and serve straight away with side dishes of chutney, sliced tomatoes, natural yogurt combined with coarsely-chopped salted peanuts and finely-chopped celery sprinkled with lemon juice.

Scottish mince

Serves 4 to 6

2oz (50gm) butter

2 medium onions, chopped

4oz (100gm) carrots, coarsely grated

1½lb (¾ kilo) raw minced beef

2 level tablespoons medium oatmeal

1 level tablespoon tomato paste

¾ pint (375ml) beef stock

salt and pepper to taste

1. Melt butter in a saucepan. Add onions and carrots and fry gently until soft and pale gold.
2. Add beef and fry a little more briskly until well-browned, breaking it up with a fork all the time.
3. Stir in oatmeal and tomato paste then gradually blend in stock.
4. Season to taste with salt and pepper and bring to boil, stirring.
5. Lower heat and cover pan.
6. Simmer gently for 45 minutes, stirring occasionally.
7. Serve hot with creamed potatoes and a green vegetable.

Savoury stuffed apples

Serves 4

Make up Scottish mince, as above, halving all the ingredients. When cooked, stir in 1 level tablespoon seedless raisins and 1 level tablespoon flaked almonds. Core 4 medium cooking apples and place in a deep heat-proof dish. Fill centres with minced beef, spooning any surplus around apples. Pour ¼ pint (125ml) well-seasoned beef stock into dish then cover with buttered aluminium foil. Bake in centre of moderate oven, 350 deg F or gas 4 (180 deg C), for 35 to 45 minutes or until apples are tender. Serve straight away, garnished with parsley and a bay leaf in each apple.

Steak with port and peaches

Serves 4

8oz (200gm) button mushrooms

2½oz (62gm) butter

salt and pepper to taste

1 large can (approximately 2lb or 1 kilo) cling peach halves

4 rump or fillet steaks, each about 6oz (150gm)

6 tablespoons port

4 slices bread, fried in butter and kept hot

1 tablespoon double cream

watercress or parsley to garnish

1. Brown mushrooms quickly in half the butter. Season to taste with salt and pepper.
2. Heat peaches in their own syrup. Strain and keep warm.
3. Melt remaining butter in another, larger pan and quickly brown steaks on both sides.
4. Remove from pan and keep warm.
5. Add port to juices in the pan and bring to boil.
6. Replace steaks, add mushrooms and drained peaches and simmer 5 minutes.
7. Serve steaks on slices of fried bread, garnished with peaches and mushrooms.
8. Add cream to sauce and bring to the boil.
9. Cover each steak with a little sauce and serve remainder in a sauceboat.
10. If liked, decorate dish with a little watercress or parsley and serve straight away.

Right: savoury stuffed apples garnished with bay leaves.
Below: steak with port and peaches

Beef loaf

Serves 4 to 6

1½lb (¾ kilo) raw minced beef
3oz (75gm) fresh white breadcrumbs
1 medium onion, finely grated
1 tablespoon tomato ketchup
½ level teaspoon mixed herbs
1 level teaspoon made mustard
¼ level teaspoon garlic salt (optional)
1 large egg, beaten
¼ pint (125ml) beef stock or water
salt and pepper to taste

1. Pre-heat oven to moderate, 350 deg F or gas 4 (180 deg C).
2. Combine meat with all remaining ingredients and mix thoroughly.
3. Shape into a 3-inch high loaf and place on foil-lined baking tray.
4. Bake in centre of oven for approximately 1 hour.
5. Serve hot with vegetables and accompany with a suitable sauce. Alternatively, serve cold, garnished with gherkins, olives, watercress and tomatoes and accompany with a mixed salad.

Note
1. Any left-over loaf makes an excellent sandwich filling.
2. If preferred, use 2lb (1 kilo) raw minced beef plus a packet of meat loaf seasoning mix.

Above: beef loaf with mixed salad. Below: classic hamburger

Classic hamburgers

Serves 4

1lb (½ kilo) raw minced beef
1 small onion, grated
1 standard egg, beaten
½ level teaspoon salt
½ level teaspoon pepper
1½oz (37gm) butter or margarine

1. Mix all ingredients, except butter or margarine, well together.
2. Divide into 4 equal portions and shape into cakes, 1 inch thick.
3. Fry in hot butter or margarine for 8 to 10 minutes, turning twice.
4. Remove from pan and serve hot with chips, vegetables to taste and tomato ketchup. Alternatively, place between sliced hamburger buns with fried onions and fried tomato slices. Serve with chips and salad.

Meat balls in mushroom sauce

Serves 4

Make up classic hamburger recipe, as above, but divide mixture into 16 equal sized pieces and shape into balls. Make up ½ pint (250ml) mushroom pouring sauce (see page 95). Add meat balls and simmer very gently for 20 minutes. Serve with rice, noodles or creamed potatoes and green vegetables to taste.

Chilli con carne

Serves 6

12oz (300gm) long grain rice
1½ pints (¾ litre) water
1½ level teaspoons salt
1½lb (¾ kilo) raw minced beef
1 garlic clove, chopped
3 tablespoons salad oil
salt and chilli powder
1lb (½ kilo) tomatoes, skinned
1½ pints (approximately ¾ litre) beef stock
1 can (approximately 1lb or ½ kilo) red kidney beans, drained

1. Put rice, water and salt into saucepan.
2. Bring to the boil and stir once.
3. Lower heat, cover tightly and simmer 15 minutes or until rice is tender and fluffy and liquid absorbed.
4. Meanwhile, fry meat and garlic in the oil.
5. Add salt to taste then spice heavily with chilli powder.
6. Add tomatoes and stock, bring to boil and lower heat.
7. Simmer 10 minutes, add beans and heat through a further 5 minutes.
8. Serve on bed of rice.

Lattice beef pie

Serves 6

short crust pastry made with 6oz (150gm) flour (see page 108)
1oz (25gm) dripping
1 large onion, chopped
1lb (½ kilo) raw minced beef, as lean as possible
6oz (150gm) mushrooms, sliced
6 tablespoons tomato ketchup
¼ pint (125ml) water
3 level dessertspoons cornflour
½ level teaspoon garlic salt (optional)
salt and pepper to taste
2 large tomatoes, skinned and sliced
beaten egg for brushing

1. Pre-heat oven to moderately hot, 375 deg F or gas 5 (190 deg C).
2. Roll out pastry and use to line an 8-inch shallow heatproof dish. Reserve trimmings.
3. Heat dripping in pan. Add onion and fry gently until pale gold.
4. Add meat and mushrooms, and fry until well-browned, breaking up the meat with a fork all the time.
5. Remove from heat and stir in ketchup, water, cornflour, garlic salt (if used) and salt and pepper to taste.
6. Transfer to pastry-lined dish then top with slices of tomato.
7. Add a lattice design of pastry strips cut from trimmings, moisten tips with water and press well on to lining pastry to seal.
8. Brush with beaten egg then bake in centre of oven for 45 minutes. Serve hot.

Above: chilli con carne with rice. Below: lattice beef pie

Beef galantine

Dutch meat balls

Serves 4

1lb (½ kilo) raw minced beef

1 medium onion, very finely chopped

1 level tablespoon finely-chopped parsley

1oz (25gm) fresh white breadcrumbs

¼ level teaspoon garlic powder

pinch of nutmeg

salt and pepper to taste

2 standard eggs

toasted breadcrumbs for coating

4oz (100gm) Dutch butter for frying

parsley to garnish

1. Combine beef with onion, parsley, fresh breadcrumbs, garlic powder, nutmeg, salt and pepper to taste and 1 beaten egg. Mix thoroughly.
2. Shape into 8 even-sized balls with damp hands.
3. Dip balls in second beaten egg then toss in toasted crumbs.
4. Heat butter in a frying pan until it sizzles. Add coated beef balls and fry until crisp and golden all over, turning frequently.
5. Lower heat and fry over a medium heat for approximately 15 to 20 minutes or until meat balls are cooked through. Turn frequently.
6. Serve on a bed of freshly-cooked wide noodles, garnished with parsley.

Marinated and grilled beef

Serves 4 to 6

2lb (1 kilo) beef skirt

4 tablespoons Worcestershire sauce

2 tablespoons salad oil

4 tablespoons dry cider

juice of ½ lemon

salt to taste

2oz (50gm) butter, melted

1 small onion, finely grated

1 level teaspoon Continental mustard

6 midget gherkins, very finely chopped

2 tablespoons double cream

1. Place beef in a glass or enamel dish.
2. To make marinade, beat 3 tablespoons Worcestershire sauce with oil, cider, lemon juice and salt to taste.
3. Pour over beef. Cover and leave to marinate between 4 to 6 hours, turning twice.
4. To make grilling sauce, beat all remaining ingredients well together.
5. Remove beef from marinade and place in grill pan.
6. Spread with sauce and grill for a total of 20 minutes under a hot grill, turning at least 3 times and brushing beef every time with more sauce.
7. To carve, transfer to a board and cut into fairly thin diagonal slices.
8. Serve with jacket or roast potatoes and vegetables to taste.

Corned beef Alaska

Serves 4

1 large can (12oz or 300gm) corned beef

1 tablespoon tomato ketchup

1½lb (¾ kilo) freshly-boiled potatoes

1oz (25gm) butter or margarine

hot milk

salt and pepper to taste

1oz (25gm) Cheddar cheese, finely grated

1. Pre-heat oven to moderately hot, 400 deg F or gas 6 (200 deg C).
2. Stand corned beef on a greased heatproof plate. Spread with ketchup.
3. Mash potatoes finely then beat to a light cream with butter or margarine and hot milk.
4. Season to taste with salt and pepper and pile over corned beef.
5. Sprinkle with cheese and bake just above centre of oven for 30 minutes or until brown and heated through.
6. Serve straight away.

Beef galantine

Serves 6 to 8

1lb (½ kilo) raw minced beef

8oz (200gm) pork sausagemeat

6oz (150gm) fresh white breadcrumbs

salt and pepper to taste

½ level teaspoon powdered allspice

1 standard egg, beaten

1 teaspoon Tabasco

½ pint (250ml) beef stock

½ pint (250ml) aspic jelly

strips of canned pimiento

2 hard-boiled eggs

parsley sprigs to garnish

1. Pre-heat oven to moderately hot, 375 deg F or gas 5 (190 deg C).
2. Brush a 2lb (1 kilo) loaf tin with melted fat then line base and sides with foil. Brush with more fat.
3. Combine beef with sausagemeat, crumbs, salt and pepper, allspice, egg, Tabasco and stock, mixing thoroughly with a fork.
4. Transfer to prepared tin, smooth top with a knife then cover with a piece of greased foil.
5. Place in a roasting tin containing 2 inches of cold water and bake in centre of oven for 2 hours.
6. Allow to cool then remove from tin. Strip off foil when cold.
7. When aspic jelly is cold and just beginning to thicken and set, brush thickly over top and sides of galantine.
8. Leave until firm and set then decorate top with a diamond design made from pimiento strips.
9. Fill in 'diamonds' with chopped egg white and sieved egg yolk then transfer to a plate.
10. Outline lower edges with parsley sprigs.

Left: Dutch meat balls with noodles
Right: corned beef Alaska

Savoy rolls with pepper sauce

Serves 4

Make as for dolmas (see this page), using Savoy cabbage leaves. When cooked, place on a bed of creamed potatoes and keep hot. Strain tomato sauce into a saucepan. Stir in 2 level tablespoons cornflour mixed to a smooth cream with 3 tablespoons cold water. Cook, stirring continuously, until sauce comes to the boil and thickens. Add 4 tablespoons chopped canned pimiento and adjust seasoning to taste. Pour round potatoes and serve straight away, garnished with pieces of red pimiento.

Cottage pie

Serves 4

1oz (25gm) butter or dripping

1 large onion, chopped

1lb (½ kilo) raw minced beef

1 level tablespoon flour

¼ pint (125ml) beef stock or water

salt and pepper to taste

1½lb (¾ kilo) freshly-boiled potatoes

1½oz (37gm) butter

2 tablespoons hot milk

beaten egg for brushing

1. Pre-heat oven to moderate, 350 deg F or gas 4 (180 deg C).
2. Heat butter or dripping in saucepan. Add onion and fry gently until pale gold.
3. Add meat and fry a little more briskly until lightly brown, breaking it up with a fork all the time.
4. Stir in flour then blend in stock or water.
5. Bring to boil and simmer 5 minutes, stirring. Season well to taste with salt and pepper.
6. Transfer to a greased dish of about 2 inches in depth.
7. Mash potatoes finely with butter then beat in milk.
8. Season to taste with salt and pepper then spoon over mince.
9. Brush lightly with beaten egg then cook in centre of oven for 30 minutes.

Note

1. To add an unusual flavour touch, add 2 or 3 teaspoons Angostura bitters to the meat mixture.
2. If preferred, cottage pie may be made with 1lb (½ kilo) cold roast beef, finely minced.

Savoy rolls with pepper sauce served on a bed of creamed potatoes

Cornish style pasties

Makes 4

8oz (200gm) topside or chuck steak

4oz (100gm) kidney

4oz (100gm) raw potato

1 medium onion

1 tablespoon water

salt and pepper to taste

short crust pastry made with 12oz (300gm) flour (see page 108)

beaten egg for brushing

1. Pre-heat oven to hot, 425 deg F or gas 7 (220 deg C).
2. Cut meat, kidney and potato into tiny cubes. Put into bowl.
3. Grate onion and add with water then season to taste with salt and pepper.
4. Divide pastry into 4 equal pieces then roll into 8-inch rounds.
5. Put equal amounts of filling on to each then moisten edges of pastry with water.
6. Bring edges of pastry together across the top of each pastry then press well together to seal.
7. Pinch into flutes with fingers then place on greased baking tray.
8. Brush with beaten egg and bake just above centre of oven for 15 minutes.
9. Reduce temperature to moderate, 325 deg F or gas 3 (170 deg C), and cook a further 50 minutes.
10. Serve hot or cold.

Dolmas or stuffed cabbage leaves

Serves 4

12 large cabbage leaves

2 pints (approximately 1¼ litre) boiling water

1 level teaspoon salt

12oz (300gm) cooked long grain rice (cooked weight)

8oz (200gm) cold roast beef, finely chopped

½ level teaspoon thyme

1 small onion, finely grated

1 can (approximately 14oz or 350gm) tomato juice

1 level teaspoon sugar

1 level tablespoon finely-chopped parsley

1 level teaspoon onion or garlic salt

pepper to taste

1 level tablespoon finely-chopped parsley to garnish

1. Pre-heat oven to moderate, 325 deg F or gas 3 (170 deg C).
2. Cover cabbage leaves with boiling water to which salt has been added.
3. Leave 3 minutes. Drain. When cool enough to handle, cut away hard part of stalk at base of each leaf.
4. To make filling, combine rice with beef, thyme and onion.
5. Put equal amounts on to cabbage leaves.
6. Fold each up like a parcel, completely enclosing filling.
7. Tie with thick thread then place close together in a heatproof dish.
8. Combine all remaining ingredients, except garnish, well together then pour into dish over cabbage leaves.
9. Cover dish with lid or foil and cook in centre of oven for 1 hour.
10. Uncover and sprinkle with parsley.
11. Serve either hot or lightly chilled.

Cottage pie

Lamb

Cuts of lamb suitable for:

Roasting
Loin, shoulder, leg, best end neck and breast.

Frying and grilling
Loin and chump chops and cutlets cut from the best end neck. Fillet of lamb cut from top of leg.

Pot-roasting
Legs and half legs and shoulders.

Boiling
Leg of lamb or mutton.

Stewing, braising, casseroling
Best end neck, middle neck, scrag and breast

Roast lamb

Allow approximately 8 to 12oz (200 to 300gm) of any cut of lamb per person. This is because lamb has a high percentage of fat and bone and an allowance must be made for this.
Cook in the centre of a moderate oven, 350 deg F or gas 4 (180 deg C), for 25 minutes per lb ($\frac{1}{2}$ kilo) and 30 minutes over. Place lamb in roasting tin with fat side uppermost. Add no additional fat unless joint is especially lean. Roast for required amount of time, basting only once or twice. Foil-wrapped joints should be loosely wrapped in foil and roasted in centre of a hot oven, 425 deg F or gas 7 (220 deg C), allowing 30 minutes per lb plus 30 minutes over. Foil should be opened up during the last 30 minutes to brown the meat.
Serve with mint sauce or jelly, green peas, roast and boiled potatoes (tiny new potatoes are traditional) and gravy.

Honey glazed lamb

Serves 6

Sprinkle a medium leg or shoulder of lamb with 1 level tablespoon flour seasoned with salt, pepper and $\frac{1}{2}$ level teaspoon cinnamon. Slice 1 large carrot and 1 large onion coarsely. Chop 2 large celery stalks. Cover base of roasting tin with vegetables then place lamb joint on top. Roast, uncovered, as directed above. After 1 hour, turn joint over and baste well with pan juices. About 30 minutes before joint is ready, take out of oven. Place joint on a plate and drain off all the fat from the tin. Replace joint, best side up, and spread with 1 level tablespoon thick honey. Pour $\frac{1}{2}$ pint (250ml) dry cider into tin and continue roasting for required amount of time, basting frequently. Stand lamb on carving board and keep hot. Gradually mix 1 level tablespoon cornflour with $\frac{1}{4}$ pint (125ml) cold water. Pour into tin. Place over moderate heat and cook, stirring, until mixture comes to boil and thickens. Simmer 2 minutes. Strain and serve with the lamb.

Roast lamb with garlic and rosemary

Serves 6 to 8

Choose a leg of lamb weighing about 4lb (2 kilo). Using a metal skewer, puncture flesh fairly deeply and insert very thin slivers of garlic into each hole. Place in roasting tin then sprinkle joint with 1 to 2 level teaspoons crushed dried rosemary (or double quantity of fresh) and roast, uncovered, as directed in recipe for roast lamb (see this page).

Crown roast of lamb

Serves 6

| 1 crown of lamb, prepared from 2 best end necks of lamb, each with 6 or 7 cutlets |
| 1oz (25gm) butter or margarine |
| 1 dessertspoon salad oil |
| $\frac{1}{2}$ medium red pepper, de-seeded and chopped |
| $\frac{1}{2}$ medium green pepper, de-seeded and chopped |
| 2 medium celery stalks |
| 1 large onion, chopped |
| 8oz (200gm) long grain rice |
| 1 pint (approximately $\frac{1}{2}$ litre) chicken stock |
| salt and pepper to taste |
| 4oz (100gm) sultanas |
| 1 medium can apricot halves, drained |

1. Ask butcher to prepare a crown roast.
2. Pre-heat oven to moderately hot, 375 deg F or gas 5 (190 deg C).
3. Stand crown roast in a baking tin and cover completely with foil.
4. Roast near top of oven for 1$\frac{1}{4}$ hours, uncovering for the last half an hour.
5. Heat butter or margarine and oil in large pan. Add red and green pepper, celery and onion. Fry for 7 minutes or until golden.
6. Add rice and fry a further 2 minutes, turning all the time.
7. Pour in stock and season to taste with salt and pepper.
8. Bring to boil, stir twice with a fork and cover.
9. Lower heat and simmer 10 minutes.
10. Add sultanas and continue to cook for a further 10 minutes or until rice grains have absorbed all the moisture and are plump and tender.
11. Remove crown from oven and place on a warm platter.
12. Fill centre with rice mixture then arrange the rest in a border round the edge of the crown.
13. Garnish with apricot halves then put a cutlet frill on the top of each bone.

Note
Alternatively, fill crown with a freshly-cooked cauliflower or choose a suitable stuffing from the selection on pages 106, 107. Put stuffing into the crown 30 minutes before it is ready.

Crown roast of lamb

Lamb hot pot

Serves 4

| 2lb (1 kilo) middle neck of lamb |
| 1lb ($\frac{1}{2}$ kilo) potatoes, thinly sliced |
| 8oz (200gm) onions, thinly sliced |
| 3 medium celery stalks, cut into diagonal strips |
| 2 carrots, thinly sliced |
| 2 level tablespoons chopped parsley |
| salt and pepper to taste |
| chicken stock or water |
| $\frac{1}{2}$oz (12gm) butter or margarine |

1. Pre-heat oven to moderate, 350 deg F or gas 4 (180 deg C).
2. Divide lamb into neat pieces and trim away surplus fat.
3. Fill a large, lightly-greased casserole dish with alternate layers of lamb and vegetables, beginning and ending with potatoes and sprinkling parsley, salt and pepper between layers.
4. Half-fill dish with stock or water then dot top with flakes of butter or margarine.
5. Cover with lid and cook in centre of oven for 1$\frac{1}{2}$ hours.
6. Uncover and continue to cook until top layer of potatoes are brown and meat is tender.
7. Serve straight away.

Lancashire hot pot

Serves 4

Make as for lamb hot pot, above, using 1$\frac{1}{2}$lb ($\frac{3}{4}$ kilo) best end neck of lamb cutlets, 2 sliced lamb's kidneys and the same amount of potatoes and onions. Omit all other vegetables and the parsley, but put 8 to 10 oysters in the middle of the lamb and vegetables.

Lamb rosettes served on a bed of vegetables

Lamb rosettes

Serves 2 to 3

1lb ($\frac{1}{2}$ kilo) potatoes

1 red pepper

2 medium celery stalks

2 medium carrots

$\frac{1}{4}$ pint (125ml) dry cider

salt and pepper to taste

1 large lamb breast, boned, rolled and tied

parsley to garnish

1. Pre-heat oven to moderately hot, 400 deg F or gas 6 (200 deg C).
2. Slice potatoes fairly thickly.
3. Halve red pepper, remove seeds and fibres and cut flesh into thin strips.
4. Cut celery into diagonal slices then cut each carrot lengthwise into 4 long strips.
5. Put vegetables into roasting tin, add cider then sprinkle with salt and pepper to taste.
6. Place lamb on top, and cover tin with foil.
7. Roast in centre of oven for 1 hour.
8. Uncover and continue to roast until meat and vegetables are tender.
9. Arrange vegetables in a warm dish.
10. Cut lamb into slices and place on top of vegetables.
11. Garnish with parsley and serve straight away.

Fruit and nut lamb roast

Serves 8

a leg of lamb weighing 3 to 4lb (1$\frac{1}{2}$ to 2 kilo), already boned

1 medium onion

2oz (50gm) Brazil nuts

$\frac{1}{2}$ teacup parsley

1 can (approximately 1lb or $\frac{1}{2}$ kilo) apricot halves

4oz (100gm) fresh white breadcrumbs

$\frac{1}{2}$ level teaspoon salt

good shake of pepper

1 teaspoon lemon juice

1 level teaspoon orange peel, grated

1 standard egg, beaten

1oz (25gm) butter, melted

1. Pre-heat oven to moderate, 350 deg F or gas 4 (180 deg C).
2. Remove as much surplus fat as possible from lamb.
3. To make stuffing, chop onion, nuts and parsley.
4. Drain apricots (syrup may be kept for sauces and drinks) and chop roughly.
5. Add to onion mixture with crumbs, salt, pepper, lemon juice and orange peel.
6. Bind with beaten egg and melted butter then pack stuffing loosely into meat cavity.
7. Re-shape joint and hold in place with string or skewers.
8. Roast, uncovered, as directed in recipe for roast lamb (see page 59).
9. Serve hot with gravy, baked jacket potatoes, broccoli and carrots.

Navarin of lamb

Serves 4

2lb (1 kilo) best end of neck, divided into cutlets

3 dessertspoons melted dripping

1 level tablespoon flour

$\frac{3}{4}$ pint (375ml) water

2 level tablespoons tomato paste

2 level teaspoons salt

6 small carrots

3 small turnips, diced

1 dozen small onions or shallots

1lb ($\frac{1}{2}$ kilo) small potatoes

1 small packet frozen peas

3 level tablespoons chopped parsley

1. Trim excess fat away from cutlets.
2. Heat dripping in large pan. Add cutlets and fry until well sealed and golden. Remove to a plate.
3. Stir flour into rest of fat. Cook 2 minutes without browning.
4. Gradually blend in water. Add tomato paste and salt.
5. Cook, stirring, until mixture comes to boil.
6. Replace cutlets, lower heat and cover. Simmer very gently for 45 minutes, stirring occasionally.
7. Add carrots, turnips, onions or shallots and potatoes.
8. Cover and continue to cook slowly for a further 30 minutes.
9. Add peas and cook 5 minutes.
10. Transfer to a warm dish and sprinkle generously with parsley. Serve straight away.

Braised lamb breast

Serves 2 to 3

1oz (25gm) dripping

1lb (½ kilo) small carrots

1 large green pepper, de-seeded and cut into strips

1 large onion, chopped

1 breast of lamb, boned but not rolled

salt and pepper

hot water

1. Heat dripping in a flameproof casserole.
2. Add vegetables and cover. Fry slowly for 10 minutes or until pale gold.
3. Uncover and stand lamb on top.
4. Sprinkle with salt and pepper then add sufficient hot water just to cover vegetables.
5. Cover and simmer gently for 1 to 1½ hours or until meat is tender.
6. Uncover, skim off excess fat then cook in centre of hot oven, 425 deg F or gas 7 (220 deg C), for 15 to 25 minutes to brown meat.
7. Serve with creamed potatoes and brussels sprouts or cabbage.

Braised lamb breast

Haricot lamb

Serves 4

4oz (100gm) haricot beans, soaked overnight

1½oz (37gm) dripping or margarine

2 medium onions, chopped

1 medium turnip, diced

2 to 2½lb (1 to 1¼ kilo) middle neck of lamb

1oz (25gm) flour

1½ pints (approximately ¾ litre) water

2 level teaspoons salt

pepper to taste

1. Drain beans.
2. Melt dripping or margarine in saucepan. Add onions and turnip and fry gently until pale gold.
3. Meanwhile, divide meat into neat pieces and coat with flour.
4. Add to pan and fry fairly briskly until well-sealed and brown.
5. Add all remaining ingredients and bring to boil.
6. Lower heat and cover pan.
7. Simmer gently for 2 hours or until lamb and beans are tender, stirring occasionally.
8. Serve with boiled potatoes and a green vegetable.

Mixed grill

Serves 4

4 loin chops

4 lamb's kidneys, skinned

salt and pepper to taste

1½oz (37gm) butter, melted

4 chipolata sausages

12 button mushrooms

4 medium tomatoes, halved

4 rashers back bacon

watercress

potato crisps

savoury butter to taste (see page 101)

1. Put chops and kidneys into grill pan. Sprinkle with salt and pepper then brush with butter.
2. Place under pre-heated hot grill and grill 4 minutes. Turn.
3. Add sausages and mushrooms to pan. Sprinkle with salt and pepper then brush with more butter. Grill 5 minutes.
4. Turn all ingredients. Add tomatoes and bacon and brush with more butter.
5. Grill 5 minutes.
6. Transfer to a large platter and garnish with watercress and potato crisps. Put a pat of savoury butter on to each chop and serve straight away.

Ragoût of lamb

Serves 4

1oz (25gm) dripping or margarine

1 large onion, chopped

2oz (50gm) lean bacon, finely chopped

1 large carrot, finely grated

2lb (1 kilo) middle neck of lamb

2 level tablespoons flour, well-seasoned with salt and pepper

¾ pint (375ml) water

1 tablespoon canned red pimiento, chopped

lemon slices

1. Melt dripping or margarine in saucepan.
2. Add onion, bacon and carrot. Fry gently until pale gold.
3. Meanwhile, cut lamb into neat pieces and remove as much surplus fat as possible.
4. Coat meat with seasoned flour and fry fairly briskly until pieces are well-sealed and brown.
5. Pour in water and bring to boil, stirring. Adjust seasoning to taste.
6. Lower heat and cover pan. Simmer gently for 1 to 1½ hours or until meat is tender, stirring occasionally.
7. Serve on a platter surrounded with freshly-boiled rice and garnish with pimiento and lemon.

Ragoût of lamb served with rice

Chilli lamb

Serves 4

2lb (1 kilo) middle neck of lamb

1½oz (37gm) margarine or bacon dripping

8oz (200gm) onions, chopped

1 garlic clove, chopped

1½oz (37gm) flour, well-seasoned with salt

1lb (½ kilo) tomatoes, skinned and chopped

1 to 3 level teaspoons chilli powder (depending on taste)

shake of Tabasco

1 level dessertspoon golden syrup

½ pint (250ml) water

1. Divide lamb into neat pieces and trim off surplus fat.
2. Heat margarine or dripping in large pan. Add onions and garlic and fry gently until pale gold.
3. Coat lamb with seasoned flour. Add to pan and fry until brown and well-sealed.
4. Add tomatoes, chilli powder, Tabasco, syrup and water.
5. Bring to the boil, stirring, then adjust seasoning to taste.
6. Lower heat and cover.
7. Simmer gently for 1½ hours or until meat is tender, stirring occasionally.
8. Serve with freshly-boiled rice or boiled potatoes.

Shashlik or shish kebab

Serves 4

1 to 1½lb (½ to ¾ kilo) lamb fillet, cut from leg

4 tablespoons vinegar

4 tablespoons salad oil

2 bay leaves, crumbled

1 medium onion, coarsely chopped

1 garlic clove, chopped

½ level teaspoon salt

freshly-milled black pepper

8 rashers back bacon, rolled

16 button mushrooms

8 whole tomatoes, skinned

1. Cut meat into 1-inch cubes and put into glass dish.
2. Beat vinegar and oil well together. Stir in bay leaves, onion, garlic, salt and pepper to taste.
3. Pour over lamb, cover and leave to marinate in the refrigerator for a good 6 hours, turning twice.
4. Thread cubes of lamb on to long skewers alternately with bacon, mushrooms and tomatoes. Place in grill pan.
5. Brush with marinade and cook under pre-heated hot grill for about 15 minutes, turning frequently.
6. Serve straight away on a bed of freshly-boiled rice.

Curried lamb balls

Serves 4

1lb (½ kilo) lamb fillet, cut from leg and finely minced

1 small onion, finely minced or grated

2 level teaspoons curry powder

¼ level teaspoon garlic salt

1 level teaspoon salt

1 level tablespoon tomato paste

2oz (50gm) fresh white breadcrumbs

freshly-milled black pepper to taste

beaten egg

8 small onions, par-boiled

8 rashers streaky bacon, each rolled separately

2 tablespoons natural yogurt

1 tablespoon salad oil

1. Combine minced lamb with onion, curry powder, garlic salt, salt, tomato paste, breadcrumbs and pepper to taste.
2. Bind with beaten egg then shape into 16 small balls.
3. Thread on to skewers alternately with onions and bacon rashers.
4. Brush with yogurt, beaten with oil, and cook under a pre-heated hot grill for 15 minutes, turning frequently.
5. Serve on a bed of freshly-boiled rice.

Lamb curry

Serves 4 to 5

3lb (1½ kilo) best end neck of lamb

1½oz (37gm) margarine

1 large onion, chopped

1 garlic clove, chopped

2 level tablespoons flour

1 to 3 tablespoons curry powder (depending on taste)

½ level teaspoon each cinnamon and ginger

2 level tablespoons tomato paste

¾ pint (375ml) beef stock

8oz (200gm) carrots, grated

1 can (approximately 1lb or ½ kilo) fruit cocktail

1 to 2 level teaspoons salt

1. Cut lamb into neat pieces and trim off as much surplus fat as possible.
2. Heat margarine in saucepan. Add lamb and fry until well-sealed and brown.
3. Remove to a plate. Add onion and garlic to remaining margarine in saucepan and fry until pale gold.
4. Stir in flour, curry powder, cinnamon, ginger and tomato paste.
5. Gradually blend in stock. Cook, stirring, until sauce comes to the boil and thickens.
6. Add carrots, fruit cocktail (with syrup from can) and salt to taste.
7. Replace lamb, cover pan and simmer gently for 1 to 1½ hours or until lamb is tender.
8. Serve with freshly-boiled long grain rice and side dishes of sliced cucumber topped with natural yogurt, mango chutney and desiccated coconut.

Note

Flavour of curry is improved if it is made on one day and re-heated and served on the next.

Mutton with caper sauce

Serves 6 to 7

3lb (1½ kilo) piece of leg of mutton (or lamb if preferred)

cold water

2 level teaspoons salt

3 cloves

2 large onions

2 large carrots

1 teacup parsley

2 medium celery stalks, coarsely chopped

1 small turnip, sliced

caper sauce (see page 94)

1. Cut away excess fat from mutton.
2. Put into pan and cover with cold water.
3. Add salt and slowly bring to boil.
4. Remove any scum that rises to the top. Add vegetables.
5. Lower heat and cover. Simmer gently, allowing 25 minutes per lb (½ kilo) and 25 minutes over.
6. Transfer meat to a board, carve thinly and accompany with caper sauce.

Italian style lamb

Illustrated facing title page

Serves 6 to 7

3 tablespoons salad oil

a leg of lamb weighing between 4 and 5lb (2 to 2½ kilo)

2 medium onions, chopped

4oz (100gm) mushrooms

2 level tablespoons flour

¼ pint (125ml) dry red wine

½ pint (250ml) water

1 garlic clove, crushed

1 level teaspoon salt

2 level teaspoons paprika

8oz (200gm) tomatoes, skinned and quartered

8 stuffed olives

1 sprig of fresh rosemary

1 dozen small tomatoes

1 large orange slice and 3 stuffed olives to garnish

1. Pre-heat oven to cool, 300 deg F or gas 2 (150 deg C).
2. Heat oil in large roasting tin. Add lamb and fry fairly briskly until crisp and brown all over. Remove to a plate.
3. Add onions and mushrooms to tin and fry gently for 5 minutes.
4. Stir in flour then gradually blend in wine, water, garlic, salt, paprika, skinned and quartered tomatoes and olives.
5. Place meat on vegetables then top with a sprig of rosemary.
6. Cover with foil and cook in centre of oven for 2½ hours.
7. Uncover, stand 10 tomatoes round joint then return to oven for 20 minutes.
8. Transfer meat to a warm platter and stand tomatoes round it.
9. Spear the 2 remaining tomatoes on to a long skewer with the orange slice and olives. Spear into lamb at an angle.
10. Accompany with sauce from roasting tin (first skimmed if very fat), served separately in a sauce boat.
11. Accompany with spaghetti or rice.

Grilled lamb chops

Serves 4

4 loin or chump chops

1oz (25gm) butter, melted

salt and pepper

maître d'hôtel butter (see page 101)

watercress

1. Stand chops in grill pan and brush with melted butter.
2. Sprinkle with salt and pepper and place under a pre-heated hot grill.
3. Grill 2 minutes each side.
4. Lower heat and continue to grill a further 6 to 8 minutes, depending on thickness. Turn twice.
5. Garnish with pats of maître d'hôtel butter and watercress. Serve straight away.
6. Accompany with grilled mushrooms, tomato halves and a green vegetable.

Barbecued lamb chops

Serves 4

Cook as for grilled lamb chops (see this page), but instead of melted butter, brush the chops, as they are grilling, with 1 dessertspoon salad oil beaten with 1 dessertspoon Worcestershire sauce, ¼ to ½ level teaspoon garlic or onion salt, a shake of Tabasco, 1 tablespoon vinegar and 1 level teaspoon caster sugar.

Fried lamb chops

Serves 4

4 chump chops

salt and pepper

1oz (25gm) butter or margarine or 1 tablespoon salad oil

1. Sprinkle chops with salt and pepper.
2. Heat butter or margarine or oil in frying pan. Add chops and fry briskly for 1 minute each side.
3. Lower heat and fry more slowly for a total of 12 to 15 minutes, turning 3 times.
4. Serve with fried potatoes, fried tomatoes and mushrooms, a green vegetable and any suitable sauce (see pages 92–99).

Lamb chops Lyonnaise

Cook as above, but first brown 1 large and thinly-sliced onion in the fat or oil before frying the chops. Serve with creamed potatoes, gravy and green vegetables to taste.

Egg and crumbed lamb cutlets

Serves 4

8 lamb cutlets

salt and pepper

1 large egg

2 teaspoons water

lightly-toasted breadcrumbs

2oz (50gm) lard or dripping or 4 tablespoons salad oil for frying

watercress

wedges of orange

1. Sprinkle chops with salt and pepper.
2. Dip in egg beaten with water then toss in crumbs.
3. Leave to stand 15 minutes for coating to harden.
4. Heat lard or dripping or oil in a frying pan.
5. Add chops and fry briskly for 1 minute each side or until crisp.
6. Lower heat and continue to fry a little more slowly for a total of 10 minutes, turning twice.
7. Drain on soft kitchen paper and transfer to a d'oily lined platter.
8. Garnish with watercress and orange wedges and serve straight away with vegetables to taste and any suitable sauce (see pages 92–99).

Moussaka

Serves 4 to 6

2 large aubergines

salt

6 tablespoons salad oil

2 large onions, sliced

2 garlic cloves, crushed

1lb (½ kilo) cold cooked lamb, minced

2 level tablespoons fresh white breadcrumbs

2 level tablespoons tomato paste

¼ pint (125ml) chicken stock

2 level tablespoons chopped parsley

8oz (200gm) tomatoes, skinned and
   chopped

pepper to taste

½ pint (250ml) freshly-made coating
   cheese sauce (see page 94)

1 egg yolk

2oz (50gm) Cheddar cheese, grated

paprika

1. Cut unpeeled aubergines into ¼ inch thick slices. Put on large plate and sprinkle with salt. Leave 45 minutes then drain, rinse and dry.
2. Pre-heat oven to moderate, 350 deg F or gas 4 (180 deg C).
3. Fry aubergine slices until pale gold on both sides in 4 tablespoons oil. Drain on soft kitchen paper.
4. Add rest of oil to pan. Add onions and garlic and fry gently until pale gold.
5. Stir in lamb, crumbs, tomato paste, stock, parsley, tomatoes and salt and pepper to taste. Simmer 5 minutes.
6. Line a lightly-greased square or oblong heatproof dish with half the aubergine slices.
7. Top with meat mixture then cover with rest of aubergine slices.
8. Coat completely with cheese sauce to which egg yolk has been added.
9. Sprinkle with cheese, dust lightly with paprika and cook in centre of oven for 30 to 40 minutes or until golden brown.
10. Serve hot.

Moussaka

Lamb blanquette

Serves 4 to 6

1½lb (¾ kilo) fillet of lamb, cut from leg

4 cloves

1 large onion

2 medium celery stalks

1 large carrot

1 small bay leaf

cold water

2 level teaspoons salt

1½oz (37gm) butter

1½oz (37gm) flour

4 tablespoons single cream

1 egg yolk

1 dessertspoon lemon juice

1 level tablespoon chopped parsley

1. Cut lamb into cubes, remove surplus fat and put meat into a saucepan.
2. Press cloves into onion and add to pan with celery, carrot and bay leaf.
3. Cover ingredients with cold water (use minimum of 1 pint or approximately ½ litre) and add salt.
4. Bring to the boil and lower heat.
5. Cover and simmer for 1½ hours or until meat is tender.
6. Lift meat out of saucepan with a perforated spoon and put into a dish. Keep hot.
7. Strain liquor in which lamb was cooked and reserve ¾ pint (375ml).
8. Melt butter in saucepan. Stir in flour and cook 2 minutes without browning.
9. Gradually blend in strained lamb liquor.
10. Cook, stirring, until sauce comes to the boil and thickens.
11. Add lamb and simmer 5 minutes.
12. Beat cream with egg yolk and lemon juice.
13. Stir into pan of lamb and re-heat gently without boiling.
14. Transfer to a warm serving dish and sprinkle with parsley.
15. Serve straight away with freshly-boiled rice or new potatoes.

Irish stew

Serves 4

2 to 2½lb (1 to 1¼ kilo) middle neck of
   lamb

1lb (½ kilo) potatoes, sliced

8 to 12oz (200 to 300gm) onions,
   thinly sliced

salt and pepper

¾ pint (375ml) water

3 level tablespoons finely-chopped
   parsley to garnish

1. Divide lamb into neat pieces and trim away surplus fat.
2. Put meat and vegetables in layers in a large saucepan, sprinkling salt and pepper between layers.
3. Add water then slowly bring to boil.
4. Remove any scum that rises to the top then lower heat.
5. Cover pan and simmer gently for 1½ to 2 hours or until meat is tender.
6. Serve piping hot, sprinkled with parsley.

Lamb cutlets with apricots

Serves 4

2oz (50gm) butter, softened

2 level teaspoons rosemary

8 lamb cutlets

salt and pepper

8oz (200gm) dried apricots, soaked
   overnight, drained and chopped

2oz (50gm) sultanas, soaked overnight,
   drained and chopped

juice of ½ lemon

1 can (8oz or 200gm) apricot halves,
   drained

4oz (100gm) cottage cheese

1. Beat butter and rosemary well together and spread over each cutlet.
2. Season with salt and pepper.
3. Grill cutlets as given in recipe for grilled lamb chops (see page 63), allowing a total of 6 to 8 minutes and turning twice.
4. Meanwhile, place dried apricots, sultanas and lemon juice into saucepan.
5. Simmer 2 to 3 minutes.
6. Arrange cutlets down centre of a warm platter and top each with apricot sultana mixture.
7. Garnish with canned apricot halves filled with cottage cheese and serve straight away.

Lamb and tomato casserole

Serves 4 to 5

6oz (150gm) long grain rice

2 medium onions, finely chopped

2 medium celery stalks, chopped

3lb (1½ kilo) scrag end neck of lamb

1 can condensed tomato soup

¾ pint (375ml) water

1 level teaspoon basil

salt and pepper to taste

1. Pre-heat oven to moderate, 325 deg F or gas 3 (170 deg C).
2. Put rice into lightly-greased casserole dish which is shallow rather than tall.
3. Add onions and celery and mix well together.
4. Divide lamb into neat pieces and trim off surplus fat.
5. Stand meat on top of rice mixture.
6. Beat soup and water well together and pour into dish over lamb.
7. Sprinkle with basil and salt and pepper to taste.
8. Cover closely and cook in centre of oven for 1½ hours.
9. Uncover and continue to cook for a further 30 minutes to brown meat.
10. Serve straight away.

Lamb cutlets with apricot halves filled with cottage cheese

Above: roast pork and apple sauce. Below: stuffed roast pork served with roast potatoes, broccoli, apple sauce and gravy

Pork

Cuts suitable for:

Roasting
Leg, loin, fillet, spare rib, blade and hand and spring.

Grilling and frying
Chops, cutlets and fillet.

Boiling
Fresh or salted belly and hand and spring.

Stewing, braising, casseroling
Spare rib and hand and spring. The more expensive, prime cuts may be used as well.

Roast pork

Allow 8 to 12oz (200 to 300gm) pork per person.
Cook pork with bone in centre of hot oven, 450 deg F or gas 8 (230 deg C), for 15 minutes. Reduce heat to moderately hot, 375 deg F or gas 5 (190 deg C), and continue to roast for required amount of time, allowing 25 minutes per lb (½ kilo) and 25 minutes over. If meat is boneless and rolled, cook in moderately hot oven only, allowing 35 minutes per lb (½ kilo) and 35 minutes over. Place joint in roasting tin with skin side (which should be scored) uppermost. For crisp and golden-brown crackling, rub skin with oil and salt. If joint has a high proportion of fat, stand it on a grid in the roasting tin to prevent meat from sitting in a sea of melted grease. Foil-wrapped pork should be loosely wrapped in foil and roasted in centre of hot oven, 425 deg F or gas 7 (220 deg C), for required amount of time, allowing 35 minutes per lb (½ kilo) and 35 minutes over. Foil should be opened up for last 30 minutes to brown the meat. Where crisp crackling is required, it is better to cook the pork uncovered.
Serve with sage and onion stuffing (see page 106), gravy, roast and boiled potatoes, apple sauce (see page 102) and vegetables to taste.

Stuffed roast pork

Stuff joint with home-made or packet sage and onion stuffing or any other suitable stuffing to taste (see pages 106–107) and roast as directed for roast pork, above. Serve with roast potatoes and broccoli.

Crown roast of pork

Ask butcher to prepare a crown of pork from the ribs cut from each side of a loin of pork (6 ribs on each). Place in roasting tin and cover tops of bones with cubes of fat to prevent them from burning. Fill centre with any suitable stuffing (see pages 106–107) and cook in centre of moderately hot oven, 375 deg F or gas 5 (190 deg C), allowing 30 minutes per lb (½ kilo) and 30 minutes over. Baste frequently. Transfer to a carving board and top each bone with a cutlet frill. Accompany with gravy, boiled and roast potatoes, any suitable meat sauce and green vegetables to taste.

Grilled pork chops

Serves 4

4 pork chops, each about 6oz (150gm)

salt and pepper to taste

1oz (25gm) butter, melted

1. Sprinkle chops with salt and pepper and place in grill pan. Brush with butter.
2. Place under pre-heated grill and grill 9 to 10 minutes, depending on thickness.
3. Turn chops over, sprinkle with more salt and pepper and brush with butter.
4. Grill a further 9 to 10 minutes.

Crunchy-topped grilled chops

Serves 4

Grill 4 chops as directed in recipe for grilled pork chops, above. About 5 minutes before they are ready, spread one side of each with a mixture of 2 level teaspoons dried mustard, 4 level teaspoons Demerara sugar, 1oz (25gm) chopped salted peanuts, ½ teaspoon Worcestershire sauce, 1 teaspoon vinegar, ½ level teaspoon salt and 1 teaspoon melted butter. Return to grill and continue to cook until golden brown. Serve with cored apple rings, lightly fried on both sides in a little butter.

Hawaiian pork chops

Serves 4

Grill 4 pork chops as directed in recipe for grilled pork chops (see this page), brushing fairly thickly with ½oz (12gm) melted butter mixed with 1 dessertspoon syrup from can of pineapple, ¼ level teaspoon salt and shake of pepper. Meanwhile, cut 2 medium bananas lengthwise and well-drain 4 canned pineapple rings. Fry both bananas and pineapple in butter until golden on both sides. Remove from pan, arrange on grilled chops then garnish with watercress.

Fried pork chops

Serves 4

1oz (25gm) lard or dripping

4 pork chops, each about 6oz (150gm)

1. Heat lard or dripping in frying pan.
2. Add chops and brown briskly on both sides.
3. Lower heat and fry a total of 15 minutes, turning twice.

Pork chops with paprika sauce

Serves 4

4 pork chops, each about 6oz (150gm)

1oz (25gm) flour, well-seasoned with salt and pepper

1oz (25gm) butter or margarine

1 carton (¼ pint or 125ml) soured cream

2 tablespoons lemon juice

5 tablespoons chicken stock

2 teaspoons caster sugar

1 level teaspoon onion salt

2 level tablespoons chopped parsley

salt and pepper to taste

1 level teaspoon paprika

1. Pre-heat oven to moderate, 350 deg F or gas 4 (180 deg C).
2. Coat chops with seasoned flour then fry in the butter or margarine until golden brown on both sides.
3. Transfer to a casserole dish.
4. Mix all remaining ingredients well together.
5. Spoon over chops then cover with lid or aluminium foil.
6. Cook in centre of oven for 45 minutes or until chops are tender.

Pork cutlets

Serves 4

1lb (½ kilo) pork fillet

2 level tablespoons flour, well-seasoned with salt and pepper

1 large egg

2 tablespoons water

fresh white breadcrumbs

deep oil for frying

lemon slices to garnish

1. Cut fillet into 4 slices and beat until very thin with a rolling pin. Dust each with seasoned flour.
2. Dip in egg, beaten with water, then toss in breadcrumbs.
3. Heat a pan of deep oil until a cube of bread, dropped into it, turns golden brown in 1 minute and floats to the top.
4. Add cutlets, one or two at a time, and fry for 8 minutes, allowing them to float about in the oil.
5. Remove from pan, drain thoroughly on soft kitchen paper and serve garnished with lemon.

Sweet-sour pork

Serves 4

1oz (25gm) butter

1 tablespoon salad oil

1 medium onion, thinly sliced

1 garlic clove, chopped

4oz (100gm) mushrooms

12oz (300gm) pork fillet

1 level tablespoon flour, well-seasoned with salt and pepper

6oz (150gm) cooked green beans, canned, frozen or fresh

1 medium can (approximately 13oz or 325gm) pineapple chunks

1 level tablespoon soft brown sugar

1 level tablespoon cornflour

3 tablespoons vinegar

freshly-cooked noodles for serving

1. Heat butter and oil in pan.
2. Add onion and garlic and fry gently until soft but not brown.
3. Slice mushrooms. Cut pork into thin strips and coat with flour.
4. Add mushrooms and pork to pan. Cover and cook gently for 10 minutes, stirring occasionally.
5. Add beans. Drain pineapple and reserve syrup. Add pineapple chunks to pan.
6. Mix sugar and cornflour to a smooth paste with vinegar. Stir in pineapple syrup and add to pan.
7. Cook, stirring, until mixture boils. Lower heat and cover then simmer for 7 minutes.
8. Line a warm serving dish with noodles then pile sweet-sour pork on top. Serve straight away.

Sweet-sour pork

Cider braised spare rib

Serves 4

2lb (1 kilo) spare ribs, divided into neat portions

2 level tablespoons plain flour, well-seasoned with salt and pepper

2oz (50gm) lard or dripping

1 large onion, chopped

2 celery stalks, chopped

1 turnip, diced

1 small parsnip, diced

1lb (½ kilo) potatoes, thickly sliced

salt and pepper to taste

¼ pint (125ml) dry cider

¼ pint (125ml) chicken stock

1. Pre-heat oven to moderate, 350 deg F or gas 4 (180 deg C).
2. Coat spare ribs with well-seasoned flour and fry briskly in the lard or dripping until brown on both sides.
3. Remove to a plate. Add onion, celery, turnip and parsnip to rest of fat in pan and fry gently until pale gold.
4. Arrange potato slices over base of casserole dish. Season with salt and pepper then cover with fried vegetables.
5. Arrange chops on top, season with more salt and pepper then pour cider and stock into dish.
6. Cover with lid or foil and cook in centre of oven for 1 to 1¼ hours or until pork is cooked through.

Spiced pork fillet

Serves 4

1lb (½ kilo) pork fillet

1oz (25gm) butter

1 large onion, finely chopped

1 green pepper, de-seeded and chopped

salt and pepper

1 small can (8oz or 200gm) apricot halves

6oz (150gm) soft brown sugar

4 level tablespoons apricot jam

2 tablespoons Worcestershire sauce

4 tablespoons malt vinegar

2 tablespoons lemon juice

1 level teaspoon dry mustard

2 level teaspoons cornflour

1. Cut pork fillets into ½ inch thick slices.
2. Melt butter in large frying pan. Add onion and pepper and fry gently for 5 minutes.
3. Add pork slices. Season to taste with salt and pepper and fry slowly for 10 minutes, turning once.
4. Meanwhile, make sauce. Drain apricots and reserve syrup.
5. Put sugar, jam, Worcestershire sauce, vinegar, lemon juice and mustard into a saucepan. Stir over a low heat until sugar dissolves.
6. Mix cornflour to a smooth paste with a little of the apricot syrup.
7. Add to sauce with rest of syrup. Cook, stirring, until sauce comes to boil and thickens. Add apricots and simmer 2 minutes.
8. Arrange pork and vegetables on a serving dish and coat with sauce.
9. Serve with plain boiled rice or noodles.

Pork and vegetable stewpot

Pork and vegetable stewpot

Serves 4

1½oz (37gm) lard or dripping

1 large onion, sliced

4 medium celery stalks, chopped

1 large cooking apple, peeled, cored and sliced

1½lb (¾ kilo) loin pork, cubed

2 level tablespoons flour, well-seasoned with salt, pepper and dry mustard

½ pint (250ml) chicken stock

¼ pint (125ml) tomato juice

1 level tablespoon tomato paste

¼ level teaspoon dried sage

salt and pepper to taste

1 small onion, thinly sliced into rings, and 1 medium celery stalk, cut into fairly thin diagonal slices, to garnish

1. Heat lard or dripping in saucepan.
2. Add onion, celery and apple and fry gently until soft and pale gold.
3. Meanwhile, coat pork with seasoned flour.
4. Add to pan and fry fairly briskly until well-sealed and brown.
5. Pour in stock and tomato juice then cook, stirring continuously, until mixture comes to boil and thickens.
6. Stir in tomato paste and sage then adjust seasoning to taste.
7. Lower heat and cover pan. Simmer gently 1 to 1½ hours or until meat is tender, stirring occasionally.
8. About 20 minutes before pork is ready, cook thinly-sliced onion rings and celery in boiling salted water until just tender.
9. Transfer stewed pork to warm dish and garnish with onion rings and celery.
10. Serve with boiled potatoes and freshly-boiled cabbage tossed with butter.

Polish hunter's stew

Serves 4

1lb (½ kilo) canned or bottled sauerkraut, drained

1 bay leaf

½ pint (250ml) water

1lb (½ kilo) white cabbage, shredded

4oz (100gm) streaky bacon, chopped

2oz (50gm) lard or dripping

1 large onion, chopped

8oz (200gm) raw lean pork, cut into small cubes

1 level tablespoon flour, well-seasoned with salt and pepper

4oz (100gm) lean ham, cut into strips

2oz (50gm) mushrooms, sliced

2 Frankfurter sausages, sliced

2 level tablespoons tomato paste

¼ pint (125ml) red wine

1 garlic clove, chopped

salt and pepper to taste

1. In a large saucepan, put sauerkraut, bay leaf, water and shredded cabbage. Bring to boil and lower heat. Cover and simmer 30 minutes.
2. Fry bacon in its own fat until crisp. Add to cabbage mixture.
3. Add lard or dripping to remaining bacon fat in pan. Add onion and fry very slowly for 5 minutes.
4. Meanwhile, coat pork with seasoned flour. Add to onion and fry a little more briskly until well-sealed and brown.
5. Add onion and pork to cabbage and simmer very gently for 45 minutes, stirring frequently.
6. Stir in ham, mushrooms, sausages, tomato paste, wine, garlic and salt and pepper to taste.
7. Cover and simmer a further 30 minutes.
8. Serve with freshly-boiled potatoes or rye bread.

Rainbow pork

Serves 4

6oz (150gm) long grain rice

8oz (200gm) halibut, skinned and boned

salt and pepper

few drops of Worcestershire sauce

juice of ½ lemon

1oz (25gm) flour

salad oil

2 large bananas, peeled and halved

4 canned peach halves

4oz (100gm) butter

16 glacé cherries

4 thin slices pork fillet

6oz (150gm) peeled shrimps

5 tablespoons dry sherry

1oz (25gm) flaked almonds

12 stuffed olives

10oz (250gm) mushrooms

½ pint (250ml) Italian tomato sauce (see page 102)

1. Cook rice in plenty of boiling salted water for 12 minutes. Drain thoroughly and keep hot.
2. Cut halibut into 4 pieces.
3. Mix together ½ level teaspoon salt, pepper to taste, Worcestershire sauce and lemon juice in a shallow dish.
4. Add fish, cover and leave to marinate in a cold place for 1 hour.
5. Coat with flour then fry in 2 tablespoons oil until golden, turning once.
6. In a separate pan, fry bananas and peach halves gently in 2oz (50gm) butter for 5 minutes. Add cherries for last 2 minutes of cooking time.
7. Remove fish from pan and keep hot.
8. Using same pan, add 2 tablespoons oil.
9. Heat until hot, add pork and fry gently until cooked through, turning once.
10. Put shrimps in a small pan with sherry and ½oz (12gm) butter and simmer until half the liquid has evaporated.
11. Combine pork with halibut and keep hot.
12. Fry almonds until golden in 1 tablespoon oil.
13. Pile rice in centre of a hot serving dish and scatter shrimps, almonds and olives on top.
14. Arrange fish, pork and fruit around the edge.
15. Finally, fry mushrooms in rest of butter and 1 tablespoon oil for 3 minutes and add to serving dish.
16. Serve with tomato sauce.

Rainbow pork

Pork roll served with peas and tomatoes

Pork loaf

Serves 8

crushed cornflakes

1lb ($\frac{1}{2}$ kilo) lean pork, minced

8oz (200gm) pork sausagemeat

3oz (75gm) fresh white breadcrumbs

2 standard eggs, beaten

2 level tablespoons chopped parsley

$\frac{1}{4}$ level teaspoon each garlic and celery salt

1 level teaspoon sage or thyme

good shake of pepper

$\frac{1}{4}$ level teaspoon salt

1. Pre-heat oven to moderate, 350 deg F or gas 4 (180 deg C).
2. Well-grease a 2lb (1 kilo) loaf tin and brush base and sides thickly with crushed cornflakes.
3. Mix all remaining ingredients well together then transfer mixture to prepared tin.
4. Press down well then cover with greased foil.
5. Bake in centre of oven for 1 hour.
6. Turn out and serve cold with salad.

Pork roll

Serves 8

Make pork loaf as given in previous recipe. Shape into a thick sausage and wrap in short crust or rough puff pastry (see pages 108 or 110) to give a giant sausage roll. Moisten edges of pastry with water and press well together to seal. Stand roll on a baking tray with joins underneath and brush with beaten egg. Decorate with pastry leaves and brush with more egg. Bake just above centre of hot oven, 425 deg F or gas 7 (220 deg C), for 15 minutes. Reduce temperature to moderate, 325 deg F or gas 3 (170 deg C), and continue to bake for a further 1$\frac{1}{4}$ hours, covering pastry with greaseproof paper during the last half hour if it seems to be browning too much. Serve with peas and tomatoes.

Pork with pease pudding

Serves 4

2lb (1 kilo) salted belly of pork

cold water

2 medium onions

2 medium carrots

1 small turnip

1 celery stalk

2 peppercorns

pease pudding (see page 153)

1. Put pork into a saucepan and cover with cold water. Bring to boil and drain.
2. Cover with more water then add vegetables and peppercorns.
3. Bring to boil and simmer very gently for 2 hours.
4. Drain thoroughly, cut in slices and serve hot with pease pudding.

Scandinavian style meat balls

Serves 4

1lb ($\frac{1}{2}$ kilo) lean pork

1 medium onion

1 large slice white bread

3 tablespoons milk

1 to 2 level teaspoons salt

pepper to taste

1 small egg, beaten

deep fat or oil for frying

1. Cut pork and onion into cubes and finely mince.
2. Soak bread in the milk and beat into pork mixture with salt, pepper to taste and the egg.
3. When evenly combined, shape into about 16 balls.
4. Heat fat or oil until a cube of bread, dropped into it, turns golden brown in 1 minute and floats to the top.
5. Add pork balls and fry 5 to 6 minutes or until golden brown and cooked through.
6. Drain on soft kitchen paper and serve straight away with Italian tomato or onion sauce (see pages 102 or 95).

Bacon

Cuts suitable for:

Grilling and frying
Back rashers, streaky rashers, bacon chops and gammon rashers and steaks.

Boiling
Back in the piece, collar, hock, slipper and middle and corner gammon.

Baking
Hock, and middle and corner gammon.

Stewing and braising
Collar, hock and slipper.

Danish crackle crisp

Serves 10

Wash and dry a 4 to 5lb (2 to 2½ kilo) piece of Danish corner gammon. Using a sharp knife, score rind into a small diamond pattern. Put gammon into a large saucepan. Cover with cold water and bring to the boil. Drain (this removes excess salt). Stand gammon in a roasting tin and roast in centre of moderate oven, 350 deg F or gas 4 (180 deg C), allowing 20 minutes per lb (½ kilo) and 20 minutes over. Baste once or twice with pan juices. Remove from oven (crackling will be crisp) and serve hot with redcurrant sauce and vegetables to taste, or cold with salad.

Danish crackle crisp

Redcurrant sauce

Over a low heat, melt 4oz (100gm) redcurrant jelly in ½ pint (250ml) red wine. Meanwhile, blend 2 level teaspoons arrowroot with 1 tablespoon cold water. Add to redcurrant mixture and cook, stirring, until sauce comes to the boil, thickens and clears.

Brisbane fruity gammon

Brisbane fruity gammon

Serves 6 to 8

Cover a 3lb (1½ kilo) piece of gammon with cold water. Bring to boil. Drain. Cover with fresh water and bring to the boil. Lower heat and cover. Simmer slowly, allowing 20 minutes per lb (½ kilo) and 20 minutes over. Drain, leave to stand 10 minutes then carefully peel off rind. Score fat into a diamond pattern and spread with 1oz (25gm) fresh white breadcrumbs mixed with 1 level teaspoon dry mustard, 1 level dessertspoon Demerara sugar and 1oz (25gm) melted butter. Transfer to a roasting tin and surround with 1 can (approximately 1lb or ½ kilo) quartered pears and peaches (stuck with cloves if liked), including syrup from can. Cook in centre of hot oven, 425 deg F or gas 7 (220 deg C), for 20 minutes, basting frequently. Serve hot with vegetables.

Irish bacon with cherry sauce

Serves 6 to 8

Cook 3lb (1½ kilo) gammon as given in previous recipe for Brisbane fruity gammon. Do not surround joint with canned fruit while in the oven but add ¼ pint (125ml) stock for basting. Meanwhile, strain 1 small can (8oz or 200gm) red cherries and and make up syrup to ¼ pint (125ml) with cold water if necessary. Stone cherries without breaking. Pour syrup into a saucepan with 2 level tablespoons cranberry sauce and 1 tablespoon lemon juice. Cook gently until cranberry sauce melts then bring to boil and continue boiling until mixture is syrupy. Chop half the cherries and add to sauce. Press cocktail onions into rest of cherries then spear into diamonds of bacon fat. Garnish with watercress and serve hot, accompanied with the cherry sauce.

Irish bacon decorated with cherries and cocktail onions

Apple and bacon pie

Serves 4

1lb (½ kilo) bacon forehock

cold water

short crust pastry made from 8oz (200gm) flour (see page 108)

1 large onion, chopped

1 large cooking apple, peeled, cored and chopped

2 tablespoons cider

1 level tablespoon soft brown sugar

pepper to taste

beaten egg for brushing

1. Pre-heat oven to hot, 425 deg F or gas 7 (220 deg C).
2. Cut bacon into small cubes. To remove excess salt, cover with cold water, bring to the boil and drain. Repeat once more if very salty.
3. Roll out about two-thirds of the pastry and use to line an 8-inch pie plate.
4. Combine bacon with onion, cooking apple, cider, brown sugar and pepper to taste.
5. Transfer to pastry-lined plate.
6. Moisten edges of pastry with water then cover with lid, rolled from rest of pastry.
7. Press edges well together to seal then decorate by fluting.
8. Brush with beaten egg and make a hole in the top to allow steam to escape.
9. Cut trimmings into leaves and arrange on top of pie. Brush with more egg.
10. Cook just above centre of oven for 15 minutes.
11. Reduce temperature to moderate, 350 deg F or gas 4 (180 deg C), and bake a further 1 hour.
12. Serve hot or cold.

Crumbed bacon served cold with orange salad

Crumbed bacon with orange salad

Serves 6 to 8

Cook 3lb (1½ kilo) boned and rolled forehock bacon as given in recipe for Brisbane fruity gammon (see page 71) but do not roast in oven. Drain bacon thoroughly and leave 10 minutes. Strip off skin then press about 2 to 3 level tablespoons toasted breadcrumbs on to fat. Serve cold and accompany with orange salad made by tossing well together 1 shredded lettuce, 2 sliced oranges, 1 level tablespoon chopped parsley and 6 tablespoons French dressing (see page 161).

Apple and bacon pie

Grilled gammon steaks

Serves 4

4 gammon steaks, each ¼ inch thick and about 6oz (150gm) in weight

melted butter

1. Remove rinds from gammon steaks with scissors then snip fat at close intervals all the way round each steak to prevent it from curling as it cooks.
2. Brush with melted butter and place under pre-heated hot grill.
3. Grill 7 minutes then turn steaks over.
4. Brush with more butter and continue to grill a further 7 minutes or until gammon is cooked through.
5. Serve steaks as they are or garnished with fried canned pineapple rings, fried canned peach halves or fried banana halves.

Devilled gammon steaks

Serves 4

Prepare as given in recipe for grilled gammon steaks, (see opposite), but instead of brushing steaks with melted butter, spread with 1oz (25gm) softened butter beaten with ½ level teaspoon curry powder, shake of Tabasco, ¼ level teaspoon ground ginger, 1 teaspoon Worcestershire sauce and 1 teaspoon chutney. Grill, turn, spread with more devilled mixture then finish cooking.

Ginger glazed gammon steaks

Serves 4

Prepare as given in recipe for grilled gammon steaks, (see opposite), but brush with 1oz (25gm) melted butter mixed with 1 level dessertspoon soft brown sugar and 1 level teaspoon powdered ginger.

Bacon hot pot

Serves 6

2½lb (1¼ kilo) forehock

cold water

2 medium carrots, sliced

2 medium celery stalks, coarsely chopped

1lb (½ kilo) potatoes, cut into chunks

8oz (200gm) turnips, cut into chunks

1lb (½ kilo) onions, sliced

stock

1 small packet frozen peas

1. Pre-heat oven to moderately hot, 375 deg F or gas 5 (190 deg C).
2. Put bacon into a saucepan and cover with cold water.
3. Slowly bring to boil then drain (this removes excess salt).
4. Leave 10 minutes and remove rind. Stand joint in casserole dish and surround with carrots, celery, potatoes, turnips and onions.
5. Pour in just sufficient stock to reach to the top of the vegetables, then cover with lid or aluminium foil.
6. Cook in centre of oven for 1¾ hours.
7. Uncover, add peas and continue to cook for a further 15 minutes.

Bacon medley pie

Bacon medley pie

Serves 4

1 can condensed mushroom soup

1 tablespoon Worcestershire sauce

12oz (300gm) cooked bacon, cut into ½-inch cubes

2 hard-boiled eggs, chopped

4oz (100gm) mushrooms and stalks, sliced

short crust pastry made with 6oz (150gm) flour (see page 108)

beaten egg for brushing

1. Pre-heat oven to hot, 425 deg F or gas 7 (220 deg C).
2. Combine soup with Worcestershire sauce, bacon, eggs and mushrooms.
3. Transfer mixture to 2 pint (approximately 1¼ litre) pie dish with rim.
4. Moisten edge of dish with water then line with strips of pastry.
5. Roll out rest of pastry into a lid and use to cover pie.
6. Press edges of lid and lining well together to seal then decorate by fluting.
7. Brush with beaten egg and bake just above centre of oven for 25 minutes or until golden brown.
8. Serve straight away.

Sausagemeat and bacon roly poly

Serves 4 to 6

6oz (150gm) sausagemeat

6oz (150gm) lean boiled bacon, finely minced

1 medium onion, chopped

1 level teaspoon mixed herbs

1 teaspoon Worcestershire sauce

suet crust pastry made with 8oz (200gm) flour (see page 110)

1. Combine sausagemeat, bacon, onion, herbs and Worcestershire sauce well together.
2. Roll out pastry into an 8 inch by 10 inch oblong.
3. Cover with meat mixture to within ½ inch of edges.
4. Moisten edges with water then roll up like a Swiss roll, starting from one of the shorter sides.
5. Wrap in double thickness of greased greaseproof paper or aluminium foil and steam steadily for 2½ hours.
6. Unwrap, cut into slices and serve with gravy.

Veal

Cuts of veal suitable for:

Roasting
Leg, loin, boned shoulder and boned breast.

Grilling and frying
Chops, cutlets and fillet cut from the top of the leg.

Pot roasting
Leg, shoulder and boned and rolled breast.

Stewing, braising
Knuckle, neck, breast and shoulder.

Roast veal

Allow 8 to 12oz (200 to 300gm) veal with bone or 6 to 8oz (150 to 200gm) veal without bone.
Roast veal with bone in the centre of a moderately hot oven, 375 deg F or gas 5 (190 deg C), for 25 minutes per lb ($\frac{1}{2}$ kilo) and 25 minutes over. Veal off the bone or stuffed and rolled, 35 minutes per lb ($\frac{1}{2}$ kilo) and 30 minutes over. Place veal in roasting tin and, because veal is a fairly dry meat, either brush heavily with melted butter or margarine or cover with rashers of streaky bacon. Roast for required amount of time, basting frequently and removing bacon rashers during the last 30 minutes.
Foil-wrapped joints should be loosely wrapped in foil and cooked in the centre of a hot oven, 425 deg F or gas 7 (220 deg C), for the length of time given for unwrapped joints. Allow only 15 to 20 minutes overtime. Foil should be opened up during the last 30 minutes to brown the meat.
Serve with gravy, grilled bacon rolls, wedges of lemon, roast and creamed potatoes and other vegetables to taste.

Pot roasted veal

Serves 4

1$\frac{1}{2}$ to 2lb ($\frac{3}{4}$ to 1 kilo) boned breast or shoulder of veal

1oz (25gm) bacon dripping or butter

salt and pepper to taste

1 onion, sliced

2 tablespoons water

1. Pre-heat oven to moderate, 350 deg F or gas 4 (180 deg C).
2. Tie boned breast or shoulder at close intervals to keep joint in shape. If liked, stuff first, choosing any suitable stuffing from the selection on pages 106-7.
3. Heat dripping or butter in flameproof casserole. Add veal and brown briskly all over.
4. Season to taste with salt and pepper then add onion and water.
5. Cover closely and cook in centre of oven for 2 to 2$\frac{1}{2}$ hours or until veal is tender and cooked through.
6. Uncover during the last 30 minutes to brown meat then serve cut in thick slices with creamy mashed potatoes and vegetables to taste.

Marinated veal roast

Serves 4 to 6

Put 2$\frac{1}{2}$ to 3lb (1$\frac{1}{4}$ to 1$\frac{1}{2}$ kilo) boned veal breast or shoulder into a glass or enamel dish. Cover with a marinade made from 5 tablespoons dry red wine, 5 tablespoons water, 1 tablespoon vinegar, 1 sliced onion, 1 chopped garlic clove, 6 peppercorns, 1 bay leaf and 2 level teaspoons salt. Cover and leave the veal in a cold place for 24 hours, turning it over several times. Remove from marinade, wipe dry, roll and/or tie. Roast as directed in recipe for roast veal (see this page).

Wiener schnitzel

Serves 4

4 slices veal fillet, each 4oz (100gm)

flour, well-seasoned with salt and pepper

1 large egg

2 teaspoons water

fresh white breadcrumbs for coating

deep fresh oil for frying

lemon wedges to garnish

1. Beat fillets until very thin or ask your butcher to do this for you.
2. Make small cuts round the edge of each fillet to prevent meat from curling up as it cooks.
3. Coat veal with flour then dip in egg, beaten with water.
4. Toss in crumbs then leave veal for 15 minutes so that coating hardens.
5. Heat oil until a cube of bread, dropped into it, turns golden brown in one minute and floats to the top.
6. Add veal, 2 pieces at a time.
7. Fry for 8 to 10 minutes, allowing escalopes to float about in the oil.
8. Drain on soft kitchen paper and serve garnished with lemon wedges.

Wiener schnitzel Holstein

Serves 4

Prepare and cook veal fillets as directed in Wiener schnitzel above, then top each with a fried egg.

Escalopes Milanese

Serves 4

Prepare and cook veal fillets as directed in Wiener schnitzel, above. Transfer to grill pan and cover each with one slice of mild ham. Top thickly with finely-grated Parmesan cheese and then flakes of butter. Place under a pre-heated grill and leave until cheese begins to melt.

Baked veal chops

Serves 4

1oz (25gm) butter

4 large veal chops, each 4 to 6oz (100 to 150gm)

4oz (100gm) sultanas

4oz (100gm) dried apricots, quartered

juice of 3 large oranges

$\frac{1}{2}$ level teaspoon curry powder

1 level teaspoon salt

freshly-milled black pepper

parsley to garnish

1. Pre-heat oven to moderate, 350 deg F or gas 4 (180 deg C).
2. Heat butter in flameproof casserole.
3. Add chops and fry briskly for 1 minute per side.
4. Sprinkle with sultanas and apricots.
5. Beat orange juice with curry powder and salt.
6. Pour into dish over chops then grind black pepper over each.
7. Cover closely with lid or aluminium foil and cook in centre of oven for 45 minutes to 1 hour. Serve garnished with parsley.

Veal in paprika sauce

Serves 4

1$\frac{1}{2}$ to 2lb ($\frac{3}{4}$ to 1 kilo) stewing veal, cut into 1-inch cubes

2 level tablespoons flour, well-seasoned with salt and pepper

2oz (50gm) lard or dripping

2 large onions, chopped

1 medium green pepper, de-seeded and chopped

8oz (200gm) tomatoes, skinned and chopped

1 level tablespoon paprika

1 garlic clove, finely chopped

$\frac{1}{4}$ pint (125ml) water

1 level tablespoon tomato purée

1 to 2 level teaspoons salt

$\frac{1}{4}$ to $\frac{1}{2}$ pint (125 to 250ml) soured cream

1. Coat veal with seasoned flour.
2. Heat lard or dripping in a heavy saucepan.
3. Add onions and green pepper and fry gently, with lid on pan, for 10 to 15 minutes or until pale gold.
4. Add veal and fry a little more briskly until pieces are well-sealed and golden.
5. Add all remaining ingredients except soured cream.
6. Bring to boil, stirring. Lower heat and cover pan.
7. Simmer gently for 1$\frac{1}{2}$ to 2 hours or until meat is cooked through and tender, stirring occasionally.
8. Blend in soured cream and serve with freshly-boiled rice or noodles.

Baked veal chops sprinkled with sultanas and apricots

Veal stew with dumplings

Serves 4

1½ to 2lb (¾ to 1 kilo) stewing veal, cut into 1-inch cubes

2 level tablespoons flour, well-seasoned with salt and pepper

2oz (50gm) lard or dripping

1 tablespoon oil

2 medium onions, chopped

2 medium carrots, thinly sliced

2 medium celery stalks, thinly sliced

¾ pint (375ml) chicken stock

2 dessertspoons lemon juice

salt and pepper to taste

8oz (200gm) fresh white breadcrumbs

4 tablespoons milk

2oz (50gm) butter or margarine, melted

1 standard egg, beaten

1. Coat meat with seasoned flour.
2. Heat lard or dripping and oil in a saucepan. Add onions, carrots and celery and fry gently, with lid on pan, for 10 minutes.
3. Add veal cubes and fry a little more briskly until well-sealed and brown.
4. Pour in stock, lemon juice and salt and pepper, and bring to boil, stirring.
5. Lower heat and cover pan. Simmer 1½ hours or until meat is tender, stirring occasionally.
6. About 20 minutes before meat is ready, make dumplings.
7. Soak crumbs in milk then beat in all remaining ingredients, and seasoning to taste.
8. Shape into 8 balls and cook in boiling salted water for 5 minutes.
9. Drain and add to stew.
10. Serve straight away.

Veal escalope garni

Serves 2

2 slices veal fillet, each about 4oz (100gm)

1oz (25gm) flour, well-seasoned with salt and pepper

3 tablespoons oil

1oz (25gm) butter

4oz (100gm) mushrooms, sliced

squeeze of lemon juice

8oz (200gm) French beans, topped and tailed

½ small cauliflower, divided into florets

8oz (200gm) sprouts

6 small carrots

1 large potato, par-boiled and cut into rounds

parsley to garnish

1. Coat fillets with seasoned flour.
2. Heat oil in the pan, add fillets and brown quickly on both sides.
3. Cover and fry slowly until tender—about 10 minutes.
4. Add butter, mushrooms and lemon juice to pan.
5. Cover and cook a further 5 minutes.
6. Meanwhile, cook beans, cauliflower, sprouts and carrots in individual pans of boiling, salted water until just tender.
7. Sauté potato in a little oil and butter until golden.
8. Place fillets on a hot serving dish, top with mushrooms, drain vegetables and arrange, with fried potatoes, in piles round meat. Garnish with parsley.

Veal and tomato stewpot

Illustrated on page 45

Serves 8

8oz (200gm) streaky bacon, chopped

2lb (1 kilo) stewing veal, cubed

4 level tablespoons flour

salt and pepper to taste

1lb (½ kilo) onions, chopped

4 tablespoons salad oil

1 can (about 1lb or ½ kilo) tomatoes

1 wine glass red wine

3 tablespoons vinegar

1 pint (approximately ½ litre) beef stock

3 carrots, thinly sliced

1 bay leaf

2 cloves

1lb (½ kilo) long grain rice

2 pints (approximately 1¼ litre) water

parsley to garnish

1. Sprinkle bacon and veal with flour, salt and pepper.
2. Fry onions in the oil until golden.
3. Add floured bacon and veal and fry until brown on all sides.
4. Add tomatoes, wine, vinegar, stock, carrots, bay leaf and cloves.
5. Bring to boil and lower heat.
6. Cover and simmer for 1½ hours or until meat is tender.
7. About 20 minutes before meat is cooked, put rice, water and 2 level teaspoons salt into a saucepan.
8. Bring to boil and stir once.
9. Lower heat and cover.
10. Cook 15 minutes or until rice is tender and liquid absorbed.
11. Arrange rice on a platter and top with veal stew. Garnish with parsley and serve straight away.

Veal escalope garni

Veal with peaches

Serves 4

1 can (1lb or ½ kilo) cling peaches

2oz (50gm) butter

2lb (1 kilo) boned veal breast

2 large onions, sliced and separated into rings

salt and pepper

1 bay leaf

½ level teaspoon dried thyme

1 level tablespoon chopped parsley

1 small bottle Maraschino cherries

1. Pre-heat oven to moderately hot, 375 deg F or gas 5 (190 deg C).
2. Drain peaches and reserve syrup.
3. Melt butter in flameproof casserole.
4. Add veal and brown on all sides.
5. Remove from pan and leave on one side.
6. Add onion rings to remaining butter in pan and fry gently until pale gold.
7. Replace veal, season to taste with salt and pepper then add bay leaf, thyme and parsley.
8. Pour peach syrup into pan and bring to the boil.
9. Cover and cook in centre of oven for about 1½ to 2 hours or until meat is tender.
10. Add drained peaches and cherries, and continue to cook for a further 15 minutes.

Veal rolls Espagnole

Serves 4

4 slices veal fillet, each 4oz (100gm)

4oz (100gm) fresh white breadcrumbs

2oz (50gm) ham, finely chopped

1 small onion, grated

½ level teaspoon mixed herbs

½ level teaspoon finely-grated lemon peel

1 level teaspoon paprika

salt and pepper to taste

2oz (50gm) butter, melted

beaten egg to bind

Espagnole sauce (see page 97)

1. Beat veal fillet until very thin or ask butcher to do this for you.
2. Combine crumbs with ham, onion, herbs, lemon peel and paprika.
3. Season to taste with salt and pepper then add 1oz (25gm) melted butter.
4. Stirring with a fork, add sufficient beaten egg to bind loosely.
5. Spread equal amounts of crumb mixture on to each fillet then roll up.
6. Tie with fine string or thick thread.
7. Heat rest of butter in a pan. Add veal rolls and fry fairly briskly until brown all over.
8. Add Espagnole sauce then simmer gently for 45 minutes to 1 hour or until veal is tender, stirring occasionally.
9. Lift rolls out of sauce, remove string then transfer to a warm serving dish.
10. Coat with sauce and serve with creamy mashed potatoes and green vegetables to taste.

Veal with peaches and cherries

Marsala veal chops

Serves 4

1oz (25gm) butter

4 loin chops, each about 4 to 6oz (100 to 150gm)

cut clove of garlic (optional)

salt and pepper

3 tablespoons Marsala

2 tablespoons double cream

1 heaped tablespoon finely-chopped parsley

1. Heat butter in frying pan.
2. Rub chops with cut clove of garlic (if used) then season to taste with salt and pepper.
3. Fry briskly in the butter for 1 minute per side then lower heat.
4. Cover pan and continue to cook for a further 15 to 20 minutes, turning once.
5. Remove chops to a warm dish and keep hot.
6. Add Marsala and cream to pan and heat through gently without boiling, stirring well.
7. Add parsley, adjust seasoning to taste then pour over chops.
8. Serve straight away.

Vitello tonnato

Serves 4

12oz (300gm) cold cooked veal, thinly sliced

¼ pint (125ml) home-made mayonnaise (see page 99)

½ can (approximately 3oz or 75gm) tuna, drained and finely mashed

a little chicken stock

lemon juice

6 anchovy fillets

1 level tablespoon capers

1. Arrange slices of veal on a serving dish.
2. Combine mayonnaise with tuna then mix to a creamy consistency with stock and lemon juice. The sauce should be about the same thickness as slightly-whipped double cream.
3. Spoon over veal, covering it completely.
4. Chill between 6 to 8 hours in the refrigerator.
5. Before serving, garnish with anchovy fillets and capers.
6. Serve with salad.

Veal casserole

Italian ossi buchi

3lb (1½ kilo) leg of veal, sawn through into 2-inch pieces

salt and pepper

1oz (25gm) butter

3 dessertspoons olive oil

1 large onion, chopped

2 garlic cloves, chopped

¼ pint (125ml) dry white wine

¼ pint (125ml) chicken stock

8oz (200gm) tomatoes, skinned and chopped

1 level tablespoon cornflour

2 tablespoons cold water

1 level teaspoon finely-grated lemon peel

2 level teaspoons chopped parsley

1. Season meat with salt and pepper.
2. Heat butter and oil in large, shallow pan. Add onion and 1 clove of garlic and fry gently for 10 minutes or until pale gold.
3. Add pieces of veal and fry about 10 minutes turning them over once.
4. Pour wine and chicken stock into pan then add tomatoes and 1 to 2 level teaspoons salt.
5. Slowly bring to boil. Lower heat and cover.
6. Simmer gently for 1½ hours or until meat is tender.
7. Arrange pieces of veal on a warm serving dish and keep hot.
8. Mix cornflour to a smooth cream with cold water.
9. Add to tomato mixture in saucepan.
10. Cook, stirring, until sauce comes to the boil and thickens. Simmer 2 minutes.
11. Adjust seasoning to taste then pour over veal.
12. Sprinkle with grated lemon peel mixed with remaining garlic and parsley and serve straight away with risotto (see page 135) or with plain boiled rice.

Fricassee of veal

Serves 4

2lb (1 kilo) stewing veal, cut into 1-inch cubes

½ pint (250ml) water

¼ pint (125ml) dry white wine

4 cloves

1 large onion

1 blade mace

1 large parsley sprig

3oz (75gm) streaky bacon, chopped

salt

2oz (50gm) butter

4oz (100gm) button mushrooms

1½oz (37gm) flour

pepper to taste

4 tablespoons double cream

1 dessertspoon lemon juice

8 rolls of grilled bacon

4 wedges lemon

parsley to garnish

1. Put veal into saucepan with water and wine.
2. Press cloves into onion and add to pan with mace and parsley. Slowly bring to boil and remove scum.
3. Fry bacon gently in its own fat until soft.
4. Add to pan with 1 level teaspoon salt.
5. Lower heat and cover. Simmer gently for 1½ to 2 hours or until veal is tender.
6. Strain and reserve ¾ pint (375ml) veal liquor.
7. Melt butter in a saucepan. Add mushrooms and fry 5 minutes. Stir in flour and cook further 2 minutes.
8. Gradually blend in veal liquor.
9. Cook, stirring, until sauce comes to the boil and thickens.
10. Replace veal and adjust seasoning to taste. Heat through 5 minutes.
11. Stir in cream and lemon juice and serve straight away on a bed of freshly-boiled rice.
12. Garnish with bacon rolls, lemon and parsley.

Veal blanquette

Serves 4

Make exactly as for fricassee of veal (see previous recipe), but after heating through for 5 minutes at the end, stir in ¼ pint (125ml) double cream beaten with 2 egg yolks and 1 dessertspoon lemon juice. Warm through, stirring gently, but on no account allow mixture to boil.

Veal casserole

Serves 4

1½ to 2lb (¾ to 1 kilo) stewing veal, cut into 1-inch cubes

2 level tablespoons flour, well-seasoned with salt and pepper

1½oz (37gm) bacon dripping

1 large onion, chopped

4 medium celery stalks, cut into 1-inch lengths

3 medium carrots, sliced

3oz (75gm) lean bacon, diced

¼ pint (125ml) dry white wine or cider

¼ pint (125ml) chicken stock

¼ level teaspoon finely-grated lemon peel

4 small onions, halved

1. Pre-heat oven to moderate, 350 deg F or gas 4 (180 deg C).
2. Coat veal with the seasoned flour.
3. Heat dripping in a flameproof casserole, add veal and fry until pieces are well-browned. Remove to plate.
4. Add onion, celery, carrots and bacon and fry gently for 10 minutes or until pale gold.
5. Replace veal then add all remaining ingredients.
6. Cover closely and cook in centre of oven for 2 hours.

Offal

Cuts suitable for:

Roasting
Lamb's and calf's heart.

Grilling and frying
Calf's and lamb's liver, calf's and lamb's kidney, lamb's sweetbreads (frying only).

Stewing, braising and casseroling
Oxtail, ox and calf's heart, ox and calf's sweetbreads. Ox, pig's, sheep's and calf's kidney. Ox, lamb's and pig's liver.

Boiling
Salted and pickled tongue and dressed tripe.

Poaching
Brains.

Stewed oxtail

Serves 4

1 oxtail

2oz (50gm) lard or dripping

2 medium onions, chopped

3 medium carrots, sliced

1 small turnip, diced

2 level tablespoons tomato paste

bouquet garni (1 bay leaf, 4 peppercorns, 4 parsley sprigs and 4 cloves) tied in muslin bag

1½ pints (¾ litre) beef stock

2 level teaspoons salt

pepper to taste

2 level tablespoons cornflour

3 tablespoons cold water

2 to 3 tablespoons dry sherry

2 level tablespoons chopped parsley

1. Divide oxtail into neat pieces. Wash and wipe dry.
2. Heat lard or dripping in large saucepan.
3. Add onions, carrots and turnip and fry gently, with lid on pan, for 5 minutes.
4. Add oxtail and fry a little more briskly until pieces are well-sealed and brown.
5. Stir in tomato paste, bouquet garni, beef stock and salt and pepper to taste.
6. Bring to boil, stirring. Lower heat and cover.
7. Simmer gently for 3½ to 4 hours or until oxtail is tender.
8. Remove bouquet garni. When contents of pan are cold, transfer to refrigerator and leave overnight.
9. Before serving, remove hard layer of fat on the surface.
10. Bring oxtail to the boil. Mix cornflour to a smooth cream with cold water and add.
11. Cook, stirring, until stew comes to the boil and thickens.
12. Simmer 5 minutes. Add sherry and tansfer to a warm serving dish.
13. Sprinkle with parsley and accompany with creamed mashed potatoes and green vegetables to taste.

Oxtail and chestnut casserole

Serves 4

4oz (100gm) dried chestnuts, soaked overnight

1 oxtail

2 level tablespoons flour, well-seasoned with salt and pepper

2oz (50gm) lard or dripping

1 medium onion, chopped

½ pint (250ml) dry cider

¾ pint (375ml) beef stock

salt and pepper to taste

1 level teaspoon mixed herbs

12 small onions or shallots

4oz (100gm) lean bacon, chopped

1lb (½ kilo) potatoes

1. Drain chestnuts and break each in half.
2. Divide oxtail into joints and coat with seasoned flour.
3. Heat 1oz (25gm) lard or dripping in saucepan. Add onion and fry very gently until pale gold.
4. Add oxtail and fry a little more briskly until well-sealed and brown.
5. Pour cider and stock into pan. Season to taste with salt and pepper and add herbs.
6. Bring to boil, stirring. Lower heat and cover pan.
7. Simmer gently for 2½ to 3 hours, stirring occasionally.
8. Add chestnuts, onions or shallots, bacon and whole potatoes.
9. Cover and cook a further 30 minutes.
10. When contents of pan are cold, transfer to the refrigerator and leave overnight.
11. Before serving, remove hard layer of fat on the surface then re-heat oxtail.
12. Serve with green vegetables to taste.

Note
If preferred, use 8oz (200gm) fresh chestnuts, boiled and skinned, instead of dried ones.

Grilled kidneys

Serves 4

8 lamb's kidneys

about 1 tablespoon melted butter

salt and pepper to taste

1. Peel kidneys then cut each in half horizontally to give 2 thin slices. Remove cores, wash well and dry with paper towels.
2. Place in grill pan, cut sides down.
3. Brush with butter then sprinkle with salt and pepper.
4. Grill under medium heat for 5 minutes. Turn kidneys over, brush with more butter then sprinkle with more salt and pepper.
5. Serve with grilled and fried bacon, mushrooms, tomatoes and/or fried bread.

Kidneys in wine sauce

Serves 4

1 to 1½lb (½ to ¾ kilo) ox, sheep's or pig's kidney

2 level tablespoons flour, well-seasoned with salt, pepper and dry mustard

1½oz (37gm) bacon dripping or lard

1 large onion, chopped

2 level tablespoons tomato paste

½ pint (250ml) beef stock

½ pint (250ml) dry red wine

1 level teaspoon sugar

½ level teaspoon mixed herbs

8oz (200gm) button mushrooms

1. Cut kidney into 1-inch cubes and coat with seasoned flour.
2. Heat dripping or lard in saucepan. Add onion and fry gently until soft and gold.
3. Add kidney and fry a little more briskly until pieces are well-sealed and brown.
4. Stir in tomato paste then add stock and wine.
5. Cook, stirring, until mixture comes to the boil and thickens.
6. Add sugar and herbs. Lower heat and cover pan. Simmer gently for 1 hour or until kidney is tender. Stir occasionally.
7. Add mushrooms and cook a further 10 minutes.
8. Serve with creamed potatoes or freshly-boiled rice.

Kidney, bacon and sausage hot pot

Serves 4

8oz (200gm) ox kidney

6oz (150gm) lean bacon rashers

8oz (200gm) pork sausages

1lb (½ kilo) potatoes

2 medium leeks, trimmed and washed

4 medium tomatoes, skinned

1 large cooking apple, peeled and cored

salt and pepper

¼ pint (125ml) beef stock

½oz (12gm) butter or margarine

1. Pre-heat oven to moderate, 350 deg F or gas 4 (180 deg C).
2. Cut kidney into small cubes. Wash and wipe dry with paper towels.
3. Roll up bacon rashers. Separate sausages.
4. Thinly slice potatoes, leeks, tomatoes and apple.
5. Cover base of casserole dish with half the potatoes, leeks, tomatoes and apple. Sprinkle with salt and pepper to taste.
6. Arrange kidney, rolled bacon rashers and sausages on top.
7. Cover with rest of apples, tomatoes and leeks and season well with salt and pepper.
8. Arrange rest of potato slices on the top.
9. Pour stock into dish then dot with flakes of butter or margarine.
10. Cover with lid or aluminium foil and cook in centre of oven for 1¼ hours. Uncover and continue to cook for a further 30 minutes or until top is golden brown.

Fried liver

Serves 4

¾ to 1lb (300gm to ½ kilo) calf's or lamb's liver

1 level tablespoon flour, well-seasoned with salt and pepper

1½oz (37gm) butter or margarine for frying

1. Cut liver into slices, ½ inch thick. Wash and wipe dry with paper towels. Coat with seasoned flour.
2. Heat butter or margarine in frying pan.
3. Add liver and fry briskly on both sides for 1 minute.
4. Lower heat and fry a little more slowly for 6 to 7 minutes, turning once.
5. Serve straight away.

Fried liver with onions

Serves 4

Prepare liver as directed in recipe for fried liver, above. Slowly fry 8oz (200gm) sliced onions in 2oz (50gm) hot butter or margarine until soft and pale gold. Add liver and fry, with onions, as directed.

Crumbed and fried liver

Serves 4

Coat liver with flour as directed in recipe for fried liver (see this page). Dip slices in 1 standard egg beaten with 2 teaspoons cold water then toss in toasted breadcrumbs. Fry in 2oz (50gm) hot butter or bacon dripping for 8 to 9 minutes, turning once. Drain on soft kitchen paper and serve with wedges of lemon.

Grilled liver

Serves 4

¾ to 1lb (300gm to ½ kilo) calf's or lamb's liver

melted butter or olive oil

salt and pepper to taste

1. Cut liver into slices, ½ inch thick. Wash and wipe dry with paper towels.
2. Put into grill pan and brush with butter or oil.
3. Sprinkle with salt and pepper and grill under a medium heat for 4 to 5 minutes.
4. Turn slices over, brush with more butter or oil and sprinkle with salt and pepper.
5. Grill a further 4 to 5 minutes.
6. Serve straight away.

Liver fritters

Serves 4

6oz (150gm) cooked liver, finely minced

1 level tablespoon finely-chopped parsley

1 recipe savoury fritter batter (see page 105)

deep oil for frying

1. Gently fold liver and parsley into fritter batter.
2. Heat oil until a cube of bread, dropped into it, turns golden brown in one minute and floats to the top.
3. Add dessertspoons of fritter mixture to the oil and fry for 5 minutes or until well-puffed and golden.
4. Drain on soft kitchen paper then serve straight away with freshly-scrambled eggs.

Liver fritters with scrambled eggs

Liver and bacon stewpot

Liver and bacon stewpot

Serves 4

12oz (300gm) ox, sheep's or pig's liver

2 level tablespoons flour, well-seasoned with salt and pepper

1½oz (37gm) lard or dripping

1 large onion, chopped

6oz (150gm) lean bacon, chopped

1 green pepper, de-seeded and cut into strips

6oz (150gm) green beans

¾ pint (375ml) beef stock

1 tablespoon vinegar

2 teaspoons Worcestershire sauce

salt and pepper to taste

1. Cut liver into small cubes and coat with seasoned flour.
2. Heat lard or dripping in a saucepan.
3. Add onion, bacon and pepper and fry gently, with lid on pan, for 10 minutes.
4. Add coated liver and fry a little more briskly until pieces are well-sealed and brown.
5. Stir in beans then pour in stock, vinegar and Worcestershire sauce.
6. Bring to boil, stirring, then season to taste with salt and pepper.
7. Lower heat and cover pan.
8. Simmer gently for approximately 1 hour or until liver is tender, stirring occasionally. Serve with creamy mashed potatoes and green vegetables to taste.

Roast hearts with forcemeat

Serves 4

4 lamb's or calf's hearts

stuffing to taste (see pages 106-7)

3 level tablespoons well-seasoned flour

2oz (50gm) lard or dripping

¾ pint (375ml) beef stock

2 tablespoons red wine (optional)

1. Pre-heat oven to moderate, 325 deg F or gas 3 (190 deg C).
2. Wash hearts thoroughly and cut away tubes, excess fat and gristle.
3. Cut through centre divisions to give one cavity in each heart.
4. Fill with stuffing, then tie hearts with thick thread so that they keep their shape.
5. Coat with flour then fry in the lard or dripping until crisp and golden all over.
6. Place upright in casserole. Add stock and wine, if used, cover with lid or foil and cook in centre of oven for 2 to 2½ hours or until tender, basting at least twice.
7. Serve with liquor from casserole, creamy mashed potatoes and redcurrant jelly.

Rum-braised heart

Serves 4

1½lb (¾ kilo) ox heart

2 level tablespoons flour

2oz (50gm) lard or dripping

1 large onion, finely chopped

2 medium celery stalks, chopped

2 medium carrots, sliced

2 level tablespoons redcurrant jelly

1 level teaspoon prepared English mustard

¼ pint (125ml) red or rosé wine

¼ pint (125ml) beef stock

1 to 2 tablespoons rum

1 tablespoon seedless raisins

salt and pepper to taste

1. Pre-heat oven to moderate, 350 deg F or gas 4 (180 deg C).
2. Slice heart then coat with flour.
3. Heat lard or dripping in flameproof casserole.
4. Add onion, celery and carrots and fry gently, with lid on pan, for 10 minutes.
5. Add slices of heart and fry a little more briskly until well-sealed and golden.
6. Add redcurrant jelly, mustard, wine, stock, rum and raisins.
7. Slowly bring to boil, stirring.
8. Season to taste with salt and pepper then cover with lid.
9. Put into centre of oven and cook 2 hours or until heart is tender.
10. Serve with freshly-boiled potatoes and green vegetables to taste.

Brains with black butter sauce

Serves 4

4 sheep's brains	
2 tablespoons vinegar	
salt and pepper	
2 peppercorns	
3 cloves	
1 blade mace	
freshly-made black butter sauce (see page 101)	

1. Cover brains with cold water and leave to soak 2 hours, changing water twice.
2. Cover with lukewarm water for 5 minutes to remove blood.
3. Carefully remove skin and fibres and wash once again.
4. Put into saucepan with vinegar, water to cover, salt and pepper to taste, the peppercorns, cloves and mace.
5. Slowly bring to boil, lower heat and cover.
6. Poach very gently for 20 minutes.
7. Lift brains out of water, drain thoroughly and cut each in half.
8. Put on to a warm platter and coat with black butter sauce.
9. Accompany with creamed potatoes.

Tripe with onions

Serves 4

2lb (1 kilo) dressed tripe	
8oz (200gm) onions	
¾ pint (375ml) milk	
¼ pint (125ml) water	
1 level teaspoon salt	
1½oz (37gm) butter or margarine	
1½oz (37gm) flour	
pinch of nutmeg	
white pepper to taste	

1. Wash tripe very thoroughly then cut into 2-inch squares. Slice onions.
2. Put both into saucepan with milk, water and salt.
3. Slowly bring to boil. Lower heat and cover pan.
4. Simmer gently 1 hour or until tripe is tender. Drain, reserving liquor.
5. Melt butter or margarine in saucepan. Add flour and cook 2 minutes without browning.
6. Gradually blend in tripe liquor.
7. Cook, stirring, until sauce comes to boil and thickens.
8. Replace tripe and onions then add nutmeg and pepper to taste.
9. Heat through 5 minutes, add salt if necessary then serve with plain boiled potatoes.

Fried tripe with Parmesan cheese

Serves 4

Cook 2lb (1 kilo) tripe in boiling salted water for approximately 1 hour or until tender. Drain thoroughly and cut into 2-inch pieces. Wipe each with soft kitchen paper. Sprinkle lightly with garlic salt and white pepper then fry in 2oz (50gm) butter and 1 tablespoon olive oil until golden. Remove from pan, drain on soft paper towels and sprinkle heavily with grated Parmesan cheese. Serve straight away and accompany with French bread.

Fried sweetbreads

Serves 4

1lb (½ kilo) sweetbreads	
water	
lemon juice	
1 large egg	
2 teaspoons water	
toasted breadcrumbs	
2oz (50gm) butter or margarine	
2 tablespoons olive oil	
wedges of lemon and parsley to garnish	

1. Soak sweetbreads in lukewarm water for 1 hour. Drain.
2. Put into saucepan and cover with cold water. Add a squeeze of lemon juice and bring to boil. Boil 5 minutes.
3. Drain and rinse under cold water then remove skin and grizzle.
4. Wipe sweetbreads dry with soft kitchen paper.
5. Coat with egg, beaten with water, then toss in crumbs. Leave to stand 15 minutes for coating to harden.
6. Heat butter or margarine and oil in pan. Add sweetbreads and fry 4 to 5 minutes or until crisp and golden.
7. Drain on soft kitchen paper and serve hot with suitable sauce (see pages 92–99).
8. Garnish with lemon and parsley.

Sweetbreads suprême

Serves 4

Prepare sweetbreads as given in recipe for fried sweetbreads, above. After removing skin and grizzle, put sweetbreads into a saucepan and add ½ pint (250ml) water, ¼ pint (125ml) milk, 1 onion stuck with 4 cloves, 1 sliced carrot and salt and pepper to taste. Cover and simmer gently for 30 minutes. Strain and reserve liquor. Melt 1½oz (37gm) butter in a saucepan. Stir in 1½oz (37gm) flour and cook 2 minutes without browning. Gradually blend in reserved liquor. Cook, stirring, until sauce comes to boil and thickens. Replace sweetbreads and simmer 5 minutes. Beat 4 tablespoons double cream with an egg yolk and squeeze of lemon. Add to sweetbreads and re-heat gently without boiling. Adjust seasoning to taste and serve on freshly-made toast.

Boiled ox tongue

Serves 12

1 fresh or pickled ox tongue, about 5lb or 2½ kilo in weight	
cold water	
2 large onions	
2 carrots	
2 celery stalks	
4 cloves	
1 bay leaf	
2 peppercorns	
handful of parsley	

1. Remove excess fat from root end of tongue.
2. Put into cold water and slowly bring to boil. Drain.
3. Cover with fresh cold water then add all remaining ingredients.
4. Bring to boil and lower heat. Cover and simmer gently for about 6 hours if tongue is fresh, 3 to 3½ hours if pickled.
5. Drain and leave until cool enough to handle.
6. Strip off skin then remove tubes, bones, grizzle and fat from root end.

Tongue with Madeira or mustard sauce

Serves about 12

Cook fresh tongue as directed for boiled ox tongue, above. Carve into slices and serve hot with Madeira or mustard sauce (see pages 95, 98).

Cold tongue

Serves 12

Cook fresh or pickled tongue as directed for boiled ox tongue, above. After stripping off skin and removing tubes, bones, grizzle and fat, press into a 6 or 7-inch round cake tin, curving tongue to shape. Cover with a second dish or plate then weigh down with a heavy garden stone. Leave until cold, turn out of tin and carve thinly. Accompany with salad.

Poultry

1. The breast of a fresh chicken should be plump and the breast bone flexible. Feet should be soft and clean and the legs smooth. Turkeys should look white and plump with supple feet. Ducks and geese should have creamy white skin and plump breasts.

2. Frozen birds with brown patches should be avoided, as this indicates that they have freezer burn through bad or over-storage.

3. Fresh birds should be kept unwrapped in the refrigerator for up to 36 hours. Jointed poultry should be kept no longer than 24 hours.

4. Frozen birds should be thawed completely before cooking. Speedy de-frosting is the most satisfactory method and the best way to do this is to stand the unwrapped bird in a sink filled with water from the hot tap.

5. It is essential to remove the giblet bag in the body cavity before cooking the bird itself.

6. Allow 3 to 4oz (75 to 100gm) stuffing to every lb ($\frac{1}{2}$ kilo) of oven-ready bird. Put stuffing into bird just before roasting; in no circumstances stuff any bird the previous day or in fact any time in advance, because even if kept in the refrigerator, cold air is unable to penetrate through to the centre of the bird and the warm atmosphere inside the body cavity causes the growth of bacteria.

7. For the same reasons, never slow roast the Christmas bird through the night.

8 Allow approximately 12oz (300gm) ovenready chicken, turkey and capon (neutered cockerel) per person; 1lb ($\frac{1}{2}$ kilo) duck or goose per person.

9 As the proportion of meat to bone is greater in large birds than in small ones, a big bird is a more economical proposition.

Roast chicken

Allow 12oz (300gm) per person. Roast in centre of moderately hot oven, 400 deg F or gas 6 (200 deg C), for 20 minutes per lb ($\frac{1}{2}$ kilo) and 20 minutes over. Put chicken into roasting tin and brush with melted butter, dripping or oil. Season with salt and pepper. Roast for required amount of time, basting frequently. If chicken is unwrapped, a few rashers of streaky bacon may be draped over the breast to keep it moist but should be removed $\frac{1}{2}$ an hour before the chicken is cooked.

Foil-wrapped chicken should be loosely wrapped in aluminium foil and roasted as unwrapped birds, allowing 2 minutes extra per lb ($\frac{1}{2}$ kilo) and 22 minutes over. The foil should be opened up during the last 30 minutes to brown the breast.

Serve with gravy, bread sauce (see page 103), grilled bacon rolls, grilled chipolata sausages, roast and boiled potatoes and vegetables to taste.

Note
If preferred, chicken may be roasted in a transparent roasting bag in which it will brown and keep moist without basting.

Roast chicken with herbs

Cream 3oz (75gm) softened butter with $\frac{1}{2}$ level teaspoon tarragon, 1 level teaspoon French mustard and 1 level tablespoon finely-chopped parsley. Put half the butter inside the body cavity of the bird then spread remainder over the chicken breast. Roast as directed above, basting frequently.

Roast chicken joints

Put joints into a roasting tin, skin side uppermost and sprinkle with salt and pepper. Brush generously with melted butter then roast in centre of moderately hot oven, 400 deg F or gas 6 (200 deg C), for 40 to 50 minutes or until crisp and cooked through.

Chicken roasted in a transparent roasting bag will brown and keep moist without basting

Almond buttered chicken

Almond buttered chicken

Serves 8

4 baby chickens, each about 2lb (1 kilo) in weight

6oz (150gm) slightly salted butter

1 tablespoon olive oil

4oz (100gm) flaked almonds

parsley to garnish

1. Pre-heat oven to moderately hot, 375 deg F or gas 5 (190 deg C).
2. Halve chickens by cutting through breast and backbone with a sharp knife or kitchen scissors.
3. Melt butter in large frying pan. Add oil.
4. Fry chicken, 2 halves at a time, until crisp and golden.
5. Transfer to a large baking tin and baste generously with melted butter and oil from frying pan.
6. Roast near top of oven for approximately 45 minutes, basting frequently with melted butter and oil.
7. About 5 minutes before chicken is ready, fry almonds until light gold in remaining butter and oil in frying pan. Remove from pan and drain.
8. Arrange chicken on a large warm platter and garnish with parsley and almonds.

Chicken Maryland

Serves 4

4 medium joints roasting chicken

2 level tablespoons flour, well-seasoned with salt and pepper

1 large egg

2 teaspoons cold water

toasted breadcrumbs

deep oil for frying

6oz (150gm) sweetcorn kernels

coating batter (see page 105)

halved bananas, fried in butter, and gravy to accompany

watercress to garnish

1. Coat chicken with seasoned flour, then dip in egg beaten with the water.
2. Toss in crumbs and leave to stand for about 15 minutes for coating to harden.
3. Heat oil until a cube of bread, dropped into it, turns golden in 1 minute and floats to the top.
4. Add joints and fry 10 to 15 minutes.
5. Remove from pan, drain thoroughly and keep hot.
6. To make corn fritters, stir corn into batter. Drop about 16 dessertspoons of mixture into the hot oil and fry 4 to 5 minutes or until puffy and golden brown. Remove from pan and drain on soft kitchen paper.
7. Arrange chicken on a d'oily-lined platter with the hot fritters and fried bananas.
8. Accompany with gravy, and garnish with watercress.

Grilled chicken joints

Serves 4

4 medium joints roasting chicken

2oz (50gm) butter, melted

salt and pepper

1 tablespoon lemon juice

½ level teaspoon paprika

watercress or parsley to garnish

1. Wash and wipe joints with paper towels then place in grill pan, skin sides down.
2. Brush generously with butter then sprinkle with salt and pepper.
3. Grill 5 minutes. Turn joints over, brush with more butter then sprinkle with more salt and pepper.
4. Continue to grill a further 25 to 30 minutes or until tender, turning frequently and brushing with more melted butter.
5. Transfer to a warm serving dish and keep hot.
6. Add lemon juice and paprika to grill pan juices.
7. Pour over chicken and garnish with watercress or parsley.

Note

If liked, joints may be first rubbed over with a cut clove of garlic.

Fried chicken

Serves 4

4 medium joints roasting chicken

2 level tablespoons flour, well-seasoned with salt and pepper

2oz (50gm) butter or margarine or bacon dripping

1. Wash and wipe joints then coat with seasoned flour.
2. Heat butter or margarine or bacon dripping with oil in a large frying pan.
3. Add joints, skin side up.
4. Fry briskly on both sides for 5 minutes.
5. Lower heat and cover. Cook gently for a further 20 minutes. Uncover and continue to cook a further 10 to 15 minutes or until joints are golden brown.
6. If liked, accompany with fried bananas, corn-on-the-cob, sliced tomatoes and peas.

Fried chicken with fried bananas, corn-on-the-cob, sliced tomatoes and peas

West African style chicken

Serves 4

Fry chicken joints as given in recipe for fried chicken, above. Use only 1½oz (37gm) butter or margarine and 1 dessertspoon salad oil for frying. Remove chicken joints from pan after 10 minutes and leave on one side. Add 1 medium chopped onion and 1 crushed garlic clove to remaining butter and oil in pan. Fry gently 5 minutes. Stir in 2 level tablespoons peanut butter, 1 can (approximately 1lb or ½ kilo) tomatoes, 1 level teaspoon sugar, 1 small bay leaf, 1 teaspoon Worcestershire sauce and 1 to 2 level teaspoons salt. Bring to boil, stirring, and simmer 10 minutes. Mix 1 level dessertspoon cornflour to a thin cream with 2 to 3 dessertspoons cold water. Add to tomato mixture in pan and cook, stirring, until sauce comes to boil and thickens. Replace chicken joints, baste with sauce then cover with lid. Lower heat and simmer 40 to 50 minutes or until chicken is tender, stirring frequently. Serve garnished with parsley, with creamy mashed potatoes and green vegetables to taste.

Creamy chicken curry garnished with parsley and grapes and served with rice

Creamy chicken curry

Serves 4

Fry chicken joints as given in recipe for fried chicken (see this page), but remove from pan after 10 minutes. Transfer to a plate and leave on one side. Add 2 medium chopped onions to rest of fat and oil in pan and fry gently until pale gold. Stir in 1 level tablespoon flour, 2 to 3 level tablespoons curry powder, ½ level teaspoon each powdered ginger and cinnamon, 1 to 2 level teaspoons salt and 2 coarsely-grated medium carrots. Gradually blend in ¾ pint (375ml) chicken stock and 1 small can evaporated milk made up to ½ pint (250ml) with cold water. Cook, stirring, until sauce comes to the boil and then replace chicken. Lower heat and simmer very gently for ¾ to 1 hour, stirring frequently. About 10 minutes before curry is ready, add 8oz (200gm) peeled, halved and de-seeded green grapes. Serve with freshly-boiled rice, garnished with parsley.

West African style chicken served with creamed potatoes

Sweet-sour chicken

Serves 4

2 small carrots, very thinly sliced

1 small green pepper, de-seeded and cut into strips

4 level tablespoons finely-chopped canned pineapple

6 spring onions, chopped

4 tablespoons syrup from can of pineapple

1 tablespoon Soy sauce

1 level tablespoon clear honey

1oz (25gm) soft brown sugar

4 tablespoons vinegar

2 level tablespoons cornflour

½ pint (250ml) chicken stock

salt and pepper

1oz (25gm) blanched almonds

1oz (25gm) butter

1 freshly-roasted chicken, uncooked weight about 3½lb (1¾ kilo)

1. Put carrots into saucepan with green pepper, pineapple and spring onions.
2. Stir in pineapple syrup, Soy sauce, honey, sugar and vinegar.
3. Slowly bring to boil then simmer 5 minutes.
4. Meanwhile, blend cornflour to a smooth cream with the chicken stock.
5. Add to pan and cook, stirring, until sauce comes to the boil and thickens. Season with salt and pepper. Add almonds and butter. Leave over very low heat.
6. Quickly cut the chicken into bite-size pieces and put into a warm serving dish.
7. Coat with sweet-sour sauce and serve straight away with freshly-boiled rice or noodles.

Chicken braise with olives

Serves 4 to 6

1 roasting chicken, about 3lb (1½ kilo) in weight

flour

2oz (50gm) butter

1 dessertspoon salad oil

1 large onion, finely chopped

2 large celery stalks, finely chopped

1lb (½ kilo) small carrots

¼ pint (125ml) chicken stock

1 wine glass dry white wine or cider

¼ level teaspoon marjoram

2 level teaspoons salt

1 medium lemon, sliced

1 dozen black olives

parsley to garnish

1. Wash and dry chicken with paper towels then coat chicken all over with flour.
2. Heat butter and oil in large flameproof casserole.
3. Add chicken and fry fairly briskly until crisp and brown all over. Remove to a plate.
4. Add onion, celery and carrots to remaining fat and oil in pan and fry about 7 minutes or until well-browned.
5. Add stock, wine or cider, marjoram and salt.
6. Bring to boil and replace chicken, breast uppermost. Lower heat and cover pan.
7. Simmer gently for 1½ hours or until chicken is just tender.
8. Pre-heat oven to moderately hot, 400 deg F or gas 6 (200 deg C).
9. Uncover casserole and add lemon slices and olives.
10. Put into centre of oven and cook, uncovered, for 30 to 40 minutes or until breast is golden brown.
11. Garnish with parsley and serve with freshly-boiled potatoes.

Chicken fricassee

Serves 4

8 small or 4 large joints roasting chicken

cold water

4 cloves

1 large onion

1 blade mace

1 medium carrot, sliced

2 to 3 level teaspoons salt

pepper to taste

2oz (50gm) butter or margarine

4oz (100gm) lean bacon, chopped

2oz (50gm) flour

½ pint (250ml) milk

1 level tablespoon chopped parsley

½ level teaspoon finely-grated lemon peel

1. Put chicken into large saucepan.
2. Pour in cold water to cover.
3. Press cloves into onion and add to pan with mace, carrot, salt and pepper to taste.
4. Bring to boil, remove scum then lower heat.
5. Cover pan and simmer very gently for 1 hour or until chicken is tender.
6. Remove chicken from pan and cut into bite-size pieces. Strain stock and reserve ½ pint (250ml).
7. Heat butter or margarine in saucepan. Add bacon and fry gently for 5 minutes.
8. Stir in flour and cook 2 minutes.
9. Gradually blend in chicken stock and milk.
10. Cook, stirring, until sauce comes to the boil and thickens then add chicken.
11. Adjust seasoning to taste and heat through for 5 to 10 minutes.
12. Transfer to a warm serving dish and sprinkle with parsley mixed with lemon peel.
13. Serve with freshly-boiled rice.

Chicken pie

Serves 4 to 6

Choose same quantity of boiling fowl as given in recipe for chicken fricassee, (see previous recipe). Simmer for 2½ to 3 hours adding an extra ¼ pint (125ml) water. Continue as for chicken fricassee then leave mixture until completely cold. Transfer to 1½ pint (¾ litre) pie dish and cover with puff or short crust pastry (see pages 108 and 112). Brush with egg and bake near top of oven, 425 deg F or gas 7 (220 deg C), for 25 to 30 minutes or until golden brown.

Hunter's chicken

Serves 4

4 medium joints roasting chicken

4 level tablespoons flour, well-seasoned with salt and pepper

1½oz (37gm) butter or margarine

3 dessertspoons salad oil

1 large onion, chopped

1 garlic clove

4 level dessertspoons tomato paste

12oz (300gm) tomatoes, skinned

¼ pint (125ml) dry white wine

2 tablespoons brandy

1 level dessertspoon sugar

1 bay leaf

½ level teaspoon mixed herbs

salt and pepper to taste

6oz (150gm) mushrooms

1. Coat chicken with seasoned flour.
2. Heat butter or margarine and salad oil in large saucepan. Add chicken and fry until golden brown all over. Remove to a plate.
3. Add onion and garlic to remaining butter and oil in pan and fry gently until pale gold.
4. Stir in tomato paste then add tomatoes and wine.
5. Pour brandy into a ladle and set alight.
6. Add to pan when flames have subsided.
7. Stir in sugar, bay leaf and herbs then slowly bring to the boil, stirring. Adjust seasoning to taste.
8. Replace chicken, cover pan and lower heat.
9. Simmer very gently for 30 minutes, stirring occasionally. Add mushrooms and simmer a further 30 minutes or until chicken is tender.
10. Serve with freshly-boiled spaghetti tossed in butter.

Marengo chicken

Serves 4

Make exactly as for hunter's chicken, above, but add 4oz (100gm) stoned black olives and ½ teacup chopped parsley with the mushrooms.

Chicken braise with olives

Guinea fowl in wine sauce garnished with grapes

Guinea fowl in wine sauce

Serves 4

2 guinea fowl and giblets, each about 2lb (1 kilo) in weight

1½ pints (¾ litre) water

salt

1 bay leaf

1 onion, sliced

1 medium celery stalk, coarsely chopped

3 sprigs parsley

6oz (150gm) butter, softened

8 rashers streaky bacon

3 level tablespoons flour

½ bottle dry white wine

pepper to taste

lemon juice

8oz (200gm) green grapes, skinned and with pips removed

parsley to garnish

1. To make stock, simmer guinea fowl giblets for 1 hour with water, 1 level teaspoon salt, bay leaf, onion, celery and 1 sprig parsley. Strain and reserve ¾ pint (375ml) stock.
2. Pre-heat oven to moderately hot, 375 deg F or gas 5 (190 deg C).
3. Put a large knob of butter and a parsley sprig into each guinea fowl.
4. Spread remaining butter over birds and transfer to roasting tin.
5. Cover breasts with rashers of streaky bacon and roast for 1 hour in the centre of the oven until golden brown and tender, basting frequently.
6. When cooked, remove bacon then transfer birds to a warm dish. Keep hot.
7. Carefully pour off fat from roasting tin, leaving behind about 1 tablespoon.
8. Add flour and place tin over a low heat.
9. Cook 2 or 3 minutes, scraping residue from tin and mixing thoroughly.
10. Gradually stir in reserved giblet stock and the wine. Simmer 10 minutes.
11. Season to taste, adding a little lemon juice if necessary.
12. Strain sauce into a heated sauceboat and arrange grapes round the guinea fowls on serving dish. Garnish with parsley.

Chicken curry

Serves 6

1oz (25gm) desiccated coconut

1 pint (approximately ½ litre) hot water

1 boiling fowl weighing about 4lb or 2 kilo

2 tablespoons salad oil

1 large onion, chopped

2 garlic cloves, chopped

2 to 3 level tablespoons curry powder

1 level tablespoon flour

2 level tablespoons tomato paste

juice of ½ lemon

½ level teaspoon cinnamon

½ level teaspoon ginger

pinch of Cayenne pepper

1 bay leaf

2 level tablespoons mango chutney

2 level teaspoons salt

2 level tablespoons sultanas

1. Put coconut into bowl. Cover with hot water and leave on one side.
2. Cut chicken into joints and remove excess fat. Wash and wipe dry with paper towels.
3. Fry in the hot oil until golden. Remove to plate.
4. Add onion and garlic to remaining oil in pan and fry gently until pale gold.
5. Stir in curry powder, flour, tomato paste and lemon juice then strain in coconut water, discarding coconut.
6. Add all remaining ingredients and bring to the boil, stirring.
7. Replace chicken, lower heat and cover.
8. Simmer very gently for 2½ to 3 hours. or until chicken is tender, stirring frequently.
9. Serve with freshly-boiled rice and side dishes of natural yogurt, thinly-sliced cucumber and grated carrots mixed with French dressing (see page 161), and chopped salted cashews.

Coq au vin

Serves 4

4 medium joints roasting chicken

4 level tablespoons flour, well-seasoned with salt and pepper

2oz (50gm) butter or bacon dripping

1 tablespoon olive oil

1 to 2 garlic cloves

1 large onion, chopped

8oz (200gm) lean bacon, chopped

1 dozen small onions or shallots

1 teacup parsley, finely chopped

1 bay leaf

½ pint (250ml) red wine

¼ pint (125ml) chicken stock

salt and pepper to taste

6oz (150gm) button mushrooms

1. Pre-heat oven to moderate, 350 deg F or gas 4 (180 deg C).
2. Coat chicken with seasoned flour.
3. Heat butter or dripping and oil in flameproof casserole.
4. Add chicken and fry briskly until golden brown. Take out of casserole and remove to a plate.
5. Add garlic, onion and bacon and fry gently until pale gold.
6. Stir in any left-over coating flour then add onions or shallots, parsley, bay leaf, wine and stock.
7. Bring to boil, stirring, then adjust seasoning to taste.
8. Replace chicken, add mushrooms then cover closely with lid or foil.
9. Cook in centre of oven for 1 hour or until chicken is tender.
10. Serve with freshly-boiled whole potatoes.

Roast turkey

Allow 12oz (300gm) raw weight of turkey per person for birds up to 16lb (approximately 7 kilo). For turkeys weighing over this, allow 8oz (200gm) per person. Roast in centre of a moderate oven, 350 deg F or gas 4 (180 deg C), allowing 25 minutes per lb (½ kilo) for turkeys weighing between 6 and 12lb (3 and 6 kilo); 20 minutes per lb (½ kilo) for turkeys weighing between 12 and 16lb (approximately 5½ and 7 kilo); 18 minutes per lb (½ kilo) for turkeys weighing between 16 and 25lb (7 and 11 kilo). Fill crop and body cavity of bird with 2 different stuffings (see pages 106–107). Place in roasting tin and brush generously with melted butter, margarine or bacon dripping. Season well to taste with salt and pepper and roast as directed above, basting frequently.

Foil-wrapped turkeys should be cooked in the centre of a hot oven, 425 deg F or gas 7 (220 deg C), for the same length of time as unwrapped birds. The foil should be opened up during the last 30 minutes to brown the breast.

Serve with gravy, bread and cranberry sauces (see pages 102 and 103), chipolata sausages, bacon rolls, roast and boiled potatoes and other vegetables to taste.

Using left-over turkey

Turkey cutlets

Serves 4

Cut 4 large slices off breast and coat with egg and toasted breadcrumbs. Fry quickly in butter and/or margarine until golden on both sides. Drain thoroughly and serve with wedges of lemon and a sharp sauce such as tartare (see page 100).

Turkey mornay

Serves 4

Cut 8 to 12oz (200 to 300gm) cold turkey into dice. Combine with ½ pint (250ml) mornay sauce (see page 96). Transfer to buttered heatproof dish and sprinkle top generously with grated Cheddar cheese. Re-heat and brown near top of hot oven, 425 deg F or gas 7 (220 deg C), for 15 minutes. Serve with crisp toast.

Curried turkey

Serves 4

Combine 8 to 12oz (200 to 300gm) cooked diced turkey with curry sauce (see page 103). Simmer gently for 20 minutes then serve on a bed of freshly-boiled rice. Accompany with a crisp salad tossed with French dressing (see page 161).

Turkey à la king

Serves 4

Combine 8 to 12oz (200 to 300gm) cooked diced turkey with ½ pint (250ml) white coating sauce (see page 94). Add 4oz (100gm) sliced and butter-fried mushrooms, 1 level tablespoon chopped canned pimiento, 2 tablespoons sherry and plenty of salt and pepper to taste. Simmer gently for 15 minutes then stir in 4 tablespoons single cream beaten with 1 egg yolk. Re-heat gently without boiling and serve with freshly-made toast.

Fried turkey cakes

Serves 4

Combine 8 to 12oz (200 to 300gm) finely-minced turkey with 1lb (½ kilo) freshly-mashed potatoes. Add 1 small grated onion, 1 level tablespoon finely-chopped parsley, 1 level teaspoon prepared mustard and plenty of salt and pepper to taste. Bind with a little beaten egg. Shape into 8 cakes, coat lightly with flour then dip in beaten egg. Toss in breadcrumbs and fry in hot lard, butter or bacon dripping until crisp and golden on both sides. Serve piping hot with suitable sauce (see pages 92–99), and green vegetables to taste.

Roast duckling served with peas, baby carrots, cranberry sauce and garnished with fresh cherries

Roast duckling

Serves 4

Wash a 4lb (2 kilo) duckling (ovenready weight) and dry thoroughly inside and out with paper towels. Stand duckling on rack in roasting tin and prick skin all over with a fork so that fat runs freely. Sprinkle fairly heavily with salt (for a crisp skin) then roast in centre of moderately hot oven, 375 deg F or gas 5 (190 deg C), for 2 hours. Do not baste. Serve with gravy, apple or cranberry sauce (see pages 102, 103), roast and boiled potatoes, green peas, baby carrots, and garnished with cocktail cherries.

Roast duckling portions

Serves 4

Allow 1 duckling portion per person. Prepare as for roast duckling, above, but roast for 1 hour only.

Apple-stuffed roast duckling

Serves 4

Prepare and roast duckling as for roast duckling, above, but first pack into body cavity 2 or 3 large peeled, cored and quartered cooking apples. Serve with gravy, red cabbage and boiled potatoes.

Roast duckling portions served with peas, cranberry sauce and garnished with cherries and orange slices

Duckling with orange sauce

Serves 4

Prepare and roast duckling as for roast duckling (see opposite). Remove bird from roasting tin, transfer to a warm platter and keep hot. Pour off all but 1 tablespoon fat from roasting tin. Stand tin over a medium heat and stir in 1 level tablespoon flour. Cook 2 minutes. Gradually blend in juice from 2 large oranges, finely-shredded orange peel from 1 orange, 5 tablespoons dry red wine, 2 level tablespoons redcurrant jelly, 2 to 3 tablespoons brandy and salt and pepper to taste. Cook over a low heat, stirring continuously, until sauce comes to the boil and thickens. Simmer 2 minutes and, if too thick, thin down with a little boiling water. Pour over duck then garnish with orange slices and watercress.

Duck with brandy and cherries

Prepare and roast duckling as for roast duckling (see opposite). Remove bird from roasting tin, transfer to a platter and keep hot. Pour off all but 1 tablespoon fat from roasting tin. Stand tin over a medium heat and stir in 1 level tablespoon flour. Cook 2 minutes. Gradually blend in $\frac{1}{4}$ pint (125ml) gravy, 4 tablespoons brandy, 1 tablespoon lemon juice, 4 heaped tablespoons canned black cherries (pitted), 2 tablespoons syrup from cherry can and plenty of pepper and salt to taste. Cook, stirring, until sauce comes to boil and thickens. Simmer 2 minutes then pour over duckling. Garnish with fresh mandarin segments.

Roast goose

Prepare as for roast duckling (see opposite), but cook in centre of moderately hot oven, 400 deg F or gas 6 (200 deg C), allowing 20 minutes per lb ($\frac{1}{2}$ kilo).

Game

This is in season mainly during the early autumn and early winter months. At other times, game is protected by law and the killing of it is prohibited. There is no close season for hare, rabbit and pigeons but the sale of hare is not allowed between March and July. To improve flavour and tenderness, all game birds should be hung by the legs for varying amounts of time and this is best done in a cool, dry and airy place until the tail and breast feathers pull out easily. Afterwards, the birds should be plucked, drawn and trussed as for poultry but the feet should not be removed. Young game birds are best roasted, while older ones should be casseroled, stewed or braised.

Partridge is in season from 1 September to 1 February and should be hung 7 to 8 days.

Pheasant is in season from 1 October to 1 February and should be hung 7 to 8 days.

Grouse is in season from 12 August to 10 December and should be hung 4 to 5 days.

Woodcock is in season from 1 October to 31 January and should be hung 4 to 5 days.

Snipe is in season from 12 August to 31 January and should be hung 5 to 8 days.

Pigeons have no close season and should be hung 2 to 3 days.

Rabbit has no close season and should be hung 4 to 5 days.

Hare is in season from August to February and should be hung 7 to 8 days.

Venison is in season from June to 31 December and should be hung 7 to 14 days.

Water game Wild duck and goose are in season from 1 September to 20 February and should be hung 2 to 3 days. (Inland season ends on 21 January.)

Note
Hanging times given are a general guide only. So much depends on personal taste —some people like their game very high while others do not—and the weather is also an important consideration. Obviously, when the weather is warm and muggy, game matures more quickly than in cold, frosty weather and should be hung for a shorter length of time.

Roast pheasant

Serves 4

2oz (50gm) rump steak

1 pheasant, plucked, drawn and trussed

6 rashers streaky bacon

2 to 3oz (50 to 75gm) butter, melted

flour for dredging

watercress

thin gravy

2oz (50gm) butter-fried breadcrumbs

bread sauce (see page 103)

thin chips

tossed green salad

1. Pre-heat oven to moderately hot, 400 deg F or gas 6 (200 deg C).
2. Put steak inside pheasant (to keep bird moist) then place in roasting tin.
3. Cover breast with bacon rashers then brush generously with melted butter.
4. Roast 30 minutes, basting frequently.
5. Remove bacon rashers, baste bird with melted butter and sprinkle with flour. Baste with butter again.
6. Return to oven and roast a further 20 minutes.
7. Transfer to a warm serving platter and remove string.
8. Garnish with watercress then serve with gravy, fried crumbs, bread sauce, chips and salad.

Roast partridge

Serves 4

Put 2 walnut-sized pieces of butter into 2 plucked, drawn and trussed partridges. Cook as for roast pheasant (see previous recipe). Garnish and serve with same accompaniments.

Roast grouse

Serves 4

Roast 2 grouse in a similar way as for roast partridge, above, but leave in the oven a total of 40 minutes. Garnish and serve with same accompaniments but include also cranberry sauce (see page 102).

Salmi of game

Serves 4

Roast 1 pheasant or 2 partridges as directed in recipes above, but for 20 minutes only; roast 2 grouse for 15 minutes only. Divide birds into neat joints. Put ¾ pint (375ml) Espagnole sauce (see page 97) into saucepan. Add ¼ pint (125ml) port, 1 tablespoon redcurrant jelly and salt and pepper to taste. Cook slowly, uncovered, until sauce is reduced by about a third. Add pieces of bird, cover pan and cook gently for 15 to 20 minutes or until tender. Transfer to a warm serving dish and garnish with triangles of butter-fried bread.

Fricassee of rabbit

Serves 4

Make as for chicken fricassee (see page 86), using 1 jointed rabbit instead of the chicken. In addition to the parsley and grated lemon peel, garnish with small triangles of toast. To reduce the somewhat strong flavour of the rabbit, soak for 2 hours in salted water and juice of ½ lemon before cooking.

Jugged hare

1 hare

2oz (50gm) bacon dripping or butter

2 medium onions, chopped

2 medium carrots, thinly sliced

2 medium celery stalks, chopped

1½ pints (¾ litre) chicken stock

bouquet garni (1 blade mace, 1 bay leaf, 3 parsley sprigs, 4 peppercorns and 4 cloves) tied in muslin bag

2 level teaspoons salt

1 tablespoon wine vinegar

1½oz (37gm) flour

4 tablespoons cold water

reserved blood from hare

2 level tablespoons redcurrant jelly

4 tablespoons port

parsley, lemon and thyme stuffing (see page 106) and redcurrant jelly

1. Pre-heat oven to moderate, 350 deg F or gas 4 (180 deg C).
2. Joint hare, wash well then dry thoroughly on paper towels.
3. Heat dripping or butter in flameproof casserole.
4. Add hare and fry until pieces are well-browned. Remove to a plate.
5. Add onions, carrots and celery to remaining dripping or butter in saucepan.
6. Fry gently until pale gold.
7. Add stock, bouquet garni, salt and vinegar.
8. Slowly bring to boil.
9. Add hare, cover with lid or foil and cook in centre of oven for 3 to 3½ hours or until tender.
10. Remove from oven and place over low heat.
11. Mix flour to a smooth paste with cold water then stir in blood.
12. Add to casserole with redcurrant jelly and port.
13. Simmer 2 minutes then serve topped with 12 stuffing balls, fried gently in a little dripping until crisp and golden.
14. Accompany with redcurrant jelly.

Raised game pie

Serves approximately 8

hot water crust pastry (see page 111)

12oz (300gm) pork sausagemeat

12oz (300gm) rump steak, cubed

1lb ($\frac{1}{2}$ kilo) cooked and boned game, cubed

2oz (50gm) lean ham, cubed

1 level teaspoon salt

white pepper

$\frac{1}{2}$ pint (250ml) aspic jelly made up with stock instead of water

beaten egg

1. Pre-heat oven to hot, 425 deg F or gas 7 (220 deg C).
2. Roll out two-thirds of the pastry.
3. Use to line a 7-inch greased and loose-bottomed round cake tin or raised pie mould.
4. Press sausagemeat over base then fill with steak, game and ham, sprinkling salt and pepper between layers.
5. Pour half the liquid aspic jelly into pie.
6. Moisten edges of pastry with water then cover with lid, rolled from rest of pastry.
7. Brush with beaten egg then decorate top with pastry leaves. Brush with more egg.
8. Make a small hole in the centre to allow steam to escape then bake in centre of oven for 20 minutes.
9. Reduce temperature to moderate, 350 deg F or gas 4 (180 deg C), and bake a further 2 hours. Cover top of pie with a sheet of greaseproof paper if pastry appears to be browning too much.
10. Remove pie from oven then, using a small funnel, pour rest of liquid jelly through hole in the top.
11. Leave in the cool for 12 hours then remove from tin or mould just before serving.

Roast pigeons

Serves 4

4 pigeons, plucked, drawn and trussed

2oz (50gm) butter

4 rashers streaky bacon

4 slices butter-fried bread

watercress

gravy

1. Pre-heat oven to hot, 425 deg F or gas 7 (220 deg C).
2. Put a walnut-sized piece of butter into each pigeon.
3. Stand birds in roasting tin and brush with rest of butter, melted.
4. Put a rasher of bacon over each pigeon.
5. Roast in centre of oven for 15 minutes.
6. Remove bacon, brush with more butter and return to oven for a further 10 minutes.
7. Serve on slices of freshly-fried bread.
8. Garnish with watercress and accompany with gravy.

Quails flambé with peaches and grapes

Pigeon hot pot

Serves 4

4 pigeons, cleaned and halved

4 level tablespoons flour, well-seasoned with salt and pepper

1oz (25gm) butter, melted

1 tablespoon olive oil

2oz (50gm) lean bacon

1 small onion, chopped

1 celery stalk, chopped

1 pint (approximately $\frac{1}{2}$ litre) stock

4 tablespoons port

salt and pepper to taste

1. Pre-heat oven to moderately hot, 375 deg F or gas 5 (190 deg C).
2. Coat pigeons with flour.
3. Heat butter and oil in flameproof casserole. Add pigeons and fry until golden brown and crisp. Remove to plate.
4. Add bacon, onion and celery to pan and fry gently until pale gold.
5. Add stock and slowly bring to boil.
6. Stir in port, season with salt and pepper then replace pigeons.
7. Cover and cook in centre of oven for 1 hour.
8. Serve with creamed potatoes, cranberry sauce (see page 102), and green vegetables to taste.

Quails flambé

Serves 6

6 ovenready quails

salt and pepper

3oz (75gm) butter

6 rashers streaky bacon

1 can (2lb or 1 kilo) cling peaches

5 tablespoons brandy

8oz (200gm) green grapes, peeled

6 slices bread, freshly fried in butter and kept warm

1. Pre-heat oven to hot, 450 deg F or gas 8 (230 deg C).
2. Season quails with salt and pepper.
3. Put a small piece of butter into each, using a total of 1$\frac{1}{2}$oz (37gm).
4. Wrap each quail in a rasher of bacon.
5. Brown in rest of butter for 5 to 6 minutes in flameproof casserole.
6. Cover and continue to cook for 10 minutes in centre of oven.
7. Heat peaches in their syrup and strain carefully.
8. Heat brandy in a small saucepan.
9. Remove casserole from oven. Add hot peach halves and grapes.
10. Sprinkle the quails with hot brandy and set alight.
11. Replace cover and return casserole to the oven for a further 5 minutes.
12. Arrange fried bread on a large platter.
13. Place the quails on top then garnish with peach halves and grapes.
14. Add a tablespoon of hot water to the pan juices and sprinkle this sauce over the grapes.
15. Serve straight away.

Sauces, batters, stuffings and pastry

Sauces

One evening a little while ago I had guests for dinner and served grilled sole with a rather super sauce which was the creation of an overseas friend—a keen and very clever young cook—who was staying with us at the time. Fortunately, I served this masterpiece separately in a sauceboat because when I offered it to one of my guests she smiled sweetly and said, "No, thank you. I don't want to spoil the flavour of the fish!"

Sadly, this reflects all too often the attitude of so many people towards sauces and, as a result, our food suffers. Continental cooks make and serve a vast array of sauces more frequently and with greater aplomb than we do, knowing that far from dulling the flavour of food, sauces play an important part in enhancing and improving it.

Sauces, which seem to be surrounded by an aura of misplaced mystique are, in fact, relatively uncomplicated affairs requiring conscientiousness and enthusiasm from the cook rather than technical expertise and chef-like skill. The majority of sauces are only variations of a few basic recipes and having mastered those, one can make almost any sauce from the simplest to the most advanced. To prove this I give here recipes for the basics with as many variations as space permits. I firmly believe that with an accurate recipe and a bit of practical guidance, any cook can make any sauce, provided he or she is keen enough to try.

Before I begin the actual recipes, a word about re-heating sauces: if a sauce, with a flour or cornflour base, is made in advance of when it is actually required, it should be tipped into a basin, covered with a piece of wet greaseproof paper (when the paper is lifted off the skin on top will come away with it) and cooled as quickly as possible. If the pan is covered with a lid and the sauce kept hot, steam will cause a breakdown in the consistency of the sauce and it will subsequently be thinner than expected. Re-heating a sauce over direct heat is also unwise because there is a tendency for the sauce to stick and burn on the base of the pan. The best method is to stand the basin of sauce in a saucepan of gently simmering water and whisk the sauce continuously until it is sufficiently hot. Alternatively the sauce may be re-heated in the top of a double saucepan.

Curry sauce (see page 103)

Basic pouring and coating white sauces

Cornflour pouring sauce (savoury)

Makes ½ pint or 250ml

A light and easily digested sauce for serving with baked, grilled and steamed fish, pies made with poultry and white meat, fish cakes, rissoles, plain boiled potatoes and other root vegetables.

½oz (12gm) or 1 level tablespoon cornflour

½ pint (250ml) cold milk

a walnut-sized piece of butter or margarine

salt and pepper to taste

1. Mix cornflour to a smooth cream with 3 tablespoons cold milk.
2. Bring rest of milk to boil and pour gradually on to cornflour cream, stirring briskly all the time.
3. Return to saucepan and add the butter or margarine.
4. Cook over low heat, stirring continuously with a wooden spoon, until sauce comes to the boil and thickens.
5. Simmer for 1 minute only then season to taste with salt and pepper.

Cornflour pouring sauce (sweet)

Makes ½ pint or 250ml

Serve with steamed and baked puddings, over hot stewed fruits and with pies and turnovers.

Make exactly as for savoury pouring sauce above, but omit salt and pepper and add 1 level tablespoon caster or granulated sugar after the sauce has come to the boil and thickened.

Cornflour coating sauce (savoury or sweet)

Makes ½ pint or 250ml

Make exactly as for cornflour pouring sauce above (savoury or sweet recipe, as required), but double the quantity of cornflour used.

Basic white savoury pouring sauce (roux method)

Makes ½ pint or 250ml

A slightly richer sauce which may be used with the same dishes as the cornflour sauce.

½oz (12gm) butter or margarine

½oz (12gm) flour

½ pint (250ml) cold milk

salt and pepper to taste

1. Melt the butter or margarine in a saucepan over a gentle heat.
2. Stir in flour and cook slowly for 2 minutes, stirring mixture (or roux) all the time.
3. Remove from heat. Using a wooden spoon or whisk, blend in milk gradually.
4. When milk has been added and the sauce is smooth, return to heat.
5. Cook slowly, stirring or whisking continuously, until sauce comes to the boil and thickens.
6. Simmer gently for 3 minutes so that the starch grains in the flour are thoroughly cooked.
7. Season to taste with salt and pepper.

Basic white sweet pouring sauce (roux method)

Makes ½ pint or 250ml

Make exactly as for previous recipe, but omit salt and pepper and add 1 level tablespoon caster sugar after sauce has come to the boil and thickened.

Basic white sweet or savoury coating sauce (roux method)

Makes ½ pint or 250ml

Make exactly as for basic white pouring sauce above (savoury or sweet recipe, as required) but increase the quantity of butter or margarine used to 1oz (25gm), and also increase flour to 1oz (25gm).

Note
Although all milk has been recommended in the recipes, ½ milk and ½ stock may be used, provided the stock complements the dish with which the sauce is to be served. For example, when making sauce for a chicken dish, use ½ milk and ½ chicken stock; for a fish dish, ½ milk and ½ fish stock; for a vegetable dish, ½ milk and ½ vegetable water and so on.

The variations

Anchovy sauce

Suitable for all fish dishes and also for serving with fried veal escalopes.
Make up ½ pint (250ml) pouring or coating white sauce (see this page). After sauce has come to the boil and thickened, add 2 level teaspoons anchovy essence, 2 very finely-chopped anchovy fillets, 2 teaspoons lemon juice and pepper to taste. If necessary, tint sauce pale pink with red food colouring. Re-heat gently before serving.

Caper sauce

Traditionally served with skate, mackerel, herrings and roast mutton.
Make up ½ pint (250ml) pouring or coating white sauce (see this page). After sauce has come to the boil and thickened, stir in 1 to 2 level tablespoons finely-chopped capers, 1 tablespoon vinegar, a pinch of sugar and salt and pepper to taste.

Cheese sauce

An internationally popular sauce which can be served with meat, bacon, poultry, fish, egg and vegetable dishes—especially good with cauliflower. Although the usual cheese to use is strong Cheddar, crumbled Lancashire may be used instead and makes a pleasant change. Other cheeses to try are Parmesan (½ quantity only will be necessary), grated Gruyère or grated Gouda. I sometimes make this sauce with ½ Cheddar or Lancashire cheese and ½ Danish blue. The result is an unusually flavoured sauce which goes well with white fish dishes.
To make a basic cheese sauce, make up ½ pint (250ml) pouring or coating white sauce (see this page). After sauce has come to the boil and thickened, add 2 to 4oz (50 to 100gm) grated cheese to taste, ½ level teaspoon prepared mustard, ½ teaspoon Worcestershire sauce, a very light shake of cayenne pepper and salt to taste. Stir over very low heat until cheese melts.

Egg sauce

A mild sauce for fish and poultry dishes.
Make up ½ pint (250ml) pouring or coating white sauce (see this page). After sauce has come to the boil and thickened, add 2 chopped hard-boiled eggs, a pinch of nutmeg and salt and pepper to taste. Re-heat gently before serving.

Cauliflower with cheese sauce

Mushroom sauce

Another popular sauce that goes well with fish, egg, cheese, poultry, white meat and vegetable dishes.

Make up ½ pint (250ml) pouring or coating white sauce (see opposite page). After sauce has come to the boil and thickened, add 2 to 3oz (50 to 75gm) mushrooms, which have been first sliced and fried in a little butter or margarine.

Onion sauce

One of my own particular favourites with roast lamb although the sauce goes equally well with boiled bacon, mutton and ham dishes.

Make up ½ pint (250ml) pouring or coating white sauce (see opposite page). After sauce has come to the boil and thickened, add 2 cooked and chopped medium onions, a sprinkling of nutmeg and salt and pepper to taste. Re-heat gently before serving.

Mustard sauce

Ideal with grilled and fried herrings and mackerel and also good with bacon, ham, cheese and offal dishes.

Make up ½ pint (250ml) pouring or coating white sauce (see opposite page). After sauce has come to the boil and thickened, stir in 1 to 2 level teaspoons prepared mustard, 1 dessertspoon wine or cider vinegar and salt and pepper to taste. Re-heat gently before serving.

Parsley sauce

A mild sauce for poached, baked, steamed and grilled fish, boiled mutton and ham and bacon dishes.

Make up ½ pint (250ml) pouring or coating white sauce (see opposite page). After sauce has come to the boil and thickened, add 3 to 5 level tablespoons very finely-chopped parsley and salt and pepper to taste.

Note on freezing sauces

The basic white pouring or coating sauce may be deep frozen in a domestic deep freeze. Simply make up a double or even treble quantity of sauce and pour into ice cube trays fitted with standard dividers. When frozen solid, take out of trays, put into tightly covered containers or plastic bags and return to freezer. To use, take out as many sauce cubes as are required and melt them down in a basin over a saucepan of hot water or in the top of a double saucepan. To make the variations given, stir in additions when the sauce is hot.

Béchamel sauce

This is a classic sauce which is said to have been created in France during the reign of Louis XIV. It is, in fact, an elaboration of the basic white sauce given previously but is no more complicated or difficult to make. Straightforward béchamel, served just as it is without additions, may be used to coat poached, grilled, baked or steamed fish dishes, poultry dishes, egg dishes and vegetables. It may also be combined with cooked meat, fish, eggs or vegetables and used as a filling for pies, flans, tartlets and vol-au-vents. Although this sauce and its variations may be re-heated in exactly the same way as the other white sauces previously given, any variety containing eggs should be freshly made and served because re-heating could cause separation and curdling. Béchamel sauce may be frozen and re-heated as described on previous page.

Basic béchamel sauce

Makes ½ pint or 250ml

½ pint (250ml) milk

1 medium onion, peeled and quartered

1 small carrot, peeled and thickly sliced

½ small celery stalk, coarsely chopped

1 level dessertspoon coarsely-chopped parsley

2 cloves

½ small bay leaf

1 blade mace (optional)

4 white peppercorns

1oz (25gm) butter

1oz (25gm) flour

salt and pepper to taste

1. Put milk into saucepan with remaining ingredients except butter, flour and salt and pepper.
2. Slowly bring to boil, stirring continuously.
3. Remove from heat and cover pan.
4. Leave for 1 hour. Strain.
5. Melt butter in clean saucepan.
6. Stir in flour and cook slowly for 2 minutes, stirring mixture (or roux) all the time. Remove from heat.
7. Using a wooden spoon or whisk, blend in milk gradually.
8. When all the milk has been added and the sauce is smooth, return to heat.
9. Cook slowly, stirring or whisking continuously, until sauce comes to the boil and thickens.
10. Simmer gently for 3 minutes so that the starch grains in the flour are thoroughly cooked.
11. Season to taste with salt and pepper.

Béchamel sauce

The variations

Chaud-froid sauce

This literally means hot-cold sauce because it is a combination of hot béchamel and cold aspic jelly. It is the traditional sauce used for coating cold buffet foods such as whole cooked salmon, hams, cooked chickens, cooked turkeys, and portions of cooked fish and poultry.
Make up ½ pint (250ml) béchamel sauce (see left) and combine it with ¼ pint (125ml) double strength aspic jelly which should still be in liquid form. Leave in the cool until mixture thickens sufficiently to coat the back of a spoon. Use as required.

Hot horseradish sauce

Deliciously piquant with hot roast beef, beef grills, baked beef loaves, grilled trout, grilled mackerel and herrings and grilled salmon steaks.
Make up ½ pint (250ml) béchamel (see this page). After sauce has come to the boil and thickened, stir in 2 level dessertspoons grated horseradish, 2 teaspoons lemon juice, ½ level teaspoon caster sugar, 3 tablespoons double cream and salt and pepper to taste.

Mornay sauce

A famous luxury cheese sauce which is splendid with poached, steamed and grilled white fish dishes, gammon steaks, shellfish, chicken, turkey and veal.
Make up ½ pint (250ml) béchamel sauce (see this page). After sauce has come to the boil and thickened, stir in 2oz (50gm) very finely-grated Parmesan cheese or Gruyère cheese, a shake of cayenne pepper, a pinch of dry mustard and salt to taste. Re-heat just long enough for cheese to melt.

Mock hollandaise or Dutch sauce

For those who find a true hollandaise too rich and too high in calories, this sauce makes an admirable substitute and can be used to coat poached and grilled fish of all kinds, poultry, cauliflower, broccoli and hot asparagus.
Make up ½ pint (250ml) béchamel sauce (see this page). After sauce has come to the boil and thickened, stir in 1 dessertspoon strained lemon juice, 1 egg yolk beaten with 3 tablespoons double cream and salt and pepper to taste. Re-heat without boiling.

Hot tartare sauce

A well-flavoured, tangy sauce for fried and baked fish dishes—it makes a change from the more conventional cold version.
Make up ½ pint (250ml) béchamel sauce (see opposite). After sauce has come to the boil and thickened, stir in 1 dessertspoon lemon juice, 2 level tablespoons finely-chopped parsley, 2 level tablespoons finely-chopped gherkins, 1 level tablespoon finely-chopped capers and salt and pepper to taste. Re-heat gently without boiling. If liked, one egg yolk beaten with 2 table-spoons single cream may be stirred into the sauce with the other ingredients.

Velouté sauce

This is another basic classic sauce with its own variations and differs from béchamel in that it is made from clear white stock—chicken, veal or fish—instead of milk, and the roux of butter and flour is cooked until it is 'blond' or the colour of straw. The sauce itself is simmered for an hour, strained and then enriched with cream. Velouté sauce, which is mild and delicate, may be served with chicken, veal or fish dishes and the stock used should be chosen accordingly.

Basic velouté sauce

Makes ½ pint or 250ml

1oz (25gm) butter

1oz (25gm) flour

½ pint (250ml) chicken, veal or fish stock

1oz (25gm) button mushrooms, sliced

1 dessertspoon lemon juice

2 tablespoons double cream

salt and white pepper to taste

1. Melt butter in a saucepan over a moderate heat.
2. Add flour and cook, stirring continuously, until fat and flour (the roux) become the colour of pale straw—about 5 minutes.
3. Remove pan from heat. Using a wooden spoon or whisk, blend in stock gradually.
4. When all the stock has been added and the sauce is smooth, return to heat.
5. Cook slowly, stirring or whisking continuously until sauce comes to the boil and thickens.
6. Transfer to basin or top of double saucepan and place over gently boiling water.
7. Add mushrooms then cover.
8. Leave over boiling water for 45 minutes, stirring occasionally.
9. Strain into a clean saucepan and add lemon juice.
10. Re-heat slowly, remove from heat then stir in cream and salt and pepper to taste.

Chicken with suprême sauce

The variations

Estragon or tarragon sauce

A subtly flavoured sauce for grilled, poached and steamed white fish dishes.
Make up ½ pint (250ml) velouté sauce (see this page) and add ¼ level teaspoon dried or 1 level teaspoon fresh chopped tarragon with the mushrooms.

Suprême sauce

This is an aristocratic variation of velouté sauce but is richer and creamier and luxurious with white fish and poultry dishes.
Make up ½ pint (250ml) velouté sauce (see left) and after straining, stir in 2 egg yolks beaten with 3 tablespoons double cream, ½oz (12gm) butter, 1 teaspoon lemon juice and salt and pepper to taste. Re-heat briefly but on no account allow the sauce to boil or curdling will result.

Flamande sauce

A rich, mustard-flavoured sauce for ham steaks, roast beef and hot shellfish.
Make up ½ pint (250ml) suprême sauce (see above) but increase egg yolks to 3 and cream to 4 tablespoons. Stir in 1 to 2 level teaspoons prepared mustard just before serving.

Classic brown or Espagnole sauce

This is a full-flavoured sauce which can be served with all meat dishes, offal, sausages and game and used in place of gravy in dishes such as shepherd's pie. Like its white counterpart, this sauce has many well-known variations which follow the basic recipe.

Basic brown or Espagnole sauce

Makes 1 pint or approximately ½ litre

2 tablespoons salad oil or 2oz (50gm) meat or bacon dripping

2oz (50gm) bacon, chopped

1 large onion, coarsely chopped

1 medium celery stalk, coarsely chopped

2oz (50gm) button mushrooms, sliced

1 large carrot, thickly sliced

1½oz (37gm) flour

1 pint (approximately ½ litre) beef stock

1 level tablespoon tomato paste

2 medium tomatoes, skinned and chopped

1 bay leaf

2 heaped tablespoons coarsely-chopped parsley

4 black peppercorns

1 level teaspoon meat or yeast extract (optional)

salt and pepper to taste

1. Heat oil or dripping in heavy-based saucepan.
2. Add bacon, onion, celery, mushrooms and carrot.
3. Cover and fry gently for 10 minutes, shaking pan frequently.
4. Stir in flour and cook over low heat, stirring continuously, until fat and flour (roux) turns a deep gold.
5. Remove from heat and gradually add stock.
6. Cook, stirring all the time with a wooden spoon, until sauce comes to the boil and thickens.
7. Add all remaining ingredients except salt and pepper.
8. Cover and simmer very gently for 45 minutes, stirring occasionally. Alternatively, pour sauce into a casserole dish, cover and cook in centre of moderate oven, 350 deg F or gas 4 (180 deg C), for 2 hours.
9. Strain sauce, skim off fat with a metal spoon and season to taste with salt and pepper.
10. Re-heat before serving.

The variations

Bordelaise sauce

Makes 1 pint or approximately ½ litre

A robust sauce for grilled meats, rissoles and offal.
Make up classic brown sauce (see page 97) then strain, skim, season and keep hot. Put ¼ pint (125ml) dry red wine into a saucepan with 1 small, very finely-chopped onion. Cook, uncovered, until wine is reduced by half. Strain into brown sauce. Add a pinch of dried tarragon and thyme (or ¼ level teaspoon mixed herbs), a teaspoon of lemon juice and 1 level tablespoon finely-chopped parsley. Re-heat before serving.

Chasseur or hunter's sauce

Makes 1 pint or approximately ½ litre

A beautifully flavoured full-bodied sauce which is particularly good with roast duck and goose, offal, gammon and steaks.
Make up classic brown sauce (see page 97) then strain, skim, season and keep hot. Slowly fry 1 small chopped onion in ½oz (12gm) butter until soft but not brown. Add 2oz (50gm) finely-chopped mushrooms and stalks, 5 tablespoons dry white wine and 2 level teaspoons tomato paste. Stir in brown sauce, adjust seasoning to taste then simmer for 5 minutes, stirring. Add 1 dessertspoon finely-chopped parsley.

Piquant sauce

Makes 1 pint or approximately ½ litre

A tangy sauce which, in a way, is the brown equivalent of sauce tartare. Serve it with cold meats, hot roast pork, ham and bacon dishes, rissoles and croquettes.
Make up classic brown sauce (see page 97) then strain, skim, season and keep hot. Slowly fry 1 small chopped onion in ½oz (12gm) butter until soft but not brown. Add 4 tablespoons wine vinegar and cook, uncovered, until liquid is reduced by half. Stir in brown sauce, cover and slowly simmer for 10 minutes. Stir in 2 level tablespoons finely-chopped gherkins, 1 level dessertspoon finely-chopped capers and 1 level tablespoon finely-chopped parsley. Re-heat for 2 to 3 minutes.

Madeira sauce

Makes 1 pint or approximately ½ litre

One of the best-known sauces in the world for meat and game dishes.
Make up classic brown sauce (see page 97) then strain, skim, season and pour into saucepan. Simmer, uncovered, until sauce is reduced by about a third, stirring frequently. Add 6 to 8 tablespoons Madeira and gently re-heat without boiling.

Poivrade sauce

Makes 1 pint or approximately ½ litre

A peppery sauce for beef grills and roasts and game.
Make up classic brown sauce (see page 97) then strain, skim, season and keep hot. Cook 1 small chopped onion in 6 tablespoons wine vinegar and 3 tablespoons dry red wine until the liquid is reduced by half. Strain into brown sauce then add 6 to 8 finely-crushed black peppercorns. Re-heat gently.

Reforme sauce

Makes 1 pint or approximately ½ litre

A very well-known sauce created during the 19th century by a master chef, Alexis Soyer. It is a sauce full of character and though originally intended for lamb cutlets, it is equally good with pork chops and gammon steaks.
Make up classic brown sauce (see page 97) then strain, skim, season and keep hot. Add 1 tablespoon redcurrant jelly, 3 tablespoons port and 1 level dessertspoon finely-chopped gherkins. Re-heat slowly for 10 minutes, stirring until jelly melts. Add the white of one hard-boiled egg, cut into thin matchstick-sized pieces.

Classic brown sauce with the added ingredients for orange sauce

Bigarade or orange sauce

Makes 1 pint or approximately ½ litre

The very best sauce with roast duckling.
Make up classic brown sauce (see page 97) then strain, skim, season and keep hot. Add 2 level teaspoons coarsely-grated orange peel, the juice of 1 small orange and 1 lemon, 3 tablespoons dry red wine and 1 level teaspoon brown sugar. Simmer, uncovered, for 10 minutes.

Hollandaise sauce

One of the greatest sauces of all and in a class by itself. Its mildness, delicacy and subtle richness put hollandaise at once into the gourmet class and I know of no better sauce than this for poached Scotch salmon, salmon trout, poached sole, halibut and turbot, broccoli, asparagus and hot globe artichokes. Although hollandaise is considered a difficult sauce to make it will only misbehave if badly handled and all it really asks for is patience and care. There are several different recipes for hollandaise—including one made in an electric blender which works very well and certainly saves time. The first recipe is the one I always make, the second is the traditional recipe and the last is the blender. Hollandaise sauce is always served warm—never hot.

Basic hollandaise sauce (method 1)

Serves 4 to 6

4oz (100gm) unsalted butter

3 egg yolks

3 tablespoons boiling water

3 tablespoons strained lemon juice

1 tablespoon wine vinegar

a pinch of sugar

salt and pepper to taste

1. Very slowly melt the butter and leave on one side until lukewarm.
2. Put egg yolks into a glass or pottery pudding basin and place over a saucepan of gently simmering water. In no circumstances allow the water to boil rapidly or the sauce will curdle.
3. Add 1 tablespoon boiling water and whisk until yolks begin to thicken.
4. Add second tablespoon of water and whisk until yolks thicken again.
5. Repeat with last tablespoon of boiling water.
6. In a separate saucepan, heat lemon juice, vinegar and sugar to lukewarm.
7. Beat into egg yolks and water.
8. Whisking continuously, add ½ the melted butter, *a teaspoon at a time.*
9. When the sauce is thick and fluffy (the consistency of softly-whipped cream), add remaining butter in a thin, continuous stream, whisking all the time.
10. Serve straight away.

Note
If the sauce seems to be on the thin side, the water in the saucepan may not be hot enough to cook the egg yolks sufficiently to thicken the sauce. Increase the heat slightly and whisk until the sauce thickens. If, on the other hand, the sauce is too thick, add 1 or 2 teaspoons cold water.

Basic hollandaise sauce (method 2)

Serves 4 to 6

4oz (100gm) unsalted butter, softened

3 tablespoons lemon juice

1 tablespoon wine vinegar

6 tablespoons water

3 egg yolks

salt and pepper to taste

a pinch of caster sugar

1. Cut butter into 12 small cubes.
2. Put lemon juice, vinegar and 4 teaspoons water into a small saucepan.
3. Boil briskly until only 2 tablespoons of liquid remain. Stir in rest of water. Pour into glass or pottery pudding basin.
4. Add egg yolks and stand basin over a saucepan of gently simmering water. In no circumstances allow the water to boil rapidly or the sauce will curdle.
5. Whisk until egg yolks begin to thicken.
6. Add butter, one cube at a time, and whisk until each cube has melted. By the time all the butter has been added, the sauce should be thick enough to coat the back of a spoon.
7. Season to taste with salt, pepper and sugar.
8. Serve straight away.

Hollandaise sauce (blender method)

Serves 4 to 6

6oz (150gm) unsalted butter

3 dessertspoons strained lemon juice

1 dessertspoon wine vinegar

3 egg yolks

a pinch of granulated sugar

¼ to ½ level teaspoon salt

white pepper to taste

1. Put butter into a pan and heat slowly until hot and foamy.
2. In a separate saucepan bring lemon juice and vinegar to the boil. Put into blender with egg yolks, sugar, salt and pepper.
3. Cover and blend for 6 seconds.
4. Uncover and with blender set at high speed, add hot butter in a thin, continuous stream.
5. Blend until sauce is thick—35 to 45 seconds.
6. Serve straight away.

Asparagus with hollandaise sauce

The variations

Béarnaise sauce

Perhaps the most celebrated sauce of all for steaks.

Put 2 tablespoons dry white wine and 2 tablespoons tarragon vinegar into a saucepan. Add 1 small finely-chopped onion and 1 level teaspoon finely-chopped parsley. Boil briskly until only 2 tablespoons of liquid remain. Strain, then add 2 teaspoons cold water. Make up any of the recipes for hollandaise sauce (see page 98 and this page) using the tarragon flavoured liquid to replace liquid in basic recipe. Just before serving, stir in 1 level teaspoon very finely-chopped fresh tarragon or ½ level teaspoon dried tarragon.

Palois sauce

Serves 4 to 6

This is to roast and grilled lamb what béarnaise sauce is to beef steaks. This time the predominant flavour of the hollandaise is mint instead of tarragon.

Follow the recipe for béarnaise sauce, above, but use wine vinegar instead of tarragon and add 2 level teaspoons very finely-chopped fresh mint just before serving.

Mayonnaise

Mayonnaise is the only uncooked coating sauce in the classic range and one which requires as much patience to make well as hollandaise sauce does. However, if the directions are carefully followed failure is unlikely, although the mayonnaise may not work well if made during thundery weather. Mayonnaise is, in its simplest form, a thick glossy emulsion of oil, egg yolks, acid and seasoning and although purists insist on olive oil, any good quality salad oil may be used instead of, or in conjunction with, the more traditional olive oil. I use half corn oil and half olive oil because I prefer the blander flavour which this combination gives. Mayonnaise may be made by hand or in the mixer and there is an excellent recipe for a blender mayonnaise as well. For best results, all ingredients should be at room temperature.

Basic mayonnaise

Makes ½ pint or 250ml

2 egg yolks

½ level teaspoon salt

½ level teaspoon dry or prepared mustard

¼ level teaspoon caster sugar

¼ level teaspoon Worcestershire sauce (optional)

2 dessertspoons strained lemon juice

½ pint (250ml) salad oil

2 dessertspoons wine or cider vinegar

1 tablespoon boiling water

1. Put egg yolks into a bowl rinsed in hot water and quickly dried.
2. Add salt, mustard, sugar, Worcestershire sauce (if used) and 1 dessertspoon lemon juice.
3. Beat thoroughly.
4. Still beating continuously, begin adding oil *drop by drop*.
5. When the mayonnaise begins to thicken add second dessertspoon of lemon juice.
6. Still beating, continue adding oil drop by drop until mayonnaise is consistency of whipped cream.
7. Stir in 1 dessertspoon vinegar then add remaining oil in a slow and thin steady stream, beating all the time.
8. Add last dessertspoon of vinegar with boiling water (which prevents separation).
9. Either use straight away or put into an airtight container with lid and leave in the least cold part of the refrigerator up to 10 days.

Note

Should the mayonnaise curdle—which it will do if the oil is cold and/or has been added too quickly—put a fresh egg yolk into a clean warm basin and gradually add the curdled mayonnaise to it —*drop by drop*. When it begins to thicken and looks as if it is stable, add the curdled mayonnaise a little more quickly.

Blender mayonnaise

Makes ½ pint or 250ml

1 large egg
½ level teaspoon prepared mustard
½ to 1 level teaspoon salt
¼ level teaspoon sugar
½ teaspoon Worcestershire sauce
shake of white pepper
½ pint (250ml) salad oil
2 dessertspoons strained lemon juice
2 dessertspoons wine or cider vinegar
1 tablespoon boiling water

1. Put egg, mustard, salt, sugar, Worcestershire sauce and pepper into blender goblet.
2. Cover and blend until smooth.
3. Uncover. With blender at medium speed, add half the oil in a slow, thin trickle.
4. Stop machine and add lemon juice. Cover and blend until smooth.
5. Uncover. Slowly add rest of oil with vinegar and blend until thick and smooth.
6. Stir in boiling water to prevent separation.
7. Either use straight away or put into an airtight container with lid and leave in the least cold part of the refrigerator up to 10 days.

The variations

Cocktail sauce

A pink-tinted piquant sauce for seafood cocktails and avocado pear halves.
Make up ½ pint (250ml) mayonnaise (see page 99 and above). Stir in 2 level tablespoons tomato paste, 1 teaspoon Worcestershire sauce, 2 to 3 level teaspoons horseradish sauce and a large pinch of cayenne pepper. To heighten the colour, 1 level teaspoon paprika should be stirred in.

Louis sauce

A rich sauce for seafood salads (especially crab) and green salads.
Make up ½ pint (250ml) mayonnaise (see page 99 and this page). Stir in 1 to 3 tablespoons chilli sauce (depending on how hot you like your sauce to be), 4 tablespoons softly whipped cream, ½ a medium de-seeded green pepper, very finely chopped, 2 level teaspoons finely-grated onion and 1 tablespoon lemon juice.

Tartare sauce

The traditional sauce for fried fish.
Make up ½ pint (250ml) mayonnaise (see page 99 and this page). Stir in 3 level tablespoons finely-chopped gherkins, 3 level dessertspoons finely-chopped capers and 2 dessertspoons finely-chopped parsley.

Corn-on-the-cob with melted butter sauce

Remoulade sauce

An intriguing sauce for cold roast beef, lamb and veal, cold poultry, fish salads and hard-boiled eggs.
Make up ½ pint (250ml) mayonnaise (see page 99 and this page). Stir in 3 very finely-chopped anchovy fillets, 1 level teaspoon continental mustard, 2 level teaspoons finely-chopped parsley, 1 level teaspoon fresh or ½ level teaspoon dried tarragon, 2 level teaspoons finely-chopped gherkins and 2 level teaspoons finely-chopped drained capers.

Thousand island sauce

An exciting sauce with a miscellany of colourful ingredients. It is particularly good with fish salads, green salads and egg salads and, like Louis sauce, it comes from the United States.
Make up ½ pint (250ml) mayonnaise (see page 99 and this page). Stir in 2 finely-chopped hard-boiled eggs, 1 to 2 dessertspoons chilli sauce, 3 dessertspoons tomato ketchup, 1 level dessertspoon very finely-grated onion and 1 level tablespoon finely-chopped parsley.

Melted butter sauces

These are very simple sauces made, as their name would suggest, almost exclusively from butter. They are used for pouring over such foods as hot asparagus and broccoli, corn on the cob, brains and fish and have a characteristic richness and fragrance which gives them their distinction. To make these successfully, clarified butter should, whenever possible, be used because it contains no milky solids. To clarify butter, simply melt the required amount of butter in a saucepan then leave it for about 15 minutes or until any sediment sinks to the bottom. Strain off the butter carefully and use as required.

Brown butter sauce

Serves 4 to 6

For hot asparagus, broccoli, cauliflower and brains.

4oz (100gm) clarified butter

1. Put butter into a small pan and stand it over a low heat until butter turns deep gold.
2. Remove from heat and serve.

Butter sauce with lemon and parsley

Serves 4 to 6

This is very similar to the plain brown butter sauce except that it is sharpened with lemon juice and flavoured with parsley. It is excellent with all steamed and poached fish dishes and with hot boiled chicken.
Make up the brown butter sauce as directed in previous recipe. Remove from heat and stir in 1 dessertspoon lemon juice, 2 level dessertspoons finely-chopped parsley and a shake of white pepper.

Black butter sauce

Serves 4 to 6

This sauce, with its nutty flavour, may be served with all poached and steamed fish dishes, vegetables such as cauliflower and over poached eggs.

4 oz (100gm) clarified butter

1 teaspoon lemon juice

1. Put butter into a small pan and stand it over a low heat until butter turns a fairly dark brown.
2. Remove from heat and stir in lemon juice.
3. Serve straight away.

Butter sauce and capers

Serves 4 to 6

Very good with skate and brains.
Make up the black butter sauce as in previous recipe then add 2 level teaspoons finely-chopped capers with the teaspoon lemon juice.

Savoury butters

Pats or squares of savoury butters, when placed on hot food, melt over it and in so doing add moisture, flavour and richness. Not sauces in the strict sense of the word but useful substitutes, which is why they are included in this section. To make these butters, choose unsalted or slightly salted lactic butter (which is more delicate than salted butter) and make sure it is soft; butter taken straight from the refrigerator is hard to cope with and wastes time. Once the savoury butters have been made, stand them on a square of foil and either form them into a block or thin sausage shape. Wrap in foil and chill until firm. Cut the block into cubes or the sausages into pats and put one or two cubes or pats on to the hot food immediately before serving.

Anchovy butter

Serves 4 to 6

Excellent with grilled and baked fish, grilled veal chops and beef steaks.

2oz (50gm) butter, softened

anchovy fillets, very finely chopped

teaspoon lemon juice

Pinch each paprika and white pepper

1. Beat butter to a soft cream.
2. Gradually beat in all remaining ingredients.
3. Shape, wrap and chill.

Colbert butter

Serves 4 to 6

For grilled fish and beef grills.
Make as for anchovy butter (see above) but instead of anchovies, add 1 level teaspoon very finely-chopped parsley and $\frac{1}{4}$ to $\frac{1}{2}$ level teaspoon meat extract with the lemon juice.

Curry butter

Serves 4 to 6

A savoury butter which harmonises well with grilled chicken, grilled or baked pork chops and shellfish.
Make as for anchovy butter (see this page) but instead of anchovies, add 1 to 2 level teaspoons curry powder and a shake of tabasco sauce. Increase the lemon juice to 2 teaspoons.

Savoury butters: top, anchovy, centre, curry and devilled, and in the foreground, maître d'hôtel

Devilled butter

Serves 4 to 6

A hot one for grilled gammon steaks, pork and lamb chops, grilled fish and shellfish. Make as for anchovy butter (see this page) but instead of anchovies and lemon juice, add 1 level teaspoon dry mustard, $\frac{1}{2}$ teaspoon Worcestershire sauce, a pinch of cayenne pepper, $\frac{1}{4}$ level teaspoon paprika and 1 teaspoon vinegar.

Garlic or onion butter

Serves 4 to 6

Delicious on all meat grills.
Make as for anchovy butter (see this page) but instead of anchovies add 1 level teaspoon garlic or onion salt with the lemon juice.

Horseradish butter

Serves 4 to 6

Especially for grilled steaks, grilled trout, grilled herrings and grilled mackerel.
Make as for anchovy butter (see this page) but instead of anchovies, add 2 level teaspoons very finely-grated horseradish and a pinch of dried mustard with the lemon juice.

Maître d'hôtel butter

Serves 4 to 6

A classic butter for fish.
Make as for anchovy butter (see this page) but instead of anchovies, add 1 to 2 level teaspoons finely-chopped parsley with the lemon juice.

Mustard butter

Serves 4 to 6

For all pork and bacon grills, shellfish and grilled fish such as herrings, mackerel, trout and salmon. Even for sausages!
Make as for anchovy butter (see this page) but instead of anchovies, add 1 to 2 level teaspoons prepared continental mustard with the lemon juice.

Hungarian butter

Serves 4 to 6

A prettily coloured and appetising butter for veal, shellfish, ham and bacon.
Make as for anchovy butter (see this page) but instead of anchovies, add 1 level teaspoon paprika and 1 level teaspoon finely-grated onion with the lemon juice.

Miscellaneous sauces

Bolognese sauce

Serves 4

½oz (12gm) butter or margarine

1 dessertspoon salad oil

1 medium onion, finely chopped

2oz (50gm) bacon, chopped

1 medium carrot, coarsely grated

1 medium celery stalk, finely chopped

2oz (50gm) mushrooms, sliced

12oz (300gm) lean minced beef

8oz (200gm) tomatoes, skinned and chopped

2 level tablespoons tomato paste

2 level teaspoons granulated sugar

1 bay leaf

½ pint (250ml) stock or water

1 wine glass dry red wine

1 level teaspoon dried basil

salt and pepper to taste

1. Heat butter or margarine and oil in a saucepan.
2. Add onion, bacon, carrot, celery and mushrooms and fry gently, with lid on pan, until onion is pale gold—about 10 minutes.
3. Add beef and fry a little more briskly until brown, turning beef and breaking it up with a fork all the time.
4. Add all remaining ingredients and slowly bring to the boil, stirring.
5. Cover and simmer gently for 1 hour, stirring occasionally.
6. Serve with any freshly-cooked pasta.

Bolognese sauce

Italian tomato sauce

Serves 4

A thick sauce which is well-flavoured and excellent with pasta, lamb and veal dishes.

2lb (approximately 1 kilo) tomatoes, skinned

1oz (25gm) butter or margarine

1 tablespoon salad oil

1 medium onion, chopped

1 level tablespoon cornflour

½ to 1 level teaspoon dried basil

1 level dessertspoon finely-chopped parsley

2 level teaspoons granulated sugar

salt and pepper to taste

1. Chop tomatoes and either rub through a sieve or liquidise in blender.
2. Heat butter or margarine and oil in saucepan. Add onion and fry gently until soft and pale gold—about 7 minutes.
3. Stir in cornflour then add tomatoes.
4. Slowly bring to boil, stirring.
5. Add all remaining ingredients.
6. Cover pan and simmer gently for 45 minutes, stirring frequently.

Apple sauce

Serves 4 to 6

1lb (approximately ½ kilo) cooking apples

3 tablespoons water

pinch of salt

2 level teaspoons sugar

a walnut-sized piece of butter

1. Peel, core and slice apples.
2. Put into saucepan with water and salt.
3. Cook, covered, until apples are very soft.
4. Beat until smooth with sugar and butter.
5. Serve hot or cold.

Note
Alternatively, hot apples may be put into blender goblet with all remaining ingredients and blended until smooth.

Mint sauce

Serves 4

4 to 5 level tablespoons finely-chopped mint

1 level dessertspoon granulated sugar

2 tablespoons boiling water

2 tablespoons wine vinegar

¼ level teaspoon salt

1. Put mint and sugar into a basin.
2. Add water and stir until sugar dissolves.
3. Stir in vinegar and salt and leave until cold.

Note
Alternatively, put all ingredients into blender goblet and blend until mint is finely chopped.

Cranberry sauce

Serves 4 to 6

A sweet-sour sauce which is delicious with turkey, poultry, duck and pork.

6oz (150gm) granulated sugar

¼ pint (125ml) water

8oz (200gm) fresh cranberries

1. Put sugar and water into saucepan.
2. Stand saucepan over low heat until sugar dissolves.
3. Bring to the boil then add cranberries.
4. Cook briskly until skins burst and pop open—2 to 3 minutes.
5. Lower heat and simmer a further 8 minutes.
6. Serve hot or cold.

Gooseberry sauce

Serves 4

An old-fashioned sauce, popular in the Victorian era with grilled and fried mackerel, roast duck and roast goose. It is a sweet-sharp sauce and complements the rich foods with which it is traditionally served.

8oz (200gm) green gooseberries, topped and tailed

2 tablespoons water

½ level teaspoon finely-grated lemon peel

2 level tablespoons granulated sugar

a small piece of butter

1. Put gooseberries into saucepan with water.
2. Bring to boil, lower heat and cover pan.
3. Simmer slowly until fruit is very soft.
4. Remove from heat and beat until pulpy with all remaining ingredients.
5. Serve hot or cold.

Cumberland sauce (hot)

Serves 4 to 6

This is a richly-flavoured and spicy-sweet sauce with a fruity piquancy. It is ideal with pork, gammon, offal dishes, roast goose and roast duckling.

½ level teaspoon prepared mustard

1 level tablespoon soft brown sugar

¼ level teaspoon powdered ginger

pinch of cayenne pepper

½ level teaspoon salt

½ pint (250ml) dry red wine

3 cloves

1 level tablespoon cornflour

2 tablespoons cold water

4 level tablespoons redcurrant jelly

1 level teaspoon each orange and lemon peel

juice of 1 small orange and 1 small lemon

1. Put mustard, sugar, ginger, pepper and salt into saucepan.
2. Mix to a smooth liquid with a little of the wine. Add rest of wine and cloves.
3. Bring to boil over low heat, stirring continuously all the time.
4. Cover and simmer slowly for 10 minutes.
5. Mix cornflour to a smooth cream with water. Add a little wine mixture.
6. Return to saucepan and cook, stirring all the time, until sauce comes to the boil and thickens.
7. Add all remaining ingredients.
8. Leave over low heat until redcurrant jelly has melted and sauce is hot.

Cumberland sauce (cold)

Serves 4

This is similar to hot Cumberland sauce but is a cold and strained version, usually served with cold game, ham and other cold meats.

¼ pint (125ml) dry red wine

4 tablespoons redcurrant jelly

finely grated peel and juice of 1 small lemon and 1 small orange

1 small onion, finely grated

½ level teaspoon prepared mustard

3 cloves

¼ level teaspoon powdered ginger

salt and pepper to taste

1. Put all ingredients into a saucepan.
2. Slowly bring to boil, stirring.
3. Lower heat and cover.
4. Simmer gently for 20 minutes.
5. Strain and leave until completely cold before serving.

Horseradish sauce (cold)

Serves 4

For hot roast beef, smoked trout and duckling.

¼ pint (125ml) double cream

1 tablespoon cold milk

2 level tablespoons finely-grated horseradish

1 teaspoon wine vinegar

1 teaspoon lemon juice

pinch of caster sugar

½ to 1 level teaspoon salt

white pepper

1. Beat cream and milk together until thick.
2. Stir in all remaining ingredients.
3. Serve straight away.

Curry sauce

Illustrated on page 93

Serves 4 to 6

This sauce may be made up and frozen in a domestic deep freeze then re-heated when wanted with cold cooked meat or poultry. It may also be re-heated by itself and used to coat hard-boiled eggs and cooked vegetables, and may even be combined with freshly-boiled rice.

1oz (25gm) butter or margarine

1 tablespoon salad oil

1 large onion, very finely chopped

1 to 2 garlic cloves, finely chopped

1 to 3 level tablespoons curry powder (depending on taste)

1 level tablespoon cornflour

2 level tablespoons tomato paste

½ level teaspoon each powdered ginger and cinnamon

3 cloves

1 bay leaf

2 level tablespoons sweet pickle

1 level teaspoon salt

1 teaspoon Worcestershire sauce

½ teaspoon tabasco sauce (omit for less hot sauce)

juice of ½ lemon

¾ pint (375ml) stock or water

1. Heat butter or margarine and oil in saucepan.
2. Add onion and garlic and fry gently until pale gold.
3. Stir in all remaining ingredients except stock.
4. Cook, stirring, for 5 minutes.
5. Remove from heat and gradually blend in stock or water.
6. Slowly bring to boil, stirring.
7. Cover pan and simmer very gently for 45 minutes, stirring frequently.

Note

1 to 2 level tablespoons seedless raisins or sultanas and 1 chopped cooking apple may be added as well.

Bread sauce

Serves 4 to 6

Traditionally served with roast poultry.

4 cloves

1 large onion

6 white peppercorns

1 blade mace

1 small bay leaf

2 large parsley sprigs

½ pint (250ml) milk

2oz (50gm) fresh white breadcrumbs

½oz (12gm) butter

3 tablespoons single or double cream

seasoning to taste

1. Press cloves into onion.
2. Put into saucepan with peppercorns, mace, bay leaf, parsley and milk.
3. Slowly bring to boil, stirring.
4. Lower heat, cover pan and simmer slowly for 20 minutes.
5. Strain hot milk on to breadcrumbs.
6. Add butter and cream and return mixture to saucepan.
7. Season to taste with salt and pepper and leave over a low heat until thick, stirring continuously.

Gravy

Gravies are usually made with pan juices and fat, flour and stock or water and are traditionally served with meat and poultry. It is customary to serve thin gravies with beef and poultry; thicker ones with lamb, veal and pork.

Thick gravy

Serves 4

3 tablespoons pan juices

1 level tablespoon flour

½ pint (250ml) stock or water

salt and pepper to taste

1. Pour off all but 3 tablespoons fat and juices from roasting pan.
2. Stand pan over low heat and stir in flour. Cook 2 minutes.
3. Gradually blend in stock or water.
4. Cook, stirring continuously, until gravy comes to the boil and thickens.
5. Simmer 3 minutes then season to taste with salt and pepper.

Thin gravy

Make exactly as thick gravy but reduce flour to 1 level dessertspoon.

Sweet sauces

Custard sauce

Serves 4

What memories of childhood this evokes! I can still taste and see my grandmother's gargantuan trifles, steeped in home-made wine and sweet enough to please any child's heart. And always on the top a mammoth layer of egg and milk custard, garlanded with thick golden cream and wisps of grated chocolate to complete the magic. When time permits, I still make custard sauce for trifles or serve it warm with steamed puddings, stewed fruits and pies.

| 2 standard eggs plus 1 egg yolk |
| 1 level tablespoon caster sugar |
| ½ pint (250ml) milk |
| ¼ to ½ teaspoon vanilla essence |
| pinch of salt |

1. Put the eggs, egg yolk and sugar into the top of a double saucepan or into a basin placed over a saucepan of gently simmering water.
2. Bring milk just up to the boil and pour on to egg mixture.
3. Cook, stirring continuously, until custard thickens sufficiently to coat the back of the spoon. This is a fairly long process and can take up to 20 minutes.
4. Pour custard at once into a cold bowl (to prevent further cooking) and stir in vanilla and salt.

Note
In no circumstances allow the water beneath the custard to over-heat, or the custard itself may boil and subsequently curdle.

Chocolate sauce (1)

Serves 4 to 6

A hot sauce for steamed and baked ginger, chocolate, coffee and dried fruit puddings.

| 2 level tablespoons cornflour |
| ½ pint (250ml) cold milk |
| 2oz (50gm) chopped plain chocolate or chocolate dots |
| 1 level tablespoon granulated sugar |
| ½ teaspoon vanilla essence |

1. Mix cornflour to a smooth cream with a little cold milk.
2. Put rest of milk into a saucepan with chocolate.
3. Heat slowly until chocolate melts then combine with cornflour cream.
4. Return to saucepan. Cook, stirring continuously, until sauce comes to the boil and thickens.
5. Add all remaining ingredients.
6. Cook over low heat, stirring, for 3 minutes.
7. Serve straight away.

Baked sponge puddings with jam sauce

Chocolate sauce (2)

Serves 4 to 6

A deep brown, bitter-sweet hot sauce for ice cream and ice cream sundaes.

| 2oz (50gm) soft brown sugar |
| 1 level tablespoon golden syrup |
| 1oz (25gm) butter |
| 3 level dessertspoons cocoa powder, sifted |
| 2 tablespoons single cream or top of the milk |
| 1 teaspoon vanilla essence |

1. Put all ingredients into a heavy-based saucepan.
2. Stir over low heat until all ingredients have melted.
3. Still stirring, bring to boil and boil steadily for 4 minutes.
4. Serve hot.

Jam or marmalade sauce

Serves 4 to 6

A clear sauce for steamed and baked sponge puddings.

| 6 level tablespoons jam or marmalade |
| 1 level dessertspoon arrowroot |
| ¼ pint (125ml) cold water |
| 1 level tablespoon granulated sugar |
| squeeze of lemon juice |

1. Put jam or marmalade into a saucepan and leave over low heat until melted.
2. Mix arrowroot to a smooth cream with a little cold water. Blend in rest of water then add to jam.
3. Cook slowly, stirring, until sauce comes to the boil and thickens.
4. Remove from heat, add sugar and lemon juice and stir until sugar dissolves.

Rum or brandy sauce

Serves 4 to 6

A popular sauce for Christmas and other rich puddings and for mince pies and tarts.

| 2 level tablespoons cornflour |
| ½ pint (250ml) cold milk |
| 3 level dessertspoons granulated sugar |
| ¼ to ½oz (6 to 12gm) butter |
| 1 to 2 tablespoons rum or brandy |

1. Mix cornflour to a smooth cream with a little of the cold milk.
2. Bring rest of milk to boil and combine with cornflour cream.
3. Return mixture to saucepan. Cook, stirring continuously, until sauce comes to boil and thickens.
4. Add all remaining ingredients.
5. Cook over low heat, stirring, for 3 minutes.
6. Serve straight away.

Vanilla sauce

Serves 4 to 6

Make exactly as previous recipe but add 1 teaspoon vanilla essence instead of rum or brandy.

Rum butter sauce

Serves 4 to 6

This is a solidified sauce of butter, sugar, alcohol and flavouring and traditionally served with Christmas and other rich puddings.

| 4oz (100gm) butter, softened |
| 2oz (50gm) caster sugar |
| 2oz (50gm) icing sugar, sifted |
| 2 tablespoons dark rum |
| 1oz (25gm) ground almonds |
| pinch of mixed spice |

1. Beat butter and sugars to a light cream.
2. Gradually beat in rum then stir in almonds.
3. Transfer to a small serving dish and sprinkle top lightly with mixed spice.

Brandy butter sauce

Make exactly as previous recipe, substituting brandy for rum. Sprinkle sauce with cinnamon instead of mixed spice.

Batters

The word batter comes from the French verb 'battre' meaning to beat. Theoretically, batters should be beaten hard and long in order to incorporate as much air as possible into the mixture so that the resulting pudding or pancake will be light. In practice though, it has been found by many experts that conscientious beating makes comparatively little difference and that most batters respond in exactly the same way whether they have been beaten for a long time or a short time. I waver somewhere between theoretical facts and practical application and usually beat my batters until a wealth of bubbles collect on the surface which may take anything from 3 to 5 minutes. To short-cut the whole process, I often put all the batter ingredients into the blender goblet and blend them for about 50 seconds.

It is customary to leave prepared batter to stand for a while before cooking to give flour grains an opportunity to soften and in turn make the pancakes or pudding finer in texture. However, because the combination of flour, eggs and milk is a happy breeding ground for bacteria, it is advisable to leave the batter to stand for no longer than 30 minutes and even so it is best to leave it in the coolest part of the refrigerator and keep it well-covered.

Batter, with the addition of oil or melted butter—about 1 dessertspoon oil or ½oz (12gm) butter or margarine, melted, to every 4oz (100gm) flour—becomes much more velvety in texture. Plain flour is the usual flour to use for batters although self-raising flour can be used for pancakes.

Pancake and fritters

Pouring batter

This is suitable for pancakes or Yorkshire pudding.

Basic pouring batter

4oz (100gm) plain flour
½ level teaspoon salt
1 standard egg
½ pint (250ml) cold milk
1 dessertspoon salad oil or ½oz (12gm) butter or margarine, melted

1. Sift flour and salt into a bowl.
2. Add unbeaten egg.
3. With a wooden spoon, gradually beat in half the milk and continue beating until batter is smooth and air bubbles collect on the surface.
4. Very gently fold in rest of milk with oil or melted fat.
5. Cover and refrigerate for 15 to 30 minutes.

Note
This quantity is sufficient for 7 to 8 pancakes or a family-sized Yorkshire pudding.

Popovers

These are individual batter puddings baked in bun tins in a hot oven, 425 deg F or gas 7 (220 deg C) for 20 to 25 minutes. The basic pouring batter will make 24 popovers. Popovers may be served with beef and gravy or with golden syrup as a sweet.

Coating batter

The standard batter for coating pieces of meat, fish, fruit and vegetables.
Make exactly as pouring batter (see this page) but reduce the milk to ¼ pint (125ml).

Savoury fritter batter

This is a light but puffy and crisp batter, also used for coating food. Sometimes pieces of finely-chopped meat, fish, chicken and vegetables (or a combination of ingredients) are folded into the batter and teaspoons of the mixture are fried in deep fat to give savoury fritters. The batter is made from flour, oil, water and egg white only and as a little goes a long way, 2oz (50gm) flour is a satisfactory amount for an average quantity of food to be coated.

Basic savoury fritter batter

2oz (50gm) plain flour
pinch of salt
shake of pepper
4 tablespoons lukewarm water or stock
1 tablespoon salad oil
1 egg white

1. Sift flour, salt and pepper into a bowl.
2. Mix to a smooth, thick batter with water or stock and oil.
3. Beat egg white to a stiff snow.
4. Fold into batter mixture with a metal spoon.
5. Use straight away.

Sweet fritter batter

This is as crisp and as light as savoury fritter batter and is usually used to coat pieces of fresh or canned fruits such as pineapple, banana, apple rings, and peach and apricot halves.
Make this batter in exactly the same way as the savoury one but omit pepper and sieve flour with salt and 2 level teaspoons sifted icing sugar. Use water only for mixing. The quantity should be sufficient for approximately 6 large pineapple rings but when making more than 6 fruit fritters, it is advisable to double all the batter ingredients.

Stuffings

Stuffings are useful as not only do they add to the flavour of foods, but they also make them go further and, in the case of poultry and boned joints, help them stay a good shape. Breadcrumbs usually form the base for stuffings, although sausagemeat, rice and chestnuts are often used either as a substitute or in addition to the crumbs. In general, stuffings swell up during cooking and therefore should always be packed loosely inside poultry and joints. Using beaten egg to bind produces a firmer stuffing than milk or stock but either is satisfactory. Avoid making crumb stuffings too wet as they will become heavy and/or stodgy. The best are those which are crumbly but at the same time firm enough to hold their shape when drawn together with the fingertips. Allow 2 to 3oz (50 to 75gm) stuffing per lb (½ kilo) meat, fish or poultry. Surplus stuffing should be put into a greased heatproof dish and baked with the meat. Alternatively, it may be rolled into small balls and placed round a joint of meat or poultry for approximately 1 hour. Always stuff meat, poultry and fish *immediately before cooking*.

Parsley, lemon and thyme stuffing

For veal, poultry, cutlets of fish and whole fish such as haddock.

4oz (100gm) fresh white breadcrumbs

1oz (25gm) finely-shredded suet

1 level tablespoon finely-chopped parsley

finely grated peel of ½ small lemon

½ level teaspoon thyme

salt and pepper to taste

1 standard egg, beaten

milk or stock (if necessary)

1. Combine crumbs with suet, parsley, lemon peel, thyme and salt and pepper to taste.
2. Bind with the beaten egg, adding milk or stock only if necessary.

Sage and onion stuffing

For pork.

2 medium onions

4oz (100gm) breadcrumbs

1 to 2 level teaspoons dried sage

salt and pepper to taste

1oz (25gm) butter, melted

milk or stock (if necessary)

1. Cook onions in boiling salted water until tender. Drain and chop finely.
2. Put into bowl with crumbs, sage and salt and pepper to taste.
3. Bind with melted butter, adding milk or stock only if necessary.

Pork with sage and onion stuffing

Sausagemeat stuffing

For poultry.

1lb (½ kilo) pork or beef sausagemeat

4oz (100gm) fresh white breadcrumbs

1 level teaspoon dry mustard

1 medium onion, grated

1 level tablespoon chopped parsley

½ to 1 level teaspoon dried mixed herbs

salt and pepper to taste

2 tablespoons stock, water or milk

1. Combine all ingredients well together by kneading thoroughly.
2. Use as required.

Chestnut stuffing

Although traditionally used for turkey, I have found that this stuffing is just as good for duckling and goose.

1 can (approximately 1lb or ½ kilo) unsweetened chestnut purée

8oz (200gm) fresh white or brown breadcrumbs

1 medium onion, finely grated

2oz (50gm) melted bacon dripping or butter

salt and pepper to taste

2 standard eggs, beaten

a little milk (if necessary)

1. Combine chestnut purée with crumbs, onion, melted dripping or butter and salt and pepper to taste.
2. Bind with eggs and milk only if necessary.

Note
1. If using dried chestnuts, allow 8 to 12oz (200 to 300gm) and soak overnight. Cook until tender, drain and mash as finely as possible.
2. If using fresh chestnuts, allow 2lb (1 kilo). Make a cut in the skins and drop into a saucepan of rapidly boiling water. Cook until tender (30 to 40 minutes). Drain, peel and mash as finely as possible.

Piquant rice stuffing

A delicious stuffing for poultry.

1 medium onion, finely chopped

1 medium green pepper, de-seeded and finely chopped

4oz (100gm) lean bacon, chopped

1 tablespoon salad oil

2 large tomatoes, skinned and chopped

1 tablespoon soft brown sugar

1 level tablespoon finely-chopped parsley

8oz (200gm) boiled rice (cooked weight)

seasoning to taste

1. Slowly fry onion, pepper and bacon in the oil until onion is pale gold. Remove from heat.
2. Stir in all remaining ingredients. Leave until cold before using.

Bacon stuffing

For meat, fish and poultry.

4oz (100gm) lean bacon, chopped

1oz (25gm) butter or margarine

4oz (100gm) fresh white breadcrumbs

1 teaspoon Worcestershire sauce

½ level teaspoon dried mixed herbs

salt and pepper to taste

milk (if necessary)

1. Fry bacon for 5 minutes in the butter or margarine.
2. Stir in crumbs, Worcestershire sauce, mixed herbs and salt and pepper to taste.
3. Bind with a little milk if necessary.

Prune and pork stuffing

A sumptuous, subtly-flavoured stuffing for poultry.

4oz (100gm) prunes

1 wine glass dry white wine

6oz (150gm) lean pork, finely minced

1 egg yolk

1 tablespoon brandy

1 level tablespoon finely-chopped parsley

½ level teaspoon sage (optional)

1 dozen toasted almonds, coarsely chopped

salt and pepper to taste

1. Soak prunes in wine overnight.
2. Remove stones from prunes and chop flesh finely.
3. Combine with pork, egg yolk, brandy, parsley, sage (if used), almonds and salt and pepper to taste.

Liver and orange stuffing

For goose and guinea-fowl.

1oz (25gm) butter or margarine

1 teaspoon salad oil

1 rasher streaky bacon, chopped

1 small onion, chopped

8oz (200gm) lamb or chicken, cubed

6oz (150gm) prunes, soaked overnight then stoned and chopped

finely-grated peel and juice of 1 medium orange

juice of ½ medium lemon

salt and pepper to taste

1. Heat butter or margarine and salad oil in pan.
2. Add bacon, onion and liver and fry gently until onion is pale gold.
3. Mince finely and combine with prunes, orange peel, orange and lemon juices and salt and pepper to taste.

Potato and liver stuffing

An unusual stuffing for goose and duckling.

2lb (1 kilo) potatoes, freshly cooked

2oz (50gm) butter, softened

1 large onion, finely grated

liver from goose or duckling, chopped

2 standard eggs, beaten

3 level tablespoons finely-chopped parsley

1 level teaspoon dried mixed herbs

salt and pepper to taste

1. Mash potatoes finely then combine with all remaining ingredients.
2. Leave until cold before using.

Stuffed rolled bacon

Tomato and olive stuffing

For fish, poultry, veal and lamb.

4oz (100gm) fresh white breadcrumbs

3 medium skinned tomatoes, chopped

2 medium celery stalks, finely chopped

8 to 12 stuffed olives, sliced

1oz (25gm) butter, melted

salt and pepper to taste

milk (if necessary)

1. Combine crumbs with tomatoes, celery, olives and butter.
2. Season to taste with salt and pepper and bind with milk if necessary.

Note
If preferred, 2 level tablespoons finely-chopped gherkins may be used instead of the olives.

Mushroom and onion stuffing

For fish, meat and poultry.

1oz (25gm) butter or margarine

2 teaspoons salad oil

4oz (100gm) mushrooms, sliced

1 small onion, grated

4oz (100gm) fresh white breadcrumbs

1 level dessertspoon finely-chopped parsley

salt and pepper to taste

milk (if necessary)

1. Heat butter or margarine and oil in pan.
2. Add mushrooms and onions and fry 5 minutes.
3. Stir in crumbs, parsley and salt and pepper to taste.
4. Bind with a little milk if necessary.

Apple and raisin stuffing

For duck, goose, pork, bacon joints and lamb.

4oz (100gm) fresh white breadcrumbs

4 medium cooking apples

1 small onion, grated

3 level tablespoons seedless raisins

1 level tablespoon caster sugar

salt and pepper to taste

1oz (25gm) butter, melted

a little stock or milk (if necessary)

1. Put crumbs into bowl.
2. Peel, core and chop apples. Add to crumbs with onion, raisins and sugar.
3. Season to taste with salt and pepper.
4. Bind with butter and stock or milk only if necessary.

Cashew and hazelnut stuffing

For meat and poultry.

6oz (150gm) cashew nuts, finely ground

6oz (150gm) hazelnuts, finely ground

1 medium onion, finely grated

½ level teaspoon dried mixed herbs

salt and pepper to taste

1 standard egg, beaten

1. Put nuts, onion and herbs into bowl.
2. Season to taste with salt and pepper then bind with the egg.

Apple, cranberry and orange stuffing

For all poultry dishes.

2 large cooking apples

1 can (8oz or 200gm) cranberry sauce

1 level teaspoon finely-grated orange peel

1. Peel, core and chop apples.
2. Combine with cranberry sauce and orange peel.

Packet stuffings

These make an excellent substitute for home-made stuffings when time is short, and may be varied by the addition of 1 or 2 level tablespoons chopped fresh parsley, 1 or 2 level tablespoons chopped celery, 1 or 2 level tablespoons tomato paste and 1 to 2oz (25 to 50gm) coarsely-chopped nuts, such as walnuts or salted peanuts. The packet stuffings may be used as directed but can also be rolled into small balls and either fried or baked or added to stews and casseroles instead of dumplings.

Pastry

Tender, golden-crisp and melt-in-the-mouth pastry is not the result of a chance meeting between flour, fat, liquid and sometimes egg. On the contrary, good pastry is dependent more on the correct proportion of these ingredients to each other than anything else and while some cooks get superb pastry by throwing everything into a bowl and never weighing a thing, most of us do need more careful guide lines in order to succeed.

Short crust pastry

This is the most popular pastry of all and probably the simplest to make. The standard proportion is half fat to flour (for example 4oz or 100gm fat to 8oz or 200gm flour) plus 1 to 1½ teaspoons cold water to every oz or 25gm of flour used. The correct flour to use is plain and for best results, the fats should be a mixture of half margarine or butter and half lard or cooking fat. All butter or all margarine tends to produce a slightly tougher pastry.

The amount of salt used does depend, to a certain extent, on personal taste but a safe margin is 1 level teaspoon to every 8oz or 200gm flour.

The ingredients and utensils should be as cold as possible and the fats should first be cut into the sifted flour and salt and then lightly rubbed in with the fingertips only—using the palms of the hands, which are warmer, can cause heavy pastry. The water should be sprinkled all at once on top of the dry ingredients and then the pastry mixed together with a round-topped knife. At this stage it will still be crumbly and should be drawn together into a ball with the fingertips.

Kneading helps to make the pastry smooth but this should be kept to a minimum and done quickly and lightly. Wrapping it in foil and chilling it for 30 minutes makes rolling out easier but this is not vital, except in hot weather.

The pastry should be rolled out on an evenly-floured surface with light forward strokes—not in all directions—and never turned over.

Stretching the pastry to make it fit is dangerous because it will shrink back during cooking and lose its shape. It is much better to patch if necessary (pastry sticks to itself if it is first moistened with water) rather than stretch it.

Self-raising flour can be used if the pastry is to be used to cover a pie or tart but not if it is to be baked empty in the form of a flan or tartlet cases. This is because the pastry would puff up too much, partially lose its shape and leave insufficient room for the filling.

The term 'bake blind' refers to pastry flans and tarts which are baked empty and filled later. To 'bake blind' the pastry is rolled out and used to line a flan tin, then the raw pastry is pricked lightly all over with a fork. Line the base and sides with a piece of foil—this holds the pastry down and stops it from rising as it cooks. Alternatively, line with grease-proof paper and fill the centre with dried beans to weight down the pastry.

Sugar, if in direct contact with pastry, makes it soggy and therefore before adding a pastry covering to a fruit pie, make sure the top layer is fruit only and not fruit with a sprinkling of sugar. To prevent sunken pies, the fillings should be cold and not too liquidy. They should also be well-domed to support the pastry.

Short crust responds best to a brisk oven and the starting temperature should be 425 deg F or gas 7 (220 deg C). The best position in the oven is one shelf above the centre.

Basic short crust pastry

Use for tarts, flans, pies, turnovers, pasties and patties.

4oz (100gm) plain flour
½ level teaspoon salt
1oz (25gm) butter or margarine
1oz (25gm) lard or cooking fat
4 to 6 teaspoons cold water to mix

1. Sift flour and salt into a bowl.
2. Cut in fats finely then rub into flour with fingertips until mixture resembles fine breadcrumbs.
3. Add all the water at once then mix to a crumbly dough with round-topped knife.
4. Draw together with fingertips.
5. Turn out on a thinly-floured surface and knead quickly and lightly until smooth.
6. Wrap in foil and refrigerate 30 minutes before using.

Sweet short crust

Make as basic short crust pastry (above) but sift 1 to 1½oz (25 to 37gm) icing sugar with the flour.

Note

Icing sugar is more satisfactory than caster because being so fine, it melts quickly and does not cause speckles.

Rich flan pastry

Make as basic short crust pastry (see this page) but sift the flour with 1 level dessert-spoon icing sugar, increase butter by ½oz (12gm) and mix with one egg yolk and 2 to 3 teaspoons cold water. Refrigerate for at least 45 minutes before rolling out and shaping.

Easy-mix pastry

This is short crust pastry made with oil and although richer than the basic pastry, it is useful for those who must, for health reasons, omit animal fats from their diets. It is also very easy to make but is more suited to savoury dishes than sweet ones.

2½ tablespoons salad oil
1 tablespoon cold water
4oz (100gm) plain flour
½ level teaspoon salt

1. Beat the oil and water well together.
2. Sift together flour and salt.
3. Using a fork, gradually stir into oil and water to form a dough.
4. Roll out between 2 lightly-floured sheets of greaseproof paper or between 2 sheets of waxed paper.

Fork-mix pastry

This is a very quickly-made short crust which eliminates rubbing-in altogether.

4oz (100gm) plain flour
½ level teaspoon salt
2oz (50gm) whipped-up white cooking fat
3 dessertspoons cold water

1. Sift together flour and salt.
2. Put 1 rounded tablespoon into bowl.
3. Add cooking fat and water and whisk with a fork for 30 seconds.
4. Add rest of flour, stirring to form a firm dough.
5. Knead lightly on a thinly-floured surface.
6. Wrap in foil and refrigerate 30 minutes before using.

Cheese pastry

Use for savoury flans, pies, turnovers, pasties and patties.

Make as for basic short crust pastry but sift 1 level teaspoon dry mustard with the salt and add 2oz (50gm) very finely-grated strong Cheddar cheese to the rubbed-in ingredients.

Danish apple flan (see page 167) made with short crust pastry

Rich cheese pastry

Use for cheese biscuits, cheese straws, savoury flans and tartlets.

4oz (100gm) plain flour

¼ to ½ level teaspoon dry mustard

½ level teaspoon salt

shake of cayenne pepper

1½oz (37gm) cooking fat

1oz (25gm) butter

2oz (50gm) very finely-grated Cheddar cheese (preferably stale)

1 egg yolk

2 to 3 teaspoons cold water

1. Sift flour, mustard, salt and pepper into bowl.
2. Cut in fats finely then rub into flour with fingertips until mixture resembles fine breadcrumbs.
3. Add cheese and toss ingredients lightly together.
4. Beat egg yolk and water together.
5. Add, all at once, to dry ingredients then mix to crumbly dough with round-topped knife.
6. Draw together with fingertips.
7. Turn out on to thinly-floured surface and knead quickly and lightly until smooth.
8. Wrap in foil and refrigerate about 30 minutes before using.

Suet crust pastry

Suet crust is a hearty pastry used for many traditional British dishes such as steak and kidney pudding, roly poly, dumplings and spotted Dick. The pastry itself is simply a mixture of flour, salt, suet and water and it is the only pastry which depends on a raising agent for lightness. The proportion of fat to flour is the same as in short crust but the water requirement is greater and the usual amount is ¼ pint (125ml) to every 8oz (200gm) flour. Although self-raising flour may be used, this is a fine flour more suited to cakes. Therefore, I would advise strong, plain flour with the addition of baking powder in the proportion of 3 level teaspoons to every 8oz (200gm) flour. The best suet to use is that which surrounds beef kidney, although any fresh beef suet is suitable. The suet must be skinned and very finely chopped if the pastry is to work well and the easiest way to do it is to mix the coarsely-chopped suet with 1 or 2 tablespoons of the weighed flour and baking powder (to prevent sticking) and then continue to chop until the suet is in very fine pieces. Simpler still, of course, is to use packet suet which is already shredded. Suet crust pastry should be rolled out slightly more thickly than short crust and should always be eaten hot—cold suet crust tastes greasy and hard. When steaming or boiling puddings made with suet crust, the water must bubble continuously, otherwise the pastry will be heavy. Like short crust, this pastry will shrink back if it has been stretched to fit.

110

Basic suet crust pastry

Use for sweet and savoury puddings and roly poly.

8oz (200gm) self-raising flour or 8oz (200gm) plain flour plus 3 level teaspoons baking powder

1 level teaspoon salt

4oz (100gm) finely-chopped or shredded suet

¼ pint (125ml) cold water

1. Sift flour (or flour and baking powder) with salt into bowl.
2. Add suet and toss ingredients lightly together.
3. Using a round-bladed knife, mix to a soft dough with cold water.
4. Turn out on to a thinly-floured surface and knead lightly until smooth. Shape into a ball.
5. Cover with a bowl and leave to stand for 10 minutes before using.

Rough puff pastry

This is a simplified and speedier version of flaky pastry and makes a very good substitute for most dishes where flaky would normally be used. Because of the way it is made, the flakes tend to be uneven and therefore it is unsatisfactory for vol-au-vents, patties and mille feuilles. The flour must always be plain and the fat a mixture of butter or margarine with lard or cooking fat. The proportion of fat to flour is higher than for the other pastries and the standard amount is 6oz (150gm) fat to 8oz (200gm) flour. It requires more water than short crust and the average quantity for 8oz (200gm) flour is ¼ pint (125ml). A squeeze of lemon juice is also advisable as this gives the pastry more elasticity and makes it easier to roll. When making rough puff, it is essential for the fat to be firm and it should therefore be taken straight from the refrigerator. Rough puff must always be rolled evenly with light forward strokes and rolling over the edges should be avoided. This pastry must never be stretched either, as it will lose both its shape and puffiness. A hot oven, 425 deg F or gas 7 (220 deg C), is required for rough puff pastry.

Basic rough puff pastry

8oz (200gm) plain flour

1 level teaspoon salt

3oz (75gm) butter or margarine

3oz (75gm) lard or cooking fat

¼ pint (125ml) cold water

squeeze of lemon juice

1. Sift flour and salt into bowl.
2. Cut fats into ½-inch cubes.
3. Stir into flour without breaking up the cubes but making sure each one is coated with flour.
4. Add water and lemon juice.
5. With a round-bladed knife, mix to a fairly stiff dough.
6. Draw together with fingertips then turn out on to a floured surface.
7. Roll into a rectangle 3 times as long as it is wide.
8. Fold the bottom third up and the top third over (like an envelope).
9. Seal open edges of pastry by pressing lightly together with a rolling pin.
10. Slip into a polythene bag and chill for 15 minutes.
11. With the folds to the right and left and with sealed edges top and bottom, roll out pastry into a rectangle as before.
12. Fold, seal and refrigerate.
13. Repeat twice more.
14. Refrigerate 30 minutes before using.
15. Roll out to ¼ inch in thickness.

Suet strudel (see page 175) made with suet crust pastry

Flaky pastry

This is another popular pastry for sweet and savoury pies, patties, turnovers and sausage rolls and may also be used for pastries such as cream slices and cream horns. It is not a particularly easy pastry to make and requires considerable care and patience. The proportion of fat to flour is exactly the same as for rough puff (6oz or 150gm fat to 8oz or 200gm plain flour) and best results are obtained with a mixture of butter or margarine with lard or cooking fat. The fat should be softer than for rough puff but not on the point of melting. The lightness and flakiness of this pastry is dependent mainly on the way fat and air are incorporated and also the way it is rolled. It must be rolled lightly, with even, forward strokes so that the air pockets formed between the pieces of fat and folds of pastry are not broken down. It is essential to 'rest' the pastry in the refrigerator for at least 20 minutes after each folding so that the fats have an opportunity of becoming firm again. Rolling over the edges should be avoided and this pastry should always be baked in a hot oven, 450 deg F or gas 8 (230 deg C), on an ungreased baking sheet.

Cream horn (see page 223) made with flaky pastry

Basic flaky pastry

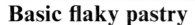

| 8oz (200gm) plain flour |
| 1 level teaspoon salt |
| 3oz (75gm) butter or margarine |
| 3oz (75gm) lard or cooking fat |
| 7 tablespoons cold water |
| 2 teaspoons lemon juice |

1. Sift flour and salt into a bowl.
2. Divide fats into 4 equal portions.
3. Rub one portion finely into sifted flour.
4. Mix to a fairly soft dough with water and lemon juice.
5. Turn out on to a floured surface and knead lightly until smooth.
6. Slip into a polythene bag and refrigerate for 20 minutes.
7. Roll into a rectangle 3 times as long as it is wide. Starting from the end farthest away from you, cover two-thirds of the pastry with flakes of fat, using second portion only. Sprinkle lightly with flour.
8. Fold the bottom third up and the top third over (like an envelope) completely enclosing fat.
9. Seal open edges of pastry by pressing lightly together with a rolling pin.
10. Slip into a polythene bag and refrigerate 30 minutes.
11. With folds to the right and left and with sealed edges top and bottom, roll out pastry into a rectangle as before.
12. Cover two-thirds of the pastry with third portion of fat, as before, and sprinkle lightly with flour.
13. Fold, seal and refrigerate for 30 minutes.
14. Repeat process, using last portion of fat.
15. Fold, seal and refrigerate for 1 hour.
16. Roll out to between $\frac{1}{4}$ and $\frac{1}{2}$ inch in thickness, and use as required.

Hot water crust pastry

This is a good, satisfying pastry capable not only of supporting itself but also the filling it contains. It is made in a different way from other pastries and requires warmth rather than cold for its success. It is the traditional pastry used for game, veal and ham and pork pies. The pies are known as raised pies because they can be shaped or raised by hand (quite a difficult operation) but for ease the pastry is frequently moulded round a cake tin or baked in a decorative and hinged raised pie mould. Making the pastry is fairly easy. More difficult is the moulding which must be done fairly quickly while the pastry is still warm. Because hot water crust must be cooked for a long time (at least long enough for the meat inside to become tender) it is generally thicker than other pastries and requires two different oven temperatures. A moderately hot oven, 400 deg F or gas 6 (200 deg C), for the first 30 minutes, followed by a moderate temperature, 350 deg F or gas 4 (180 deg C), for the rest of the cooking time. As meat fillings tend to shrink and leave gaps, it is customary to fill up these pies—through a hole in the top—with liquid jelly while the pie itself is still hot. As the pie cools the jelly sets and when cut open, there is appetising jelly intermingled with cooked meat. Raised pies look best—and indeed taste best—if made a day before required.

Basic hot water crust pastry

| 1lb ($\frac{1}{2}$ kilo) plain flour |
| 3 level teaspoons salt |
| 1 egg yolk |
| 6oz (150gm) lard or cooking fat |
| 8 tablespoons water |
| 4 tablespoons milk |

1. Sift flour and salt into a bowl. Make well in centre.
2. Drop in egg yolk and cover with some of the flour.
3. Put lard or cooking fat, water and milk into a saucepan. Heat gently until fat melts.
4. Bring to boil and add all at once to flour, mixing to a dough with a wooden spoon.
5. Turn out on to a thinly-floured surface and knead until smooth and crack-free. Shape into a ball.
6. Stand dough in a basin over a saucepan of gently simmering water. Cover and leave 30 minutes to rest.
7. Shape three-quarters of the dough into a pie but leave remaining quarter (for the lid) in the basin so that it keeps warm until you are ready to use it.

Note
Hot water crust should be moulded to about $\frac{1}{4}$ inch in thickness.

Cream bun (see page 224) made with choux pastry

Choux pastry

This pastry is unique in that it is made entirely in a saucepan, is neither rolled nor moulded and is richer both in fat and eggs than any other pastry. Choux pastry is the traditional pastry to use for cream puffs, éclairs, gateau St Honoré and, on the savoury side, for cheese aigrettes and one variety of gnocchi. Well-made choux pastry puffs up to about three times its original size, leaving a golden crisp shell with a hollow centre. Choux pastry depends entirely on air for its lightness and this is built into the mixture when the eggs are incorporated. Oven temperature is important too and if the pastry is to hold its shape and not collapse when taken out of the oven, it should be baked in a fairly brisk oven, 400 deg F or gas 6 (200 deg C).

Basic choux pastry

2½oz (62gm) plain flour

pinch of salt

2oz (50gm) butter or best table margarine

¼ pint (125ml) water

2 standard eggs, well beaten

1. Sift flour and salt on to a plate.
2. Put butter or margarine with water into a saucepan. Heat slowly until fat melts.
3. Bring to a rolling boil. Remove from heat and add flour *all at once*.
4. Beat until mixture is smooth and sufficiently thick to leave sides of pan clean and form a ball in the centre.
5. Very gradually add eggs, beating thoroughly after each addition.
6. Continue beating until mixture is smooth and shiny and firm enough to hold soft peaks when lifted with a spoon.
7. Use immediately.

Puff pastry

This is the classic of the pastry family, and has a characteristic richness, lightness and crisp flakiness which distinguishes it from all other pastry. It is tricky to make and demands time and patience. Ideally, it should be prepared a day before required so that it has plenty of time to rest and become firm. Equal amounts of fat and plain flour are always used and unsalted butter is the best choice, not only for flakiness but also for appearance and texture. The success of this pastry depends almost entirely on the way it is rolled and those who know they have a heavy hand should, to avoid disappointment, settle for frozen puff pastry which is totally reliable. Puff pastry should be placed on an ungreased and slightly damp baking tray and baked in a hot oven, 450 deg F or gas 8 (230 deg C).

Basic puff pastry

8oz (200gm) plain flour

1 level teaspoon salt

8oz (200gm) unsalted butter

8 tablespoons chilled water

2 teaspoons lemon juice

1. Sift flour and salt into bowl.
2. Rub in ½oz (12gm) butter.
3. Mix to a soft dough with water and lemon juice.
4. Turn out on to a floured surface and knead lightly until smooth.
5. Slip into a polythene bag and leave to rest in a cool place for 30 minutes.
6. Meanwhile, put rest of butter into a clean cloth and work it with the hands until it is soft and pliable and the same texture as the dough. Shape fat into a square measuring approximately 5½ inches.
7. Roll out pastry into an oblong measuring 12 inches by 6 inches.
8. Place butter on lower half then bring top half over, completely enclosing butter.
9. Press the open edges well together to seal.
10. Turn the pastry so that the fold is either to the left or right and gently roll into a strip 3 times as long as it is wide.
11. Fold, seal, roll and refrigerate as for flaky pastry, repeating these processes a total of 7 times altogether.
12. Return pastry to polythene bag and refrigerate for a minimum of 2 hours and for a maximum of 12.
13. Roll out to ½ inch in thickness and bake in a hot oven, 450 deg F or gas 8 (230 deg C).

Miscellaneous pastries

Cottage cheese pastry

This slightly resembles rough puff but is much quicker to make and somewhat richer. It is excellent as a covering for sweet and savoury pies and is equally good if used for sausage rolls and jam turnovers.

4oz (100gm) plain flour

pinch of salt

4oz (100gm) butter, chilled

4oz (100gm) cottage cheese

1. Sift flour and salt into a bowl.
2. Add butter and cut it into flour until it is in pieces no larger than small peas.
3. Rub cheese through a sieve directly on to flour and butter.
4. Mix well with a knife and then draw mixture together with fingertips.
5. Wrap in foil and refrigerate for a minimum of 8 hours.
6. Roll out to about ⅛ inch in thickness and bake in a hot oven, 450 deg F or gas 8 (230 deg C).

Mock puff pastry

This is a recipe I worked out years ago and it defies all the accepted rules of good pastry-making! But it works well, is meltingly light and crisp and is a pastry I make more often than any other.

8oz (200gm) self-raising flour

1 level teaspoon salt

3oz (75gm) butter or margarine

3oz (75gm) lard or cooking fat

5 tablespoons cold milk

1. Sift flour and salt into bowl.
2. Add fats and cut into flour until they are in pieces no larger than peas.
3. Mix to a stiff dough with cold milk.
4. Draw together with fingertips and wrap in a piece of foil.
5. Refrigerate for a minimum of 2 hours.
6. Roll out. fairly thinly (but fractionally thicker than short crust) and bake in a hot oven, 425 deg F or gas 7 (220 deg C).

Cherry mille feuille (see page 200) made with puff pastry

113

Lunch and supper dishes

In this chapter you will find a pot pourri of egg, cheese, pasta, rice and nut dishes, suitable for mid-week lunches, informal suppers—and snacks at any time of the day. Classic favourites such as macaroni cheese, cheese soufflé, French omelet and curried eggs are included, and so too are many less familiar specialities. Quite a number of the recipes use no meat, so vegetarians and others seeking a change from meat, fish and poultry should find a varied selection of dishes to please them.

Welsh rarebit

Serves 4

4 large slices white or brown bread

1oz (25gm) butter or margarine, softened

1 level teaspoon made mustard

1 teaspoon Worcestershire sauce

8oz (200gm) strong Cheddar cheese, finely grated

1 tablespoon milk or cream

salt and pepper to taste

1. Toast bread on one side only.
2. Beat butter or margarine to a light cream then add all remaining ingredients.
3. Beat until smooth.
4. Spread untoasted sides of bread with equal amounts of cheese mixture then brown under a hot grill.
5. Serve straight away.

Tomato rarebit

Serves 4

Make as for Welsh rarebit, above, but add 3 level teaspoons tomato paste to cheese mixture.

Buck rarebit

Serves 4

Make as for Welsh rarebit, above, but top each slice of toast with a poached or fried egg.

Pale ale rarebit

Serves 4

Make as for Welsh rarebit, above, but substitute 3 dessertspoons pale ale for the milk.

Meatball fritters

Serves 4

1lb (½ kilo) lean minced beef

1 small onion, grated

1 standard egg, beaten

½ level teaspoon mixed herbs

salt and pepper to taste

savoury fritter batter (see page 105)

deep fat or oil for frying

8 to 12oz (200 to 300gm) freshly-boiled spaghetti

1oz (25gm) butter

Italian tomato sauce (see page 102)

parsley to garnish

1. Combine beef with onion, egg, herbs and salt and pepper to taste.
2. Shape into 20 small balls then coat with fritter batter.
3. Heat deep fat or oil until a cube of bread, dropped into it, turns pale gold in 1 minute and floats to the top.
4. Add meat balls, about 5 at a time, and fry 5 to 6 minutes.
5. Drain thoroughly on soft kitchen paper and keep hot.
6. Toss spaghetti with butter then transfer to a warm dish.
7. Top with meat balls then coat with tomato sauce.
8. Serve straight away, garnished with chopped parsley.

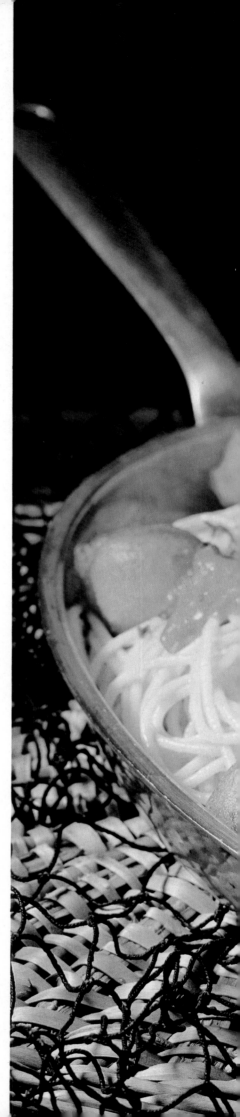

Meatball fritters with spaghetti and tomato sauce

Above: pilchard pancakes au gratin served on a bed of spinach and garnished with mandarin orange slices.
Below: Australian pancake layer

116

Curried eggs

Serves 4

2oz (50gm) butter or margarine

1 medium onion, peeled and chopped

1 medium eating apple, peeled, cored and finely chopped

2 level tablespoons flour

1 to 2 level tablespoons curry powder

¾ pint (375ml) vegetable stock or water

1 packet (8oz or 200gm) cream cheese

2 level tablespoons sultanas

2 level tablespoons mango chutney

6 hard-boiled eggs, freshly cooked

8oz (200gm) freshly-boiled rice (raw weight)

lemon slices to garnish

1. Melt butter or margarine in saucepan. Add onion and fry gently until pale gold.
2. Add apple and fry a further 2 to 3 minutes or until soft.
3. Stir in flour and curry powder. Cook 2 minutes.
4. Gradually blend in ½ pint (250ml) vegetable stock or water.
5. Beat rest of stock or water very gradually into cheese and add to saucepan.
6. Cook, stirring, until sauce comes to boil and thickens.
7. Lower heat and cover. Simmer 20 minutes.
8. Add sultanas and chutney and continue to cook for a further 5 minutes.
9. Shell and halve eggs and add to sauce.
10. Arrange rice on warm platter. Top with curried eggs and garnish with lemon slices.

Chicken and walnut pancakes

Serves 4

Pouring batter (see page 105)

½ pint (250ml) freshly-made white or béchamel sauce (see pages 94, 96)

8oz (200gm) cold cooked chicken, coarsely chopped

2oz (50gm) walnuts, coarsely chopped

1 teaspoon Worcestershire sauce

salt and pepper to taste

2oz (50gm) Cheddar cheese, grated

1. Brush an 8-inch heavy frying pan with lard or cooking fat and heat until hot.
2. Pour in enough batter to cover base of pan thinly.
3. Cook until underside is golden. Turn over and cook other side until golden. Remove from pan and keep warm.
4. Continue to make pancakes in this way, until all the batter mixture is used up.
5. Combine half the sauce with chicken, walnuts, Worcestershire sauce and salt and pepper to taste. Heat through gently for 5 minutes.
6. Put equal amounts on to pancakes. Roll up and transfer to a heatproof dish.
7. Coat with rest of sauce then sprinkle with cheese.
8. Brown under a hot grill and serve straight away.

Curried eggs with rice

Pilchard pancakes au gratin

Serves 3 to 4

Make pancakes as given in recipe for chicken and walnut pancakes (see this page), but use 2oz (50gm) flour, 1 small egg and ¼ pint (125ml) milk. Cook pancakes in a small pan and keep them warm by stacking one on top of the other in a folded tea-towel. To make filling, melt 1oz (25gm) butter in a saucepan. Add 1 medium onion, chopped, and fry until pale gold. Add 2 skinned and chopped tomatoes and 1 can (8oz or 200gm) drained and flaked pilchards. Season well to taste with salt and pepper then put equal amounts on to pancakes. Roll up and place stuffed pancakes on a bed of freshly-cooked hot spinach. Sprinkle generously with 2oz (50gm) grated Cheddar cheese and brown under a hot grill. If liked, garnish with drained mandarin oranges, lemon and parsley.

Pancake tower coated with sauce

Pancake tower

Serves 4

Make as for chicken and walnut pancakes (see this page), but stack pancakes one on top of the other, with chicken mixture sandwiched between. Coat with sauce, sprinkle with cheese and reheat and brown just above centre of hot oven, 450 deg F or gas 8 (230 deg C), for 10 minutes.

Australian pancake layer

Serves 4

Make pancakes as for chicken and walnut pancakes (see this page). Keep warm. Coarsely grate 1 large peeled and cored eating apple and combine with 8oz (200gm) cream cheese and 8oz (200gm) sultanas. Spread mixture on to pancakes then pile one on top of the other. Sprinkle grated cheese on top, garnish with parsley, then cut into wedges like a cake. Serve straight away.

Egg and potato casserole

Egg and vegetable curry

Serves 4

1 large packet frozen mixed vegetables

1 large onion, chopped

1 garlic clove, chopped

1 tablespoon salad oil

1 level tablespoon curry powder

2 level teaspoons flour

$\frac{3}{4}$ pint (375ml) water or vegetable stock

1 bay leaf

1 small lemon, washed and sliced

salt and pepper to taste

8oz (200gm) freshly-cooked long grain rice (raw weight)

8 hard-boiled eggs, freshly cooked

2 tomatoes, cut into wedges

1. Cook mixed vegetables until tender then drain. Keep on one side.
2. Fry onion and garlic in the oil until pale gold.
3. Stir in curry powder and flour and cook slowly for 1 minute.
4. Gradually blend in water or stock. Cook, stirring continuously, until sauce comes to boil and thickens.
5. Add bay leaf and lemon. Season to taste with salt and pepper. Cover and simmer 30 minutes.
6. Arrange rice on warm platter. Halve eggs and place them on top. Keep hot.
7. Remove bay leaf and lemon from sauce. Add vegetables and warm through for 5 minutes.
8. Pour over eggs and rice then garnish with wedges of tomatoes.

Note
If liked, accompany with side dishes of sliced bananas sprinkled with lemon juice and cubes of cucumber tossed with French dressing (see page 161) or natural yogurt.

Egg and vegetable curry accompanied with sliced bananas and cucumber

Egg and potato casserole

Serves 6

2lb (1 kilo) potatoes, peeled and diced

1 large onion, thinly sliced

4 rashers lean bacon, chopped

salt and pepper to taste

$\frac{1}{4}$ pint (125ml) milk

1oz (25gm) butter

6 standard eggs

1. Pre-heat oven to moderately hot, 400 deg F or gas 6 (200 deg C).
2. Put potatoes, onion slices and bacon in layers in a 3 to 4 pint (1$\frac{3}{4}$ to 2$\frac{1}{2}$ litre) buttered casserole dish which is shallow rather than tall.
3. Begin and end with a layer of potatoes and sprinkle salt and pepper between layers.
4. Pour milk into dish and top with flakes of butter.
5. Cover with lid or aluminium foil and cook in centre of oven for 1 hour.
6. Remove from oven, uncover and make 6 wells in the potato mixture with the back of a spoon.
7. Break an egg into each and return casserole to oven for a further 6 to 8 minutes or until eggs are just set.
8. Serve straight away.

Anchovy cheese scramble

Serves 4

2oz (50gm) butter

1 small onion, chopped

3oz (75gm) Gruyère cheese, grated

3oz (75gm) Cheddar cheese, grated

4 tablespoons dry white wine

6 standard eggs

1 level tablespoon finely-chopped parsley

pinch of grated nutmeg

pinch of Cayenne pepper

4 large slices hot buttered toast

12 anchovy fillets to garnish

1. Heat butter in pan.
2. Add onion and fry until pale gold.
3. Reduce heat to very low. Add cheese and wine and stir gently until cheese melts.
4. Continue to cook until mixture bubbles then add 4 eggs beaten with 2 yolks, parsley, nutmeg and Cayenne pepper.
5. Stir continuously until mixture thickens, then remove from heat.
6. Beat remaining egg whites to a stiff snow.
7. Fold into scrambled cheese mixture and pile equal amounts on to toast.
8. Garnish with anchovy fillets and serve straight away.

Note
If preferred, parsley, watercress or strips of green pepper may be used as a garnish instead of anchovies.

Anchovy cheese scramble on toast

Cheese soufflé

Serves 4

2oz (50gm) butter or margarine

2oz (50gm) flour

½ pint (250ml) milk

1 level teaspoon made mustard

½ to 1 level teaspoon salt

pinch of Cayenne pepper

4oz (100gm) strong Cheddar cheese, grated

4 standard eggs, separated

1. Well-butter a 2 pint (1¼ litre) straight-sided soufflé dish.
2. Pre-heat oven to moderately hot, 375 deg F or gas 5 (190 deg C).
3. Melt butter or margarine in large sauce-pan.
4. Stir in flour and cook 1 minute without browning.
5. Very gradually whisk in milk then cook for about 2 to 3 minutes, stirring continuously, until mixture thickens sufficiently to form a ball and leave sides of pan clean.
6. Remove from heat and cool 3 minutes then beat in mustard, salt, Cayenne pepper, cheese and egg yolks.
7. Continue beating until mixture is smooth and glossy.
8. Beat egg whites to a stiff snow and gently and lightly fold into cheese mixture.
9. Transfer to prepared dish and cook in centre of oven for 45 minutes or until soufflé is well-risen and golden.
10. Remove from oven and serve straight away.

Note
Do not open the oven door while the soufflé is cooking or it will collapse.

Ham soufflé

Serves 4

Make as for cheese soufflé, above, but add 4oz (100gm) minced ham instead of the cheese.

Chicken soufflé

Serves 4

Make as for cheese soufflé (see this page), but use half the amount of mustard and add a large pinch of nutmeg. Instead of cheese, add 4oz (100gm) minced cooked chicken.

Haddock soufflé

Serves 4

Make as for cheese soufflé (see this page), but add 4oz (100gm) cooked and finely-mashed smoked haddock instead of the cheese. If liked, add 1 level tablespoon finely-chopped parsley or scissor-snipped chives as well.

Stuffed anchovy eggs in tomato halves garnished with anchovies and olives

Salmon soufflé

Serves 4

Make as for cheese soufflé (see this page), but add 4oz (100gm) drained and very finely-mashed canned red salmon instead of the cheese. Include also ½ teaspoon anchovy essence and 2 teaspoons lemon juice.

Stuffed anchovy eggs

Serves 4

4 large eggs

1 small can (2oz or 50gm) anchovy fillets

2 large tomatoes, skinned

1oz (25gm) butter, softened

salt and pepper to taste

4 stuffed olives

1. Hard-boil eggs and cool. Remove shells.
2. Cut a slice from each end of each egg and squeeze out the yolks.
3. Press yolks through a fine nylon sieve into bowl.
4. Separate anchovy fillets and reserve half for garnishing. Chop remainder finely and add to yolks.
5. Halve tomatoes. Remove pulp and sieve.
6. Add to egg yolk mixture with butter.
7. Beat thoroughly until smooth then season to taste with salt and pepper.
8. Pipe yolk mixture into egg whites then pipe remaining mixture into tomato halves.
9. Stand an egg in each tomato half then garnish with anchovies and olives. Serve with brown bread and butter.

French omelet garnished with tomato and parsley

French omelet

Serves 1

3 standard eggs

2 teaspoons water

salt and pepper to taste

½oz (12gm) butter

tomato and parsley to garnish

1. Beat eggs and water lightly together.
2. Season to taste with salt and pepper.
3. Heat butter in a 7-inch omelet pan.
4. As soon as butter sizzles and begins to turn brown, pour in egg mixture.
5. Shake pan over heat for about 20 seconds then draw edges of omelet towards centre of pan with a knife. At the same time tilt pan in all directions so that uncooked egg runs back to edges and gets cooked.
6. When under side is golden and top still moist (about 1 to 1½ minutes) fold omelet in half or thirds and slide out on to a plate.
7. Serve immediately, garnished with tomato and parsley.

Note
If an omelet pan is not available, use a non-stick pan (plus the butter which is necessary for flavour) or a thick-based frying pan. If using the latter, 'prove' it first to stop the egg mixture from sticking. To do this, cover the base of the pan with salt and stand it over a low heat. Add a tablespoon of salad oil and rub salt and oil into pan with a thick pad of kitchen paper. Continue for about 4 to 5 minutes then wipe clean with fresh paper. Alternatively, rub base and sides of pan with a piece of green bacon fat. An omelet pan should be wiped clean after use with kitchen paper—washing is unnecessary.

Herb omelet

Serves 1

Make as for French omelet, above, but add 2 level teaspoons each, finely-chopped parsley and scissor-snipped chives to the beaten eggs before cooking.

Cheese omelet

Serves 1

Make as for French omelet, above, but add 1 to 2oz (25 to 50gm) very finely-grated Cheddar cheese to the beaten eggs before cooking. Alternatively, put a line of grated cheese on to the cooked omelet before folding.

Savoury soufflé omelet

Serves 1

2 large eggs, separated

2 teaspoons cold water

salt and pepper to taste

1. Beat egg yolks, water and salt and pepper together until pale and creamy.
2. Whisk egg whites to a stiff snow and gently fold beaten yolks into them with a large metal spoon.
3. Melt butter in a 7-inch pan and heat until it begins to sizzle and turn brown.
4. Spoon in egg mixture and level top with a knife.
5. Stand pan over a medium heat for 3 to 4 minutes or until base is golden and firm. Do not move egg mixture at all.
6. Remove from heat and place pan under a pre-heated grill.
7. Leave 2 to 3 minutes or until top is firm and set.
8. Fold in half and slide out of pan on to a warm plate.
9. Serve immediately.

Eggs Florentine

Serves 4

1 large can (approximately 1lb or ½ kilo) spinach purée

3 tablespoons double cream

½oz (12gm) butter

salt and pepper to taste

4 large eggs

½ pint (250ml) cheese or Mornay sauce (see pages 94 and 96)

2oz (50gm) strong Cheddar cheese, grated

1. Put spinach into saucepan with cream and butter.
2. Cook over a low heat until all the liquid evaporates. Stir frequently and season to taste with salt and pepper.
3. Arrange in shallow heatproof dish and keep hot.
4. Poach eggs and place on top of spinach.
5. Coat with sauce then sprinkle with cheese.
6. Brown under a pre-heated hot grill and serve straight away.

Danish egg and bacon cake

Serves 2

8oz (200gm) streaky bacon

4 standard eggs

2 level tablespoons plain flour

8 tablespoons milk

salt and pepper to taste

scissor-snipped chives to garnish

1. Fry bacon slowly in its own fat until crisp. Remove from pan and keep warm.
2. Beat eggs lightly then stir in flour and milk.
3. Season to taste with salt and pepper.
4. Pour off all but a dessertspoon of bacon fat from pan.
5. Heat pan over a moderate heat then pour in egg mixture.
6. Cover pan and cook slowly until eggs are set.
7. Place bacon on top, sprinkle with chives and serve straight away from the pan.

Spanish tortilla (omelet)

Serves 2

1½oz (37gm) butter

1 teaspoon olive oil

1 medium onion, chopped

3 medium potatoes, cooked and diced

4 standard eggs

4 teaspoons water

salt and pepper to taste

1. Heat butter and oil in 8-inch frying pan.
2. Add onion and fry until pale gold.
3. Add potatoes and fry a further 5 minutes, turning frequently.
4. Beat eggs with water and salt and pepper to taste.
5. Pour into pan and cook slowly until base of omelet is golden brown and firm.
6. Place under pre-heated hot grill and leave for ½ to 1 minute or until top is set.
7. Slide out on to a plate and cut into 2 portions.

Note

2 level tablespoons chopped canned pimiento (well-drained) may be added with the potatoes.

Oeufs en cocotte

Serves 4

1½oz (37gm) butter

1 large onion, thinly sliced

4oz (100gm) mushrooms and stalks, sliced

8 standard eggs

salt and pepper to taste

1. Pre-heat oven to moderate, 350 deg F or gas 4 (180 deg C).
2. Butter 4 individual heatproof dishes.
3. Melt 1oz (25gm) butter in a pan. Add onion slices and fry very gently for 7 minutes or until pale gold.
4. Add mushrooms and fry a further 4 minutes.
5. Transfer equal amounts to prepared dishes.
6. Break 2 eggs into each then season to taste with salt and pepper.
7. Melt remaining butter and spoon over eggs.
8. Place dishes in a large roasting tin containing about 1 inch of hot water.
9. Cook in centre of oven for 8 to 10 minutes or until whites are just set.
10. Serve straight away with freshly-made toast.

Danish blue cheese tart

Serves 4 to 6

short crust pastry made with 8oz (200 gm) flour (see page 108)

2oz (50gm) butter

8oz (200gm) onions, chopped

1½oz (37gm) flour

½ pint (250ml) cold milk

4oz (100gm) Danish blue cheese, crumbled

salt and pepper to taste

watercress to garnish

1. Pre-heat oven to hot, 425 deg F or gas 7 (220 deg C).
2. Roll out pastry and use to line an 8-inch flan ring on a baking tray. Reserve trimmings.
3. Heat butter in pan. Add onions and fry gently until soft but not brown.
4. Stir in flour and cook 2 minutes without browning.
5. Gradually blend in milk. Cook, stirring continuously, until sauce comes to boil and thickens. Simmer 2 minutes.
6. Add cheese and salt and pepper to taste and pour into prepared flan case.
7. Decorate top with strips of pastry rolled and cut from trimmings then bake in centre of oven for 15 minutes.
8. Reduce temperature to moderate, 350 deg F or gas 4 (180 deg C), and continue to bake a further 15 to 20 minutes or until pastry is golden brown.
9. Remove flan ring and serve tart hot or cold, garnished with watercress.

Left: Danish blue cheese tart with sliced tomatoes.
Right: Danish egg and bacon cake sprinkled with chives

Cheddar ham flan

Serves 4 to 6

short crust pastry made with 6oz (150gm) flour (see page 108)

1 medium onion, finely chopped

1oz (25gm) butter

2oz (50gm) lean ham, chopped

1 standard egg plus 1 egg yolk

1 small can evaporated milk

1 level teaspoon made mustard

salt and pepper to taste

2oz (50gm) Cheddar cheese, coarsely grated

1. Pre-heat oven to moderately hot, 375 deg F or gas 5 (190 deg C).
2. Roll out pastry and use to line an 8-inch fluted flan ring on an ungreased baking tray.
3. Fry onion in butter for 2 to 3 minutes.
4. Add ham and continue to fry until onion is soft and lightly coloured.
5. Beat the egg and egg yolk well then add onion, ham, milk, mustard, salt and pepper to taste and most of the cheese.
6. Pour into pastry case and sprinkle remaining cheese over top.
7. Bake just above centre of oven for 35 to 40 minutes or until golden brown.
8. Serve hot or cold.

Note

If liked, decorate top with 3 small rolls of ham and sprays of watercress.

Left: Cheddar ham flan decorated with ham rolls and sprays of watercress. Below: crispy cheese puffs

Egg and onion flan

Serves 4

short crust pastry made with 4oz (100 gm) flour (see page 108)

1 large onion, chopped

1oz (25gm) butter or margarine

2 standard eggs

¼ pint (125ml) single cream

salt and pepper to taste

1. Pre-heat oven to moderately hot, 425 deg F or gas 7 (220 deg C).
2. Roll out pastry and use to line a 7-inch flan ring on an ungreased baking tray.
3. Prick lightly then line with aluminium foil to prevent pastry from rising as it cooks.
4. Bake near top of oven for 15 minutes. Take out of oven and carefully remove foil. Lower temperature to moderate, 350 deg F or gas 4 (180 deg C).
5. Gently fry onion in the butter or margarine until pale gold and soft. Take out of pan and use to cover base of pastry case.
6. Beat eggs with cream and salt and pepper to taste.
7. Strain into flan case over onion.
8. Cook in centre of oven for 30 to 40 minutes or until filling is set.
9. Serve hot or cold.

Cheese flan

Serves 4

Make as for egg and onion flan, above, but cover base of flan case with 2 to 3oz (50 to 75gm) grated Gruyère or Cheddar cheese.

Crispy cheese puffs

Serves 4

2oz (50gm) finely-shredded suet

¼ pint (125ml) water

2oz (50gm) plain flour, sifted

2 standard eggs, beaten

2oz (50gm) Cheddar cheese, finely grated

½ to 1 level teaspoon salt

pinch of Cayenne pepper

½ level teaspoon prepared mustard

deep fat or oil for frying

1. Put suet into saucepan and melt over a low heat.
2. Add water and bring to the boil.
3. Add flour and then cook, stirring all the time, until mixture thickens sufficiently to form a ball and leave sides of pan clean.
4. Remove from heat. Cool slightly then gradually beat in eggs and continue beating until mixture is very smooth and shiny.
5. Add cheese, salt, pepper and mustard and beat into mixture.
6. Heat pan of deep oil or fat until a bread cube, dropped into it, turns golden in 1 minute and floats to the top.
7. Lower heaped teaspoons of cheese mixture into pan and fry until well-puffed and golden.
8. Drain on soft kitchen paper then serve straight away.
9. If liked, accompany with a crisp salad and suitable savoury sauce (see sauce section, starting page 92).

Swedish onion pie

Swedish onion pie

Serves 4

rough puff pastry made with 8oz (200 gm) flour (see page 110)

6oz (150gm) streaky bacon, chopped

3 medium onions, sliced

2 standard eggs, beaten

½ pint (250ml) onion sauce (see page 95)

salt and pepper to taste

a little beaten egg for brushing

½ to 1 level teaspoon caraway seeds

1. Pre-heat oven to hot, 450 deg F or gas 8 (230 deg C).
2. Roll out just under two-thirds of the pastry and use to line a 1 pint (approximately ½ litre) pie dish.
3. Fry bacon very gently in its own fat until soft. Add onions and continue to fry slowly until pale gold.
4. Stir in eggs, onion sauce and salt and pepper to taste.
5. Remove from heat, mix thoroughly and leave until almost cold.
6. Pour into pastry-lined dish. Moisten edge of lining pastry with water.
7. Cover with lid, rolled from rest of pastry. Press edges of pastry well together to seal.
8. Brush with egg and sprinkle with caraway seeds.
9. Bake in centre of oven for 15 minutes.
10. Lower temperature to moderate, 325 deg F or gas 3 (170 deg C), and continue to cook for a further 30 to 40 minutes.
11. Serve hot.

Cheese and walnut roast

Serves 4

8oz (200gm) walnuts

6oz (150gm) fresh brown breadcrumbs

3oz (75gm) Cheddar cheese, finely grated

1 medium onion, finely grated

2 level teaspoons salt

2 level tablespoons finely-chopped parsley

5 tablespoons hot milk

1 level teaspoon prepared mustard

1 level tablespoon tomato paste

pepper to taste

½oz (12gm) butter

1. Pre-heat oven to moderate, 350 deg F or gas 4 (180 deg C).
2. Line baking tray with foil and lightly butter.
3. Grind nuts finely and put into bowl.
4. Add all remaining ingredients except butter and mix thoroughly.
5. Shape into a loaf 3 inches high and stand it on prepared tray.
6. Dot top with flakes of butter and bake in centre of oven for 45 minutes.
7. Cut into slices and serve with mustard or tomato sauce (see pages 95, 102) and a green salad tossed with French dressing (see page 161).

Spaghetti pancake

Serves 4

8oz (200gm) spaghetti

2 standard eggs, beaten

4oz (100gm) Cheddar cheese, grated

4oz (100gm) luncheon meat or corned beef, diced

salt and pepper to taste

2 tablespoons salad oil

tomato and parsley to garnish

1. Cook spaghetti in plenty of boiling salted water for 10 to 12 minutes. Drain.
2. Put into large bowl and add eggs, cheese, luncheon meat or corned beef. Season to taste with salt and pepper. Mix thoroughly.
3. Heat oil in a medium-sized frying pan then add spaghetti mixture.
4. Cook gently until base is brown and set then slide out on to a heatproof plate.
5. Place under a pre-heated hot grill and cook until top is golden and bubbly.
6. Garnish with tomato slices and parsley and serve straight away.

Spaghetti pancake garnished with tomato slices

Spaghetti Neapolitan

Serves 4

1lb (½ kilo) spaghetti

1 tablespoon olive oil or 1oz (25gm) butter

Italian tomato sauce made with 2lb 1 kilo) tomatoes (see page 102)

grated Parmesan cheese

1. Cook spaghetti in a large pan of boiling salted water for about 15 minutes or until just tender. Do not overcook, or spaghetti will taste soggy.
2. Drain thoroughly and toss either with oil or butter.
3. Put equal amounts on to 4 individual plates and top each with hot tomato sauce.
4. Serve straight away and pass cheese separately.

Lasagne with fish sauce

Classic lasagne verdi

Serves 6

8oz (200gm) lasagne verdi (green lasagne)

3oz (75gm) Cheddar cheese, grated

3oz (75gm) Parmesan cheese, grated

1 pint (approximately ½ litre) freshly-made béchamel sauce (see page 96)

freshly-made bolognese sauce (see page 102)

1oz (25gm) butter

1. Pre-heat oven to moderately hot, 400 deg F or gas 6 (200 deg C).
2. Cook lasagne in plenty of boiling salted water for 12 to 14 minutes. Drain. Rinse in cold water, drain very thoroughly and place each piece on soft kitchen paper.
3. Well butter a large heatproof dish which is shallow rather than deep.
4. Add half the Cheddar and half the Parmesan cheese to the béchamel sauce. Fill dish with alternate layers of lasagne, bolognese and béchamel sauce.
5. Finish with a layer of béchamel sauce then sprinkle rest of cheese on top.
6. Dot with flakes of butter then re-heat and brown near top of oven for 30 minutes.
7. Serve straight away.

Lasagne with fish sauce

Serves 4

4oz (100gm) lasagne verdi (green lasagne)

8oz (200gm) smoked cod fillet

¾ pint (375ml) freshly-made coating cheese sauce (see page 94)

salt and pepper to taste

2oz (50gm) Cheddar cheese, grated

1. Pre-heat oven to moderately hot, 400 deg F or gas 6 (200 deg C).
2. Cook lasagne in plenty of boiling salted water for 12 to 14 minutes. Drain. Rinse in cold water, drain very thoroughly and place each piece on soft kitchen paper.
3. Poach cod in unsalted water for 7 to 10 minutes. Drain thoroughly and flake fish with 2 forks.
4. Cover a well-buttered heatproof dish with alternate layers of lasagne, cod and cheese sauce, beginning with lasagne and ending with cheese sauce. Sprinkle salt and pepper to taste between layers.
5. Cover top with grated Cheddar cheese then re-heat and brown towards top of oven for 35 to 40 minutes.

Creamed salmon savouries

Macaroni cheese

Serves 4

6oz (150gm) elbow macaroni

1½oz (37gm) butter or margarine

1oz (25gm) flour

½ pint (250ml) milk

6oz (150gm) Cheddar cheese, grated

1 level teaspoon Worcestershire sauce

1 level teaspoon made mustard

pinch of Cayenne pepper

salt to taste

1 level tablespoon toasted breadcrumbs

1. Cook macaroni in plenty of boiling salted water until just tender—about 10 to 15 minutes, or as directed on the packet. Drain, reserving ½ pint (250ml) macaroni water.
2. Melt 1oz (25gm) butter or margarine in saucepan.
3. Stir in flour and cook 2 minutes without browning.
4. Gradually blend in macaroni water and milk.
5. Cook, stirring continuously, until sauce comes to the boil and thickens. Simmer 2 minutes.
6. Stir in 4oz (100gm) cheese, Worcestershire sauce, mustard, Cayenne pepper, salt to taste and the macaroni.
7. Mix thoroughly then transfer to a 2 to 2½ pint (approximately 1¼ to 1½ litre) buttered heatproof dish.
8. Sprinkle rest of cheese and breadcrumbs over the top then add flakes of remaining butter.
9. Brown under a hot grill and serve straight away.

Cauliflower cheese

Serves 4

1 medium cauliflower

1oz (25gm) butter or margarine

1oz (25gm) flour

¼ pint (125ml) milk

5oz (125gm) Cheddar cheese, grated

1 level teaspoon made mustard

pinch of nutmeg

shake of Tabasco (optional)

salt and pepper to taste

1. Trim cauliflower and cook whole in boiling salted water until tender. Drain and reserve ¼ pint (125ml) cauliflower water. Keep cauliflower hot.
2. Melt butter or margarine in saucepan. Add flour and cook 2 minutes without browning.
3. Gradually blend in cauliflower water and milk.
4. Cook, stirring continuously, until sauce comes to boil and thickens. Simmer 2 minutes.
5. Stir in 4oz (100gm) cheese, mustard, nutmeg, Tabasco (if used) and salt and pepper to taste.
6. Transfer cauliflower to buttered heatproof dish.
7. Coat with sauce then sprinkle rest of cheese on top.
8. Brown under a hot grill and serve straight away.

Creamed salmon savouries

Serves 4

1 packet (8oz or 200gm) cream cheese

1 can (approximately 8oz or 200gm) red salmon, drained

1 small onion, grated

1 level dessertspoon finely-chopped parsley

2oz (50gm) fresh white or brown breadcrumbs

salt and pepper to taste

1 large egg

2 teaspoons water

toasted breadcrumbs

deep fat or oil for frying

lemon wedges and parsley to garnish

1. Beat cheese until smooth.
2. Remove bones and skin from salmon and mash fish finely.
3. Gradually beat into cheese with onion, chopped parsley, fresh crumbs and salt and pepper to taste.
4. Turn out on to a lightly-floured surface and shape into a long roll.
5. Cut into 16 equal-sized pieces and roll into balls.
6. Coat with egg, beaten with water, then toss in toasted breadcrumbs.
7. Heat pan of deep fat or oil until a cube of bread, dropped into it, turns golden brown in 1 minute and floats to the top.
8. Add balls, a few at a time, and fry until golden and crisp.
9. Remove from pan, drain on soft kitchen paper and transfer to a warm serving platter.
10. Garnish with lemon and parsley and serve hot or cold.

Golden mushroom puffs

Serves 4

8oz (200gm) button mushrooms

1oz (25gm) flour, seasoned with salt, pepper and dry mustard

4oz (100gm) plain flour

½ level teaspoon salt

good shake of pepper

1 standard egg

¼ pint (125ml) light ale

pinch of nutmeg

deep oil for frying

parsley and tomatoes to garnish

1. Wash and dry mushrooms then coat with seasoned flour.
2. Sift flour and salt into bowl. Add pepper.
3. Mix to a thick, smooth batter with unbeaten egg and three-quarters of the ale, stirring briskly without beating. Stir in rest of ale.
4. Add mushrooms and toss gently in the batter until all are well coated.
5. Heat pan of deep oil until a cube of bread, dropped into it, turns golden brown in 1 minute and floats to the top.
6. Add mushrooms, a few at a time, and fry until golden brown.
7. Drain on soft kitchen paper and serve hot, garnished with parsley and tomatoes.
8. Accompany with Italian tomato sauce (see page 102) and a crisp green salad.

Glazed chestnuts and mushrooms

Serves 4

8oz (200gm) dried chestnuts

2oz (50gm) granulated sugar

4 tablespoons water

2 teaspoons lemon juice

2oz (50gm) butter

¼ level teaspoon salt

4 to 6oz (100 to 150gm) button mushrooms

1. Cover chestnuts with cold water and leave to soak overnight. Drain thoroughly.
2. Put sugar and water into a saucepan and leave over a low heat until sugar dissolves.
3. Bring to boil and boil gently until syrup turns a deep gold.
4. Remove from heat and stir in lemon juice, butter and salt.
5. Add sufficient water *just* to cover chestnuts.
6. Put lid on to pan and simmer 10 minutes. Uncover and cook briskly until almost no liquid remains.
7. Add mushrooms, cover and simmer for 3 minutes.
8. Transfer to a serving dish and accompany with a crisp salad and wedges of mild cheese.

Nut loaf

Serves 4

6oz (150gm) cashew nuts

6oz (150gm) peanuts

4oz (100gm) fresh white breadcrumbs

1 medium onion, grated

1 small garlic clove, finely chopped

1 level teaspoon mixed herbs

½ level teaspoon finely-grated lemon peel

1 level teaspoon yeast extract

2 standard eggs, beaten

4 tablespoons hot water

1 level teaspoon salt

pepper to taste

½oz (12gm) butter, melted

1. Pre-heat oven to moderate, 350 deg F or gas 4 (180 deg C).
2. Well butter a 1½ pint (¾ litre) heatproof dish.
3. Grind nuts finely and put into bowl with crumbs, onion, garlic, herbs, lemon peel and yeast extract.
4. Add eggs, water, salt, pepper and melted butter. Mix thoroughly.
5. Transfer to prepared dish and bake in centre of oven for 30 minutes.
6. Serve with spinach purée and baked tomatoes.

Left: golden mushroom puffs. Below: glazed chestnuts and mushrooms

Eggburger rolls

Serves 4

2oz (50gm) butter

1 small onion, chopped

1 small garlic clove, chopped

1 level tablespoon smooth peanut butter

2 level tablespoons tomato paste

½ level teaspoon dried basil

½ level teaspoon salt

good shake of pepper

4 soft hamburger rolls

4 rashers streaky bacon, chopped

4 small eggs

parsley to garnish

lettuce leaves

1. Pre-heat oven to moderately hot, 400 deg F or gas 6 (200 deg C).
2. Heat 1oz (25gm) butter in a pan. Add onion and garlic and fry gently until soft but not brown.
3. Stir in peanut butter, tomato paste and basil then season with salt and pepper.
4. Cut tops off rolls and remove most of the soft insides. (Reserve for breadcrumbs.)
5. Brush insides of rolls with ½oz (12gm) butter, melted.
6. Place rolls on baking tray and heat through near top of oven for 5 to 7 minutes.
7. Meanwhile, fry bacon in its own fat until crisp.
8. Remove rolls from oven and spread insides with onion/tomato mixture. Sprinkle with fried bacon.
9. Break an egg into each then top with flakes of remaining butter.
10. Return to oven and cook about 8 to 10 minutes or until egg whites are just set.
11. Garnish with parsley then replace roll tops.
12. Serve straight away, on a lettuce-lined platter.

Mixed nut cakes

Serves 4

2oz (50gm) hazelnuts

2oz (50gm) walnuts

3oz (75gm) fresh brown breadcrumbs

1 medium onion, finely grated

1 level dessertspoon finely-chopped parsley

1 level teaspoon yeast extract

1 large egg, beaten

1 tablespoon hot water

½ to 1 level teaspoon salt

½ to 1 level teaspoon paprika

oil or margarine for frying

1. Finely grind nuts and put into bowl.
2. Add all remaining ingredients except oil or margarine.
3. Stir thoroughly to mix and leave to stand for 10 minutes.
4. Shape into 8 cakes and fry in hot oil or margarine until golden brown and crisp on both sides.
5. Serve straight away with baked jacket potatoes, a green vegetable to taste and apple or gooseberry sauce (see page 102).

Eggburger rolls

Southern hash

Serves 4

2oz (50gm) butter or margarine

8oz (200gm) onions, chopped

1 medium green pepper, de-seeded and chopped

12oz (300gm) raw minced beef

6oz (150gm) tomatoes, skinned and chopped

6oz (150gm) long grain rice

1 level teaspoon chilli powder

½ pint (250ml) stock or vegetable water

salt and pepper to taste

1. Heat butter or margarine in a saucepan.
2. Add onions and green pepper. Fry gently until soft and just beginning to brown.
3. Add meat and cook a little more briskly until brown, breaking meat up with a fork all the time.
4. Add all remaining ingredients and bring to boil.
5. Stir once, lower heat and cover pan.
6. Simmer 15 to 20 minutes or until rice grains have absorbed all the moisture.
7. Toss lightly with a fork and serve straight away.

Nutty fries

Corn and sausagemeat casserole

Serves 4

1lb (½ kilo) pork sausagemeat

4oz (100gm) carrots, weighed after peeling

1 can (approximately 12oz or 300gm) sweetcorn kernels, undrained

1 can condensed tomato soup

1 level tablespoon chopped parsley

1. Pre-heat oven to moderate, 350 deg F or gas 4 (180 deg C).
2. Put sausagemeat into a saucepan and brown over a medium heat, breaking the meat up with a fork all the time.
3. Drain off excess fat from pan.
4. Cut carrots into matchstick strips.
5. Add to pan with sausagemeat and all remaining ingredients.
6. Mix thoroughly, then transfer to buttered 1½ pint (approximately ¾ litre) casserole dish.
7. Cover and cook in centre of oven for 40 minutes.

Nutty fries

Serves 2

4 large slices white or brown bread

crunchy peanut butter

yeast extract

1 large egg

2 tablespoons milk

butter or margarine for frying

tomato and parsley to garnish

1. Spread bread slices thickly with peanut butter then cover lightly with yeast extract.
2. Sandwich together in pairs and remove crusts.
3. Cut each sandwich into 4 triangles.
4. Beat egg and milk well together.
5. Soak each triangle in the egg and milk for ¼ minute each side.
6. Fry in hot butter or margarine until golden and crisp, turning twice.
7. Drain on soft kitchen paper and garnish with tomato and parsley.
8. Eat while hot.

Corn and sausagemeat casserole

131

Haddock and corn au gratin with tomato slices

Haddock and corn au gratin

Serves 4

12oz (300gm) smoked haddock fillets

¼ pint (125ml) plus 5 tablespoons evaporated milk

1½oz (37gm) butter or margarine

1½oz (37gm) flour

6oz (150gm) canned sweetcorn, well-drained

4oz (100gm) Cheddar cheese, grated

salt and pepper to taste

3 large tomatoes, skinned and halved

1oz (25gm) fresh white breadcrumbs

parsley to garnish

1. Put fish into shallow pan, cover with water and poach gently for 10 to 15 minutes.
2. Drain and reserve liquor. Flake fish with 2 forks, discarding skin and bones if any.
3. Make up milk to 1 pint (approximately ½ litre) with fish liquor and water.
4. Melt butter or margarine in saucepan. Add flour and cook 2 minutes without browning.
5. Gradually blend in milk mixture. Cook, stirring continuously, until sauce comes to the boil and thickens.
6. Add fish, sweetcorn and 3oz (75gm) cheese.
7. Season to taste with salt and pepper then stir over very low heat until cheese melts.
8. Transfer to a 2½ pint (approximately 1½ litre) buttered heatproof dish.
9. Arrange tomato slices round edge of dish then sprinkle with rest of cheese and crumbs.
10. Brown under a pre-heated hot grill and serve straight away, garnished with parsley.

Devilled egg mayonnaise

Serves 4

6 hard-boiled eggs

1 small can (3oz or 75gm) dressed crab

1 level teaspoon curry paste

½ to 1 teaspoon chilli sauce

juice of 1 medium lemon

½ pint (250ml) mayonnaise (see page 99)

salt to taste

1 small lettuce

cucumber slices, stuffed olives and pieces of lobster (optional) to garnish

1. Halve eggs lengthwise.
2. Remove yolks and press through a nylon sieve into a bowl.
3. Add crab, curry paste, chilli sauce and squeeze of lemon.
4. Mix to creamy texture with 2 to 4 tablespoons mayonnaise.
5. Place eggs, cut sides down, on 4 individual plates lined with lettuce.
6. Coat with rest of mayonnaise mixed with rest of lemon juice then garnish with cucumber, olives and pieces of lobster (if used).

Stuffed potatoes

Serves 2

2 freshly-baked large jacket potatoes (see page 152)

6 tablespoons hot milk

1oz (25gm) butter

salt and pepper to taste

4oz (100gm) cottage cheese

4oz (100gm) peeled prawns

parsley to garnish

1. Cut tops off potatoes and scoop insides into saucepan.
2. Mash finely then add milk, butter and salt and pepper to taste.
3. Beat over low heat until light, fluffy and very hot then stir in cheese and prawns. Heat through gently.
4. Pile back into potato shells, garnish with parsley and serve straight away.

Right: jacket potato stuffed with cheese and prawns.
Below: devilled egg mayonnaise garnished with cucumber, olives and lobster pieces

Cheese fondue

Fondue

Serves 6 to 8

2 level tablespoons cornflour

6 tablespoons Kirsch

1 large garlic clove

1 pint (approximately ½ litre) dry white wine (Rhine, Moselle or Swiss)

1½lb (¾ kilo) Gruyère cheese, grated

8oz (200gm) Emmenthal cheese, grated

1 large crusty French loaf, cubed

1. Mix cornflour to a smooth cream with Kirsch.
2. Rub inside of thick and heavy flame-proof casserole with cut clove of garlic.
3. Add wine and heat gently until it begins to bubble.
4. Mix cheeses together then add a large handful and cook until melted, stirring continuously.
5. Repeat until all the cheese has been added.
6. Cook until mixture just comes to the boil then add cornflour and Kirsch.
7. Cook, stirring, until cheese mixture bubbles again then simmer a further 3 minutes.
8. Transfer casserole to a plate warmer or spirit stove and keep hot.
9. Spear cubes of bread on to forks (one fork per person), dip into fondue and swirl round until pieces of bread are thickly coated with mixture.
10. Eat straight away and accompany with lemon tea or black coffee.

Cream cheese and chive tarts

Makes 12

short crust pastry made with 4oz (100 gm) flour (see page 108)

8oz (200gm) curd cheese

1 level dessertspoon cornflour

1 dessertspoon single cream

2 level tablespoons scissor-snipped chives

1 level teaspoon Worcestershire sauce

½ level teaspoon paprika

pinch of Cayenne pepper

½ level teaspoon continental mustard

1 large egg, separated

salt to taste

1. Pre-heat oven to hot, 450 deg F or gas 8 (230 deg C).
2. Roll out pastry thinly.
3. Cut into 12 rounds with a 3-inch cutter and use to line 12 fairly deep bun tins.
4. Beat cheese with cornflour, cream, chives, Worcestershire sauce, paprika, Cayenne pepper, mustard and egg yolk.
5. Season to taste with salt then fold in egg white, beaten to a stiff snow.
6. Transfer equal amounts to pastry-lined tins.
7. Put into centre of oven and reduce temperature to moderate, 350 deg F or gas 4 (180 deg C).
8. Bake 20 minutes and remove from oven.
9. Cool slightly then lift tarts out of tins.
10. Serve hot or cold.

Pilau

Serves 4

2 tablespoons salad oil

1 large onion, chopped

12oz (300gm) long grain rice

1½ pints (approximately ¾ litre) chicken stock

1oz (25gm) sultanas

1 level teaspoon finely-grated orange peel

1 level teaspoon salt

2oz (50gm) flaked almonds, lightly toasted

1. Heat oil in large pan.
2. Add onion and fry slowly until soft and pale gold.
3. Add rice and fry a further minute, turning all the time.
4. Pour in stock then add sultanas, orange peel and salt.
5. Bring to boil, lower heat and cover.
6. Simmer 15 to 20 minutes or until rice grains are plump and fluffy and have absorbed all the moisture.
7. Add almonds and stir rice with a fork.
8. Serve straight away with any egg dish, cheese, roast lamb or poultry.

Creamed mushroom puff

Serves 4

8oz (200gm) mushrooms

2oz (50gm) butter

2oz (50gm) flour

½ pint (250ml) milk

4 tablespoons cream

3 standard eggs, separated

½oz (12gm) Parmesan cheese, grated

½ level teaspoon salt

pinch of Cayenne pepper

1. Well-butter a 2 pint (approximately 1¼ litre) soufflé dish.
2. Pre-heat oven to moderately hot, 375 deg F or gas 5 (190 deg C).
3. Thinly slice mushrooms and stalks.
4. Melt butter in saucepan. Add mushrooms and cook gently, covered, until soft—about 4 minutes.
5. Add flour and cook 2 minutes.
6. Gradually blend in milk and cream. Cook slowly, stirring, until mixture comes to the boil and thickens sufficiently to form a ball and leave sides of pan clean.
7. Beat in egg yolks, cheese, salt and Cayenne pepper.
8. Beat egg whites to a stiff snow and fold into mixture with a large metal spoon.
9. Transfer to prepared dish and bake in centre of oven for 40 to 45 minutes or until well-risen, puffy and golden. Serve straight away with a salad.

Shirred eggs

Serves 4

4 tablespoons double cream

4 heaped tablespoons grated Gruyère cheese

8 standard eggs

½oz (12gm) butter, melted

salt and pepper to taste

1. Pre-heat oven to hot, 425 deg F or gas 7 (220 deg C).
2. Butter 4 shallow heatproof dishes.
3. Put a tablespoon of cream and cheese into each.
4. Break 2 eggs into each dish over cream and cheese.
5. Spoon melted butter over the eggs then season to taste with salt and pepper.
6. Cook near top of oven for 5 minutes or until whites are just set.
7. Serve straight away and accompany with crisp toast.

Risotto

Serves 4

3 dessertspoons olive oil

1 large onion, grated

12oz (300gm) long grain rice

2½ pints (1½ litre) chicken stock or vegetable water

2 level teaspoons salt

pepper to taste

2oz (50gm) butter

2oz (50gm) Parmesan cheese, grated

1. Heat oil in large saucepan. Add onion and fry gently until pale gold.
2. Add rice and fry a further 2 minutes, turning all the time.
3. Pour stock or vegetable water into pan then add salt and pepper to taste.
4. Bring to the boil, stir once or twice then cover pan.
5. Lower heat and simmer 15 to 20 minutes or until rice grains have absorbed all the moisture.
6. Add butter and cheese and toss gently with a fork until both have melted.
7. Serve straight away with a crisp green salad.

Creamed mushroom puff

Left: savoury triangles. Above: cream cheese and peach topper

Savoury triangles

Serves 4 to 6

| 12oz (300gm) self-raising flour |
| 1 level teaspoon baking powder |
| 1 level teaspoon dry mustard |
| 1 level teaspoon salt |
| 2 level teaspoons curry powder |
| 3oz (75gm) butter or margarine |
| 2oz (50gm) salted peanuts, chopped |
| 1 large egg |
| ¼ pint (125ml) cold milk |
| a little beaten egg for brushing |

1. Pre-heat oven to hot, 425 deg F or gas 7 (220 deg C).
2. Well grease a large baking tray.
3. Sift flour, baking powder, mustard, salt and curry powder into a bowl.
4. Rub in butter or margarine finely.
5. Beat egg and milk well together and add all at once to dry ingredients.
6. Mix to a soft dough with a round-topped knife.
7. Turn out on to a floured surface and knead lightly until smooth.
8. Pat into a circle measuring ¾ inch in thickness and transfer to prepared baking tray.
9. Brush with beaten egg then mark into 12 triangles with the back of a knife.
10. Bake just above centre of oven for 15 to 20 minutes or until well-risen and golden.
11. Transfer to a wire cooling rack and leave until lukewarm.
12. Separate into triangles by breaking gently apart with the fingers then serve while still warm with butter, yeast extract, cheese and tomatoes.

Cream cheese and peach topper

Serves 1

Butter a slice of Pumpernickel or wholemeal bread with butter. Cover thickly with cream cheese then top with lettuce leaves and 2 well-drained canned peach slices.

Cheese and walnut ham rolls garnished with tomatoes, cucumber and watercress

Cheese and walnut ham rolls

Serves 4

| 4 hard-boiled eggs |
| 2oz (50gm) walnuts, chopped |
| 8oz (200gm) cottage cheese with chives |
| salt and pepper |
| 4 large slices cooked ham |
| tomato wedges, cucumber slices and watercress to garnish |

1. Shell eggs and chop.
2. Add walnuts and cheese and mix well together.
3. Season to taste with salt and pepper then spread equal amounts on to slices of ham.
4. Roll up loosely then place on 4 individual plates.
5. Garnish with tomatoes, cucumber and watercress.

Vegetables and salads

Vegetables

Now that greengrocers, supermarkets and market stalls are packed throughout the year with colourful, fresh vegetables from every part of the globe, it is possible to make the vegetable course one of the most exciting and interesting parts of the meal. The following ABC tells you something about each variety of vegetable, and gives cooking methods and recipe suggestions.

Apart from adding flavour, colour and balance to meals, most vegetables are also highly nutritious. Many are rich in vitamins A and C and also important minerals, so they make their own valuable contribution to sound eating and good health.

All green vegetables should be bought as fresh as possible and eaten fairly soon after purchase in order to get the greatest benefit from the vitamin C content. Other vegetables—such as potatoes, carrots, parsnips, turnips and swedes—can be stored for a short time and are best kept on racks in a cool, dry and airy place such as a pantry or larder. Alternatively, most vegetables will stay fresh and crisp if stored in the least cold part of the refrigerator until required, usually the bottom shelf, but even so it is advisable never to buy more than two or three days' supply at a time.

The following useful hints should help you make the most of your vegetables:
1. Because most of the vitamins and other nutrients lie directly under the skin, always peel vegetables thinly.
2. Wash vegetables just before cooking and never leave them to soak (except where specified in a particular recipe) as this results in loss of vitamins.
3. Make sure vegetables to be boiled are uniform in size, otherwise some pieces will be cooked sooner than others.
4. Cook vegetables so that they are ready exactly on time for the meal. Cooking the vegetables in advance and then keeping them warm destroys vitamins, flavour and colour.
5. Most vegetables, unless they are young, tender and in prime condition, benefit from a pinch of sugar added to the cooking water.
6. Avoid the use of too much salt as this also causes loss of flavour. Allow about 1 level teaspoon to every pint (approximately ½ litre) water.
7. Never add bicarbonate of soda as a means of retaining colour when cooking green vegetables because it kills off the vitamin C and makes the vegetables mushy. In hard water areas, 1 teaspoon vinegar or lemon juice added to every pint (approximately ½ litre) water sometimes helps to keep the vegetables a good colour.
8. It is usual to cover vegetables while they are boiling, although to retain colour, flavour and texture, greens of all kinds, onions and leeks, parsnips and turnips and raw beets should be left uncovered.
9. Never overcook vegetables. They are better in every respect cooked until only just tender and then very thoroughly drained.
10. Fried vegetables should never be covered and kept hot because they will lose their crispness and rapidly become soft, soggy and greasy.

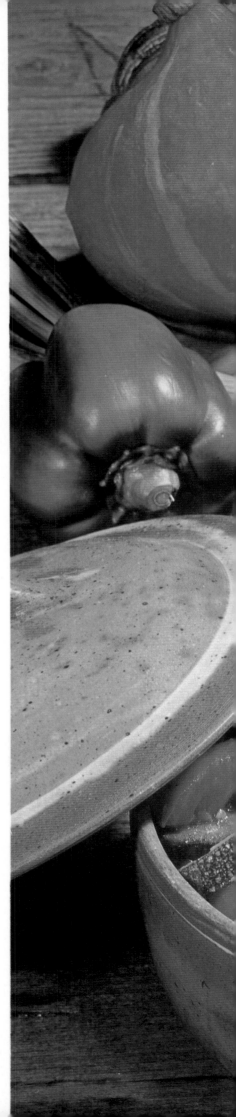

Ratatouille (see page 146)

138

Artichokes-globe

These thistle-like vegetables, a favourite food during the reign of Henry VIII, are usually served as an hors d'oeuvre, either hot with hollandaise sauce or cold with French dressing (see pages 98 and 161). The most highly esteemed part of the artichoke is the heart, which lies below the softly fuzzy centre known as the choke. To the uninitiated, eating artichokes may present problems, so here are a few tips to save embarrassment. Peel off one leaf at a time and dip the pale, tender end in sauce or dressing. Pass it through the teeth then discard the leaf. Continue in this way until you reach a cone of very pale leaves in the centre. Hold the cone and lift it off the artichoke, then gently remove the inedible fuzzy part which constitutes the choke. You will then be left with the heart which should be coated with sauce or dressing and eaten with a knife and fork.

To cook globe artichokes

Allow 1 medium artichoke per person. Ensure that the leaves are a healthy green colour and are fairly close together. Spreading, purply leaves indicate that the artichokes are overgrown and/or stale. Cut off stems and remove the first two rows of leaves, which are often tough and woody. Cut tips off rest of leaves with kitchen scissors. (A slow job, this, but it does add a professional touch!) Soak for 30 minutes in cold salted water then drain very thoroughly. Stand the artichokes upright in saucepan and add about 3 inches of boiling water and 1 level teaspoon salt for every 4 artichokes. Cover and boil gently for 30 to 40 minutes or until leaves pull out easily. Drain them upside down and serve hot or cold to taste.

Artichokes-Jerusalem

These look like knobbly potatoes and are available during the winter months. They contain less starch than potatoes, are easy to digest and are excellent both in soup and as a vegetable in sauce.

To cook artichokes

Allow about ½lb (200gm) artichokes per person. Peel thinly or scrape with a stainless knife. Drop each one into a bowl of cold water as it is ready to prevent browning. Drain. Transfer to saucepan of boiling salted water. Add 1 teaspoon vinegar or lemon juice (to stop discoloration) and cook for approximately 30 minutes or until tender. Drain thoroughly and toss with butter. Serve sprinkled with chopped parsley.

Note

Artichokes may be pressure cooked at 15lb (7 kilo) pressure for 7 minutes.

Asparagus

This is a delicate, luxury vegetable usually available during late spring and early summer. Asparagus is a member of the lily family, and in its wild state, was much favoured as a vegetable by the ancient Greeks and Romans. It was cultivated as early as the 17th century in the United Kingdom and a hundred years ago was sold

Asparagus

in the street markets under the name of 'sparrowgrass'. In the middle of the last century, asparagus tongs were invented to 'add to the elegance of the dinner table' and the word 'grass' is still used in Covent Garden to describe asparagus.

To cook asparagus

Allow approximately 8 to 12 stalks per person; a few less if very thick. Cut ends off each stick, then scrape the white parts only (avoiding the tips) with a knife. Wash well. Ideally asparagus should be cooked upright in a tall saucepan, but for practical purposes it is easier to lay the asparagus flat in a roasting tin or large frying pan containing about 2 inches of boiling salted water. Cover with a lid or piece of aluminium foil and boil fairly gently for 12 to 15 minutes. Drain very thoroughly (preferably on a soft tea towel) and serve hot with melted butter or hollandaise sauce, (see page 98), or very cold with French dressing (see page 161) or mayonnaise (see page 99). To eat asparagus, lift up each stick in turn and dip the tip into sauce or dressing. Eat the tip and as much of the stem as is edible and still soft.

Aubergines or egg-plants

Aubergines look like elongated pears with shiny, purple skins. They came originally from India and were sometimes known as 'mad-apples' or 'raging' apples. They are a versatile vegetable with a distinctive, delicate flavour and team well with eggs, fish, meat and other vegetables as, for example, in ratatouille.

Aubergines have a high water content and therefore it is advisable to dehydrate the slices partially before frying or baking. To do this, cut the aubergines into ½-inch thick slices, put them on to a plate and sprinkle with salt. Cover and leave to stand in a cool place for about one hour when much of the moisture should have come out. Rinse and wipe dry. When estimating quantities, allow about ½ a medium aubergine per person.

To cook aubergines

1. Shallow-fried aubergine slices
Dip slices in milk then coat lightly with flour. Fry briskly in a little salad oil (or a mixture of butter and oil) until crisp on both sides. Drain on kitchen paper and sprinkle with salt.

2. Batter-fried aubergine slices
Dip slices in well-seasoned fritter batter (see page 105) then lower them carefully into hot, deep fat or oil. Fry until golden then lift out of pan and drain thoroughly.

Note

Instead of batter, the slices may be egg and crumbed and fried in deep fat as above.

3. Baked aubergine slices
Stand aubergine slices on a lightly buttered baking tray. Sprinkle with lemon juice and salt and pepper to taste. Pour over a little melted butter then grate a little onion on top. Bake in centre of moderately hot oven, 400 deg F or gas 6 (200 deg C), for 12 to 15 minutes.

Beans—broad

Broad beans are one of the oldest vegetables in cultivation. They were enjoyed by the early Egyptians and Greeks and it is likely that they were introduced to Britain by the Romans.

Young, small and tender beans—alas, not easy to find in shops any more but still home-grown by keen gardeners—can be cooked and eaten with the pods as well and are delicious coated with melted butter. Mature beans have to be shelled before cooking and as the pods are on the large side, allow about ¾lb (300gm) per person. Broad beans are in season throughout the summer but are at their best from May to July.

To cook broad beans

Shell beans and cook, covered, in boiling salted water for 15 to 25 minutes, according to size. Drain thoroughly and either toss with butter or combine with parsley sauce (see page 95). Serve with roast and grilled meats and poultry.

Note

Alternatively, mix some chopped boiled bacon with the beans and combine with white sauce.

Beans—French or dwarf

These should be bought while still young, tender and 'snappy'—in other words the beans should be fresh enough to break cleanly without strings hanging down on either side. As there is relatively little waste with this vegetable, allow between 4 to 6oz (100 to 150gm) per person.

To cook French or dwarf beans

Top and tail beans and cook whole and uncovered in boiling salted water for 15 to 20 minutes or until tender. Drain thoroughly and return to saucepan. Add a knob of butter and pepper to taste. Toss lightly and serve while still hot with meat, fish, poultry and egg dishes.

Beans—scarlet runners

Scarlet runners were originally grown for bouquets of flowers because of the brilliant colour of the small blooms. No one had thought of the pods as being edible until a gardener from Chelsea, towards the end of the 18th century, discovered that the beans themselves were delicious to eat.

To cook scarlet runners

Allow 1 to 1½lb (½ to ¾ kilo) beans for four people. Top and tail beans then remove strings from sides. Cut beans into thin, diagonal slices then cook, uncovered, in boiling salted water for 15 to 20 minutes or until tender. Drain thoroughly, return to saucepan and toss with butter.

Beetroot

A sweet-tasting root vegetable which always goes well with meat, fish, poultry and egg dishes. Large, full-grown beetroots are best served cold and sliced with salads. But young, small beetroots are delicious as a hot vegetable coated with melted butter or a savoury sauce.

To cook beetroot

Wash carefully in lukewarm water, and trim tops to leave about 1 inch of stem—do not cut the roots. Either boil in salted water, or place beetroots on a baking tray in a moderate oven, 325 deg F or gas 3 (170 deg C). Cooking time can be from 1 to 4 hours, depending on the size of beetroots. When the skins slide easily off, the beetroots are ready.

Broccoli

Broccoli is Italian in origin and a close relation of the cauliflower. It can be either white or purple-headed and should be bought according to the size required. A medium-sized broccoli serves about 4.

To cook broccoli

Strip off outer leaves and cut a deep cross in the stalk. Wash broccoli head quickly under cold running water then put into a saucepan containing about 3 inches of boiling salted water. Make sure the head is upright. Cover and boil steadily for about 20 minutes or until tender. Drain thoroughly. Either coat with melted butter or hollandaise sauce (see page 98). Serve with fish, egg, meat, cheese and poultry dishes.

Broccoli—green sprouting

This is often sold loose by weight. Allow about ½lb (¼ kilo) per person. Wash thoroughly and cook, covered, in boiling salted water for about 15 minutes or until tender. Drain and coat with melted butter or hollandaise sauce (see page 98).

Brussels sprouts

These are a variety of the cabbage, and it is likely that sprouts originated in or near Brussels—hence their name. They have been known since the 13th century but were not introduced to Britain until the early 1800s.

To cook Brussels sprouts

Remove any marked or withered leaves. Cut a cross in the base of each sprout then wash thoroughly. Drop into a pan of boiling salted water and cook, uncovered, for 12 to 15 minutes; sprouts should be tender but still reasonably crisp in the centre. Drain thoroughly and return to saucepan. Add a large knob of butter and toss gently. Serve with all meat and poultry dishes.

Cabbage

Cabbage originated from the European wild variety, and was popular with Greeks, Romans and the ancient Egyptians. It has been grown in Britain for many centuries. There are many kinds of cabbages but roughly speaking they can be divided into three principal categories: green, white and red. The green is popular for boiling, the white for boiling and also for salads such as cole slaw, and the red for pickling and cooking continental-style. Allow about 4oz (100gm) firm cabbage—such as Savoy or Dutch—per person; about 6 to 8oz (150 to 200gm) spring greens. Choose firm, hard heads of cabbage with as few discoloured leaves as possible. Spring greens should be a good colour and also fairly firm to the touch.

To cook cabbage

Remove and discard all the woody and/or discoloured outer leaves of the cabbage. Cut in half, remove the centre stalk then shred the cabbage finely. Plunge into a saucepan containing about 1 inch rapidly boiling salted water. Cook, uncovered, for 10 to 15 minutes or until cabbage is just tender. Avoid over-cooking. Drain thoroughly, return to saucepan and toss with butter. Serve straight away.

Note

Alternatively, cut cabbage into 4 wedges, remove centre piece of stalk from each and plunge into 2 inches of rapidly boiling salted water. Cook, uncovered, for 15 to 20 minutes. Drain thoroughly, transfer to a warm serving dish and pour melted butter over each wedge. If liked, dust very lightly with nutmeg or freshly-milled black pepper.

To cook spring greens

Separate leaves, wash thoroughly and shred coarsely, cutting away pieces of hard stalk. Drop into a saucepan of briskly boiling water and cook, uncovered, for 10 to 15 minutes. Drain thoroughly and toss with butter.

Carrots

Carrots have an interesting history. They were eaten as vegetables by the ancient Greeks but not until the 16th century did they find their way to Britain, and it is probable that they were introduced by the Flemish who were, by all accounts, enthusiastic and successful market gardeners! During the subsequent reigns of James I and Charles I, the feathery leaves were put to good use. They ornamented ladies' head-dresses and were also used as table decorations!

To prepare carrots, scrape new ones (after first removing tops) or scrub with a stiff brush under cold running water. Leave whole. Peel old carrots thinly then cut into thinnish slices, small dice, or 2-inch long sticks. Allow about 4oz (100gm) per person and serve with all main dishes.

To cook carrots

Cook new and old carrots in boiling salted water. Allow about 15 minutes for new carrots; from 20 to 40 minutes for old ones. Keep the saucepan covered. Drain, return to pan and toss with butter. Serve sprinkled with finely-chopped parsley.

Note

Alternatively, pressure cook carrots for 5 minutes at 15lb (7 kilo) pressure.

Oven-cooked carrots

Put carrots into a casserole dish with ½ to 1oz (12 to 25gm) butter or margarine, 3 dessertspoons water and 1 level teaspoon salt to every lb (½ kilo). Cover and cook in the centre of a moderate oven, 350 deg F or gas 4 (180 deg C), for about 1 hour or until tender. Uncover and sprinkle with parsley.

To bake carrots round a joint of meat

Par-boil carrots in boiling salted water for 10 minutes. Drain thoroughly. Stand carrots in roasting tin round joint and baste with hot fat. Bake for 1 to 1½ hours.

Cauliflower

Choose cauliflowers with firm white heads and with the florets pressed tightly together. Spreading and discoloured cauliflowers are likely to lack flavour and be watery when cooked. Choose a medium-sized one for four people.

To cook cauliflower

Strip off outer leaves and cut a deep cross in the stalk. Wash cauliflower thoroughly then stand it upright in about 3 inches of boiling salted water. Add 1 dessertspoon lemon juice or a tablespoon of milk which helps to keep the cauliflower white. Cover and cook steadily until the stalk part is just tender—about 12 to 15 minutes. Drain thoroughly, put into a warm serving dish and coat with melted butter. Alternatively, coat with white, cheese or hollandaise sauce (see pages 94 and 98). Serve with meat, fish, poultry and egg dishes.

Note

1. Pressure cook a whole cauliflower for 7 minutes at 15lb (7 kilo) pressure.
2. If preferred, divide head into florets and cook in boiling salted water for 7 to 10 minutes.

Celeriac

This is a variety of celery with the root shaped like a turnip. This is the part which is eaten. It is particularly popular in Germany, sliced and boiled and eaten cold with French dressing (see page 161). In Britain, it is more usual to boil celeriac and serve it hot in a white or hollandaise sauce (see page 98), or simply with melted butter.

To cook celeriac

Allow 4 to 6oz (100 to 150gm) per person and choose small rather than large roots. Peel them thickly as the outside is apt to be coarse and stringy. Cut into slices, thick sticks or dice and wash well. Transfer to a pan of boiling salted water and add a dessertspoon of lemon juice (to prevent discoloration). Cover and cook over a medium heat until tender—20 to 40 minutes according to age of celeriac. Drain well then combine with white or hollandaise sauce (see pages 94 and 98). Serve with meat, poultry, egg and fish dishes.

Celery

Celery is another vegetable with an ancient history and was referred to in Homer's Odyssey as 'selinon'. It was introduced to Britain by the Italians round about the middle of the 17th century and has been widely cultivated ever since. Cold winters are supposed to produce the best celery and certainly any which have been frost-bitten are crisp and deliciously flavoured. Imported celery, greener than British and often larger, is now available all the year round, and can be used in summer salads.

To cook celery

Allow either 1 small head or 3 large sticks per person. Remove leaves, then scrub the sticks well, discarding any that are discoloured and badly bruised. Cut sticks into 2-inch lengths. Cook, covered, in boiling salted water (to which a squeeze of lemon juice has been added) until tender—30 to 45 minutes depending on the coarseness of the celery. Drain thoroughly then toss with butter.

Note

1. Alternatively, coat with white, cheese, parsley or hollandaise sauce (see pages 94, 95, 98). Serve with all main course dishes.
2. Celery may be pressure cooked for about 7 minutes at 15lb (7 kilo) pressure.

Oven-cooked celery

Prepare celery as above. Put into casserole dish with 1oz (25gm) butter or margarine, 3 dessertspoons water and 1 level teaspoon salt for every 12 sticks. Cover and cook in centre of moderate oven, 350 deg F or gas 4 (180 deg C), for approximately 1 hour or until tender. Uncover and sprinkle with chopped parsley. Serve with all main course dishes.

Chicory

This is a distinctive-tasting vegetable which may be used cold in salads or hot in a sauce. Allow one head per person and make sure that the leaves are firm and white and tipped with very light yellow.

To cook chicory

Wash chicory heads quickly under cold running water. Cut a slice off the base of each then remove core with a pointed knife (this is important because it is the core which makes the chicory taste bitter). Put into a saucepan containing boiling salted water. Add 1 dessertspoon lemon juice (which preserves the white colour) and cook for 15 to 20 minutes or until tender. Drain thoroughly and either coat with melted butter or with white, cheese, parsley or hollandaise sauce (see pages 94, 95, 98).

Corn-on-the-cob

Corn was introduced into Europe by Christopher Columbus and its cultivation spread more quickly than almost any other crop. The younger the corn the better the flavour so whenever possible, choose cobs where the leaves are a fresh green colour and the kernels pearly white verging on cream. The cobs should also be plump and well-rounded and the silks or tassels which grow at the top of the cobs should be brown in colour. Corn-on-the-cob—fresh, frozen or canned—goes well with meat, poultry, fish, cheese and egg dishes.

To cook corn

Remove husks and silk from corn then put into a large frying pan containing 2 inches of boiling water. No salt this time because it hardens the kernels. Cover and boil briskly for 5 to 7 minutes. Drain thoroughly and serve very hot with plenty of butter and salt and pepper.

Courgettes

These belong to the marrow family but they are considerably smaller and do not require peeling. They can be fried, boiled or cooked in conjunction with other vegetables. Allow 4 to 6oz (100 to 150gm) per person.

To cook courgettes

Top and tail courgettes, wash thoroughly then cut into slices. Drop into a saucepan of boiling salted water. Cover and cook 10 to 15 minutes or until tender. Drain thoroughly and toss with melted butter. Sprinkle thickly with parsley and serve with all main course dishes.

Cucumber

Cucumbers were mentioned in the Bible and were originally cultivated in Eastern countries. Records show that they were grown in England during the reign of Edward III but subsequently died out for some time and then appeared again during the reign of Henry VIII. During the 17th and 18th centuries they were referred to as 'cowcumbers'. Cucumbers are usually served raw but they can also be cooked in water and tossed in butter to make an unusual and tasty accompaniment to poultry, white meat and fish dishes. Allow half a medium-sized cucumber per person, when using as a cooked vegetable.

To cook cucumber

Peel cucumber and cut into dice. Drop the dice into about 1 inch of boiling salted water. Cover and cook gently for approximately 10 minutes. Drain thoroughly, toss with butter and dust lightly with pepper and/or a little nutmeg.

Endive

There are two principal kinds of endive: one has green crinkly leaves, the other slightly smoother leaves. Both types have almost white centres. Endive has a slightly bitter taste and is more popular abroad than in Britain. It is usually eaten raw in salads though can be cooked in the same way as lettuce. Allow one head of endive per person when cooked; the same quantity will serve four people, when used raw.

To cook endive

Wash endive thoroughly then remove any bruised and discoloured outer leaves. Chop up and put into a saucepan of boiling salted water. Cook, uncovered, for 20 to 30 minutes. Drain very thoroughly and return to saucepan. Toss with butter and freshly-milled pepper to taste.

Fennel

The fennel available in shops is known as Florence fennel and tastes faintly of aniseed. Eaten raw, it lends a subtlety to salads but it can also be cut up and cooked in exactly the same way as for celery and used as a hot vegetable accompaniment to white meat, fish and poultry dishes. The side stems should be removed and kept for salads and the bulbous remainder used for cooking. Allow one medium head of fennel per person if cooked; the same amount will serve four people, if used in salads.

Kohl-rabi

This vegetable belongs to the cabbage family. It grows above ground and has a turnip-shaped root (the part which is eaten) and a crown of green leaves.

To cook kohl-rabi

Allow 2 small kohl-rabi per person. Remove crown leaves then peel the roots. Wash well. Drop into a saucepan of boiling salted water, add a dessertspoon of lemon juice and cook gently, uncovered, until just tender—30 to 45 minutes depending on size. Drain thoroughly and toss with butter. Serve sprinkled with chopped parsley.

Note

1. The green leaves can be boiled separately and served as a vegetable in their own right.
2. Cooked kohl-rabi can be allowed to get cold, then sliced or diced and tossed with French dressing (see page 161).

Leeks

Leeks, members of the onion family, were once so widely grown in Britain that gardens were known as 'leac-tums' and gardeners as 'leac-wards'! When buying leeks, choose small to medium-sized ones in preference to large. Allow two leeks per person.

To cook leeks

Strip off outer leaves then remove tops and all but 2 inches of the green leaves from each leek. Slit leeks lengthwise and wash thoroughly under cold running water to remove grit. Shake dry. Put into a large frying pan containing 2 inches of boiling water and cook, partially covered, for 15 to 20 minutes or until tender. Drain thoroughly and coat with white or cheese sauce (see page 94). Serve with main course dishes.

Lettuce

According to Herodotus, lettuces were served to Persian royalty more than 400 years B.C. which makes them one of the oldest established vegetables on record. In Great Britain lettuces are used mainly for salads but they can also be braised in a similar way as for leeks. For this method of cooking, choose one small cos lettuce per person. Remove all outer leaves and cut away stalks. Cook in exactly the same way as for braised leeks (see page 148) but leave in the oven for about 30 minutes. Serve with poultry, fish and egg dishes and white meat.

Marrow

Choose marrows which are medium in size and with dark green, mottled skins. Oversize marrows (the mammoth ones of which gardeners are so proud) are sometimes very watery and lack the flavour of the smaller ones. Allow one medium marrow for four people.

To cook marrow
Peel thinly and cut marrow into 1-inch slices. Remove seeds then cut each slice into small cubes. Cook in about 1 inch boiling salted water for 15 minutes. Drain thoroughly, toss with butter, then sprinkle with freshly-milled black pepper to taste. Alternatively, coat with white, cheese or tomato sauce (see pages 94 or 102). Serve with meat, poultry and fish dishes.

To steam marrow
Cut into cubes as above and stand cubes in a colander over a saucepan of gently boiling water. Sprinkle with salt and pepper then steam for 20 to 30 minutes or until tender. Toss with butter or coat with sauce.

Mushrooms

Mushrooms were known to the Pharaohs, who believed they had magical powers, and also to the ancient Chinese who regarded them as having health-giving properties. Today, cultivated mushrooms are available all the year round and there are three types from which to choose: button mushrooms which are small, unopened and firm; cup mushrooms which are riper and more open; flat mushrooms which are larger than the other two and fully open. The small buttons can be used whole in sauces, raw in salads and as a garnish. The cups can be sliced and used for soups, stews, casseroles, as a vegetable and for stuffing. The flats can be used whole as a vegetable and also for stuffing. Never buy large quantities of mushrooms at a time as they deteriorate fairly quickly. It is safer to buy little and often, allowing 2 to 3oz (50 to 75gm) per person if used as a vegetable; half that quantity will be sufficient if used as a garnish. Cultivated mushrooms are usually clean and need very little pre-cooking preparation. Cut off and discard tops of stalks then simply wipe the mushrooms with a clean, damp cloth or wash under cold running water. Drain thoroughly before use. If cup and flat mushrooms happen to be earthy, peel off the outer skin before washing, starting from the outside edges and working towards the centre. Field mushrooms should always be peeled and washed thoroughly to get rid of earth and grit. As a vegetable, mushrooms can be served with all meat, poultry, fish, egg and cheese dishes.

To cook mushrooms
1. Grilled mushrooms (Serves 4)
Stand about 12oz (300gm) prepared mushrooms in grill pan, stalks uppermost. Dot each with small pieces of butter. Grill 2 minutes. Turn them over. Grill further 1 to 2 minutes. Sprinkle with salt and pepper and serve straight away.

2. Baked mushrooms (Serves 4)
Pre-heat oven to moderately hot, 375 deg F or gas 5 (190 deg C). Stand about 12oz (300gm) prepared mushrooms in buttered baking dish, stalks uppermost. Dot each with small pieces of butter. Sprinkle with salt and pepper then cover with lid or piece of foil. Cook in centre of oven for 20 minutes.

3. Fried mushrooms (Serves 4)
Heat 2oz (50gm) butter and 1 teaspoon salad oil in a frying pan. Add 12oz (300gm) prepared mushrooms and fry briskly, shaking pan frequently, for 5 minutes. Remove from heat, season to taste with salt and pepper and serve straight away, either on toast or to accompany meat, poultry, fish, egg and cheese dishes.

Mushrooms

Onions

The onion, a member of the lily family, must be one of the oldest and most widely cultivated vegetables in the world. There are several types of onion; the large, mild and slightly sweet kind known as Spanish; the smaller variety which is stronger than Spanish and which can be used for almost all culinary purposes; and the tiny ones which are used whole either for pickling or for adding to a variety of savoury dishes. There are also spring onions, normally used in salads, and shallots, a variety of small onion which is said to have been brought to Britain by the Crusaders. When choosing onions, be sure that they are firm and the skins feathery. Those with sprouts shooting from them should be avoided as this indicates staleness. When serving onions as an accompanying vegetable, allow one onion per person.

There are several pet theories put out as to how one can avoid crying when peeling onions. How effective these are is another matter but peeling them under cold water helps, as does holding a slice of bread between the teeth.

To cook onions
1. Boiled onions
Remove roots and peel onions. Cook, uncovered, in boiling salted water until tender—30 to 45 minutes, depending on size. Drain thoroughly and either coat with melted butter and freshly-milled black pepper to taste or coat with white or cheese sauce (see page 94). Serve with meat, poultry, egg and cheese dishes.

2. Baked onions
Pre-heat oven to moderately hot, 375 deg F or gas 5 (190 deg C). Remove roots and peel onions. Cook, uncovered, in boiling salted water for 10 minutes. Drain thoroughly. Stand onions in baking dish containing about 1 inch hot fat, dripping or oil or a mixture of butter and oil. Baste onions with the fat then cook near top of oven for 30 to 45 minutes or until tender and golden. Serve with all meat and poultry roasts and grills.

3. Fried onions
Peel and thinly slice as many onions as are required. Cover base of frying pan to depth of $\frac{1}{4}$ inch with oil, a mixture of butter and oil or good beef dripping. Heat until hot, add onions and fry over a medium heat until golden brown, stirring frequently. Drain thoroughly and serve with roasts, grills and fried meat dishes.

Parsnips

These are in season from late summer through to the following spring. When buying parsnips, avoid those with discoloured 'shoulders' and with blemishes and fangs. Misshapen parsnips, provided they are fresh and in good condition, are quite satisfactory to use for soups, stews and mashing. When served whole as a vegetable, choose well-shaped parsnips of medium size and allow approximately one whole parsnip per person.

To cook parsnips
1. Boiled parsnips
Peel parsnips, wash them, then cut into quarters lengthwise. Remove hard centre core then either leave parsnips as they are or cut into slices or strips. Put into boiling salted water to which a dessertspoon of lemon juice has been added. Cook, uncovered, for 30 minutes or until tender. Drain thoroughly and toss with melted butter. Serve with all meat and poultry dishes and fried fish dishes.

2. Creamed parsnips
Cook as above. Drain thoroughly and stand parsnips over low heat. Mash finely adding a large knob of butter and, if liked, freshly-milled black pepper to taste. Serve while still very hot with meat, fish, poultry, egg and cheese dishes.

3. Roast parsnips
Prepare parsnips as for boiling but leave in quarters. Par-boil in boiling salted water for 10 minutes. Drain thoroughly. Stand them round a joint of meat or poultry for about 1 hour, basting once or twice with fat.

4. Baked parsnips
Peel and core parsnips and cut into slices. Put into a casserole with $\frac{1}{2}$ to 1oz (12 to 25gm) butter or margarine, 3 dessertspoons water and 1 level teaspoon salt to every 1lb ($\frac{1}{2}$ kilo). Cover and cook in the centre of a moderately hot oven, 350 deg F or gas 4 (180 deg C), for about 1 hour or until tender. Uncover and sprinkle with chopped parsley.

5. Fried parsnips
Par-boil parsnip slices in boiling salted water for 15 minutes. Drain thoroughly then coat with beaten egg and crumbs. Leave to stand for 10 minutes for coating to harden slightly. Fry in deep hot fat or oil until crisp and golden. Drain on soft kitchen paper and serve with all main course dishes.

Peas

Peas were known to the Greeks and Romans and, according to Sanskrit writings, were also grown in Northern India. Some sources claim that peas were introduced from Southern Europe into Britain during the reign of Henry VIII.

To cook peas

Allow ½lb (¼ kilo) peas in the pod per person. Shell just before cooking. Cook, uncovered, in a small quantity of boiling salted water to which a sprig of fresh mint, ½ teaspoon lemon juice, ½ teaspoon sugar and salt to taste have been added. Allow 10 to 15 minutes' cooking time. Drain thoroughly, return to saucepan and toss with butter. Serve with all main course dishes.

Note

1. For a more pronounced flavour, add about ½ dozen pea pods to the cooking water.
2. Pressure cook peas for 2 minutes at 15lb (7 kilo) pressure.

Peppers

The most widely used and commonly available peppers in Britain are the green ones, although the red and yellow varieties can be found as well. Sweet peppers, which are also known as pimientos and capsicums, are packed with vitamin C and make a valuable contribution to the diet whether eaten raw or cooked. Raw peppers have a very distinctive and strong flavour and, for the uninitiated, should be used in sparing quantities when added to salads. Cooked peppers, however, are milder—a lot of the harshness is lost in the cooking process. The seeds inside peppers are very hot and as they can be painful to lips and eyes if they come in contact, they should be removed very carefully. When buying peppers for salads, allow about a medium one for four people. When buying them for cooking, allow one per person.

Potatoes

Potatoes were brought to England by Sir Walter Raleigh, after his expedition of discovery to North America in the latter part of the 16th century. For a long time afterwards, potatoes were reared only in the gardens of the nobility and were regarded as exotic plants of unusual character. During the reign of James I potatoes were grown in small quantities for the royal household, were considered to be a delicacy and cost 2s per lb. Potatoes remained scarce for well over a hundred years afterwards and not until the 18th century did their cultivation spread throughout Britain.

To cook potatoes

1. Boiled potatoes

Allow 4 to 8oz (100 to 200gm) per person. Peel old potatoes as thinly as possible. Scrape new ones. Wash. Drop into cold water as each one is peeled to prevent discoloration. Cut old potatoes into even-sized pieces. Leave new potatoes whole but if on the large side, cut in half. Put potatoes into saucepan with sufficient cold water to cover and 1 level teaspoon salt to every lb (½ kilo). Bring to boil and remove scum. Lower heat and cover. Cook old potatoes until just tender—about 20 to 30 minutes. Cook new potatoes for about 10 minutes less. Drain thoroughly and return to saucepan. Toss new potatoes with melted butter and a sprig of mint. Transfer to serving dish, remove mint and sprinkle with chopped parsley. Do the same with old potatoes but omit mint. Alternatively pressure cook potatoes for 5 minutes at 15lb (7 kilo) pressure.

2. Potatoes en chemise

These are potatoes boiled in their skins and both new and old potatoes (the latter should not be too big) can be cooked in this way. Wash and scrub thoroughly and cook in boiling salted water as above. Drain. To serve, put the potatoes in a basket lined with a clean table napkin; people then skin their own potatoes at the table and smother them with melted butter. The advantages? No time involved in peeling and the flavour of the potatoes is better.

3. Mashed potatoes

Cook old potatoes as previously directed. Drain thoroughly. Return to saucepan and stand saucepan over low heat. Mash potatoes finely with a fork or masher and continue mashing until potatoes are dry and floury. Remove from heat and use as required.

4. Creamed potatoes

Cook and mash old potatoes as directed in previous recipe. Leave saucepan over low heat then, using a whisk or large metal fork, beat in ½ to 1oz (12 to 25gm) butter or margarine and 2 to 3 tablespoons milk for every lb (½ kilo) of potatoes. Continue beating until potatoes are snowy-white and creamy. Pile into a serving dish and ridge with prongs of a fork. Sprinkle with chopped parsley before serving.

Pumpkin

Pumpkin is related to the vegetable marrow but is usually round, not elongated, and it has bright orange flesh. A pumpkin can grow to a very large size and is therefore frequently sold by the piece. When buying pumpkin to serve as a vegetable, allow 8oz (200gm) per person. Apart from its savoury uses (it can be combined with other vegetables and added to soups, casseroles and stews), pumpkin can also form the basis of a sweet, spicy pie which is extremely popular in the United States and for which a recipe is included in the pudding section of this book (see page 164).

To cook pumpkin

1. Boiled pumpkin

Peel pumpkin and remove seeds. Cut flesh into cubes and cook, covered, in boiling salted water for 15 minutes. Drain thoroughly and either toss with butter or coat with white, cheese or parsley sauce. (see pages 94 and 95.)
Serve with all main course dishes.

2. Roast pumpkin

Prepare pumpkin as above but cook in boiling salted water for only 5 minutes. Drain thoroughly and wipe dry with soft kitchen paper. Stand pumpkin round a joint of meat or poultry and roast for 1 hour.

Radishes

Radishes probably originated in southern Asia and although there are many varieties grown abroad, probably the most familiar are the bright red crisp radishes with snow-white trimmings and middles, and a characteristic 'bite'. They are tasty and refreshing in mixed salads but are just as good simply dipped in salt and eaten alone with bread and butter. Because crispness and flavour are their chief merit, radishes are rarely cooked.

Salsify

This is the root of a plant called a vegetable oyster and is parsnip-shaped though longer and thinner. It has a faint taste of oysters—hence its name. It may be cooked in exactly the same way as for parsnips (see page 143), and when estimating quantities allow 4 to 6oz (100 to 150gm) per person.

Seakale

This is a mild and delicate vegetable which tastes faintly of asparagus and looks like celery. It is in fact grown in much the same way as celery and may be eaten raw, either in salads or with cheese at the end of a meal, or cooked. It grows wild on the sea coasts of western Europe and southern England. Seakale goes very well with fish, goose, poultry and white meat dishes.

To cook seakale

Allow 8oz (200gm) per person. Wash seakale thoroughly, taking care to remove all grit, then cut off the ends and tie the seakale into 4 bundles with cotton thread. Lower into boiling salted water to which a dessertspoon of lemon juice has been added. Cook, covered, for 20 to 30 minutes. Drain thoroughly, remove threads and serve with white or hollandaise sauce (see pages 94, 98). Alternatively, pressure cook seakale for 5 minutes at 15lb (7 kilo) pressure.

Sorrel

Sorrel is a leafy vegetable with a distinctive acid tang and is widely used on the continent, both raw and cooked. In small quantities, it makes an interesting flavour addition to green salads, sauces and soups and may also be cooked and served as a vegetable, either by itself or in conjunction with spinach. Allow 6 to 8oz (150 to 200gm) sorrel per person and choose leaves which are young, bright green and tender.

To cook sorrel

Wash leaves thoroughly under cold running water and remove stalks only if they look tough. Put into a large saucepan with ¼ level teaspoon sugar but no additional liquid; there should be enough clinging to the leaves after washing. Cook, uncovered, for 10 to 15 minutes until soft, stirring frequently. Drain thoroughly, return to saucepan and heat through with a large knob of butter and salt and pepper to taste. Serve with all main course dishes.

Spinach

Spinach came originally from Persia. It was known and eaten by French monks during the 14th century but it was another 300 years or so before it reached Britain. Spinach is richer in vitamin A than other green vegetables and contains as much vitamin C as cabbage. Spinach may be served with all main course dishes and goes particularly well with eggs, poultry, fish and white meats.

To cook spinach
1. Boiled spinach
Allow 8oz (200gm) per person. Wash leaves very thoroughly under cold running water to remove grit then cut away any coarse stalks. Put into a saucepan with a pinch of sugar but no additional liquid—there should be enough clinging to the leaves after washing. Cook, stirring all the time, until spinach comes to the boil then lower heat and cook gently, uncovered, for 10 to 15 minutes or until tender. Drain thoroughly, return to saucepan and re-heat with butter and salt and pepper to taste.

2. Creamed spinach
In order to make this dish the cooked spinach must be rubbed through a sieve which is a slow and tedious job. Therefore I would recommend buying either frozen chopped spinach or canned spinach purée and heating through with cream and seasonings. For those with blenders the problem is solved. Simply put the cooked spinach into the blender goblet, add 3 or 4 tablespoons double cream, seasoning to taste and blend until smooth. Re-heat gently without boiling.

Swedes

Swedes—or Swedish turnips to be exact—originated from a type of thick, rooted cabbage. They are a large vegetable with a distinctive flavour and yellow flesh and are in season from August through to late spring the following year. They may be served as a vegetable or added to stews, casseroles and soups. Allow 4 to 6oz (100 to 150gm) per person.

To cook swedes
1. Boiled swedes
Peel thickly—as the skin is tough—and either slice or dice, keeping the pieces immersed in cold water to prevent discoloration. Put into a saucepan containing boiling salted water and a dessertspoon of lemon juice or vinegar. Cover and cook for about 45 minutes or until tender. Drain thoroughly then mash with butter, salt and pepper to taste and a light sprinkling of nutmeg. Serve with meat grills and roasts.

Note
Alternatively, pressure cook swedes for 10 minutes at 15lb (7 kilo) pressure.

2. Roast swedes
Prepare swedes as in previous recipe and cook in boiling salted water (plus lemon juice or vinegar) for 20 minutes. Drain thoroughly. Stand swedes round a joint of meat, baste with dripping and roast for 1 to 1¼ hours.

Tomatoes

Tomatoes, once known as love apples and apples of paradise, originated in South America and were brought to Europe either by the Italians or the Spaniards round about the second half of the 16th century. In Great Britain they were regarded only as decorative and somewhat frivolous plants and not until the 19th century were they

Tomatoes—delicious in a salad (see page 154).

grown commercially and accepted as a food. Tomatoes are, to be strictly accurate, a fruit but usage has placed them in the vegetable category. Tomatoes may be eaten either cooked or raw, made into soups, sauces, purée and juice, added to stews, casseroles, hot-pots and pies, used as a garnish for all sorts of savoury dishes and turned into chutney.

To skin tomatoes
Many recipes call for skinned tomatoes and here is a very simple and reliable method to do this. Put tomatoes into a bowl. Cover with boiling water and leave for 1 minute. Drain and cover with cold water. When tomatoes are cool enough to handle, lift out of bowl and slip off the skins. The tomatoes may also be speared on to a fork and rotated over a lit gas jet. The skins burst and then may be peeled off with a knife.

To cook tomatoes
1. Whole baked tomatoes
Allow 2 medium tomatoes per person. Pre-heat oven to moderately hot, 375 deg F or gas 5 (190 deg C). Cut a cross on top of each (not stalk side) with a knife. Stand tomatoes in lightly-buttered baking dish, stalk sides down, and sprinkle with salt and pepper. Top each tomato with a small piece of butter and bake just above centre of oven for 15 minutes. Serve with main course dishes.

2. Baked tomato halves
Allow 2 medium tomatoes per person. Pre-heat oven to moderately hot, 375 deg F or gas 5 (190 deg C). Halve tomatoes horizontally. Stand them in a lightly-buttered baking dish. Sprinkle with salt, pepper, a pinch of sugar and, if wished, a little dried basil. Dot with flakes of butter and cook near top of oven for 12 to 15 minutes. Serve with any main course dish or with cooked breakfasts.

3. Grilled tomatoes
Allow 2 medium tomatoes per person. Cut in half as in previous recipe. Stand halves in lightly-buttered grill pan, cut sides uppermost. Sprinkle with salt, pepper and a pinch of sugar then dot with flakes of butter. Grill about 7 minutes under medium heat. Serve with any main course dish or with cooked breakfasts.

4. Fried tomatoes
Allow 2 medium tomatoes per person. Cut each tomato into 4 thick slices. Heat a little bacon dripping or butter in a frying pan. Add tomato slices and fry gently for 3 to 4 minutes, turning once. Serve with any main course dish or with cooked breakfasts.

Turnips

Turnips were a familiar vegetable to the ancient Greeks and Romans and in all probability were introduced to Britain by the Flemish during the 16th century. The globular turnips are considered to have a more distinctive flavour and greater sweetness than the elongated variety. Small to medium young turnips are preferable to large ones (which may be tough and woody) and they should look fresh and clean enough to eat raw. Allow 4 to 6oz (100 to 150gm) per person.

To cook turnips
Peel turnips and drop into bowl of cold water to prevent discoloration. Drain and transfer to a saucepan of boiling salted water. Add 1 or 2 teaspoons lemon juice or vinegar and 1 level teaspoon sugar. Cook, uncovered, for 20 or 30 minutes or until tender. Drain thoroughly, return to pan and toss with butter and freshly-milled pepper to taste. Alternatively, combine turnips with white, cheese or parsley sauce (see pages 94 and 95). Turnips team particularly well with lamb.

Note
Alternatively, pressure cook turnips for 5 minutes at 15lb (7 kilo) pressure.

Watercress

During the reign of Queen Elizabeth I, watercress grew wild by the side of streams and was considered a pick-me-up, a blood cleanser and antidote against lethargy, and enthusiastically recommended by Culpepper, a famous herbalist of the day. It was not until 1808 that the first watercress beds were constructed in Kent. Dark green watercress is a vitamin-packed vegetable with a characteristic crispness and distinctive flavour. It is normally eaten raw in salads or used as a garnish but it may also be cooked in exactly the same way as for spinach (see this page), and served with the same dishes. It makes a delicious soup and if finely chopped and mixed with parsley, can be added to omelette and scrambled egg mixtures. Its preparation is quick and easy; simply trim the stalks and wash the watercress under cold running water. Allow one bunch for 4 to 6 people when used in salads; one bunch per person if cooked like spinach.

Yams or sweet potatoes

These look like something between Jerusalem artichokes and ordinary potatoes and appear to have been widely used by British cooks in the 17th century. They are extremely popular in America. They are faintly perfumed and sweet and are a good source of vitamin A. Yams are an acquired taste but well worth trying. When estimating quantities allow 8oz (200gm) per person. They may be boiled, baked, roasted or fried in exactly the same way as for potatoes.

Ratatouille

Illustrated on page 139

Serves 4

2 tablespoons salad oil
1oz (25gm) butter
1 large onion, thinly sliced
1 garlic clove, finely chopped
8oz (200gm) tomatoes, skinned and chopped
2 medium green peppers, de-seeded and cut into strips
1lb (½ kilo) courgettes or young marrow
2 medium aubergines
1 to 2 level teaspoons salt
freshly-milled pepper to taste
4 level tablespoons chopped parsley

1. Heat salad oil and butter in large saucepan.
2. Add onion and garlic and fry gently until pale gold.
3. Add tomatoes and peppers and cover pan.
4. Wash and dry unpeeled courgettes and slice. Alternatively, peel marrow and cut into cubes.
5. Thinly slice unpeeled aubergines, first cutting away stalk end.
6. Add courgettes or marrow and aubergines to saucepan with salt and pepper to taste and the parsley.
7. Cover and simmer very gently for approximately 1 hour, stirring occasionally.
8. Serve hot with meat, egg and poultry dishes.

Note
Alternatively, pressure cook ratatouille for 15 minutes at 15lb (7 kilo) pressure. Cool down, uncover and cook a further 10 minutes to reduce liquid.

Baked crumbed aubergines

Serves 4

2 medium aubergines
2 tablespoons salad oil
4 level tablespoons fresh white bread-crumbs
1 garlic clove
2 tablespoons hot milk
1 level tablespoon finely-chopped parsley
salt and pepper to taste
about 1oz (25gm) butter or margarine

1. Pre-heat oven to moderately hot, 400 deg F or gas 6 (200 deg C).
2. Halve aubergines lengthwise and make diagonal slashes in the flesh with a knife.
3. Heat oil in shallow pan. Put in aubergine halves, cut sides down. Fry gently for 10 minutes.
4. Meanwhile, put crumbs into bowl. Chop garlic very finely and add to crumbs with hot milk, parsley and salt and pepper to taste. Mix thoroughly.
5. Stand aubergines, cut sides up, in baking dish. Cover tops with equal amounts of crumb mixture then dot with flakes of butter or margarine.
6. Cook in centre of oven for 30 minutes.

Broad beans Portugaise

Serves 4

3lb (1½ kilo) broad beans
1 garlic clove, chopped
2 medium tomatoes, skinned and chopped
2 tablespoons olive oil
4 tablespoons hot water
½ level teaspoon dried basil
½ level teaspoon salt
½ level teaspoon sugar
pepper to taste

1. Shell beans and put into saucepan with all remaining ingredients.
2. Cover and simmer gently for 20 minutes or until beans are tender, stirring occasionally.
3. Serve with roast and grilled meats and poultry.

French-style beans

Cook French or dwarf beans as directed on page 140. After draining, wash and dry saucepan and rub inside with a cut clove of garlic. Add a generous knob of butter, return beans to a low heat and toss gently for 3 to 4 minutes.

French beans à l'anglaise

Serves 4

Arrange 1 to 1½lb (½ to ¾ kilo) freshly-cooked French or dwarf beans in a warm serving dish. Coat with 2oz (50gm) melted butter then sprinkle heavily with finely-chopped parsley.

Jacket beetroots with butter

Serves 4

8 small beetroots
salt and pepper
1oz (25gm) butter, melted

1. Pre-heat oven to moderate, 325 deg F or gas 3 (170 deg C).
2. Trim beetroot tops, leaving about 1 inch of stem.
3. Stand beetroots on baking tray and cook in centre of oven for approximately 1 hour or until tender.
4. Rub off skins then stand beetroots in warm serving dish.
5. Sprinkle with salt and pepper then coat with butter.
6. Serve hot with meat and egg dishes.

Creamed curried beets

Serves 4

8 small raw beetroots
4 tablespoons double cream
salt and pepper to taste
1 level teaspoon curry powder
1 level dessertspoon finely-grated onion
1 teaspoon lemon juice

1. Trim beetroot tops, leaving about 1 inch of stem. Take care not to bruise the skins or the beets will 'bleed' and lose flavour and colour.
2. Wash beets thoroughly, put into saucepan and cover with boiling water.
3. Simmer, uncovered, for 1 to 1½ hours or until tender. Drain and rub off skins. Cut into quarters and return to clean saucepan.
4. Stand saucepan over low heat and add all remaining ingredients. Heat through gently.
5. Serve with poultry and fish dishes.

Note
Small beetroots may be pressure cooked at 15lb (7 kilo) pressure for 12 minutes. Larger ones at the same pressure for 20 minutes.

Sweet-sour beetroot

Serves 4 to 6

An unusual recipe for cooked beetroot. Try it hot or cold with cold cooked meats, poultry and game.

1lb (½ kilo) cooked beetroot
2oz (50gm) Demerara sugar
3 tablespoons malt vinegar
3 tablespoons undiluted orange squash
pinch of cinnamon
salt and pepper to taste
2 level teaspoons cornflour
1 dessertspoon cold water

1. Dice beetroot.
2. Put sugar, vinegar and squash into saucepan and stand it over low heat until sugar dissolves.
3. Add beetroot, cinnamon and salt and pepper to taste.
4. Mix cornflour to a smooth cream with cold water.
5. Add to beetroot mixture.
6. Cook, stirring continuously, until mixture comes to boil.
7. Simmer for 2 minutes then serve hot or cold.

Beetroots in vinegar

Serves 4

2 medium beetroots, cooked
about 2 tablespoons vinegar

1. Slice beetroots, put into bowl and add vinegar.
2. Cover and chill lightly before serving.

Cauliflower cheese garnished with prawns

Carrots à l'Orleans

Serves 4

1lb (½ kilo) carrots

4 tablespoons chicken stock

1 level tablespoon soft brown sugar

½ level teaspoon salt

1oz (25gm) butter

1. Cut peeled and washed carrots into slices.
2. Cook in boiling salted water for 7 minutes. Drain thoroughly and return to pan.
3. Add stock, sugar and salt and cook fairly briskly, shaking pan frequently, until carrot slices are golden and glazed and until little or no liquid remains.
4. Add butter and toss.
5. Serve straight away with meat, poultry, egg, fish and cheese dishes.

Cauliflower cheese

Serves 4

1 medium cauliflower, freshly cooked

½ pint (250ml) hot cheese sauce (see page 94)

2oz (50gm) Cheddar cheese, grated

paprika

1. Put drained cauliflower into a serving dish.
2. Coat with cheese sauce.
3. Sprinkle with grated cheese and paprika.
4. Either brown under a grill or in a hot oven, 425 deg F or gas 7 (220 deg C), for 15 minutes.

Note

For a luxury touch add prawns to the cheese sauce before pouring it over the cauliflower.

Cauliflower with almond butter crumbs

Serves 4

1 medium cauliflower, prepared for boiling

2oz (50gm) butter

3 level tablespoons fresh white bread-crumbs

1oz (25gm) flaked almonds

1. Cook cauliflower in boiling salted water, as explained on page 141.
2. Five minutes before it is ready, melt butter in a small frying pan.
3. Add crumbs and almonds.
4. Fry over a medium heat until golden.
5. Drain cauliflower and put into a warm serving dish.
6. Coat with almond crumb mixture and any remaining butter from pan.
7. Serve with meat, fish and poultry dishes.

Cauliflower fritters

Serves 4

Divide a medium cauliflower, cooked, into florets. Coat with fritter batter (see page 105) or toss in beaten egg and fine breadcrumbs. Lower into a pan of hot deep fat or oil and fry until pieces turn golden. Drain on soft kitchen paper and serve straight away with meat, poultry, fish, egg and cheese dishes.

Braised celery

Serves 4

4 small heads of celery

2 rashers streaky bacon, chopped

½oz (12gm) butter or margarine

1 small onion, grated

1 medium carrot, thinly sliced

stock or water

salt and pepper to taste

1. Pre-heat oven to moderate, 350 deg F or gas 4 (180 deg C).
2. Remove leaves from celery. Wash celery heads thoroughly and hold together by tying each with thick thread.
3. Put bacon with butter or margarine into pan. Heat until fat melts.
4. Add onion and carrot and fry, covered, until vegetables are pale gold.
5. Transfer contents of pan to oblong heatproof dish.
6. Add celery and half cover with stock or water.
7. Season to taste with salt and pepper and cover with lid or foil. Cook in centre of oven for 1 to 1½ hours or until tender.
8. Remove strings, transfer celery to a serving dish and spoon over vegetable liquid in which it was cooked.
9. Serve with all main course dishes.

Corn fritters

Serves 4 to 6

4oz (100gm) self-raising flour

1 level teaspoon salt

1 standard egg

¼ pint (125ml) cold milk

8 to 10 level tablespoons corn kernels, canned, or frozen and thawed

3 to 4 tablespoons oil for frying

1. Sift flour and salt into bowl.
2. Make well in centre. Add unbeaten egg and half the milk.
3. Beat thoroughly to form a thick, creamy batter.
4. Beat in rest of milk then stir in corn.
5. Heat oil in pan. Add tablespoons of fritter mixture then fry until crisp and golden turning once.
6. Drain on soft kitchen paper and serve hot with fried chicken.

Baked corn

Allow 1 corn-on-the-cob per person. Pre-heat oven to moderately hot, 400 deg F or gas 6 (200 deg C). Remove husks and silk from corn. Stand cobs on a baking tray and brush heavily with melted butter. Put into centre of oven and bake for 30 minutes or until golden, turning once. Sprinkle with salt and freshly-milled pepper and serve extra butter separately.

Fried courgettes

Serves 4

4 medium courgettes

salt

3 level tablespoons flour, well-seasoned with salt and pepper

1oz (25gm) butter or 3 tablespoons salad oil

little chopped parsley

1. Top and tail courgettes. Wash them well and cut into slices.
2. Put on to a flat plate. Sprinkle with salt and leave to stand for 30 minutes.
3. Rinse slices and wipe them dry with soft kitchen paper.
4. Coat slices with seasoned flour.
5. Fry, a few at a time, in hot butter or oil until golden on both sides.
6. Drain on soft kitchen paper.
7. Transfer to a serving dish and sprinkle with chopped parsley.

Leeks au jus

In this, the leeks are cooked French style, with stock used instead of water (see page 142). After the leeks are tender, remove to a serving dish and keep hot. Boil stock briskly until it is reduced to about 4 tablespoons then pour over the leeks. Sprinkle with chopped parsley and serve straight away.

Braised leeks

Braised leeks

Serves 4

1oz (25gm) butter or margarine

1 medium carrot, sliced

2 rashers streaky bacon, chopped

1 celery stalk, chopped

4 medium leeks, trimmed and washed

½ to 1 level teaspoon salt

½ to 1 level teaspoon mixed herbs

¼ pint (125ml) stock

1. Pre-heat oven to moderate, 350 deg F or gas 4 (180 deg C).
2. Melt butter or margarine in saucepan. Add carrot, bacon and celery.
3. Cover and fry gently for 10 minutes or until vegetables start to turn colour.
4. Transfer to oblong casserole dish and top with leeks.
5. Sprinkle with salt and herbs then pour stock into dish.
6. Cover and cook in centre of oven for 45 minutes.

Creamed mushrooms

Serves 4

12oz (300gm) button or cup mushrooms

1oz (25gm) butter

1 level tablespoon cornflour

½ pint (250ml) cold milk

large pinch marjoram

1 dessertspoon lemon juice

salt and pepper to taste

1. Prepare mushrooms by washing or wiping with a clean, damp cloth. Leave buttons whole; cut cups into slices of even size.
2. Heat butter in saucepan. Add mushrooms and fry briskly for 5 minutes.
3. Stir in cornflour then gradually blend in milk.
4. Cook, stirring, until mixture comes to boil and thickens. Simmer 1 minute.
5. Add marjoram and lemon juice and season to taste with salt and pepper.
6. Serve on toast for a light meal or use as an accompaniment to meat and poultry grills and roasts, fish dishes and egg dishes.

148

Stuffed mushrooms

Serves 4

8 large flat mushrooms

salad oil

stuffing to taste (see stuffings section, page 106)

1oz (25gm) butter or margarine

8 rounds toast or fried bread

1. Pre-heat oven to moderately hot, 375 deg F or gas 5 (190 deg C).
2. Stand mushrooms on buttered baking tray.
3. Brush lightly with oil.
4. Pile equal amounts of stuffing on to each mushroom then top with flakes of butter.
5. Cook, uncovered, near top of oven for 15 to 20 minutes.
6. Stand each mushroom on a round of hot toast or fried bread.
7. Serve as a meal starter or as an accompaniment to meat and poultry roasts and grills.

Sweet-sour red cabbage

Serves 4

Another continental cabbage dish which goes admirably with roast duckling, goose and pork. One word of warning though when cutting up red cabbage: it stains the hands badly so I would advise wearing rubber gloves or else shredding the cabbage in the shredder attachment of an electric mixer.

1 firm red cabbage about 2lb (1 kilo) in weight

2oz (50gm) lard or bacon dripping

3 level tablespoons granulated sugar

1 medium onion, grated

½lb (200gm) cooking apples, chopped

½ pint (250ml) water

1 to 2 level teaspoons salt

½ to 1 level teaspoon caraway seeds

1 level tablespoon cornflour

4 tablespoons vinegar

1. Shred cabbage finely and wash under cold running water.
2. Heat lard or dripping in a large saucepan.
3. Add cabbage, sugar, onion, apples, water, salt, caraway seeds and cornflour mixed to a cream with vinegar.
4. Stand saucepan over medium heat. Bring mixture slowly to the boil, stirring. Cover.
5. Reduce heat and simmer slowly for 1½ to 2 hours, topping up with boiling water if cabbage seems to be drying out, and stirring occasionally.

Note
The flavour of cabbage is improved if the vegetable is cooked one day and then re-heated and served the next.

Marrow au gratin

Serves 4

1 medium marrow

1 garlic clove

little Parmesan cheese, grated

2oz (50gm) butter or margarine

salt and pepper

3 tablespoons milk

little nutmeg, grated

2 tablespoons fine dried breadcrumbs

1. Pre-heat oven to moderately hot, 400 deg F or gas 6 (200 deg C).
2. Prepare marrow as for boiling. Cook in boiling salted water for 7 minutes. Drain.
3. Rub the inside of a fairly large casserole dish with cut clove of garlic.
4. Melt 1oz (25gm) of the butter and use to brush inside of casserole dish.
5. Fill with layers of marrow and Parmesan cheese, sprinkling salt and pepper between layers.
6. Pour milk into dish then dot top with flakes of the remaining butter.
7. Sprinkle lightly with nutmeg followed by crumbs.
8. Bake near top of oven for 15 to 20 minutes.
9. Serve with meat roasts and grills, fish dishes and omelettes.

Stuffed marrow

Serves 4

1 medium marrow

1lb (½ kilo) minced beef

6 level tablespoons fresh white breadcrumbs

1 medium onion, grated

1 level tablespoon tomato paste

½ level teaspoon dried basil or mixed herbs

1 level teaspoon salt

pepper to taste

4 tablespoons stock or water

1. Pre-heat oven to moderate, 350 deg F or gas 4 (180 deg C).
2. Peel marrow thinly and cut in half lengthwise.
3. Remove seeds and cook marrow halves in boiling salted water for 10 minutes.
4. Meanwhile, combine minced beef with all remaining ingredients.
5. Drain marrow thoroughly.
6. When cool enough to handle, fill the cavities with meat mixture.
7. Put halves, side by side, in a buttered baking dish (meat filling should be uppermost).
8. Pour stock or warm water into dish and cover with piece of buttered foil.
9. Cook in centre of oven for ¾ to 1 hour or until marrow is tender and meat is cooked.

Sweet-sour red cabbage

Hot sauerkraut

Serves 4 to 6

Sauerkraut, cooked in central European style, must be one of the tastiest cabbage dishes in the world and I know of no finer accompaniment to Frankfurter sausages and bacon dishes. To say that my recipe is one hundred per cent authentic would be untrue because almost every continental family has its own version. The one I give is an amalgamation of about four different recipes collected from German, Austrian and Polish friends and it has always been praised by those more conversant than I am with the traditional art of sauerkraut-making!

6 to 8oz (150 to 200gm) streaky bacon, chopped

1oz (25gm) lard or bacon dripping

1 large onion, finely chopped

1 large cooking apple, peeled, cored and finely chopped

2lb (1 kilo) sauerkraut, undrained

3 level tablespoons granulated sugar

½ to 1 level teaspoon caraway seeds

½ pint (250ml) water

salt and pepper to taste

1. Put bacon and lard or dripping into saucepan. Heat until fat melts.
2. Add onion. Cover pan and fry gently for 7 to 10 minutes or until onion just starts to brown.
3. Add all remaining ingredients.
4. Stir well to mix then slowly bring to boil, stirring.
5. At once lower heat. Cover and simmer very gently for 1½ to 2 hours, topping up with boiling water if sauerkraut seems to be drying out, and stirring occasionally.
6. Serve very hot.

Note
For a luxury touch, add ¼ pint (125ml) dry white wine with the ½ pint (250ml) water.

Pois à la bonne femme

Serves 4

1oz (25gm) butter or margarine

1 bunch spring onions, trimmed

4oz (100gm) back bacon, chopped

1 level tablespoon flour

½ pint (250ml) stock

2lb (1 kilo) peas in the pod

salt and pepper

1. Heat butter or margarine in saucepan. Add whole onions and bacon.
2. Cover pan and fry gently for 10 minutes.
3. Stir in flour. Cook 2 minutes.
4. Gradually blend in stock.
5. Cook, stirring, until liquid comes to the boil and thickens.
6. Add peas and salt and pepper to taste.
7. Cover. Cook, stirring occasionally, until peas are tender and liquid is reduced by half.
8. Serve with meat and poultry dishes.

Casseroled onions

Serves 4

20 small onions

little flour

salt and pepper

1oz (25gm) butter

5 tablespoons stock

2 tablespoons dry white wine or dry cider

2 level tablespoons chopped parsley

1. Pre-heat oven to moderately hot, 375 deg F or gas 5 (190 deg C).
2. Remove roots and peel onions.
3. Toss onions lightly in flour, well-seasoned with salt and pepper.
4. Melt butter in flameproof casserole.
5. Add onions and fry gently until golden brown all over.
6. Add stock and wine or cider.
7. Cover and cook in centre of oven for 30 minutes or until tender.
8. Uncover and sprinkle with chopped parsley.
9. Serve with meat and poultry roasts and grills, fried fish dishes and egg dishes.

French fried onions

Serves 4

Peel and thinly slice 2 large onions. Separate slices into rings. Soak in ½ pint (250ml) milk and water (¼ pint — 125ml — each) for 30 minutes. Drain thoroughly by standing the onion rings on soft kitchen paper. Coat each ring with self-raising flour well-seasoned with salt and pepper. Lower, a few at a time, into deep hot fat or oil and fry until crisp and golden—about 2 to 3 minutes. Lift out of pan, drain on soft kitchen paper and serve straight away.

Spanish pepper dish

Baked stuffed onions

Serves 4

4 large onions, peeled

4 level tablespoons fresh white bread-crumbs

4 level tablespoons grated Cheddar cheese or cold cooked minced meat

a large pinch of mace

½ level teaspoon mixed herbs

salt and pepper to taste

a little milk if necessary

1 level tablespoon lightly-toasted bread-crumbs

1oz (25gm) butter or margarine

about ¼ pint (125ml) stock

1. Pre-heat oven to moderately hot, 400 deg F or gas 6 (200 deg C).
2. Cook onions in boiling salted water for 10 minutes.
3. Drain thoroughly and carefully remove centres, leaving ¼ inch thick walls round each onion.
4. Chop centres fairly finely and combine with breadcrumbs, cheese or meat, mace, herbs and salt and pepper to taste. Add a little milk to bind if mixture is at all on the dry side.
5. Mix thoroughly then spoon into onion shells.
6. Stand onions in a buttered baking dish.
7. Sprinkle tops with toasted breadcrumbs then dot with flakes of butter.
8. Pour sufficient stock into dish to come a quarter of the way up the onions.
9. Bake, uncovered, in centre of oven for about 30 minutes or until onions are tender and golden.
10. Serve as an hors d'oeuvre, as an accompaniment to meat and poultry grills and roasts, or as a light lunch or supper dish.

Spanish pepper dish

Serves 4

1 small green pepper

1 small onion

1½oz (37gm) butter

4 standard eggs

salt and pepper to taste

8 level tablespoons fresh white bread-crumbs

1½oz (37gm) Cheddar cheese, grated

a little extra butter

1. Pre-heat oven to hot, 425 deg F or gas 7 (220 deg C).
2. Well-butter 4 individual heatproof dishes.
3. De-seed and chop green pepper. Chop the onion.
4. Fry both in the butter until pale gold then divide equally among 4 dishes.
5. Break an egg into each then season to taste with salt and pepper.
6. Mix crumbs and cheese well together and sprinkle over eggs.
7. Dot with flakes of butter then cook near top of oven for 10 minutes.
8. Serve straight away.

Stuffed peppers

Serves 4

4 medium green peppers

1oz (25gm) butter, margarine or dripping

1 medium onion, grated

8oz (200gm) raw minced beef

3oz (75gm) rice, freshly-boiled (weighed before cooking)

8 tablespoons stock or water

1 teaspoon Worcestershire sauce

½ level teaspoon savory, thyme or mixed herbs

1oz (25gm) extra butter or margarine

1. Pre-heat oven to moderately hot, 375 deg F or gas 5 (190 deg C).
2. Cut tops off peppers and remove inside fibres and seeds.
3. Cover with boiling water and leave to stand 5 minutes.
4. Lift peppers out of water, turn upside down and drain very thoroughly.
5. Melt first 1oz (25gm) butter in saucepan. Add onion and fry for 5 to 7 minutes or until it turns pale gold.
6. Add meat and fry a little more briskly for 5 minutes, breaking it up with a fork all the time.
7. Add rice, 4 tablespoons stock, Worcestershire sauce and herbs. Mix thoroughly.
8. Fill the peppers with the meat mixture then stand them in a baking dish and add rest of stock.
9. Dot top of each with butter or margarine then cook in centre of oven for 20 to 30 minutes or until peppers are completely tender and the filling is heated through.

Italian-style pepper stew

Serves 4

4 medium peppers

2 tablespoons olive oil (or other salad oil to taste)

1 large onion, finely chopped or coarsely grated

1 garlic clove, chopped (optional)

12oz (300gm) tomatoes

1 level teaspoon salt

1. Cut tops off peppers and remove inside fibres and seeds. Wash peppers and cut into strips.
2. Heat oil in saucepan. Add onions and garlic and fry gently, with lid on pan, for 5 minutes.
3. Add peppers and fry a further 5 minutes.
4. Add tomatoes and salt.
5. Bring to boil, cover pan and lower heat.
6. Simmer gently for 30 minutes, stirring occasionally.
7. Serve with meat, poultry, egg and fish dishes.

Cheese and potato balls

Cheese and potato balls

Serves 4

1lb (½ kilo) freshly-boiled potatoes

1 standard egg, beaten

1 level teaspoon prepared mustard

salt and pepper to taste

4oz (100gm) Cheddar cheese, grated

1. Pre-heat oven to hot, 425 deg F or gas 7 (220 deg C).
2. Mash potatoes finely.
3. Beat in egg and mustard.
4. Season to taste with salt and pepper.
5. Leave to cool slightly then shape into fairly small balls.
6. Roll each one in cheese then transfer to lightly-greased baking tray.
7. Bake near top of oven for 15 to 20 minutes or until crisp and golden.
8. Serve with fish or poultry dishes.

Potatoes Anna

Serves 4

1½lb (¾ kilo) potatoes

4oz (100gm) butter, melted

salt and pepper

1. Pre-heat oven to moderately hot, 375 deg F or gas 5 (190 deg C).
2. Peel, wash and dry potatoes and cut into paper-thin slices.
3. Brush a 1½ to 2 pint (¾ to 1 kilo) heatproof dish or cake tin heavily with melted butter.
4. Cover base with a layer of potatoes, making sure the slices overlap.
5. Brush with more butter and sprinkle with salt and pepper.
6. Repeat the layering with rest of potatoes, butter and salt and pepper, pressing each layer down with the hand.
7. Cover with greased aluminium foil.
8. Cook in centre of oven for 1½ hours.
9. Turn out on to a heatproof plate brushed with butter (the potatoes should hold together) and return dish to oven for 15 to 20 minutes or until potatoes are lightly brown.
10. Serve with all main course dishes.

Purée or mousseline potatoes

Cook and mash potatoes as for mashed potatoes (see page 144). With pan over very low heat, gradually beat in ¼ pint (125ml) hot milk and 1oz (25gm) butter to every lb (½ kilo) potatoes. Beat vigorously until potatoes are light in texture and the consistency of softly whipped cream. Serve very hot with all main course dishes.

Duchesse potatoes

Pre-heat oven to moderately hot, 400 deg F or gas 6 (200 deg C). Cook potatoes as directed on page 144. Drain thoroughly and either mash very finely or rub through a sieve. Lump-free potatoes are essential for the success of this dish. Return potatoes to saucepan and stand them over a very low heat. For every lb (½ kilo) potatoes, add 1oz (25gm) butter or margarine, 2 egg yolks and 1 dessertspoon milk. Beat until completely smooth and well-blended. Transfer to forcing bag fitted with a large star-shaped tube and pipe rosettes or whirls of potato mixture on to a greased baking tray. Brush with lightly-beaten egg white and bake near top of oven for about 15 minutes or until golden brown.
If wanted as a garnish, pipe potato in a border round a large heatproof plate. Brush with egg white and bake as above.

Quick duchesse potatoes

For quick to prepare and beautifully smooth duchesse potatoes, make up a packet of instant mashed potatoes, according to directions on packet, then beat in 1 beaten egg.

Sauté potatoes

Serves 4

1½lb (¾ kilo) potatoes

2 tablespoons salad oil

2oz (50gm) butter or margarine

salt

1. Cook potatoes in boiling salted water for 7 minutes. Drain thoroughly and allow to cool.
2. Cut into ¼-inch thick slices or large dice.
3. Heat oil and butter or margarine in a frying pan.
4. Add potatoes and fry until golden on all sides.
5. Drain on soft kitchen paper.
6. Sprinkle lightly with salt and serve with poultry, meat, fish, cheese and egg dishes.

Lyonnaise potatoes

Serves 4

Sauté potatoes as in previous recipe.
After draining and sprinkling with salt, combine with 1 large onion, thinly sliced and fried in a little butter or margarine until golden. Serve with meat, poultry and egg dishes.

Potato chips

There are many recipes given for chips and though the majority call for raw potatoes, I always par-boil mine first. Less frying time is then needed and the chips seem to get much crisper. The first choice for deep frying is oil because it leaves no greasy after-taste. Next best is lard, or a mixture of lard and oil, and finally good-quality beef dripping.
Allow at least 8oz (¼ kilo) of potatoes per person.
1. Peel and wash potatoes and cut them in half lengthwise.
2. Cook in boiling salted water for 7 minutes.
3. Drain and leave to cool.
4. Cut potatoes into ½-inch thick slices. Cut slices into ½-inch wide strips.
5. Heat oil or fat until a chip dropped into it bubbles up to the top immediately.
6. Put chips—not too many at once—into a chip basket then lower into hot oil or fat.
7. Fry steadily for 7 to 10 minutes or until golden and crisp, shaking basket gently from side to side.
8. Drain on soft kitchen paper then transfer to serving dish. Keep hot but do not cover.
9. Repeat with rest of chips.
10. Transfer to serving dish and sprinkle with salt.
11. Serve straight away.

Oven-cooked chips

Serves 4

Useful on days when one can't face the smell of frying!
1. Pre-heat oven to hot, 450 deg F or gas 8 (230 deg C).
2. Peel and wash 4 large potatoes.
3. Cut into ½-inch wide strips and soak in cold water for 10 minutes.
4. Drain and dry thoroughly.
5. Put into roasting tin—in a single layer—and pour over either 3 tablespoons oil or 2oz (50gm) melted dripping, butter or margarine.
6. Turn potatoes over and over with a spoon until they are evenly coated with oil or fat.
7. Bake near top of oven for 30 to 40 minutes or until crisp and golden, turning two or three times.
8. Remove from tin and drain on soft kitchen paper.
9. Sprinkle with salt and serve straight away.

Note
These chips may be made with par-boiled potatoes or cold cooked potatoes. Oven-cook the par-boiled potatoes for 25 minutes and the cooked potatoes for 15 to 20 minutes.

Baked jacket potatoes

Serves 4

4 medium potatoes

a little oil

butter or soured cream

watercress sprigs

1. Pre-heat oven to moderately hot, 400 deg F or gas 6 (200 deg C).
2. Brush baking tray with oil.
3. Wash, scrub and dry potatoes. Prick skins all over with a fork.
4. Put on to prepared tray and brush potatoes with oil (this helps to make the skins tender).
5. Bake just above centre of oven for 1½ to 2 hours or until potatoes feel soft when pressed between the fingers. Remove from oven.
6. Cut a cross on the top of each with a sharp knife then, holding the potato in a tea towel, squeeze gently until the cross opens at all 4 points.
7. Fill the cut with a large piece of butter or top with soured cream and garnish with watercress.
8. Serve straight away.

Stuffed jacket potatoes

Prepare and bake potatoes as in previous recipe. When potatoes are tender, cut in half lengthwise and spoon insides into bowl. Mash finely with about 1 to 1½oz (25 to 37gm) butter or margarine and sufficient milk or single cream to make mixture creamy but not wet. Add 2 to 4oz (50 to 100gm) grated Cheddar cheese and season to taste with salt, pepper and dry mustard. Pile back into potato shells and sprinkle with a little more grated cheese. Return to baking tray and bake near top of oven for 15 to 20 minutes or until golden brown. Garnish with parsley and serve straight away.

Potato croquettes

Serves 4

Combine 1lb (½ kilo) freshly-boiled and mashed potatoes with 1oz (25gm) butter or margarine, 1 small beaten egg and seasonings to taste. A little chopped parsley, finely snipped chives, grated Cheddar cheese or very finely chopped ham may be added as well, if wished. When cool enough to handle, divide the mixture into 8 equal-sized pieces and shape into cakes or rolls. Coat with beaten egg and bread-crumbs. Leave to set for 10 minutes and coat with egg and crumbs again. Leave for 15 minutes so that coating hardens and croquettes do not break while they are being cooked. Fry in about 1 inch of hot dripping oil, lard or cooking fat until crisp and golden, turning once. Drain on soft kitchen paper and serve with all main course dishes, for breakfast with fried bacon and eggs, or for high tea with cold meat and salad.

Straw chips

Serves 4

These are delicious served with roast poultry and game and deserve to be made more often than they are.

| 1 to 1½lb (½ to ¾ kilo) potatoes |
| deep oil or fat for frying |

1. Peel and wash potatoes and slice thinly.
2. Slice into narrow strips, about double the thickness of a matchstick.
3. Soak in cold water for 30 minutes.
4. Drain thoroughly and dry in a clean tea towel.
5. Heat oil or fat until 2 chips, dropped into it, bubble to the top immediately.
6. Put chips, not too many at once, into basket.
7. Lower basket into hot oil or fat and fry about 7 minutes or until chips are crisp and golden.
8. Remove from basket and drain on soft kitchen paper.
9. Transfer to serving dish. Keep hot but do not cover.
10. Repeat with rest of chips.
11. Transfer to serving dish and sprinkle with salt.
12. Serve straight away.

Stuffed tomatoes

Serves 4

| 4 large or 8 medium tomatoes |
| 3 level tablespoons fresh white bread-crumbs |
| 1 small onion, finely chopped |
| 1 level tablespoon chopped parsley |
| 1 level tablespoon melted bacon dripping or butter |
| 1 teaspoon Worcestershire sauce |
| salt and pepper to taste |
| 1oz (25gm) stale Cheddar cheese, finely grated |

1. Pre-heat oven to moderately hot, 400 deg F or gas 6 (200 deg C).
2. Cut tops off tomatoes and scoop insides into bowl, removing hard cores. Turn tomatoes upside down to drain on soft kitchen paper.
3. Add crumbs, onion, parsley, dripping or butter, Worcestershire sauce and salt and pepper to taste to tomato pulp.
4. Mix thoroughly then spoon into tomato halves.
5. Transfer to lightly greased baking tray then sprinkle tomatoes with cheese.
6. Cook near top of oven for 15 to 20 minutes.

Turnips à la crème

Cook turnips as on page 145; drain thoroughly. Return turnips to saucepan and stand them over a low heat. Mash finely, add a large knob of butter and 3 or 4 tablespoons of double cream. Adjust seasoning to taste and beat until turnips are light and smooth in texture. Serve piping hot with meat roasts and grills.

Stuffed tomatoes

Sugar-glazed turnips

Cook turnips as directed on page 145. Drain and dry thoroughly. Heat about 2oz (50gm) butter in a frying pan with 2 teaspoons olive oil. Add turnips and sprinkle with salt, pepper and sugar (it is the sugar which helps to give the turnips a shiny glaze). Stand frying pan over a low heat and fry, turning frequently, until turnips are a warm gold. Sprinkle with very finely chopped parsley and serve straight away with meat dishes.

Pease pudding

Serves 4

| 8oz (200gm) split peas, pre-soaked overnight in plenty of cold water |
| 1 level teaspoon salt |
| 1oz (25gm) butter |
| 2 egg yolks |
| salt and pepper to taste |

1. Put peas into saucepan.
2. Cover with cold water then add salt.
3. Slowly bring to boil, lower heat and cover.
4. Simmer gently for 2 to 2½ hours, topping up with extra boiling water if necessary and stirring occasionally.
5. Remove from heat, drain and mash finely with butter.
6. Beat in egg yolks and season to taste with salt and pepper.
7. Transfer to greased heatproof dish and cook in centre of moderate oven, 350 deg F or gas 4 (180 deg C), for 30 minutes
8. Serve with boiled ham or bacon.

Salads

Once upon a time, salads added up to little more than lettuce, cucumber and tomato salad in summer, and cabbage, carrot and cole slaw in winter. Now, however, with fresh vegetables available in plenty all the year round, it is possible to make and enjoy delicious, exciting salads at any time, with texture, colour and flavour of ingredients carefully balanced.

The essential requirements for tip-top salads are as-fresh-as-possible ingredients, a chopping board, an ultra sharp vegetable knife, a grater and, for tossed salads, a salad bowl large enough to hold the ingredients in comfort. The bowl may be wood, glass or plastic, whichever you prefer. For formal salads, where ingredients should be arranged with artistic panache, a large flat plate or platter or very shallow bowl is preferable to the normal deep salad bowl. One warning about salads with French dressings: please add the dressing at the very last moment, otherwise the greenery will wilt beyond recognition and the appetising crispness will be lost. Also, do not drown the salad with dressing—use just enough to coat the ingredients thinly; too much and the salad will be dismal and soggy.

Careful washing—particularly of greenery—is, of course, essential to get rid of insects, grit and earth, but drying is equally important. If you do not have a proper salad shaker, you can dry lettuce quite successfully by putting the greenery into a colander, standing another colander on top and shaking both together up and down over the kitchen sink or in the garden. Alternatively, stand the greenery in the middle of a large, clean tea towel, gather up the ends of the towel and shake as before.

Garnishes

Finishing touches in the form of attractive garnishes do much to brighten up salads. Here are a few ideas to try.

Radish flowers
Top and tail radishes then carefully make 6 cross cuts into each, leaving one end intact. Drop into a bowl of iced water and refrigerate 1 to 2 hours or until radishes open out like flowers.

Radish concertinas
Choose longish radishes. Top and tail then cut each into several slices without actually cutting through the radish. Put into water and refrigerate as for radish flowers (see above).

Celery curls
Cut well-washed celery stalks into 2-inch lengths. 'Fringe' each by making cuts—close together—along the length of each to within ½ inch of one end. Drop into a bowl of cold water and refrigerate for an hour or two, or until celery 'fringes' curl.

Scalloped cucumber
Wash and dry an unpeeled cucumber. Run a fork from top to bottom so that it cuts into the skin and removes it. Do this all the way round. When sliced, the cucumber will have prettily serrated edges.

Cucumber hats
Cut peeled or unpeeled cucumber into very thin slices. Make a slit in each slice from outside edge. to centre. Put one cut edge over the other then twist into a cone or hat.

Cucumber twists
Cut peeled or unpeeled cucumber into very thin slices, then slit each from centre to outside edge Twist each piece in opposite directions to form an 'S' shape.

Waterlily tomatoes
Wash and dry tomatoes. With a sharp knife, make small vandyke or V-shaped cuts round the middle of each, making sure the cuts come right to the centre. Gently pull the two halves apart.

Side salads

These are usually served as an accompaniment to hot and cold main courses and consist of vegetable or vegetable and fruit combinations mixed or coated with an appropriate dressing.

Tomato salad

Serves 4

8 large tomatoes, skinned

2 heaped tablespoons chopped parsley

French or other dressing to taste (see page 161)

1. Slice tomatoes thinly and arrange over base of large plate or platter.
2. Sprinkle generously with parsley then coat with dressing.
3. Serve straight away.

Note
The tomato salad may be sprinkled with a mixture of chopped parsley and scissor-snipped chives or topped with chopped parsley and very thin onion rings.

Cucumber salad

Serves 4

1 medium cucumber

French or other dressing to taste (see page 161)

2 heaped tablespoons finely-chopped parsley

1. Peel cucumber and cut into very thin slices.
2. Put into shallow salad bowl.
3. Add dressing and toss together.
4. Sprinkle with parsley.

Summer salad medley

Serves 4 to 6

4 oz (100gm) green grapes, halved and pipped

4oz (100gm) black grapes, halved and pipped

2oz (50gm) hazelnuts

6 medium tomatoes, skinned and sliced

2 medium oranges, peeled and thinly sliced

4oz (100gm) button mushrooms, sliced

¼ cucumber, sliced

1 small onion, thinly sliced

watercress

3 lemon slices

French dressing (see page 161)

1. Arrange grapes, hazelnuts, tomatoes and oranges in lines on a serving dish.
2. Garnish with all remaining vegetables and lemon.
3. Coat with dressing and chill lightly before serving.

Summer salad medley

Tossed green salad

Serves 4

1 garlic clove

1 lettuce

French dressing (see page 161)

1. Peel garlic clove then cut in half.
2. Rub cut sides round the inside of salad bowl.
3. Wash lettuce and shake leaves dry.
4. Tear into bite-size pieces with fingers. Add dressing just before serving and toss gently with salad servers.

Note
1. Other greens, such as watercress, mustard and cress and well-washed endive may be added to the lettuce.
2. Rubbing the salad bowl with garlic may be omitted if preferred.

Watercress and orange salad

Serves 4

1 bunch watercress

2 medium oranges

1 small onion, peeled

French or other dressing to taste (see page 161)

1. Trim stalks then wash watercress under cold running water.
2. Shake dry and use to cover base of plate or platter.
3. Peel oranges and cut into thin slices. Arrange over watercress in overlapping rings.
4. Cut onion into slices then separate slices into rings.
5. Use to garnish salad.
6. Coat with dressing just before serving.

Grapefruit and green pepper salad

Serves 4

Especially good with poultry and liver.

2 medium grapefruit

1 small green pepper, washed and dried

8oz (200gm) cold cooked potatoes

1 medium onion

1 tablespoon salad oil

1 dessertspoon wine vinegar

salt and pepper to taste

1. Peel grapefruit and divide into slices by cutting out flesh in between membranes.
2. Put into salad bowl.
3. Remove fibres and seeds from pepper then cut flesh into thin strips.
4. Cut potatoes into small dice.
5. Slice onion and separate slices into rings.
6. Put pepper, potatoes and onion rings into bowl with the grapefruit.
7. Add oil, vinegar and salt and pepper to taste.
8. Toss lightly together.
9. Refrigerate about 30 minutes before serving.

Banana and raisin salad

Serves 4

4 large bananas

2oz (50gm) flaked almonds

2 large carrots, coarsely grated

2oz (50gm) seedless raisins

French dressing (see page 161)

1 medium lettuce

1 level tablespoon finely-chopped parsley

1. Peel bananas and slice into bowl.
2. Add almonds, carrots, raisins and French dressing.
3. Toss lightly but thoroughly.
4. Pile into lettuce-lined bowl and sprinkle with chopped parsley.

Tutti frutti salad

Serves 4

A French-dressed fruit salad which is very suitable for serving with poultry and game dishes.

4oz (100gm) black or green grapes

1 large orange

2 canned pineapple rings

4 medium bananas

French dressing (see page 161)

1. Peel grapes and remove pips. Put into bowl.
2. Peel orange and cut flesh into segments between membranes. Chop pineapple. Slice bananas.
3. Put orange segments, pineapple and bananas into bowl with grapes.
4. Add French dressing and toss ingredients lightly together.

Salad Flamingo

Serves 4

1 hard-boiled egg

2oz (50gm) Cheddar cheese

2 large eating apples

lemon juice

4 large bananas

2 large tomatoes, skinned and sliced

mayonnaise or salad cream to accompany (see page 99 or 161)

1. Slice hard-boiled egg.
2. Grate cheese.
3. Peel and core apples and cut into slices. Arrange on flat serving dish. Sprinkle with lemon juice.
4. Slice bananas and stand them on top of apples. Sprinkle with lemon juice.
5. Garnish alternately with egg and tomato slices then sprinkle with cheese.
6. Accompany with mayonnaise or salad cream.

In the foreground, individual lunch salad (see page 159) and salad flamingo. In the background, banana and raisin salad, and tutti frutti salad

Pepper salad

Serves 4

2 red or green peppers (or one of each)

3 celery stalks, well-washed

1 small onion

French or other dressing to taste (see page 161)

1. Wash peppers and wipe dry. Remove inside fibres and seeds and cut peppers into fine strips. Put into bowl.
2. Cut celery into thin diagonal slices. Finely grate or chop onion. Add both to bowl.
3. Toss with dressing and chill lightly before serving.

Salad Louisette

Serves 4

A charming salad, especially for poultry and fish dishes.

1 medium lettuce

6oz (150gm) white grapes

4 medium tomatoes, skinned

5 tablespoons French or other dressing to taste (see page 161)

1. Wash lettuce and shake leaves dry.
2. Tear into bite-size pieces and put into salad bowl.
3. Peel grapes. Cut in half and remove pips.
4. Cut tomatoes into thin wedges.
5. Add grapes and tomatoes with dressing to salad bowl.
6. Toss gently and serve straight away.

Beetroot salad

Serves 4

Excellent with meat, fish and poultry dishes.

2 medium beetroots, cooked

2 hard-boiled eggs

1 level tablespoon chopped watercress

5 tablespoons French or other dressing to taste (see page 161)

1. Peel beetroots and slice thinly. Arrange over base of platter.
2. Chop eggs coarsely and scatter on top of beetroot.
3. Sprinkle with watercress then coat with dressing.
4. Serve straight away.

Green bean salad

Serves 4

Appetising with meat and poultry.

1 garlic clove

12oz (300gm) cooked green beans, fresh, frozen or canned

6 tablespoons French or other dressing (see page 161)

paprika or chilli powder

1. Cut garlic clove in half and rub cut side against inside of salad bowl.
2. Drain beans thoroughly and put into bowl.
3. Toss gently with dressing then sprinkle with paprika or chilli powder.
4. Serve straight away.

Curried endive salad

Serves 4

A mild salad which partners well with poultry and white meat dishes.

2 heads of chicory

1 recipe curry dressing (see page 161)

paprika

1. Strip off outer leaves of chicory. If bruised or in any way damaged then wash heads under cold running water.
2. Cut a slice off the base of each then remove cores with a pointed knife (to prevent bitterness).
3. Peel off leaves, one by one, and put into bowl.
4. Add dressing and toss gently until all leaves are lightly coated.
5. Sprinkle with paprika and chill lightly before serving.

Russian salad

Serves 4

A traditional favourite for cold meats and poultry. Fresh or frozen vegetables give the best flavour although canned mixed ones, well-drained first, may be used to save time.

½ medium lettuce

8oz (200gm) cold cooked potatoes

8oz (200gm) cold cooked carrots

6oz (150gm) cold cooked peas

6oz (150gm) green beans, sliced

1 level tablespoon drained and chopped capers or chopped gherkins

mayonnaise or variation (see page 99)

2 hard-boiled eggs, sliced

1. Wash lettuce and shake leaves dry. Use to line 4 individual plates.
2. Dice potatoes and carrots. Put into bowl with peas, beans and capers or gherkins.
3. Toss with sufficient mayonnaise to coat thoroughly.
4. Mound on top of lettuce then garnish each with egg slices.
5. Serve straight away.

Button mushroom salad

Serves 4

8oz (200gm) button mushrooms

French or other dressing to taste (see page 161)

¼ to ½ level teaspoon dried basil

a few whole leaves of washed lettuce

1 heaped tablespoon finely-chopped parsley

1. Wash mushrooms and wipe dry.
2. Either leave whole or slice.
3. Combine with dressing to which basil has been added.
4. Toss thoroughly, transfer to lettuce-lined bowl and sprinkle with parsley.
5. Serve straight away.

Apricot, tomato and parsley salad

Serves 4

An intriguing salad for poultry and game dishes.

1 small can (8oz or 200gm) apricot halves

4 large tomatoes, skinned

1 level tablespoon finely-chopped parsley

1 level tablespoon salted Cashew nuts

3 tablespoons French or other dressing to taste (see page 161)

few lettuce leaves

1. Drain apricots and cut into quarters.
2. Cut tomatoes into wedges.
3. Put both into bowl with parsley, nuts and dressing.
4. Mix thoroughly together. Chill lightly.
5. Just before serving, arrange in serving bowl lined with lettuce.

Cole slaw

Serves 4 (generously)

1 small head white cabbage (or other variety to taste)

4 tablespoons French dressing (see page 161)

3 level tablespoons mayonnaise or variation (see page 99)

1. Wash cabbage, cut into quarters and remove hard cores. Cut the quarters into the finest possible shreds with a sharp knife.
2. Put into a large bowl.
3. Beat dressing with mayonnaise until smooth.
4. Add to cabbage and toss until all pieces are completely coated.
5. Serve straight away.

Note

1. To vary, use finely-shredded red cabbage instead of white or an equal mixture of red and white.
2. For speed, cabbage may be grated instead of shredded.
3. Any left-over slaw may be put into an air-tight container and refrigerated for up to 2 days.

Pineapple slaw

Make in exactly the same way as for cole slaw (see above) but add 4 to 6 level tablespoons finely-chopped fresh or canned pineapple to the cabbage. Use the same quantity of French dressing and mayonnaise or variation.

Carrot and raisin slaw

Make in exactly the same way as for cole slaw (see above) but add 2 large finely-grated carrots and 2 to 3 tablespoons seedless raisins to the cabbage. Increase both the French dressing and mayonnaise or variation by 1 tablespoon.

157

Potato salad

Serves 4

Yesterday's cold cooked potatoes, although adequate, do not make the best potato salad in the world. Much better are potatoes which have been freshly boiled—in their skins for preference—then peeled and diced and mixed, while still warm, with the chosen dressing.

1lb (½ kilo) cooked potatoes, lukewarm

¼ pint (125ml) mayonnaise or variation (see page 99)

salt and pepper to taste

2 level dessertspoons chopped chives

1. Cut potatoes into small dice.
2. Put into bowl and add mayonnaise or variation.
3. Mix gently with a spoon and season to taste with salt and pepper.
4. Pile into a serving dish and sprinkle with chives.
5. Serve straight away.

Note
To vary, add any of the following:
1. One or 2 level dessertspoons finely-chopped onions or spring onions.
2. One level tablespoon chopped parsley.
3. Two rashers chopped and fried bacon.

Potato salad

Main meal salads

Pork, mushroom and almond salad

Serves 4

grated peel and juice of 1 medium orange

2 teaspoons lemon juice

2 level tablespoons sultanas

¼ pint (125ml) mayonnaise or variation (see page 99)

12oz (300gm) cold pork, diced (or diced luncheon meat)

3 medium celery stalks

8oz (300gm) button mushrooms

½ a small cucumber

1oz (25gm) blanched, split and toasted almonds

1 small lettuce, washed and shaken dry

1. Combine orange peel and juice with lemon juice and sultanas. Leave to stand at room temperature for 1 hour.
2. Gradually beat in mayonnaise and continue beating until mixture is smooth.
3. Put diced pork or luncheon meat into large bowl.
4. Cut celery into thin diagonal strips. Slice mushrooms. Peel cucumber and cut into small dice. Add to bowl with almonds.
5. Toss all ingredients with the fruit and mayonnaise mixture.
6. Line salad bowl with lettuce then pile mixture on top.
7. Serve straight away.

Salad nicoise

A full flavoured Mediterranean-style salad which tastes as good as it looks.

1 round lettuce

8oz (200gm) cold cooked potatoes

1 small packet frozen green beans, cooked and drained

1 medium can (175gm) salmon or tuna

8 anchovy fillets

1 dozen black olives

2 hard-boiled eggs, shelled and quartered

4 medium tomatoes, skinned and cut into wedges

6 tablespoons French or other dressing to taste (see page 161)

1. Wash lettuce and shake leaves dry. Use to line fairly shallow salad bowl.
2. Dice potatoes and put into salad bowl over lettuce. Sprinkle with beans.
3. Drain salmon or tuna and use 2 forks to flake flesh. Arrange on top of vegetables.
4. Garnish attractively with anchovies, olives, eggs and tomatoes.
5. Pour dressing over salad and serve straight away.

Salad in bread crust

Mixed meat and vegetable salad

Serves 4

1lb (½ kilo) freshly-boiled potatoes

8oz (200gm) cooked green beans

1 level tablespoon finely-chopped onion

4oz (100gm) salami

4oz (100gm) cold roast beef, veal or chicken

2 medium celery stalks

French or other dressing to taste (see page 161)

1 large carrot, finely grated

1 large tomato, skinned and cut into 8 wedges

1. Cut potatoes into dice and put into bowl with beans and onion.
2. Coarsely chop salami and cold meat or chicken. Cut celery into thin diagonal strips.
3. Add to bowl with dressing.
4. Toss ingredients well together to mix.
5. Garnish with mounds of grated carrot and tomato wedges.
6. Serve straight away.

Individual lunch salads

Serves 4

4oz (100gm) curd cheese

2 level tablespoons finely-chopped salted peanuts

1 medium lettuce

4 large bananas

French dressing (see page 161)

fresh strawberries and watercress to garnish

1. Divide cheese into 8 portions and shape into balls. Roll in nuts.
2. Wash lettuce and shake leaves dry. Arrange on 4 individual plates.
3. Top each with 2 cheese balls.
4. Halve bananas lengthwise and stand them on plates.
5. Sprinkle with French dressing then garnish with strawberries and watercress.

Salad in bread crust

Serves 4

6oz (150gm) butter or margarine

1 large sliced loaf, 2 to 3 days old

6oz (150gm) cold cooked meat, cut into strips

1lb ($\frac{1}{2}$ kilo) tomatoes, skinned and sliced

8 cooked baby beets

8oz (200gm) broad beans, cooked

6 rounded tablespoons cooked sweet corn

1lb ($\frac{1}{2}$ kilo) new potatoes

mayonnaise (see page 99)

chopped parsley or scissor-snipped chives

French dressing (see page 161)

1. Pre-heat oven to moderate, 350 deg F or Gas 4 (180 deg C).
2. Brush tin measuring 12 inches by 8 inches with some of the butter or margarine.
3. Remove crusts from bread. Spread slices with remaining butter or margarine.
4. Line base of tin with bread and butter.
5. Cut rest of bread slices in half. Arrange round edge of tin, slightly overlapping and with corner of each half slice showing above tin.
6. Put another tin or heatproof dish inside to hold the bread in place then add a weight or large garden stone to keep it down.
7. Bake just above centre of oven for 30 minutes.
8. Remove inside tin or dish and return bread cast to oven for a further 15 to 20 minutes or until bread is golden and crisp round the edges. Leave until cold.
9. Cover base with strips of meat then arrange tomatoes over the top in 2 crosswise lines to give 4 divisions.
10. Fill 1 division with halved beets, 1 with beans, 1 with sweetcorn and the last with potatoes.
11. Coat potatoes with mayonnaise and sprinkle with parsley or chives.
12. Sprinkle rest of salad with dressing and serve straight away.

Lobster salad

Lobster salad

Serves 4

1 medium lettuce, washed, dried and shredded

2 medium lobsters

mayonnaise or variation (see page 99)

$\frac{1}{2}$ small cucumber, peeled and sliced

2 hard-boiled eggs, finely-chopped

paprika

1. Arrange lettuce over base of serving dish.
2. Remove meat from lobsters and large claws. Keep the green meat (which is the liver) and mix with the lobster meat. If there is any coral present, keep on one side for garnishing.
3. Combine lobster with sufficient mayonnaise to moisten pieces thoroughly.
4. Pile on top of lettuce.
5. Garnish with small lobster claws, slices of cucumber, mounds of chopped egg and the coral.
6. Dust lightly with paprika and serve straight away.

Note
1. Alternatively, pile lobster meat (first mixed with mayonnaise as above) into washed and dried lobster shells. Stand on a bed of shredded lettuce tossed with French or other dressing to taste. Garnish as above.
2. For simplicity, halve the lobsters. Stand them on a bed of lettuce. Garnish with slices of cucumber and watercress and serve mayonnaise separately.

Croûton cheese salad

Serves 4

1 garlic clove

3 large slices white bread

2oz (50gm) butter, margarine or bacon dripping (or mixture of fats)

salt

1 large crisp lettuce

1 small onion, grated

4oz (100gm) button mushrooms, sliced

6oz (150gm) Dutch cheese, cut into small cubes

3oz (75gm) lean ham, cut into strips

6 tablespoons French or other dressing to taste (see page 161)

1. Cut garlic clove in half and rub cut side round inside of salad bowl.
2. Cut bread into cubes and fry in the fat until crisp and golden on all sides. Drain on soft kitchen paper then sprinkle with salt.
3. Wash lettuce and dry. Shred and put into salad bowl.
4. Add onion, mushrooms, cheese, ham, fried bread and dressing.
5. Toss all ingredients thoroughly together and serve straight away.

Oriental salad

Serves 4

An interesting combination of rice, chicken, mandarins and almonds which makes a colourful and substantial main course meal.

1 medium lettuce

3 medium celery stalks

12oz (300gm) freshly-cooked long grain rice (6oz or 150gm raw)

8 to 12oz (200 to 300gm) cold cooked chicken, cut into strips

1 can mandarins, drained

2oz (50gm) flaked almonds, toasted

yogurt dressing (see opposite page)

3 level tablespoons chopped canned pimiento

1. Wash lettuce and shake leaves dry. Use to line salad bowl.
2. Chop celery finely and put into large bowl.
3. Add rice, chicken, half the drained mandarins and the almonds.
4. Add dressing and toss gently to combine.
5. Pile on top of lettuce then garnish with remaining drained mandarins and the pimiento.
6. Serve straight away.

Curried haddock and rice salad

Serves 4

12oz (300gm) smoked haddock, cooked and flaked

8oz (200gm) button mushrooms, sliced

4oz (100gm) freshly-cooked long grain rice (2oz or 50gm raw)

2 level tablespoons drained and chopped canned pineapple

1 level teaspoon curry powder

1 level dessertspoon chutney

3 tablespoons French or other dressing to taste (see opposite page)

few leaves of lettuce

2 level tablespoons desiccated coconut

4 slices of lemon

1 hard-boiled egg, sliced

1. Put fish into bowl. Add mushrooms, rice, pineapple, curry, chutney and dressing.
2. Toss thoroughly to mix.
3. Line salad bowl with lettuce and pile fish mixture on top.
4. Sprinkle with coconut then garnish with lemon and egg slices.
5. Serve straight away.

Beefy rice salad

Beefy rice salad

Serves 4

12oz (300gm) long grain rice, cooked weight

12oz (300gm) cold cooked beef, diced

¼ pint (125ml) vinegar

1 level teaspoon dry mustard

4 gherkins, finely chopped

½ level teaspoon salt

2 level teaspoons sugar

lettuce

2 hard-boiled eggs, sliced

1 onion, sliced

2 tomatoes, cut into wedges

1. Combine rice with beef.
2. Beat vinegar, mustard, gherkins, salt and sugar well together and add.
3. Toss well together and chill a minimum of 1 hour.
4. Before serving, arrange on lettuce-lined platter and garnish with eggs, onion slices and tomatoes.

Crab Louis

Serves 4

A luxurious salad which originated from the west coast of America.

1 medium lettuce

12oz (300gm) fresh, frozen or canned crabmeat

Louis sauce (see page 100)

2 hard-boiled eggs, sliced

1 level tablespoon chopped parsley or scissor-snipped chives

1. Wash lettuce and shake leaves dry.
2. Tear into bite-size pieces and put into salad bowl.
3. Flake crabmeat and arrange on top of lettuce.
4. Coat thickly with Louis sauce.
5. Garnish with egg slices then sprinkle with parsley or chives.
6. Serve straight away.

Note
To make this a more economical dish, use half crabmeat and half cooked and flaked white fish such as cod or haddock.

Salad dressings

Basic French dressing (sauce vinaigrette)

4 tablespoons olive or salad oil
$\frac{1}{4}$ to $\frac{1}{2}$ level teaspoon salt
$\frac{1}{4}$ level teaspoon caster sugar
$\frac{1}{4}$ level teaspoon dry or $\frac{1}{2}$ level teaspoon prepared mustard
shake of white pepper
2 tablespoons wine or cider vinegar (or half vinegar and half lemon juice)

1. Beat oil with salt, sugar, mustard and pepper.
2. Gradually beat in vinegar, or vinegar and lemon juice, and continue beating until mixture thickens slightly and forms an emulsion.

Note
1. All the ingredients may be put into a screw-topped jar and shaken vigorously together until they thicken as above.
2. For those with blenders, simply put all the ingredients into the goblet and blend for about 20 seconds.

Blue vein cheese dressing

An excellent dressing for green salads of all kinds.
Make as basic French dressing, but beat oil, salt, sugar, mustard and pepper into 1oz (25gm) finely-mashed blue vein cheese before adding vinegar.

Horseradish dressing

A good dressing for meat salads, and for side salads served to accompany beef grills and roasts.
Make up recipe for basic French dressing, then stir in 1 to 3 level dessertspoons grated horseradish (depending on strength preferred) right at the end.

Ravigotte dressing

This is a classic and piquant dressing which adds zest and flavour interest to all manner of tossed salads, including those containing red meat, game and fish. Make up recipe for basic French dressing. Right at the end, stir in 2 level dessertspoons finely-grated onion, 1 chopped hard-boiled egg, 1 level dessertspoon drained and chopped capers, 1 level tablespoon finely-chopped parsley and a pinch of dried tarragon.

Italian dressing

A good dressing for tossed salads which are being served to accompany Italian-style dishes.
Make up recipe for basic French dressing, then stir in 2 level tablespoons grated Parmesan cheese right at the end.

Green dressing (salsa verde)

Also Italian in origin, this is a flavourful dressing for all green and mixed salads and more robust salads containing meat and fish.
Make up recipe for basic French dressing. Right at the end, stir in 3 very finely-chopped anchovy fillets, 1 very finely-chopped garlic clove, 2 level dessertspoons drained and chopped capers and 4 level tablespoons very finely-chopped parsley.

Home-cooked salad cream

A useful and fairly economical dressing which may be used as a substitute for mayonnaise. It can be stored up to 4 days in the refrigerator and can take all sorts of additions including paprika, chopped parsley or scissor-snipped chives, grated orange or lemon peel, grated onion and even finely-chopped walnuts or Cashews.

2 level teaspoons prepared mustard
3 level dessertspoons flour
2 level dessertspoons caster sugar
$\frac{1}{2}$ to 1 level teaspoon salt
4 dessertspoons wine or cider vinegar
2 dessertspoons lemon juice
6 tablespoons cold water
1 large egg
4 tablespoons single cream
white pepper to taste
a few drops of yellow food colouring

1. Put mustard, flour, sugar and salt into a basin.
2. Gradually mix to a smooth paste with vinegar, lemon juice and water.
3. Beat egg thoroughly and add.
4. Stand basin over a saucepan of gently simmering water.
5. Whisk with a wire whisk or large fork until mixture thickens to the consistency of whipped cream.
6. Remove from heat and continue whisking until smooth.
7. Stir in cream, pepper to taste and just sufficient colouring to give dressing a golden glow.
8. Cover with a sheet of wet greaseproof paper and leave until cold.
9. Peel off paper (the skin will come away with it) and either use straight away or transfer dressing to a basin, cover with foil and leave in the refrigerator until required.

Basic yogurt dressing

A not-too-rich dressing, for all types of tossed salads, potato salad and Russian salad.

1 carton ($\frac{1}{4}$ pint or 125ml) natural yogurt
2 tablespoons single cream
1 dessertspoon fresh lemon juice
1 level teaspoon caster sugar
salt and pepper to taste

1. Put all ingredients into a bowl and beat well together.
2. Use as required.

Yogurt curry dressing

Make up basic yogurt dressing then beat in 1 to 2 level teaspoons curry powder and $\frac{1}{2}$ level teaspoon paprika.

Yogurt herb dressing

Make up basic yogurt dressing then beat in 1 level tablespoon scissor-snipped chives and 1 level tablespoon chopped parsley.

Soured cream dressing

A semi-rich and ultra smooth dressing which lends its own subtle flavour and texture to salads of meat, poultry, fish and eggs and tossed salads of all kinds.

1 carton ($\frac{1}{4}$ pint or 125ml) soured cream
3 tablespoons milk
1 tablespoon lemon juice
$\frac{1}{2}$ level teaspoon caster sugar
$\frac{1}{4}$ level teaspoon salt
pepper to taste

1. Put all ingredients into a bowl and beat well together.
2. Use as required.

Soured cream dressing with cucumber

Make up soured cream dressing then stir in 3 level tablespoons finely-chopped cucumber and a pinch of nutmeg.

Soured cream dressing with mustard

Make up soured cream dressing then stir in 1 level teaspoon prepared mustard and $\frac{1}{2}$ teaspoon Worcestershire sauce.

Puddings and desserts

A pudding can be anything you want it to be from a gala-gay and festive centrepiece to a down-to-earth family favourite. Because so many families—and mine is one of them—regard a meal as incomplete if there is no sweet to bring it to a conclusion, I have tried in this section to cater for every occasion, every season, every taste, every pocket and every age. There are recipes for steamed and baked puddings; for assorted jellies, soufflés and mousses; for Pavlovas and meringues; for open and closed pies, tarts and flans; for trifles, fools and fruit-filled shortcakes; for ice creams and ice cream desserts. Also included are a number of quicky ideas for cooks in a hurry together with some rich and fanciful concoctions to make at leisure for extra special occasions.

Gooseberry and ginger fool

Serves 4

1lb ($\frac{1}{2}$ kilo) gooseberries, topped and tailed

4 tablespoons water

4oz (100gm) granulated sugar

$\frac{1}{2}$ pint (250ml) custard, freshly made as directed on the packet

1 level teaspoon ground ginger

$\frac{1}{4}$ pint (125ml) double cream

green food colouring

pieces of crystallised ginger

1. Reserve 8 gooseberries for decoration. Cook remainder slowly with the water until very soft and pulpy.
2. Add sugar and stir until dissolved.
3. Simmer gently until most of the liquid has evaporated, stirring frequently.
4. Combine with custard then leave until cold.
5. Beat half the cream until softly stiff and fold into gooseberry mixture.
6. Tint pale green with food colouring then transfer to 4 sundae glasses.
7. Whip rest of cream until thick.
8. Spoon equal amounts on to each fool then garnish with pieces of fresh ginger and whole gooseberries.
9. Chill thoroughly before serving.

Note
If preferred, the fool may be made with apples or rhubarb instead of the gooseberries. Ginger may be omitted and the fool garnished with whipped cream and chopped nuts.

Raspberry velvet

Serves 4 to 6

1 can (1lb or $\frac{1}{2}$ kilo) raspberries

1 raspberry jelly

$1\frac{1}{2}$oz (37gm) low fat instant milk granules

3 tablespoons cold water

4 teaspoons lemon juice

$\frac{1}{4}$ pint (125ml) double cream

1. Strain raspberries and reserve syrup.
2. Put a few of the better-shaped raspberries aside for decoration then crush remainder finely.
3. Stand jelly in saucepan then add raspberry syrup made up to $\frac{1}{2}$ pint (250ml) with cold water.
4. Leave over low heat until melted.
5. Pour a little jelly into a $1\frac{1}{2}$ pint ($\frac{3}{4}$ litre) mould, first rinsed with cold water or lightly oiled, and leave until set.
6. Beat milk granules until thick with water and lemon juice.
7. Stir into cool liquid jelly with raspberry purée.
8. Lightly whip half the cream then fold into jelly mixture.
9. When smooth and evenly combined, spoon into mould on top of already-set jelly.
10. Chill until firm and set.
11. Unmould on to a plate and decorate with rest of cream—whipped until thick—and the raspberries.

Raspberry velvet, gooseberry and ginger fool decorated with cream, gooseberries and fresh ginger, and blackcurrant cheesecake (see page 164)

Blackcurrant cheesecake

Illustrated on previous page

Serves 8

1oz (25gm) butter

1 level tablespoon golden syrup

5oz (125gm) digestive biscuits, crushed

½ pint (250ml) milk

3 eggs, separated

1oz (25gm) caster sugar

½oz (12gm) gelatine

2 tablespoons water

8oz (200gm) cream cheese

finely-grated peel and juice of 1 lemon

1 can (approximately 1lb or ½ kilo) blackcurrants

2 level teaspoons arrowroot

1. Grease a 6-inch square or 7-inch round, loose-bottomed cake tin.
2. Melt butter and syrup in saucepan then stir in biscuits.
3. Press over base of cake tin and leave in a cool place to harden.
4. Very gently heat milk and egg yolks in a saucepan, stirring until thickened.
5. Add sugar and cool.
6. Dissolve gelatine in 2 tablespoons water over gentle heat.
7. Beat cheese until smooth then gradually stir in thickened milk and eggs, grated lemon peel, 3 teaspoons lemon juice and dissolved gelatine.
8. Whisk well until beginning to thicken.
9. Beat egg whites until stiff, fold into cheese mixture then pour into prepared tin. Leave to set.
9. Drain syrup from blackcurrants.
10. Blend 4 tablespoons with the arrowroot then stir over a gentle heat until mixture thickens and clears.
11. Add blackcurrants, mix well and leave to cool.
12. Remove cake from tin (but leave on base) and stand on a plate or cake board.
13. Spoon blackcurrants over the top.

Apple pie

Serves 4 to 6

2½lb (1¼ kilo) cooking apples

4 to 8oz (100 to 200gm) caster sugar (exact quantity will depend on sourness of fruit)

4 cloves (optional)

short crust, rough puff or flaky pastry (see pages 108, 110 or 111)

beaten egg for brushing

extra caster sugar

1. Pre-heat oven to hot, 425 deg F or gas 7 (200 deg C).
2. Peel and core apples. Cut into slices.
3. Fill a 2 pint (1¼ litre) lipped pie dish with alternate layers of apple slices and sugar, beginning and ending with fruit. Add cloves, if used.
4. Roll out pastry and cut into an oval approximately 1½ inches larger all the way round than the top of the dish.
5. Moisten lip of dish with water then line with a strip of pastry, cut from trimmings. Moisten strip with more water.
6. Cover with pastry lid, pressing edges well together to seal.
7. Flake up edges by cutting with the back of a knife then press into flutes.
8. Brush with beaten egg then make a small hole in the top to allow steam to escape.
9. Decorate with pastry leaves, rolled and cut from rest of trimmings, then brush with more egg.
10. Bake just above centre of oven for 15 minutes.
11. Reduce temperature to moderate, 350 deg F or gas 4 (180 deg C), and continue to bake for a further 45 minutes, covering pastry with a piece of greaseproof paper halfway through if it seems to be browning too much.
12. Remove from oven and sprinkle with caster sugar.
13. Serve hot with cream, custard or ice cream.

Apple pie

Pear and apricot pie

Serves 4 to 6

Make as for apple pie, (see previous recipe), using 2lb (1 kilo) peeled, cored and sliced cooking pears, 8oz (200gm) dried apricots (soaked overnight) and only 4oz (100gm) sugar. Add ¼ to ½ level teaspoon cinnamon instead of cloves.

Apple and rhubarb pie

Serves 4 to 6

Make as for apple pie (see this page), using 1½lb (¾ kilo) apples and 1lb (½ kilo) cut up rhubarb. A little chopped crystallised or preserved ginger may be used instead of the cloves.

Apple and blackberry pie

Serves 4 to 6

Make as for apple pie (see this page) using 2lb (1 kilo) apples and 8oz (200gm) blackberries.

Pumpkin pie

Serves 6 to 8

short crust pastry made with 6oz (150gm) flour (see page 108)

1lb (½ kilo) pumpkin (prepared weight)

2 standard eggs, beaten

4oz (100gm) caster sugar

4 tablespoons single cream

1 level teaspoon mixed spice

1 level teaspoon powdered cinnamon

¼ level teaspoon salt

1. Pre-heat oven to hot, 425 deg F or gas 7 (220 deg C).
2. Roll out pastry and use to line a buttered 8-inch pie plate. Prick lightly with a fork all over.
3. Line base and sides with aluminium foil to prevent pastry from rising as it cooks.
4. Bake towards top of oven for 15 minutes. Carefully remove foil and return pastry to oven for a further 5 to 10 minutes or until golden brown.
5. Peel pumpkin and remove inside seeds and fibres. Cut into cubes.
6. Put cubes into a colander and steam over boiling water for about 30 minutes or until very soft. Drain, put into bowl and mash very finely.
7. Add all remaining ingredients and mix thoroughly.
8. Pour into pastry case and put into centre of oven for 15 minutes.
9. Reduce temperature to moderate, 350 deg F or gas 4 (180 deg C), and continue cooking for 30 to 40 minutes or until pumpkin filling is set.
10. Serve warm with cream.

Above: pear and apricot pie. Below: apple and rhubarb pie

Apple and sultana soured cream pie decorated with walnuts

Apple and sultana soured cream pie

Serves 6 to 8

short crust pastry made with 8oz (200gm) flour (see page 108)

8oz (200gm) sultanas

¼ pint (125ml) sweet sherry

3 medium cooking apples, peeled, cored and sliced

2 standard eggs

6oz (150gm) caster sugar

1 tablespoon lemon juice

¼ pint (125ml) soured cream

1 level teaspoon mixed spice

1oz (25gm) walnuts, finely chopped

1. Pre-heat oven to moderately hot, 400 deg F or gas 6 (200 deg C).
2. Roll out pastry and use to line an 8-inch fluted flan ring on an ungreased baking tray. Reserve pastry trimmings.
3. To make filling, simmer sultanas in the sherry for 5 minutes.
4. Arrange apples over base of flan case.
5. Beat eggs and sugar well together.
6. Stir in lemon juice, soured cream, spice, sultanas and sherry.
7. Pour mixture into flan case over apples then decorate with a trellis of pastry strips, cut from rolled trimmings.
8. Sprinkle with walnuts and bake in centre of oven for 10 minutes.
9. Reduce temperature to moderate, 325 deg F or gas 3 (170 deg C), and bake a further 30 to 35 minutes.
10. Serve lukewarm.

Fruit crumble

Serves 4

1lb (½kilo) stewed fruit or 1 can fruit pie filling

6oz (150gm) plain flour

pinch of salt

3oz (75gm) butter or margarine

3oz (75gm) caster or soft brown sugar

1. Pre-heat oven to moderately hot, 375 deg F or gas 5 (190 deg C).
2. Put fruit or pie filling into a buttered heatproof dish.
3. Sift flour and salt into bowl. Rub in butter or margarine finely.
4. Add sugar and toss ingredients lightly together to mix.
5. Sprinkle thickly over fruit in dish.
6. Bake just above centre of oven for 25 to 30 minutes or until crumble is pale gold.
7. Serve hot with cream or custard.

Note

If preferred, crumble may be made with raw fruit instead of cooked. Layer 1lb (½ kilo) prepared fruit (apples, black-currants, gooseberries, rhubarb, damsons, plums) in a greased heatproof dish with 4 to 6oz (100 to 150gm) sugar, ending with fruit. Cover with crumble topping then bake in a moderate oven, 325 deg F or gas 3 (170 deg C), 45 minutes to 1 hour.

Pear and ginger tarts

Serves 8 to 9

short crust pastry made with 4oz (100gm) flour (see page 108)

4oz (100gm) granulated sugar

5 tablespoons water

3 large dessert pears

1oz (25gm) preserved ginger

½ level teaspoon finely-grated orange peel

1. Pre-heat oven to hot, 425 deg F or gas 7 (220 deg C).
2. Roll out pastry on floured surface and cut into 8 or 9 rounds with a 3-inch biscuit cutter.
3. Use to line 8 or 9 fairly deep bun tins. Prick pastry lightly all over with a fork then line each with a square of aluminium foil to prevent pastry from rising as it cooks.
4. Bake near top of oven for 7 minutes. Remove foil and return pastry to oven until golden brown and crisp. Transfer to a wire cooling rack.
5. Dissolve sugar in the water over a low heat.
6. Meanwhile, peel pears and cut into small cubes. Chop ginger.
7. Add both to sugar and water with grated orange peel.
8. Boil gently until pears are tender and liquid becomes thick and syrupy.
9. Remove from heat and spoon mixture into baked pastry cases.
10. Serve hot or cold with whipped cream or ice cream.

Traditional mince pies

Makes 12

short crust pastry made with 8oz (200gm) flour (see page 108)

12oz (300gm) mincemeat

beaten egg for brushing

icing sugar

1. Pre-heat oven to hot, 425 deg F or gas 7 (220 deg C).
2. Roll out pastry and cut into 12 rounds with a 3½-inch biscuit cutter and 12 rounds with a 2½-inch cutter.
3. Use larger rounds to line 12 fairly deep bun tins.
4. Fill with equal amounts of mincemeat then cover with remaining rounds.
5. Brush with egg then bake in centre of oven for 20 to 25 minutes or until golden brown.
6. Remove from tins and dredge with sifted icing sugar.
7. Serve hot with cream, ice cream, custard or any other suitable sweet sauce.

Mince tarts with rum butter

Makes 12

short crust pastry made with 6oz (150gm) flour (see page 108)

12oz (300gm) mincemeat

rum butter sauce (see page 104)

1. Pre-heat oven to hot, 425 deg F or gas 7 (220 deg C).
2. Roll out pastry and cut into 12 rounds with a 3½-inch fluted biscuit cutter.
3. Use to line 12 deep bun tins.
4. Put equal amounts of mincemeat into each.
5. Bake near top of oven for 20 to 25 minutes or until pastry is golden brown.
6. Transfer to a wire cooling rack.
7. When completely cold, pipe a whirl of rum butter sauce on each.

Pear and ginger tarts

Snow-peaked mincemeat flan decorated with pieces of cherry and angelica, mince pies with almond paste, mince tarts topped with a whirl of rum butter sauce, and traditional mince pies

Mince pies with almond paste

Makes 12

Make as for mince tarts with rum butter, left, but cover top of each tart with a round of almond paste (see page 217).

Snow-peaked mincemeat flan

Serves 6 to 8

short crust pastry made with 6oz (150gm) flour (see page 108)

1lb (½ kilo) mincemeat

1 egg white

2oz (50gm) caster sugar

glacé cherries

leaves cut from angelica

1. Pre-heat oven to moderately hot, 400 deg F or gas 6 (200 deg C).
2. Roll out pastry and use to line an 8-inch fluted flan ring on a baking tray.
3. Fill with mincemeat.
4. Bake near top of oven for 25 minutes. Remove from oven.
5. Beat egg white to a stiff snow. Gradually add half the sugar and continue beating until meringue is very shiny and stands in high, firm peaks. Fold in remaining sugar.
6. Pipe a border of meringue rosettes all the way round edge of flan then decorate with small pieces of cherries and angelica.
7. Return to oven for a further 5 minutes or until meringue is pale gold. Remove flan ring. Serve hot.

Danish apple flan

Serves 8

short crust pastry made with 8oz (200gm) flour (see page 108)

2lb (1 kilo) freshly stewed and sweetened apples (without too much liquid)

2oz (50gm) sultanas

1 level tablespoon cornflour

2 level tablespoons apricot jam

finely-grated peel of 1 small orange

2 to 4 teaspoons Angostura bitters

1. Pre-heat oven to moderate, 350 deg F or gas 4 (180 deg C).
2. Roll out pastry and use to line an 8-inch flan ring on an ungreased baking tray. Reserve trimmings.
3. Beat apples until smooth then stir in all remaining filling ingredients.
4. Cool then transfer to flan case.
5. Decorate with lattice design of pastry strips, cut from rolled trimmings.
6. Bake in centre of oven for 50 to 60 minutes or until golden brown.
7. Remove flan ring. Serve flan warm with cream.

Syrup tart

Serves 4 to 6

short crust pastry made with 6oz (150gm) flour (see page 108)

2 level tablespoons fresh white bread-crumbs

4 level tablespoons golden syrup

½ level teaspoon finely-grated lemon peel

2 tablespoons lemon juice

1. Pre-heat oven to moderately hot, 400 deg F or gas 6 (200 deg C).
2. Roll out pastry and use to line an 8-inch, lightly-buttered heatproof plate. Trim away surplus pastry and reserve.
3. Combine crumbs with syrup and lemon peel then stir in lemon juice.
4. Spread over pastry to within 1 inch of edges.
5. Roll out remaining pastry and cut into thin strips.
6. Arrange in trellis design over pie and press well on to edges of pastry to seal (the strips will hold better if edge of pie is first moistened with water).
7. Bake just above centre of oven for 30 to 35 minutes or until pastry is golden brown.
8. Serve with cream or custard.

Chocolate bakewell tart

Chocolate bakewell tart

Serves 6 to 8

short crust pastry made with 8oz (200gm) flour (see page 108)

3 level tablespoons apricot or raspberry jam

3oz (75gm) butter or margarine, softened

3oz (75gm) caster sugar

½ teaspoon almond essence

1 large egg

1oz (25gm) ground almonds

2oz (50gm) self-raising flour, sifted

2 level tablespoons cocoa powder, sifted

1. Pre-heat oven to moderately hot, 400 deg F or gas 6 (200 deg C).
2. Roll out pastry and use to line an 8-inch fluted flan ring on a baking tray. Reserve trimmings.
3. Spread jam over base.
4. Cream butter or margarine with sugar and essence until light and fluffy.
5. Beat in egg thoroughly.
6. Stir in almonds then gently fold in sifted dry ingredients with a metal spoon.
7. Transfer to pastry-lined flan ring and smooth top with a knife.
8. Decorate with pastry strips, rolled and cut from trimmings.
9. Bake in centre of oven for 15 minutes.
10. Lower temperature to moderate, 350 deg F or gas 4 (180 deg C), and bake a further 20 to 25 minutes or until a wooden cocktail stick, inserted into centre, comes out clean.
11. Serve hot with cream.

Almond lattice pie

Almond lattice pie

Serves 6 to 8

short crust pastry made with 8oz (200gm) flour (see page 108)

2 level tablespoons marmalade

4oz (100gm) butter, softened

4oz (100gm) caster sugar

½ teaspoon each almond and vanilla essences

2 standard eggs

4oz (100gm) ground almonds

1oz (25gm) semolina

1. Pre-heat oven to hot, 425 deg F or gas 7 (220 deg C).
2. Roll out pastry and use to line an 8-inch fluted flan ring on a baking tray. Reserve trimmings.
3. Spread base with marmalade.
4. Cream butter, sugar and essences together until light and fluffy.
5. Beat in whole eggs, one at a time.
6. Fold in almonds and semolina with a metal spoon then transfer mixture to prepared flan case.
7. Smooth top with a knife then decorate with a lattice of pastry strips, rolled and cut from trimmings.
8. Put into centre of oven then reduce temperature at once to moderately hot, 375 deg F or gas 5 (190 deg C).
9. Bake 45 to 50 minutes or until golden.
10. Remove from oven and serve hot or cold.

Hazelnut lattice pie

Serves 6 to 8

Make as for almond lattice pie, above, but spread base with raspberry jam instead of marmalade. Use 4oz (100gm) hazelnuts instead of the almonds.

Wine-baked apples

Serves 6

6oz (150gm) stoned raisins

½ bottle sweet white wine

6 cooking apples

1 level teaspoon grated lemon peel

3 level tablespoons sugar

1½oz (37gm) butter

1. Pre-heat oven to moderately hot, 375 deg F or gas 5 (190 deg C).
2. Soak raisins in the wine for 20 minutes.
3. Wash and core apples, taking care not to cut through blossom end, then peel them one-third of the way down.
4. Put into a well-buttered baking dish just large enough to hold them.
5. Fill cavities with raisins then sprinkle generously with grated lemon peel and sugar.
6. Dot with flakes of butter and slowly pour remaining wine over them.
7. Bake in centre of oven for 1 hour, or until apples are tender, occasionally basting with wine to keep them moist.

Apricots flambé

Serves 6

1 large can apricot halves

finely-grated peel of 1 medium orange

6 tablespoons brandy or dark rum

¼ pint (125ml) double cream

1 tablespoon milk

1. Put apricots with syrup from can and orange peel into a saucepan.
2. Bring just up to the boil and remove from heat.
3. Pour brandy or rum into a saucepan, warm slightly then set alight.
4. Pour immediately over the apricots.
5. Serve while still hot and accompany with the cream, whipped until just thick, with the milk.

Apricot Charlotte

Serves 6

3oz (75gm) butter

3oz (75gm) soft brown sugar

1 level teaspoon cinnamon

6oz (150gm) fresh white breadcrumbs

1 large can apricots, drained

¼ pint (125ml) syrup from can of apricots

finely-grated peel of ½ medium orange

1. Pre-heat oven to moderately hot, 375 deg F or gas 5 (190 deg C).
2. Melt butter in a saucepan. Add sugar, cinnamon and crumbs.
3. Stir over a low heat until crumbs have absorbed all the butter.
4. Fill a 1½ pint (¾ litre) buttered heatproof dish with alternate layers of crumb mixture and fruit, ending with a layer of crumbs.
5. Bake towards top of oven for 20 to 25 minutes or until top is crisp and golden.
6. Serve hot with whipped cream, and syrup warmed through with orange peel.

Above: wine-baked apples. Below: apricots flambé

Apple Charlotte

Serves 6

Make as for apricot charlotte, (see page 169), but increase sugar to 4oz (100gm) and use 1lb (½ kilo) peeled, cored and sliced cooking apples instead of the apricots. Omit syrup and orange peel. Bake in centre of moderate oven, 350 deg F or gas 4 (180 deg C), for approximately 45 minutes to 1 hour.

Crêpes Suzette

Serves 4

pouring batter (see page 105)

3oz (75gm) butter

2oz (50gm) caster sugar

finely-grated peel and juice of 1 medium orange

juice of 1 lemon

3 tablespoons cointreau or grand marnier

2 tablespoons brandy

1. Brush a large frying pan with melted white cooking fat and heat until hot.
2. Pour in sufficient batter to cover base thinly.
3. Cook until golden brown, turn pancake over and cook second side until mottled with brown.
4. Repeat, using rest of pancake batter (8 pancakes).
5. Fold each pancake in half then in half again.
6. Melt butter in frying pan. Add all remaining ingredients except brandy. Bring just up to the boil and lower heat.
7. Add pancakes and heat through gently, turning twice.
8. Warm brandy in a small saucepan.
9. Pour over pancakes and set alight.
10. Serve as soon as the flames have subsided.

Pancakes with lemon and sugar

Serves 4

Make pancakes as directed in recipe for Crêpes Suzette (see this page), but do not fold. Sprinkle with lemon juice and sugar, roll up and serve straight away.

Banana pancakes

Serves 4

Make pancakes as directed in recipe for Crêpes Suzette (see this page), but do not fold. Combine 1oz (25gm) caster sugar with 1 level teaspoon cinnamon. Slice 3 or 4 medium bananas, sprinkle with lemon juice then toss in sugar and cinnamon mixture. Put equal amounts on to pancakes, roll up and serve straight away.

Locksmith's apprentices

Banana fritters

Serves 4 to 6

deep oil for frying

1lb (½ kilo) bananas

sweet fritter batter (see page 105)

icing sugar

1. Heat oil until a cube of bread, dropped into it, turns golden brown in 1 minute and floats to the top.
2. Cut each banana into 3 pieces.
3. Coat with batter then fry, a few at a time, until crisp and golden.
4. Drain thoroughly on soft kitchen paper then dust heavily with sifted icing sugar.
5. Serve straight away.

Locksmith's apprentices

Makes 12

12 large prunes, soaked overnight

12 blanched almonds

deep oil for frying

sweet fritter batter (see page 105)

2oz (50gm) caster sugar

1oz (25gm) grated chocolate

1. Drain prunes. Make a slit in each, remove stones then insert almonds into cavities.
2. Heat oil until a cube of bread, dropped into it, turns golden brown in 1 minute and floats to the top.
3. Coat prunes with batter then fry, a few at a time, until crisp and golden.
4. Drain then dust heavily with caster sugar.
5. Sprinkle chocolate over the top of each and serve straight away.

170

Banana toad

Serves 4

4 tablespoons melted butter

4 large or 6 medium bananas

2 level tablespoons soft brown sugar

pancake batter (see page 105)

cinnamon or mixed spice

1. Pre-heat oven to hot, 425 deg F or gas 7 (220 deg C).
2. Pour butter into a 9-inch square tin or heatproof dish.
3. Put into oven and heat until hot.
4. Slice bananas lengthwise then add to hot butter in tin or dish.
5. Sprinkle with sugar then pour in batter.
6. Bake near top of oven for 20 minutes.
7. Reduce temperature to moderately hot, 400 deg F or gas 6 (200 deg C), and bake a further 20 to 30 minutes or until batter is well-risen and golden brown.
8. Serve with jam sauce (see page 104).

Apple toad

Serves 4

Make as for banana toad, above, using 1lb (½ kilo) peeled, cored and thickly-sliced apples instead of bananas. Increase sugar to 4oz (100gm) and use either caster or soft brown.

Rhubarb toad

Serves 4

Make as for banana toad, above, using 1lb (½ kilo) cut up rhubarb instead of bananas. Increase sugar to 4 to 6oz (100 to 150gm) and use either caster or soft brown. Sprinkle with ground ginger instead of cinnamon or spice.

Banana toad with jam sauce

Lemon puddings garnished with chopped lemon peel

Steamed date pudding

Serves 4

6oz (150gm) self-raising flour

pinch of salt

3oz (75gm) margarine, cooking fat or lard

3oz (75gm) soft brown sugar

3oz (75gm) stoned dates, finely chopped

1 standard egg, beaten

5 to 6 tablespoons cold milk to mix

1. Sift flour and salt into bowl.
2. Rub in fat finely then add sugar and dates.
3. Mix to a fairly soft consistency with egg and milk, stirring briskly without beating.
4. Transfer to well-greased 2 pint (1¼ litre) pudding basin and cover with double thickness of greased greaseproof paper or aluminium foil.
5. Steam steadily for 1½ to 2 hours or until pudding is well-risen and firm.
6. Turn out on to a warm dish and serve with custard.

Steamed chocolate raisin pudding

Serves 4

Make as for steamed date pudding, above, but sift 5oz (125gm) self-raising flour with ½oz (12gm) each, cornflour and cocoa powder. Add 2oz (50gm) chopped seedless raisins instead of dates.

Baked jam or syrup pudding

Serves 4

Make as for steamed date pudding (see this page), using caster sugar instead of brown. Omit fruit and add 1 level teaspoon vanilla essence with the egg and milk. Put 2 level tablespoons jam or golden syrup into a 2 pint (1¼ litre) pie dish. Add pudding mixture, smoothing top with a knife. Bake just above centre of moderately hot oven, 350 deg F or gas 4 (180 deg C), for 1 to 1¼ hours or until a wooden cocktail stick, inserted into centre, comes out clean.

Lemon puddings

Serves 4

2oz (50gm) self-raising flour

2oz (50gm) fresh white breadcrumbs

2oz (50gm) finely-shredded suet

2oz (50gm) caster sugar

grated peel and juice of 1 lemon

1 standard egg, beaten

1. Sift flour into bowl. Add breadcrumbs, suet and sugar.
2. Add lemon peel (reserving a little for decoration), juice and egg. Stir briskly.
3. Transfer mixture to 4 individual (¼ pint or 125ml) plastic or foil pudding basins.
4. Cover securely with greased foil or double thickness of greased greaseproof paper and steam steadily for 1 to 1¼ hours.
5. Turn out of basins, garnish with a little chopped lemon peel. Serve with custard.

Sultana layer pudding served with cream

Rich Christmas pudding

Makes approximately 3 medium-sized puddings

6oz (150gm) plain flour

2 level teaspoons mixed spice

1 level teaspoon each cinnamon, nutmeg and ginger

1 level teaspoon salt

12oz (300gm) fresh white breadcrumbs

12oz (300gm) finely-shredded suet

12oz (300gm) soft brown sugar

1lb (½ kilo) seedless raisins

1lb (½ kilo) sultanas

1lb (½ kilo) currants

8oz (200gm) stoned dates, chopped

8oz (200gm) mixed chopped peel

4oz (100gm) walnuts or blanched almonds, chopped

1 large carrot, peeled and grated

1 large cooking apple, peeled and grated

finely-grated peel of 1 large orange

6 large eggs, beaten

4 level tablespoons black treacle

¼ pint (125ml) stout

1. Sift flour, spices and salt into large bowl or small clean bucket.
2. Aad crumbs, suet, sugar, raisins, sultanas, currants, dates, mixed peel, nuts, carrot, apple and fresh orange peel. Toss all ingredients lightly together.
3. Stir in eggs, treacle and stout.
4. Cover and leave to stand overnight.
5. Stir thoroughly to mix then transfer to three 3 pint (1¾ litre) well-greased pudding basins.
6. Cover securely with double thickness of greased greaseproof paper or aluminium foil and steam steadily for 8 hours, topping up saucepan with extra boiling water every hour, to ensure that level of water remains fairly constant.
7. Cool puddings to lukewarm then carefully turn out of basins.
8. Wrap in clean foil when completely cold then store in a cool dry place until required.
9. Before serving, transfer to greased basins and steam each pudding for 3 hours. Garnish with holly, and serve with rum butter sauce (see page 104).

Note

If preferred, make 2 smaller puddings by halving all the ingredients and steaming mixture in two 2 pint (1¾ litre) basins.

Steamed suet pudding

Serves 6

6oz (150gm) self-raising flour

pinch of salt

2oz (50gm) fresh white breadcrumbs

4oz (100gm) finely-shredded suet

3oz (75gm) caster sugar

1 standard egg, beaten

7 to 8 tablespoons milk to mix

1. Sift flour and salt into a bowl.
2. Add crumbs, suet and sugar then mix to a fairly soft consistency with the egg and milk, stirring briskly without beating.
3. Transfer to a 2 pint (1¼ litre) pudding basin and cover with double thickness of greased greaseproof paper or aluminium foil.
4. Steam steadily for 2½ to 3 hours, topping up saucepan with extra boiling water as and when necessary.
5. Turn out on to a warm dish and serve with any suitable sweet sauce.

Fruit pudding

Serves 6

Make as for steamed suet pudding, above, sifting 1 level teaspoon mixed spice with the flour and salt, and adding 4oz (100gm) mixed dried fruit with the sugar.

Sultana layer pudding

Serves 4

8oz (200gm) sultanas

2 tablespoons sweet sherry

3oz (75gm) finely-shredded suet

2oz (50gm) self-raising flour

3oz (75gm) fresh white breadcrumbs

3oz (75gm) caster sugar

4 to 5 tablespoons cold water to mix

1. Soak sultanas in the sherry for 3 to 4 hours.
2. Put suet, flour, crumbs and sugar into bowl.
3. Mix to a dropping consistency with the cold water, stirring briskly without beating.
4. Put a layer of suet mixture into base of well-greased 2 pint (1¼ litre) pudding basin.
5. Add a layer of sultanas, another layer of suet mixture, then the rest of the fruit and finally the remaining suet mixture.
6. Cover with double thickness of greased foil or greased greaseproof paper and steam steadily for 3½ hours, topping up saucepan with more boiling water as and when necessary.
7. Turn out on to a warm dish and serve with cream or custard.

Light Christmas pudding

Makes two 2lb (1 kilo) puddings

8oz (200gm) self-raising flour
1 level teaspoon mixed spice
8oz (200gm) suet
8oz (200gm) fresh white breadcrumbs
8oz (200gm) seedless raisins
8oz (200gm) sultanas
8oz (200gm) currants
4oz (100gm) mixed chopped peel
4oz (100gm) soft brown sugar
8oz (200gm) golden syrup
grated peel and juice of 1 orange and 1 lemon
3 standard eggs, beaten
½ wine glass white rum
milk to mix if necessary
little icing sugar

1. Sift flour and spice into bowl.
2. Add suet, crumbs, dried fruit, peel and sugar.
3. Mix thoroughly with syrup, grated peel and juice of orange and lemon, beaten eggs and rum.
4. Stir in a little milk if mixture is very stiff then transfer to two 2lb (1 kilo) well-greased basins.
5. Cover securely with double thickness of greased greaseproof paper or aluminium foil and steam steadily for 6 hours, topping up saucepan with extra boiling water as and when necessary.
6. Leave until lukewarm then turn out of basins.
7. Wrap in clean foil when cold and store in a cool dry place until required.
8. Before serving, transfer to greased basins, cover and steam for 2 hours.
9. Dust lightly with icing sugar, and garnish with holly.

Steamed sponge pudding

Serves 4

4oz (100gm) self-raising flour
pinch of salt
4oz (100gm) butter or margarine, softened
4oz (100gm) caster sugar
1 teaspoon vanilla essence
2 standard eggs

1. Sift together flour and salt.
2. Cream butter or margarine with sugar and essence until light and fluffy.
3. Beat in eggs, one at a time, adding a tablespoon of sifted flour with each.
4. Fold in rest of flour then transfer mixture to a 1½ pint (¾ litre) greased pudding basin.
5. Cover with double thickness of greased greaseproof paper or aluminium foil and steam steadily for 1½ hours or until well-risen and firm.
6. Turn out on to a warm dish and accompany with any suitable sweet sauce.

Above: rich Christmas pudding with rum butter sauce
Below: light Christmas pudding dusted with icing sugar

173

Lemon or orange pudding

Serves 4

Make as for steamed sponge pudding (see page 173), adding 1 level teaspoon orange or lemon peel instead of the vanilla essence.

Steamed syrup ginger sponge

Serves 4

Make as for steamed sponge pudding (see page 173), sifting flour and salt with 2 to 3 teaspoons ground ginger. After beating in eggs, add ½oz (12gm) finely-chopped preserved ginger. Put 2 level tablespoons golden syrup into basin before adding pudding mixture.

Baked sponge puddings

Serves 4

If preferred, any of the 3 previous puddings may be transferred to a well-greased 1½ pint (¾ litre) pie dish and baked in centre of moderate oven, 350 deg F or gas 4 (180 deg C), for ¾ to 1 hour or until a wooden cocktail stick, inserted into centre, comes out clean.

Eve's pudding

Serves 4 to 6

Peel, core and thinly slice 1lb (½ kilo) cooking apples. Layer into a 2½ pint (approximately 1½ litre) greased heatproof dish (more shallow than deep) with 4oz (100gm) caster sugar. Make up steamed sponge pudding mixture (see page 173) and put into dish over apples. Smooth top evenly with a knife then bake in centre of moderate oven, 325 deg F or gas 3 (170 deg C), for 1½ to 1¾ hours or until a wooden cocktail stick, inserted into centre, comes out clean. Serve from the dish and accompany with cream or custard.

Zabaglione

Serves 4

4 egg yolks

2oz (50gm) icing sugar, sifted

4 tablespoons Marsala

1. Put egg yolks and sugar into a basin over saucepan of hot water.
2. Beat until thick.
3. Add Marsala and continue beating until mixture is almost twice its original volume and very light in texture.
4. Transfer to 4 warm glasses and accompany with sponge fingers.
5. Serve straight away.

174

Autumn fruit sponge

Serves 8

4oz (100gm) butter or margarine, softened

4oz (100gm) caster sugar

½ teaspoon almond essence

2 standard eggs

4oz (100gm) self-raising flour, sifted

8 canned apricot halves

about 1 dozen large prunes, soaked for a few hours in very hot water

2 tablespoons syrup from can of apricots

little caster sugar to serve

1. Pre-heat oven to moderate, 325 deg F or gas 3 (170 deg C).
2. Well-grease an 8-inch loose-bottomed round cake tin.
3. Cream butter or margarine, sugar and essence together until light and fluffy then beat in eggs, one at a time, adding a tablespoon of flour with each.
4. Gently fold in rest of flour with a large metal spoon.
5. Transfer to prepared tin then cover top with apricot halves, cut sides down.
6. Stone prunes and arrange in between apricots. Brush fruit with apricot syrup.
7. Bake in centre of oven for 45 minutes to 1 hour or until a wooden cocktail stick, inserted into centre, comes out clean.
8. Carefully remove from tin. Serve hot, dusted with caster sugar, and accompanied with cream or custard.

Winter pudding

Serves 4

5oz (125gm) butter

2oz (50gm) soft brown sugar

1 dozen glacé cherries

12 dried apricots, soaked overnight then drained

2oz (50gm) angelica, chopped

4oz (100gm) cooked prunes, stoned

3oz (75gm) caster sugar

2 standard eggs

1oz (25gm) ground almonds

3oz (75gm) self-raising flour

1. Pre-heat oven to moderate, 325 deg F or gas 3 (170 deg C).
2. Well butter a 2 pint (1¼ litre) ovenproof dish.
3. Melt 2oz (50gm) butter and pour into dish. Sprinkle with sugar then cover with 6 halved cherries, half the apricots, half the angelica and half the prunes.
4. Chop remaining fruit fairly finely.
5. Cream rest of butter with sugar until light and fluffy.
6. Beat in eggs then stir in chopped fruit with almonds.
7. Fold in flour lightly then transfer mixture to prepared dish.
8. Bake in centre of oven for 1¼ to 1½ hours or until a wooden cocktail stick, inserted into centre, comes out clean.
9. Turn out on to a warm plate and serve hot with cream or custard.

Autumn fruit sponge

Winter pudding

Mock suet strudel

Serves 4 to 6

6oz (150gm) self-raising flour
3oz (75gm) finely-shredded suet
3 standard eggs
2oz (50gm) butter
2oz (50gm) plus 1 level tablespoon caster sugar
2oz (50gm) cake crumbs
1 level teaspoon cinnamon
1 level teaspoon finely-grated lemon peel
4oz (100gm) mixed dried fruit
1 egg white

1. Pre-heat oven to moderately hot, 375 deg F or gas 5 (190 deg C).
2. Sift flour into bowl. Add suet then mix to a stiff dough with 2 eggs.
3. Knead lightly until smooth then roll into a rectangle measuring 8 inches by 10 inches. Moisten edges with water.
4. To make filling, cream butter and 2oz (50gm) sugar well together.
5. Beat in remaining egg then stir in cake crumbs, cinnamon, lemon peel and dried fruit.
6. Spread over pastry to within 1 inch of edges then roll up like a Swiss roll, starting from one of the longer sides.
7. Press edges and joins well together to seal then place in buttered baking dish. Brush with egg white then sprinkle with remaining sugar.
8. Cover with foil and bake in centre of oven for 35 to 40 minutes.
9. Uncover and return to oven for a further 5 to 10 minutes or until golden brown.
10. Serve hot with custard.

Caramel queen pudding

Pineapple upside-down pudding

Serves 6

6oz (150gm) butter or margarine, softened
4oz (100gm) soft brown sugar
1 small can pineapple slices
2 glacé cherries, halved
4oz (100gm) self-raising flour
½ level teaspoon cinnamon
4oz (100gm) caster sugar
2 standard eggs

1. Pre-heat oven to moderate, 350 deg F cr gas 4 (180 deg C).
2. Well grease a 7-inch round cake tin.
3. Melt 2oz (50gm) butter and use to cover base of tin then sprinkle brown sugar on top.
4. Drain pineapple and arrange on top of butter and sugar mixture.
5. Put half a cherry, cut side uppermost, into centre of each slice of pineapple.
6. Sift together flour and cinnamon.
7. Cream remaining butter or margarine and caster sugar together until light and fluffy then beat in eggs, one at a time, adding a tablespoon of flour mixture with each.
8. Fold in rest of flour with a large metal spoon then transfer to prepared tin.
9. Bake in centre of oven for approximately 45 minutes or until a wooden cocktail stick, inserted into centre, comes out clean.
10. Turn out on to a warm platter and serve hot with cream or custard.

Caramel queen pudding

Serves 4 to 6

3oz (75gm) golden syrup
½oz (12gm) butter
½ pint (250ml) milk
2oz (50gm) fresh white breadcrumbs
2 standard eggs, separated
½ teaspoon vanilla essence
2oz (50gm) caster sugar

1. Pre-heat oven to moderate, 325 deg F or gas 3 (170 deg C).
2. Put syrup into saucepan with butter.
3. Cook until a deep golden colour.
4. Add milk then slowly bring to boil, stirring continuously.
5. Stir in breadcrumbs then leave mixture to cool slightly.
6. Beat in egg yolks and essence then transfer to a 1 pint (approximately ½ litre) buttered heatproof dish.
7. Bake in centre of oven for 30 minutes. Remove from oven.
8. Beat egg whites to a stiff snow. Gradually add half the sugar and continue beating until meringue is shiny and stands in high, firm peaks. Gently fold in rest of sugar.
9. Pile in little heaps on top of pudding then return to oven for a further 15 to 20 minutes or until meringue is lightly flecked with gold.
10. Serve hot with single cream.

Crunchy grape meringue flan

Crunchy grape meringue flan

Serves 6 to 8

2oz (50gm) butter

3oz (75gm) soft brown sugar

3oz (75gm) Demerara sugar

8 level tablespoons golden syrup

8oz (200gm) bran buds

¼ pint (125ml) double cream, whipped until thick

8oz (200gm) green grapes, halved and pipped

2oz (50gm) black grapes, halved and pipped

10 small meringues

2 level tablespoons apricot jam for glazing

1. Place the butter, sugars and syrup in a saucepan.
2. Dissolve slowly over low heat.
3. Simmer 2 to 3 minutes then add to bran buds. Stir well to mix.
4. Press over base and sides of an 8-inch fluted flan ring on an oiled baking tray.
5. Leave in a cool place until firm then spread cream over base.
6. Arrange meringues round edge of flan then place green grapes in the centre.
7. Stand black grapes in between meringues.
8. Brush grapes with hot apricot jam and leave to cool.

Pear and blackberry tartlets

Serves 8

short crust pastry made with 4oz (100gm) flour (see page 108)

4 dessert pears

lemon juice

4oz (100gm) fresh blackberries

redcurrant jelly

2oz (50gm) ground almonds

4oz (100gm) icing sugar, sifted

½ teaspoon almond essence

1 egg, beaten

1. Pre-heat oven to hot, 425 deg F or gas 7 (220 deg C).
2. Roll out pastry and cut into approximately 8 rounds with a 3-inch biscuit cutter.
3. Use to line 8 fairly deep bun tins. Prick lightly all over then line each with a piece of foil to prevent pastry from rising as it cooks.
4. Bake near top of oven for 7 minutes. Remove foil then return tartlets to the oven until golden brown.
5. Remove from tins and cool on a wire rack.
6. Peel pears, cut into quarters and remove cores. Sprinkle with lemon juice.
7. Fill tartlet cases with pear quarters and blackberries then coat heavily with warmed redcurrant jelly.
8. To make decoration, combine almonds and sugar then mix to a firm but pliable paste with essence and beaten egg.
9. Roll out on sugared surface then cut into 8 leaves with a knife.
10. Mark in veins then put a leaf on to each tartlet.

Mixed fruit sponge flan

Serves 8

2 standard eggs

2oz (50gm) caster sugar

2oz (50gm) plain flour, sifted

1 tablespoon warm water

2 tablespoons lemon juice

3 tablespoons clear honey

½ pint (250ml) water

3 eating apples

3 dessert pears

½ a lemon jelly

1oz (25gm) crystallised ginger, chopped

glacé cherries

1. Pre-heat oven to hot, 450 deg F or gas 8 (230 deg C).
2. Well-grease and flour a 9-inch sponge flan tin.
3. Put eggs and sugar into a bowl over saucepan of hot water.
4. Beat until mixture is very thick, the consistency of whipped cream and at least twice its original volume.
5. Gently fold in flour alternately with warm water.
6. Transfer to prepared tin and bake in centre of oven for approximately 9 minutes or until well-risen and golden.
7. Turn out on to wire cooling rack covered with a clean, folded tea-towel. Leave until cold.
8. Put lemon juice, honey and water into saucepan and bring to boil.
9. Peel, core and thickly slice apples and pears. Poach in the honey syrup until tender but not broken. Drain the fruit.
10. Stand flan on serving plate and sprinkle with a little honey syrup.
11. Fill with fruit slices.
12. Make up jelly to ½ pint (250ml) with rest of honey syrup.
13. Pour into a saucepan and place over a low heat until dissolved. Leave until cold and just beginning to thicken and set.
14. Sprinkle ginger over fruit then arrange halved or quartered glacé cherries on top.
15. Carefully pour over the half-set jelly and leave until firm.
16. If liked, accompany with cream.

Pear and blackberry tartlets

Almond pear flan

Serves 6 to 8

6oz (150gm) plain flour

2oz (50gm) ground almonds

pinch of salt

3oz (75gm) butter

3 level dessertspoons caster sugar

1 standard egg, beaten

1 to 2 dessertspoons cold water

1 can (approximately 1lb or ½ kilo) pear halves

1 can (approximately 13oz or 325gm) crushed pineapple

1 level tablespoon arrowroot

¼ teaspoon almond essence

a little whipped cream

toasted almonds

1. Pre-heat oven to moderately hot, 400 deg F or gas 6 (200 deg C).
2. Sift flour, ground almonds and salt into bowl.
3. Rub in butter finely.
4. Stir in sugar then mix to a stiff paste with egg and water. Knead lightly.
5. Roll out on floured surface and use to line an 8-inch fluted flan ring on an ungreased baking tray.
6. Prick lightly with a fork then line with aluminium foil to prevent pastry from rising as it cooks.
7. Bake towards top of oven for 15 minutes. Remove flan ring and foil then return flan to oven until pastry is cooked through— about 10 to 15 minutes.
8. Remove from oven and leave to cool on wire rack.
9. Drain syrup from cans of pears and pineapple and reserve ½ pint (250ml).
10. Blend arrowroot to smooth paste with some of the measured syrup then stir in remainder. Add almond essence.
11. Transfer to saucepan and cook, stirring, till the glaze is smooth and coats the back of a spoon.
12. Arrange pears and pineapple in flan case then coat with arrowroot glaze.
13. Just before serving, decorate with piped whipped cream and toasted almonds.

Above: mixed fruit sponge flan. Below: almond pear flan

Semolina pudding

Serves 4

1 pint (approximately ½ litre) milk

2oz (50gm) semolina

1oz (25gm) caster sugar

½oz (12gm) butter

½ teaspoon vanilla essence (optional)

1. Pour milk into saucepan.
2. Add semolina and cook, stirring continuously, until pudding comes to the boil and thickens.
3. Simmer 5 minutes.
4. Remove from heat and beat in all remaining ingredients.
5. Transfer to 4 warm dishes and serve straight away.

Continental vanilla pudding with fruit

Serves 4

Make as for semolina pudding (see page 177). Transfer mixture to 4 dishes and chill. Before serving, top with canned raspberries, strawberries or blackberries.

Rice pudding

Serves 4

2oz (50gm) round grain pudding rice

1oz (25gm) caster sugar

1 pint (approximately ½ litre) milk

1 long strip of lemon peel

grated nutmeg

a little butter or margarine

1. Pre-heat oven to cool, 300 deg F or gas 2 (150 deg C).
2. Put rice into buttered 1½ pint (¾ litre) pie dish.
3. Add sugar then pour in milk.
4. Stir thoroughly to mix then add strip of lemon peel.
5. Sprinkle top with grated nutmeg then add flakes of butter or margarine.
6. Bake in centre of oven for 2 to 2½ hours, stirring in skin 2 or 3 times during the first hour of cooking.

Hot vanilla soufflé

Serves 4

2oz (50gm) butter or margarine

2oz (50gm) flour

½ pint (250ml) warm milk

2 level tablespoons caster sugar

1 teaspoon vanilla essence

3 large eggs, separated, plus 1 extra white

1. Pre-heat oven to moderately hot, 375 deg F or gas 5 (190 deg C).
2. Well-butter a 2 to 2½ pint (1¼ to 1½ litre) straight-sided soufflé dish.
3. Melt butter or margarine in a saucepan. Stir in flour and add milk. Cook, stirring, until mixture thickens sufficiently to form a ball in the centre of the pan, leaving sides clean.
4. Remove from heat and cool slightly, then beat in sugar, essence and egg yolks.
5. Beat egg whites to a stiff snow and gently fold into egg yolk mixture with a large metal spoon.
6. When evenly combined, pour into soufflé dish.
7. Cook in centre of oven for 45 minutes and serve straight away with cream.

Chocolate or coffee soufflé

Serves 4

Make as for vanilla soufflé, above, dissolving 2oz (50gm) plain chocolate or 3 level teaspoons instant coffee in the milk and omitting vanilla essence.

Hot lemon or orange soufflé

Serves 4

Make as for vanilla soufflé (see this page), omitting vanilla and adding 2 level teaspoons grated lemon or orange peel instead.

Bread and butter pudding

Serves 4 to 6

6 thin slices white bread, with crusts removed

2oz (50gm) butter

2oz (50gm) currants

2oz (50gm) caster sugar

3 standard eggs

¾ pint (375ml) milk

1. Pre-heat oven to moderate, 325 or gas 3 (170 deg C).
2. Butter bread evenly then cut each slice into 4 squares.
3. Arrange half the squares in a buttered 2 pint (1¼ litre) heatproof dish.
4. Sprinkle with all the currants and half the sugar.
5. Cover with remaining bread squares, buttered sides uppermost, then sprinkle with remaining sugar.
6. Beat eggs and milk well together then strain into dish over bread.
7. Leave to stand for 30 minutes then bake in centre of oven for ¾ to 1 hour or until the top of the pudding is crisp and golden.
8. Serve hot.

Coffee ice cream

Serves 4 to 6

2 standard eggs, separated

2oz (50gm) icing sugar, sifted

2 tablespoons liquid coffee essence

¼ pint (125ml) double cream

single cream for serving (optional)

1. Set refrigerator control to coldest setting at least 1 hour before making ice cream.
2. Wash and dry 2 ice cube trays or a 1½ pint (¾ litre) shallow tin.
3. Whisk egg whites to a stiff snow then gradually whisk in sifted icing sugar.
4. Beat egg yolks and coffee essence well together then gently fold into egg whites.
5. Beat double cream until thick then fold into coffee mixture.
6. Transfer to ice cube trays or shallow tin and freeze in freezing compartment of refrigerator until mixture is firm.
7. To serve, scoop into dishes and, if liked, pour single cream over the top of each.
8. Accompany with wafers.

Note

1. Unlike most ice creams, this one requires no beating—to break up ice crystals—halfway through freezing.
2. Remember to return refrigerator control back to normal setting after ice cream is made.

Vanilla ice cream

Serves 4 to 6

Make as for coffee ice cream, above, increasing icing sugar by ½oz (12gm) and substituting 2 teaspoons vanilla essence for the coffee essence.

Blackcurrant ice cream

Serves 4 to 6

Make as for coffee ice cream, above, substituting 2 tablespoons blackcurrant syrup for the coffee essence.

Dishes of coffee ice cream served with wafers and single cream

Mandarin baked Alaska

Custard ice cream

Serves 6

$\frac{1}{4}$ pint (125ml) single cream

2 large eggs, beaten

2oz (50gm) icing sugar, sifted

2 teaspoons vanilla essence

$\frac{1}{4}$ pint (125ml) double cream

1. Set refrigerator control to coldest setting at least 1 hour before making ice cream.
2. Put single cream, eggs and icing sugar into the top of a double saucepan or into a basin over a saucepan of gently simmering water.
3. Cook, stirring continuously, until custard thickens sufficiently to coat the back of a spoon but do not allow it to boil.
4. Remove from heat and leave until completely cold. Stir in essence.
5. Beat double cream until softly stiff then fold custard into it.
6. Transfer to 1 or 2 empty ice cube trays.
7. Freeze until ice cream has frozen $\frac{1}{2}$ inch round sides of trays.
8. Tip into bowl, break up with a fork then beat gently until smooth.
9. Return to ice cube trays and freeze until firm.

Chocolate ice cream

Serves 6

Make as for custard ice cream (see previous recipe), adding 2oz (50gm) plain chocolate, melted, to the hot custard.

Fruit cream ice

Serves 6 to 8

$\frac{1}{2}$ pint (250ml) fresh fruit purée made from strawberries or raspberries

4oz (100gm) icing sugar, sifted

$\frac{1}{2}$ pint (250ml) double cream

1. Set refrigerator control to coldest setting at least 1 hour before making ice cream.
2. Combine purée and icing sugar well together.
3. Beat cream until thick then gently fold in fruit purée.
4. Transfer to 2 empty ice cube trays and freeze until ice cream has frozen about $\frac{1}{2}$ inch round sides of trays.
5. Tip into a well-chilled bowl, break up with a fork then beat gently until smooth.
6. Return to trays and chill until firm.

Mandarin baked Alaska

Serves 6

a 7-inch sponge flan case

1 tin mandarin oranges

2 tablespoons curaçao, grand marnier or cointreau

3 egg whites

6oz (150gm) caster sugar

1 family block raspberry ripple ice cream

Maraschino cherry to decorate

1. Pre-heat oven to hot, 450 deg F or gas 8 (230 deg C).
2. Place sponge flan case on an ovenproof plate.
3. Arrange drained mandarin oranges round the edge and spoon a little of the syrup and liqueur over sponge.
4. Leave to stand 20 minutes.
5. Beat egg whites to a stiff snow.
6. Add half the sugar and continue beating until meringue is very stiff and shiny.
7. Fold in rest of sugar with a large metal spoon.
8. Stand ice cream in centre of flan case.
9. Spread completely with the meringue, making sure there are no gaps anywhere.
10. Flash bake near top of oven for 2 minutes.
11. Top with a cherry and serve.

179

Ice cream sponge

Serves 6

1 sponge sandwich (see page 215)

1 family block vanilla ice cream

4 tablespoons chocolate sauce (see page 104)

2oz (50gm) walnuts, chopped

1. Stand one half of the sponge cake on a serving dish.
2. Top with scoops or tablespoons of ice cream.
3. Cover with second half of cake.
4. Drizzle chocolate sauce over the top then sprinkle with walnuts.
5. Serve straight away.

Ice cream with butterscotch sauce

Serves 6

1 small can evaporated milk

4oz (100gm) soft brown sugar

1 teaspoon vanilla essence

2oz (50gm) butter

1 family block vanilla ice cream

1oz (25gm) walnuts, finely chopped

1. To make sauce, put evaporated milk, sugar, vanilla essence and butter into pan.
2. Heat gently, stirring all the time, until sugar dissolves and butter melts.
3. Bring to boil and boil steadily for 10 minutes or until sauce is fairly thick, stirring occasionally.
4. Divide ice cream equally among 4 sundae glasses.
5. Coat with hot butterscotch sauce and sprinkle with walnuts.
6. Serve straight away.

Note

Left-over sauce may be kept in the refrigerator and heated through gently before serving.

Butterscotch banana split sundaes

Serves 4

Make butterscotch sauce as directed in previous recipe. Split 4 bananas lengthwise then place on 4 individual plates. Sandwich together with tablespoons of vanilla or coffee ice cream and coat with butterscotch sauce. Top with softly-whipped cream and sprinkle with chopped walnuts and chopped glacé cherries. Serve straight away.

Coupe rouge

Coupe rouge

Serves 4

1 family block vanilla ice cream

4oz (100gm) small strawberries

4oz (100gm) raspberries

4oz (100gm) redcurrants

4 teaspoons Maraschino syrup

1. Place a scoop of ice cream in each of 4 glasses.
2. Sprinkle with a few strawberries, reserving 4 berries, top with another layer of ice cream then the raspberries.
3. Finish with a further scoop of ice cream and decorate with strings of redcurrants.
4. Top each with a whole strawberry and a teaspoon of the syrup.
5. Serve straight away with wafer biscuits.

Romanoff pineapple

Serves 4

1 small pineapple

8oz (200gm) strawberries, hulled and halved

1 family block vanilla ice cream

4 tablespoons Kirsch (optional)

1. Cut the pineapple into quarters and remove hard cores.
2. Remove the flesh from each section and cut into cubes.
3. Arrange the cubes with strawberry halves on each portion of pineapple.
4. Top with scoops of ice cream then decorate with a strawberry.
5. Sprinkle with Kirsch and serve immediately.

Left: ice cream sponge with chocolate sauce and walnuts.
Right: Romanoff pineapple decorated with strawberries

Knickerbocker glory

Knickerbocker glories

Serves 4

½ strawberry or raspberry flavour jelly

boiling water

1 can (approximately 1lb or ½ kilo) fruit cocktail

6 to 8 heaped tablespoons vanilla ice cream

4 heaped teaspoons whipped cream

4 glacé cherries

1. Make up jelly to ½ pint (250ml) with boiling water.
2. Stir until dissolved then leave in the cold until firm and set.
3. About 10 minutes before serving, tip jelly on to a sheet of damp greaseproof paper. Chop into small pieces with a knife dipped in cold water.
4. Divide jelly equally among 4 sundae glasses. Spoon approximately half the can of fruit cocktail (with syrup) into glasses over jelly.
5. Add equal amounts of ice cream to each then fill with rest of fruit cocktail and syrup.
6. Top each with cream and a cherry and serve straight away.

Peach melba

Serves 4

2 large peaches

4oz (100gm) granulated sugar

5 tablespoons hot water

1 teaspoon vanilla essence

4oz (100gm) fresh raspberries

1oz (25gm) icing sugar, sifted

either bought or home-made vanilla ice cream

1. Cover peaches with boiling water and leave 2 minutes. Drain and cover with cold water.
2. When cool enough to handle, slip skins off peaches and cut peaches in half.
3. Dissolve sugar in the water and add vanilla essence and peaches. Poach gently for 5 minutes, then leave until completely cold.
4. Rub raspberries through a fine sieve then sweeten with icing sugar.
5. Divide ice cream among 4 sundae glasses.
6. Top each with a poached peach half, then coat with sieved raspberries.
7. Serve straight away.

Right: prune and ice cream whip
Below: easy jewel dessert

Prune and ice cream whip

Serves 4

1 pint (approximately ½ litre) thick custard, made as directed on the packet

1 large can prunes, drained and stoned

1 family block rich vanilla ice cream

approximately 1oz (25gm) chopped almonds, toasted

1. Put custard into bowl.
2. Sieve prunes to a purée or blend in liquidiser until smooth. Add to custard.
3. Cool and chill in the refrigerator.
4. Just before serving, beat in half quantity of ice cream.
5. Divide mixture equally among 4 individual glasses.
6. Top each with a scoop of remaining ice cream and sprinkle with toasted nuts.
7. Serve straight away.

Easy jewel dessert

Serves 4

1 family block vanilla, Cornish or Italian ice cream

2 chocolate flake bars

2 candy sticks, coarsely crushed

sprig of mint or flower to decorate

1. Stand ice cream on chilled serving plate.
2. Break chocolate bars into small pieces and toss lightly with the crushed candy sticks.
3. Sprinkle over the ice cream and decorate with sprig of mint or flower.
4. Serve straight away.

Pear Hélène

Pear Hélène

Serves 2

2 large dessert pears, peeled, cored and halved

2 tablespoons lemon juice

2oz (50gm) plain chocolate

4 level tablespoons golden syrup

½oz (12gm) butter

4 heaped tablespoons vanilla ice cream

Maraschino cherries to decorate

1. Sprinkle pear halves with lemon juice to prevent discoloration.
2. To make chocolate sauce, place chocolate, syrup and butter in a basin over a saucepan of hot water. Leave until melted, stirring once or twice.
3. Beat well until smooth and glossy and leave until cold.
4. Place 2 tablespoons vanilla ice cream into 2 sundae glasses and arrange a pear half on either side.
5. Coat with chocolate sauce and decorate each with a cherry.
6. Serve straight away.

Lemon sorbet

Serves 6 to 8

8oz (200gm) granulated sugar

¾ pint (375ml) water

4 medium lemons, washed and dried

2 egg whites

1oz (25gm) caster sugar

1. Set refrigerator control to coldest setting at least 1 hour before making sorbet.
2. Put sugar and water into a saucepan.
3. Peel lemons thinly. Add rind to saucepan.
4. Heat gently, stirring, until sugar dissolves.
5. Squeeze juice from lemons and add to sugar in saucepan.
6. Strain into bowl and leave until cold.
7. Pour into 2 empty ice cube trays and freeze until half-frozen.
8. Beat egg whites to a stiff snow then beat in caster sugar.
9. Tip sorbet into a bowl and break up with a fork.
10. Gently fold in beaten egg whites.
11. When mixture is smooth and evenly combined, return to trays and freeze until firm.
12. Spoon into dishes and serve straight away.

Orange sorbet

Serves 6 to 8

Make as for lemon sorbet, above, using only ¼ pint (125ml) water and ½ pint (250ml) fresh orange juice. Add finely-grated peel of 1 orange to sugar, water and orange juice in saucepan. When sugar has dissolved, add to juice of 1 large lemon. Do not strain.

Cream meringues

Serves 6

2 egg whites

pinch of cream of tartar or squeeze of lemon juice

4oz (100gm) caster sugar

2 level teaspoons cornflour

¼ pint (125ml) double cream

1 tablespoon milk

1. Pre-heat oven to very cool, 225 deg F or gas ¼ (110 deg C).
2. Brush a fairly large baking tray with oil then line with greaseproof paper. Leave paper unoiled.
3. Put egg whites and cream of tartar or lemon juice into a clean dry bowl and beat until very stiff.
4. Gradually add half the sugar and continue beating until meringue is very shiny and stands in high, firm peaks.
5. Gently beat in a further ounce (25gm) sugar.
6. Lastly fold in rest of sugar and cornflour with a large metal spoon.
7. Spoon or pipe 12 ovals of mixture on to prepared tray.
8. Cook in centre of oven for 2 to 2½ hours until meringues are dry and crisp and the colour of the palest straw. Turn off oven.
9. Carefully peel meringues away from paper then place meringues upside down on a clean tray.
10. Return to oven and leave a further hour then cool on a wire rack.
11. Before serving, sandwich meringues together with the cream, beaten until thick with the milk.

Note

Meringues may be stored indefinitely in an airtight tin but once cream-filled, should be eaten on the same day.

Lemon water ice

Serves 4

2oz (50gm) golden syrup

3oz (75gm) granulated sugar

¾ pint (375ml) water

1 large lemon

¼oz (6gm) powdered gelatine

1. Set refrigerator control to coldest setting at least 1 hour before making water ice.
2. Put syrup, sugar and ½ pint (250ml) water in a saucepan.
3. Add thinly-peeled rind of lemon and heat together gently to dissolve sugar, stirring continuously.
4. Bring to boil and simmer gently for 5 minutes.
5. Meanwhile, dissolve gelatine over low heat in remaining ¼ pint (125ml) water and lemon juice.
6. Strain syrup mixture on to gelatine and allow to cool.
7. Pour into empty ice cube tray then transfer to freezing compartment of refrigerator.
8. Leave until thick and beginning to set.
9. Stir quickly with a fork then leave to set until firm.
10. Transfer to 4 individual glasses and serve straight away.

Butterscotch almond whip

Serves 4

5oz (125gm) golden syrup

1oz (25gm) butter

1 pint (approximately ½ litre) milk

1½oz (37gm) cornflour

1 standard egg, separated

1 teaspoon vanilla essence

4 heaped teaspoons whipped cream

toasted almonds

1. Put syrup and butter into a heavy saucepan and cook until deep golden brown.
2. Slowly add ¾ pint (375ml) milk and stir over gentle heat until butterscotch is melted.
3. Blend cornflour with remaining milk.
4. Combine with the hot liquid and continue to cook until thick and smooth.
5. Remove from heat, cool a little then beat in egg yolk and vanilla essence.
6. Cool again then fold in stiffly-beaten egg white.
7. Pour into 4 individual glass dishes and chill.
8. Before serving, decorate with whipped cream and almonds.

Quick raspberry cream

Serves 4

4 level tablespoons golden syrup

8oz (200gm) fresh raspberries

1 large can creamed rice pudding

4 tablespoons whipped cream

1. Place a level tablespoon of syrup into each of 4 sundae glasses.
2. Reserve about 20 berries for decoration.
3. Crush remainder and beat into rice.
4. Fold in cream then pile into glasses on top of syrup.
5. Decorate with whole raspberries and chill 1 hour before serving.

Bananas with raspberry cream

Serves 4

8oz (200gm) fresh raspberries

¼ pint (125ml) double cream

2 level tablespoons icing sugar, sifted

1 dessertspoon Kirsch or grand marnier

4 large bananas

1. Crush raspberries or liquidise in blender.
2. Beat cream with icing sugar and liqueur until thick. Fold in raspberry purée.
3. Slice bananas into 4 sundae glasses.
4. Pile raspberry mixture over each then chill at least ½ an hour before serving.

Easy summer soufflé

Serves 6

1 packet (8oz or 200gm) cream cheese

1 large can condensed milk

juice of ½ orange

grated peel of ½ lemon

juice of 1 lemon

2 tablespoons lime juice cordial

½oz (12gm) gelatine

3 tablespoons boiling water

2 egg whites

½oz (12gm) pistachio nuts, chopped

1. Put a 4-inch strip of folded greaseproof paper round a ¾ pint (375ml) soufflé dish lightly brushed with oil.
2. Make sure paper extends 3 inches above rim of dish.
3. Tie on to dish with thick thread or fine string then brush inside of strip with oil.
4. Beat cheese until smooth.
5. Gradually stir in condensed milk, orange juice, lemon peel, lemon juice and lime cordial.
6. Dissolve gelatine in the boiling water.
7. Add to cream cheese mixture and leave in a cool place until just beginning to thicken and set.
8. Beat egg whites to a stiff snow and gently fold into cheese mixture.
9. Pour into prepared soufflé dish and chill until firm and set.
10. Before serving, carefully remove paper and decorate top with a border of chopped nuts.

Left: butterscotch almond whip decorated with whipped cream and almonds, quick raspberry cream, and lemon water ice
Right: easy summer soufflé

185

Prune soufflé

Prune soufflé

Serves 6 to 7

1 level tablespoon gelatine

2 tablespoons cold water

8oz (200gm) stewed prunes or can of equivalent weight

¼ pint (125ml) double cream

6 tablespoons single cream

3 egg whites

2 level tablespoons caster sugar

1oz (25gm) walnuts, finely chopped

1. Put a 4-inch strip of folded greaseproof paper round a ¾ pint (375ml) soufflé dish lightly brushed with oil, making sure paper extends 3 inches above rim. Tie on to dish with thick thread or fine string then brush inside of strip with oil.
2. Soak gelatine in water for 5 minutes.
3. Put into saucepan with 3 tablespoons prune liquor and place over low heat until dissolved.
4. Reserve 4 prunes for decoration.
5. Stone remainder and put into blender with rest of prune liquor. Blend until smooth.
6. Combine with melted gelatine and leave in a cool place until just beginning to thicken and set.
7. Reserve about one-third of the double cream.
8. Beat remainder with single cream until softly stiff.
9. Whisk egg whites to a stiff snow.
10. Add sugar and continue whisking until meringue stands in stiff peaks.
11. Fold cream and meringue alternately into prune mixture then transfer to prepared dish (mixture should reach almost to top of paper).
12. Chill until firm and set.
13. Just before serving, remove paper and press walnuts against sides.
14. Beat rest of cream until thick and pile on to centre of soufflé.
15. Decorate with reserved prunes, halved and stoned.

Lemon soufflé

Serves 6

3 level teaspoons gelatine

2 tablespoons cold water

3 large eggs, separated

3oz (75gm) caster sugar

finely-grated peel and juice of 1 medium lemon

¼ pint (125ml) double cream

1oz (25gm) walnuts, finely chopped

whipped cream

sugar-coated jellied lemon slices

1. Prepare a ¾ pint (375ml) soufflé dish as for easy summer soufflé (see page 185).
2. Soak gelatine in the cold water for 5 minutes. Transfer to saucepan and place over a very low heat until gelatine has dissolved.
3. Put egg yolks and sugar into a bowl and beat until very thick and almost white in colour.
4. Gently stir in dissolved gelatine with lemon peel and juice.
5. Leave in the cold until just beginning to thicken and set.
6. Beat egg whites to a stiff snow. Whip cream until thick.
7. Fold alternately into gelatine mixture.
8. Transfer to prepared dish (mixture should come at least halfway up the paper) and chill until firm and set.
9. Before serving, carefully remove paper then press walnuts against the sides.
10. Decorate top with whipped cream and pieces of lemon slices.

Orange soufflé

Serves 6

Make as for lemon soufflé, above, substituting the finely-grated peel and juice of 1 large orange for the lemon. Decorate with orange slices instead of the lemon.

Coffee soufflé

Serves 6

Make as for lemon soufflé (see this page), dissolving 3 level teaspoons instant coffee with the gelatine and water and omitting the lemon.

Chocolate soufflé

Serves 6

Make as for lemon soufflé (see this page), adding 2oz (50gm) melted and cooled plain chocolate instead of the lemon.

Chocolate mousse

Serves 4

4oz (100gm) plain chocolate

1oz (25gm) butter

1 teaspoon vanilla essence

4 large eggs, separated

4 heaped dessertspoons whipped cream

4 level teaspoons chopped walnuts, hazelnuts or pistachios

1. Break up chocolate and put with butter and vanilla into a basin over a saucepan of hot water. Leave until melted, stirring once or twice.
2. Remove basin from saucepan then beat in egg yolks.
3. Beat egg whites to a stiff snow and gently fold into chocolate mixture.
4. When mixture is smooth and evenly combined, transfer to 4 wine-type glasses.
5. Chill at least 2 hours.
6. Before serving, decorate each with cream and nuts.

Mocha mousse

Serves 4

Make as for chocolate mousse (see previous recipe), but add 1 dessertspoon very strong coffee instead of the vanilla.

Strawberry or raspberry mousse

Serves 6

3 large eggs, separated

3oz (75gm) caster sugar

½ pint (250ml) strawberry or raspberry purée, made from canned, fresh or frozen fruit

4 level teaspoons gelatine

2 tablespoons water

2 tablespoons Kirsch or cointreau

1 tablespoon lemon juice

¼ pint (125ml) double cream

6 fresh strawberries or raspberries

1. Put egg yolks and sugar into a bowl and whisk until thick and almost white in colour.
2. Beat in fruit purée.
3. Soften gelatine for 3 minutes in the cold water. Transfer to saucepan and place over a low heat until dissolved.
4. Add to fruit mixture with Kirsch or cointreau and the lemon juice.
5. Leave in the cold until just beginning to thicken and set.
6. Beat egg whites to a stiff snow. Whip cream until softly stiff.
7. Fold alternately into cream mixture.
8. Transfer to 6 sundae glasses and chill until firm and set.
9. Before serving, decorate with cream and fresh strawberries or raspberries.

Orange rose creams

Peach or apricot mousse

Serves 6

Make as for strawberry mousse (see previous recipe), using ½ pint (250ml) thick peach or apricot purée made from drained canned fruit. Use sherry instead of the Kirsch or cointreau. Decorate with chopped glacé cherries and/or chopped crystallised ginger.

Orange rose creams

Serves 4

2 almond macaroons

½ can mandarin oranges

1 egg white

3 level dessertspoons caster sugar

¼ pint (125ml) double cream

1 tablespoon milk

3 dessertspoons orange and rose hip syrup

a little green food colouring

green leaves for decoration

1. Break up macaroons and put into 4 sundae glasses.
2. Top with equal amounts of mandarins and syrup from the can.
3. Beat egg white to a stiff snow.
4. Add sugar and continue beating until mixture is shiny and stands in high, firm peaks.
5. Whip cream and milk together until thick. Stir in orange and rose hip syrup then colour pale green with food colouring.
6. Fold cream mixture into beaten egg white.
7. Pile into glasses over macaroons and fruit.
8. Chill thoroughly but eat within 4 hours of making.
9. Just before serving, decorate with fresh green leaves (lemon balm or mint).

Lemon meringue pie

Serves 4 to 6

short crust pastry made with 6oz (150gm) flour (see page 108)

3 level teaspoons cornflour

6oz (150gm) caster sugar

finely-grated peel and juice of 2 large lemons

¼ pint (125ml) water

2 standard eggs, separated

½oz (12gm) butter

1. Pre-heat oven to hot, 425 deg F or gas 7 (220 deg C).
2. Roll out pastry and use to line a 7-inch flan ring on an ungreased baking tray.
3. Prick lightly all over then line with foil to prevent pastry from rising as it cooks.
4. Bake near top of oven for 20 minutes. Carefully remove foil and return pastry to oven for a further 10 minutes or until crisp and gold. Remove from oven then carefully lift off flan ring. Reduce oven temperature to cool, 300 deg F or gas 2 (150 deg C).
5. Mix cornflour and 2oz (50gm) sugar to a smooth cream with lemon juice and water. Stir in lemon peel.
6. Cook, stirring continuously, until mixture comes to the boil and thickens. Simmer 2 minutes.
7. Remove from heat and cool slightly. Beat in egg yolks and butter and pour into flan case.
8. Beat egg whites to a stiff snow. Gradually add half the remaining sugar and continue beating until meringue is shiny and stands in high, firm peaks.
9. Gently fold in rest of sugar then pile meringue over lemon filling, making sure it reaches edges of pastry.
10. Bake in centre of oven for 30 minutes or until meringue is pale gold.
11. Serve cold.

Pavlova

Serves 6 to 8

4 egg whites

¼ level teaspoon cream of tartar

10oz (250gm) caster sugar

2 level teaspoons cornflour

1 teaspoon vinegar

passionfruit

½ pint (250ml) double cream

2 tablespoons milk

1. Pre-heat oven to cool, 250 deg F or gas ½ (130 deg C).
2. Draw a 9-inch circle on double thickness of greaseproof paper.
3. Turn paper over and place on well-oiled baking tray. Sprinkle paper with water.
4. Beat egg whites and cream of tartar to a stiff snow.
5. Add half the sugar and continue beating until meringue is very shiny and stands in high, firm peaks.
6. Fold in remaining sugar with cornflour and vinegar.
7. Pile meringue on to greaseproof paper to cover the shape drawn.
8. Bake in centre of oven for 1½ hours or until Pavlova is firm on the outside and a pale biscuit colour.
9. Leave to cool for 20 minutes then transfer to a serving dish, bottom side up. Peel away paper being careful when handling as the meringue is very brittle, especially when hot.
10. Beat cream until thick, then fold in passionfruit pulp.
11. Fill Pavlova with passionfruit-cream mixture and serve.

Apricot or strawberry Pavlova

Serves 6 to 8

Make as for Pavlova in previous recipe, but in place of passionfruit use well-drained canned apricots, cut in quarters, to add to cream. Put some apricot quarters aside for garnishing. Fresh strawberries or raspberries can also be used instead of passionfruit in the same way.

Pineapple rice mould

Serves 4 to 6

1 pineapple jelly

1 can (10oz or 250gm) pineapple cubes

1 large can rice pudding

¼ pint (125ml) double cream

1oz (25gm) walnuts, finely chopped

1. Make up jelly to ½ pint (250ml) with pineapple syrup and water if necessary.
2. Leave over a low heat until dissolved then combine with rice pudding.
3. When cold and just beginning to thicken and set, fold in two-thirds of the drained pineapple cubes.
4. Transfer to a 1½ to 2 pint (¾ to 1¼ litre) fancy mould first rinsed with cold water or lightly oiled.
5. Chill until firm and set then unmould on to a platter.
6. Whip cream until thick and pipe in a heavy border on top of mould.
7. Fill centre with remaining pineapple cubes then sprinkle cream with nuts.

Right: Pavlova
Below: pineapple rice mould

Crème brûlée

Serves 6 to 8

4 egg yolks

½ pint (250ml) double cream

¼ pint (125ml) single cream

1 level teaspoon cornflour

2oz (50gm) caster sugar

1 teaspoon vanilla essence

extra caster sugar

1. Pre-heat oven to moderate, 325 deg F or gas 3 (170 deg C).
2. Beat egg yolks and the creams well together.
3. Put into top of double saucepan or into a basin over a saucepan of hot water.
4. Add cornflour and 2oz (50gm) caster sugar.
5. Cook, stirring frequently, until custard thickens sufficiently to coat the back of a spoon, but in no circumstances allow mixture to boil.
6. Stir in essence then pour mixture into a 1 pint (approximately ½ litre) lightly-buttered heatproof dish.
7. Place dish in roasting tin containing 1 inch of cold water and cook in centre of oven for ¾ to 1 hour or until custard is firm and set.
8. When completely cold, cover top with a thick layer of caster sugar.
9. Leave under pre-heated hot grill until sugar turns a deep gold and begins to caramelise.
10. Remove from grill then chill thoroughly before serving.

Floating islands

Serves 4

2 large eggs, separated, plus 2 extra egg yolks

4oz (100gm) caster sugar

1 pint (approximately ½ litre) milk

1 level teaspoon cornflour

1 teaspoon vanilla essence

1. Beat egg whites to a stiff snow. Add half the sugar and continue beating until meringue is very shiny and stands in firm peaks.
2. Pour milk into a saucepan and heat over a low heat until hot, stirring continuously. Do not allow to boil.
3. Add tablespoons of meringue and poach gently in the milk for 5 minutes, turning once.
4. Carefully lift out of milk with a perforated spoon and place on a clean, folded tea-towel.
5. Beat yolks then add to milk with rest of sugar and cornflour.
6. Transfer to top of double saucepan or to large basin over saucepan of gently simmering water.
7. Cook until custard thickens sufficiently to coat the back of a spoon, stirring frequently. Add vanilla.
8. Pour into serving dish and arrange meringues on top.
9. Chill before serving.

Caramel cream

Serves 4 to 6

2oz (50gm) granulated sugar

4 tablespoons water

4 large eggs plus 2 extra egg yolks

3 level dessertspoons caster sugar

1 teaspoon vanilla essence

1 pint (approximately ½ litre) evaporated milk diluted with water

single cream

1. Pre-heat oven to moderate, 325 deg F or gas 3 (170 deg C).
2. Well-butter a 1½ pint (¾ litre) pie dish.
3. To make caramel, dissolve granulated sugar in the water. Bring to the boil, then boil without stirring until mixture turns a deep gold.
4. Pour into prepared dish and quickly tilt in all directions so that base is completely covered with caramel.
5. Beat eggs, yolks, sugar and essence well together.
6. Bring milk just up to boil, whisking gently.
7. Beat into egg mixture then strain into prepared dish.
8. Stand dish in roasting tin containing 1 inch of cold water.
9. Cook in centre of oven for 1 hour or until custard is firm and set.
10. When completely cold, transfer to refrigerator and chill thoroughly.
11. Before serving, loosen edges of custard and turn out on to a dish.
12. Serve with single cream.

Baked egg custard

Serves 4 to 6

Make as for caramel cream (see previous recipe), but omit the caramel. Use only 3 large eggs to the pint (or approximately ½ litre) of milk. Sprinkle top lightly with nutmeg before baking. Serve hot or cold.

Peach trifles

Serves 4

Prepare custard as in recipe for floating islands (see this page), using 1 large egg and an extra yolk, 2oz (50gm) caster sugar and ½ level teaspoon each cornflour and vanilla essence. Leave until cold. Put 4 slices of jam-filled Swiss roll into 4 individual glasses. Moisten with sweet sherry then cover with canned peach slices followed by liquid lemon jelly. Leave until set. Pour equal amounts of custard on to each and refrigerate until set. Just before serving, cover completely with softly-whipped cream then sprinkle with grated plain chocolate or nuts.

Cream-topped apricot trifle

Serves 8

1 jam-filled Swiss roll

1 can (approximately 1lb or ½ kilo) apricots

6 tablespoons sweet sherry

1 pint (approximately ½ litre) custard, freshly made as directed on packet and sweetened to taste

½ pint (250ml) double cream

2 level tablespoons caster sugar

9 glacé cherries

a few blanched and toasted almonds

1. Cut Swiss roll into slices and put into serving dish.
2. Moisten with a little syrup from can of apricots and the sherry. Arrange drained apricots on top.
3. Cover with custard and leave until completely cold.
4. Beat cream until thick with the sugar.
5. Swirl over custard then decorate with cherries and almonds.
6. Chill at least 1 hour before serving.

Syllabub

Serves 4 to 6

¼ pint (125ml) sweet sherry

finely-grated peel and juice of 1 medium lemon

2oz (50gm) caster sugar

½ pint (250ml) double cream

1. Put sherry, lemon peel and juice into bowl. Add sugar. Cover.
2. Leave to stand in the refrigerator for a minimum of 3 hours.
3. Add cream and whip until mixture forms soft peaks.
4. Transfer to 4 glasses and serve straight away.

Cherry syllabub

Serves 6

Make as for syllabub, above. Divide 1 can (approximately 14oz or 350gm) cherry pie filling among 6 glasses. Top with syllabub then decorate with leaves of angelica. Serve straight away, accompanied with sponge finger biscuits.

Old English lemon possett

Serves 6

Make as for syllabub, above, using sweet white wine instead of sherry. After beating in cream, gently and lightly fold in 2 stiffly-beaten egg whites. Transfer to 6 glasses and serve straight away.

Above: cream-topped apricot trifle. Below: cherry syllabub

Banana coeur à la crème

Serves 8 to 10

1lb (½ kilo) cottage cheese

2 packets (each 200gm) cream cheese

8oz (200gm) caster sugar

large pinch of salt

4 teaspoons vanilla essence

2 medium bananas

lemon juice

1 medium orange, sliced

1. Carefully sieve cottage cheese, making sure all excess whey or liquid is drawn off.
2. Beat the two cheeses together then stir in sugar and salt.
3. Continue beating until mixture is smooth, fluffy and well-blended. Add vanilla.
4. Line a heart-shaped cake tin or mould with a piece of damp muslin.
5. Fill with the cheese mixture and chill 2 or 3 hours until firm.
6. Unmould on to a platter and remove muslin.
7. Slice bananas and sprinkle with lemon juice to prevent discoloration.
8. Outline edge of mould with halved orange slices then top with bananas.

Pinwheel surprise

Serves 8 to 10

1 Swiss roll

2 standard eggs

3oz (75gm) caster sugar

¼ level teaspoon salt

6 tablespoons milk

4 level teaspoons gelatine

3 tablespoons boiling water

1 teaspoon vanilla essence

2oz (50gm) desiccated coconut

½ pint (250ml) double cream, whipped

glacé cherries

angelica

shredded coconut

1. Line base of spring form tin with aluminium foil.
2. Cut Swiss roll into ½-inch thick slices and stand them on end around the side of the tin, allowing each slice to fit firmly against the next.
3. Separate eggs. Beat yolks with sugar and salt.
4. Heat milk until it just reaches boiling point.
5. Add yolk mixture and cook over low heat until it thickens, stirring continuously.
6. Remove from heat.
7. Dissolve gelatine in the boiling water and add to custard mixture.
8. Add vanilla and desiccated coconut. Cool.
9. Beat egg whites until stiff and stir into mixture with two-thirds of the whipped cream.
10. Pour into prepared tin and decorate top with rest of cream, cherries, angelica and shredded coconut.
11. Chill until firm then unclip sides of tin.

Above: banana coeur à la crème. Below: pinwheel surprise

Spiral strawberry mould

Chilled orange cups

Serves 4

4 large oranges

1 orange flavour jelly

1 can mandarin oranges

4 heaped tablespoons vanilla ice cream, softened

1. Cut tops off oranges by serrating with a sharp knife.
2. Squeeze out all the juice and reserve.
3. Scrape pulp and membranes out of oranges and discard.
4. Make up jelly to ¾ pint (375ml) with mandarin syrup and orange juice.
5. Leave over a low heat until jelly dissolves.
6. When cold and just beginning to thicken and set, beat briskly until light and foamy.
7. Beat in ice cream then fold in all but 8 mandarins.
8. Spoon equally into orange cups and chill until firm and set.
9. Decorate each with 2 mandarins before serving.

Note
If there is too much jelly mixture for the oranges, set it separately in a small serving dish.

Pear nut cream

Serves 4

7 canned pear halves, drained

7 Maraschino cherries

1 large can rice pudding

2 level teaspoons gelatine

4 tablespoons syrup from can of pears

¼ pint (125ml) double cream

1 teaspoon vanilla essence

1oz (25gm) walnuts, chopped

1 chocolate flake bar

1. Fill each pear half with a cherry and place round edge of glass serving dish, cut sides against glass.
2. Tip rice into a basin.
3. Put gelatine and syrup into a saucepan and place over a low heat until gelatine dissolves.
4. Stir into rice pudding.
5. Beat cream until thick. Fold into rice pudding with vanilla essence and walnuts.
6. Spoon into dish over pears and refrigerate until softly set. Serve garnished with flaked chocolate.

Spiral strawberry mould

Serves 8

2 strawberry jellies

1 can (approximately 1lb or ½ kilo) spiral pineapple slices

water

4oz (100gm) strawberries

1. Make up jellies to 2 pints (1¼ litre) with pineapple syrup and water.
2. Put into saucepan and stir over a low heat until dissolved.
3. Leave until cold.
4. Reserve 3 pineapple spirals and a few whole strawberries for decoration.
5. Chop remainder and stir into half-set jelly.
6. Turn into a 2½ pint (approximately 1½ litre) fancy mould and chill until firm and set.
7. Unmould on to a platter and decorate top with a whole pineapple spiral and a whole strawberry. Arrange pieces of cut-up pineapple and rest of strawberries round lower edge.

Hawaiian fingers

Serves 4

1 can (1¼lb or ⅝ kilo) pineapple fingers

8oz (200gm) caster sugar

3 tablespoons water

2oz (50gm) desiccated coconut

6oz (150gm) ginger nuts

1. Drain pineapple fingers thoroughly on kitchen paper.
2. Place sugar and water in a saucepan and dissolve slowly over low heat.
3. Bring to boil and boil until mixture turns golden brown.
4. Dip ends of pineapple fingers into syrup then coat with coconut.
5. Transfer to a serving dish and surround with ginger nuts.

Hawaiian fingers surrounded by ginger nuts, chilled orange cups decorated with mandarin pieces, and pear nut cream garnished with flaked chocolate

Above: coffee mould with chocolate sauce. Left: peach shortcake with whipped cream

Peach shortcakes

Serves 6

8oz (200gm) self-raising flour

pinch of salt

3oz (75gm) butter

1oz (25gm) caster sugar

1 standard egg, beaten

cold milk

1 can (approximately 1lb or ½ kilo) peach slices, drained

¼ pint (125ml) double cream

1 tablespoon milk

1 level dessertspoon caster sugar

1. Pre-heat oven to hot, 425 deg F or gas 7 (220 deg C).
2. Sift flour and salt into bowl.
3. Rub in 2oz (50gm) butter finely. Add sugar and toss ingredients lightly together.
4. Put egg into measuring cup and make up to ¼ pint (125ml) with cold milk.
5. Add all at once to dry ingredients and mix to a soft dough with a round-topped knife.
6. Turn out on to lightly-floured surface and knead gently until smooth.
7. Roll out to ½ inch in thickness and cut into 6 rounds with a 3-inch cutter.
8. Transfer to a lightly-buttered tray.
9. Bake towards top of oven for 10 to 15 minutes or until well-risen and golden.
10. Cool on a wire rack then gently break rounds apart with fingers when lukewarm.
11. Butter thickly with remaining butter then sandwich together with two-thirds of the peach slices. Place on individual plates.
12. Beat cream with milk and sugar until thick.
13. Pile on top of shortcakes then decorate with remaining peach slices.
14. Serve straight away.

Raspberry or strawberry shortcakes

Serves 6

Make as for peach shortcakes (see previous recipe), using 8oz (200gm) sliced strawberries or whole raspberries instead of peach slices.

Coffee mould

Serves 6

1 level teaspoon cornflour

3 standard eggs, separated

¾ pint (375ml) hot milk

1½oz (37gm) caster sugar

3 level teaspoons instant coffee granules

6 tablespoons boiling water

1 level tablespoon gelatine

1. Put cornflour, egg yolks, hot milk and sugar into basin over saucepan of gently simmering water.
2. Cook until custard thickens, stirring, but do not allow mixture to boil.
3. Meanwhile, put coffee, water and gelatine into a saucepan and leave over a low heat until gelatine dissolves.
4. Stir into custard then leave in the cool until just beginning to thicken and set.
5. Beat egg whites to a stiff snow and fold into coffee custard then transfer to 2 pint (1¼ litre) fancy mould, first rinsed with cold water or lightly oiled.
6. Chill until firm and set then unmould on to a platter. If wished, serve with a chocolate sauce (see page 104).

Chocolate mould

Serves 6

Make as for coffee mould, above, but dissolve 2oz (50gm) plain chocolate (chopped first) in the milk. Omit coffee.

Peaches and cream layer dessert

Danish peasant girl with veil

Serves 6

3oz (75gm) butter

8oz (200gm) fresh white breadcrumbs

3oz (75gm) Demerara sugar

1½lb (¾ kilo) cooking apples

water

juice of ½ lemon

granulated sugar to taste

¼ pint (125ml) double cream

1oz (25gm) plain chocolate, grated

1. Melt butter in a saucepan. Add breadcrumbs and fry gently until pale gold, stirring frequently.
2. Combine with Demerara sugar and leave on one side.
3. Peel, core and slice apples and cook in 3 to 4 tablespoons water and lemon juice until soft and pulpy.
4. Beat in granulated sugar to taste and leave until completely cold.
5. Fill a serving dish with alternate layers of crumb mixture and apples, beginning and ending with crumbs.
6. Whip cream until thick. Pile on top of crumbs then sprinkle with grated chocolate.
7. Chill thoroughly before serving.

Peaches and cream layer dessert

Serves 6

9oz (225gm) plain flour

6oz (150gm) butter

3oz (75gm) caster sugar

beaten egg

½ pint (250ml) double cream

2 tablespoons milk

3 tablespoons clear honey

finely-grated peel of 1 lemon

1 can (approximately 1lb or ½ kilo) peach slices, drained

1. Pre-heat oven to cool, 300 deg F or gas 2 (150 deg C).
2. Sift flour into bowl. Rub in butter finely then add sugar.
3. Mix to a stiff paste with beaten egg. Divide into 3 equal portions and roll each out into an 8-inch circle.
4. Place on lightly-greased baking trays and prick lightly with a fork.
5. Bake just above centre of oven for 50 minutes or until very pale gold. Cool on a wire rack.
6. Beat cream and milk together until thick then stir in half the honey and lemon peel. Put 2 to 3 tablespoons on one side.
7. Reserve 6 peach slices for decoration. Chop remainder and fold into cream.
8. Sandwich the biscuit rounds together with peaches and cream then glaze by brushing with remaining honey.
9. Decorate with reserved cream and rest of peach slices.
10. Chill lightly before serving.

Tasmanian shortcakes

Serves 6

6oz (150gm) butter

3oz (75gm) caster sugar

9oz (225gm) plain flour

a little beaten egg for brushing

2 eating apples, cored and sliced thinly

½oz (12gm) extra butter, melted

2 level tablespoons apricot jam, warmed

1oz (25gm) walnuts, chopped

1. Pre-heat oven to moderately hot, 375 deg F or gas 5 (190 deg C).
2. Cream butter and sugar until light and fluffy.
3. Stir in flour, kneading gently to bind.
4. Press into a 6-inch square tin and bake in centre of oven for 25 to 30 minutes.
5. Remove from oven, cut into 6 pieces and brush with beaten egg.
5. Arrange apple slices in overlapping rows on top of each piece of shortcake.
6. Brush with a little melted butter and return to oven for a further 10 minutes.
7. When cool, brush with apricot jam and sprinkle with chopped walnuts.

Tasmanian shortcakes with apple slices and chopped walnuts

Sunset pears

Serves 6

6 even-sized dessert pears

1 pint (approximately ½ litre) plus 4 tablespoons water

8oz (200gm) granulated sugar

1 vanilla pod or ½ teaspoon vanilla essence

12oz (300gm) fresh or frozen blackcurrants

8oz (200gm) fresh or frozen raspberries

¼ pint (125ml) double cream

1 tablespoon milk

a few toasted almonds for decoration

1. Peel pears, leaving them whole with the stalks intact.
2. Put 1 pint (approximately ½ litre) water and 4oz (100gm) sugar into pan.
3. Stir over gentle heat until sugar dissolves.
4. Add vanilla pod or essence then add pears. Poach approximately 20 minutes or until pears are just cooked through—do not over-cook.
5. Meanwhile put blackcurrants, raspberries, 4 tablespoons water and rest of sugar into saucepan.
6. Cook slowly until mixture is soft, pulpy and purée-like.
7. Lift pears into a bowl and coat with cooked puréed fruit.
8. Leave to cool then chill thoroughly in refrigerator.
9. To serve, divide the fruit purée among 6 individual glass dishes.
10. Stand a whole pear (which will be a deep pink colour) on top.
11. Whip cream and milk together until thick. Pipe round pears then scatter toasted almonds on top.
12. Serve very cold.

Mandarin yogurt cooler

Serves 4

1 tin mandarins

½oz (12gm) gelatine

2½oz (62gm) caster sugar

1 pint (approximately ½ litre) natural yogurt

juice of 1 medium lemon

¼ pint (125ml) double cream

1. Drain mandarins and strain syrup into saucepan.
2. Add gelatine and stir over low heat until dissolved.
3. Add sugar and leave mixture until cold and just on the point of setting.
4. Combine with yogurt and lemon juice.
5. Reserve a few mandarins for decoration. Chop remainder and stir into yogurt mixture.
6. Transfer to individual sundae glasses and leave to set.
7. Before serving, decorate with cream, whipped until thick, and reserved mandarins.
8. Serve with crisp biscuits.

Opposite: sunset pears with whipped cream and toasted almonds.
Below: banana Alaska flambé

Banana Alaska flambé

Serves 4

2 egg whites

4 level tablespoons caster sugar

4 large bananas

1 family block coffee ice cream, frozen hard

2 tablespoons dark rum

1. Pre-heat oven to hot, 450 deg F or gas 8 (230 deg C).
2. Beat egg whites to a stiff snow. Add half the sugar and continue beating until meringue is very shiny and stands in high peaks.
3. Gently fold in rest of sugar.
4. Slice half the bananas into a heatproof dish.
5. Stand ice cream on top then slice rest of bananas and add.
6. Cover completely with meringue, making sure there are no gaps between ice cream and sides of dish.
7. Flash bake near top of oven until golden—about 2 minutes only.
8. Remove from oven, gently pour rum over the top then set alight.
9. Serve immediately.

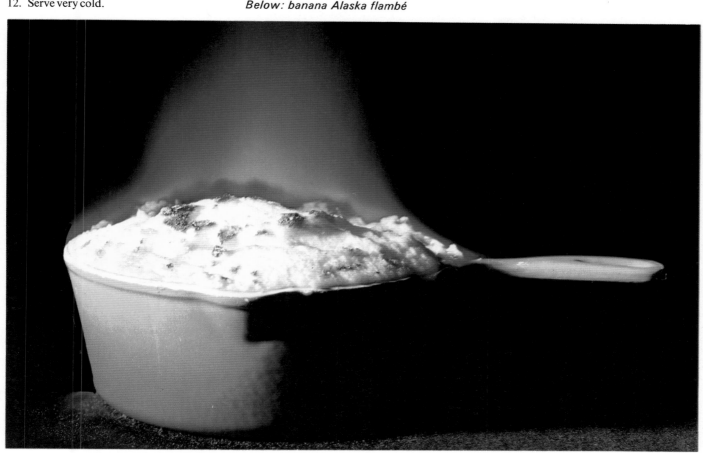

Cherry mille feuilles

Serves 4 to 6

puff pastry made with 8oz (200gm) flour (see page 112) or 1 large packet frozen puff pastry, thawed.

½ pint (250ml) double cream

1 tablespoon milk

2 level tablespoons caster sugar

1 can (approximately 1lb or ½ kilo) Italian red cherries, drained and stoned

icing sugar, sifted

1. Pre-heat oven to hot, 450 deg F or gas 8 (230 deg C).
2. Roll out pastry into ¼ inch in thickness, or roll out frozen pastry as directed.
3. Cut into 3 strips, each measuring approximately 8 inches by 4 inches.
4. Place strips on damp baking tray and bake just above centre of oven for 10 to 15 minutes or until well-puffed and golden.
5. Cool on a wire rack.
6. Before serving, whip cream with milk and sugar until thick.
7. Spread one pastry slice with half the cream then place half the cherries on top.
8. Add second slice of pastry and cover with cream and cherries as before.
9. Top with third slice of pastry and dust heavily with sifted icing sugar.
10. Cut into slices and serve.

Above: cherry mille feuilles. Below: profiteroles

Profiteroles

Serves 6

Make as for cream buns (see page 224). Pile cream-filled buns into a serving dish then coat with hot chocolate sauce (see page 104). Serve when sauce is cold.

Choux boat

Serves 6 to 8

choux pastry (see page 112)

1 can (approximately 1lb or ½ kilo) fruit cocktail

½ pint (250ml) double cream

icing sugar, sifted

1. Pre-heat oven to moderately hot, 400 deg F or gas 6 (200 deg C).
2. Spoon freshly-made choux pastry in a 10 inches by 2 inches line on a greased baking tray.
3. Bake in centre of oven for 20 minutes.
4. Reduce temperature to 375 deg F or gas 5 (190 deg C) and bake a further 20 to 25 minutes.
5. Cool on a wire rack then split open.
6. Drain fruit. Beat cream until thick.
7. Combine fruit and cream well together then pile into choux boat.
8. Dust top with sifted icing sugar and serve straight away.

Choux boat

Teatime cookery

Cakes

There are five important points to bear in mind when choosing ingredients for cake-making:

1. Choose good-quality flour and keep supplies of both plain and self-raising. Although the latter is the more popular choice, plain flour on its own or with varying amounts of baking powder is better for some of the richer cakes.

2. Caster sugar should always be used for the majority of cakes unless otherwise specified. Where a richer colour is preferred, soft brown sugar may be used instead.

3. Standard eggs are a good average size and should be used unless otherwise stated.

4. Butter always gives the best flavour but for reasons of economy, half butter and half margarine may be used. Lard or cooking fat makes a reasonable substitute for margarine but should be kept for fairly plain cakes.

5. All ingredients for cake-making should be at room temperature—never taken straight from the refrigerator.

Methods of making

Rubbing in
This method is used for plainer cakes and the fat is rubbed into the flour with the fingertips until the mixture resembles fine breadcrumbs. The usual proportion is half fat and sugar to flour so that for 8oz (200gm) flour, 4oz (100gm) each of fat and sugar should be used. In some cases, the proportion of fat and sugar to flour is a little less.

Creaming
This method is used for richer mixtures such as Madeira cake, Victoria sandwich and Christmas cakes. The softened fat and sugar are beaten together—either with a wooden spoon or electric beaters—until they become very pale in colour, light and fluffy in texture and almost double their original volume. The proportion varies according to the cake being made but can be anything from half fat and sugar to flour, up to equal amounts of fat, sugar and flour. As the proportion of fat and sugar to flour increases, so less raising agent is needed and this is where plain flour plus a small amount of baking powder is often recommended for certain recipes. Softened fat makes the task of creaming easier but do not let the fat become over-soft and then oily or the cakes will be heavy.

One-bowl method
This is a method of cake-making where all the ingredients are put into one bowl and creamed together for 3 to 4 minutes by hand or about 1½ to 2 minutes with an electric mixer. It saves a considerable amount of time but is only suitable for recipes containing whipped-up cooking fat or best quality or luxury margarine. In cakes made by this method, it is usual to add a little extra baking powder even if self-raising flour has already been used.

Flake cream sandwich (see page 214), malted loaf (see page 214), cherry basket cakes (see page 214) and farmhouse cake (see page 212)

Whisking

This method is used for fatless sponges and Swiss rolls. The proportion of eggs, sugar and flour is usually equal and a sponge cake baked in two 7-inch tins is generally made from 3oz (75gm) plain flour, 3oz (75gm) sugar and 3 eggs. The eggs and sugar are put into a bowl over a saucepan of hot water, and then whisked with a hand whisk or electric beaters continuously until they are the consistency of softly-whipped cream and at least twice their original volume. Thorough whisking is essential in order to aerate the mixture and make it rise satisfactorily.

Melting

This is a method used for gingerbreads, parkins and honey cakes. The fat, sugar and syrup are melted together in a saucepan before being added to the dry ingredients with the eggs and milk.

Faults in cake-making

Rubbed-in mixtures

Heavy—too much liquid. Fat oily. Oven not hot enough. Insufficient baking powder used with plain flour.
Texture full of holes—fat not rubbed in finely enough. Too much beating or stirring after liquid was added.
Crust hard and sugary—too much sugar used. Cake overcooked.

Creamed mixtures

Heavy and close—insufficient creaming of fat and sugar. Insufficient beating after each egg was added. Not enough baking powder used. Oven either too hot or too cool.
Texture full of holes—flour beaten into creamed mixture instead of being folded in.

Rubbed-in and creamed mixtures

Top cracked and peaked in centre—too hot an oven. Cake tin too small. Tin placed too near top of oven. Insufficient liquid added.
Cake sinks in the centre—mixture over-wet. Too much baking powder. Oven too cool or too hot. Tin placed too low down in oven. Insufficient baking time allowed. Oven door opened too often.
Fruit sinks to the bottom of cake—fruit wet or damp. Too much liquid added—mixture should be stiff so that it is able to support the weight of the fruit. Using self-raising flour instead of plain or adding too much baking powder with the plain flour. Opening and closing the oven door during the first hour or two of baking.

Whisked mixtures

Close and biscuity—insufficient whisking of eggs and sugar. Flour stirred in instead of being folded in.
Slightly wet and sticky—too much sugar used. Oven too hot or too cool. Cakes insufficiently cooked.
Deep sponge sinks—self-raising flour used or baking powder added to plain flour. Oven too hot. Cake insufficiently cooked.

Melted mixtures

Cake sinks in centre—too much raising agent used. Too much syrup and/or treacle. Oven too hot. Tin placed too high up in oven.
Top shiny—texture close—mixture over-beaten.
Top cracked — texture dry—insufficient liquid. Too much raising agent used. Oven too hot. Tin placed too high up in oven.

To test when cakes are cooked

For sponge and sandwich cakes, press surface lightly with the fingertips. If it springs back and leaves no mark, the cakes are cooked sufficiently.
For deep cakes, insert a cocktail stick or fine knitting needle into the centre. If it comes out clean with no cake mixture sticking to it, then the cake has cooked for long enough.

Victoria sandwich

Makes about 8 portions

4oz (100gm) butter or margarine

4oz (100gm) caster sugar

1 teaspoon vanilla essence (optional)

2 standard eggs

4oz (100gm) self-raising flour, sifted

raspberry jam and/or whipped cream

little icing sugar, sifted

1. Pre-heat oven to moderate, 350 deg F or gas 4 (180 deg C).
2. Well grease two 7-inch sandwich tins and line bases with greased greaseproof paper.
3. Cream butter or margarine with sugar and vanilla essence until light and fluffy.
4. Gradually beat in eggs, one at a time, adding a tablespoon of flour with each.
5. Gently fold in rest of flour with a metal spoon then divide mixture equally between prepared tins.
6. Bake near centre of oven for 20 to 25 minutes or until well-risen and golden.
7. Turn out on to a wire rack, strip off paper and leave until cold.
8. Sandwich together with raspberry jam and/or whipped cream and dust top lightly with sifted icing sugar.

Nut sandwich

Makes about 8 portions

Make as for Victoria sandwich, above, adding 2oz (50gm) very finely-chopped walnuts, hazelnuts or toasted almonds before folding in the flour. Sandwich cakes together with sweetened whipped cream or butter cream and dust top with sifted icing sugar.

Victoria sandwich

Lemon or orange sandwich

Makes about 8 portions

Make as for Victoria sandwich (see page 204), adding 1 level teaspoon very finely-grated orange or lemon peel before folding in the flour. Sandwich cakes together with sweetened whipped cream and/or apricot jam or lemon curd. Dust top with sifted icing sugar.

Cup cakes

Makes 10 to 12

Make as for Victoria sandwich (see page 204), then divide mixture equally among 10 to 12 paper cake cases in ungreased bun tins. Bake in centre of fairly hot oven, 375 deg F or gas 5 (190 deg C), for about 20 minutes or until well-risen and golden. Cool on a wire rack.

Fairy cakes

Makes 10 to 12

Make as for cup cakes, above, adding 2oz (50gm) currants before folding in the flour.

Chocolate frosted layer cake

Chocolate frosted layer cake

Makes about 10 portions

Make as for Victoria sandwich (see page 204), but increase fat, flour and sugar to 6oz (150gm) each and use 3 standard eggs instead of 2. Bake cakes in two 8-inch sandwich tins and leave until cold. To make chocolate frosting, melt 2oz (50gm) table margarine in 6 tablespoons boiling water. Gradually combine with 4 level tablespoons cocoa powder. Beat chocolate mixture into 1lb (½ kilo) sifted icing sugar. Continue beating until mixture is smooth and well-combined. Cut each cake in half and sandwich together with chocolate frosting. Spread rest of frosting over top and sides of cake and chill lightly before serving.

American frosted sandwich

American frosted sandwich

Makes about 10 portions

Make as for Victoria sandwich (see page 204), but increase fat, flour and sugar to 6oz (150gm) each and use 3 standard eggs instead of 2. Bake cakes in two 8-inch sandwich tins then leave until cold. To make American frosting, put 1lb (½ kilo) granulated sugar and ¼ pint (125ml) water into a saucepan. Stir over low heat until sugar dissolves. Bring to boil and boil briskly until a little of the syrup forms a firm ball when dropped into very cold water. Meanwhile, beat 2 egg whites and a good pinch of cream of tartar to a very stiff snow. Whisking continuously, add syrup to whites in a slow, steady stream. Add vanilla and continue whisking until icing is cold and thick enough to spread. Sandwich cakes together with a little of the frosting plus some fresh raspberries, redcurrants, chopped strawberries or blackberries. Quickly cover top and sides with rest of frosting, swirling it on with a knife. Leave until icing is firm before cutting cake.

Chocolate coconut cake

Makes about 8 portions

Make as for Victoria sandwich (see page 204), using 3½oz (87gm) self-raising flour, sifted with ½oz (12gm) cocoa powder and soft brown sugar instead of white. Leave until cold. Make up half quantity of chocolate frosting as given for chocolate frosted layer cake, left. Sandwich both cakes together with frosting then spread remainder over top and sides. Press about 1oz (25gm) desiccated coconut against the sides then decorate top with bands of sifted icing sugar. Chill lightly before serving.

Marzipan petal gateau

Makes about 10 portions

Make as for Victoria sandwich (see page 204), but increase fat, flour and sugar to 6oz (150gm) each and use 3 standard eggs instead of 2. Bake cakes in two 8-inch sandwich tins. Leave until cold then sandwich together with 2 tablespoons lemon curd. To make lemon butter cream, beat 3oz (75gm) softened butter with 6oz (150gm) sifted icing sugar, 1 level teaspoon finely-grated lemon peel and 2 teaspoons lemon juice. Continue to beat until mixture is light and fluffy. Spread round sides of cake then roll in about 2oz (50gm) chopped walnuts. To make almond paste, put 4oz (100gm) each ground almonds, sifted icing sugar and caster sugar into bowl. Mix to a stiff paste with 1 egg yolk, ½ teaspoon almond essence and few drops of vanilla essence. Work in a little yellow food colouring and knead until mixture is evenly coloured and smooth. Roll out thinly on a board lightly dusted with sifted icing sugar. Cut into rounds with a 1-inch cutter, ¾-inch cutter and ½-inch cutter. Pinch up to make petals then arrange in overlapping circles on top of cake, starting from the outside edge with the largest petals and working inwards. Fill in centres with tiny coloured sweets.

Marzipan petal gateau

Frosted grape layer sandwich

Easter cockerel cake

Makes about 10 portions

Make as for Victoria sandwich (see page 204), but bake in one fairly deep 8-inch sandwich tin for about 45 to 50 minutes then leave until cold. Make up almond paste as given for marzipan petal gateau (see page 205). Knead until smooth then roll out evenly on surface dusted with sifted icing sugar. Spread top of cake with a little lemon curd then cover with almond paste. Reserve trimmings. Cut cake in half and spread cut outside edges with lemon curd. Cover with strips of almond paste. Stand 'tail' and 'body' portions of cake on a board, as shown in photograph. Make leg and foot from almond paste and place against body as shown. Outline body, wing, eye and foot with piped lines of glacé icing, made by mixing a little sifted icing sugar to a fairly thick paste with cold water or lemon juice. Soak long thin strips of angelica in warm water until softened and use to decorate the tail. Make the comb and beak from crystallised flower petals.

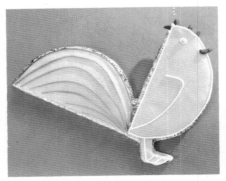

Easter cockerel cake

Raspberry cream layer sandwich

Makes about 8 portions

Make as for Victoria sandwich (see page 204), and leave until cold. Whip $\frac{1}{2}$ pint (250ml) double cream with 2 tablespoons milk and 2 level tablespoons caster sugar until thick. Stir in 1 teaspoon vanilla essence. Sandwich cakes together with half the cream and 6oz (150gm) raspberries. Cover top of cake with remaining cream and stud with more raspberries, using about 6oz (150gm). Chill lightly before serving.

Frosted grape layer sandwich

Makes about 10 portions

Make as for Victoria sandwich (see page 204), but increase fat, flour and sugar to 6oz (150gm) each and use 3 standard eggs instead of 2. Bake cakes in three 7-inch sandwich tins then leave until cold. Halve 3oz (75gm) black grapes and 3oz (75gm) green grapes, first reserving 3 small bunches of each for decoration. Remove pips from halved grapes and discard. Beat $\frac{1}{2}$ pint (250ml) double Devon cream, 2 tablespoons milk and 2 level tablespoons caster sugar until thick. Put two-thirds into a bowl and gently fold in the halved grapes. Sandwich cakes together with the cream and grapes then swirl remaining cream on top. Refrigerate about 30 minutes. Just before serving, beat 1 egg white until foamy. Dip reserved bunches of grapes into egg white then toss in caster sugar. Place on top of cake.

Coffee frosted walnut cake

Makes about 10 portions

Make as for Victoria sandwich (see page 204), but increase fat, flour and sugar to 6oz (150gm) each and use 3 standard eggs instead of 2. Bake cakes in two 8-inch sandwich tins and leave until cold. To make coffee frosting, dissolve 2 level teaspoons gelatine in $\frac{1}{4}$ pint (125ml) hot, strong coffee and leave until cold. Beat egg white to a stiff snow. Gradually beat in coffee mixture alternately with 8oz (200gm) sifted icing sugar and continue beating until mixture thickens to a spreading consistency. Quickly stir in 2oz (50gm) chopped walnuts. Sandwich cakes together with frosting then spread remainder over top and sides. Decorate top with walnut halves and glacé cherries.

Above: coffee frosted walnut cake
Right: raspberry cream layer sandwich

Mandarin layer cake

Makes about 10 portions

Make as for Victoria sandwich (see page 204), but increase fat, sugar and flour to 6oz (150gm) each and use 3 standard eggs instead of 2. Bake cakes in two 8-inch sandwich tins then leave until cold. Make up vanilla butter cream by beating 6oz (150gm) softened butter with 12oz (300gm) sifted icing sugar, 4 dessertspoons cold milk and 1 teaspoon vanilla essence. Take a third of the butter cream and stir in 3 tablespoons drained and chopped mandarins. Use to sandwich cakes together. Colour remaining butter cream pale orange with food colouring and spread two-thirds over top and sides of cake. Roll sides in 6 to 8 level tablespoons finely-chopped nuts, crushed biscuit crumbs or crushed breakfast cereal. Pipe remaining butter cream on top of cake then decorate with well-drained mandarins. Chill lightly before serving.

Coffee crunch cakes

Makes about 6

3oz (75gm) quick-cooking oats

3 egg whites

5oz (125gm) caster sugar

2oz (50gm) ground almonds

½ teaspoon almond essence

3oz (75gm) butter

6oz (150gm) icing sugar, sifted

1 tablespoon very strong coffee

1. Pre-heat oven to moderate, 350 deg F or gas 4 (180 deg C).
2. Well-grease a Swiss roll tin measuring approximately 8 inches by 12 inches.
3. Grill oats until lightly brown, turning frequently.
4. Beat egg whites to a stiff snow.
5. Fold in oats, sugar, almonds and essence.
6. When smooth and evenly combined, transfer to prepared tin, spreading mixture evenly with a knife.
7. Bake in centre of oven for 20 minutes. Remove from oven then reduce heat to cool, 300 deg F or gas 3 (150 deg C).
8. Cut mixture into rounds with a 2½-inch cutter, but leave rounds in the tin.
9. Return to oven and bake a further 20 minutes.
10. Remove rounds and leave on one side. Crush trimmings and return to oven for a further 20 minutes or until well-browned.
11. To make butter cream, beat butter to a soft cream. Gradually beat in icing sugar alternately with coffee.
12. Sandwich rounds together in pairs with coffee cream then spread remainder over top and sides.
13. Coat with crushed trimmings then decorate with chocolate buttons or other chocolate shapes.

Chocolate cream gateau, strawberry mountain cake, mushroom gateau, mandarin layer cake and coffee crunch cakes

Chocolate cream gateau

Makes about 10 portions

Make as for Victoria sandwich (see page 204), but increase fat, flour and sugar to 6oz (150gm) each and use 3 standard eggs instead of 2. Bake cakes in two 8-inch sandwich tins then leave until cold. Make up chocolate butter cream by beating to a light and fluffy cream 6oz (150gm) softened butter with 12oz (300gm) sifted icing sugar, 3oz (75gm) melted and cooled plain chocolate, 1 dessertspoon milk and 1 teaspoon vanilla essence. Sandwich cakes together with about a quarter of the butter cream then spread some of the remainder over top and sides. Roll sides in puffed breakfast cereal then pipe rows of cream in rosettes on top of cake. Decorate with about 6 small chocolate biscuits, lightly sprinkled with sifted icing sugar.

Strawberry mountain cake

Makes about 10 portions

Make as for Victoria sandwich (see page 204), but increase fat, flour and sugar to 6oz (150gm) each and use 3 standard eggs instead of 2. Bake cakes in two 8-inch sandwich tins then leave until cold. Cut a 4-inch circle out of one of the layers and leave, with the outer ring, on one side. Whip ½ pint (250ml) double cream with 2 tablespoons milk and 4 level tablespoons caster sugar until thick. Divide in half. Add 8oz (200gm) chopped strawberries to half the cream. Pile thickly over uncut layer of cake, building it up in the centre. Stand ring of cake on top then place 4-inch round in the centre so that it rests on the cream mixture and stands above top of other cake. Pipe rows of whipped cream attractively on the cake then decorate with 6 to 8oz (150 to 200gm) fresh strawberries. Sift icing sugar lightly over the top and chill for about 30 minutes before serving.

Mushroom gateau

Makes about 10 portions

Make as for Victoria sandwich (see page 204), but increase fat, sugar and flour to 6oz (150gm) each and use 3 standard eggs instead of 2. Bake cakes in two 8-inch sandwich tins then leave until cold. Whip ½ pint (250ml) double cream with 2 tablespoons milk and 2 level tablespoons caster sugar until thick. Sandwich cakes together with apricot jam and approximately a quarter of the cream. Spread top and sides with rest of cream then roll sides in 6 to 8 level tablespoons crushed sweet biscuits. Cover top with 1oz (25gm) desiccated coconut, coloured green with a little food colouring. Decorate with 'mushrooms' and stalks made from white marshmallows. For brown effect, brush marshmallows with a little strong coffee. Chill lightly before serving.

Easter bonnet cake

Easter bonnet cake

Makes about 8 portions

4oz (100gm) butter or margarine, softened

4oz (100gm) caster sugar

½ teaspoon almond essence

2 standard eggs

2oz (50gm) self-raising flour

1 level dessertspoon cocoa powder

2oz (50gm) ground almonds

3oz (75gm) butter, softened

1lb 3oz (475gm) icing sugar, sifted

a little water or strained lemon juice

chocolate buttons

1. Pre-heat oven to moderate, 350 deg F or gas 4 (180 deg C).
2. Brush two 7-inch sandwich tins with butter. Line bases with greaseproof paper and brush with more butter.
3. Cream butter or margarine with caster sugar and almond essence until light and fluffy.
4. Beat in eggs, one at a time.
5. Sift flour and cocoa and fold into creamed ingredients with ground almonds.
6. Transfer to prepared tins and bake in centre of oven for 25 minutes or until well-risen and golden.
7. Turn out on to wire cooling rack and peel away paper.
8. To make butter cream, cream softened butter and 3oz (75gm) icing sugar until light and fluffy and use to sandwich cakes together.
9. To make glacé icing, mix 8oz (200gm) icing sugar to a thick icing with a little water or lemon juice.
10. Stand cake on wire rack and pour over the icing.
11. Allow to set then repeat, using rest of icing sugar.
12. When set, place cake on board and spread glacé icing around the edge to form brim of hat.
13. Decorate with chocolate buttons and tie a ribbon round the cake.

Black Forest cake

Makes about 12 to 14 portions

4oz (100gm) plain flour

2oz (50gm) butter (for base)

1oz (25gm) hazelnuts, finely ground

9oz (225gm) icing sugar, sifted

beaten egg to mix

2 level tablespoons black cherry jam

5oz (125gm) self-raising flour

1oz (25gm) cocoa powder

6oz (150gm) butter or margarine, softened (for cake)

6oz (150gm) soft brown sugar

1 teaspoon vanilla essence

3 standard eggs

1 can (1lb or ½ kilo) black cherries

3 tablespoons Kirsch or brandy

½ pint (250ml) double cream

1 level tablespoon caster sugar

2 teaspoons very strong black coffee

1 level tablespoon cocoa powder, sifted

2 tablespoons boiling water

4oz (100gm) butter, softened (for coating)

1 teaspoon vanilla essence

about 2 to 3oz (50 to 75gm) plain chocolate, grated

glacé cherries, tossed in caster sugar

walnut halves

1. Pre-heat oven to moderately hot, 400 deg F or gas 6 (200 deg C).
2. To make base, sift plain flour into bowl. Rub in butter finely. Add hazelnuts and 1oz (25gm) icing sugar.
3. Mix to stiff paste with egg. Wrap in foil and refrigerate about 15 minutes.
4. Turn out on to a floured surface and roll into an 8-inch round. Transfer to baking tray and bake just above centre of oven for 15 to 20 minutes or until pale gold.
5. Remove from oven and transfer to wire cooling rack. Spread with jam when cold. Reduce oven temperature to moderate, 350 deg F or gas 4 (180 deg C).
6. To make cakes, brush two 8-inch sandwich tins with melted butter and line the bases with buttered greaseproof paper.
7. Sift together self-raising flour and cocoa powder. Cream butter or margarine with soft brown sugar and essence until light and fluffy.
8. Beat in eggs, one at a time, adding a tablespoon of sieved dry ingredients with each.
9. Fold in rest of dry ingredients with a metal spoon then transfer to prepared tins.
10. Bake in centre of oven for 25 to 30 minutes or until well-risen and firm.
11. Turn out on to a wire cooling rack, strip off paper then moisten cakes with 2 tablespoons syrup from can of cherries mixed with the Kirsch or brandy. Leave until completely cold.
12. Halve cherries and remove stones. Drain thoroughly.
13. Beat cream and sugar together until thick. Divide into 2 portions and flavour one with coffee.
14. Sandwich cake together with the plain portion of whipped cream and the canned cherries. Place on top of jam-covered base.
15. To make chocolate butter cream, mix cocoa to a smooth paste with boiling water and leave until completely cold.
16. Beat butter and remaining icing sugar to a light and fluffy cream. Gradually beat in cooled cocoa and vanilla essence.
17. Cover top and sides of cake with butter cream then press grated chocolate against the sides.
18. Pipe whirls of whipped coffee cream on top of cake then decorate with cherries and walnut halves.
19. Chill lightly before serving.

Cherry walnut chocolate gateau

Makes about 12 portions

Make chocolate layer cake as for Black Forest cake, left. Leave until cold. Melt 3oz (75gm) plain chocolate in a basin over a saucepan of hot, but not boiling water. Spread out thickly on to a large sheet of waxed paper and leave until firm and set. Meanwhile, make chocolate butter cream. Mix 1 level tablespoon cocoa to a smooth paste with 2 tablespoons boiling water and leave until cold. Beat 6oz (150gm) softened butter and 12oz (300gm) sifted icing sugar to a light and fluffy cream. Beat in cooled cocoa. Sandwich cakes together with a little of the butter cream then spread more butter cream over top and sides. Colour 1 heaped tablespoon butter cream dark brown with gravy browning. Put into icing bag fitted with a writing tube and pipe lines across the cake. For feather design, draw a skewer alternately up and down the cake across the piped lines. Cover sides with about 2oz (50gm) finely-chopped walnuts then, using remaining butter cream, pipe rosettes round top edge of cake. Cut chocolate on waxed paper into 1½-inch squares then cut the squares into triangles. Use, with glacé cherries tossed in icing sugar, to decorate top of cake. Chill lightly before serving.

Brandied almond layer torte

Makes about 8 to 9 portions

3oz (75gm) plain flour

3 large eggs

3oz (75gm) caster sugar

1oz (25gm) ground almonds

8oz (200gm) butter

1lb (½ kilo) icing sugar, sifted

½ to 1 teaspoon almond essence

1 tablespoon hot water

1 tablespoon brandy

3oz (75gm) flaked almonds, lightly toasted

1. Pre-heat oven to moderate, 350 deg F or gas 4 (180 deg C).
2. Brush a 7-inch round cake tin with melted butter. Line base and sides with greaseproof paper and brush with more melted butter.
3. Sift flour twice on to a plate.
4. Put eggs and sugar into a bowl over a large saucepan of hot water.
5. Whisk continuously until mixture thickens to the consistency of softly-whipped cream and is twice its original volume.
6. Using a metal spoon, gently and lightly fold in ground almonds and flour.
7. When mixture is smooth and well-blended, transfer to prepared tin.
8. Bake in centre of oven for 45 minutes or until well-risen and golden.
9. Leave in tin 5 minutes then turn out on to a wire cooling rack. Carefully peel away paper and leave cake until cold.
10. To make butter cream, beat butter to a soft cream. Gradually add icing sugar, essence, hot water and brandy and continue beating until mixture is light and fluffy.
11. Cut cake into 3 layers and sandwich together with butter cream.
12. Spread more butter cream over top and sides then stud with toasted almonds.
13. Chill lightly before serving.

Brandied almond layer torte

Above: Black Forest cake. Below: cherry walnut chocolate gateau

Orange layer torte

Makes about 8 to 9 portions

Make as for brandied almond layer torte (see page 210), but transfer mixture to two well-buttered 7-inch sandwich tins, with the bases lined with buttered greaseproof paper. Bake 20 minutes in centre of moderate oven, 350 deg F or gas 4 (180 deg C). Turn out on to wire cooling rack and carefully peel away paper. Leave until cold. Drain 1 can mandarins. Reserve 5 segments and chop remainder. To make lemon butter cream, beat 4oz (100gm) butter and 1 level teaspoon finely-grated lemon peel to a soft cream. Gradually add 8oz (200gm) sifted icing sugar alternately with 2 dessertspoons lemon juice and continue beating until mixture is light and fluffy. Slice each cake into 2 layers. Sandwich first two layers together with butter cream. Spread top with apricot jam then cover with chopped mandarins. Add third layer of cake then spread with more butter cream. Finally add last layer of cake. Decorate top with 5 heaped teaspoons of butter cream then press a mandarin segment into each.

Danish almond cake

Makes about 10 portions

6oz (150gm) Danish butter

8oz (200gm) caster sugar

3 standard eggs

2oz (50gm) ground almonds

8oz (200gm) self-raising flour, sifted

2 tablespoons cold milk

4oz (100gm) almonds, blanched and roughly chopped

1 level tablespoon plain flour

1 tablespoon single cream

1. Pre-heat oven to moderately hot, 375 deg F or gas 5 (190 deg C).
2. Well-butter an 8-inch loose-bottomed cake tin. Line base with greased grease-proof paper.
3. Cream butter and 6oz (150gm) sugar together until light and fluffy.
4. Beat in whole eggs, one at a time.
5. Stir in ground almonds then gently fold in self-raising flour alternately with milk.
6. Transfer to prepared tin and bake in centre of oven for 1 hour.
7. Put chopped almonds, remaining caster sugar, plain flour and cream into a saucepan. Slowly bring to boil, stirring.
8. Spread over top of cake then return to oven for a further 10 to 15 minutes or until a wooden cocktail stick, inserted into centre of cake, comes out clean.
9. Leave in tin 15 minutes then turn out and cool on a wire rack.

Danish spiced butter cake

Makes about 12 portions

6oz (150gm) plain flour

1½ level teaspoons baking powder

½ level teaspoon mixed spice

6oz (150gm) Danish butter, softened

6oz (150gm) caster sugar

3 standard eggs

1oz (25gm) mixed chopped peel

1oz (25gm) almonds, blanched and split

1. Pre-heat oven to moderately hot, 375 deg F or gas 5 (190 deg C).
2. Grease and line a Swiss roll tin measuring approximately 8 inches by 12 inches.
3. Sift together flour, baking powder and spice.
4. Cream butter and sugar together until light and fluffy.
5. Beat in whole eggs, one at a time, adding a tablespoon of sifted dry ingredients with each.
6. Stir in peel then gradually fold in rest of flour.
7. Spread into prepared tin then cover top with rows of almonds.
8. Bake for 30 to 40 minutes or until well-risen and golden brown.
9. Leave in tin 10 minutes then cut into 12 squares and cool on a wire rack.

Cherry cake

Makes about 10 portions

4oz (100gm) glacé cherries

8oz (200gm) self-raising flour

2oz (50gm) fine semolina

4oz (100gm) butter

4oz (100gm) caster sugar

2 standard eggs, beaten

1 teaspoon vanilla essence

2 to 3 tablespoons cold milk

1. Pre-heat oven to moderate, 350 deg F or gas 4 (180 deg C).
2. Well-grease a 2lb (1 kilo) loaf tin.
3. Quarter glacé cherries. Wash well to remove syrup then dry thoroughly.
4. Sift flour and semolina into bowl. Add butter and rub in finely with fingertips.
5. Add sugar and cherries and toss ingredients lightly together.
6. Mix to a fairly stiff batter with eggs, vanilla and milk, stirring briskly without beating.
7. Transfer to prepared tin and bake in centre of oven for about 1 hour until well-risen and golden or until a wooden cocktail stick, inserted into centre, comes out clean.
8. Leave in tin 15 minutes then turn out and cool on a wire rack.

Sand cake

Makes about 10 portions

4½oz (112gm) plain flour

4oz (100gm) cornflour

2 level teaspoons baking powder

10oz (250gm) butter, softened

6oz (150gm) caster sugar

3 standard eggs

1 teaspoon lemon juice

1. Pre-heat oven to moderately hot, 375 deg F or gas 5 (190 deg C).
2. Well-butter and lightly flour an 8-inch deep ring tin.
3. Sift together flour, cornflour and baking powder.
4. Cream butter and sugar together until light and fluffy.
5. Beat in whole eggs, one at a time, adding a tablespoon of sifted dry ingredients with each.
6. Fold in rest of dry ingredients with a large metal spoon then lastly add lemon juice.
7. Transfer to prepared tin and bake in centre of oven for ¾ to 1 hour or until well-risen and golden.
8. Leave in tin for 15 minutes then turn out and cool on a wire rack.

Farmhouse cake

Illustrated on page 203

Makes about 8 portions

6oz (150gm) self-raising flour

pinch of salt

4oz (100gm) butter or margarine

4oz (100gm) caster sugar

3oz (75gm) currants

3oz (75gm) sultanas

1oz (25gm) mixed chopped peel

2 large eggs

3 tablespoons milk

little caster sugar to decorate

1. Pre-heat oven to moderate, 350 deg F or gas 4 (180 deg C).
2. Well-grease and line base and sides of a 7-inch round cake tin with greased greaseproof paper.
3. Sift flour and salt into bowl.
4. Rub in butter or margarine finely then stir in sugar and dried fruit.
5. Mix to a dropping consistency with beaten eggs and milk, stirring briskly without beating.
6. Transfer mixture to prepared tin and bake in centre of oven for 1 to 1¼ hours or until a wooden cocktail stick, inserted into centre, comes out clean.
7. Leave in tin to cool slightly before turning out on to a wire rack. Cover top with a little caster sugar.

Note
It is better to keep the cake at least 1 day before cutting.

In the background: orange layer torte, squares of Danish spiced butter cake and sand cake. In the foreground: Danish almond cake and cherry cake

Malted loaf

Illustrated on page 203

Makes about 8 portions

8oz (200gm) self-raising flour

pinch of salt

2oz (50gm) soft brown sugar

2oz (50gm) stoned dates, chopped

2oz (50gm) mixed dried fruit

2oz (50gm) malted milk drink powder

2 tablespoons golden syrup, melted

about ¼ pint (125ml) milk and water, mixed

1. Pre-heat oven to moderate, 350 deg F or gas 4 (180 deg C).
2. Well-grease a 1lb (½ kilo) loaf tin.
3. Sift dry ingredients into bowl. Add fruit and malted milk drink powder.
4. Stir in syrup and enough liquid to make a dropping consistency.
5. Pour into prepared tin and bake in centre of oven for about 1 hour or until wooden cocktail stick, inserted into centre, comes out clean.

Note

Keep loaf in an airtight tin for 1 day before eating. Slice thinly and spread with butter.

Cherry basket cakes

Illustrated on page 203

Makes 6 cakes

2oz (50gm) butter or margarine, softened

2oz (50gm) caster sugar

1 standard egg

2oz (50gm) self-raising flour

1 level dessertspoon cocoa powder

pinch of salt

3oz (75gm) butter

6oz (150gm) icing sugar, sifted

½ teaspoon vanilla essence

2 teaspoons milk

6 glacé cherries, sliced

6 strips of angelica about 3 inches long

1. Pre-heat oven to moderately hot, 375 deg F or gas 5 (190 deg C).
2. Cream butter or margarine and sugar until light and fluffy.
3. Beat in egg. Fold in flour sifted with cocoa and salt.
4. Add 1 or 2 teaspoons milk if necessary to give a soft dropping consistency.
5. Place a paper case in each of 6 bun tins.
6. Put equal amounts of cake mixture into each.
7. Bake in centre of oven for about 15 minutes or until well-risen and golden. Cool on a wire rack.
8. To make butter cream, beat butter to a light, fluffy cream with icing sugar. Beat in vanilla essence and milk.
9. Pipe rosettes of butter cream on to top of cakes then decorate each with 'flowers' of cherries. Attach a handle of angelica to each.

Flake cream sandwich

Illustrated on page 203

Makes about 8 to 10 portions

4oz (100gm) plain flour

2 level tablespoons cocoa powder

2 level teaspoons baking powder

4oz (100gm) butter or margarine, softened

4oz (100gm) caster sugar

2 standard eggs

4oz (100gm) butter, softened

6oz (150gm) icing sugar, sifted

2 dessertspoons milk

5 chocolate flake bars

5 walnut halves

1. Pre-heat oven to moderately hot, 375 deg F or gas 5 (190 deg C).
2. Well-grease a Swiss roll tin measuring approximately 12 inches by 8 inches then line with greased greaseproof paper.
3. Sift together dry ingredients.
4. Cream butter or margarine and sugar until light and fluffy.
5. Beat in whole eggs then fold in dry ingredients.
6. Transfer mixture to prepared tin and bake in centre of oven for 25 to 30 minutes or until well-risen and golden.
7. Turn out on to a wire cooling rack.
8. To make butter cream, beat butter and icing sugar together until light and fluffy then beat in milk.
9. Cut cake in half and sandwich together with butter cream.
19. Either pipe or spread remaining butter cream thickly over top of cake.
11. Decorate with flake bars and walnuts.

Chocolate rum cake

Chocolate rum cake

Makes about 8 to 10 portions

5oz (125gm) plain flour

1oz (25gm) cocoa powder

2 level teaspoons baking powder

5oz (125gm) soft brown sugar

2 standard eggs, separated

6 tablespoons salad oil

8 tablespoons milk

1 teaspoon vanilla essence

4 tablespoons rum

¼ pint (125ml) double cream

2 level tablespoons icing sugar, sifted

about 10 walnut halves

1. Pre-heat oven to moderate, 350 deg F or gas 4 (180 deg C).
2. Well-grease and line an 8-inch square tin.
3. Sift flour, cocoa and baking powder into bowl. Stir in brown sugar.
4. Add egg yolks, oil, 6 tablespoons milk and vanilla and beat to a smooth batter.
5. Beat egg whites to a soft snow and fold into batter with a large metal spoon.
6. Transfer to prepared tin and bake in centre of oven for 1¼ hours until well-risen and golden or until a wooden cocktail stick, inserted into centre, comes out clean.
7. Leave in tin 10 minutes then turn out on to a wire rack. Make several holes in the cake with a skewer then pour in the rum. Leave cake until completely cold.
8. Beat cream, remaining milk and icing sugar together until thick. Pile on top of cake then decorate with walnut halves.

Cherry flan cake

Cherry flan cake

Makes about 10 portions

short crust pastry made with 8oz (200gm) flour (see page 108)

4oz (100gm) glacé cherries

3oz (75gm) soft, luxury margarine

3oz (75gm) caster sugar

2 large eggs

2oz (50gm) self-raising flour

2oz (50gm) ground almonds

½ teaspoon almond essence

2 tablespoons apricot jam, warm and sieved

4 heaped tablespoons icing sugar, sifted

a little lemon juice

2 almonds

1. Pre-heat oven to moderate, 350 deg F or gas 4 (180 deg C).
2. Roll out pastry and use to line an 8-inch fluted flan ring on an ungreased baking tray. Trim off surplus pastry and reserve.
3. Line base with halved cherries, reserving 1 whole cherry.
4. To make filling, put margarine, caster sugar, egg, ground almonds and essence into a bowl. Beat until well-mixed— 2 to 3 minutes.
5. Spread into pastry case over cherries then decorate with strips of pastry cut from rolled pastry trimmings.
6. Bake in centre of oven for 45 minutes or until well-risen.
7. Remove from oven and brush top completely with melted jam. Leave until cold then remove flan ring.
8. Mix icing sugar to a thick icing with a little lemon juice.
9. Spread on to middle of cake then decorate with almonds. Stand reserved cherry in the centre.

Cherry marshmallow bars

Makes about 36

4oz (100gm) butter

3 level dessertspoons cocoa powder

4oz (100gm) icing sugar, sifted

1 egg, beaten

1 teaspoon vanilla essence

3½oz (87gm) desiccated coconut

6oz (150gm) digestive biscuits, crushed

6 tablespoons cold water

1lb (½ kilo) caster sugar

1 level tablespoon gelatine

6 tablespoons boiling water

4oz (100gm) glacé cherries, chopped

½ to 1 teaspoon oil of peppermint

4oz (100gm) plain chocolate, melted

1. Brush a Swiss roll tin measuring approximately 12 inches by 8 inches with oil. Line with greaseproof paper, allowing it to stand about 2 inches above edge of tin. Brush paper with oil.
2. Put butter, cocoa powder and icing sugar into the top of a double saucepan or into a basin over a saucepan of gently-simmering water.
3. Stir until butter melts then add egg, essence, coconut and biscuits. Mix thoroughly then spread thickly over base of prepared tin.
4. To make topping, put cold water and caster sugar into a basin and beat with electric beaters for 5 minutes at high speed.
5. Dissolve gelatine in the boiling water and beat into sugar and water. Continue beating until mixture becomes very thick and white.
6. Fold in cherries and peppermint then quickly spread over crushed biscuit base. Leave until set.
7. Drizzle melted chocolate over the top, leave until firm then cut into approximately 36 pieces.

Sponge sandwich

Makes 6 to 8 portions

3oz (75gm) plain flour

3 large eggs

3oz (75gm) caster sugar

raspberry jam

little caster sugar to decorate

1. Pre-heat oven to moderate, 350 deg F or gas 4 (180 deg C).
2. Well-grease two 7-inch sandwich tins. Line bases with greased greaseproof paper.
3. Sift flour twice on to a plate.
4. Put eggs and sugar into a bowl over a large saucepan of hot water.
5. Whisk continuously until mixture thickens to consistency of softly-whipped cream and is twice its original volume.
6. Using a metal spoon, gently and lightly fold in flour.
7. When evenly combined, transfer to prepared tins.
8. Bake in centre of oven for 20 minutes or until well-risen and golden.
9. Turn out on to a wire cooling rack covered with a clean tea-towel (to prevent wire from cutting into delicate surface of cakes) and carefully peel away paper.
10. Sandwich cakes together with raspberry jam when completely cold, then sprinkle top lightly with caster sugar.

Swiss roll

Makes about 6 to 8 portions

Make as for sponge sandwich, above, but transfer mixture to a greased and lined Swiss roll tin measuring approximately 8 inches by 12 inches. Bake just above centre of hot oven, 425 deg F or gas 7 (220 deg C), for 8 to 9 minutes or until well-risen and golden. Turn out on to a sheet of sugared greaseproof paper on a damp tea-towel. Peel away lining paper then cut away crisp edges of cake. Spread Swiss roll with jam (about 3 level tablespoons) then roll up, starting from one of the shorter sides. Hold in place for about 1 minute then leave until completely cold before cutting.

Cherry marshmallow bars

Frangipan flan

Frangipan flan

Makes about 10 portions

short crust pastry made with 4oz (100gm) flour (see page 108)

1 level tablespoon lemon curd or raspberry jam

2oz (50gm) butter, softened

2oz (50gm) caster sugar

1 standard egg

2oz (50gm) ground almonds

1½ teaspoons almond essence

½oz (12gm) self-raising flour

8oz (200gm) icing sugar, sifted

5 to 6 teaspoons hot water

4 glacé cherries

8 leaves cut from angelica

1. Pre-heat oven to moderately hot, 375 deg F or gas 5 (190 deg C).
2. Roll out pastry and use to line a 7-inch flan ring on a baking tray. Spread base with lemon curd or jam.
3. Cream butter and caster sugar until light and fluffy.
4. Beat in whole egg then stir in almonds, ½ teaspoon essence and flour.
5. Transfer to flan case then bake in centre of oven for about 30 minutes or until golden and firm. Remove from oven. Leave until cold then lift off flan ring.
6. To make icing, put icing sugar into a bowl and gradually mix to a fairly stiff icing with remaining essence and water.
7. Spread over top of flan and leave until set.
8. Before serving, decorate with cherries and leaves of angelica.

Mocha fudge cake

Makes about 10 portions

10oz (250gm) plain flour

1 level teaspoon bicarbonate of soda

½ level teaspoon cream of tartar

2oz (50gm) cocoa powder

large pinch of salt

4oz (100gm) cooking fat

7 tablespoons very strong black coffee

7oz (175gm) soft brown sugar

4oz (100gm) caster sugar

1 teaspoon vanilla essence

¼ pint (125ml) milk, soured with 1 dessertspoon lemon juice

2 large eggs, beaten

4oz (100gm) plain chocolate

½ pint (250ml) double cream

6oz (150gm) icing sugar, sifted

2oz (50gm) hazelnuts

1. Pre-heat oven to moderate, 350 deg F or gas 4 (180 deg C).
2. Brush two 8-inch sandwich tins with melted fat. Line bases with rounds of greaseproof paper. Brush paper with more fat.
3. Sift dry ingredients into bowl.
4. Melt cooking fat in the coffee. Stir in brown and caster sugars and essence.
5. Add to dry ingredients alternately with milk and eggs.
6. Stir briskly, without beating, until smooth then divide equally between prepared tins.
7. Bake just above centre of oven for 35 to 40 minutes or until cakes are well-risen and springy when pressed lightly with the fingertips.
8. Leave in tins 5 minutes then turn out on to a wire cooling rack.
9. Strip off paper and leave until cold. Cut each cake into 2 layers.
10. Break up chocolate and put into a basin over a saucepan of hot water. Leave until melted, stirring once or twice. Remove basin from saucepan of water and leave chocolate to cool.
11. Beat cream until just thick. Gradually stir in icing sugar and cooled chocolate.
12. Sandwich cake together with chocolate cream then spread remainder over top.
13. Decorate with whole hazelnuts and chill lightly before serving.

Christmas ring cake

Makes about 8 to 10 portions

4oz (100gm) soft, luxury margarine

4oz (100gm) caster sugar

1 level dessertspoon clear honey

1 level teaspoon finely-grated orange peel

½ teaspoon vanilla essence

5oz (125gm) self-raising flour

½ level teaspoon baking powder

2 standard eggs

3 tablespoons cold milk

6oz (150gm) granulated sugar

1 egg white

3 tablespoons cold water

½ teaspoon vanilla essence

1. Pre-heat oven to moderate, 350 deg F or gas 4 (180 deg C).
2. Brush an 8-inch deep ring tin with melted fat.
3. Put margarine, caster sugar, honey, peel, vanilla, flour, baking powder, eggs and milk into a mixing bowl and beat until well blended—about 4 minutes.
4. Transfer to ring tin and bake in centre of oven for 45 minutes until well-risen and golden.
5. Leave in tin 5 minutes then turn out on to a wire cooling rack. Leave until completely cold.
6. To make frosting, put all remaining ingredients into a basin over a saucepan of boiling water. Whisk approximately 7 minutes or until frosting is very white and thick enough to leave a trail.
7. Swirl over cake with a large knife and leave to set.
8. Transfer to a silver cake board or platter lined with aluminium foil.
9. Arrange Christmas decorations round the edge then stand a coloured candle in the centre.

Christmas ring cake

Christmas cake

Family size

8oz (200gm) plain flour

1 level teaspoon mixed spice

1 level teaspoon cinnamon

$\frac{1}{4}$ level teaspoon grated nutmeg

1 level teaspoon cocoa powder

8oz (200gm) butter, softened

8oz (200gm) soft brown sugar (dark variety)

4 standard eggs

1 tablespoon black treacle

1$\frac{1}{2}$lb ($\frac{3}{4}$ kilo) mixed fruit (currants, sultanas and seedless raisins)

4oz (100gm) dates, finely-chopped

4oz (100gm) mixed chopped peel

4oz (100gm) walnuts or blanched almonds, finely chopped

finely-grated peel of 1 medium orange

2 tablespoons brandy or sherry

1. Pre-heat oven to cool, 275 deg F or gas 1 (140 deg C).
2. Brush a 9-inch round cake tin or 8-inch square cake tin with melted butter. Line base and sides with a double thickness of greaseproof paper. Brush paper with melted butter. Tie a strip of double brown paper round outside of tin to prevent cake mixture from burning.
3. Sift flour, spice, cinnamon, nutmeg and cocoa into a bowl.
4. Cream butter and sugar together until light and fluffy.
5. Gradually beat in eggs, one at a time, adding a tablespoon of sieved dry ingredients with each.
6. Stir in treacle, dried fruit, dates, peel, nuts and grated orange peel.
7. Fold in remaining dry ingredients with a metal spoon then transfer mixture to prepared cake tin.
8. Hollow out centre slightly then bake just below centre of oven for 6 hours or until a fine knitting needle or skewer, inserted into centre of cake, comes out clean.
9. Leave in tin until lukewarm then turn out on to a wire cooling rack. Make holes in the cake with a knitting needle or skewer and pour over the brandy or sherry.
10. When completely cold, wrap in foil and store in an airtight tin at least 2 weeks before covering with almond paste.

Christmas cake

Almond paste

8oz (200gm) ground almonds

8oz (200gm) icing sugar, sifted

8oz (200gm) caster sugar

2 egg yolks

1 teaspoon almond essence

$\frac{1}{2}$ teaspoon vanilla essence

1 teaspoon lemon juice

1. Put almonds and both sugars into a bowl.
2. Mix to a stiff paste with egg yolks, essences and lemon juice.
3. Draw together with fingertips then knead until smooth on a board lightly dusted with sifted icing sugar.
4. To cover cake, brush top and sides with melted apricot jam.
5. Roll just under half the almond paste into a round or square, depending on the shape of the cake. Use to cover top.
6. Roll out remaining paste into a strip— the same depth as the cake—and wrap round sides. Press all edges and joins well together to seal.
7. Cover lightly and leave to harden overnight. Next day, wrap in foil and leave 1 week before icing with royal icing.

Royal icing

3 egg whites

$\frac{1}{2}$ teaspoon lemon juice

1$\frac{1}{2}$lb ($\frac{3}{4}$ kilo) icing sugar, sifted

$\frac{1}{2}$ teaspoon glycerine

1. Put egg whites into a clean, dry bowl. Add lemon juice.
2. Whisk until foamy. Gradually beat in icing sugar and glycerine (the glycerine prevents icing from hardening up too much).
3. Continue beating until icing is very white and firm enough to stand in peaks when beaters are lifted out of bowl.
4. Stand cake on cake board. Swirl icing over top and sides then flick upwards with the blade of a knife or back of a teaspoon so that it stands in peaks.
5. Add suitable Christmas decorations as wished.

Plastic icing

As an alternative to royal icing, the cake may be covered with 'plastic' icing which is an Australian speciality. For the recipe I give, I have to thank Margaret Donnelley, a home economist from Perth, Australia, with whom I had the pleasure of working some years ago and who demonstrated this icing to me.

| 1 level dessertspoon gelatine |
| 3 dessertspoons cold water |
| 4oz (100gm) granulated sugar |
| 6 tablespoons hot water |
| 1 dessertspoon lemon juice |
| 1 to 2 teaspoons vanilla essence |
| 1oz (25gm) white cooking fat |
| 1 to 1½lb (½ to ¾ kilo) icing sugar, sifted |

1. Combine gelatine and cold water.
2. Put granulated sugar, hot water and lemon juice into a small saucepan. Bring to boil, stirring.
3. Cover and boil 2 minutes. Uncover and continue to boil a further 4 to 5 minutes or until a little of the syrup, dropped into a cup of very cold water, forms a soft ball. Remove from heat.
4. Add gelatine, vanilla essence and cooking fat. Stir until gelatine dissolves. Cool to lukewarm.
5. Put half the icing sugar into a bowl. Add gelatine mixture and stir thoroughly.
6. Gradually work in rest of sugar, kneading with fingers until icing becomes smooth and pliable.
7. Transfer to a plastic bag and leave overnight at kitchen temperature.
8. Next day, turn out on to a surface dusted with sifted icing sugar and roll out fairly thinly into a round large enough to cover top and sides of cake.
9. Brush almond paste with melted syrup then cover with icing, pressing it on to cake with fingers dipped in icing sugar.
10. Mould or cut trimmings into assorted Christmas shapes, paint green or red with food colouring and place on cake, securing with a little syrup.

Note
1. This icing may be used to cover any special occasion cake and then royal icing used for piping on decorations.
2. Plastic icing moulds well and therefore is ideal for making miniature decorative flowers.
3. Colouring may be kneaded into the icing itself or painted on afterwards.

Easter simnel cake

Family size

Make up cake mixture and almond paste as given for Christmas cake (see page 217). Put half the cake mixture into a greased and paper-lined 9-inch round or 8-inch square cake tin. Roll one-third of the almond paste into a round or square the same size as the tin and place on top of cake mixture. Cover with rest of cake mixture and bake as for Christmas cake. When completely cold, brush top of cake with melted jam or syrup and cover with half the remaining almond paste, rolled into a round or square. Shape rest of almond paste into 11 balls and place round edge of cake. Brush with a little beaten egg white and brown quickly under a hot grill. Decorate with Easter decorations such as chicks, tiny sugar or chocolate Easter eggs and rabbits.

Fruited cobblestone cake

| Makes about 10 to 12 portions |
| 6oz (150gm) soft, luxury margarine |
| 6oz (150gm) caster sugar |
| 3 standard eggs, beaten |
| 2oz (50gm) glacé cherries, quartered |
| 4oz (100gm) sultanas |
| 1oz (25gm) angelica, chopped |
| 8oz (200gm) plain flour and ½ level teaspoon baking powder, sifted together |
| 4oz (100gm) glacé cherries, halved |
| 4 level tablespoons apricot jam, warmed and sieved |

1. Pre-heat oven to moderate, 325 deg F or gas 3 (170 deg C).
2. Brush a 2lb (1 kilo) loaf tin with melted fat. Line base and sides with greaseproof paper and brush with more fat.
3. Place all ingredients except halved cherries and jam together in mixing bowl and beat with a wooden spoon until well-mixed (3 to 4 minutes).
4. Transfer mixture to prepared tin then cover top with rows of halved cherries.
5. Bake in centre of oven for 1¾ to 2 hours or until a wooden cocktail stick, inserted into centre, comes out clean.
6. Leave in tin 5 minutes then turn out on to a cooling rack.
7. Glaze top by brushing with apricot jam.
8. Store in an airtight tin when cold.

Boiled fruit cake

| Makes about 12 to 14 portions |
| 12oz (300gm) plain flour |
| 2 level teaspoons baking powder |
| ½ level teaspoon bicarbonate of soda |
| 1 level teaspoon mixed spice |
| 1 level teaspoon cinnamon |
| 6oz (150gm) mixture of margarine and lard |
| 4oz (100gm) soft brown sugar |
| 6oz (150gm) golden syrup |
| ¼ pint (125ml) plus 4 tablespoons water |
| 12oz (300gm) mixed dried fruit (currants, sultanas and raisins) |
| 2oz (50gm) chopped mixed peel |
| 2 standard eggs, beaten |

1. Pre-heat oven to moderate, 325 deg F or gas 3 (170 deg C).
2. Well-grease and line a 7-inch round cake tin.
3. Sift dry ingredients into a bowl.
4. Put all remaining ingredients, except eggs, into a saucepan.
5. Slowly bring to boil, stirring, then simmer for 5 minutes. Leave until cool.
6. Add to dry ingredients with eggs.
7. Mix thoroughly then transfer to prepared cake tin.
8. Bake in centre of oven for approximately 2 hours or until a wooden cocktail stick, inserted into centre, comes out clean.
9. Leave in tin until lukewarm then turn out on to a wire cooling rack.
10. Store in an airtight tin when cold.

Note
This is a very moist cake which improves with keeping.

Rock cakes

| Makes about 10 |
| 8oz (200gm) self-raising flour |
| 4oz (100gm) butter or margarine (or mixture) |
| 3oz (75gm) caster sugar |
| 4oz (100gm) currants |
| 1 standard egg, beaten |
| 1 or 2 dessertspoons cold milk |

1. Pre-heat oven to moderately hot, 400 deg F or gas 6 (200 deg C).
2. Well-grease a large baking tray.
3. Sift flour into bowl and rub in butter or margarine (or mixture) finely.
4. Add sugar and currants and toss ingredients lightly together.
5. Using a fork, mix to a very stiff batter with egg and milk.
6. Pile 10 rocky heaps on to prepared tray—leaving room between each as they spread slightly—and bake just above centre of oven for 15 to 20 minutes or until golden brown.
7. Cool on a wire rack and store in an airtight tin when cold.

Fruited cobblestone cake

Madeira cake

Makes about 10 to 12 portions

6oz (150gm) butter or margarine (or mixture), softened

6oz (150gm) caster sugar

1 level teaspoon finely-grated lemon peel

3 standard eggs

8oz (200gm) plain flour and 1½ level teaspoons baking powder, sifted together

2 tablespoons cold milk

1 thin strip of candied citron peel

1. Pre-heat oven to moderate, 325 deg F or gas 3 (170 deg C).
2. Brush a 7-inch round cake tin or 2lb (1 kilo) loaf tin with melted butter or margarine. Line base and sides with grease-proof paper. Brush with more melted butter or margarine.
3. Cream butter or margarine (or mixture) with sugar and lemon peel until light and fluffy.
4. Beat in whole eggs, one at a time, adding a tablespoon of sifted dry ingredients with each.
5. Fold in rest of flour alternately with milk then transfer to prepared tin.
6. Stand citron peel in the middle then bake cake in centre of oven for 1½ to 1¾ hours or until a wooden cocktail stick, inserted into centre, comes out clean.
7. Leave in tin 10 minutes then turn out on to a wire cooling rack.
8. Strip off paper when cake is completely cold.
9. Store in an airtight tin.

Note
If preferred, 1 teaspoon vanilla essence may be used instead of grated lemon peel.

Coconut cake

Makes about 10 portions

Make as for Madeira cake, above, but stir in 2oz (50gm) desiccated coconut after beating in the eggs. Increase milk to 3 tablespoons instead of 2.

Genoa cake

Makes about 10 to 12 portions

Make as for Madeira cake, above, but after beating in eggs stir in 8oz (200gm) sultanas, 4oz (100gm) chopped mixed peel, 2oz (50gm) chopped glacé cherries, 2oz (50gm) chopped blanched almonds and the finely-grated peel of ½ lemon. Transfer to prepared tin and cover top with 1oz (25gm) split almonds. Bake 30 minutes longer.

Ginger cake

Makes 10 portions

Make as for Madeira cake (see above), but after beating in eggs stir in 3 to 4oz (75 to 100gm) chopped preserved ginger and sift the flour with 1 to 2 level teaspoons ginger.

Rich Madeira cake

Makes about 10 to 12 portions

Make as for Madeira cake (see above), but increase butter and sugar by 2oz (50gm) each and use 1 more standard egg. Use plain flour only and omit baking powder and milk completely.

Marble cake

Marble cake

Makes about 10 to 12 portions

Make as for rich Madeira cake, left, but after beating in eggs divide mixture into 3 equal parts. Fold 2½oz (62gm) flour into one part and colour pink with red food colouring. Fold 2½oz (62gm) flour sifted with ½oz (12gm) cocoa powder into second part, alternately with 1 dessertspoon cold milk. Fold 2½oz (62gm) flour into third part but otherwise leave plain. Drop alternate tablespoons of the three mixtures into a greased and lined 7-inch round cake tin and bake as for Madeira cake (above, left).

From left to right: malted tea bread, spicy tea bread and walnut orange tea bread

Malted tea bread

Makes about 20 slices

8oz (200gm) plain flour

3 level teaspoons baking powder

pinch of salt

4oz (100gm) golden syrup

4oz (100gm) malt extract

1½oz (37gm) cooking fat

6 tablespoons milk

1 standard egg, beaten

4oz (100gm) sultanas

1. Pre-heat oven to moderate, 325 deg F or gas 3 (170 deg C).
2. Well-grease a 2lb (1 kilo) loaf tin.
3. Sift together flour, baking powder and salt.
4. Put syrup, malt extract and cooking fat into a saucepan and melt over a gentle heat.
5. Remove from heat and stir in milk, egg and sultanas.
6. Gradually beat in to dry ingredients.
7. Transfer to prepared tin and bake in centre of oven for 1¼ hours.
8. Leave in tin until lukewarm then turn out on to a wire cooling rack.
9. Store in an airtight tin when cold and leave 1 to 2 days before eating.
10. Serve the loaf sliced and buttered.

Spicy tea bread

Makes about 20 slices

10oz (250gm) self-raising flour

1 level teaspoon mixed spice

½ level teaspoon each, cinnamon and ginger

4oz (100gm) soft brown sugar

6oz (150gm) sultanas

2oz (50gm) mixed chopped peel

2oz (50gm) margarine

6oz (150gm) golden syrup

1 large egg, beaten

6 tablespoons milk

1. Pre-heat oven to moderate, 325 deg F or gas 3 (170 deg C).
2. Well-grease a 2lb (1 kilo) loaf tin.
3. Sift flour, spice, cinnamon and ginger into a bowl.
4. Add sugar, sultanas and peel.
5. Melt margarine and syrup over low heat. Stir into dry ingredients with egg and milk.
6. Transfer to prepared tin and bake in centre of oven for 1½ hours. Leave in tin until lukewarm.
7. Turn out on to a wire cooling rack.
8. Store in an airtight tin when cold and leave 2 days before cutting.
9. Serve the loaf sliced and buttered.

Walnut orange tea bread

Makes about 20 slices

10oz (250gm) self-raising flour

4oz (100gm) soft brown sugar

4oz (100gm) walnuts, chopped

2 level teaspoons finely-grated orange peel

2oz (50gm) margarine

6oz (150gm) golden syrup

1 large egg, beaten

6 tablespoons milk

1. Pre-heat oven to moderate, 325 deg F or gas 3 (170 deg C).
2. Well-grease a 2lb (1 kilo) loaf tin.
3. Sift flour into bowl. Add sugar, walnuts and orange peel.
4. Melt margarine and syrup over low heat. Stir into dry ingredients with egg and milk.
5. Transfer to prepared tin and bake in centre of oven for 1¼ hours. Leave in tin until lukewarm.
6. Turn out on to a wire cooling rack and store in an airtight tin when cold.
7. Leave 2 days before cutting and serve the loaf sliced and buttered.

Dundee cake

Makes about 12 to 15 portions

8oz (200gm) plain flour

1 level teaspoon mixed spice

8oz (200gm) butter, softened

8oz (200gm) caster sugar

4 standard eggs

1 level teaspoon grated lemon peel

1oz (25gm) blanched almonds, chopped

12oz (300gm) mixed dried fruit (currants, sultanas and seedless raisins)

4oz (100gm) chopped mixed peel

2oz (50gm) glacé cherries, chopped

2oz (50gm) almonds, blanched and split

1. Pre-heat oven to cool, 300 deg F or gas 2 (150 deg C).
2. Brush an 8-inch round cake tin with melted butter. Line base and sides with greaseproof paper. Brush with more butter.
3. Sift flour and spice together.
4. Cream butter with sugar until light and fluffy.
5. Beat in whole eggs, one at a time, adding a tablespoon of sifted dry ingredients with each.
6. Stir in lemon peel, chopped almonds, dried fruit, mixed peel and glacé cherries.
7. Fold in rest of dry ingredients then transfer mixture to prepared tin.
8. Smooth top with knife then cover with blanched and split almonds.
9. Bake in centre of oven for approximately 3½ hours or until a wooden cocktail stick, inserted into centre, comes out clean.
10. Leave in tin until lukewarm then turn out and cool on a wire rack.
11. Store in an airtight tin when cold.

Family raisin cake

Makes about 8 to 10 portions

8oz (200gm) self-raising flour

pinch of salt

4oz (100gm) margarine or cooking fat (or mixture)

4oz (100gm) caster sugar

3oz (75gm) seedless raisins

1 level teaspoon grated lemon peel

1 large egg, beaten

5 to 6 tablespoons cold milk

1. Pre-heat oven to moderate, 350 deg F or gas 4 (180 deg C).
2. Brush a 6-inch round cake tin or 1lb (½ kilo) loaf tin with melted fat.
3. Sift flour and salt into a bowl. Rub in margarine or cooking fat (or mixture).
4. Add sugar, raisins and lemon peel and toss ingredients lightly together.
5. Mix to a dropping consistency with beaten egg and milk, stirring briskly without beating.
6. Transfer to prepared tin and bake in centre of oven for about 1¼ hours until well-risen and golden brown or until a wooden cocktail stick, inserted into centre of cake, comes out clean.
7. Leave in tin 10 minutes then turn out on to a wire cooling rack.
8. Store in an airtight tin when cold.

Cinnamon date cake

Makes about 8 to 10 portions

Make as for family raisin cake (previous recipe), but sift flour and salt with 1 to 2 level teaspoons cinnamon. Add 4oz (100gm) chopped dates instead of raisins and omit lemon peel.

Mixed fruit cake

Makes about 8 to 10 portions

Make as for family raisin cake (see below left), but add 6oz (150gm) mixed dried fruit instead of the raisins.

Linzertorte (Austrian jam flan)

Makes about 8 to 10 portions

6oz (150gm) plain flour

1 level teaspoon cinnamon

6oz (150gm) butter, softened

6oz (150gm) finely-ground hazelnuts

6oz (150gm) caster sugar

1 standard egg, beaten

raspberry jam

a little beaten egg yolk for brushing

icing sugar

1. Sift flour and cinnamon into bowl.
2. Rub in butter then add hazelnuts and sugar.
3. Add beaten egg then draw mixture together with fingertips. Knead lightly until smooth.
4. Wrap in foil and chill dough for 1 to 2 hours.
5. Pre-heat oven to moderate, 350 deg F or gas 4 (180 deg C).
6. Stand an 8-inch flan ring on an ungreased baking tray.
7. Line base and sides thickly with three-quarters of the dough, moulding it evenly with the fingertips.
8. Fill with raspberry jam.
9. Roll out rest of dough on a floured surface and cut into strips.
10. Arrange in lattice design over top of flan.
11. Brush strips and edges with beaten egg then bake in centre of oven for 45 minutes or until golden brown.
12. Remove from oven and dredge sifted icing sugar thickly over the top. Remove flan ring when lukewarm.
13. Leave until completely cold before cutting.

Note

If preferred, a mixture of hazelnuts, walnuts and unblanched almonds may be used, although this is not traditional.

Uncooked chocolate fudge cake

Makes about 30 portions

8oz (200gm) plain chocolate

1lb (½ kilo) plain biscuits

3oz (75gm) caster sugar

2oz (50gm) glacé cherries, chopped

2oz (50gm) glacé pineapple, chopped

2oz (50gm) walnuts, chopped

2oz (50gm) hazelnuts, chopped

2oz (50gm) butter

1 small can evaporated milk

2 standard eggs, beaten

1 teaspoon vanilla essence

1. Line a 2lb (1 kilo) loaf tin with aluminium foil.
2. Break up chocolate into a basin over a saucepan of hot water and leave until melted, stirring once or twice.
3. Put biscuits into a polythene bag and crush fairly finely with a rolling pin. Tip into bowl and add sugar, cherries, pineapple and nuts.
4. Put butter and milk into a saucepan and place over a low heat until butter has melted.
5. Add to crumb mixture with melted chocolate, beaten eggs and vanilla. Stir very well to mix.
6. Transfer to prepared tin. Smooth top with a knife and refrigerate for 12 hours.
7. To serve, lift cake out of tin and cut off as many slices as are needed. Cut slices into fingers and store rest of cake—wrapped in foil—in the refrigerator.

Chocolate brownies

Makes 20

3oz (75gm) plain flour

1½ (37gm) cocoa powder

½ level teaspoon baking powder

4oz (100gm) butter or margarine, softened

8oz (200gm) soft brown sugar

1 teaspoon vanilla essence

2 large eggs

1. Pre-heat oven to moderate, 350 deg F or gas 4 (180 deg C).
2. Well-grease a Swiss roll tin measuring approximately 12 inches by 8 inches.
3. Sift together flour, cocoa powder and baking powder.
4. Cream butter or margarine, sugar and vanilla essence together until light and fluffy.
5. Beat in eggs one at a time, adding a tablespoon of sifted dry ingredients with each.
6. Fold in rest of dry ingredients with a large metal spoon.
7. Spread into prepared tin and bake just above centre of oven for 30 minutes or until well-risen and golden.
8. Cut into 20 fingers while still warm then remove from tin and cool on a wire rack.
9. Store in an airtight tin when cold.

Austrian sachertorte

Makes about 10 to 12 portions

10oz (250gm) plain chocolate

1 tablespoon strong black coffee

2½oz (62gm) plain flour

7oz (175gm) butter, softened

10oz (250gm) icing sugar, sifted

5 large eggs, separated

2½oz (62gm) ground almonds

apricot jam

8 teaspoons warm water

1. Pre-heat oven to moderate, 350 deg F or gas 4 (180 deg C).
2. Brush an 8-inch round cake tin with melted butter. Line base and sides with greaseproof paper and brush with more butter.
3. Break up 6oz (150gm) chocolate and put it and coffee into a basin over a saucepan of hot water. Leave until melted, stirring once or twice. Remove basin from pan and leave chocolate to cool.
4. Sift flour twice.
5. Cream 5oz (125gm) butter with 3oz (75gm) icing sugar until light and fluffy.
6. Beat in egg yolks then stir in almonds and cooled chocolate.
7. Beat egg whites to a stiff snow. Gradually add 3oz (75gm) icing sugar and continue beating until meringue is very stiff and shiny.
8. Gently fold into chocolate mixture alternately with flour.
9. When evenly combined, transfer to prepared tin.
10. Bake in centre of oven for approximately 1 hour or until a wooden cocktail stick, inserted into centre, comes out clean.
11. Leave in tin 15 minutes then turn out on to a wire cooling rack. Peel away paper carefully.
12. When cake is cold, cut in half horizontally and sandwich together with apricot jam. Spread more jam over top and sides.
13. To make icing, break up remaining chocolate and put it and remaining butter into basin over saucepan of hot water. Leave until melted, stirring once or twice.
14. Remove basin from saucepan then stir in remaining icing sugar and water.
15. Continue stirring until smooth then spread over top and sides of cake.
16. Leave until icing is set before cutting the cake.

Note

If liked, the top of the cake may be decorated with whirls of whipped cream and/or crystallised violet petals.

Cheesecake tart

Makes 6 to 8 portions

rich flan pastry made with 6oz (150gm) flour (see page 108)

8oz (200gm) curd cheese

1oz (25gm) cornflour

3 standard eggs, separated

2oz (50gm) caster sugar

finely-grated peel of ½ lemon

2 teaspoons lemon juice

½ teaspoon vanilla essence

4 tablespoons double cream

1. Pre-heat oven to moderately hot, 375 deg F or gas 5 (190 deg C).
2. Stand an 8-inch flan ring on an ungreased baking tray.
3. Roll out pastry and use to line flan ring.
4. Put cheese into a bowl. Stir in cornflour, egg yolks, sugar, lemon peel, lemon juice, and vanilla essence. Mix thoroughly.
5. Beat egg whites to a stiff snow. Beat cream until softly stiff.
6. Fold alternately into cheese mixture with a large metal spoon.
7. Transfer to flan case and bake in centre of oven for 35 minutes.
8. Turn off heat and leave cake to cool completely in the oven.

Note

1. If liked, 2oz (50gm) raisins or sultanas may be added to the cheese mixture before egg whites and cream are folded in.
2. Top may be dredged with sifted icing sugar.

Cinnamon apple cake

Makes about 10 to 12 portions

8oz (200gm) self-raising flour

pinch of salt

1 to 2 level teaspoons cinnamon

¼ level teaspoon bicarbonate of soda

4oz (100gm) golden syrup

4oz (100gm) margarine

4oz (100gm) soft brown sugar

2 large cooking apples

2oz (50gm) walnuts, chopped

2 standard eggs, beaten

½ teaspoon vanilla essence

1. Pre-heat oven to moderate, 350 deg F or gas 4 (180 deg C).
2. Well-grease a 2lb (1 kilo) loaf tin.
3. Sift flour, salt, cinnamon and bicarbonate of soda into bowl.
4. Put syrup, margarine and sugar into a saucepan. Leave over a very low heat until margarine melts.
5. Meanwhile, peel apples and grate fairly coarsely into the flour mixture.
6. Add walnuts, eggs and essence with syrup mixture and stir briskly to mix.
7. Transfer to prepared tin and bake in centre of oven for 1¼ hours or until a wooden cocktail stick, inserted into centre, comes out clean.
8. Turn out on to a wire cooling rack and leave until completely cold.
9. To serve, cut in slices and spread with butter.

Cheesecake tart

222

Gingerbread

Makes about 20 portions

10oz (250gm) plain flour

2 to 3 level teaspoons ground ginger

2 level teaspoons cinnamon

1 level teaspoon mixed spice

1 level teaspoon bicarbonate of soda

4oz (100gm) cooking fat

4oz (100gm) soft brown sugar

6oz (150gm) black treacle

6oz (150gm) golden syrup

2 standard eggs, beaten

$\frac{1}{4}$ pint (125ml) boiling water

1. Pre-heat oven to moderate, 350 deg F or gas 4 (180 deg C).
2. Brush a 10-inch square cake tin with melted cooking fat. Line base and sides with greaseproof paper. Brush with more fat.
3. Sift flour, ginger, cinnamon, spice and bicarbonate of soda into a bowl.
4. Put fat, sugar, treacle and syrup into a saucepan and melt over a low heat.
5. Add to dry ingredients with eggs and water.
6. Stir briskly without beating to combine then transfer to prepared tin.
7. Bake in centre of oven for approximately 45 minutes or until a wooden cocktail stick, inserted into centre, comes out clean.
8. Leave in tin until lukewarm then turn out on to a wire cooling rack and leave until cold.
9. Store in an airtight tin when cold.

Parkin

Makes about 20 portions

6oz (150gm) plain flour

1 level teaspoon bicarbonate of soda

1 level teaspoon cinnamon

1 level teaspoon ground ginger

6oz (150gm) medium oatmeal

3oz (75gm) cooking fat

4oz (100gm) chopped mixed peel

2oz (50gm) soft brown sugar

8oz (200gm) golden syrup

1 standard egg, beaten

2 tablespoons milk

1. Pre-heat oven to moderate, 325 deg F or gas 3 (170 deg C).
2. Well-grease a Yorkshire pudding tin measuring about 8$\frac{1}{2}$ inches by 6$\frac{1}{2}$ inches. Line base with greased greaseproof paper.
3. Sift flour with bicarbonate of soda, cinnamon and ginger. Add oatmeal.
4. Rub in cooking fat finely then add peel and sugar.
5. Mix to a soft consistency with syrup, egg and milk, stirring briskly without beating.
6. Transfer to prepared tin and bake in centre of oven for 1 hour.
7. Leave in tin 15 minutes then turn out on to a wire cooling rack.
8. Store in an airtight tin when completely cold and leave at least 1 day before cutting.

Cream horns

Cream horns

Makes 12

flaky pastry made with 8oz (200gm) flour (see page 111) or 1 large packet frozen puff pastry

milk for brushing

caster sugar

raspberry or strawberry jam

$\frac{1}{2}$ pint (250ml) double cream

2 tablespoons milk

2 level tablespoons icing sugar, sifted

1. Pre-heat oven to hot, 450 deg F or gas 8 (230 deg C).
2. Brush 12 cream horn tins with melted butter.
3. Roll out pastry thinly and cut into 12 strips, each about 1 inch wide.
4. Moisten one side of each strip with water.
5. Wind pastry strips (moist side inside) round tins, starting from the pointed end of each and overlapping pastry slightly.
6. Transfer to a wetted baking tray and leave to rest for 30 minutes.
7. Bake in centre of oven for 10 minutes.
8. Remove from oven, brush with milk and sprinkle with sugar. Return to oven for a further 7 minutes or until golden brown.
9. Remove from oven and transfer to a wire cooling rack.
10. Leave until lukewarm then gently remove tins.
11. Just before serving, put a heaped teaspoon of jam into each pastry horn then fill with cream, whipped until thick with the milk and icing sugar.

Note
If liked, put half a flake bar into each cream horn.

Florentines

Makes 12

3$\frac{1}{2}$oz (87gm) butter

4 tablespoons milk

4oz (100gm) icing sugar, sifted

1$\frac{1}{2}$oz (37gm) plain flour

2oz (50gm) chopped mixed peel

1oz (25gm) sultanas

2oz (50gm) glacé cherries

3oz (75gm) flaked almonds

1 teaspoon lemon juice

4oz (100gm) plain chocolate

1. Pre-heat oven to moderately hot, 375 deg F or gas 5 (190 deg C).
2. Brush 2 large baking trays with oil then cover with rice paper.
3. Put 3oz (75gm) butter, milk and sugar into a saucepan and leave over a low heat until butter melts.
4. Remove from heat and stir in all other ingredients except chocolate and remaining butter. Leave until completely cold.
5. Put equal amounts of mixture—well apart to allow for spreading—on to prepared trays.
6. Bake just above centre of oven for 12 minutes or until pale gold.
7. Leave until lukewarm, then carefully lift Florentines off trays, removing surplus rice paper round each.
8. Cool on a wire rack.
9. Break up chocolate and put it and remaining butter into a basin over a saucepan of hot water. Leave until melted, stirring once or twice.
10. Spread rice paper sides of Florentines with melted chocolate and, when half set, mark into wavy lines with a fork.
11. Leave until chocolate has set completely before eating.

Walnut squares

Makes about 18

2 standard eggs

4oz (100gm) caster sugar

4oz (100gm) golden syrup

3oz (75gm) butter or margarine

3oz (75gm) self-raising flour, sifted

4oz (100gm) walnuts, finely chopped

$\frac{1}{2}$ teaspoon vanilla essence

icing sugar

1. Pre-heat oven to moderate, 325 deg F or gas 3 (170 deg C).
2. Well-butter a Swiss roll tin measuring approximately 12 inches by 8 inches.
3. Put eggs and sugar into a bowl over a saucepan of hot water and whisk continuously until thick.
4. Melt syrup and butter or margarine then add to eggs and sugar.
5. Fold in flour, walnuts and essence.
6. When mixture is evenly combined, transfer to prepared tin.
7. Bake in centre of oven for 40 minutes.
8. Cool in the tin then cut into about 18 squares.
9. Dredge thickly with sifted icing sugar.

Chocolate éclairs

Makes 12

1 recipe choux pastry (see page 112)

½ pint (250ml) double cream

2 tablespoons milk

6oz (150gm) plus 4 level tablespoons icing sugar, sifted

3oz (75gm) plain chocolate

1oz (25gm) butter

6 dessertspoons warm water

1 teaspoon vanilla essence

1. Pre-heat oven to moderately hot, 400 deg F or gas 6 (200 deg C).
2. Brush a baking tray with melted butter.
3. Transfer choux pastry to a forcing bag fitted with a ½-inch plain tube.
4. Pipe 12 lengths on to prepared tray, each about 4 inches long.
5. Bake just above centre of oven for approximately 25 to 30 minutes or until well-risen and golden.
6. Remove from oven and make a slit in the side of each.
7. Transfer to a wire rack and leave until completely cold.
8. Fill each with cream, beaten until thick with the milk and 4 level tablespoons icing sugar.
9. To make icing, break up chocolate and put it and butter into basin over saucepan of hot water. Leave until melted, stirring once or twice.
10. Add water and essence then gradually beat in remaining icing sugar.
11. Leave about 15 minutes for icing to set slightly then spread over tops of éclairs.
12. Leave icing to set before serving.

Coffee éclairs

Makes 12

Make as for chocolate éclairs, above, but cover tops with coffee icing made by mixing 8oz (200gm) sifted icing sugar with about 3 dessertspoons hot strong coffee.

Cream buns

Makes 14

Make as for chocolate éclairs, above, but pipe 14 balls of mixture—well apart—on to a buttered baking tray. Bake just above centre of oven for 25 to 30 minutes or until well-puffed and golden. Remove from oven, make slits in each then leave on a wire rack until cold. Fill with sweetened whipped cream then dredge tops with sifted icing sugar.

Chocolate or coffee cream buns

Makes 14

Make as for cream buns, above, but after filling with cream, cover tops with the chocolate or coffee icing as given for chocolate or coffee éclairs.

Brandy snaps

Makes about 12

2oz (50gm) plain flour

1 level teaspoon ginger

2oz (50gm) caster sugar

2oz (50gm) golden syrup

2oz (50gm) butter

1 teaspoon lemon juice

1. Pre-heat oven to moderate, 325 deg F or gas 3 (170 deg C).
2. Well-grease 2 large baking trays.
3. Sift flour and ginger into bowl.
4. Put sugar, syrup and butter into a saucepan and leave over a very low heat until melted.
5. Stir in lemon juice then add to dry ingredients. Mix thoroughly.
6. Drop teaspoons of mixture—about 6 inches apart to allow for spreading—on to a baking tray.
7. Bake 8 minutes or until lacy in appearance and golden.
8. Remove from oven and leave to stand for 1 minute.
9. Lift off trays with palette knife and quickly roll round the greased handle of a wooden spoon.
10. Repeat until all the mixture has been used.
11. Leave on a wire rack until completely cold then either serve plain or fill with sweetened whipped cream.

Note
If the brandy snaps harden up too much before rolling, return them to the oven for about 1 minute.

Flapjack

Makes about 12

6oz (150gm) rolled oats

4oz (100gm) soft brown sugar

3oz (75gm) butter or margarine

2oz (50gm) golden syrup

1. Pre-heat oven to moderate, 350 deg F or gas 4 (180 deg C).
2. Well-grease an 8-inch square tin.
3. Put oats and sugar into bowl and mix well together.
4. Put butter or margarine and syrup into a saucepan and melt over a low heat.
5. Add oats and sugar, mix thoroughly then transfer to prepared tin.
6. Bake in centre of oven for 25 to 30 minutes or until golden brown.
7. Remove from oven. Cool slightly then cut into approximately 12 fingers.
8. Remove from tin and transfer to a wire rack.
9. Store in an airtight tin when cold.

Cream bun

Macaroons

Makes about 18

2 egg whites

4oz (100gm) ground almonds

8oz (200gm) caster sugar

½oz (12gm) fine semolina

½ teaspoon each, almond and vanilla essences

a little extra egg white for brushing

18 blanched almonds

1. Lightly oil 2 baking trays and line with rice paper.
2. Beat egg whites until foamy then stir in ground almonds, sugar, semolina and essences.
3. Beat thoroughly then pipe or spoon 18 small mounds on to prepared trays.
4. Brush tops with egg white then top each with an almond.
5. Bake in centre of cool oven 300 deg F or gas 2 (150 deg C) for 20 to 25 minutes or until macaroons are pale gold.
6. Leave on tins for 5 minutes then carefully lift off.
7. Remove surplus rice paper round edge of each macaroon then cool on a wire rack.
8. Store in an airtight tin when cold.

Plain biscuits

Makes about 24

8oz (200gm) plain flour

pinch of salt

4½oz (112gm) butter

4oz (100gm) caster sugar

beaten egg

1. Pre-heat oven to moderate, 350 deg F or gas 4 (180 deg C).
2. Grease 2 baking trays.
3. Sift flour and salt into bowl.
4. Rub in butter finely.
5. Add sugar and toss lightly together.
6. Mix to a stiff dough with beaten egg.
7. Knead lightly until smooth and turn out on to a floured surface.
8. Roll out to about ⅛ inch in thickness and cut into approximately 20 to 24 rounds with a 2½-inch bicuit cutter.
9. Transfer to prepared trays and bake just above centre of oven for 15 to 20 minutes or until pale gold.
10. Cool on a wire rack and store in an airtight tin when cold.

Currant biscuits

Makes about 24

Make as for plain biscuits, above, but add 2oz (50gm) currants with the sugar.

Lemon or orange biscuits

Makes about 24

Make as for plain biscuits, above, but add 1 level teaspoon finely-grated lemon or orange peel with the sugar.

Nut biscuits

Makes about 24

Make as for plain biscuits, (see this page), but add 1 to 2oz (25 to 50gm) very finely-chopped walnuts or toasted almonds with the sugar.

Ginger nuts

Makes about 24

6oz (150gm) plain flour

2 level teaspoons ginger

1 level teaspoon mixed spice

½ level teaspoon cinnamon

¼ level teaspoon ground cloves

2oz (50gm) butter or margarine

4oz (100gm) soft brown sugar

3oz (75gm) golden syrup

1. Pre-heat oven to moderate, 350 deg F or gas 4 (180 deg C).
2. Grease 2 baking trays.
3. Sift together flour, ginger, spice, cinnamon and cloves.
4. Cream butter or margarine with sugar and syrup until light and fluffy.
5. Gradually stir in dry ingredients and mix to a firm dough with a fork.
6. Divide mixture into 24 even-sized balls and place on prepared baking trays.
7. Flatten slightly with prongs of a fork and bake in centre of oven for 15 to 20 minutes or until crisp and golden.
8. Remove from trays and transfer to a wire cooling rack. Store in an airtight tin when cold.

Melting moments

Makes about 24

4oz (100gm) butter, softened

3oz (75gm) caster sugar

1 egg yolk

1 teaspoon vanilla essence

4oz (100gm) self-raising flour

1oz (25gm) cornflour

rolled oats

1. Pre-heat oven to moderately hot, 375 deg F or gas 5 (190 deg C).
2. Well-grease 2 baking trays.
3. Cream butter with sugar until light and fluffy then beat in egg yolk and vanilla.
4. Sift flour and cornflour together and stir into creamed mixture with a fork.
5. Divide mixture into 24 equal pieces and roll into balls.
6. Toss in oats then transfer to prepared trays, leaving room between each as they spread.
7. Bake just above centre of oven for 15 to 20 minutes.
8. Leave to cool for 5 minutes then transfer to a wire cooling rack. Store in an airtight tin when cold.

Nut cookies

Makes about 16

2oz (50gm) butter, softened

2oz (50gm) caster sugar

½ teaspoon vanilla essence

1oz (25gm) walnuts, finely chopped

4oz (100gm) self-raising flour, sifted

1. Pre-heat oven to moderately hot, 375 deg F or gas 5 (190 deg C).
2. Grease a large baking tray.
3. Cream butter, sugar and vanilla essence together until light and fluffy.
4. Using a fork, stir in walnuts and flour and continue to stir until ingredients are thoroughly combined.
5. Transfer 16 heaped teaspoons to prepared baking tray, leaving room between each as they spread.
6. Bake just above centre of oven for 8 to 10 minutes or until pale gold.
7. Transfer to a wire cooling rack and store in an airtight tin when cold.

Chocolate dot cookies

Makes 16

Make as for nut cookies, above, adding 2oz (50gm) chocolate dots instead of the nuts.

Chocolate cookies

Makes 16

Make as for nut cookies, above, but use 3½oz (87gm) self-raising flour sifted with ½oz (12gm) cocoa powder. Omit nuts.

Coconut pyramids

Makes 12

3 egg whites

4oz (100gm) caster sugar

8oz (200gm) desiccated coconut

1 level tablespoon ground rice

1 teaspoon vanilla essence

6 glacé cherries, halved

1. Pre-heat oven to cool, 300 deg F or gas 2 (150 deg C).
2. Lightly-oil a large baking tray then line with rice paper.
3. Beat egg whites to a stiff snow then slowly whisk in half the sugar.
4. Fold in rest of sugar, coconut, ground rice and essence.
5. Shape 12 equal amounts into pyramids and place on prepared trays. Top each with half a cherry.
6. Bake in centre of oven for 30 to 35 minutes or until pale gold.
7. Leave on tray 5 minutes then carefully lift off, removing surplus rice paper round edges of each.
8. Cool on a wire rack then store in an airtight tin when cold.

Danish rings

Makes about 12

3oz (75gm) Danish butter, softened

2oz (50gm) golden syrup

3oz (75gm) plain flour, sifted

1oz (25gm) ground almonds

1 teaspoon vanilla essence

1. Pre-heat oven to moderate, 325 deg F or gas 3 (170 deg C).
2. Well-grease a large baking tray.
3. Cream butter with syrup until very light then stir in flour, almonds and vanilla essence.
4. When mixture is evenly combined, put into a forcing bag fitted with a large star-shaped pipe.
5. Pipe 12 rings of mixture on to prepared tray.
6. Bake in centre of oven for 20 minutes or until pale gold.
7. Transfer to a wire cooling rack and store in an airtight tin when cold.

Finnish biscuits

Makes 24

4oz (100gm) plain flour

¼ level teaspoon baking powder

2½oz (62gm) Danish butter

1½oz (37gm) caster sugar

about 1 tablespoon beaten egg

milk for brushing

granulated sugar

12 almonds, blanched and split

1. Pre-heat oven to moderately hot, 375 deg F or gas 5 (190 deg C).
2. Well-grease a large baking tray.
3. Sift flour and baking powder into a bowl.
4. Rub in butter finely then add sugar.
5. Mix to a stiff paste with beaten egg.
6. Knead lightly until smooth then roll into a long sausage of approximately 1½ inches in diameter.
7. Flatten slightly with a rolling pin then cut into ½-inch diagonal slices.
8. Transfer to baking tray and brush with milk.
9. Sprinkle with sugar and top each with half an almond.
10. Bake in centre of oven for 15 minutes.
11. Cool on a wire rack and store in an airtight tin when cold.

Spicy nut biscuits

Makes 24

Make as Finnish biscuits (previous recipe), but roll mixture out thinly on a lightly-floured surface. Cut into rounds with a 1½-inch cutter and transfer to a greased baking tray. Brush with a little beaten egg or milk and sprinkle each with cinnamon, caster sugar and a few flaked almonds. Bake in centre of oven for 7 to 8 minutes. Cool on a wire cooling rack and store in an airtight tin when cold.

Crunchy peanut cookies

Makes about 30

2oz (50gm) butter, softened

2oz (50gm) crunchy peanut butter

3oz (75gm) soft brown sugar

1 teaspoon vanilla essence

5oz (125gm) self-raising flour

1. Pre-heat oven to moderate, 350 deg F or gas 4 (180 deg C).
2. Grease a large baking tray.
3. Cream butter, peanut butter, sugar and vanilla essence together until light and fluffy.
4. Stir in flour with a fork.
5. Transfer 30 equal amounts to prepared baking tray, leaving room between each as they spread.
6. Flatten slightly with prongs of a fork then bake just above centre of oven for 10 to 12 minutes.
7. Transfer to a wire cooling rack and store in an airtight tin when cold.

Butter shortbread

Makes 8 portions

6oz (150gm) plain flour

4oz (100gm) butter

2oz (50gm) caster sugar

1. Pre-heat oven to moderate, 325 deg F or gas 3 (170 deg C).
2. Sift flour into a bowl.
3. Rub in butter then add caster sugar.
4. Draw mixture together with fingertips and knead very lightly until smooth.
5. Press into a 7-inch sandwich tin then prick all over with a fork.
6. Ridge edge with prongs of a fork then bake in centre of oven for about 35 to 40 minutes or until the colour of pale straw.
7. Leave until lukewarm then cut into 8 triangles.
8. Remove from tin and cool on a wire rack.

Refrigerator cookies

Makes about 48 to 60

8oz (200gm) plain flour

1 level teaspoon baking powder

4oz (100gm) butter

4oz (100gm) caster sugar

1 teaspoon vanilla essence

1 standard egg, beaten

a little cold milk if necessary

1. Sift flour and baking powder together.
2. Grease 2 large baking trays.
3. Cream butter, sugar and vanilla essence until light and fluffy then beat in egg.
4. Stir in dry ingredients then draw mixture together with a fork, adding a little milk if dough is on the dry side.
5. Shape into a long roll of about 1½ inches in diameter and wrap in aluminium foil.
6. Refrigerate overnight then cut roll into thin slices.
7. Transfer to prepared baking trays—allowing room between each as they spread—and bake just above centre of moderately hot oven, 375 deg F or gas 5 (190 deg C), for about 10 minutes or until pale gold.
8. Transfer to a wire cooling rack and store in an airtight tin when cold.

Note
The biscuits need not all be baked at once. Unwrap, slice as many biscuits as are required from the roll and bake as directed above. Re-wrap roll in foil and leave in the refrigerator (up to 1 week) until more biscuits are required.

Chocolate refrigerator cookies

Makes about 48 to 60

Make as for refrigerator cookies, above, but use 6½oz (162gm) plain flour sifted with 1½oz (37gm) cocoa powder and 1 level teaspoon baking powder.

Peanut refrigerator cookies

Makes about 48 to 60

Make as for refrigerator cookies, above, but add 2oz (50gm) finely-chopped salted peanuts after beating in the egg.

Danish rings, Finnish biscuits decorated with whole almonds, and spicy nut biscuits

Scones

Baked scones

Pointers to success:
1. Work speedily.
2. Add liquid all at once to the dry ingredients.
3. Knead only long enough to make scone dough smooth.
4. Roll quickly and lightly.
5. Cut out with cutter dipped in flour.
6. Transfer to lightly-greased baking tray and bake immediately.
7. Leave until lukewarm before breaking each scone gently in half with the fingers. Cutting with a knife makes scones doughy.
8. Whenever possible, make and eat scones on same day.

Plain scones

Makes about 9

8oz (200gm) self-raising flour

½ level teaspoon salt

1 to 2oz (25gm to 50gm) butter or margarine

¼ pint (125ml) cold milk

beaten egg or milk for brushing

1. Pre-heat oven to hot, 450 deg F or gas 8 (230 deg C).
2. Lightly grease a baking tray.
3. Sift flour and salt into bowl.
4. Rub in fat finely.
5. Add all the milk and mix to a soft dough with a round-topped knife.
6. Turn out on to surface dusted with flour and knead lightly until smooth.
7. Roll out lightly to ½ inch in thickness and cut into 9 rounds with a 2½-inch biscuit cutter dipped in flour.
8. Transfer to prepared tray and bake just above centre of oven for approximately 10 minutes or until well-risen and golden.
9. Cool on a wire rack.

Note
Instead of self-raising flour, sift 8oz (200gm) plain flour with 4 level teaspoons baking powder or with 2 level teaspoons cream of tartar and 1 level teaspoon bicarbonate of soda.

Tea scones

Makes about 16 to 18

Make as for plain scones (see above), adding 1oz (25gm) caster sugar and 2oz (50gm) dried fruit (currants, sultanas or chopped seedless raisins) after rubbing in fat. Cut into 16 or 18 rounds with a 1½-inch fluted biscuit cutter. Bake 7 to 10 minutes.

Sweet scones

Makes about 9

Make as for plain scones (see this page) adding 1oz (25gm) caster sugar after rubbing in the butter or margarine.

Scone round

Makes about 10

Make either plain scones, sweet scones or tea scones (see above). Roll into a round ¾ inch thick and transfer to greased tray. Mark into 10 triangles with a knife. Brush with beaten egg or milk and bake near top of oven, 425 deg F or gas 7 (220 deg C), for 15 to 20 minutes. Leave 10 minutes, then gently break into triangles.

Wholemeal scones

Makes about 9

Make as for plain scones (see left), using 4oz (100gm) each plain and wholemeal flour sifted with 3 level teaspoons baking powder. If liked, 1 level tablespoon caster sugar may be added to the rubbed-in ingredients.

Cheese scones

Makes about 8

Make as for plain scones (see left), but sift 1 level teaspoon dry mustard with the flour. Add 2 to 3oz (50 to 75gm) very finely-grated Cheddar cheese before adding the liquid. Roll out to just over ½ inch in thickness. Bake for 10 minutes.

Potato scones

Makes about 12 to 14

8oz (200gm) self-raising flour

2 level teaspoons salt

12oz (300gm) freshly-boiled potatoes (drained weight)

2oz (50gm) butter or margarine

cold milk if necessary

1. Pre-heat oven to hot, 425 deg F or gas 7 (220 deg C).
2. Sift flour and salt into bowl.
3. Mash potatoes finely with the butter.
4. Gradually work in sifted flour, adding a little milk if mixture is too dry to hold together.
5. Turn out on to a floured surface and knead lightly until smooth.
6. Roll out to ½ inch in thickness and cut into 12 or 14 rounds with a 2½-inch biscuit cutter.
7. Transfer to a greased baking tray and bake near top of oven for 15 minutes or until well-risen and golden.
8. Remove from oven, spread tops with butter and serve straight away.

Note
Alternatively, scones may be cut as above and then fried on a hot greased griddle or a greased and heated heavy frying pan for 5 minutes per side.

Griddle scones

Pointers to success:
1. If using a frying pan, make sure it is a heavy one and that the base is thick and smooth.
2. Do not add more egg or milk than the quantities recommended in the recipe or the batter mixture will be too thin and the scones will spread out like pancakes.
3. To prevent sticking, cover the base of the pan or griddle with a thin layer of salt plus a dessertspoon of oil. Place over a low heat and rub salt and oil into base of pan with a pad of soft kitchen paper. Wipe clean with fresh paper before use.
4. Do not allow pan or griddle to over-heat or scones will be burnt on the outside and raw in the middle.

Plain scones and fruit bread (see page 230)

Dropped scones or Scotch pancakes

Makes about 12

4oz (100gm) self-raising flour

pinch of salt

1 level tablespoon caster sugar

1 standard egg

1 dessertspoon melted butter

¼ pint (125ml) milk

1. Sift flour and salt into bowl. Add sugar.
2. Mix to a thick, smooth and creamy batter with egg, butter and two-thirds of the milk, stirring briskly without beating.
3. Gently stir in rest of milk.
4. Drop dessertspoon of mixture from tip of spoon into greased and heated frying pan or griddle.
5. Fry 2 to 3 minutes or until bubbles rise to the surface and begin to break.
6. Turn over with a knife and cook a further 2 minutes.
7. Stack in a folded tea-towel to keep warm then serve straight away with butter and jam, honey or golden syrup.

Note

If savoury scones are preferred, increase salt to ¼ level teaspoon and omit sugar.

Welsh cakes

Makes about 15

6oz (150gm) plain flour

1½ level teaspoons baking powder

½ level teaspoon nutmeg

3oz (75gm) butter

2oz (50gm) caster sugar

3oz (75gm) currants and sultanas

1 standard egg, beaten

milk to mix

1. Sift flour, baking powder and nutmeg into bowl.
2. Rub in butter finely.
3. Add sugar and dried fruit.
4. Mix to a stiff dough with beaten egg and a little cold milk if necessary.
5. Turn out on to floured surface and knead lightly until smooth.
6. Roll out to ¼ inch in thickness and cut into about 15 rounds with a 2½-inch biscuit cutter.
7. Cook in lightly-greased and heated heavy frying pan or griddle for 4 to 5 minutes each side. Cool to lukewarm then split and butter.

Bread, rolls and buns

Cooking with yeast:

1. Fresh or dried yeast give equal success and 2 level teaspoons dried should be allowed for every ½oz (12gm) of fresh yeast recommended in the recipe.
2. To reconstitute dried yeast, dissolve a teaspoon of sugar in a little of the measured warm liquid. Sprinkle yeast granules on top and leave in the warm for about 20 minutes or until frothy. Add to the dry ingredients with remaining liquid.
3. Unless otherwise specified, use strong plain flour—it absorbs more liquid and makes the loaf or whatever you are making larger and lighter.
4. Dough may be left to rise to suit individual needs and time. For a very slow rise, leave 24 hours in the refrigerator but allow to reach room temperature before shaping. For an overnight rise, leave dough in the larder overnight. For a slow rise, leave dough 1 to 2 hours in the kitchen. For a fast rise, 30 to 40 minutes in a warm place.
5. To prevent a skin forming on uncooked dough, cover with greased polythene or slip bowl and/or tins inside greased polythene bags.

Easy brown bread

Makes two 1lb (½ kilo) loaves

1 level teaspoon sugar

¾ pint (375ml) warm water

1 level tablespoon dried yeast

1lb (½ kilo) wholemeal flour

8oz (200gm) strong plain flour

3 level teaspoons salt

1 level dessertspoon caster sugar

little milk for brushing

1. Dissolve teaspoon of sugar in ¼ pint (125ml) water. Sprinkle yeast on top and leave in a warm place for 20 minutes or until frothy.
2. Sift flours, salt and caster sugar into a bowl.
3. Mix to a soft, scone-like dough with yeast liquid and remaining water, adding a little white flour if dough is very sticky.
4. Turn out on to a floured surface and divide into 2 equal pieces.
5. Knead quickly until smooth then shape to fit two 1lb (½ kilo) well-greased loaf tins.
6. Cover with greased polythene and leave to rise until dough reaches tops of tins. Pre-heat oven to hot, 450 deg F or gas 8 (230 deg C).
7. Brush loaves with milk and bake in centre of oven for 30 to 40 minutes.
8. Cool on a wire rack.

White bread

Makes two 2lb (1 kilo) loaves or three 1lb (½ kilo) loaves

1oz (25gm) fresh yeast or 1 level tablespoon dried yeast

1½ pint (approximately ¾ litre) warm water

3lb (1½ kilo) strong plain flour

6 level teaspoons salt

2oz (50gm) butter, margarine or lard

milk or beaten egg and milk for brushing

1. Well-grease two 2lb (1 kilo) loaf tins or three 1lb (½ kilo) loaf tins.
2. Blend fresh yeast with ½ pint (250ml) warm water. If using dried yeast, dissolve 1 teaspoon sugar in ½ pint (250gm) water and sprinkle yeast on top. Leave in a warm place for 20 minutes or until frothy.
3. Sift flour and salt into bowl. Rub in fat finely.
4. Work to a dough with yeast liquid and remaining water.
5. Knead dough on floured surface for 10 to 15 minutes or until smooth and elastic and no longer sticky.
6. Return to bowl, cover with greased polythene and leave to rise until double in size.
7. Turn out on to floured surface, knead lightly and shape to fit tins.
8. Cover loaves with greased polythene and leave to rise until dough reaches tops of tins. Pre-heat oven to hot, 450 deg F or gas 8 (230 deg C).
9. Brush loaves with milk or beaten egg and milk. Bake in centre of oven for 30 to 40 minutes or until loaves shrink slightly from sides of tins and the crust is a warm gold.
10. Turn out and cool on a wire rack.

Milk loaves

Make as above, using half warm water and half warm milk. The texture will be a little closer and the crust softer.

Note

Instead of fresh milk, diluted evaporated milk or low fat milk granules made up with water, may be used.

Fancy rolls

Clover rolls

Makes 8

Take ½lb (¼ kilo) risen white bread dough and, after kneading lightly, divide into 24 equal pieces. Shape each into a small ball and put 3 together into 8 well-greased bun tins. Cover with greased polythene and leave until rolls reach tops of tins. Brush with beaten egg, sprinkle with poppy seeds and bake near top of hot oven, 450 deg F or gas 8 (230 deg C), for 15 to 20 minutes or until golden brown. Remove from tins and cool on a wire rack.

Knot rolls

Makes 8

Take ½lb (¼ kilo) risen white bread dough and, after kneading lightly, divide into 8 equal pieces. Roll each into a 10-inch long strand and tie loosely into a knot. Place on greased baking tray, cover with greased polythene and leave to rise until rolls have doubled in size. Brush with beaten egg and bake as for clover rolls, above.

Plait rolls

Makes 8

Take ½lb (¼ kilo) risen white bread dough and, after kneading lightly, divide into 8 equal pieces. Divide each piece again into 3 pieces and roll into 6-inch long strips. Plait together. Place on greased baking tray, cover with greased polythene and leave to rise until rolls have doubled in size. Brush with beaten egg and bake as for clover rolls, above.

Fruit bread

Illustrated on page 229

Makes 1 loaf

Take 1lb (½ kilo) risen white bread dough and put into bowl. Add 2oz (50gm) softened butter or margarine, 2oz (50gm) caster sugar, 4oz (100gm) dried fruit and 1 level teaspoon mixed spice. Work extra ingredients into dough by squeezing and kneading with the hands until thoroughly mixed. Transfer to 1lb (½ kilo) well-greased loaf tin. Cover with greased polythene and leave to rise until loaf reaches top of tin. Bake in centre of hot oven, 425 deg F or gas 7 (220 deg C), for 40 minutes until golden brown. Turn out on to a wire rack and glaze top by brushing with golden syrup.

Knot rolls and clover rolls

Enriched white dough

This is a useful dough as it forms the basis for a variety of buns and may also be turned into various shapes of rolls and fancy loaves. In addition, re-constitution is unnecessary if dried yeast is used.

| 1lb (½ kilo) strong plain flour |
| 1 level teaspoon sugar |
| ½oz (12gm) fresh yeast or 1 level teaspoon dried yeast |
| ¼ pint (125gm) plus 5 tablespoons warm milk |
| 1 level teaspoon salt |
| 2oz (50gm) butter or margarine |
| 1 large egg, beaten |

1. Sift 5oz (125gm) flour into bowl. Add sugar, yeast and milk and mix well. Leave in a warm place for 15 to 20 minutes or until frothy.
2. Meanwhile, sieve rest of flour and salt into another bowl. Rub in butter or margarine finely.
3. Add to yeast mixture with three-quarters of the beaten egg. Turn out on to lightly-floured surface and knead thoroughly for 15 minutes or until smooth and elastic. The dough will be sticky at first, but tightens up during kneading.
4. Cover with greased polythene and leave to rise until double in size.
5. Turn out on to floured surface and knead evenly until smooth.

Cottage loaf

1. Shape three-quarters of the dough, as given in above recipe, into a ball and place on greased baking tray.
2. Roll rest of dough into a smaller ball and place on top.
3. Cover with greased polythene and leave until loaf doubles in size.
4. Brush with rest of beaten egg then bake in centre of moderately hot oven, 375 deg F or gas 5 (190 deg C), for 45 to 50 minutes until golden brown and base of loaf sounds hollow when tapped. Cool.

Note
Other shaped loaves may be made if preferred.

Lardy cake

Makes 1 large cake

Take half the risen white bread dough and, after kneading lightly, roll into a ¼ inch thick strip, 3 times as long as it is wide. Cover with 1½oz (37gm) lard, putting it on to dough in small flakes. Sprinkle with 1oz (25gm) each caster sugar and sultanas then roll up loosely like a Swiss roll. Roll out into a strip again and cover with lard, sugar and sultanas as before. Repeat once more. Roll out into an oblong and press into a well-greased tin measuring approximately 8 inches by 10 inches. Criss-cross the top by scoring with a very sharp knife. Cover with greased polythene and leave to rise until dough doubles in size. Bake in centre of hot oven 425 deg F or gas 7 (220 deg C) for 30 minutes. Turn out and glaze with 1 level tablespoon granulated sugar boiled in 1 tablespoon milk for 1 minute.

Harvest plait

Makes 1 loaf

Take 1lb (½ kilo) risen white bread dough and, after kneading lightly, divide into 4 pieces. Roll 3 of the pieces into strands measuring approximately 20 inches in length and join together at one end. Place on greased baking tray and plait strands together, tucking ends underneath. Brush with beaten egg. Take fourth piece of dough and divide in two. Roll into 2 strands, each 20 inches in length. Join at one end and twist both strands loosely together. Arrange along centre of plait and tuck ends underneath. Cover with greased polythene and leave to rise until loaf doubles in size. Brush with beaten egg and bake in centre of hot oven, 450 deg F or gas 8 (230 deg C), for 30 to 40 minutes until golden brown and base of loaf sounds hollow when tapped. Cool on a wire rack.

Yorkshire tea cakes

Makes 6

Make as for enriched white dough (see above), but add 1oz (25gm) caster sugar and 2oz (50gm) currants to rubbed-in ingredients. After dough has risen, turn out on to floured surface and knead lightly. Divide into 6 equal pieces and shape each into a 6-inch round. Transfer to greased baking tray and cover with greased polythene. Leave to rise until double in size then bake just above centre of moderately hot oven, 400 deg F or gas 6 (200 deg C), for 20 minutes. Cool on a wire rack then split in half and butter. Alternatively, split in half then toast and butter.

Hot cross buns

Makes 12

Make as for enriched white dough (see page 231), but when you sift flour with salt, add 1½ level teaspoons mixed spice, ½ level teaspoon cinnamon and ¼ level teaspoon ground cloves. Add 4oz (100gm) currants, 2oz (50gm) chopped mixed peel and 2oz (50gm) caster sugar to rubbed-in ingredients. Knead, cover and leave to rise. Turn out on to floured surface and knead lightly until smooth. Divide into 12 equal pieces and shape each into a ball. Transfer to greased baking tray, cover with greased polythene and leave to rise until double in size. Cut a cross on top of each bun, or make crosses with strips of short crust pastry (see page 108), then bake in centre of hot oven, 425 deg F or gas 7 (220 deg C), for 20 to 25 minutes or until well-risen and golden. Cool on a wire rack.

Bath buns

Makes 14

Make as for enriched white dough (see page 231), but add 6oz (150gm) sultanas and 2oz (50gm) chopped mixed peel to the rubbed-in ingredients. After dough has risen, turn out on to a floured surface and knead lightly until smooth. Put 14 tablespoons dough (which need not be even) on to greased baking trays. Cover with greased polythene and leave to rise until buns double in size. Brush with egg beaten with a little water then sprinkle each with coarsely-crushed cube sugar. Bake just above centre of hot oven, 425 deg F or gas 7 (220 deg C), for 20 to 25 minutes. Cool on a wire rack.

Chelsea buns

Makes 15

Make up enriched white dough (see page 231), and after it has risen turn out on to floured surface and knead lightly until smooth. Roll out into a rectangle measuring 10 inches by 16 inches. Brush with 1oz (25gm) melted butter then sprinkle with 6oz (150gm) currants and 3oz (75gm) caster sugar. Roll up like a Swiss roll, starting from one of the shorter sides, then cut into 15 slices. Place on large greased baking tray, cover with greased polythene and leave to rise until double in size. Bake in centre of hot oven, 425 deg F or gas 7 (220 deg C), for 20 minutes or until golden brown. Remove from oven and glaze tops by brushing with 2 level tablespoons caster sugar boiled in 2 tablespoons milk for 2 minutes.

Chelsea Christmas tree

Chelsea Christmas tree

Serves 8

Make up Chelsea buns as given, left, but sprinkle dough with 2oz (50gm) sultanas, 2oz (50gm) each, quartered red and green glacé cherries, 3oz (75gm) Demerara sugar and ½ level teaspoon mixed spice. Roll up and cut into 19 slices. Arrange on a large greased baking tray as shown in photograph, using 4 rounds for the 'tub', and remainder for the tree. Cover and leave to rise until double in size then bake as Chelsea buns 20 to 25 minutes. Remove from oven and glaze with 1 tablespoon golden syrup. When completely cold, transfer to a cake board. Tie a band of red ribbon round the 'tub' and arrange a star of tinsel on the top of the tree. Mix a little sifted icing sugar to a thick icing with a little warm water and drizzle over the tree.

Doughnuts

Makes 16

Make up enriched white dough (see page 231), and after dough has risen turn out on to floured surface. Knead lightly until smooth then divide into 16 equal pieces. Shape into balls, cover with greased polythene and leave to rise until double in size. Press a hole into each with a finger then fill with jam. Pinch up edges of dough so that jam is completely enclosed. Heat a pan of deep fat or oil until a bread cube, dropped into it, turns brown in 1 minute. Add doughnuts, a few at a time, and fry 4 to 5 minutes or until golden. Remove from pan, drain thoroughly and toss in caster sugar.

Hot cross buns

Brioches

Makes 12

3 level teaspoons caster sugar

3 dessertspoons lukewarm water

2 level teaspoons dried yeast

8oz (200gm) plain flour

½ level teaspoon salt

2 standard eggs, beaten

2oz (50gm) butter, melted and cooled

beaten egg for brushing

1. Dissolve 1 level teaspoon sugar in the water and sprinkle yeast on top.
2. Leave in a warm place for 20 minutes or until frothy.
3. Sift flour and salt into bowl. Add remaining sugar then mix to a soft dough with the yeast liquid, eggs and butter.
4. Turn out on to floured surface and knead about 7 minutes or until dough is smooth and no longer sticky.
5. Cover with greased polythene and leave dough to rise until double in size.
6. Turn out on to floured surface and knead lightly until smooth. Heat oven to hot, 450 deg F or gas 8 (230 deg C).
7. Divide three-quarters of the dough into 12 equal pieces and shape into balls. Transfer to 12 buttered 3-inch fluted brioche tins.
8. Roll rest of dough into 12 small balls and place on top of brioches, holding them in place with a little beaten egg.
9. Cover with greased polythene and leave until dough reaches tops of tins. Brush with egg.
10. Bake in centre of oven for 10 minutes or until golden brown.
11. Turn out on to a wire cooling rack and serve warm with butter.

Croissants

Make up enriched white bread dough (see page 231), using water instead of milk. Roll into a rectangle measuring 20 inches by 6 inches by ¼ inch thick. Cover top two-thirds of dough with 2oz (50gm) hard butter or margarine, putting it on to dough in flakes. Fold in 3, envelope style, by bringing the plain part over the centre and the top third over. Seal edges by pressing with a rolling pin. Turn dough so that the folded edges are to the right and left. Repeat rolling, covering with butter or margarine and folding twice more. Transfer to greased polythene bag and refrigerate 30 minutes. Roll out into a 20-inch strip then fold and roll 3 times more. Return to greased polythene bag and refrigerate 1 hour. Roll into a rectangle measuring about 22 inches by 13 inches. Trim away edges with a sharp knife then cut dough in half lengthwise. From each half, cut 6 equal triangles. Brush with egg, beaten with a little water and ½ level teaspoon caster sugar, and roll each triangle up loosely, starting from the end opposite the point. Place on an ungreased baking tray, cover with greased polythene and leave to rise for about 30 minutes or until croissants are light and flaky. Brush with egg mixture and bake in centre of hot oven, 425 deg F or gas 7 (220 deg C), for 20 minutes. Serve warm.

Danish pastries

Makes 16

1 level teaspoon and 1 level tablespoon caster sugar

5 tablespoons warm water

1 level teaspoon dried yeast

8oz (200gm) plain flour

pinch of salt

1oz (25gm) Danish butter

1 standard egg, beaten

5oz (125gm) Danish butter, softened

1. Dissolve 1 level teaspoon caster sugar in the warm water, sprinkle yeast on top and leave in a warm place for about 20 minutes or until frothy.
2. Sift flour and salt into a bowl and rub in 1oz (25gm) butter.
3. Add remaining sugar, egg and yeast liquid and work to a soft dough.
4. Turn out on to floured board and knead very lightly until smooth. Transfer to greased polythene bag and leave in the cool for 10 minutes.
5. Shape remaining butter into a rectangle measuring 3 inches by 10 inches. Roll out dough into a 10-inch square.
6. Stand butter in the middle of the square then bring the 2 pieces of dough on either side of the butter to the centre, overlapping them slightly and completely enclosing the butter.
7. Seal top and bottom edges by pressing with a rolling pin.
8. Roll into an oblong strip, 3 times as long as it is wide.
9. Fold evenly in 3, transfer to a polythene bag and rest in the cool for 10 minutes.
10. Repeat rolling, folding and resting twice more. Finally rest dough for 10 minutes.
Cut dough into 4 equal pieces, and use in the following ways:

Pin wheels

Roll out a quarter of the dough into a rectangle measuring 6 inches by 4 inches. Brush with a little milk then sprinkle with caster sugar, cinnamon and sultanas and/or currants. Roll up, starting from the shorter sides. Cut into 4 slices. Transfer to greased baking tray.

Stars

Roll out a quarter of the dough and cut into 4 squares, each measuring 3 inches. Make 2½-inch diagonal cuts from each corner towards the centre then bring alternate corners to the middle, overlapping points slightly. Transfer to greased baking tray.

Cocks' combs

Roll out a quarter of the dough fairly thinly and cut into 4 strips, each measuring approximately 4½ inches by 5 inches. Spread half the width of each strip with a little almond paste (see page 217), placing it ½ inch above edge. Moisten edge with a little water then fold in half. Make 8 cuts in the folded side of each. Transfer to greased tray, opening out cuts slightly.

Crescents

Roll out a quarter of the dough fairly thinly and cut into 4 equal triangles. Put a small ball of almond paste (see page 217), just above the base of each triangle then roll up towards the base of each triangle then crescents and transfer to greased baking tray.

To prove and bake

Brush all pastries with egg, beaten with a little water and 1 level teaspoon caster sugar. Leave in a slightly warm place for 20 minutes or until puffy. Bake towards top of hot oven, 425 deg F or gas 7 (220 deg C), for 12 to 15 minutes.

To decorate

Pin wheels and crescents
Spread with a little glacé icing, made by mixing sifted icing sugar to a fairly thin icing with lemon juice or water. Sprinkle with toasted almonds.

Stars
Put a little thick custard on to the centre of each then top with a blob of red jam.

Cocks' combs
Leave plain or, after brushing with egg mixture, sprinkle with a few almond flakes before baking.

A selection of Danish pastries

Sweets and candies

To me, making sweets and candies at home is 'hobby cooking': a thoroughly enjoyable and satisfying pastime in which the whole family—except the very young—can happily and creatively take part. Creamy fudge, munchy caramels, old-fashioned honeycomb, assorted toffees and toffee apples, multi-coloured fondants, pink and white coconut ice, smooth and rich chocolate truffles and marzipan fruits . . . all delectable, mouthwatering concoctions that are as much fun to make as they are to eat. And if the sweets are prettily boxed and gaily ribboned, they make highly acceptable and original gifts, especially at Christmas.

But before you reach for sugar and saucepan, there are a few important rules relating to sweet-making which you should know about. These are:

1. When sweets require boiling, choose a deep, heavy saucepan with thick base.
2. Use a large wooden spoon or spatula for stirring. Metal spoons get very hot and uncomfortable to hold.
3. Make sure there is an enamel plate nearby to rest the spoon between stirrings.
4. When making fudge, toffees, caramels or any other sweet which sets fairly rapidly, butter a tin beforehand (a small roasting tin is ideal) so that the mixture can be poured into it as soon as it is ready.
5. Never leave a pan of sweet mixture unattended. The contents may boil over suddenly or catch on the base of the pan and burn.

Ideally, a sugar thermometer should be used when making sweets because it registers accurately the temperature of the mixture and gives a reliable indication as to whether the mixture has cooked for the correct length of time. However, if you do not have a sugar thermometer, the following tests give reasonably satisfactory results:

For fudges and some fondants
Boil until a little of the mixture, dropped into a cup of very cold water, forms a soft ball which flattens when lifted out of the cup. (Approximately 238 deg F to 240 deg F or 115 deg C.)

For soft caramels, soft toffees and some candies
Boil until a little of the mixture, dropped into a cup of very cold water, forms a hard but pliable ball. (Approximately 250 deg F or 121 deg C.)

For semi-hard toffees
Boil until a little of the mixture, dropped into a cup of very cold water, forms hard threads which bend without breaking. (Approximately 280 deg F or 138 deg C.)

For hard toffees and caramels, butterscotch and nut brittle
Boil until a little of the mixture, dropped into a cup of very cold water, forms hard threads which are brittle and crack easily. (Approximately 300 deg F or 149 deg C.)

For hard caramels
Boil until a little of the mixture (which should be a deep golden brown), dropped into a cup of very cold water, becomes very brittle. (Approximately 312 deg F or 156 deg C.)

Chocolate coconut ice (see page 240)

236

Vanilla fudge

Makes about 48 pieces

1lb (½ kilo) granulated or cube sugar

2oz (50gm) golden syrup

2oz (50gm) butter

¼ pint (125ml) undiluted evaporated milk

1 teaspoon vanilla essence

1. Well-butter or oil a tin measuring approximately 7 inches square.
2. Put sugar, syrup, butter and milk into a heavy saucepan.
3. Heat slowly, stirring all the time, until sugar dissolves and butter melts.
4. Bring to boil and cover with lid. Boil 2 minutes then uncover.
5. Continue to boil steadily, stirring frequently, until a little of the mixture forms a soft ball when dropped into a cup of cold water.
6. Stir in vanilla essence and cool to lukewarm.
7. Beat hard until thick and creamy then transfer to prepared tin. Spread smoothly with a knife.
8. Mark into squares and leave until set.
9. Cut up and remove from tin when cold.

Walnut fudge

Makes about 48 pieces

Make exactly as for vanilla fudge, above, but add 2 to 3oz (50 to 75gm) chopped walnuts before beating.

Cherry fudge

Makes about 48 pieces

Make exactly as for vanilla fudge (see this page), but add 2 to 3oz (50 to 75gm) chopped glacé cherries before beating.

Toasted coconut fudge

Makes about 48 pieces

Make exactly as for vanilla fudge (see this page), but add 2oz (50gm) lightly-toasted desiccated coconut before beating.

Fruit fudge

Makes about 48 pieces

Make exactly as for vanilla fudge (see this page), but add 1oz (25gm) chopped crystallised ginger, 1oz (25gm) chopped glacé pineapple and 1oz (25gm) chopped seedless raisins before beating.

Chocolate fudge

Makes about 48 pieces

Make exactly as for vanilla fudge (see this page), adding 1oz (25gm) cocoa powder and 4 tablespoons water with the sugar, syrup and butter. Use 1 small can sweetened condensed milk instead of the evaporated. If liked, 2 to 3oz (50 to 75gm) chopped nuts may be added before beating.

Brazil nut fudge

Makes about 48 pieces

4oz (100gm) shelled Brazil nuts

1lb (½ kilo) Demerara sugar

1oz (25gm) golden syrup

3oz (75gm) butter

½ pint (250ml) milk

1 tablespoon Angostura bitters

1. Well-butter or oil a tin measuring approximately 7 inches square.
2. Slice Brazil nuts and leave on one side.
3. Put sugar, syrup, butter and milk into a heavy saucepan.
4. Heat slowly, stirring all the time, until sugar dissolves and butter melts.
5. Bring to boil and cover with lid. Boil 2 minutes then uncover.
6. Continue to boil, stirring frequently, until a little of the mixture forms a soft ball when dropped into cold water.
7. Stir in Angostura bitters and cool to lukewarm.
8. Add nuts and beat hard until thick and creamy. Transfer to prepared tin and smooth top with a knife.
9. Mark into squares and leave until set.
10. Cut up and remove from tin when cold.

Uncooked coffee hazelnut fudge

Makes about 54 pieces

3oz (75gm) butter

3 tablespoons liquid coffee essence

1 tablespoon evaporated milk

2oz (50gm) hazelnuts, chopped

1lb (½ kilo) icing sugar, sifted

1. Well-butter or oil a tin measuring approximately 8 inches square.
2. Put butter and coffee essence into a large saucepan and melt over a low heat.
3. Add evaporated milk and hazelnuts then gradually stir in icing sugar.
4. When mixture is smooth, spread into prepared tin and leave until set.
5. Cut into squares when cold.

Uncooked chocolate fudge

Makes about 54 pieces

4oz (100gm) plain chocolate

2oz (50gm) butter

3 tablespoons evaporated milk

2 teaspoons vanilla essence

1lb (½ kilo) icing sugar, sifted

1. Well-butter or oil a tin measuring approximately 8 inches square.
2. Break up chocolate and put into a basin over a saucepan of hot, but not boiling, water. Add butter.
3. Leave until chocolate and butter have melted, stirring once or twice.
4. Stir in milk and vanilla essence.
5. Gradually work in icing sugar.
6. When mixture is smooth, spread into prepared tin and leave until set.
7. Cut into squares when cold.

Chocolate toffee cups

Makes about 14

3oz (75gm) plain chocolate

2oz (50gm) butter

2 level tablespoons golden syrup

2 level tablespoons instant low-fat milk granules

14 chocolate buttons

1. Break up chocolate and put into a small basin over a saucepan of hot, but not boiling, water. Leave until melted.
2. Coat the insides of 14 fluted paper sweet cases with melted chocolate, using either the end of a teaspoon or child's paint brush to 'paint' on the chocolate.
3. Leave until chocolate has set.
4. Put butter and syrup into a saucepan and place over a low heat until melted.
5. Add milk granules.
6. Slowly bring to boil, stirring continuously, and continue to boil until mixture turns a deep gold.
7. Stir to cool slightly then spoon into chocolate cases. The chocolate will melt a little but hardens up later.
8. When toffee has half-set, press a chocolate button into each.
9. Leave until completely firm before eating.

Almond logs

Makes about 25

2oz (50gm) butter, softened

2oz (50gm) caster sugar

1 level dessertspoon cocoa powder, sifted

3oz (75gm) ground almonds

6oz (150gm) stale cake crumbs, rubbed through sieve

2 to 3 dessertspoons rum or sherry

4 level tablespoons apricot jam, sifted

1 dessertspoon boiling water

3oz (75gm) almonds, toasted and chopped

1. Cream butter and sugar together until light and fluffy.
2. Stir in cocoa, ground almonds and cake crumbs.
3. Add sufficient rum or sherry to bind the mixture well together.
4. Divide into approximately 25 even-sized pieces and form into log shapes. Stand the logs on a sheet of greaseproof paper.
5. Brush all over with jam mixed with boiling water.
6. Roll logs in the toasted, chopped nuts then stand them in fluted paper sweet cases.

Raspberry creams

Makes about 32

1 egg white

2 level tablespoons raspberry jam

2 teaspoons raspberry milk shake syrup

1lb ($\frac{1}{2}$ kilo) icing sugar, sifted

8 glacé cherries, quartered

1. Put egg white into bowl with jam and raspberry syrup.
2. Beat until well mixed and frothy.
3. Gradually stir in icing sugar and continue stirring until mixture is very well blended and stiff.
4. Shape mixture into about 32 balls then stand them on a tray or sheet of greaseproof paper dusted with sifted icing sugar.
5. Flatten with a knife then stand a piece of cherry on top of each.
6. Leave about 1 day for creams to become firm and set.

Peppermint creams

Makes about 20

1 egg white

1 teaspoon oil of peppermint

10 to 12oz (250 to 300gm) icing sugar, sifted

1. Beat egg white until fluffy.
2. Add oil of peppermint.
3. Gradually stir in icing sugar, adding sufficient to form a very stiff mixture (the exact amount depends on size of egg white).
4. Turn mixture on to surface thickly dusted with sifted icing sugar and roll out to $\frac{1}{4}$ inch in thickness.
5. Cut into rounds with a 1-inch cutter.
6. Gather trimmings together, knead lightly and re-roll and re-cut until all the mixture is used up.
7. Leave for about 1 day for creams to become firm and set.

Chocolate toffee cups, chocolate fudge and almond logs

Chocolate peppermint toppers

Makes about 20

Make up peppermint creams, left. When firm and set, dip a pastry brush into melted plain chocolate and use to brush over tops of creams.

Vanilla creams

Makes about 20

Make exactly as for peppermint creams, left, adding 1 teaspoon vanilla essence instead of the oil of peppermint. Before rolling out, work a little red, yellow, green or orange food colouring into the mixture.

239

Mocha walnut creams

Makes about 25

1oz (25gm) soft, luxury margarine

2oz (50gm) walnuts, finely chopped

$\frac{1}{2}$ teaspoon vanilla essence

finely grated peel of 1 small lemon

8oz (200gm) icing sugar and 1oz (25gm) cocoa powder, sifted together

2 tablespoons strong black coffee

pieces of walnuts for decoration

1. Put all ingredients into a bowl.
2. Beat briskly until smooth and evenly combined.
3. Transfer equal amounts to 25 fluted paper sweet cases.
4. Stand a piece of walnut on each and leave until set.

Tutti frutti candy

Makes about 30 pieces

8oz (200gm) granulated sugar

4 tablespoons milk

1oz (25gm) soft, luxury margarine

1 level dessertspoon golden syrup

2 tablespoons sweetened condensed milk

2oz (50gm) glacé cherries, chopped

2oz (50gm) chopped mixed peel

1. Well-butter or oil a tin measuring approximately 7 inches square.
2. Put sugar, milk, margarine and syrup into a heavy saucepan.
3. Heat slowly, stirring all the time, until sugar dissolves.
4. Bring to boil and cover with lid.
5. Boil 2 minutes then uncover.
6. Add condensed milk and continue to boil steadily, stirring frequently, until a little of the mixture forms a soft ball when dropped into cold water.
7. Stir in cherries and peel and leave until lukewarm.
8. Beat until mixture starts to thicken then pour into prepared tin.
9. Leave until cold then cut into squares.

Coconut snowballs

Makes about 16

1oz (25gm) soft, luxury margarine

1 level tablespoon clear honey

1$\frac{1}{2}$oz (37gm) icing sugar, sifted

1 teaspoon vanilla essence

2oz (50gm) desiccated coconut

red food colouring

extra desiccated coconut and pieces of glacé cherries for decoration

1. Put margarine, honey, icing sugar, vanilla essence, coconut and a few drops of red food colouring into a bowl.
2. Beat with a wooden spoon until well combined.
3. Roll into approximately 16 balls and toss in coconut.
4. Decorate each with a piece of cherry.

Mocha walnut creams, coconut snowballs, chocolate truffles and tutti frutti candy

Pink and white coconut ice

Makes about 54 pieces

$\frac{1}{4}$ pint (125ml) milk (or milk and water mixed)

1lb ($\frac{1}{2}$ kilo) granulated sugar

6oz (150gm) desiccated coconut

1 teaspoon vanilla essence

a few drops of red food colouring

1. Well-butter or oil a tin measuring approximately 8 inches square.
2. Put milk (or milk and water) and sugar into a large, heavy saucepan.
3. Heat slowly, stirring all the time, until sugar dissolves.
4. Bring to boil and cover with lid. Boil 2 minutes then uncover.
5. Continue to boil steadily, stirring once or twice, until a little of the mixture forms a soft ball when dropped into cold water.
6. Remove from heat and add coconut and vanilla.
7. Beat fairly briskly until mixture begins to turn cloudy and thicken.
8. Pour half into prepared tin.
9. Colour remainder pale pink with food colouring and spread quickly over the white layer.
10. Leave until cold and firm then cut into squares.

Chocolate coconut ice

Illustrated on page 237

Makes about 54 pieces

Make exactly as for pink and white coconut ice, left, but after adding coconut and vanilla, divide mixture into two. Add 1 dessertspoon sifted cocoa powder to one half and beat until thick. Spread into prepared tin. Colour remainder pale pink, beat until thick and spread over chocolate layer.

Peppermint coconut ice

Makes about 54 pieces

Make exactly as for pink and white coconut ice, but add $\frac{1}{2}$ teaspoon oil of peppermint and a little green food colouring instead of red food colouring to the second portion.

Chocolate truffles

Makes about 16

6oz (150gm) plain chocolate

1oz (25gm) soft, luxury margarine

1 egg yolk

1oz (25gm) walnuts, finely chopped

4oz (100gm) icing sugar, sifted

3 teaspoons brandy

chocolate vermicelli to coat

1. Break up chocolate and put into a basin over a saucepan of hot, but not boiling, water.
2. Leave until melted, stirring once or twice.
3. Add margarine, egg yolk, walnuts, icing sugar and brandy and beat for 2 to 3 minutes or until well-mixed.
4. Refrigerate until firm then take equal amounts of mixture and roll into approximately 16 balls.
5. Coat with chocolate vermicelli then transfer to fluted paper sweet cases.

Chocolate rum truffles

Makes about 16

4oz (100gm) plain chocolate

2oz (50gm) butter

1 tablespoon rum

1oz (25gm) ground almonds

1 tablespoon double cream

6oz (150gm) icing sugar, sifted

chocolate vermicelli or drinking chocolate powder to coat

1. Break up chocolate and put into a basin over a saucepan of hot, but not boiling, water. Add butter.
2. Leave until chocolate and butter have melted, stirring once or twice.
3. Add rum, almonds, cream and icing sugar and stir well to mix.
4. Refrigerate until firm then shape into approximately 16 balls.
5. Coat with chocolate vermicelli or drinking chocolate powder then transfer to fluted paper sweet cases.

Mocha truffles

Makes about 16

Make exactly as for chocolate rum truffles, above, omitting rum and adding 1 tablespoon strong coffee instead.

Chocolate brandy truffles

Makes about 16

Make exactly as for chocolate rum truffles, above, omitting rum and adding 1 tablespoon brandy instead.

Vanilla chews

Makes about 18

1oz (25gm) butter

4 level tablespoons golden syrup

1oz (25gm) soft brown sugar

1 teaspoon vanilla essence

3½oz (87gm) instant low-fat milk granules

drinking chocolate powder to coat

1. Put butter, syrup and sugar into a saucepan.
2. Leave over a low heat until melted, stirring all the time.
3. Remove from heat and stir in vanilla and milk granules.
4. Leave until cool enough to handle then shape into 18 balls.
5. Coat with drinking chocolate powder then leave for at least 30 minutes before eating.

Lemon honey chews

Makes about 18

Make exactly as for vanilla chews, above, using clear honey instead of golden syrup and adding 1 level teaspoon finely-grated lemon peel instead of the vanilla essence.

Honeycomb

Makes between 50 and 60 pieces

8oz (200gm) golden syrup

12oz (300gm) granulated sugar

2oz (50gm) butter

1 teaspoon vinegar

2 level teaspoons bicarbonate of soda

1 teaspoon cold water

1. Well-butter or oil a large roasting tin.
2. Put syrup, sugar, butter and vinegar into a large heavy saucepan.
3. Heat slowly, stirring all the time, until sugar dissolves and butter melts.
4. Bring to boil and cover with lid. Boil 2 minutes then uncover.
5. Continue to boil steadily, stirring once or twice, until a little of the mixture, dropped into cold water, forms hard threads which are brittle and break easily.
6. Remove pan from heat then stir in bicarbonate of soda mixed with the cold water (the mixture will foam up in pan).
7. Transfer to prepared tin and leave until set before breaking up into pieces.

Marzipan balls

Makes 20

4oz (100gm) ground almonds
2oz (50gm) icing sugar, sifted
2oz (50gm) caster sugar
½ teaspoon almond essence
1 egg yolk

1. Put almonds and both sugars into a bowl.
2. Add essence and egg yolk and, using a fork, work to a stiff paste which leaves sides of bowl clean.
3. Knead until smooth with fingertips then roll equal amounts into 20 balls.
4. Transfer to fluted paper sweet cases and leave 8 hours for marzipan to harden.

Marzipan walnut sandwiches

Makes 20

Make marzipan, as above, but use only half quantities of ingredients. Sandwich 40 walnut halves together in pairs with equal amounts of marzipan. Transfer to fluted paper sweet cases and leave about 8 hours to harden.

Marzipan bananas

Makes 20

Make marzipan as given in recipe for marzipan balls, above. Colour mixture yellow by kneading in a few drops of yellow food colouring. Divide into 20 equal-sized pieces and shape into bananas. Using liquid coffee essence, paint streaks and blotches on to each then insert a clove into top end.

Marzipan oranges

Makes 20

Make marzipan as given for marzipan balls, above. Colour marzipan orange by kneading in a few drops of orange food colouring. Divide into 20 equal-sized pieces and shape into oranges. Press against sides of a grater for pitted effect then push a clove into top of each to represent the stalk.

Marzipan apples

Makes 20

Make marzipan as given in recipe for marzipan balls, above. Colour mixture green by kneading in a few drops of green food colouring. Divide into 20 equal-sized pieces and shape into apples. Dilute red food colouring with water and use a paint brush to paint rosy patches on to each apple. Push a clove into the top of each to represent the stalk.

Marzipan potatoes

Makes 20

Make marzipan as given in recipe for marzipan balls, left. Roll marzipan into 20 uneven-shaped balls and toss in drinking chocolate powder.

Caramels

Makes about 30

4oz (100gm) caster sugar
4oz (100gm) soft brown sugar
2oz (50gm) golden syrup
3oz (75gm) butter
4 tablespoons evaporated milk
3 tablespoons water
1 teaspoon vanilla essence

1. Well-butter or oil a tin measuring approximately 6 inches square.
2. Put all ingredients, except vanilla essence, into a large heavy saucepan.
3. Heat slowly, stirring all the time, until sugar dissolves and butter melts.
4. Bring to the boil and cover with lid. Boil 2 minutes then uncover.
5. Continue to boil steadily, stirring frequently, until a little of the mixture forms a hard and pliable ball when dropped into cold water.
6. Stir in essence then pour into prepared tin.
7. Cut into pieces when cold and set then wrap each in squares of waxed or cellophane paper.

Chocolate caramels

Makes about 30

Make exactly as for caramels, above, adding 2oz (50gm) plain chocolate with all the other ingredients.

Marzipan balls decorated with glacé cherries, and vanilla fudge (see page 238)

Ginger candy

Makes about 54 pieces

1lb (½ kilo) soft brown sugar
2 level teaspoons ground ginger
¼ pint (125ml) water
1oz (25gm) butter
2oz (50gm) golden syrup

1. Well-butter or oil a tin measuring approximately 8 inches square.
2. Put all ingredients into a large, heavy saucepan.
3. Heat slowly, stirring all the time, until sugar dissolves and butter melts.
4. Bring to boil and cover with lid. Boil 2 minutes then uncover.
5. Continue to boil steadily, stirring once or twice, until a little of the mixture forms a soft ball when dropped into cold water.
6. Cool 5 minutes then beat briskly until mixture becomes cloudy.
7. Spread into prepared tin and cut into squares when cold and set.

Treacle toffee

Makes about 54 pieces

1lb (½ kilo) soft brown sugar
¼ pint (125ml) water
4oz (100gm) black treacle
4oz (100gm) golden syrup
1 teaspoon vinegar
3oz (75gm) butter

1. Well-butter or oil a tin measuring approximately 8 inches square.
2. Put all ingredients into a large, heavy saucepan.
3. Heat slowly, stirring all the time, until sugar dissolves and butter melts.
4. Bring to the boil and cover with lid. Boil 2 minutes then uncover.
5. Continue to boil steadily without stirring, until a little of the mixture, dropped into cold water, forms hard threads which bend without breaking.
6. Pour into prepared tin and mark into squares when half-set.
7. Break up when cold and firm.

Peanut brittle

Makes about 48 pieces

5oz (125gm) granulated sugar

5oz (125gm) soft brown sugar

6oz (150gm) golden syrup

¼ pint (125ml) water

2oz (50gm) butter

8 to 12oz (200 to 300gm) unsalted peanuts, roughly chopped

1. Well-butter or oil a tin measuring approximately 7 inches square.
2. Put both sugars, syrup, water and butter into a large, heavy saucepan.
3. Heat slowly, stirring all the time, until sugar dissolves and butter melts.
4. Bring to the boil and cover with lid. Boil 2 minutes then uncover.
5. Continue to boil steadily without stirring, until a little of the mixture, dropped into cold water, forms hard threads which are brittle and break easily.
6. Stir in peanuts then pour mixture into prepared tin.
7. Break up with a small hammer when completely cold and set.

Vanilla toffee

Makes about 42 pieces

12oz (300gm) soft brown sugar

6oz (150gm) golden syrup

2oz (50gm) butter

¼ pint (125ml) milk

1 teaspoon vanilla essence

1. Well-butter or oil a tin measuring approximately 7 inches square.
2. Put all ingredients except vanilla into a large, heavy saucepan.
3. Heat slowly, stirring all the time, until sugar dissolves and butter melts.
4. Bring to boil and cover with lid. Boil 2 minutes then uncover.
5. Continue to boil steadily, stirring once or twice, until a little of the mixture forms a hard ball when dropped into cold water.
6. Stir in vanilla then pour into prepared tin.
7. Mark into squares when half-set then break up with a small hammer when cold.

Vanilla nut toffee

Makes about 42 pieces

Make as for vanilla toffee, above, but stir in 2oz (50gm) chopped walnuts or almonds with the vanilla.

Toffee apples

Old-fashioned toffee

Makes about 48 pieces

8oz (200gm) golden syrup

1lb (½ kilo) granulated sugar

2oz (50gm) butter

1 dessertspoon vinegar

4 tablespoons water

1. Well-butter or oil a tin measuring approximately 8 inches square.
2. Put all ingredients into a large, heavy saucepan.
3. Heat slowly, stirring all the time, until sugar dissolves and butter melts.
4. Bring to the boil and cover with lid. Boil 2 minutes then uncover.
5. Continue to boil steadily without stirring, until a little of the mixture, dropped into cold water, forms hard threads which are brittle and break easily.
6. Pour contents into prepared tin then break up with a small hammer when completely cold and set.

Everton toffee

Makes about 42 pieces

12oz (300gm) soft brown sugar

2oz (50gm) golden syrup

1 level tablespoon black treacle

3oz (75gm) butter

4 tablespoons water

1. Well-butter or oil a tin measuring approximately 6 inches square.
2. Put all ingredients into a large, heavy saucepan.
3. Heat slowly, stirring all the time, until sugar dissolves and butter melts. Bring to boil and cover with lid. Boil 2 minutes then uncover.
4. Continue to boil steadily without stirring, until a little of the mixture, dropped into cold water, forms hard threads which are brittle and break easily.
5. Pour at once into prepared tin then break up with a small hammer when completely cold and set.

Toffee apples

Makes 12

12 medium dessert apples

12oz (300gm) soft brown sugar

6oz (150gm) golden syrup

1½oz (37gm) butter

¼ pint (125ml) water

1 teaspoon lemon juice

1. Wash apples in very hot water to remove the natural oily film on their skins.
2. Dry thoroughly.
3. Remove stalks then push a wooden skewer into the stalk end of each.
4. Well-butter or oil a large baking tray.
5. Put sugar, syrup, butter, water and lemon juice into a thick and heavy saucepan.
6. Heat slowly, stirring all the time, until sugar dissolves and butter melts.
7. Bring to the boil and cover with lid. Boil 2 minutes then uncover.
8. Continue to boil steadily without stirring, until a little of the mixture, dropped into cold water, forms hard threads which are brittle and break easily.
9. Dip and twist each apple in the toffee then plunge immediately into a bowl of very cold water to harden the surface.
10. Transfer to the greased tray and leave about 15 minutes or until toffee has set completely before eating.

Note
Because the toffee gets sticky both from the atmosphere and moisture in the apples themselves, it is advisable to make and eat the toffee apples within a few hours. If, however, they have to be kept for a day or so, wrap each one in cellophane paper, twisting it round the wooden skewer and holding it in place with an elastic band.

Jams, pickles and chutneys

There is something immensely satisfying about preserving one's own fruit and vegetables from either bought or garden produce. In this chapter you will find a variety of recipes for many types of jams, jellies, chutneys and pickles......ranging from black cherry jam and lemon curd to spicy tomato relish and pickled walnuts. One of the most essential pieces of equipment for home preserving is a stout, heavy-based saucepan which is spacious enough to hold the ingredients in comfort. If the saucepan is not big enough the jam will probably boil over. Useful but not essential is a long-handled wooden spoon and a sugar thermometer which registers much higher temperatures than a medical thermometer, and gives a good indication as to when a jam or jelly has reached setting point.

Jams and jellies

1. Choose prime quality fruits that are neither over-ripe nor under-ripe. Bruised and very mature fruit may be lacking in acid and pectin and consequently the jam or jelly may not set properly.
2. Jam rises in the pan while it is boiling, so make sure the pan is no more than half full after the sugar has been added.
3. To prevent waste, do not remove scum while the jam is cooking but skim with a metal spoon after jam has reached setting point. Sometimes the addition of a small knob of butter after cooking is completed, disperses scum completely.
4. To check for setting, pour a little jam or jelly on to a saucer and leave for 2 minutes. If a skin forms on top which wrinkles when touched, then setting point has been reached. Alternatively, place a sugar thermometer upright in jam and check the temperature. If it reaches 220 deg F (approximately 110 deg C) remove jam from heat.
5. Leave the jam to cool slightly before transferring to clean, dry jars. Strawberry jam or marmalade should be left in the saucepan until a skin forms on top—this will prevent fruit and peel from sinking to the bottom of the jars.
6. Cover jam with waxed rounds while it is still hot then, when completely cold, cover with cellophane tops.
7. Store in a cool, dry place.

Plum jam

Makes approximately 5lb (2½ kilo)

3lb (1½ kilo) cooking plums
¾ pint (375ml) water
3lb (1½ kilo) granulated or preserving sugar

1. Halve plums and remove stones only if they come out easily. Otherwise leave them until later.
2. Put plums into saucepan with water. Cover and simmer 15 to 20 minutes or until very soft.
3. Add all the sugar and stir over a low heat until dissolved.
4. Bring to the boil, stirring, and boil fairly briskly until setting point is reached, removing stones as they rise to the surface. Stir frequently.
5. Remove pan from heat.
6. Skim off any scum and leave jam to cool off slightly.
7. Pot and cover.

Plum and orange jam

Makes approximately 5lb (2½ kilo)

Make as for plum jam, above, but add the coarsely-grated peel of 1 large or 2 medium oranges with the plums.

A selection of pickles and chutneys

Greengage jam

Makes approximately 5lb (2½ kilo)

Make exactly as for plum jam, (see page 244) substituting greengages for plums.

Blackcurrant jam

Makes approximately 5lb (2½ kilo)

2½lb (1¼ kilo) blackcurrants

1½ pints (approximately ¾ litre) water

3lb (1½ kilo) granulated or preserving sugar

1. Stem blackcurrants and put the currants into saucepan with water.
2. Bring to boil, cover and simmer slowly until fruit is tender—30 to 45 minutes.
3. Add all the sugar and stir over a low heat until dissolved.
4. Bring to boil, stirring.
5. Boil fairly briskly until setting point is reached, stirring frequently.
6. Remove from heat.
7. Skim off any scum and leave jam to cool off slightly.
8. Pot and cover.

Blackcurrant and redcurrant jam

Makes approximately 5lb (2½ kilo)

Make as for blackcurrant jam, above, using 1½lb (¾ kilo) blackcurrants and 1lb (½ kilo) redcurrants.

Damson jam

Makes approximately 5lb (2½ kilo)

Make exactly as for blackcurrant jam (see this page) using 2½lb (1¼ kilo) damsons instead of blackcurrants. Remove stones as they rise to the surface.

Gooseberry jam

Makes approximately 5lb (2½ kilo)

Make exactly as for blackcurrant jam (see this page) using 2½lb (1¼ kilo) topped and tailed gooseberries instead of the blackcurrants.

Gooseberry and raspberry jam

Makes approximately 5lb (2½ kilo)

Make exactly as for blackcurrant jam (see this page) but use 1½lb (¾ kilo) topped and tailed gooseberries, 1½lb (¾ kilo) raspberries and only ¼ pint (125ml) water.

Gooseberry and strawberry jam

Makes approximately 5lb (2½ kilo)

Make exactly as for blackcurrant jam (see this page) but use 1½lb (¾ kilo) topped and tailed gooseberries, 1½lb (¾ kilo) strawberries and only ¼ pint (125ml) water.

Raspberry jam

Makes approximately 5lb (2½ kilo)

3lb (1½ kilo) raspberries

3lb (1½ kilo) granulated or preserving sugar

1. Put raspberries into saucepan and crush.
2. Add sugar and stir over low heat until dissolved.
3. Bring to the boil, stirring, and boil fairly briskly until setting point is reached. Stir frequently.
4. Remove pan from heat.
5. Skim off any scum and leave jam to cool off slightly.
6. Pot and cover.

Loganberry jam

Makes approximately 5lb (2½ kilo)

Make exactly as for raspberry jam, above, substituting loganberries for raspberries.

Rhubarb and raspberry jam

Makes approximately 5lb (2½ kilo)

1½lb (¾ kilo) rhubarb, cut into 2-inch lengths

¼ pint (125ml) water

1½lb (¾ kilo) raspberries, crushed

3lb (1½ kilo) granulated or preserving sugar

1. Put rhubarb into saucepan with water.
2. Simmer until fruit is tender.
3. Add crushed raspberries and sugar and stir over low heat until sugar dissolves.
4. Bring to boil, stirring, and boil fairly briskly until setting point is reached. Stir frequently.
5. Remove pan from heat.
6. Skim off any scum and leave jam to cool off slightly.
7. Pot and cover.

Redcurrant and raspberry jam

Makes approximately 5lb (2½ kilo)

1½lb (¾ kilo) redcurrants

½ pint (250ml) water

1½lb (¾ kilo) raspberries

3lb (1½ kilo) granulated or preserving sugar

1. Stem redcurrants and put currants into saucepan with water. Simmer 10 minutes.
2. Add raspberries and cook 10 minutes.
3. Add all the sugar and stir over a low heat until dissolved.
4. Bring to boil, stirring, and boil fairly briskly until setting point is reached. Stir frequently.
5. Remove pan from heat.
6. Skim off any scum and leave jam to cool slightly.
7. Pot and cover.

Strawberry jam (1)

Makes approximately 5lb (2½ kilo)

4oz (100gm) gooseberries or redcurrants

cold water

3lb (1½ kilo) strawberries

3lb (1½ kilo) granulated or preserving sugar

1. Just cover topped and tailed gooseberries or redcurrants with water and bring to boil.
2. Lower heat and cover. Simmer until fruit is tender. Strain. Reserve liquor.
3. Lightly crush strawberries and put into saucepan with sugar and gooseberry or redcurrant liquid.
4. Stir over very low heat until sugar dissolves.
5. Bring to boil, stirring, and boil fairly briskly until setting point is reached.
6. Remove pan from heat.
7. Skim off any scum and leave jam to cool for 20 to 30 minutes.
8. Stir well then pot and cover.

Strawberry jam (2)

Makes approximately 5lb (2½ kilo)

3lb (1½ kilo) strawberries

3 tablespoons lemon juice

3lb (1½ kilo) granulated or preserving sugar

1. Put strawberries into saucepan with lemon juice.
2. Simmer 30 minutes.
3. Add all the sugar and stir over low heat until dissolved.
4. Bring to boil, stirring, and boil fairly briskly until setting point is reached.
5. Remove pan from heat.
6. Skim off any scum and leave jam to cool for 20 to 30 minutes.
7. Stir well then pot and cover.

Mixed fruit jam

Rhubarb and ginger jam

Makes approximately 5lb (2½ kilo)

3lb (1½ kilo) rhubarb (weight after trimming

3lb (1½ kilo) granulated or preserving sugar

1½oz (37gm) root ginger

4oz (100gm) preserved ginger

1. Cut rhubarb into 2-inch lengths.
2. Put into large bowl in alternate layers with sugar.
3. Cover and leave overnight.
4. Transfer rhubarb and sugar to large saucepan.
5. Hammer root ginger lightly to bruise it then tie in a muslin bag. Add to saucepan of rhubarb.
6. Bring slowly to boil, stirring.
7. Boil briskly for 15 minutes.
8. Chop or slice preserved ginger and add.
9. Boil a further 10 to 15 minutes or until rhubarb is clear and setting point is reached.
10. Remove pan from heat.
11. Skim off any scum and leave jam to cool off slightly.
12. Pot and cover.

Marrow and ginger jam

Makes approximately 5lb (2½ kilo)

3lb (1½ kilo) marrow (prepared weight)

3lb (1½ kilo) granulated or preserving sugar

1oz (25gm) root ginger

3 large lemons

1. Cut marrow into cubes and put into large basin with half the sugar.
2. Stir thoroughly to mix. Cover and leave overnight.
3. Transfer to saucepan.
4. Hammer ginger lightly to bruise it. Peel lemons thinly. Tie both the ginger and lemon peel in a piece of muslin and add to saucepan with lemon juice.
5. Stir over low heat until sugar dissolves then simmer 30 minutes.
6. Add rest of sugar, stir until dissolved then continue to boil gently until marrow is transparent—about 15 minutes.
7. Remove pan from heat.
8. Skim off any scum and leave jam to cool off slightly.
9. Pot and cover.

Note
Because marrow lacks pectin, this jam will not give a firm set.

Mixed fruit jam

Makes approximately 5lb (2½ kilo)

For this jam, choose any mixture of soft fruits. The total weight of fruit used should be 3lb (1½ kilo). Try any of the following mixtures:

(a) Gooseberries, raspberries and straw-berries

(b) Redcurrants, raspberries and rhubarb

(c) Plums, apricots, greengages and 1 or 2 peeled and sliced peaches

(d) Blackcurrants, blackberries and apples

(e) Fresh cranberries, apples and finely-grated peel of 1 or 2 oranges

1. Simmer fruits until tender in ½ pint (250ml) water.
2. Add 3lb (1½ kilo) granulated or preserving sugar and stir over a low heat until dissolved.
3. Bring to the boil, stirring, and boil fairly briskly until setting point is reached. Stir frequently.
4. Remove pan from heat.
5. Skim off any scum and leave jam to cool off slightly.
6. Pot and cover.

Fresh apricot jam

Makes approximately 5lb (2½ kilo)

3lb (1½ kilo) fresh apricots

½ pint (250ml) water

juice of 1 large lemon

3lb (1½ kilo) granulated or preserving sugar

1. Halve apricots and remove stones.
2. Put fruit into a saucepan with water and lemon juice.
3. Simmer until apricots are soft and much of the liquid has evaporated.
4. Add all the sugar and stir over a low heat until dissolved.
5. Bring to the boil, stirring, and boil steadily until setting point is reached. Stir frequently.
6. Remove pan from heat.
7. Skim off any scum and leave jam to cool off slightly.
8. Pot and cover.

Note

If liked, crack some of the apricot stones and remove kernels. Cover with boiling water, leave 1 or 2 minutes and drain. Slip the skins off the kernels, then add kernels to apricots with lemon juice.

Dried apricot jam

Makes approximately 5lb (2½ kilo)

1lb (½ kilo) dried apricots

3 pints (approximately 1¾ litre) water

juice of 1 large lemon

3lb (1½ kilo) granulated or preserving sugar

2oz (50gm) blanched almonds (optional)

1. Wash apricots thoroughly.
2. Put into large saucepan and cover with 3 pints (1¾ litre) water. Leave to soak overnight.
3. Add lemon juice and slowly bring to boil. Lower heat and cover. Simmer gently for 30 minutes.
4. Add all the sugar and stir over a low heat until dissolved.
5. Add the almonds, if used, then boil fairly briskly until setting point is reached. Stir frequently.
6. Remove pan from heat.
7. Skim off any scum and leave jam to cool off slightly.
8. Pot and cover.

Black cherry jam

Makes approximately 5lb (2½ kilo)

4lb (2 kilo) black cherries

juice of 3 large lemons

3lb (1½ kilo) granulated or preserving sugar

1. Halve cherries and remove stones.
2. Put cherries into saucepan with lemon juice.
3. Cover and simmer very gently until fruit is soft—20 to 30 minutes. Stir frequently to prevent sticking.
4. Add sugar and stir over low heat until dissolved.
5. Bring to boil and boil steadily for about 20 to 30 minutes or until setting point is reached.
6. Remove pan from heat.
7. Skim off any scum and leave jam to cool for 20 minutes.
8. Stir well then pot and cover.

Note

As cherries are lacking in pectin, this jam will not give a firm set.

Quince jam

Makes approximately 5lb (2½ kilo)

2lb (1 kilo) quinces (weight after peeling and coring)

juice of ½ lemon

1½ pints (approximately ¾ litre) water

3lb (1½ kilo) granulated or preserving sugar

1. Slice quinces and put into saucepan with lemon juice and water.
2. Cover and simmer gently until fruit is very soft and pulpy.
3. Add all the sugar and stir over low heat until dissolved.
4. Bring to boil, stirring, and boil fairly briskly until setting point is reached. Stir frequently.
5. Remove pan from heat.
6. Skim off any scum and leave jam to cool off slightly.
7. Pot and cover.

Jellies

The cooking procedures for fruit jellies are similar to those used for jam but because the characteristic quality of any jelly is clarity, only fruit juices and sugar are used. In order to obtain fruit juice, the fruit and water are simmered together first and then allowed to drip through a jelly bag or clean tea towel into a bowl. This juice is then boiled up with the sugar until setting point is reached. A word of caution: the jelly bag or cloth should not be squeezed while the fruit is dripping, or particles of fruit might be forced through which would make the jelly cloudy. To give an exact quantity of ingredients for each jelly is difficult: so much depends on the ripeness of fruit and the length of time it is allowed to drip.

However 1lb (½ kilo) sugar to every pint (approximately ½ litre) fruit juice is the proportion for all jellies and the yield from this amount could be in the region of 1½lb (¾ kilo) of jelly.

Apple jelly

4lb (2 kilo) cooking apples or garden windfalls

2 pints (approximately 1 litre) water

juice of 1 lemon

granulated or preserving sugar

1. Remove bruised parts of apples then cut into thick slices without peeling or coring.
2. Put into saucepan with water and lemon juice.
3. Simmer gently, covered, until apples are soft and pulpy—about 30 minutes.
4. Uncover and cook a little more briskly until liquid is reduced by about a third.
5. Strain through a jelly bag into a bowl and leave until dripping has stopped completely.
6. Measure the juice and allow 1lb (½ kilo) granulated or preserving sugar to every pint (approximately ½ litre).
7. Put into a saucepan and stir over a low heat until sugar dissolves.
8. Bring to the boil and boil fairly briskly until setting point is reached.
9. Remove pan from heat.
10. Skim off any scum then pot and cover.

Crab-apple jelly

Make exactly as for apple jelly, above, substituting crab-apples for cooking apples.

Spiced apple or crab-apple jelly

Add 1oz (25gm) bruised root ginger and/or 8 cloves to the fruit while it is simmering. Otherwise make exactly as for apple jelly (see this page).

Apple or crab-apple lemon jelly

Finely peel 2 medium lemons. Add peel to the fruit while it is simmering. Otherwise make exactly as for apple jelly (see this page).

Apple and blackberry jelly

Make exactly as for apple jelly (see this page), using 2lb (1 kilo) cooking apples or windfalls and 2lb (1 kilo) blackberries.

Apple and cranberry jelly

Make exactly as for apple jelly (see opposite page), using 2lb (1 kilo) cooking apples or windfalls and 2lb (1 kilo) fresh cranberries.

Apple and elderberry jelly

Make exactly as for apple jelly (see opposite page), using 2lb (1 kilo) cooking apples or windfalls and 2lb (1 kilo) elderberries. Cut the quantity of water down to 1 pint or approximately ½ litre.

Mixed currant jelly

Make exactly as for apple jelly (see opposite page), using 2lb (1 kilo) redcurrants and 2lb (1 kilo) blackcurrants. Simmer fruit for 30 minutes only.

Gooseberry jelly

Make exactly as for apple jelly (see opposite page), using 4lb (2 kilo) topped and tailed gooseberries instead of the apples.

Blackcurrant jelly

Make exactly as for apple jelly (see opposite page), using 4lb (2 kilo) stemmed blackcurrants. Increase water to 2½ pints or approximately 1½ litre.

Bramble jelly

Make exactly as for apple jelly (see opposite page), using 4lb (2 kilo) blackberries, the juice of 2 lemons and only ½ pint or approximately 250ml water.

Redcurrant jelly

Make exactly as for apple jelly (see opposite page), using 4lb (2 kilo) redcurrants instead of apples.

Raspberry jelly

Make exactly as for apple jelly (see opposite page), using 4lb (2 kilo) raspberries and only ¼ pint or 125ml water.

Mint jelly

3lb (approximately 1½ kilo) cooking apples
1 teacup mint leaves, loosely packed
1 pint (approximately ½ litre) water
1 pint (approximately ½ litre) wine or cider vinegar
granulated or preserving sugar
4 level tablespoons very finely-chopped mint
green food colouring

1. Cut apples into thick slices without peeling or coring.
2. Put into saucepan with mint leaves and water.
3. Simmer gently, covered, until apples are soft and pulpy—about 30 minutes.
4. Add vinegar and cook a further 10 minutes.
5. Strain through a jelly bag into a bowl and leave until dripping has stopped completely.
6. Measure the juice and allow 1lb (½ kilo) granulated or preserving sugar to every pint (approximately ½ litre).
7. Put into a saucepan and stir over a low heat until sugar dissolves.
8. Bring to the boil and boil fairly briskly until setting point is reached.
9. Remove pan from heat.
10. Skim off any scum then stir in chopped mint and sufficient green colouring to tint the jelly a pale green.
11. Pot and cover.

Raspberry jelly

Fruit cheeses

These are thick preserves made from fruit purée and sugar. They make delicious spreads on breads, may also be used as a filling for turnovers and patties and can be served as sweet accompaniments with meat, poultry and game. It is difficult to give an exact yield because so much depends on the amount of liquid in the fruit itself, but the basic proportion of sugar to purée is 1lb (½ kilo) granulated or preserving sugar to every pint (approximately ½ litre) purée.

Apple cheese

3lb (1½ kilo) cooking apples, garden windfalls or crab-apples
2 pints (approximately 1 litre) water
3 cloves
½ level teaspoon cinnamon
granulated or preserving sugar

1. Wash apples or crab-apples and cut up roughly.
2. Put into saucepan with all remaining ingredients.
3. Simmer gently, with lid on pan, until fruit is very soft and pulpy—about 45 minutes.
4. Rub mixture through a nylon sieve and measure purée.
5. To every pint (approximately ½ litre) allow 1lb (½ kilo) granulated or preserving sugar.
6. Put purée and sugar into a saucepan and stir over a low heat until sugar dissolves.
7. Boil slowly, over a very gentle heat, until mixture becomes *very thick*, stirring frequently. This should take between 1½ and 2 hours or until a spoon, drawn across the cheese, leaves a clean and straight line.
8. Transfer to small pots and cover while hot.
9. Leave in a cool, dry place for about 3 months before using.

Damson cheese

Make exactly as for apple cheese, above, using 3lb (1½ kilo) damsons, ½ pint (250ml) water and 1lb (½ kilo) granulated or preserving sugar to each pint (approximately ½ litre) purée.

Quince cheese

Make exactly as for apple cheese (see this page), using 3lb (1½ kilo) quinces, 1 level teaspoon citric acid, 1 level teaspoon finely-grated lemon peel, sufficient water just to cover fruit and 1lb (½ kilo) granulated or preserving sugar to every pint (approximately ½ litre) purée.

Blackcurrant cheese

Make exactly as for apple cheese (see this page), using 3lb (1½ kilo) blackcurrants, ¼ pint (125ml) water and 1lb (½ kilo) granulated or preserving sugar to every pint (approximately ½ litre) purée.

Marmalade

The success of marmalade depends chiefly on the following:
1. Bitter or Seville oranges should be used.
2. Sweet oranges should be used only in conjunction with other citrus fruits such as grapefruit and/or lemons or limes.
3. Peel should be shredded—thickly or thinly depending on taste—to tenderise it.
4. Long, slow cooking before the sugar is added to reduce the liquid and soften the peel. Without this, the marmalade is unlikely to give a satisfactory set.

Bitter orange marmalade

Makes approximately 5lb (2½ kilo)

1½lb (¾ kilo) Seville or bitter oranges

3 pints (approximately 1¾ litre) water

3 tablespoons lemon juice

3lb (1½ kilo) granulated or preserving sugar

1. Wash fruit thoroughly.
2. Cut oranges in half and squeeze out the juice and pips. Put pips into a muslin bag. Remove pith from peel and add to bag. Tie up.
3. Cut peel into strips (thickness depending on personal taste) and put into a saucepan with orange juice, bag of pips and pith, water and lemon juice.
4. Bring to boil. Lower heat, cover pan and simmer steadily for 1½ hours or until peel is very soft and liquid is reduced by about half.
5. Remove bag of pips and when cool enough to handle, squeeze well into pan of oranges.
6. Add all the sugar and stir over a low heat until dissolved.
7. Bring to the boil steadily until setting point is reached. Stir frequently.
8. Remove pan from heat.
9. Leave marmalade until a skin forms on top.
10. Stir well then pot and cover.

Sweet orange marmalade

Makes approximately 5lb (2½ kilo)

Make exactly as for bitter orange marmalade (see above), using 1½lb (¾ kilo) sweet oranges and the juice of 3 medium lemons.

Grapefruit and lemon marmalade

Makes approximately 5lb (2½ kilo)

Make exactly as for bitter orange marmalade (see above), using 1½lb (¾ kilo) grapefruit and the juice of 2 large lemons.

Mixed fruit marmalade

Makes approximately 5lb (2½ kilo)

Make exactly as for bitter orange marmalade (see this page), using 1½lb (¾ kilo) mixed citrus fruits such as 1 or 2 lemons, 1 orange and 1 grapefruit. Use whole lemons, not just the juice.

Coarse-cut dark marmalade

Makes approximately 5lb (2½ kilo)

1½lb (¾ kilo) Seville or bitter oranges

3 pints (approximately 1¾ litre) water

juice of 1 medium lemon

2½lb (1¼ kilo) granulated or preserving sugar

8oz (200gm) soft brown sugar (dark variety)

1. Wash fruit thoroughly.
2. Put into large saucepan and add water.
3. Cover and simmer 2 hours or until fruit is tender and skin may be burst easily with a skewer.
4. Lift out of pan and leave until cool enough to handle.
5. Chop fruit coarsely. Collect all the pips and tie in a muslin bag.
6. Return chopped fruit and the bag of pips to saucepan with lemon juice.
7. Add all the sugar and stir over a low heat until dissolved.
8. Bring to boil and boil steadily until setting point is reached. Stir frequently.
9. Remove pan from heat.
10. Leave marmalade until a skin forms on top.
11. Stir well then pot and cover.

Bitter orange marmalade

Miscellaneous sweet preserves

Mincemeat

Makes about 4lb (2 kilo)

8oz (200gm) currants

8oz (200gm) stoneless dates

8oz (200gm) sultanas

8oz (200gm) seedless raisins

8oz (200gm) chopped mixed peel

8oz (200gm) cooking apples, peeled and cored

3oz (75gm) blanched almonds

8oz (200gm) soft brown sugar (dark)

4oz (100gm) shredded suet

1 level teaspoon mixed spice

½ level teaspoon cinnamon

1 level teaspoon finely-grated orange peel

1 level teaspoon finely-grated lemon peel

2 tablespoons brandy or sherry

1. Mince currants, dates, sultanas, raisins, peel, apples and almonds.
2. Put into bowl and add remaining ingredients.
3. Cover and refrigerate for 2 days.
4. Stir well, put into jars and cover as for jam.

Lemon curd

Makes approximately 2lb (1 kilo)

finely-grated peel and juice of 3 large lemons

4oz (100gm) butter

3 eggs plus 1 egg yolk, beaten together

8oz (200gm) granulated sugar

1. Put all ingredients into the top of a double saucepan or into a basin over a saucepan of gently simmering water.
2. Cook, stirring frequently, until mixture thickens sufficiently to coat the back of a spoon. In no circumstances allow the curd to boil or it may separate and curdle.
3. Pour into clean, warm and dry jars and cover as for jam.
4. Store in a cool place, preferably in a refrigerator.

Note
Do not make large quantities of lemon curd as it only keeps well for 4 to 5 weeks.

Orange curd

Make exactly as for lemon curd, above, using 2 medium oranges and 1 large lemon.

Spiced apple rings

Makes about 2 to 3 pints (1 to 1½ litre)

3lb (1½ kilo) small apples

¼ pint (125ml) water

¼ pint (125ml) vinegar

12oz (200gm) caster sugar

1 level teaspoon grated orange peel

3 cinnamon sticks, each 1 inch

1 level tablespoon whole cloves

1. Peel and core apples and cut into rings. Leave in bowl of cold water to which a little vinegar or lemon juice has been added.
2. Put ¼ pint water, ¼ pint vinegar and all remaining ingredients into saucepan.
3. Cook, stirring, over a low heat until sugar dissolves.
4. Place half the apple rings in the syrup and poach slowly until tender.
5. Lift out the apple rings and pack them tightly into hot jars.
6. Cook and pack the rest of the apple rings.
7. Drain the hot syrup, and use to fill up the jars.
8. Cover when cold.

Chutneys

Chutneys, popular with cold meat and cheese, are a tangy, sweet-sour combination of chopped vegetables and/or fruits, cooked until thick with onions (for flavouring), spices, vinegar, salt, sugar and seasonings. For those who like their chutneys on the hot side, Cayenne pepper—from a pinch to 1 level teaspoon—may be used in addition to the other seasonings. All chutneys should be left to mature for at least 6 weeks before using.

Spiced apple rings, apple and pear chutney, and apple and tomato chutney (see next page)

Apple chutney

Makes about 5lb (2½ kilo)

4lb (2 kilo) cooking apples)

2lb (1 kilo) onions

2 garlic cloves (optional)

1lb (½ kilo) stoned raisins or sultanas

2 pints (approximately 1¼ litre) vinegar

1½lb (¾ kilo) soft brown sugar

1 to 2 level teaspoons salt

3 level teaspoons ground ginger

2 level teaspoons cinnamon

1 level tablespoon pickling spice, 6 cloves and 1 small bay leaf, all tied together in a muslin bag

1. Peel, core and slice apples.
2. Peel and slice onions. Peel garlic.
3. Coarsely mince apples, onions, garlic and raisins or sultanas.
4. Put into saucepan with half the vinegar.
5. Cover and simmer until fruits and vegetables are tender—about 30 minutes.
6. Add all remaining ingredients and stir until sugar dissolves.
7. Cook, uncovered, until chutney thickens to a jam-like consistency, stirring occasionally.
8. Remove bag of spices then pot and cover.

Apple and date chutney

Makes about 5lb (2½ kilo)

Make as for apple chutney (see this page), reducing apples by 1lb (½ kilo) and adding 1lb (½ kilo) stoned dates. Reduce the sugar by 8oz (200gm).

Apple and raisin chutney

Makes about 5lb (2½ kilo)

Make as for apple chutney (see this page), reducing apples by 1lb (½ kilo) and adding 1lb (½ kilo) stoned raisins. Reduce sugar by 8oz (200gm).

Gooseberry and rhubarb chutney

Makes about 5lb (2½ kilo)

Make as for apple chutney (see this page), using 2lb (1 kilo) topped and tailed gooseberries and 2lb (1 kilo) prepared rhubarb. Do not mince the ingredients but halve the gooseberries, and cut the rhubarb into 2-inch lengths. Grate the onion.

Apple and pear chutney

Makes about 5lb (2½ kilo)

Make as for apple chutney (see this page), using half apples and half cooking pears.

Plum chutney

Makes about 5lb (2½ kilo)

Make as for apple chutney (see this page), using 3lb (1½ kilo) stoned cooking plums, 1lb (½ kilo) cooking apples and 2lb (1 kilo) onions.

Plum and banana chutney

Makes approximately 5lb (2½ kilo)

Make as for apple chutney (see this page), using 2lb (1 kilo) stoned cooking plums, 1½lb (¾ kilo) bananas (weight after peeling), 1lb (½ kilo) cooking apples and 1½lb (¾ kilo) onions.

251

Green tomato chutney

Makes about 6lb (3 kilo)

5lb (2½ kilo) green tomatoes

1lb (½ kilo) onions

1 garlic clove (optional)

1 pint (½ litre) vinegar

1lb (½ kilo) soft brown sugar

1 level tablespoon pickling spice (tied in muslin bag)

1 level dessertspoon salt

1. Coarsely mince tomatoes and onions. Finely chop garlic, if used.
2. Put into saucepan with half the vinegar.
3. Cover and simmer until onions are soft.
4. Add sugar and stir until dissolved.
5. Pour in remaining vinegar then add spice and salt.
6. Cook, uncovered, until chutney thickens to a jam-like consistency, stirring occasionally.
7. Remove bag of spice then pot and cover.

Red tomato chutney

Makes about 6lb (3 kilo)

6lb (3 kilo) tomatoes, skinned

2lb (1 kilo) onions

1 garlic clove (optional)

1 pint (approximately ½ litre) vinegar

1lb (½ kilo) soft brown sugar

1 level tablespoon pickling spice (tied in muslin bag)

2 level tablespoons tomato paste

1 tablespoon Worcestershire sauce

1 to 1½ level dessertspoons salt

1. Chop tomatoes and onions. Chop garlic, if used.
2. Put into saucepan with half the vinegar.
3. Cover and simmer until onions are soft.
4. Add all remaining ingredients and stir over a low heat until sugar dissolves.
5. Cook, uncovered, until chutney thickens to a jam-like consistency. Stir occasionally.
6. Remove bag of spice then pot and cover.

Apple and tomato chutney

Make as for red tomato chutney, above, using 2lb (1 kilo) apples and 4lb (2 kilo) tomatoes.

Prune chutney

Makes about 4lb (2 kilo)

2lb (1 kilo) prunes, soaked overnight

1lb (½ kilo) onions, quartered

2oz (50gm) mustard seed and 1oz (25gm) pickling spice tied together in a muslin bag

1 level teaspoon ground ginger

½ teaspoon tabasco

1 pint (approximately ½ litre) vinegar

6oz (150gm) granulated sugar

3oz (75gm) black treacle

1. Drain prunes. Halve them and remove stones.
2. Coarsely mince prunes with onions.
3. Put into saucepan with bag of spices, ginger, tabasco and half the vinegar.
4. Cover and simmer until onions are tender.
5. Add all remaining ingredients and stir over a low heat until sugar dissolves.
6. Cook, uncovered, until chutney thickens to a jam-like consistency. Stir occasionally.
7. Remove bag of spices then pot and cover.

Dried apricot chutney

Makes about 3½lb (1¾ kilo)

12oz (300gm) dried apricots

½ pint (250ml) boiling water

1lb (½ kilo) onions, quartered

1lb (½ kilo) cooking apples, peeled, cored and sliced

½ pint (250ml) vinegar

1 level teaspoon salt

½ level teaspoon ground ginger

1 level teaspoon mixed spice

1 level teaspoon coriander

12oz (300gm) granulated or preserving sugar

1. Soak apricots overnight in the boiling water.
2. Drain and mince with onions and apples.
3. Put into saucepan with all remaining ingredients.
4. Stir over low heat until sugar dissolves.
5. Cook, uncovered, until chutney thickens to a jam-like consistency. Stir occasionally.
6. Pot and cover.

Dried apricot chutney

Mixed vegetable chutney

Makes about 5lb (2½ kilo)

1lb (½ kilo) mushrooms

12oz (300gm) green tomatoes

1 medium green pepper, de-seeded

8oz (200gm) onions

1lb (½ kilo) cooking apples, peeled, cored and sliced

2 garlic cloves

1½ pints (¾ litre) white vinegar

12oz (300gm) soft brown sugar

1. Slice mushrooms thinly.
2. Chop tomatoes, green pepper, onions and apples. Alternatively, mince coarsely.
3. Put into saucepan with half the vinegar.
4. Cover and simmer until onions and pepper are both tender.
5. Add all remaining ingredients and stir over low heat until sugar dissolves.
6. Cook, uncovered, until chutney thickens to a jam-like consistency. Stir occasionally.
7. Pot and cover.

Spicy tomato relish

Makes about 4lb (2 kilo)

1lb (½ kilo) red tomatoes, skinned

1 large green pepper

1lb (½ kilo) onions

1lb (½ kilo) cooking apples

2 garlic cloves

½ pint (250ml) vinegar

12oz (300gm) soft brown sugar

1 level tablespoon salt

1 level tablespoon paprika

2 level teaspoons prepared mustard

1 level teaspoon chilli powder

1 teaspoon Worcestershire sauce

1 can (about 6oz or 150gm) tomato paste

1. Chop tomatoes and put into saucepan. De-seed pepper and cut flesh into strips.
2. Chop or coarsely grate onions. Peel, core and slice apples. Chop garlic cloves.
3. Add green pepper, onions, apples and garlic to pan with half the vinegar.
4. Cover and simmer until onions are soft.
5. Add all remaining ingredients and stir over a low heat until sugar dissolves.
6. Cook, uncovered, until relish thickens to a jam-like consistency. Stir occasionally.
7. Remove bag of spices then pot and cover.

Pickles

Most vegetables used for pickles must be soaked in brine (a solution of salt and water in the proportion of 1lb or ½ kilo salt to 8 pints or approximately 5 litres water) and then preserved in spiced vinegar. Spiced vinegar is easily made by leaving an assortment of spices to soak in white vinegar for several weeks.

Spiced vinegar (1)

4 pints (approximately 2½ litres) white vinegar

2 level tablespoons pickling spice

1 cinnamon stick

2 dozen cloves

3 blades of mace

1 bay leaf, broken into small pieces

1. Put vinegar into a large jar.
2. Add all remaining ingredients and stir well to mix.
3. Cover with thick brown paper or treble thickness of greaseproof paper and leave for 6 to 8 weeks, stirring occasionally.
4. Strain before use.

Note

Do not cover the vinegar with a metal lid or foil.

Spiced vinegar (2)

A quick spiced vinegar may be made by using the same ingredients as for spiced vinegar (1), above—simply bring them to the boil, remove from the heat, cover them, leave to stand for 24 hours, then strain well. This makes an adequate pickling vinegar but lacks the roundness of flavour found in a spiced vinegar which has been left to mature for some weeks.

Pickled cauliflower

Divide cauliflower into small florets and put into bowl. Cover with brine. Keep cauliflower immersed in solution by covering with a plate held down by a weight or heavy garden stone. Leave to stand 24 hours then drain, rinse and drain again. Pack into jars and fill with cold spiced vinegar, leaving about a 1-inch gap at the top of each jar. Cover securely and leave for 6 to 8 weeks before using.

Pickled onions or shallots

Peel required amount of onions or shallots. Make as for pickled cauliflower, above, but leave onions or shallots to soak in the brine for 36 hours. Use cold spiced vinegar to fill the jars. Cover securely and leave 2 to 3 months before using.

Pickled beetroot

Peel required amount of cooked beetroots then put into jars. Fill with cold spiced vinegar to which salt to taste has been added. Leave about a 1-inch gap at the top of each jar. Cover securely and leave 1 to 2 weeks before using.

Piccalilli

Pickled gherkins

Soak required amount of gherkins in brine solution for 3 days. Drain well then dry. Return to bowl and cover with hot spiced vinegar. Cover closely and leave to stand in a warm place for 24 hours. Drain off vinegar, re-boil and pour over gherkins. Cover and leave to stand 24 hours. Repeat draining and covering process once more. Transfer gherkins to jars and fill with the spiced vinegar which was previously used, together with any extra if required. Leave about a 1-inch gap at the top of each jar. Cover securely and leave 4 to 6 weeks before using.

Pickled cucumber

Slice required amount of washed and dried unpeeled cucumbers. Cut into thick slices and leave to soak in brine for 24 hours. Drain thoroughly then pack into jars. Fill with spiced vinegar, leaving about a 1-inch gap at the top of each jar. Cover securely and leave 1 week before using.

Note

As pickled cucumbers do not keep well, it is advisable to use them within 7 to 10 days of making.

Pickled walnuts

Choose required amount of walnuts, making sure they are green and without shells. To test for this, prick each with a long needle. If the needle resists, it indicates that shells have begun to form and those particular walnuts should be discarded. Cover suitable walnuts with brine and leave to soak for 7 days. Change the brine and soak for a further 14 days. Wash and dry thoroughly, spread out and leave exposed to the air for 1 or 2 days or until they turn black. Transfer to jars and cover with hot spiced vinegar leaving a 1-inch gap at the top of each jar. Cover securely when cold and leave 1 to 2 months before using.

Mixed pickles

Choose cauliflower, pickling onions, French beans and cucumber. Cut the cauliflower into small florets. Peel onions, cut beans into even lengths. Cut cucumber into thick slices. Make as for pickled cauliflower (see this page) but leave vegetables in the brine for 48 hours.

Pickled red cabbage

1 large head red cabbage

dry salt

spiced vinegar

1. Shred cabbage finely, removing any bruised or discoloured leaves and the hard centre stalks.
2. Layer cabbage and dry salt in a large bowl.
3. Cover and leave overnight.
4. Rinse and drain thoroughly then loosely pack into jars.
5. Fill with cold spiced vinegar, leaving a 1-inch gap at the top of the jar.
6. Cover securely and leave for 1 week before using.

Note

Use within 4 weeks of making. If left longer, cabbage tends to loose both crispness and colour.

Piccalilli or mustard pickles

Makes about 10lb (5 kilo)

6lb (3 kilo) mixed vegetables to include cauliflower, marrow, French beans, pickling onions and cucumber

brine solution

8oz (200gm) granulated sugar

1½oz (37gm) dry mustard

1½oz (37gm) flour

1 level teaspoon ground ginger

2 level tablespoons turmeric (to give the characteristic colour of mustard pickles)

3 pints (approximately 1¾ litre) white vinegar

1. Divide cauliflower into small florets. Cut marrow into small cubes. Cut beans into even lengths. Peel onions. Slice cucumber then cut each slice into 4 wedges.
2. Immerse in brine solution, covering with a plate held down by a weight or heavy garden stone. Leave 24 hours. Drain vegetables and rinse.
3. Mix sugar with mustard, flour, ginger and turmeric. Gradually blend to a smooth cream with half the vinegar.
4. Put vegetables with rest of vinegar into a saucepan.
5. Bring to the boil. Cover and simmer 20 minutes.
6. Add blended mustard mixture. Stir thoroughly to mix then bring to the boil.
7. Boil gently for 3 minutes.
8. Pot and cover.

Home freezing

Quick freezing is one of the most convenient, reliable, and natural ways of preserving all kinds of fresh and cooked foods. An increasing number of households are investing in domestic deep freezers because a well-stocked home freezer not only makes life simpler but, in the long run, also saves time and money. One can buy in bulk, cook in bulk during quiet times of the day, store away left-overs which might otherwise be wasted and take full advantage of special cheap offers, either from local shops with a seasonal glut of fruit and vegetables or from commercial firms who offer frozen food in bulk at an appreciable discount. In addition, a freezer packed with pre-cooked meals, cakes, buns, scones, bread and ready-to-cook foods is like owning a mini supermarket—there is always something to hand for unexpected guests, or a sudden emergency.

Apart from these obvious advantages, the flavour and appearance of foods which are quick frozen remain virtually unchanged and unspoiled. Because harmful bacteria are unable to grow and multiply in a temperature of minus 18 deg C (0 deg F)—the temperature at which freezers normally operate for storage purposes—most well-packed foods can be kept safely for a reasonably long period of time.

It is important to remember that the frozen food compartment of a refrigerator and a deep freeze are not interchangeable. The frozen food compartment is useful *only* for storing packs of bought frozen foods for a short time—one week if the compartment is marked with one star, one month if marked with two stars and up to three months if marked with three stars. It should not be used for freezing fresh produce and home-cooked food because the temperature is not sufficiently low.

Choosing a deep freeze

Finding a suitable home for a new freezer can be a problem. If the kitchen is small and already over-crowded, then the deep freeze may be put elsewhere in the house or outbuildings—a garage, landing, spare room, hall or cellar are all satisfactory—provided the area is dry and well-ventilated with a suitable electric socket. There are only two styles of freezers from which to choose: chest and upright. The chest kind is like a large box with top-opening lid and is usually sold with removable baskets or open trays. It is broad rather than tall and if you are to choose this type of freezer, it is as well to check before buying that you can easily reach the bottom of it. There is hardly any loss of cold air when the lid is lifted and therefore it is very economical to run. The coldest parts are the base and sides. The upright freezer looks like a refrigerator, fitted with removable shelves and front-opening door. It takes up less floor space than the chest freezer and there is less bending and stooping involved in reaching for foods. It is easier to pack and unpack than the chest freezer but will lose cold air more quickly if the door is opened frequently.

The size—or cubic capacity—of a deep freeze should be chosen to suit the number of people in the family. One cubic foot of freezer capacity stores about 25lb (11½ kilo) of food and at least 2 cubic feet of storage space should be allowed per person. Thus a family of four would need a freezer of 8 cubic foot capacity while one person living alone would find a smaller freezer of 2 cubic foot capacity adequate.

Note: for maintenance and de-frosting always follow manufacturers' instructions.

A selection of food being prepared for freezing

Wrapping, packing and sealing

For successful results, foods to be frozen must be wrapped, packed and sealed most carefully in order to exclude as much air as possible. This is essential to stop loss of colour and flavour and also to prevent freezer 'burn' (discoloured patches on the food through dehydration). The most satisfactory closures for bags are plastic or paper-coated wire ties; special adhesive freezer tape should be used for containers. Ordinary adhesive tape is unsuitable as it becomes loose at low temperatures. Because liquids expand on freezing, an allowance should be made for this in containers—shallow containers should be filled to within $\frac{1}{2}$ inch of the top and tall containers to within 1 inch of the top.

The following is a brief guide to wrapping materials:

Polythene bags

These may be used for all foods except liquids and the most suitable are the heavy gauge ones. They should be pressed and moulded closely round foods to exclude air and then tightly closed with wire ties. If bones of meat, fish or poultry are particularly sharp and likely to pierce the bags, they should be padded first with greaseproof paper or aluminium foil.

Plastic film or sheeting

Lengths of heavy duty film may be used for wrapping round food and then sealed with freezer tape.

Self-adhesive plastic film

This is also suitable for the freezer but should be kept for small items of food which are smooth. Sharp bones can tear the film fairly easily.

Plastic containers with fitting lids

Choose square or oblong containers in preference to round ones as they take up less room. They are suitable for liquids, fruits, sauces, purées, stews, fruit and vegetables. The air-tight lids form an adequate seal.

Plastic tubs

Already-used yogurt, cottage cheese and cream tubs, together with mousse moulds in plastic, are suitable for the deep freeze, provided they are covered with plastic sheeting or aluminium foil and well-sealed with freezer tape.

Waxed containers

These may be used many times and are available in a variety of shapes and sizes. If no lids are available, cover with plastic sheeting or aluminium foil and seal with freezer tape.

Aluminium foil

This is very suitable for wrapping all foods except those containing acid but as it tears easily, use either a double thickness of standard foil or heavy duty foil.

Foil dishes

These are very useful indeed for freezing individual portions of food, cooked meals for the family, pies and puddings. If the dishes have no lids, they should be covered with foil or plastic film and sealed with freezer tape.

Labelling

Make sure foods are used in rotation and are easily identifiable, by labelling all bags and cartons with the date of freezing and contents. Special labels, which are able to withstand low temperatures, are available for this. The wording on the labels should be filled in with a waxed pencil.

Using a freezer

It is inadvisable to freeze too much food at a time because this quickly causes a temperature rise inside the cabinet. This results in an increase in running costs and a decrease in the efficiency of the freezer to freeze fast. A recommended amount of food to be frozen in any 24 hours is between 2 to 3lb (1 to $1\frac{1}{2}$ kilo) per cubic foot of space. If the freezer has a temperature control switch, this should be set as low as possible 2 or 3 hours before adding foods to be frozen, and the bags or cartons should be placed in direct contact with the coldest part of the freezer so that they are able to freeze as rapidly as possible. Provided there is no more food to be frozen, the temperature control switch should be set back to the normal storage setting of minus 18 deg C (0 deg F) after 24 hours (this is the usual time needed to freeze foods and liquids solid). The foods should then be transferred to their permanent storage area, leaving space for the next batch of items to be frozen. It is also very important to note that:

1. All foods to be frozen should be in tip-top condition.
2. All foods should be frozen as soon after preparation and/or cooking as possible.
3. All foods should be completely cold before being put into the freezer.

Foods unsuitable for freezing

These include hard-boiled eggs, all salad greens, single cream, baked egg custards, mayonnaise and salad cream, bananas, cucumber, marrow, mushrooms, onions, leeks and radishes.

Freezing vegetables

Before vegetables are frozen they must first be blanched. This arrests the action of enzymes present which would otherwise cause spoilage in colour, flavour, texture and nutritional values. Blanch vegetables as follows:

1. Choose a large saucepan which can comfortably hold a minimum of 8 pints (approximately 5 litres) of rapidly-boiling water.
2. Put 1lb ($\frac{1}{2}$ kilo) prepared vegetables into a wire basket or sieve and lower into boiling water. Blanch for the correct length of time for the particular vegetable, timing the process after the water in the saucepan *has returned to a rapid boil.*
3. Remove vegetables from pan and transfer to a large bowl of iced water or rinse several minutes under a cold tap.
4. Drain vegetables thoroughly and pack.

Note
The blanching water may be used 6 to 8 times before changing.

Asparagus

Wash in cold water. Trim to fit storage container. Leave untied for blanching. Blanch 3 minutes for small spears and 5 minutes for thick ones. Pack and seal. Store 9 months to a year.

Beans, broad

Shell. If liked, grade according to size. Blanch 3 minutes. Pack and seal. Store up to 1 year.

Beans, French

Wash thoroughly, top and tail and leave whole. Blanch 2 to 3 minutes. Pack and seal. Store up to 1 year.

Beans, runner

Top and tail and remove strings from sides. Cut into diagonal slices. Blanch 2 minutes. Pack and seal. Store up to 1 year.

Sprouts and carrots ready for freezing

Alcan Foil.

Broccoli

Choose compact heads with tender stalks. Trim stalks evenly and remove any woody parts. If using larger heads, divide into florets. Blanch 3 to 4 minutes depending on thickness of stalks. Pack and seal. Store up to 1 year.

Brussels sprouts

Choose small firm and tightly-closed sprouts. Remove outer leaves. Wash thoroughly. Blanch 4 minutes. Pack and seal. Store up to 1 year.

Cabbage

Wash thoroughly and cut into shreds. Blanch 1½ minutes. Pack and seal. Store up to 6 months.

Carrots

Choose small ones. Trim top and bottom. Wash, scrape or peel then wash again. Blanch 5 minutes. Pack and seal. Store up to 6 months.

Cauliflower

Divide into small florets and wash. Blanch 3½ minutes. Pack and seal. Store up to 8 months.

Corn on the cob

Choose young, tender corn. Remove husk and silk. Blanch 5 to 7 minutes, depending on size. Pack and seal. Store up to 1 year.

Peas

Shell. If liked, grade according to size. Blanch 1½ minutes. Pack and seal. Store up to 1 year.

Peppers, red and green

Wash in cold water. Remove stalks. Cut each in half and remove inside fibres and seeds. Cut pepper flesh into thick strips. Blanch 2 minutes. Pack and seal. Store up to 1 year.

Potatoes

Whole potatoes do not freeze very satisfactorily. Creamed potatoes, Duchesse potatoes and potato croquettes may be wrapped or packed in cartons, well-sealed and deep frozen for about 3 months. All may be re-heated in the oven without prior thawing. To freeze chips, fry until pale gold, then drain, cool and pack into cartons. Seal and freeze up to 3 months. Chips should be thawed partially before re-frying in hot fat.

Root vegetables

Peel and dice young turnips, parsnips and swedes. Blanch 3 minutes. Pack and seal. Store up to 6 months.

Spinach

Wash leaves thoroughly in several changes of cold water. Remove hard stalks. Blanch 2 minutes for batches of 2oz (50gm). Pack and seal. Store up to 1 year.

Tomatoes

These freeze best in purée form. Cover as many tomatoes as are required with boiling water. Leave 1 minute. Cover with cold water. When tomatoes are cool enough to handle, take out of bowl and slip off skins. Either rub tomatoes through a sieve or blend to a purée in liquidiser goblet. Add 1 level teaspoon salt to every 2 pints (approximately 1 litre) purée. Pack in containers and seal. Store up to 1 year.

Mixed vegetables

Blanch and prepare each vegetable according to type, preferably dicing first in the case of roots. Mix as desired then pack and seal. Store up to 6 months.

Vegetable purées

Cook turnips, carrots or parsnips until tender. Mash finely with butter, milk or cream and salt and pepper to taste. Pack, seal and store up to 3 months.

Cooking frozen vegetables

All may be cooked from the frozen state, but the number of minutes allowed for blanching should be deducted from the cooking time.

Freezing herbs

Fresh garden herbs may be deep frozen without prior blanching. Either chop or leave in sprays. Pack and seal. Store up to 1 year.

Freezing fruits

Fruits may be treated in any of three ways prior to freezing:

1. Packed with syrup, made by dissolving 8 to 10oz (200 to 250gm) granulated sugar in 1 pint (approximately ½ litre) of water and then allowing it to cool completely before using; ½ pint (250ml) of syrup is usually adequate to cover 1lb (½ kilo) of fruit.
2. Packed with dry sugar. The fruit is gently tossed and coated in approximately 4oz (100gm) caster sugar to every lb (½ kilo) of fruit.
3. Packed with neither syrup nor sugar. The whole fruits are laid out on trays or plates and left to freeze overnight. They are then transferred to cartons and well sealed before storing in the freezer. It is usual to treat fruit this way if it is required for decoration.

Storage time

All fruits may be stored up to 1 year.

Soft fruits

These include strawberries, raspberries, loganberries, mulberries, blackberries, bilberries, and red and blackcurrants. Either pack in cartons with syrup, leaving a 1-inch gap at the top of each, or toss in dry sugar before transferring to cartons. When mixed with sugar, leave only ½-inch gap at the top of each carton. Cover and seal securely before putting into the freezer.

To thaw fruit in syrup, leave unopened cartons for approximately 6 to 8 hours in the refrigerator or 2 to 4 hours at room temperature. Fruit packed with dry sugar or without syrup or sugar, thaws a little more quickly. If possible, eat the fruit just before it has thawed completely.

Strawberries can be frozen successfully

Stone fruits

These include apricots, plums, greengages, damsons and cherries. Wash and dry fruit then cut in half and remove stones where possible. Pack into cartons with syrup, leaving a 1-inch gap at the top of each. Cover and seal securely. To thaw, leave unopened cartons for 2 to 4 hours at room temperature.

Apples, puréed

Peel, slice and stew apples with a minimum of water. Leave until cold then beat to a purée with sugar to taste, or blend until smooth in liquidiser goblet. Transfer to cartons, leaving a ½-inch gap at the top of each. Cover and seal securely. To thaw, leave unopened cartons about 3 to 4 hours at room temperature.

Apples, sliced

Peel, core and slice firm cooking apples and blanch 2 minutes (see page 256). Drain, cool and pack firmly down into cartons with sugar between, allowing about 4oz (100gm) sugar to every lb (½ kilo) of prepared fruit. Leave ½-inch gap at the top of each carton then cover and seal securely. To thaw, leave unopened cartons about 3 to 4 hours at room temperature.

Gooseberries, puréed

Treat exactly as for puréed apples, above.

Gooseberries, whole

Top and tail. Pack into boxes dry, without syrup or sugar. Seal securely. Alternatively, pack into cartons with syrup, leaving a 1-inch gap at the top of each. Cover and seal. To thaw, leave unopened cartons about 3 to 4 hours at room temperature.

Grapefruit and oranges

Peel fruit, removing all traces of pith. Divide flesh into skin-free segments by cutting in between membranes. Toss in caster sugar. Pack into cartons, leaving a ½-inch gap at the top of each. Cover and seal. To thaw, leave unopened cartons 2 to 3 hours at room temperature.

Grapes

Cut in half and remove pips then prepare for freezing as for melon (see below).

Lemons

Wash and dry lemons. Grate the peel and either put into small containers with lids or wrap in pieces of plastic film. Seal securely. Squeeze juice from lemons, strain then put into containers with lids, leaving a 1-inch gap at the top of each. Cover and seal. To thaw, leave peel for 1 to 2 hours at room temperature and the juice for 2 to 3 hours.

Melon

Cut flesh into cubes. Pack into cartons with syrup, leaving a 1-inch gap at the top of each. Cover and seal. To thaw, leave unopened cartons about 6 to 8 hours in the refrigerator or 2 to 4 hours at room temperature.

Peaches

Put peaches into bowl and cover with boiling water. Leave 2 minutes. Drain. Cover with cold water and leave until cool. Slide off skins and cut peaches into slices. Quickly pack into cartons with syrup (speed is essential to avoid discoloration). If peaches float to the surface, hold them down by putting a piece of crumpled wax or greaseproof paper on top. Cover and seal. To thaw, leave unopened cartons about 3 to 4 hours at room temperature.

Pears

Choose ripe pears. Peel, quarter and core. Brush straight away with lemon juice to prevent discoloration. Pack into cartons with syrup, leaving a 1-inch gap at the top of each. Cover and seal. To thaw, leave unopened cartons about 2½ to 3 hours at room temperature.

Pineapple

Peel pineapple and cut flesh into pieces then prepare for freezing as for melon (see this page).

Rhubarb

Choose young rhubarb. Trim and cut into 1-inch lengths. Treat as soft fruit, packing into cartons with syrup or dry sugar. If sugar is used, allow 6 to 8oz (150 to 200gm) to every lb (½ kilo) of prepared fruit. Cover and seal. To thaw, leave unopened cartons about 3 to 4 hours at room temperature.

Alcan Foil.

Freezing meat

Joints

Make sure joints are in reasonable sized pieces and not over-large. If necessary, divide into 2 or even 3 smaller joints. Pad sharp bones with greaseproof paper or aluminium foil. Wrap in polythene bags, plastic film or foil. Seal carefully. Freeze beef, lamb and veal up to 1 year; pork up to 9 months.

Chops and steaks

To make separation easier, put a piece of greaseproof paper between each chop or steak. Pad bones as for joints. Wrap in polythene bags, plastic film or foil. Seal carefully. Freeze up to 1 year but pork up to 9 months only.

Offal

Trim, wash and dry thoroughly on paper towels. Wrap in polythene bags, plastic film or foil. Seal carefully. Freeze up to 3 months. Offal is best if frozen in fairly small quantities. Tripe should always be dressed before freezing and stored no longer than 2 months.

Sausages and cured bacon

Wrap in polythene bags, plastic film or aluminium foil. Seal carefully and freeze up to 2 months.

Raw minced beef

Wrap in plastic film. Seal carefully. Freeze up to 2 months.

Poultry

Pack a trussed bird inside polythene bag or wrap in plastic film or aluminium foil. Seal carefully. If bird is to be kept for no longer than 3 months, then the giblets may be wrapped in plastic film and left inside the body cavity. If the bird is to be kept longer—and poultry may be left in the freezer for up to 1 year—then the giblets should be wrapped, sealed and frozen separately.

Poultry joints

Either wrap and seal individually in plastic film or aluminium foil or stand the joints on plastic or foil trays and either wrap with film or foil. Freeze up to 1 year.

Game and duck

Treat as for trussed poultry, above, but hang game for the required amount of time *before* freezing. Freeze up to 6 months.

Thawing

Meat, offal, poultry and game should be thawed completely in their wrappings before cooking. For joints, poultry and game, allow 2 hours per lb at room temperature and 5 hours per lb in the refrigerator. For chops, steaks and small bags of offal, allow between 1 to 2 hours at room temperature.

Freezing fish

Fish to be frozen should be as fresh as possible and preferably no older than 24 hours. After scaling, the heads, fins, tails and guts should be removed. Small whole fish should be wrapped individually in plastic film or aluminium foil, well sealed then transferred to plastic bags in family-sized amounts —for example, 4 fish for a family of four. Larger fish should be cut into steaks and cutlets and also wrapped and sealed individually. Flat fish should be filleted and then the fillets placed on top of each other in groups of 2 or 4 with sheets of greaseproof paper between for easy separation. The fillets should then be wrapped and sealed in plastic film or foil. Large salmon and salmon trout should be treated as small whole fish, but the cavities left by de-gutting should be filled with greaseproof paper to keep the fish a good shape. They should then be wrapped, sealed and frozen whole. White fish may be stored up to 12 months; oily fish such as salmon, trout and herrings up to 4 months.

To thaw, leave unopened packs of fish in a cool place for about 2 to 3 hours; up to 6 hours in the refrigerator. Whole fish and thick steaks and cutlets should be allowed to thaw completely before cooking. Fillets may be cooked from the frozen state.

Freezing dairy produce

Eggs

Do not freeze eggs in their shells as they crack at low temperatures. Separate white from yolks. Pack whites in small containers but do not put more than 6 in any one container. Cover and seal. Because yolks congeal, they are best mixed with either sugar or salt, depending on whether they are later to be used for sweet or savoury dishes. Allow 3 level dessertspoons caster sugar or 1 level teaspoon salt to every 6 yolks. Pack into cartons, cover and seal. Store up to 9 months and allow whites or yolks to thaw completely in unopened containers for approximately 1 hour at room temperature.

Cream

Freeze only double cream. Whip until stiff with 1 level dessertspoon sifted icing or caster sugar to every $\frac{1}{4}$ pint (125ml). Transfer to containers, cover and seal. Store up to 1 year. Thaw between 30 minutes to 1 hour at room temperature.

Butter

Leave in original wrapping then overwrap in plastic film or aluminium foil. Seal. Unsalted butter or slightly salted lactic butter freezes better than salted butter and may be kept up to 6 months in the freezer. Salted butter should be stored no longer than 2 to 3 months as freezing tends to make it granular. To thaw, leave overnight in refrigerator or 3 to 4 hours at room temperature.

Cheeses

Soft cheeses—such as Camembert and Brie—should be wrapped in plastic film or aluminium foil, well sealed and stored up to 8 months. Grated cheese, useful for all cooking purposes, should be put into cartons, covered securely, well sealed and stored up to 3 months. To thaw, leave soft cheeses for about 6 hours at room temperature. Leave grated cheese for about 4 hours in unopened cartons.

Freezing bread and doughs

Bought bread

If sliced and wrapped in waxed paper, overwrap in aluminium foil or put into polythene bags. If unwrapped, wrap in foil or put into polythene bags. Freeze up to 4 weeks. Breads and rolls with crisp crusts should be wrapped as above but left in the freezer up to 4 days; if stored any longer the crusts might start to peel off. To thaw, leave bread in wrappers for 3 to 6 hours at room temperature or overnight in the refrigerator.

Note
1. Sliced bread may be toasted while frozen.
2. After thawing, crusty bread and rolls should be put into a hot oven, 450 deg F or gas 8 (230 deg C) for between 5 and 10 minutes. This not only refreshes them but also renews the outside crispness.

Uncooked dough

This freezes particularly successfully but it is advisable to increase the yeast in the recipe by 50 per cent as storage at very low temperatures destroys some of the yeast cells. After kneading (and before it has risen) divide into 1lb or 2lb ($\frac{1}{2}$ or 1 kilo) quantities and shape into balls. Place in large, well-greased polythene bags. Seal tightly and freeze immediately. Store plain doughs up to 8 weeks; richer doughs up to 5 weeks. To thaw, unseal bags and tie loosely at the top to allow space for rising. Leave 5 to 6 hours at room temperature or overnight in the refrigerator. When dough has risen to twice its original volume, knead lightly, shape and leave to rise for the second time and bake.

Freezing other prepared foods

Sandwiches

Prepare in the usual way but avoid using hard-boiled eggs, lettuce, tomato or cucumber in the fillings. Do not remove crusts. Cut sandwiches into halves or quarters. Wrap small amounts in plastic film or aluminium foil. Seal securely and store up to 4 weeks. To thaw, allow 2 hours at room temperature for individual sandwiches; up to 6 hours for stacks of 4 to 8 sandwiches.

Breadcrumbs

Pack into polythene bags or containers with lids. Seal. Freeze up to 3 months. As crumbs remain separate, they need not be thawed before using in puddings and stuffings. If wanted to coat food, leave at room temperature for 30 minutes.

Cakes

All cakes may be frozen satisfactorily. If not iced, wrap in plastic film or foil and seal securely. Transfer to cartons for added protection. Thaw, unopened, for 1 to 3 hours at room temperature. If cakes are iced, they should be frozen unwrapped and then wrapped in plastic film or foil when solid. All wrappings must be removed before the cakes are thawed to prevent the icing from being spoiled. As butter cream and sweetened whipped cream freeze well, layer cakes may be filled before freezing. Rich fruit cakes should not be frozen as they can be kept perfectly well in air-tight tins. All cakes may be kept up to 6 months.

Scones

As soon as freshly-baked scones are cold, transfer to polythene bags, seal well and freeze immediately. Store up to 6 months. Thaw unopened at room temperature for 1 to 2 hours. If liked, warm through in a moderately hot oven, 400 deg F or gas 6 (200 deg C) for 7 to 8 minutes before serving.

Unbaked pies and flans made from short crust pastry

Prepare large pies on foil plates or in foil dishes. Make small pies in individual foil dishes. Do not cut steam vents in lids. Freeze uncovered until solid. Cover with plastic film or foil and seal securely. Freeze flan cases, uncovered, in flan rings or foil cases until solid, remove and wrap in plastic film or foil. Seal securely. Freeze tartlet cases uncovered in bun tins. When solid, transfer to polythene bags and seal securely. Store in cartons for protection. For speed and convenience, make several pie lids, cut to fit the shape of the pie dishes and freeze unwrapped. When solid, layer several together with sheets of greaseproof paper between each, then wrap and seal in plastic film or foil. Transfer to large cartons for protection. Any of the above may be stored up to 3 months. To thaw and cook,

Steak and kidney pie ready to serve

unwrap large pies and bake without prior thawing, allowing 10 or 15 minutes' extra cooking time for thawing. Cut vents in the lid after 10 minutes' baking. Place frozen flan cases in flan rings on baking trays and bake 'blind' towards top of moderately hot oven, 400 deg F or gas 6 (200 deg C) for 20 to 25 minutes. Transfer frozen tartlet cases to bun tins and bake as flan cases for 15 minutes. For pie lids, moisten edge of pie dish with water and place frozen lid on top. Bake at 400 deg F or gas 6 (200 deg C) for 20 to 25 minutes then reduce temperature to cool, 300 deg F or gas 2 (150 deg C) and bake a further 10 to 15 minutes.

Baked pies and flans made from short crust pastry

Bake large and small pies on plates or in foil dishes. Cool as quickly as possible. Leave on plates or in dishes then wrap in double thickness of standard foil or in single thickness of heavy duty foil. Seal securely. Freeze straight away. Leave flan and tartlet cases until cold. Pack into polythene bags. Seal securely then transfer to cartons for protection. Store meat pies up to 4 months, fruit pies up to 6 months and unfilled flan and tartlet cases up to 6 months. To thaw, leave large pies at room temperature for 2 to 4 hours and flans and tartlet cases for 1 hour. If pies are to be served hot, they may be re-heated in the oven.

Unbaked pies and flans made from puff or flaky pastry

Follow directions for unbaked pies and flans made from short crust pastry (see page 108). Vol-au-vent cases should be put on to trays and frozen unwrapped. When solid, they should be wrapped and sealed in foil or polythene bags and then transferred to cartons for protection. Uncooked pastry should be put into polythene bags or wrapped in foil, sealed securely and put into freezer straight away. To thaw and cook large or small pies, unwrap and bake flaky pastry without prior thawing for 25 minutes in a hot oven, 425 deg F or gas 7 (220 deg C); puff pastry for 20 minutes at 450 deg F or gas 8 (230 deg C). If filling needs longer cooking time, reduce temperature to moderately hot, 375 deg F or gas 5 (190 deg C), and continue to cook for required time. Leave uncooked pastry for 3 to 4 hours at room temperature or overnight in the refrigerator then treat as freshly-made pastry.

Baked pies and flans made from puff or flaky pastry

Follow directions for baked pies and flans made from short crust pastry (see page 108). As baked vol-au-vent cases are fragile, pack and seal carefully in polythene bags or foil and put into a lined carton for protection. If to be served hot, re-heat in a hot oven, 450 deg F or gas 8 (230 deg C), for 5 to 7 minutes.

Sponge puddings

Make puddings as usual, cooking them in foil basins and dishes. Cool thoroughly, cover with double thickness of standard foil or single thickness of heavy duty foil and seal securely. Freeze straight away. For uncooked puddings, transfer mixture to foil basins or dishes and cover with foil. Seal securely. Store cooked puddings up to 3 months and uncooked puddings up to 1 month. To thaw, unwrap cooked puddings, re-cover with greased greaseproof paper and steam approximately 45 minutes. Thaw uncooked puddings in a similar way, steaming them for 2½ hours.

Stews and casseroles with meat

Cook in the usual way, making double or even treble quantity. Do not include celery or potatoes. Transfer to suitable sized containers or foil dishes. Cover when cold and seal securely. Freeze up to 2 months. To thaw, leave in the refrigerator for 5 hours or at room temperature for 2. Re-heat before serving, adding a top layer of sliced cooked potatoes, if wished.

Soups and sauces

Cool soups or sauces quickly and transfer to suitable sized containers, leaving a gap at the top of each for expansion. Cover and seal securely. Freeze up to 2 months. Do not freeze soups containing pieces of onion or sauces containing eggs. To thaw, leave in containers for 2 to 3 hours at room temperature. Re-heat gently, whisking all the time, until hot. If necessary, thin down with a little hot milk or water.

Ice cream

Transfer home-made ice cream to suitable sized containers. Cover and seal. Freeze up to 1 month. To thaw, leave in refrigerator for 1 to 2 hours or at room temperature for 30 minutes.

Mousses

Transfer home-made mousses to individual or family-sized containers. Cover and seal securely. Freeze up to 2 months. To thaw, leave for 6 hours in the refrigerator or for 2 hours at room temperature.

Alcan Foil.

Top: cooked sponge pudding can be stored in the deep freeze for up to three months

Right: sliced cooked potatoes may be added to a deep-frozen casserole just before re-heating

Alcan Foil.

261

Entertaining

Entertaining is one of the friendliest ways of giving enjoyment to others and few gifts can be more personal than a well-chosen meal, cooked with affection and care.

The dinner party is still one of the most popular forms of home entertaining. Every hostess undoubtedly has her own repertoire of tried and trusted menus for these occasions, but every so often a few new suggestions are welcome......so here are nine dinner party menus. I hope each menu will give you at least one new idea to try, or show a variation perhaps on an old theme.

Cheese and biscuits are an optional extra and may be served at the end of every meal if desired, although I would not recommend them after Indian or Chinese style food.

Dinner party menus

Menu 1

Serves 6

Greek taramasalata (see page 22)
Barbecued kebabs
Mixed vegetable rice
Potato almond balls
Apricots flambé (see page 169)

Barbecued kebabs

Serves 6

2lb (1 kilo) meat, from a selection of rump steak, lambs' liver and lambs' kidneys

6 long rashers streaky bacon

red wine

12 small tomatoes, skinned

button mushrooms

6 small onions, peeled

1 green pepper, de-seeded and cut into squares

2 large corn-on-the-cob, each cooked and cut into 6 thick slices

12 cocktail sausages

salad oil

garlic salt

freshly-milled pepper

about 8 to 10oz (200 to 250gm) freshly-cooked rice

8oz (200gm) frozen mixed vegetables, cooked

1 to 2oz (25 to 50gm) butter

1. Cut steak and liver into cubes. Skin and core kidneys.
2. Remove rind from bacon. Cut each rasher in half and roll up.
3. Put steak, offal and bacon rolls into a glass dish and moisten with a little wine. Cover and refrigerate for 3 hours, turning twice.
4. Thread steak, liver, kidneys, bacon, tomatoes, mushrooms, onions, green pepper squares, corn slices and cocktail sausages on to 6 kebab skewers.
5. Brush all over with salad oil then sprinkle with garlic salt and pepper.
6. Cook either over a hot barbecue or place in a grill pan and grill 2 to 3 inches below a hot grill. Cook 20 to 25 minutes, turning frequently and brushing with oil at least once more.
7. Cover a large platter with hot rice mixed with vegetables and butter.
8. Place kebabs on top and serve straight away.

Barbecued kebabs

Potato almond balls

Finely mash 1lb (½ kilo) potatoes with 1oz (25gm) butter and an egg yolk. Season to taste with salt and pepper. When cool enough to handle, shape into 12 balls and coat with flaked almonds. Put into a heavily buttered baking tin, top each with small pieces of butter and cook near top of hot oven, 425 deg F or gas 7 (220 deg C), for 15 minutes or until crisp and golden. Either serve separately with the kebabs or thread on to the skewers as well.

Note

If preferred, use instant mashed potato instead of fresh but make up with a little less liquid than specified. Add butter and egg yolk, as for fresh potato method. The mixture should not be at all wet.

Menu 2

Serves 6

Consommé Aurore (see page 11)
Wine braised beef
Whole carrots
Whole potatoes sprinkled with parsley
Salad to taste
Lemon soufflé (see page 186)

Wine braised beef

Serves 6

| 2 large onions, chopped |
| 1 garlic clove, chopped |
| 2 tablespoons salad oil |
| 3lb (1½ kilo) braising beef |
| 2 level tablespoons flour |
| ½ pint (250ml) water |
| 3 level teaspoons meat extract |
| ¼ pint (125ml) dry red wine |
| 4 level tablespoons tomato paste |
| 1 to 2 level teaspoons salt |
| freshly-milled pepper to taste |

1. Pre-heat oven to moderate, 325 deg F or gas 3 (170 deg C).
2. In large flameproof casserole, fry onions and garlic in oil until pale gold.
3. Meanwhile, cut beef into fairly large cubes.
4. Add to casserole and fry more briskly, turning with a spoon from time to time, until well-sealed and brown.
5. Stir in flour and gradually blend in water, meat extract, wine, tomato paste and salt and pepper to taste.
6. Bring to boil and cover.
7. Transfer to centre of oven and cook 2½ to 3 hours or until meat is tender.

Menu 3

Serves 6

Danish blue mousse (see page 22)
or prawn cocktail (see page 17)
Beef olives
Freshly-cooked noodles in butter
Freshly-boiled buttered carrots
Salad to taste
Apple Charlotte (see page 170)

Beef olives

Serves 6

| 1½lb (¾ kilo) topside or rump steak in one piece |
| 6oz (150gm) fresh white breadcrumbs |
| 3oz (75gm) finely-shredded suet |
| 1½ level dessertspoons chopped parsley |
| ½ level teaspoon mixed herbs |
| ½ level teaspoon finely-grated lemon peel |
| a squeeze of lemon |
| salt and pepper to taste |
| beaten egg to bind |
| 1oz (25gm) butter or margarine |
| 1 teaspoon salad oil |
| 1 medium onion, chopped |
| 1 medium carrot, thinly sliced |
| 1 level tablespoon flour |
| 1 pint (approximately ½ litre) water |
| chopped parsley to garnish |

1. Cut meat into 6 slices and flatten each by beating with a rolling pin.
2. Combine crumbs with suet, 1½ level dessertspoons parsley, herbs, lemon peel, lemon juice and salt and pepper to taste. Bind with beaten egg.
3. Put equal amounts of stuffing on to beef slices then roll each up and secure by tying with thin string or thick thread.
4. Melt butter or margarine in saucepan. Add oil and heat until hot. Add beef olives and fry briskly until well-sealed and brown. Remove from pan and transfer to a plate.
5. Add onion and carrot to pan and fry, covered, for 7 to 10 minutes or until pale gold.
6. Stir in flour and cook 2 minutes.
7. Gradually blend in water. Cook, stirring, until mixture comes to boil and thickens.
8. Replace beef olives and lower heat. Cover and simmer for 1½ to 2 hours or until meat is tender.
9. Remove string or thread, transfer to a serving dish and coat with gravy.
10. Garnish with chopped parsley.

Left: wine braised beef
Right: beef olives served with noodles and buttered whole carrots

Menu 4

Serves 8

**Double quantity of pears with
Louis sauce (see page 100)
Bacon chops with orange sauce
Baked jacket potatoes with butter
(see page 152)
Grilled tomatoes and mushrooms
Lemon meringue or pumpkin pie
(see pages 187 or 164)**

Menu 5

Serves 8

**Double quantity cream of onion soup
(see page 11)
Devilled lamb noisettes
Boiled potatoes tossed in butter
Boiled carrots tossed in butter
Gravy
Mixed fruit sponge flan (see page 176)**

Menu 6

Serves 8

**Double quantity cream of tomato soup
(see page 11)
Ham and tongue fiesta
Salad to taste
Spiral strawberry mould (see page 192)**

Bacon chops with orange sauce

Serves 8

8 short back bacon chops, each ½ inch in thickness

4 large oranges

5 tablespoons wine vinegar

3oz (75gm) granulated sugar

3 level teaspoons cornflour

salt and pepper to taste

few lettuce leaves

parsley to garnish

1. Snip fat at ½-inch intervals round each bacon chop.
2. Cook 15 minutes under a hot grill, turning frequently and reducing heat slightly after 5 minutes.
3. To make sauce, finely grate peel from 1 large orange and put into saucepan. Add juice of 3 oranges, the vinegar, sugar and cornflour.
4. Cook, whisking gently all the time, until sauce comes to the boil and thickens. Season to taste with salt and pepper and leave over a very low heat.
5. Slice remaining orange fairly thinly then slit each slice from the centre to the outside edge. Shape slices into twists.
6. Put hot bacon chops on to a lettuce-lined platter and garnish with orange twists and parsley.
7. Accompany with orange sauce, served separately in a sauce boat.

Devilled lamb noisettes

Serves 8

2oz (50gm) butter, softened

1 to 2 level teaspoons dry mustard

1 level teaspoon Worcestershire sauce

16 boned and rolled lamb cutlets (noisettes)

baked tomatoes

duchesse potatoes (see page 151)

watercress to garnish

1. Pre-heat oven to moderately hot, 375 deg F or gas 5 (190 deg C).
2. Cream butter, mustard and Worcestershire sauce well together.
3. Spread on to both sides of noisettes.
6. Transfer to roasting tin.
5. Bake near top of oven for 30 minutes, turning twice.
6. Transfer to a warm serving dish and garnish with baked tomatoes, whirls of duchesse potatoes and watercress.

Ham and tongue fiesta

Serves 8

duchesse potatoes (see page 151)

beaten egg for brushing

12oz (300gm) cooked ham, chopped

1lb (½ kilo) tongue, chopped

1½ pints (approximately ¾ litre) freshly-made white coating sauce (see page 94)

2 level teaspoons prepared mustard

1lb (½ kilo) frozen mixed vegetables, cooked as directed on packet

salt and pepper to taste

1. Pre-heat oven to hot, 425 deg F or gas 7 (220 deg C).
2. Pipe a border of duchesse potatoes round the edge of a large buttered heatproof plate. Brush lightly with egg then put into centre of oven for 10 minutes or until golden.
3. Meanwhile, add ham and tongue to sauce and heat through gently.
4. Stir in mustard and mixed vegetables then season to taste with salt and pepper. Heat through 5 minutes.
5. Remove plate from oven and fill centre with sauce mixture.
6. Serve straight away.

Bacon chops with orange sauce

Above: ham and tongue fiesta. Below: devilled lamb noisettes

Menu 7

Serves 8

**Double quantity avocados with seafood
(see page 24)
Crispy beef balls
Tomato sauce (see page 102)
Green peas
Salad to taste
Almond lattice pie (see page 168)**

Crispy beef balls

Serves 8

2lb (1 kilo) freshly-boiled potatoes
1lb (½ kilo) cold roast beef, finely minced
4 level teaspoons horseradish sauce
1 level teaspoon tomato paste
1 level teaspoon onion or garlic salt
1 level teaspoon mixed herbs
3 egg yolks
salt and pepper to taste
2 egg whites
fresh white breadcrumbs
deep oil or fat for frying
parsley sprigs and lemon wedges to garnish

1. Mash potatoes finely.
2. Stir in all beef, horseradish, tomato paste, onion or garlic salt, mixed herbs, egg yolks, and seasoning.
3. When mixture is completely cold, shape into 16 balls.
4. Coat with lightly-beaten egg whites then toss in crumbs.
5. Fry in hot oil or fat until crisp and golden.
6. Drain on soft kitchen paper and serve straight away, garnished with parsley and lemon.

Note
If preferred, 1lb (½ kilo) well-drained canned pilchards or tuna may be used instead of the meat. Corned beef makes an appetising alternative to the cold roast beef.

Menu 8

Serves 8

**Chinese crab fritters with peas in sauce
Easy sweet-sour pork
Fish Singapore
Chicken livers with almonds
Crispy fried noodles
Turnip braise
Plain boiled rice
Canned pineapple mixed with canned
mandarins
China tea**

Crispy beef balls

Chinese crab fritters

Serves 8

1 can (10oz or 250gm) bean sprouts
1 can (approximately 8oz or 200gm) crab meat
2 large eggs
3 level tablespoons cornflour
salt and pepper to taste
oil for frying
1 level tablespoon caster sugar
3 tablespoons Soy sauce
½ pint (250ml) water
1 small packet frozen peas

1. To make fritters, drain bean sprouts thoroughly. Drain crab meat and flake with 2 forks.
2. Beat eggs then add bean sprouts, crab meat, 2 level tablespoons cornflour and 1 level teaspoon salt. Season to taste with pepper.
3. Heat enough oil to cover the base of a frying pan then add tablespoons of fritter mixture. Fry until crisp and golden on both sides.
4. Remove from pan, drain thoroughly and keep hot.
5. To make sauce, mix remains of cornflour and sugar to a smooth cream with Soy sauce and water.
6. Pour into saucepan and add peas.
7. Cook, stirring, until sauce comes to the boil and thickens then season to taste with salt and pepper. Simmer 2 minutes.
8. Arrange fritters on a warm serving dish and accompany with the sauce.

Easy sweet-sour pork

Serves 8

1 large can (1lb or ½ kilo) pork luncheon meat
4 tablespoons Soy sauce
2 level tablespoons flour
fat or oil for frying
1 can (8oz or 200gm) pineapple tidbits
1 large green pepper
4 medium tomatoes, skinned
2 level tablespoons cornflour
2 tablespoons vinegar
2 tablespoons tomato ketchup
salt and pepper to taste
6oz (150gm) long grain rice (raw weight), freshly cooked

1. Cut luncheon meat into cubes. Put into bowl and add 2 tablespoons Soy sauce. Toss well to mix. Cover and leave to stand for 2 hours.
2. Toss luncheon meat cubes in flour then fry in 2 inches of hot fat or oil until crisp and golden. Remove from pan, drain thoroughly and keep hot.
3. Drain pineapple and reserve syrup. De-seed pepper and cut into strips. Cut tomatoes into wedges. Add pineapple, pepper strips and tomatoes to remaining fat or oil in pan and fry 5 minutes. Add to luncheon meat.
4. Mix cornflour to a smooth cream with vinegar. Add pineapple syrup and tomato ketchup. Cook, stirring continuously, until sauce comes to boil and thickens then simmer 1 minute. Season to taste with salt and pepper.
5. Arrange rice on a large serving dish. Top with fried pork, pineapple, pepper strips and tomatoes then coat with sweet-sour sauce.
6. Serve straight away.

Fish Singapore

Serves 8

¼ pint (125ml) vinegar
4oz (100gm) sugar
2 garlic cloves, halved
½ small cucumber, peeled and diced
1½ level teaspoons salt
2 level dessertspoons cornflour
4 tablespoons cold water
4 heaped tablespoons cooked peas
1lb (½ kilo) haddock fillet, skinned
about 3oz (75gm) flour
good shake of pepper
deep oil for frying

1. Put vinegar, sugar, garlic, cucumber and ½ level teaspoon salt into a glass dish. Cover and leave to stand for 2 hours.
2. Mix cornflour to a smooth paste with the cold water.
3. Bring vinegar mixture to the boil and blend half into the cornflour. Return to saucepan.
4. Cook, stirring, until sauce comes to the boil and thickens. Add peas and leave over a very low heat to keep hot.
5. Cut fish into 1-inch wide strips across the grain. Coat with flour mixed with rest of salt and pepper.
6. Fry in hot oil for 3 to 4 minutes or until golden and crisp.
7. Drain thoroughly and coat with sauce.

Chicken livers with almonds

Serves 8

12oz (300gm) chicken livers
1 tablespoon Soy sauce
2 tablespoons dry sherry
½ level teaspoon garlic salt
2 level tablespoons soft brown sugar
1 medium onion, finely chopped
1 can (about 10oz or 250ml) consommé
3 level tablespoons cornflour
4 tablespoons cold water
2oz (50gm) canned bamboo shoots
2oz (50gm) flaked almonds
2 tablespoons salad oil

1. Put chicken livers into a saucepan, cover with boiling salted water and simmer 3 minutes. Drain thoroughly.
2. Put Soy sauce into a glass bowl. Add sherry, garlic salt, sugar, onion and livers.
3. Mix thoroughly and cover. Leave to stand at room temperature for 1 hour.
4. Transfer to saucepan with undiluted consommé. Heat until lukewarm then stir in cornflour mixed to a smooth paste with the cold water.
5. Cook, stirring, until mixture comes to the boil and thickens. Lower heat, cover and simmer for 5 to 7 minutes.
6. Cut bamboo shoots into thin strips.
7. Fry, with the almonds, in the oil until pale gold. Remove from pan and drain.
8. Put livers and sauce in a serving dish.
9. Sprinkle with bamboo shoots and almonds and serve straight away.

In the foreground: easy sweet-sour pork, accompanied by Chinese crab fritters, turnip braise and crispy fried noodles

Crispy fried noodles

Serves 8

8oz (200gm) ribbon noodles
deep oil for frying

1. Cook noodles in plenty of boiling salted water for 5 minutes.
2. Drain, rinse under cold running water and shake thoroughly to get rid of as much surplus water as possible.
3. Place noodles on absorbent paper and dry thoroughly.
4. Transfer to chip basket and lower into hot oil.
5. Fry 4 to 5 minutes or until crisp and golden.
6. Drain thoroughly and serve straight away.

Turnip braise

Serves 8

12oz (300gm) turnips, cooked
1 dessertspoon corn oil
1 small onion, chopped
2 tablespoons Soy sauce
1 level teaspoon caster sugar
scissor-snipped chives to garnish

1. Cut turnips into small dice.
2. Put oil and onion into a pan. Fry gently for 5 minutes.
3. Add Soy sauce and sugar. Boil rapidly for 1 minute.
4. Add turnip dice and heat through for 3 minutes, turning all the time.
5. Transfer to a warm dish and sprinkle with chives.

Gosht Takhari (Indian beef curry)
Freshly-boiled long grain rice
Crisp pappadoms (obtainable from Oriental shops)
Sambals (or bowls) of any or all of the following:
Mango chutney
Lime pickle
Sliced tomatoes topped with onion
Natural yogurt
Chopped salted cashew nuts
Finish the meal with:
Fresh or canned lychees
Indian tea with lemon

Note

Pappadoms are available in packets and should be fried or grilled. They are usually crumbled over the curry and it is customary to allow 1 or 2 per person.

Gosht Takhari

Serves 8

4 tablespoons salad oil

2 large onions, chopped

2 garlic cloves, crushed

3lb (1½ kilo) stewing beef, cubed

1 pint (approximately ½ litre) water

2 large cooking apples, peeled, cored and sliced

12oz (300gm) tomatoes, skinned and chopped

2 level tablespoons tomato paste

2 medium celery stalks, chopped

salt and pepper to taste

4 to 8 level teaspoons curry powder (depending on taste)

2 level teaspoons caster sugar

3 level tablespoons flour

1 level teaspoon powdered ginger

1 level teaspoon cinnamon

¼ pint (125ml) beef stock

2 to 3 level tablespoons desiccated coconut to garnish

1. Heat oil in a large saucepan.
2. Add onions and garlic and fry very gently until pale gold.
3. Add beef and fry a little more briskly, turning all the time, until pieces are well-sealed and brown.
4. Pour in water then add apples, tomatoes, tomato paste and celery.
5. Season to taste with salt and pepper then bring to the boil.
6. Lower heat and cover pan. Simmer gently for 2 hours or until meat is tender.
7. Mix curry powder, sugar, flour, ginger and cinnamon to a paste with the stock.
8. Add to meat in saucepan and stir well.
9. Bring slowly to the boil, stirring, cover and continue to simmer a further 30 minutes, stirring occasionally.
10. Transfer to a warm dish and sprinkle with coconut.

Gosht Takhari (Indian beef curry)

Buffet parties

The buffet party—where people are able to circulate freely and help themselves to food as and when they want it—is the ideal way to entertain larger groups.

There are many types of buffets, ranging from the popular cheese and wine variety to an elaborate curry with innumerable side dishes, bowls of pearly rice and often smouldering incense to add further exotic atmosphere. But irrespective of style—or nationality—there are certain pointers to success which apply to all buffets.

1. Make sure there is an adequate supply of paper serviettes, cutlery and plates. It is better to put out too many than too few.

2. See that there is more than one cruet available, even if it means using egg cups as containers for salt and pepper.

3. Please put out some jugs of water with ice if possible. Not everyone likes beer, wine or squash.

4. Produce supplies of fresh food at regular intervals, rather than put it all out at once. There is nothing sadder than hot food which is stone cold and greasy, or cold food which is dry, discoloured and curling at the edges.

5. Rich creamy dessert cakes or fruit-filled flans should be cut into portions before being put on to the table. Few guests are completely at ease cutting their own portions.

6. If serving cakes, gateaux and similar concoctions, make sure there are wide cake servers to go with them. It is no easy task trying to balance a large wedge of cake on a narrow knife and the struggle to transfer it to a plate—without accident—can be a nerve-wracking experience.

7. No one values your furniture as much as you do. Therefore if serving any hot food and liquor on a highly prized and polished sideboard or table, cover the surface first with 2 blankets and then with a cloth. Table mats placed at strategic points are not reliable—they get moved by careless people and then the damage occurs.

*Christmas day buffet:
pork pâté de campagne, melon crescents, roast turkey and duck, and star mince pie. Recipes overleaf*

8. Even if you do not smoke, other people do, so put out plenty of ashtrays everywhere —old saucers do just as well, if you have not got a good supply of proper ashtrays.

9. Tall candles may add a decorative and romantic touch but if they get knocked over, there is always the danger of a fire starting. Settle for small decorative arrangements of flowers instead.

10. To save confusion, foods which are not instantly recognisable through being in sauce, or wrapped in pastry, or buried beneath mashed potato, should have little identification tags placed near them.

Christmas day buffet

For 6 people

Melon crescents

Illustrated on previous page

1 honeydew melon

1 can mandarin oranges

1 packet raspberry flavour jelly

water

3 dessertspoons or 1 miniature bottle Grand Marnier

1. Cut the melon in half lengthwise, remove seeds and cut out as much of the flesh as possible with a small melon ball cutter.
2. Scoop out rest of flesh with a spoon, leaving shells firm and even.
3. Refill shells with melon balls and drained mandarin segments.
4. Make up jelly to $\frac{1}{2}$ pint with syrup from can of mandarins and water if necessary.
5. Transfer to a saucepan and leave over low heat until jelly melts, stirring. Remove from heat and stir in Grand Marnier.
6. When cold and just beginning to thicken, pour into melon halves.
7. Refrigerate until firm and set.
8. Just before serving, cut into 6 wedges with a knife dipped in hot water.

Pork pâté de campagne

Illustrated on previous page

8 to 9 rashers streaky bacon

1lb ($\frac{1}{2}$ kilo) pork

8oz (200gm) lean veal

8oz (200gm) calves' liver

1 large onion

1 medium clove of garlic, crushed

1 level teaspoon marjoram

$\frac{3}{4}$ level teaspoon basil

$1\frac{1}{2}$ level teaspoons salt

grinding of black pepper

2 to 3 tablespoons cognac

2 bay leaves

1. Pre-heat oven to moderate, 350 deg F or gas 4 (180 deg C).
2. Cut off bacon rinds then use rashers to line base and sides of a 2lb (1 kilo) loaf tin or 7-inch round cake tin.
3. Finely mince pork, veal, liver and onion. Put into bowl.
4. Add garlic, marjoram, basil, salt, black pepper and cognac.
5. Transfer to prepared tin and place bay leaves on top.
6. Cover tin with foil and cook in centre of oven for 2 hours.
7. Pour away liquid, place base of another tin on top of the pâté with a weight in it, and leave until cold before turning out.
8. Cut into slices and serve with toast.

Star mince pie

Illustrated on previous page

rich flan pastry made with 8oz (200gm) flour (see page 108)

3 tablespoons sweet sherry or Grand Marnier

1 to $1\frac{1}{2}$lb ($\frac{1}{2}$ to $\frac{3}{4}$ kilo) mincemeat

beaten egg for brushing

icing sugar

1. Pre-heat oven to moderately hot, 400 deg F or gas 6 (200 deg C).
2. Roll out two-thirds of the pastry and use to line an 8 to $8\frac{1}{2}$-inch pie plate.
3. Stir sherry or Grand Marnier into the mincemeat and spread evenly over the pastry.
4. Moisten edges of pastry with cold water.
5. Roll out rest of the pastry into a lid then cut a star shape out of the centre.
6. Place lid on top of pie and press edges of pastry well together to seal.
7. Flake up with the back of a knife then press into flutes. Stand pie on baking tray.
8. Brush with beaten egg and bake near top of oven for 30 to 40 minutes or until a warm golden brown.
9. Remove from oven, sift icing sugar over the top and serve warm with cream or ice cream.

Roast turkey and roast duck

Illustrated on previous page

See recipes on pages 87 and 88

Serve turkey garnished with bacon rolls, sausages and watercress. Serve duck garnished with watercress, duchesse potatoes and peas.

Boxing day party

For about 12 people

Cheese-stuffed prunes

about 24 large prunes, soaked overnight and drained

4oz (100gm) Danish blue cheese

4oz (100gm) cream cheese

1 level teaspoon prepared mustard

1. Cut prunes in half and remove stones.
2. To make filling, mash blue cheese with fork.
3. Add cream cheese and mustard and beat until well mixed.
4. Sandwich prune halves together with a heaped teaspoon of the cheese mixture.

Savoury chicken liver pâté

1 bay leaf

8oz (200gm) streaky bacon, with rinds removed

2oz (50gm) butter

1lb ($\frac{1}{2}$ kilo) chicken livers

1 medium onion, chopped

1 level teaspoon prepared mustard

$\frac{1}{4}$ level teaspoon mixed herbs

$\frac{1}{4}$ level teaspoon thyme

salt and black pepper

1 standard egg, beaten

1. Pre-heat oven to moderate, 325 deg F or gas 3 (170 deg C).
2. Well-butter a 2 pint (approximately 1 litre) straight-sided ovenproof dish or 7-inch cake tin.
3. Place bay leaf on the base then cover base with about 6 rashers of bacon.
4. Chop rest of bacon.
5. Melt butter in a saucepan. Add chopped bacon, livers and onion. Fry, turning frequently, until livers are well-browned.
6. Mince finely then add any left-over butter and juices from pan, the mustard, herbs, thyme, salt and pepper and the beaten egg.
7. Mix very thoroughly and transfer to prepared dish or tin.
8. Smooth top with a knife, cover with foil and place in a roasting tin containing about 1 inch of water.
9. Bake in centre of oven for 1 hour.
10. Leave to cool then refrigerate overnight.
11. Turn out 2 hours before serving, then slice thinly and accompany with toast.

Ham straws

4oz (100gm) plain flour

pinch of salt

pinch of Cayenne pepper

$\frac{1}{2}$ level teaspoon dry mustard

2oz (50gm) butter or margarine

2oz (50gm) cooked ham, finely chopped

1 egg yolk

3 to 4 teaspoons cold water

few drops Tabasco sauce

1. Pre-heat oven to hot, 425 deg F or gas 7 (220 deg C).
2. Sift together flour, salt, Cayenne pepper and mustard.
3. Rub in butter or margarine finely.
4. Add ham and toss ingredients lightly together.
5. Mix to a stiff dough with egg yolk, water and Tabasco.
6. Knead lightly and roll out thinly.
7. Cut out about 8 rounds with a 2-inch cutter then remove centres with a $1\frac{1}{4}$-inch cutter.
8. Cut rest of pastry into thin strips about $\frac{1}{4}$ inch in width by 3 inches in length.
9. Place on baking tray and bake near top of oven for about 10 to 15 minutes or until crisp and lightly brown.
10. Cool on a wire rack and place a few 'straws' through each ring.

Party potato boats

6 medium/large potatoes, freshly baked in their jackets (see page 152)

2oz (50gm) butter

2 level teaspoons prepared mustard

8oz (200gm) cottage cheese with chives

4oz (100gm) streaky bacon, chopped and crisply fried

salt and pepper to taste

1. Pre-heat oven to moderately hot, 375 deg F or gas 5 (190 deg C).
2. Cut hot potatoes in half lengthwise.
3. Scoop out centres and put into large basin.
4. Mash with butter and mustard.
5. Add cottage cheese and bacon and mix well together.
6. Season to taste with salt and pepper and return to potato shells.
7. Heat through near top of oven for 15 to 20 minutes.
8. Serve straight away.

Devilled ham triangles

short crust pastry made with 8oz (200gm) flour (see page 108)

approximately 3 level teaspoons prepared mustard

4oz (100gm) ham, finely chopped

2 level tablespoons mayonnaise

milk for brushing

poppy or sesame seeds

1. Pre-heat oven to hot, 425 deg F or gas 7 (220 deg C).
2. Roll out pastry thinly and spread with mustard.
3. Cut into 24 squares, each 2 inches. Combine ham with mayonnaise. Put a little on to each square.
4. Moisten edges of pastry with water and fold over into triangles, sealing edges well together.
5. Brush with milk then sprinkle with poppy or sesame seeds.
6. Transfer to a baking tray and bake near top of oven for about 10 minutes.
7. Serve hot or cold.

Boxing day party spread: mustard-glazed gammon (see next page) surrounded by ham straws, cheese-stuffed prunes, savoury chicken liver pâté, party potato boats and devilled ham triangles

Fruity-glazed gammon

Mustard-glazed gammon

6lb (approximately 3 kilo) piece of gammon

cloves

2 level tablespoons prepared mustard

2 level tablespoons Demerara sugar

1 can (approximately 1lb or $\frac{1}{2}$ kilo) apricots

1 level tablespoon tomato ketchup

1 level tablespoon clear honey

1 tablespoon vinegar

1 dessertspoon Soy sauce

1 teaspoon Worcestershire sauce

1. Soak gammon overnight in cold water.
2. Transfer to large saucepan and cover with cold water.
3. Bring to boil and drain (this removes excess saltiness).
4. Return to pan, cover with fresh cold water and bring to the boil.
5. Lower heat and cover.
6. Simmer $2\frac{1}{4}$ hours and drain.
7. Place gammon in a roasting tin and remove skin.
8. Score fat into diamonds and stud with cloves.
9. Mix together mustard, sugar and 1 tablespoon syrup from apricots. Spread over the scored fat.
10. Bake in centre of a moderately hot oven, 375 deg F or gas 5 (190 deg C), for 30 minutes.
11. In a small pan, heat 5 tablespoons of syrup from apricots with ketchup, honey, vinegar and Soy and Worcestershire sauces.
12. Boil steadily 3 to 4 minutes, then pour over gammon 15 minutes before end of cooking time. Baste twice.
13. Stand gammon on a serving dish and surround with drained apricots.
14. Serve hot or cold.

Fruity-glazed gammon

As an alternative to mustard-glazed gammon, left, cook gammon in a similar way, but do not stud fat with cloves. Use 1 small can (approximately 8oz or 200gm) pineapple tidbits and 1 can mandarins instead of the apricots. Spike drained fruit into diamonds of gammon fat with cocktail sticks. Serve hot or cold.

A Danish buffet

Party porcupine

1. Cut 6oz (150gm) firm cheese into $\frac{3}{4}$-inch cubes.
2. Cut a slice from one end of an orange to make a firm base. Stand it on a board.
3. Pierce the cheese cubes on to cocktail sticks. Add a grape, cherry, mandarin segment or piece of pineapple to each. Press into orange to form a decorative porcupine.

Samsoe roll slices

Allow 1 slice of buttered bread per person. Cut some Samsoe cheese into thick slices and arrange in rolls on top of the bread, allowing 3 rolls each. Garnish with grapes and mandarins.

Golden shrimp savoury

Makes 16

6oz (150gm) Samsoe cheese

12oz (300gm) peeled shrimps

4 tablespoons mayonnaise

2 tablespoons soured cream

juice of 1 lemon

salt and pepper to taste

8 slices white bread, de-crusted and halved

4 egg whites

parsley to garnish

1. Pre-heat oven to moderately hot, 400 deg F or gas 6 (200 deg C).
2. Grate Samsoe cheese.
3. Reserve about a third of the peeled shrimps for garnishing. Mix remainder with mayonnaise, soured cream and lemon juice.
4. Season to taste with salt and pepper.
5. Butter bread and cover with shrimp mixture.
6. Whisk egg whites until stiff and fold in the grated cheese.
7. Pile on to bread, covering shrimp mixture completely.
8. Cook in centre of oven for 20 to 25 minutes or until golden brown.
9. Garnish with remaining shrimps and parsley. Serve hot.

Golden shrimp savoury,
party porcupine and samsoe roll slices

A selection of Danish open sandwiches

Danish open sandwiches

Allow 2 to 3 per person

Open sandwiches, the national dish of Denmark, make appetising and decorative party fare for any special occasion and are almost as much fun to prepare and arrange as they are to eat. Choose white, rye, wholemeal breads or pumpernickel and cover slices thickly with Danish butter for characteristic flavour. Then try any one of the following toppings and garnishes:

1. Tongue and salad
Cover buttered bread slices with tongue. Put a mound of Russian salad (see page 157) on to the centre of each then garnish with cucumber and tomato slices, lettuce and parsley.

2. Egg and bacon
Cover buttered bread slices with slices of hard-boiled egg. Top each with a grilled bacon rasher then garnish with slices of cucumber and tomato and watercress sprigs.

3. Mixed grill
Cover buttered bread slices with liver pâté. Top each with a grilled bacon rasher and grilled mushroom. Garnish with lettuce, tomato slices and gherkins.

4. Pork mayonnaise
Cover buttered bread slices with sliced luncheon meat. Top each with a lettuce leaf and heaped dessertspoon mayonnaise or salad cream. Garnish with orange slices, slit from centres to outside edges, and shaped into twists. Add tomato wedges and parsley.

5. Danish blue and olives
Cover buttered bread slices with lettuce leaves. Top each with Danish blue cheese then garnish with black olives.

6. Salami and onion
Cover buttered bread slices with salami then decorate with onion rings and parsley.

7. Meat and mixed vegetable
Cover buttered bread slices with slices of canned meat (corned beef or luncheon meat). Garnish with cooked carrots, small florets of cooked cauliflower, cooked peas and cucumber slices. Coat vegetables with French dressing (see page 161).

8. Cheese and radish
Cover buttered bread slices with lettuce. Top with cheese to taste then garnish each with a radish 'flower' (see page 154).

Supper buffet

For 8 people

Creamed chicken and mushrooms

8oz (200gm) quick cooking macaroni

2 cans condensed cream of mushroom soup

4 level tablespoons double cream

½ level teaspoon made mustard

8oz (200gm) cold cooked chicken, cut into bite-size pieces

4 slices of ham, rolled

cooked baby carrots, tossed in butter

1. Cook macaroni as directed on the packet. Drain.
2. Add to mushroom soup with double cream.
3. Heat through gently, whisking all the time.
4. Add mustard and chicken. Cover pan and simmer 10 minutes.
5. Transfer to a warm dish and top with ham rolls. Arrange carrots round edge of dish.

276

Scotch eggs

4 large hard-boiled eggs

1 level dessertspoon flour

12oz (300gm) pork sausagemeat

1 small onion, finely grated

2 level tablespoons quick cooking oats

1 standard egg, beaten

toasted breadcrumbs

deep oil or fat for frying

1. Shell eggs and roll them in flour.
2. Combine sausagemeat with onion and oats then divide into 4 equal portions.
3. Mould each portion round an egg, making sure the egg is evenly covered with no thin patches.
4. Coat eggs with beaten egg and crumbs and leave 15 minutes for coating to harden.
5. Lower into a pan of hot oil or fat then reduce heat slightly and fry a total of 8 minutes.
6. Remove from pan, drain on absorbent kitchen paper and leave until cold.
7. Before serving, cut in half and accompany with salad.

Macaroni cheese suprème

6oz (50gm) quick cooking macaroni

1 pint (approximately ½ litre) coating cheese sauce (see page 94)

salt and pepper to taste

1 can (about 1lb or ½ kilo) spinach purée

1 can (about 1lb or ½ kilo) canned tomatoes

3oz (75gm) Cheddar cheese, grated

1. Pre-heat oven to moderately hot, 400 deg F or gas 6 (200 deg C).
2. Cook macaroni as directed on the packet. Drain and combine with cheese sauce. Season well to taste with salt and pepper.
3. Fill a 4 pint (approximately 2½ litre) buttered heatproof dish with alternate layers of macaroni mixture, spinach purée and canned tomatoes, ending with macaroni. Place dish on a baking tray.
4. Sprinkle with grated cheese and re-heat and brown towards top of oven for 25 to 30 minutes.

Spaghetti egg quickie

Heat through 2 large cans of spaghetti in tomato sauce with 4 rashers chopped lean bacon and 4 level tablespoons chopped canned pimiento. Transfer to 8 individual dishes and top each with a poached egg.

Kidney ragout

1lb (½ kilo) ox kidney, cut into small cubes

2 level tablespoons flour, seasoned with salt and pepper

1oz (25gm) butter or margarine

1 dessertspoon salad oil

1 large onion, finely chopped

1 garlic clove, chopped

½ pint (250ml) beef stock

2 tablespoons dry sherry

1 to 2 level teaspoons salt

6oz (150gm) mushrooms and stalks

2 level tablespoons tomato ketchup

2 level tablespoons finely-chopped parsley

freshly-grilled bacon rolls

parsley sprigs

1. Coat kidney with seasoned flour.
2. Heat butter or margarine and oil in saucepan.
3. Add onion and garlic and fry gently until pale gold.
4. Add kidney and fry until pieces are brown and crisp all over.
5. Stir in all remaining ingredients except bacon rolls and parsley sprigs.
6. Bring to boil, stirring. Lower heat and cover pan.
7. Simmer gently for 1 hour or until kidneys are tender.
8. Transfer to a warm dish.
9. Garnish with bacon rolls and parsley sprigs, and accompany with either macaroni, rice or freshly-boiled potatoes and green vegetables to taste.

A supper buffet: in the background, macaroni cheese suprème and creamed chicken and mushrooms. Centre: spaghetti egg quickie and Scotch eggs, and in the foreground, kidney ragout

The any-occasion buffet

For 8 to 12 people

Minced meat puffs

Makes about 12

12oz (300gm) frozen puff pastry

beaten egg for glazing

1 can (1lb or ½ kilo) minced beef

1. Pre-heat oven to hot, 450 deg F or gas 8 (230 deg C).
2. Roll out pastry to ¼ inch in thickness. Cut into approximately 12 rounds with a 2-inch biscuit cutter.
3. Place rounds on damp baking tray then cut each half-way through centre with a 1-inch cutter.
4. Brush with egg then bake near top of oven for 10 to 15 minutes or until well-risen and golden.
5. Meanwhile, heat can of minced beef.
6. Remove puffs from oven. Lift off centre caps and remove any soft pastry left inside.
7. Fill with minced beef and serve straight away.

Note

If made ahead of time, leave filled puffs in the refrigerator. When required, heat through in a moderately hot oven, 400 deg F or gas 6 (200 deg C) for 10 minutes.

Salmon nuggets

1 can (8oz or 200gm) red salmon, drained

1lb (½ kilo) freshly-made mashed potatoes

2 level tablespoons chopped parsley

1 teaspoon Worcestershire sauce

2 teaspoons anchovy essence

squeeze of lemon juice

salt and pepper to taste

2oz (50gm) plain flour

1 standard egg, beaten

4oz (100gm) fresh white breadcrumbs

deep oil or fat for frying

1. Mash salmon finely and combine with potatoes, parsley, Worcestershire sauce, anchovy essence, lemon juice and salt and pepper to taste.
2. Shape into very small balls (40 to 45) and roll them in flour.
3. Coat with beaten egg and crumbs then fry in hot oil or fat until golden brown.
4. Remove from pan, drain on soft kitchen paper and serve straight away.

The any-occasion buffet:
in the background, from left to right, minced meat puffs, sausages and onions on sticks, and lemon scampi with tartare sauce. In the foreground, cheese-topped scone pies, salmon nuggets and cheese poppets

Cheese-topped scone pies

12oz (300gm) self-raising flour

1 level teaspoon baking powder

1 level teaspoon salt

4oz (100gm) butter, margarine or cooking fat (or mixture of fats)

½ pint (250ml) plus an extra 4 tablespoons cold milk

1 can (5oz or 125gm) tomato paste

1 teaspoon salad oil

½ level teaspoon caster sugar

½ level teaspoon flour

½ level teaspoon garlic salt

2 tablespoons water

8oz (200gm) Cheddar cheese, grated

2 small cans anchovies

about 2 dozen stuffed olives

1. Pre-heat oven to hot, 425 deg F or gas 7 (220 deg C).
2. Sift flour, baking powder and salt.
3. Rub in fat finely then mix to a soft dough with milk.
4. Turn out on to floured surface and knead lightly until smooth.
5. Roll out to just under ½ inch in thickness and cut into 12 rounds with a 2½-inch cutter.
6. Place rounds on buttered baking tray and bake near top of oven for 10 to 12 minutes or until well-risen and firm.
7. Meanwhile, put tomato paste, oil, sugar, flour, garlic salt and water into a small saucepan. Cook over a low heat for 7 minutes, stirring frequently.
8. Remove scones from oven and split in half.
9. Spread cut sides with tomato mixture then sprinkle with grated cheese.
10. Garnish each with anchovies and sliced olives then quickly brown under a hot grill.
11. Serve straight away.

Cheese poppets

choux pastry (see page 112)

¼ pint (125ml) mushroom coating sauce (see page 95)

4oz (100gm) cold cooked chicken, coarsely chopped

seasoning to taste

2oz (50gm) Cheddar cheese, finely grated

1. Pre-heat oven to moderately hot, 400 deg F or gas 6 (200 deg C).
2. Spoon walnut-sized pieces of pastry on to a greased baking tray.
3. Bake near top of oven for 20 minutes.
4. Take out of oven and slit each in half, removing any soft pastry from the centre.
5. Heat sauce with chicken and seasoning to taste.
6. Spoon equal amounts into lower half of each pastry case then cover with lid.
7. Return to baking tray, sprinkle with cheese and bake near top of oven a further 5 to 7 minutes or until cheese melts.
8. Serve straight away.

Lemon scampi

8oz (200gm) frozen scampi

1 level teaspoon finely-grated lemon peel

1 level teaspoon curry powder

savoury fritter batter (see page 105)

deep oil for frying

paprika

tartare sauce (see page 100)

1. De-frost scampi.
2. Add lemon peel and curry powder to batter. Mix thoroughly.
3. Coat scampi with batter and fry in hot oil until crisp and golden.
4. Remove from pan and drain on soft kitchen paper.
5. Sprinkle lightly with paprika then spear a cocktail stick into each.
6. Accompany with the tartare sauce.

A holiday buffet

For 12 to 15 people

Choose a large chicken, capon or medium-sized turkey and cook as instructed on pages 83, 87. Serve on a bed of rice, garnished with bacon rolls, sausages, fried onion rings and parsley.

Raised pork pie

hot water crust pastry (see page 111)

1½lb (¾ kilo) pie veal

8oz (200gm) lean ham

1 level teaspoon mixed herbs

salt and pepper

2 hard-boiled eggs, shelled

½ pint (250ml) plus 2 tablespoons stock or water

beaten egg for glazing

2 level teaspoons gelatine

1. Pre-heat oven to moderately hot, 400 deg F or gas 6 (200 deg C).
2. Roll out two-thirds of the pastry and mould over the outside of a 7-inch round cake tin, covering base and sides smoothly and evenly. Keep rest of pastry warm and covered.
3. Wrap a double thickness of greaseproof paper round pie (same depth as sides) and hold in place with fine string. Leave pie until pastry is firm then carefully remove cake tin. Stand pie on greased and floured baking tray.
4. Cut veal into small cubes. Coarsely chop ham.
5. Half-fill pie with veal and ham, sprinkling half the herbs and salt and pepper between layers.
6. Place eggs on top then fill pie with layers of veal and ham as before.
7. Pour in 2 tablespoons stock or water.
8. Moisten edges of pastry with beaten egg then cover with lid, rolled from rest of pastry.
9. Press edges well together to seal then trim off any surplus pastry with kitchen scissors. Press edges into flutes.
10. Make a large hole in the top of the pie then brush pastry with beaten egg.
11. Cut leaves from pastry trimmings and place round hole. Brush with more egg.
12. Bake pie in centre of the oven for 30 minutes.
13. Lower temperature to moderate, 350 deg F or gas 4 (180 deg C), and bake a further 1½ hours, covering pie with a sheet of damp greaseproof paper if it seems to be browning too much.
14. Remove from oven and take off band of paper. Leave pie until cold.
15. Put remaining stock or water into a saucepan and add gelatine. Stir over a low heat until dissolved. Season to taste with salt and pepper and leave until cold.
16. Using a funnel, pour into pie through centre hole until it reaches the top.
17. Leave pie one day before cutting.

French fruit tarts

Makes 18

rich flan pastry made with 8oz (200gm) flour (see page 108)

apricot jam, melted

¼ pint (125ml) double cream

well-drained canned fruit or fresh fruit to taste

2 level teaspoons cornflour

¼ pint (125ml) fruit syrup from canned fruit or same amount of diluted orange squash

1. Pre-heat oven to moderately hot, 400 deg F or gas 6 (200 deg C).
2. Roll out pastry and cut into approximately 18 rounds with a 3-inch cutter. Use to line 18 bun tins.
3. Prick well then line each with a square of foil to prevent pastry from rising as it cooks.
4. Bake near top of oven for 15 to 20 minutes or until pastry is pale gold. Remove from oven and take out foil.
5. Leave tartlets on a cooling rack until cold.
6. Brush insides with melted apricot jam.
7. Whip cream until thick and put equal amounts into pastry cases.
8. Pile canned or fresh fruit on top.
9. To make glaze, mix cornflour to a smooth cream with a little fruit syrup or diluted squash. Add rest of syrup or squash and pour into saucepan.
10. Cook, stirring, until mixture thickens. Brush over fruit when cool.

A holiday buffet: cold roast chicken, raised pork pie, French fruit tarts, coffee peach meringues and fruit wine jelly (see next page)

Coffee peach meringues

4 egg whites

8oz (200gm) caster sugar

1 tablespoon strong coffee

2 level teaspoons cornflour

½ pint (250ml) double cream

2 tablespoons milk

canned peach slices, well drained

1. Pre-heat oven to very cool, 225 deg F or gas ¼ (110 deg C).
2. Brush 2 large baking trays with oil then cover with double thickness of greaseproof paper. Do not oil paper.
3. Put egg whites into a clean, dry bowl and whisk to a stiff snow.
4. Gradually add two-thirds of the sugar and continue beating until mixture is thick and heavy and stands in high firm peaks when the beaters (or whisk) are lifted out.
5. Stir in coffee and cornflour then quickly fold in remaining sugar a little at a time with a large metal spoon.
6. Pile 14 mounds of mixture on to each baking tray, leaving a little room between each as they spread slightly.
7. Bake one tin in centre of oven, the other one shelf below, for 2 hours, changing trays round halfway through.
8. Remove from oven and lift meringues off the paper.
9. Switch off oven heat then return meringues to oven with the door open. Leave until completely dry and crisp.
10. Before serving, whip cream and milk together until thick.
11. Sandwich pairs of meringues together thickly with cream then top with peach slices.

Fruit wine jelly

Illustrated on previous page

2 raspberry or blackcurrant jellies

½ pint (250ml) boiling water

½ pint (250ml) red wine

cold water

1 can (approximately 16oz or ½ kilo) fruit cocktail

2 medium bananas, sliced

1. Dissolve jellies in the boiling water. Add wine then make up to 2 pints (approximately 1 litre) with half cold water and half syrup from can of fruit.
2. Refrigerate until just beginning to thicken and set then fold in well-drained fruit cocktail and sliced bananas.
3. Transfer to a 3 to 3½ pint (approximately 1¾ to 2 litre) fancy jelly mould first rinsed with cold water or lightly oiled. Leave in a cool place until firm and set.
4. Dip mould in boiling water for 1 or 2 minutes then turn jelly out on to a plate.
5. If liked, decorate edge with more drained fruit and serve with whipped cream.

Party dips and dunks

All serve about 10 people

Foods for dipping include crackers, savoury biscuits, fingers or squares of toast, potato crisps, thin slices of carrot and cucumber, small cauliflower florets, 2-inch lengths of celery and cooked cocktail sausages, squares of corned beef or luncheon meat on cocktail sticks, and cheese.

Fish and egg dip

Finely mash 1 can pilchards in tomato sauce with 6 very lightly-scrambled eggs. Season well to taste with salt and freshly-milled black pepper then stir in 2 level teaspoons very finely-chopped parsley and 3 tablespoons thick mayonnaise. Cover and chill lightly then transfer to serving bowl just before using.

Curried chicken dip

½ pint (250ml) thick mayonnaise

8oz (200gm) cooked chicken, very finely minced

2 to 3 level teaspoons curry powder

1 medium celery stalk, finely chopped

seasoning to taste

1 level tablespoon salted peanuts

Combine mayonnaise with chicken, curry powder and celery then season to taste with salt and pepper. Cover and lightly chill then transfer to a serving bowl just before using. Sprinkle top with peanuts.

A party dip with crisps, cheese and cheese biscuits

Cottage cheese cream dip

Combine 8oz (200gm) cottage cheese with ¼ pint (125ml) stiffly-whipped cream, 1 small finely-grated onion, 1 level teaspoon paprika, 1 small de-seeded and chopped green pepper and salt and pepper to taste. Cover and lightly chill then transfer to a serving bowl just before using.

Cottage cheese and fresh pineapple dip

Combine 8oz (200gm) cottage cheese with 6 level tablespoons finely-chopped fresh pineapple, 2 level tablespoons chopped parsley, 3 tablespoons single cream and salt and pepper to taste. Cover and lightly chill then transfer to a serving bowl just before using.

Eastern dip

Combine 2 cartons (each ¼ pint or 125ml) natural yogurt with 3 level tablespoons sweet pickle, 1 tablespoon Soy sauce, 1 level dessertspoon finely-chopped preserved ginger, 2 level tablespoons finely-chopped canned water chestnuts, 1 level tablespoon finely-chopped parsley and salt and pepper to taste. Cover and lightly chill then transfer to a serving bowl just before using.

Tuna dip

Finely flake 1 can (about 7oz or 175gm) tuna and combine with 4 tablespoons thick mayonnaise, 2 tablespoons tomato ketchup, the juice of 1 medium lemon, 1 teaspoon Worcestershire sauce, 2 level teaspoons finely-grated onion and salt and pepper to taste. Cover and lightly chill then transfer to a serving bowl just before using.

Asparagus dip

Drain and finely chop 1 can (10oz or 250 gm) asparagus. Combine with 1 carton (¼ pint or 125ml) natural yogurt, 4 tablespoons thick mayonnaise, ½ to 1 level teaspoon onion salt, a shake of Cayenne pepper, ¼ level teaspoon sugar, a squeeze of lemon and dash of Tabasco. Cover and lightly chill then transfer to a serving dish just before using.

Avocado dip

Peel 1 large ripe avocado then mash flesh finely with 2 tablespoons lemon juice. Stir in 6 tablespoons thick mayonnaise, ½ level teaspoon garlic salt and 2 level tablespoons finely-chopped stuffed olives. Cover and lightly chill then transfer to a serving bowl just before using.

Danish dip

Whip ¼ pint (125ml) double cream until thick. Stir in 3 level tablespoons Danish style caviare (lump fish), 1 small finely-grated onion, 2 chopped hard-boiled eggs, a squeeze of lemon, and salt and pepper to taste. Cover and lightly chill then transfer to a serving bowl just before serving.

Slimmers' dip

A useful party piece for those who want to celebrate but weight-watch at the same time! Put 8oz (200gm) cream cheese into bowl and soften by mashing with a fork. Dissolve 1oz (25gm) instant low fat milk granules in 3 tablespoons cold water. Beat into cheese with either 2 level tablespoons scissor-snipped chives, 1 level tablespoon grated onion, 2 to 3 level teaspoons curry powder, 2 to 3 level tablespoons chutney or 2 to 3oz (50 to 75gm) finely-chopped peeled prawns and 1 level teaspoon paprika. Transfer to a serving bowl and chill lightly. Before serving, stand bowl on a platter and surround with dunks of raw vegetables.

Slimmers' dip

Nibbles with drinks

Scalloped eggs

Makes 20

10 hard-boiled eggs

4 canned pilchards in tomato sauce

4 tablespoons soured cream

1 level teaspoon prepared mustard

salt and pepper to taste

slices of stuffed olives to garnish

1. Halve hard-boiled eggs and scoop yolks into a bowl.
2. Cut a very thin sliver off the base of each egg white half so that it stands upright without toppling.
3. If liked, serrate edges with kitchen scissors.
4. Mash pilchards and egg yolks finely together then stir in soured cream, mustard and salt and pepper to taste.
5. Return mixture to egg white halves and garnish each with olive slices.
6. Transfer to a serving dish and spear a cocktail stick into each.

Scalloped eggs

Prawn puffs

Makes approximately 32

1lb (½ kilo) raw cod or haddock

4oz (100gm) peeled prawns

juice of 1 lemon

salt and pepper to taste

1 tablespoon anchovy essence or tomato paste

5oz (125ml) self-raising flour

deep fat or oil for frying

tartare sauce (see page 100)

1. Chop raw fish.
2. Add roughly-chopped prawns, salt and pepper to taste, lemon juice and anchovy essence or tomato paste.
3. Add flour and mix thoroughly.
4. Divide mixture into 32 portions and roll into small balls.
5. Drop, a few at a time, into hot oil and fry for 3 to 4 minutes or until evenly brown. Drain on paper towels.
6. Serve on cocktail sticks and accompany with a bowl of tartare sauce for dipping.

Hot shrimp and cheese canapés

Makes 14

4oz (100gm) frozen potted shrimps

1 level tablespoon cornflour

¼ pint (125ml) milk

2oz (50gm) Cheddar cheese, grated

14 rounds French bread

lemon wedges to garnish

1. De-frost potted shrimps.
2. Blend cornflour smoothly with the milk.
3. Bring to boil, stirring, then simmer 2 to 3 minutes.
4. Add the cheese and potted shrimps (in their spiced butter) to the sauce and stir thoroughly.
5. Toast bread then pile fish mixture on top.
6. Brown under a hot grill and serve straight away, garnished with lemon.

Above: hot shrimp and cheese canapés. Below: prawn puffs

Entertaining children

Children are the most conservative of party goers! Whatever the occasion, they expect the food they are given at parties to be just the same as they have at home, but in party dress. Few children, except the very brave, will eat something they have never tasted before and many a sad Mum, determined to serve new and different food at her child's party, is only confronted at the end of the day with a mound of left-over food.

Foods which are usually popular include peanuts, crisps, baby sausages on sticks, fish fingers and chips, and hard-boiled egg halves. The dainty sandwiches which took so long to make are usually spurned. Vast quantities of orange squash, cubes of cheese, apple fritters, buttered toast spread with yeast extract, ice cream and ice lollies, biscuits and chocolate rolls—usually in that order—all go down well. Of course the birthday cake at a birthday party is a must, but it hardly ever gets eaten.

Basically, children like party fare that is simple but colourfully and gaily presented. Give them what they want, and these conservative little critics will tuck in like mad, making all the effort well worth while.

Minstrel boys

Makes 6

4oz (100gm) quick cooking oats

2 level tablespoons golden syrup

2oz (50gm) butter or margarine

2oz (50gm) caster sugar

1½oz (37gm) cocoa powder, sifted

6 ice cream cones

extra sifted cocoa powder for coating

about 3 tablespoons whipped cream

12 currants

1. Rub oats between hands until fine and powdery.
2. Heat syrup in saucepan, add oats and mix well. Cool.
3. Cream butter or margarine and sugar together until light and fluffy then stir in cocoa powder and oat mixture.
4. Mix thoroughly and shape into 6 large balls. Toss in cocoa.
5. Cut each ice cream cone in two to form a collar and tall hat.
6. Stand the cocoa balls on the necks of the cones then top with the cone hats.
7. Using a writing nozzle and icing bag, pipe in eyes, nose and mouth with the whipped cream.
8. Press a currant into the centre of each eye and refrigerate for 30 minutes before serving.

Banana crunchies

Makes 12

8oz (200gm) Demerara sugar

2 tablespoons water

2 level tablespoons golden syrup

6 bananas

cocktail sticks

breakfast cereal such as sugar puffs, lightly crushed

1. Put sugar and water into a saucepan. Dissolve over a very low heat.
2. Add 1 tablespoon syrup and boil until mixture is caramel colour—about 3 to 4 minutes.
3. Stir in remaining syrup and mix well. Remove from heat.
4. Peel bananas and cut each in half.
5. Spear a cocktail stick into each then dip in syrup mixture.
6. Coat with the cereal then leave until set on greased greaseproof paper—about 5 to 10 minutes.
7. Eat as soon as possible.

From top to bottom: banana crunchies, orange rascals, minstrel boys, biscuit spots, winter snowboys, moondrops and chocolate ruffles

284

Winter snowboys

Makes about 12

8oz (200gm) butter or margarine

3oz (75gm) icing sugar, sifted

2 teaspoons vanilla essence

8oz (200gm) self-raising flour, sifted

pinch of salt

3oz (75gm) quick cooking oats

royal icing (see page 217)

currants

glacé cherries

angelica

1. Pre-heat oven to moderate, 325 deg F or gas 3 (170 deg C).
2. Cream butter or margarine with icing sugar and vanilla essence until light and fluffy.
3. Stir in flour, salt and oats and mix thoroughly with a fork.
4. Well grease 2 large baking trays.
5. Shape oatmeal mixture into 12 balls for bodies, 12 smaller balls for heads and 48 short oblongs for arms and legs. Keep all the portions fairly small as they rise during cooking.
6. Place balls and oblongs on baking trays, joining them together to form individual snowboys.
7. Flatten each by pressing down slightly with a broad-bladed knife.
8. Bake in centre of oven for 20 to 30 minutes or until pale gold.
9. Remove from oven and cool on a wire rack.
10. When completely cold, coat with glacé icing and leave until set.
11. Mark in eyes with currants, and mouths with strips of glacé cherries.
12. Add buttons made from small triangles of angelica.

Moondrops

Makes about 30

1 teaspoon glycerine

royal icing made with 8oz (200gm) icing sugar (see page 217)

2oz (50gm) mixed dried fruit

2oz (50gm) glacé cherries, chopped

1oz (25gm) breakfast cereal

assorted food colourings

1. Stir glycerine into icing and mix thoroughly.
2. Add dried fruit, cherries and cereal. Stir well to mix.
3. Divide into portions and colour each to taste.
4. Pile teaspoons of mixture on to greased greaseproof paper and leave to set.

Biscuit spots

Take any home baked or bought biscuits and decorate each with a sugar coated chocolate drop, held in place with a little whipped cream.

Chocolate ruffles

Makes 12

6oz (150gm) plain chocolate

2 tablespoons warm water

2 teaspoons butter

breakfast cereal such as puffed wheat

1. Break up chocolate and put into a basin over a saucepan of gently-simmering water.
2. Add water and butter and leave until melted, stirring occasionally.
3. Remove basin from pan of water then stir in sufficient breakfast cereal to give a fairly stiff consistency.
4. Place heaped teaspoons of mixture on to greased greaseproof paper and leave until set.

Orange rascals

Makes 4

4 large oranges

4 level tablespoons orange jelly, chopped

4 dessertspoons vanilla ice cream

about ¼ pint (125ml) double cream, whipped

8 currants

1. Cut a slice off the top of each orange and scoop out the flesh. Chop up, removing pips and membranes, and leave on one side.
2. With a sharp knife, score lines on the front of each hollowed orange to form eyes, nose and mouth.
3. Fill oranges with chopped orange flesh, jelly and ice cream.
4. Replace tops and pipe on 'curls' of hair with the cream. Put a currant into each eye, securing it with a little cream.

Christmas snowmen cakes

Makes 6

2oz (50gm) butter or margarine, softened

2oz (50gm) caster sugar

1 large egg

2 level tablespoons cocoa powder

2oz (50gm) self-raising flour

4oz (100gm) butter, softened

4oz (100gm) icing sugar, sifted

1lb (½ kilo) marshmallows

coloured cake decoration balls

'scarves' cut from lengths of ribbon

stiff black paper

sweet cigarettes

1. Pre-heat oven to moderate, 350 deg F or gas 4 (180 deg C).
2. Well-grease 6 dariole moulds, each with 4 tablespoons liquid capacity.
3. Cream butter or margarine and caster sugar well together.
4. Beat in egg then fold in cocoa powder sifted with the flour.
5. Divide mixture equally among the moulds.
6. Tap each mould lightly to disperse air bubbles.
7. Bake in centre of oven for 20 minutes or until mixture leaves the sides of moulds and is springy to the touch.
8. Turn out on to a wire rack and leave until completely cold.
9. To make butter cream, beat butter with the icing sugar until light and fluffy.
10. Cover each cake completely with butter cream, reserving a little.
11. Leave 12 marshmallows whole and cut remainder in half with a knife dipped in hot water.
12. Press halved marshmallows over the cakes.
13. Place a whole marshmallow on the top for the neck then stick on another with butter cream, standing it upright for the head.
14. Press coloured balls into the marshmallows for the face and buttons down the front.
15. Decorate each snowman with a ribbon scarf and hat made from stiff black paper then place a cigarette in each mouth.
16. Stand snowmen in large paper cake cases or on a board dusted with icing sugar.

Christmas snowmen cakes

Toffee crunch apricot sundae

Serves 4

1 large can apricot halves, drained

4oz (100gm) glacé cherries

2oz (50gm) butter

1 level tablespoon golden syrup

1oz (25gm) caster sugar

2oz (50gm) puffed rice breakfast cereal

¼ pint (125ml) double cream, whipped

1. Liquidise or sieve the apricots to a purée.
2. Cut up the cherries, reserving 4 whole ones for decoration.
3. Heat the butter, golden syrup and sugar until melted.
4. Cook quickly until a little sets when dropped into a cup of cold water.
5. Mix with the cereal.
6. Fill 4 sundae glasses with alternate layers of apricot purée, cherries, cereal mixture and cream, finishing with cream and a whole cherry.
7. Chill lightly before serving.

Toffee apple faces

Makes 4

4 freshly-made toffee apples (see page 243)

breakfast cereal

candied sweets to decorate

1. Cover tops of toffee apples with breakfast cereal to represent hair.
2. Mark in face features with assorted-shaped sweets.
3. Stand toffee apples in paper cases and leave to harden before eating.

Fruity biscuit bars

Makes 12

4oz (100gm) pink and white marshmallows

4oz (100gm) butter

4 level tablespoons golden syrup

4oz (100gm) Rice Krispies

2oz (50gm) almonds, blanched and chopped

3oz (75gm) glacé cherries, chopped

1. Heat marshmallows with the butter until both have melted.
2. Add all remaining ingredients.
3. Mix well together.
4. Turn into greased 7-inch square tin and leave to set.
5. Turn out and cut into 12 bars when cold.

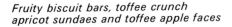

Fruity biscuit bars, toffee crunch apricot sundaes and toffee apple faces

Clown cake

Clown cake

1 level tablespoon cocoa powder

3oz (75gm) self-raising flour

3 standard eggs

3oz (75gm) caster sugar

1 tablespoon hot water

3oz (75gm) butter, softened

3oz (75gm) icing sugar, sifted

3 milk flake bars

2 sugar coated chocolate beans

2 orange jelly slices

a striped paper napkin

2 gold doilies

1. Pre-heat oven to moderate, 350 deg F or gas 4 (180 deg C).
2. Butter two 7-inch sandwich tins and line bases with rounds of greaseproof paper.
3. Sift cocoa and flour twice on to a plate.
4. Put eggs and sugar into a bowl over a saucepan of hot water.
5. Whisk continuously until mixture thickens to consistency of softly-whipped cream and is twice its original volume.
6. Using a metal spoon, fold in flour mixture and hot water.
7. Transfer to prepared tins and bake in centre of oven for 15 to 20 minutes or until well-risen and golden.
8. Turn out on to a wire cooling rack covered with a clean tea-towel (to prevent wire from cutting into delicate surfaces of cakes). Peel away paper and leave cakes until cold.
9. To make butter cream, cream butter and icing sugar together until light and fluffy.
10. With small biscuit cutter or sharp pointed knife, cut out eyes, nose and mouth shapes from one of the cakes.
11. Sandwich the cakes together with two-thirds of the butter cream and place on a doily-lined platter.
12. Using remaining butter cream, pipe lines round the eyes, nose and mouth, ending with the eyebrows.
13. Pipe a whirl of butter cream into each eye hole.
14. For hair, cut flake bars in half and press against sides of cake as shown in photograph, holding them in place with a little butter cream. Leave a gap for the hat.
15. Add chocolate beans for the eyes and orange slices for the ears.
16. Roll a paper napkin into a cone shape and secure firmly.
17. Cut out motifs from doily and stick on to the hat. Place in position on the cake.
18. Chill cake lightly before serving.

Fruit salad mould

Serves 10 to 12

2 strawberry flavour jellies or other flavours to taste

½ pint (250ml) boiling water

2 large cans (each approximately 1lb or ½ kilo) ready-to-serve custard or 1½ pints (¾ litre) freshly-made custard

1 large can fruit salad, drained

1. Dissolve jellies in boiling water.
2. Gently whisk into custard until smooth and evenly combined.
3. Pour into 3-pint (approximately 1½-litre) fancy mould, first rinsed with cold water or lightly oiled.
4. Refrigerate until firm and set.
5. Unmould on to a platter and decorate with fruit salad.

Lemon-iced cherry cake

Serves 10

1 Madeira cake (see page 219)

12oz (300gm) icing sugar

strained lemon juice

4oz (100gm) glacé cherries, halved

1. Stand cake on a wire rack.
2. To make icing, sift icing sugar into bowl.
3. Add lemon juice, a teaspoon at a time, until a stiff icing is formed.
4. Pour over top of cake and allow it to trickle down the sides.
5. When icing is set, decorate with halved glacé cherries.

Party trifle

Serves 10

8 trifle sponge cakes

a little raspberry jam

1 medium can of fruit to taste (peaches, apricots, pineapple chunks or fruit salad)

1 large can (approximately 1lb or ½ kilo) ready-to-serve custard or ¾ pint (375ml) freshly-made custard

grated chocolate

glacé cherries

strips of angelica

strips of liquorice

1. Halve sponge cakes and sandwich together with raspberry jam.
2. Cut each into 4 and arrange in serving bowl.
3. Moisten with syrup from can of fruit then arrange the drained fruit on top.
4. Cover completely with custard.
5. To decorate, mark in hair with grated chocolate.
6. Add glacé cherry eyes, outlining them with strips of angelica.
7. Add eye lashes made from thin threads of liquorice then mark in nose and mouth either with cherries, chocolate or angelica.
8. Add a bow to the hair cut from angelica and trim with a cherry.
9. Chill for about 2 hours before serving.

From top to bottom: fruit salad mould, savoury meat balls, lemon-iced cherry cake, funny face open sandwiches and party trifle

Savoury meat balls

Serves 8 to 10

1lb (½ kilo) raw minced beef

1 level teaspoon meat extract

1 level teaspoon dry mustard

1 standard egg, beaten

pinch of salt

dripping, cooking fat or oil for frying

tomato ketchup

chopped parsley to garnish

1. Mix together beef, meat extract, mustard, egg and salt to taste.
2. Shape into small balls with damp hands.
3. Fry balls in about 2 inches of dripping, cooking fat or oil until crisp and brown all over.
4. Drain on soft kitchen paper.
5. Gently warm through ketchup, transfer it to a serving dish and stand it on a warm platter. Garnish with parsley.
6. Surround with meat balls and spear a cocktail stick into each.
7. Meat balls should be dunked into the tomato dip and eaten at once.

Funny face open sandwiches

1. Allow 2 sandwiches per child.
2. Spread de-crusted slices of bread (cut into fancy shapes, if wished) first with softened butter or margarine and then with a thin layer of yeast extract for added tastiness.
3. Cover with either ham, luncheon meat, corned beef, fish or meat paste, cream cheese, finely-mashed canned salmon or mashed sardines.
4. Make funny face decorations with slices of cucumber, wedges or slices of egg and tomato, parsley, lettuce, slices of cheese, green pepper, grated carrots and watercress.

Back row, from left to right:
sea-shore sausages, halo sausages and
sausage crown salad. In the foreground:
orange cucumber sausage salad,
sausage and egg cups and
sausage and rice casserole

Sea-shore sausages

Serves 8

Line a warm serving dish with freshly-
cooked spaghetti. Cover with hot spinach
purée or finely-chopped cooked cabbage
then arrange 1lb ($\frac{1}{2}$ kilo) freshly-fried
sausages on top.

Orange cucumber sausage salad

Serves 8 to 10

1lb ($\frac{1}{2}$ kilo) sausages

6oz (150gm) long-grain rice

3 tablespoons salad oil

1 tablespoon vinegar

salt, pepper and dry mustard to taste

1 orange, peeled and cut into segments

2 large tomatoes, peeled, seeded and
roughly chopped

1 small cucumber, peeled and diced

1 level tablespoon scissor-snipped
chives

1. Fry sausages gently in frying pan for
about 20 minutes or until cooked through
and evenly browned.
2. Remove from pan and leave until cold.
3. Meanwhile, cook rice in fast boiling
salted water until tender—approximately
12 minutes. Drain.
4. Blend together oil, vinegar, salt, pepper
and mustard to taste then stir into rice.
Leave until cold.
5. Add all remaining ingredients and mix
thoroughly.
6. Pile on to a serving dish and arrange
sausages on top.

Halo sausages

Serves 8

1oz (25gm) margarine or cooking fat

1lb ($\frac{1}{2}$ kilo) pork sausages

4oz (100gm) small onions

4oz (100gm) mushrooms, quartered

3 large firm cooking apples

1. Melt fat in a large frying pan.
2. Add sausages and fry slowly for approximately 20 minutes or until well-browned all
over.
3. Remove from pan and keep hot.
4. Add onions and mushrooms to remaining fat in pan.
5. Fry gently for 8 to 10 minutes.
6. Meanwhile, prepare apples.
7. Peel and thickly slice each to give 8
slices.
8. Remove cores and add slices to frying
pan.
9. Fry very gently for 2 to 3 minutes per
side. Drain.
10. To serve, put a sausage through the
centre of each apple slice, place round
edge of serving dish and pile onion and
mushroom mixture in the centre.

Sausage and egg cups

Makes 4

½oz (12gm) cooking fat

1 small onion, finely chopped

8oz (200gm) pork sausagemeat

salt and pepper to taste

4 standard eggs

1oz (25gm) butter

1. Pre-heat oven to moderate, 350 deg F or gas 4 (180 deg C).
2. Melt fat in frying pan.
3. Add onion and fry quickly for 2 to 3 minutes.
4. Stir into sausagemeat with the salt and pepper to taste.
5. Divide into 4 portions and use to line 4 greased ramekin or individual dishes.
6. Bake in centre of oven for 20 minutes.
7. Remove from oven, break an egg into each and dot with butter.
8. Return to oven for a further 10 to 15 minutes to set the eggs.
9. Serve straight away.

Sausage crown salad

Serves 8 to 10

½oz (12gm) cooking fat

1lb (½ kilo) pork sausages

1 can (8oz or 200gm) pineapple chunks

6 gherkins, sliced

¼ pint (125ml) double cream, whipped

2 tablespoons vinegar

1. Melt cooking fat in frying pan and cook the sausages slowly for 20 minutes, turning frequently.
2. Leave until cold.
3. Strain pineapple and place chunks in a bowl with the gherkins.
4. Stir in the whipped cream and vinegar.
5. Cut sausages in half lengthwise and arrange round a deep, straight-sided dish with the cut sides outwards.
6. Fill the centre with the pineapple and gherkin mixture.

Sausage and rice casserole

Serves 8

1lb (½ kilo) cold cooked pork sausages

6oz (150gm) long-grain rice

8oz (200gm) tomatoes, skinned and sliced

6 tablespoons water

2 level tablespoons tomato ketchup

1 teaspoon Worcestershire sauce

2 hard-boiled eggs, chopped

4oz (100gm) Cheddar cheese, grated

salt and pepper to taste

1. Slice sausages.
2. Cook rice in boiling salted water until just tender—about 12 minutes. Drain.
3. Put tomatoes, water, ketchup and Worcestershire sauce into a saucepan. Bring to boil.
4. Add sausages, rice and eggs then stir in 3oz (75gm) cheese.
5. Season to taste with salt and pepper then transfer to a heatproof dish.
6. Sprinkle remaining cheese on top then brown under a hot grill.
7. Serve straight away.

Kiddy casseroles

Serves 8

A more substantial, party-style hot dish for older children.

4 cold cooked pork sausages, thinly sliced

6 standard eggs, well beaten

2 cans (each 10oz or 250gm) cream style corn

salt and pepper to taste

4 tablespoons butter or margarine, melted

stuffed green olives, sliced

1. Pre-heat oven to moderate, 325 deg F or gas 3 (170 deg C).
2. Well butter 8 individual casseroles and arrange sausage slices over base of each.
3. Combine all remaining ingredients together except olives.
4. Transfer to casseroles and bake in centre of oven for 30 to 40 minutes or until mixture is firm.
5. Mark in faces with sliced olives and serve hot.

Ice cream puffer

Serves 6

2 family bricks raspberry ripple ice cream

1 orange, sliced

6 sweet plain biscuits

4 marshmallows

1. Arrange one ice cream block on top of the other and place on an oblong platter.
2. Stand slices of orange down the long sides of the puffer to form wheels.
3. Arrange a pile of plain biscuits on top for the cabin.
4. Top the cabin with marshmallows for the funnels and serve immediately.

Above left: ice cream puffer
Above right: apple fritters
Below: kiddy casseroles

Apple fritters

Serves 8 to 10

4 large cooking apples

double quantity of sweet fritter batter (see page 105)

deep fat or oil for frying

caster sugar

1. Peel and core apples and cut each into 5 rings.
2. Coat with fritter batter.
3. Fry in hot fat or oil for 2 to 3 minutes or until crisp and golden.
4. Remove from pan and drain on soft kitchen paper.
5. Sprinkle with caster sugar and serve straight away.

Wine

The glasses used for all wine should be thin and clear so that the wine is easily recognisable. To preserve the bouquet and aroma of the drink, glasses which get narrower as they reach the rim are the best choice. However, for rosé wine, tulip-shaped glasses with outward curving rims are perfectly acceptable; this wine should always be served very well chilled.

Gentle rotation of the wine glass brings out the flavour and bouquet of the wine and therefore to avoid spills, glasses should never be more than two-thirds full.

Bottles of wine should be stored horizontally and kept in a cool, dry place.

Wine consumption is always a matter of personal taste but as a general rule, allow a minimum of 1 standard sized bottle for 4 persons. Light wine should be served first, followed by a heavy wine—never the other way round.

White wines

White wine should always be served lightly chilled in glasses with long stems. The glass should be held by the stem only because cupping the hands round the bowl warms the wine and spoils the bouquet. Dry white wine should be served with hors d'oeuvre, shellfish, white fish and white meat. Sweet white wines are best suited to the dessert course.

Rosé wines

Rosé wines should be served well chilled in long-stemmed glasses. These pleasantly light, dryish wines team well with all foods but are especially suited to salmon and salmon trout, egg, poultry and lamb dishes, and roast veal and turkey.

Red wines

Red wines should be served at average room temperature and must never be artificially warmed. The glasses for all red wines should have bulbous bowls and short stems, and as these wines respond favourably to gentle warmth, the bowls of the glasses should be held in the hands. Red wines should be uncorked an hour before serving and decanted if there is a heavy sediment at the bottom of the bottle. However, instead of decanting, the bottle may be stood upright for one or two hours, and then the wine poured very slowly into the glasses. Claret is a light-bodied red wine, well-suited to most main course dishes. Burgundy is altogether more robust and should be reserved for red meat roasts and all game dishes.

Champagne may be drunk throughout a meal provided it is fairly dry. Dry sherry is an ideal accompaniment to soup, and port or Madeira are the traditional wines to serve with cheese. Connoisseurs may select a separate wine for each course; but for most occasions one wine served throughout the meal is perfectly adequate. In this case, the wine should be chosen to complement the main course.

Drinks for all occasions

Cider punch

Serves 8 to 12

2 pints (approximately 1¼ litre) cider

1 large can (approximately 1 pint or ½ litre) orange juice

1 cinnamon stick and 6 cloves, tied in muslin bag

1 small can (approximately 8oz or 200gm) sliced peaches

4oz (100gm) granulated sugar

thinly-pared rind of 1 small lemon and 1 medium orange

¼ pint (125ml) whisky

1. Put all ingredients, except whisky, into a saucepan.
2. Bring to boil, cover and simmer over the lowest possible heat for 30 minutes.
3. Remove from heat, stir in whisky and serve straight away.

Hot toddy

Serves 6 to 8

¾ pint (375ml) water

2 level tablespoons granulated sugar

1 small can (¼ pint or 125ml) sweetened orange juice

½ pint (250ml) rum

nutmeg

1. Put all ingredients, except rum and nutmeg, into saucepan.
2. Slowly bring to boil, stirring.
3. Remove from heat, add rum and pour into glasses or mugs.
4. Sprinkle with nutmeg and serve straight away.

Icebreaker

Serves 8 to 10

2 bottles port

1 long strip lemon peel, 1 cinnamon stick and 4 cloves, tied in muslin bag

¼ level teaspoon nutmeg

8oz (200gm) granulated sugar

juice of 1 lemon

juice of 2 large oranges

¼ pint (125ml) rum

1. Put all ingredients, except rum, into saucepan.
2. Bring to boil, cover and simmer over the lowest possible heat for 30 minutes.
3. Remove from heat, stir in rum and serve straight away.

Tea punch

Serves 16

2 pints (approximately 1¼ litre) freshly-made tea, strained

1lb (½ kilo) granulated sugar

2 bottles claret

½ pint (250ml) rum

1. Pour tea into a large saucepan. Add sugar and stir over a low heat until dissolved.
2. In separate saucepan, bring claret and rum just up to the boil.
3. Remove from heat and combine with hot sweetened tea.
4. Serve straight away.

Gluhwein

Serves about 16 to 20

4 bottles dry red wine

1½lb (¾ kilo) granulated sugar

2 cinnamon sticks

1 dozen cloves

1. Put all ingredients into a saucepan.
2. Stir over low heat until sugar dissolves.
3. Bring just up to the boil, cover and simmer over the lowest possible heat for 30 minutes.
4. Serve straight away.

Hot German egg beer

Serves 6

6 standard eggs

2½ pints (approximately 1½ litre) malt beer or brown ale

8oz (200gm) sugar

finely-grated peel of 1 medium lemon

1. Put eggs into large saucepan and whisk thoroughly.
2. Add beer and sugar.
3. Place over a low heat, whisking continuously, until beer is hot but on no account allow mixture to boil.
4. Remove from heat, whisk for ½ a minute and pour into beer mugs.
5. Serve straight away with lemon peel sprinkled over each.

Spanish sangria

Serves about 12

1 small can fruit cocktail

¼ pint (125ml) brandy

1 can (approximately 1 pint or ½ litre) sweetened orange juice

2 bottles Spanish burgundy

½ large bottle soda water

1. Empty can of fruit cocktail into large bowl.
2. Stir in brandy, orange juice and burgundy.
3. Chill until required.
4. Add soda water just before serving.

Imperial punch

Serves about 16 to 18

½ level teaspoon cinnamon

½ vanilla stick

thinly-pared peel of 1 medium lemon

2 pints (approximately 1¼ litre) boiling water

10oz (250gm) granulated sugar

juice of 4 medium lemons

4 oranges, peeled and cut into segments in between membranes

1 small fresh pineapple, peeled and thinly sliced

½ to 1 bottle dark rum

2 tablespoons grenadine

1 bottle Rhine wine, chilled

1 bottle sparkling white wine, chilled

1. Put cinnamon, vanilla stick and lemon peel into boiling water. Bring to boil and simmer gently 15 minutes. Add sugar and stir until dissolved.
2. Strain into large punch bowl. Add lemon juice, oranges and pineapple.
3. Pour in rum and grenadine and leave until completely cold then add both the wines.
4. Stir well to mix and serve straight away.

Arctic circle

Arctic circle

Serves 4

4 heaped dessertspoons crushed ice

4 dessertspoons crème de menthe

Angostura bitters

1 can (approximately 1 pint or ½ litre) sweetened grapefruit juice, well-chilled

4 thin slices unpeeled cucumber

4 mint sprigs

1. Put ice into 4 tumblers.
2. Add a dessertspoon crème de menthe and 2 or 3 drops Angostura bitters to each.
3. Top up with grapefruit juice.
4. Add a slice of cucumber and mint sprig to each and serve straight away.

Orange julep

Serves about 12

2 cans (each approximately 1 pint or ½ litre) sweetened orange juice

1 dessertspoon Angostura bitters

crushed ice

2 bottles sparkling white wine

2 large oranges, unpeeled and thinly sliced

a few mint sprigs

1. Pour orange juice into large bowl.
2. Stir in all remaining ingredients except mint.
3. Stir well to mix then pour into glasses.
4. Add a sprig of mint to each and serve straight away.

Pink punch

Serves 16 to 20

ice cubes

3 bottles rosé wine, well-chilled

1 bottle gin

1 medium bottle Maraschino cherries

4 tablespoons rose hip syrup

1. Cover base of large bowl with ice cubes.
2. Add wine, gin, cherries and syrup.
3. Stir well to mix and serve straight away.

Strawberry razzmatazz

Serves 4

1 medium can pineapple pieces

4oz (100gm) strawberries

½ pint (250ml) milk

1 family brick Cornish ice cream, broken into pieces

few drops pink food colouring

whole strawberries to decorate

1. Drain pineapple pieces and reserve a few for decoration.
2. Chop pineapple and strawberries very finely.
3. Whisk with the milk, ice cream and a little colouring until frothy.
4. Pour into chilled glasses and decorate each with a strawberry and pineapple piece.

Note
Alternatively, put all ingredients into liquidiser goblet and blend until smooth and frothy.

Midsummer quencher

Midsummer quencher

Serves 6

½ pint (250ml) frozen orange juice

¼ pint (125ml) unsweetened pineapple juice

¼ pint (125ml) lemon juice

¼ pint (125ml) Maraschino juice

½ pint (250ml) ginger ale

1 level tablespoon honey

1 family brick vanilla ice cream

2 tablespoons sliced Maraschino cherries

1. Mix fruit juices, Maraschino juice, ginger ale and honey well together.
2. Chill thoroughly.
3. Add half the ice cream and stir until blended.
4. Pour into tall glasses.
5. Add a tablespoon of ice cream to each then top with cherry slices.

Strawberry razzmatazz

Green grass

Serves 4

1½ pints (approximately ¾ litre) diluted lime cordial

syrup from 1 medium can pears

juice of 1 lemon

ice cubes

4 lemon slices

1. Combine lime cordial with pear syrup and lemon juice.
2. Pour into 4 glasses and add 2 ice cubes to each.
3. Slit each lemon slice from centre to outside edge and place on rim of glasses.
4. Serve straight away.

Cherry milk shake

Serves 4

1½ pints (approximately ¾ litre) ice cold milk

4 heaped tablespoons cherry jam

4 heaped dessertspoons vanilla ice cream

1. Put ingredients into blender (half at a time) and blend until smooth and fluffy.
2. Pour into glasses and serve straight away.

Peach cream soda

Serves 4

4 heaped tablespoons vanilla ice cream

4 heaped tablespoons chopped canned peaches

4 tablespoons peach syrup from can of fruit

chilled soda water

1. Put ice cream into 4 tall glasses.
2. Add a tablespoon of chopped peaches and syrup to each.
3. Top up with soda water.
4. Stir each briskly and serve straight away.

Tomato cocktail

Serves 4

1 can (approximately 1 pint or ½ litre) chilled tomato juice

juice of 1 lemon

1 tablespoon Worcestershire sauce

salt and pepper to taste

3 tablespoons dry sherry

1. Combine tomato juice with all remaining ingredients.
2. Pour into 4 cocktail glasses and serve straight away.

Above: green grass and cherry milk shake
Below: peach cream soda and tomato cocktail

Index

T

Acknowledgments

The publishers gratefully acknowledge the generous help and co-operation given in the preparation of this book by various companies and organisations. Colour photographs are reproduced by courtesy of:

Alcan Foil
Aluminium Foils Ltd.
Angostura Aromatic Bitters
The Argentine National Meat Board
Australian Recipe Service
Bacon Advisory Bureau
Birds Eye Foods Ltd.
Borwicks Baking Powder
British Egg Information Service
British Meat Service
British Sugar Bureau
Brown and Polson
Cadbury Schweppes Food Advisory Service, Bournville, Birmingham
California Kitchens
Canned and Packaged Foods Bureau
Carnation Milk Bureau
Cherry Valley Farms Ltd.
The Cirio Co. Ltd.
Colman's Mustard
Dairy Produce Advisory Service of the Milk Marketing Board
Danish Food Centre, London
Davis Gelatine
Dutch Dairy Bureau
The Flour Advisory Bureau
Food from France (Sopexa)
Fruit Producers Council
Fyffes Bananas
Geest Food Group
Grand Marnier
Green Giant Corn
Guernsey Tomato Marketing Board
Hauser Mushrooms, Zurich
The Honey Bureau
James A. Jobling and Co. Ltd. ('Pyrosil' Cookware)
Kellogg Company of G.B. Ltd.
Kraft Kitchen
Lawry's Foods International Inc.
Lea and Perrins Worcestershire Sauce
Libby, McNeill and Libby
McDougall (Cerebos Foods Ltd.)
Malayan Pineapple Information Bureau
Parkington and Co. Ltd.
Philips Electrical Ltd.
Pilchard Food Advisory Bureau
Potato Marketing Board
Salter Houseware Ltd.
The Stork Cookery Service
Sunland Marketing Inc.
Tabasco Pepper Sauce
Tate and Lyle
Unigate Foods Ltd.
U.S. Rice Council
Wall's Ice Cream
Wall's Sausages
John West Foods Ltd.
The White Fish Kitchen
Young's Seafoods